D0378976

Presented by The
University of Colorado
CENTENNIAL
CU
1876
COMMISSION
Through The
E. Floyd Thompson Fund

# The Coloradans

# The COLORADANS

Robert G. Athearn

UNIVERSITY OF NEW MEXICO PRESS

Albuquerque

**Library of Congress Cataloging in Publication Data**

Athearn, Robert G.
The Coloradans.

Bibliography: p. 403
Includes index.
1. Colorado—History. I. Title.
F776.A9 978.8'03 76-21528
ISBN 0-8263-0427-3


Manufactured in the United States of America.
Library of Congress Catalog Card Number 76-21528
International Standard Book Number 0-8263-0427-3
*First edition*

For Eugene H. Wilson

The Coloradans owe him much . . .

# Contents

Maps viii
Illustrations viii
Prologue 1

*PART 1 The Invasion* 5

1 The New California 7
2 Cities by a Golden Gate 20
3 Seeds of a New Society 33
4 Old Institutions in a New Country 47

*PART 2 The Age of Acquisition* 63

5 The Uncertain Years 65
6 The "Selling" of Colorado 87
7 The Agricultural Towns 106
8 New Frontiers 128

*PART 3 In Search of Maturity* 147

9 The Thrust of a Developing Culture 149
10 High Country Society 171
11 The Not-So-Gay Nineties 189

*PART 4 Colorado in Midpassage* 213

12 A Time of Bounding Hopes 215
13 " 'Tis a Privilege" 239
14 In the Valley of Doubt 269
15 While the World Was at War 293

*PART 5 Colorado: Cool and Colorful* 307
16 The Rediscovery of Colorado 309
17 Cultural Crosscurrents 327
18 The Recycling of "Sell Colorado" 348

Notes 371
Acknowledgments 401
Bibliographical Essay 403
Index 417

MAPS

1 Pike's Peak Country, 1858–1861 9
2 The Tourists' Colorado, c. 1890 99
3 Colorado by Automobile, c. 1920 263
4 The Colorado Environment 349

ILLUSTRATIONS

following pages 88, 184, and 280

# Prologue

During the excitement of 1859, as thousands of miners swarmed along the approaches to the central Rockies, business and civic leaders of this newborn community decided that it merited political organization, and so they created what amounted to a rump government. They named the new territory Jefferson.

Although the organizers had acted too quickly—their creation was to be disavowed by the central government—their choice of a name demonstrated an understanding of the man to whom they owed an acknowledgment. Thomas Jefferson long had shown an interest in the Spanish-held western lands, and, after the portion of them known as Louisiana was acquired by the French in 1800, President Jefferson offered to buy it. Napoleon's government, in need of money and fearful that it might not be able to fend off the aggressive Americans, sold it in 1803 for $15 million. Included in that vast tract of land, an empire that stretched westward from the Mississippi River to the crest of the Rockies, was a piece of country that became the eastern portion of Colorado. What would later be the western section of the state was acquired by the United States as a result of the Mexican cession of 1848, but no one bothered to thank President James Polk for his efforts; not even a Colorado county bears his name.

The Spanish had known something of the area for some two hundred fifty years prior to the famed Louisiana Purchase. Beginning with Coronado's exploration of 1540, they had probed the northern reaches of Mexico, testing it for minerals, looking for passages in the mountains, and maintaining their claim to the land. During the early seventeenth century Spanish Santa Fe was founded, and in the years that followed portions of southern Colorado—the San Luis Valley, in particular—were examined. By 1706 the eastern plains of modern Colorado were claimed by Spain and the region was named the Province of San Luis. Less than a century later a part of that province became American.

Jefferson's desire to know more about the northern plains prompted the Lewis and Clark expedition. About the time this party returned to the East a young army officer named Zebulon Montgomery Pike was on his way to the central Rockies under orders to study that portion of the recent land purchase. In mid November 1806 he sighted what he described as a "small blue cloud" and upon approaching it discovered it to be the mountain that later bore his name. The party gave three cheers to the "Mexican mountains" and then moved southward along them.

In 1820 another exploring party, this one commanded by Major Stephen H. Long, returned to the area, where the major also found a mountain that would be named for him. The stories both parties brought back about the new country were interesting, but chiefly to geographers and botanists. During the three or four decades that followed the Pike and Long expeditions, other military exploration parties, led by such men as Lieutenant John C. Frémont and Captain John Gunnison, gave the American people still more detailed information about this section of the Rockies and the land that led to them. Again, their reports made fascinating reading, but, for the moment at least, few people who perused these documents believed that interest in the western country would be anything more than academic for some time to come. It was remote, cut off from the rest of the nation by the "Great American Desert" so prominent in the geographies of the day, and apparently it was of little value. The Spanish, who had searched the countryside periodically for gold, could show nothing for their efforts, and thus it appeared that the mountain region, as well as the rest of the Louisiana Purchase itself, was of no immediate value.

But that conclusion did not entirely satisfy the national curiosity. Private explorers, titled sportsmen on hunting expeditions, and fur trappers continued to travel on the high plains and into the mountains. A number of New Mexico–bound fur traders crossed southeastern Colorado in the early 1800s, and a few years later such famous pelt hunters as William H. Ashley, Jim Bridger, and others worked the northern section. Some of these entrepreneurs established fur-trading posts—invariably called forts—from which they carried on their trade with the Indians. Bent's Fort, on the lower Arkansas River, perhaps was the most famous, but also well known were such posts as Forts Lupton, Vásquez, Jackson, and St. Vrain in the South Platte River country. Across the mountains were occasional fur posts such as Fort Roubidoux in the Gunnison area and Fort Davy Crockett on the Green River.

The presence of travelers and traders was of no great concern to the Indians, who normally treated individuals or small parties as harmless passersby. Even when some of the traders built posts in Indian country the tribes did not object, for they regarded these institutions as places to exchange pelts for otherwise unavailable household and personal goods. The natives that the whites encountered along the approaches to the Rockies were primarily the Arapahoes, Cheyennes, and Kiowas, with some Comanches, Kiowa Apaches, and Jicarilla Apaches in evidence during the early period. From time to time some of the Sioux bands ventured as far from their northern homes as the South Platte grasslands, where they had close relations with the Cheyennes and Arapahoes. Perhaps the best known of the Colorado Indians were the Utes, who lived west of the mountains, were generally friendly to whites with a few notable exceptions, and were the last to retain any claim to the lands of the state.

Even when straggling groups of white settlers tried to farm along the base of the mountains, the Indians voiced few objections. Probably the first Americans who tried to till the soil did so at a location whose name well described the difficulties they encountered. The little settlement at Hardscrabble Creek, east of the Wet Mountains, began about 1840; a few years later a handful of French Canadians and their Indian wives began to raise a little corn along nearby Greenhorn Creek. During the following decade occasional ranchers settled in the area, among them Richens "Uncle Dick" Wootton and Charles Autobees. These lonely agrarians raised small grains, ran a few head of cattle, and managed to produce enough to provide a living. Now and then passing travelers, government explorers, and hunters camped on their property and bought supplies before passing on.

The federal government continued to display only a casual interest in its western real estate. Shortly after the Mexican War it offered to buy William Bent's fur post, to be converted into a fort, but when negotiations broke down the old trader moved out and blew the place to bits rather than sell. He built a new establishment not far away, and in 1859 the government leased this one, naming it Fort Wise after a prominent Virginia politician. Meanwhile, in 1852, as a protection to the settlers in the northern reaches of the territory recently acquired from Mexico, a military post named Fort Massachusetts was built in the San Luis Valley. It was poorly sited, and a few years later it was replaced by Fort Garland, built about six miles away; that establishment remains today as one of Colorado's historical tourist attractions.

The fortifications were little more than adornments or perhaps military gestures, for the soldiers stationed in them rarely were called upon to perform any duties except those of garrison routine. The years passed, and the posts drowsed, occasionally welcoming a traveler or a trader from whom the soldiers hungrily gleaned any news from the States. From time to time there was talk of gold among the trappers, but it was vague talk and none of them appeared to have any of that product for display. In 1850 some Cherokee Indians who had mined in Georgia crossed this part of the country en route to California, and one of them, named John L. Brown, made a laconic remark in his diary that gold samples had been found on the South Platte; then the party moved on.

All during the remainder of that decade the same rumor persisted, but the evidence was slim and no one seemed sure enough of it to invest in an expedition to confirm the story. California still was producing and many a prospector passed by Colorado bound for this known gold country on the Pacific Ocean. Most of them concluded that until more evidence was at hand they would not examine the streams so long ago searched by the Spanish, by itinerant fur trappers, and by gold miners bound for other diggings.

Until that time Uncle Sam's soldiers, at their far-flung and lonely outposts, could guard the land, and the Indians who traded and intermarried with the white trappers were welcome to the country Presidents Jefferson and Polk had acquired for the American people. Apparently that great purchase was being held in trust for some later and needier generation.

PART ONE

# The Invasion

# 1

# The New California

During the summer of 1858 eastern Kansas newspapers began to publish occasional items mentioning the existence of gold deposits in the westernmost part of that territory. Merchants in the Missouri River Valley, always on the lookout for more outfitting trade, displayed a great willingness to believe what they read and did what they could to spread the good word. It was, however, a surprisingly hard gospel to preach, for rumors of gold in what then was vaguely known as Pike's Peak Country had circulated for years, yet no one had brought in any hard evidence. A few people listened that autumn when an old-time fur trader named John Cantrell came back from the mountains and said that a party of Georgians led by William Green Russell had made a thousand dollars in ten days' panning. Cantrell had no gold to show, but his word was considered to be good and as his story spread, it grew.

About that time a prospector named William B. Parsons returned from Cherry Creek, a tributary of the South Platte River, bringing a few wild turkey quills filled with "dust" he and his partners had panned. He had not been particularly impressed by the find, or by the gold country's prospects; therefore he was amazed when he listened to the talk that had been generated in the river towns.[1] Although the rest of the nation showed little real interest in the matter, the eastern press noted that despite the lateness of the season several small parties had gone out to the Cherry Creek diggings, where they had laid out a cluster of small towns soon to be known as Denver. Meanwhile, during the idle winter months that followed, young men in the Middle West, many of them out of work because of the recent financial panic, talked late into the evening about the stories coming out of the West. By spring a good many of them had decided to cross the plains and see for themselves. As one of them remarked, his people were of pioneer stock "and always eager to go somewhere else."[2] In later years he admitted that few booms ever had started on slimmer evidence, but even if he had realized that fact in the spring of 1859 it would not have altered his determination to make the trip.

During those exciting weeks thousands of optimists milled about the Missouri River towns with guns, picks, blankets, and a few provisions slung over their shoulders, ready for the great gold hunt. Long lines of wagons waited at river crossings, and arriving steamboats were loaded to the gunwales. As those who had been issued their supplies left town, new customers appeared, and the merchants beamed with joy at the sight of the human stream that circulated through their shops.

For these outfitting towns the stampede triggered by rumors of gold to the west was an absolute godsend. They had experienced a recent boomlet in business as supply towns for the army's advance upon Utah in the recent Mormon "war," but when that bonanza played out and depression briefly visited the nation, times became exceedingly tight. Even if the Pike's Peak excitement produced little gold, they welcomed it, for mere rumor had brought forth a number of young hopefuls in need of outfits for their great adventure. Since talk is cheap, the merchants expended great amounts of it, and through their local editors they passed the word that a big payoff was about to be carried out at the foot of the Rockies. Before long, tellers of tales, newspapers included, vied with one another to see who could spin the most fascinating story about the golden West. Almost every town between Kansas City and Council Bluffs employed agents who collared potential miners and let them in on the worst-kept secret of the era.

To cross the plains the newly outfitted argonauts had a choice of several well-known trails. The old Platte River route had been well worn by the Oregonians, the Mormons, and the Forty-Niners, and because of forts and occasional ranches along its twisting course that familiar roadway was popular. An even older route, the Santa Fe Trail, could be followed as far as Bent's Fort; by then switching to the Cherokee Trail, travelers reached the base of the mountains near the site of Pueblo, not far south of the reported excitement. Green Russell and his party had used this trail. There were two

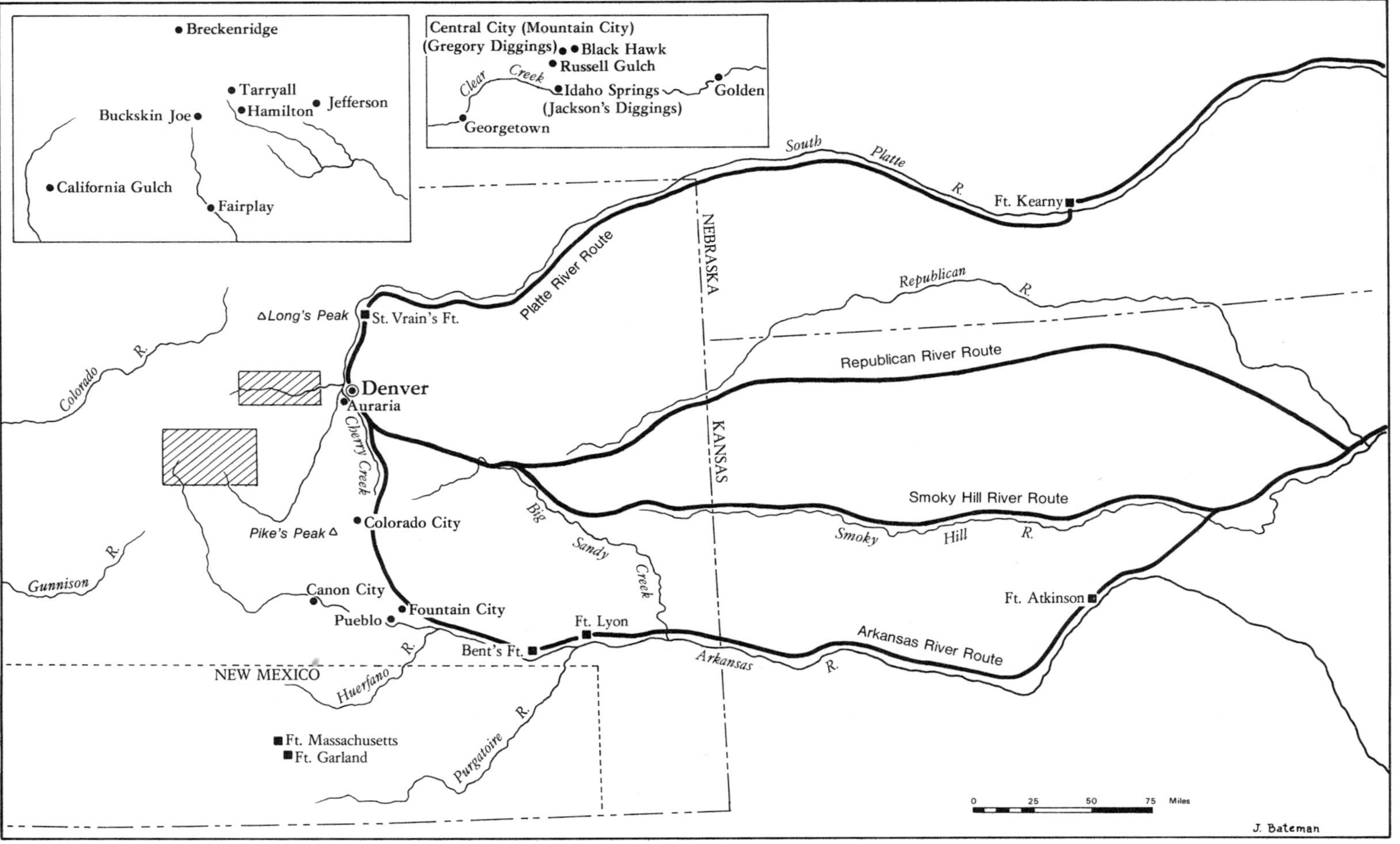


**Map 1 Pike's Peak Country, 1858-1861**

other possibilities: the Smoky Hill route that ran out along the Kansas River to the Smoky Hill Fork, a stream that had its source in eastern Colorado; or the Republican River road that paralleled the river of that name and brought its users close to Big Sandy Creek, within range of Denver. The latter was the route chosen by the Leavenworth and Pike's Peak Express Company, the first stage line to serve the new mining country.[3]

Despite the existence of these trails, those who set off for the mountains that spring, whether in well-equipped wagon groups or with the flimsiest kind of equipment, embarked upon a journey that was far from routine. For years the trappers had made the crossing, and now the river-town newspapers played down the country's aridity, the lack of fuel, and the distances between watering places; as a result a lot of innocents thought they had only to follow the sinking sun. Before long, warnings began to be heard that the ease with which the journey could be made had been exaggerated. In addition to the ordinary hardships that might be anticipated there were rumored to be cases of starvation and even of cannibalism. One old man accused some of the gold seekers of devouring his nephew when members of their party began to starve. While there were those who resisted the temptation to eat human flesh, the alternative choices provided a difficult living. Two weeks on prickly pears made many a man ready to eat almost anything. And some of them did; one group found a dead ox in an advanced state of decomposition and held their noses long enough to get down some of the putrified meat.[4]

Such tales did not slow the flood that mounted, and out into the wilderness went thousands, by horseback, in wagons, and afoot. Apparently the Great American Desert, so foreboding a patch of country in the atlases of the day, was not taken seriously, for two unaccompanied women set off from Leavenworth, driving a team of horses, and they completed the trip without incident. Old-timers blanched when they heard that one independent young woman had struck off afoot and alone, firmly declining the many proffered rides.[5] Those who were in a hurry and had a hundred dollars for fare rode the stagecoaches. That amount of money, wrote one disgruntled passenger, entitled one to "fifteen inches of seat, with a fat man on one side, a poor widow on the other, a baby in your lap, a bandbox over your head, and three or four more persons immediately in front leaning against your knees. . . ."[6] As many as a hundred thousand people were believed to have started for the "new California" that spring, but less than half of them reached it, and of those who did perhaps no more than twenty-five thousand ever witnessed actual gold panning.

There was a middle ground between the fate of those who turned to cannibalism and those who went west by coach in some discomfort but with relative speed. A young girl who made the trip by covered wagon remembered it as being reasonably uneventful and, at times, almost homelike. Tied to the rear of her family's wagon was a sheet-iron stove that was set up at mealtimes; fired by buffalo chips gathered along the way, it produced satisfactory results. Rather than hunker before an open fire and gnaw at bits of blackened meat, as many of the young bachelors did, the family tried to preserve decorum and a semblance of formality while dining. A large square of rag carpet, used in the tent at night, was spread out, and in its center was placed a box that served as a table. The spring seats of the wagon, supplemented by campstools, provided the chairs. The memory of fried pork and gravy, pancakes, and coffee served family-style on a remote prairie stayed with the lady for years after she had settled in Colorado.[7] Not all families found home life on the prairies so enticing. One discouraged woman told the folks back in Illinois that plains travel was difficult for members of her sex. Each night on the plains she had slept in a damp wagon, and she had spent most of her days in the rain. "I do not know what dry clothing is," she wrote.[8]

Group travel was not confined to family units. Single men banded together in what they termed "companies" for cheaper travel, not to mention the additional protection afforded by numbers. Some of the companies even had names to indicate organization and a common sense of purpose, or perhaps merely togetherness. They ate together, slept together, joked together, hoped together. And when they arrived at the mining country they tended to stay together, at least in subgroups of twos and threes, digging ore-bearing soil, operating sluices, retorting their gold—as a group. So their camaraderie continued, and even after they had parted company, sometimes they crossed trails and even joined up again, to continue their effort cooperatively.

The traffic was not all in one direction during those tumultuous spring weeks of 1859. Those who left a little later met a number of discouraged and even bitter farm boys who had gone out, had "seen the elephant," and were on their way home where they would tell their friends that Pike's Peak was overrated. Mottoes painted on canvas wagon tops that resolutely promised "Root, Hog, or Die!" now were replaced by a sad admission that "The Hog's Dead." Other returning slogans commented crisply, "We've Seen Him," referring to the mythical elephant. One canvas bore a short verse that explained the dilemma of those who had not dared stay at home for fear of missing the chance of a lifetime. It read:

We're "humbugged" if we stay at home,
Or "humbugged" if we leave;
There's few reports that come or go
But will some deceive.[9]

Most of the "go-backers," as they were called, tended to take their troubles philosophically, writing off the experience as another frontier venture that had failed to pay, but some of them were bitter against the promoters who had led them on. In addition to the river-town newspapers, whose editors had waxed eloquent on the subject of gold, a number of guidebooks to the promised land had appeared on the market in time for the spring rush. One of them described the way west as seen by D. C. Oakes, who earlier had made the round trip. When he set forth again that memorable spring, the author met a number of his readers who were making a footsore, hungry trip eastward. Some of them, who already had threatened to burn down a few Missouri River towns when they returned, nearly mobbed Oakes for having written such a colorful bit of prose. But they thought better of it and merely hanged him in effigy, after which they formulated an epitaph that was to become famous. It read: "Here lie the remains of D. C. Oakes; Who was the starter of this damned hoax." Except for an additional version of the couplet, one that included the name of William Byers, who was becoming well known in Denver as the editor of the *Rocky Mountain News*, the other guidebook authors failed to get equal treatment at the hands of the aggrieved; their names did not rhyme with "hoax." Meanwhile Oakes reached Colorado. Rather than becoming a rich miner he operated a sawmill and later served as an Indian agent and as a deputy U.S. land surveyor. He lived to be one of Colorado's respected pioneers.

The turmoil on the plains, characterized by the wanderings of lost, hungry men and the ebb and flow of gold seekers, some bound for the mountains and others headed for home, was capped by contradictions in the eastern press as to the validity of the gold rush itself. Each time the journalists decided that there was nothing in it, as shown by the eastward retreat of the new argonauts, reports of new finds in the mountains would rise to plague them. Overnight the mad hunt would be renewed and fresh heroes would emerge.

For example, there was the success story of a young Missourian named George A. Jackson who, after having mined in California, had returned to the Fort Laramie region during the summer of 1858. Hearing about the activity along Cherry Creek, he moved southward along the mountains, sampling the gravel in various creeks along the way. In January 1859 he found what he regarded as very encouraging pay dirt in Chicago Creek, not far from modern Idaho Springs. When the weather warmed, Jackson and some others began a serious probing of the find; as word spread that the results looked promising, a minor rush took place. Almost overnight some two hundred men were busy at the new Jackson Diggings. About the same time, word circulated among the miners that there was "color" at a place called Gold Run, on Boulder Creek, as well as at Deadwood Gulch on South Boulder Creek. The latter camp was considered "five-dollar diggings," and within a few months three hundred men were at work there.[10]

About the time these camps had settled down to routine extraction and the excitement had subsided, a new find attracted wide attention. And just in time. Hundreds of hopefuls who had stayed on despite discouragements were on the verge of concluding that they would join the "go-backer" movement. The mining country's reputation was balanced on a knife's edge, and only a piece of singularly good news would save it from possible failure.

The happy tidings came from the discovery along Clear Creek made by a Georgia miner named John H. Gregory. He had crossed the plains from Leavenworth in the summer of 1858 and, like George Jackson, spent the winter at Fort Laramie. There he heard reports of gold from the South Platte country, and he, too, began prospecting mountain streams to the south. Along Clear Creek, Gregory fell in with some other miners. The group worked its way into the mountains, sampling creek gravel all the way. On May 6 they made their big strike, and the dazed Gregory muttered, "My wife will be a lady and my children will be educated." The district that grew out of this find ultimately produced eighty-five million dollars worth of gold, but, like many a prospector, the original discoverer died a poor man.[11]

Less than a month after Gregory's strike, Green Russell and his brother, who had gone back to Georgia and had returned with equipment and 170 men, made yet another rich find, this time only about two miles southwest of Gregory Gulch. In a week 6 of the men extracted seventy-six ounces of gold worth between $16.00 and $18.00 per ounce in coin, depending upon its purity. Wages of over $200 a week for common labor were virtually unheard of in 1859.[12]

Word of these new strikes sowed more confusion on the high plains and in the river outfitting towns. Some young men who had just returned sold the remnants of their belongings for what they could get and others, just arrived and not yet discouraged, bought them from middlemen for high prices. A newspaper correspondent at Lawrence, Kansas, bitterly criticized the "sharpers," as he called these enterprising souls who lurked about the towns, ever ready to capitalize on the latest rumors and even concocting tales of their own to drive prices down so that they might buy.

Desperately, those who had a stake in the great promotion sought additional means of convincing the public that this was not just another swindle. Missouri River Valley merchants, of course, were interested in the continuation of the trade that had resulted from the spring migration, but the business and professional men who had gone out hoping to become part of a new western community were even more anxious that its birth be legitimized. Presumably the best way to accomplish this was to obtain an unbiased opinion from someone with a reputation for unimpeachable credibility.

By a happy circumstance, not just one but three such witnesses were on their way west, and all of them published accounts of what they saw. Henry Villard, a German journalist who later would come to fame in the West for his Northern Pacific Railroad, represented the Cincinnati *Daily Commercial.* Albert D. Richardson, a well-known Massachusetts journalist, and Horace Greeley, of the *New York Tribune,* completed the trio. After having looked at the "diggin's" in the spring of 1859, Richardson and Greeley wrote a joint report that was printed in the *Rocky Mountain News* of June 11. In straightforward language they reported what they had seen, admitting that fairly substantial amounts of gold were coming out of the new Gregory diggings, but they said that they knew of no other major strikes in the region. They did not say that gold was lying around loose, waiting for someone to harvest it. On the contrary, the report stressed the fact that gold mining was a serious business that required both knowledge and capital, and they decried the fact that thousands had stampeded westward under the illusion that they would get rich quickly with little effort. In his volume *Overland Journey,* Greeley pointed out that this mining region was far from any navigable waters or means of cheap transportation, that it was isolated by an arid country necessitating the importation of most foodstuffs, that the high altitudes probably would mean heavy winters and a short mining season, and, finally, that the Pike's Peak gold was so dispersed that it would be hard to wash profitably, necessitating quartz-mining equipment for successful extraction.[13]

The journalists' verification satisfied no one. Hardly had they left before Greeley, in particular, was accused of having been fooled. The scholarly-looking, bewhiskered scribe, dressed in a linen duster and limping around from a sore leg acquired on his stagecoach trip west, had peered through his rimless glasses at what the mountain men had shown him. One of the accounts that lingered after he had witnessed the proceedings was that three times more gold had been produced from the sluices than had been gathered before in an entire day's effort. Gold that had been washed was injected into the soil ready for the next sluicing, and, as the process was repeated, some astonishing results were obtained. Ovando Hollister, who published his *Mines of Colorado* a few years later, denied that the Greeley party had been "salted." The *Tribune*'s crosstown rival, the *New York Times,* chose to think otherwise. It warned eastern readers that the writings of the victimized Greeley would cause much suffering, break up many a happy home, create numerous widows and orphans, and fill the poorhouses to overflowing.[14]

To counter some of the unfavorable eastern talk, the stripling *Rocky Mountain News* tried to explain away the confusion on the ground that the spring rush had been made up principally of reckless adventurers who had struck off across the high plains without any kind of preparation or any talent for mining. Editor William Byers, therefore, was not in the least surprised that after a few days a good many of them had started for home. A New York paper remarked that the little sheet out in the Rockies certainly carried a lot of mining news, and all of it was extremely favorable. On the theory that the *News* might not as yet have a national readership, those interested in Denver's future tried another avenue of approach. They tried to plant some good news in the Mississippi Valley newspapers. For example, when Sam Hawken, the famous gunsmith from St. Louis, arrived in the mining country, his favorable account of the mines was hurried back to his hometown. Hawken admitted that he had met a few "go-backers" along the way, but claimed that he had seen no suffering on the trail and that the Indians he met were quite harmless. Since he had lived in St. Louis for thirty-seven years and was well known there, his assurance that Pike's Peak gold was no humbug carried some weight.[15]

Young Denver's propaganda efforts were not entirely convincing. Returnees shouted "liar" and "humbug" a great deal, and their complaints continued to appear in the eastern press. So did accounts of other problems in the Rockies. After the spring runoff the mountain streams dwindled and made sluice mining difficult. Primitive living conditions, poor food, and worse whiskey made daily life in the diggings less than attractive to many who were not used to hardships. Then came stories that the fabled Gregory diggings, of which so much had been made, were beginning to play out and that during the summer months the output from this camp was only about a tenth of the June production. Some who had stayed on despite stories of fraud and hoax now reluctantly concluded that it was time to "make tracks for America," as one of the discouraged prospectors put it.[16] Some of his friends, however, decided to spend the winter in Denver to see what another try might bring.

The great rush to the Rockies, as it later was called, came in not one but two big waves in 1859. The first, an early effort, commenced even before the grass was green, when the weather on the plains and in the foothills was subject to spring storms. The first of the "go-backers," therefore, started for the States in late April and early May. Many of them were on their way by May 6, when the Gregory strike was made, and they learned of it long after their arrival home. The second invasion of 1859 took place in June and July, after word of the Gregory find was received and confirmed. At that time the national press began to issue more favorable reports about the mining country, and the "go-backer" retreat momentarily was turned around as the counterattack began. However, even the second westward wave met groups of returnees, miners who had taken hope from the most recent favorable reports but who had not been so lucky as Gregory, Jackson, or Russell.

Men of stronger resolution plodded on toward the mountains, shrugging off the sorrowful tales of those they met along the way, convinced that if gold was to be found they would have as good a chance as the next man. As one of them put it, an industrious individual who was willing "to put in hard licks" when he reached the diggings could at least make a living as a miner. Some of them did. Others turned to mining-related types of business and stayed on, many of them for the rest of their lives.

Who all these people were and where they came from never will be known precisely, for a good many of them vanished before the census taker made his rounds during the next year. However, if the remnants of that great migratory army, the 34,277 who were counted in the 1860 census, are a reasonable cross section of the larger movement, some clues as to their origins are offered. Of those tallied, the greatest number of native-born gave their places of birth as Ohio, New York, Illinois, Missouri, and Indiana, in that order. The largest number of foreign-born were from Canada, followed closely by Ireland and the German states, the total of the nonnatives being 2,666. Census workers learned the occupations of about 27,000 of these newcomers; over 22,000 of them said they were miners, with laborers, carpenters, and teamsters next in number. Actually, the mining country was more heavily populated than the figures would suggest, for at that time what was listed as Colorado was merely the western portion of Kansas. Colorado itself later was made up of land from Nebraska, New Mexico, and Utah, as well as from Kansas. At that time approximately 4,000 miners lived in camps north of the 40th parallel, in what then was Nebraska, and thus they were excluded from the count.

While it is possible to learn the places of birth for those listed in the 1860 census, the document did not reveal their places of residence immediately prior to joining the ranks of the Fifty-Niners. Certainly many of them had left their hometowns and had filtered westward with the frontier movement. Then, because many of them were farmers, they had halted at the edge of the Great American Desert, unwilling to risk the vagaries of that hostile climate in their agricultural efforts. It took a gold rush to break the mental dam that held them back. Among those hunting for nuggets around the foothills of the Rockies that first summer were hundreds of people who recently had lived in Missouri, Kansas, and Nebraska.[17]

Taken as a group they were young, male Americans of northern European stock, along with some foreigners of much the same bloodlines. Being young, they had not as yet amassed much money; their main assets were their youth and their optimism. And they had a slogan: "Pike's Peak or Bust!" They believed that this was to be the big adventure of their lives, and for many of them it was. While the mountain named for Lieutenant Pike was not the actual goal of the youthful adventurers, that massive landmark symbolized the general movement. "It stood for the whole country, from Mexico to our northern line," wrote one of the prospectors. "It represented gold, and plenty of it; it spoke of influence, power and position in our middle age, and ease and comfort in our decline. I think that with the first view of the celebrated mountain we felt the first quickening of a definite purpose."[18]

Not all the "Peakers" were young; the gunsmith, Sam Hawken, boasted that at the age of sixty-seven he had walked a good part of the way west, his gun over his shoulder. He was an exception. Exceptional, also, were men possessed of any knowledge of mining. Here and there was an experienced hand who had learned his trade much earlier in Georgia or, more recently, in California, but such men were rare among the milling thousands who combed the gulches along the mountain front. Some called themselves miners, for the rudiments of panning could be acquired in a short time, but in the main their newfound knowledge quickly showed its superficiality. Augusta Tabor, the long-suffering wife of H. A. W. Tabor, looked at them and shook her head in wonderment. "I never saw a country settled up with such greenhorns as Colorado," she remarked. "They were mostly from farms and some clerks. They were all young men from 18 to 30. I was there a good many years before we saw a man with grey hair. They thought they were going to have a second California. . . ."[19]

The Fifty-Niners were not particularly bothered by the idea that they were greenhorns in the mining business. They assumed that thousands of amateur gold panners had gone to California and somehow managed to survive; Pike's Peak Country was said to be another California. In any event, many of those who headed west that spring shrugged off their lack of experience and consoled themselves with the thought that anything was better than continued unemployment at home. "We were all alike—nobody had any money—all cleaned out before we skipped out from home," admitted one of them. "No one had anything to be ashamed of; but it was a regular amalgamation of busted people, who left their country for their country's good, and their own."[20] What he said undoubtedly was true in his case, and in that of many others, but it was not true that they were all alike financially. It took money to make the move to Pike's Peak and more money to get a start there. Considerable amounts of capital were expended in the rush, and its participants were by no means invariably "busted."

Mining rushes traditionally have attracted all types, good and bad; Colorado was no exception. Eastern newspapermen and other observers who watched the stampede to the foothills of the Rockies explained that the "border countries," or the frontier, always had tended to attract the migratory and, among them, the lawless. This gold rush appeared to have drawn men from widely separated walks of life; on the streets of Denver well-dressed business and professional types mingled with some extremely disreputable-looking persons.[21] But in the pressure of the day's demands none of the Fifty-Niners gave much time to thoughts about origins and background; it was the future that counted.

# 2

# Cities by a Golden Gate

When the outriders of that restless army of prospectors reached the little Cherry Creek settlements in the early spring weeks of 1859 they came upon a sprawl of log huts known as Auraria and Denver. The names served more to identify collections of dwellings than to indicate the presence of a town, for, as yet, there were few signs of civic life. A few gloomy-looking individuals, clad in flannel and buckskin, stood around in this vacuum, wondering if they would enjoy any of the amenities of life before they went home again.[1]

Denver, soon to be heralded as the "Queen City of the Plains," grew out of the efforts of some Kansans who had reached the area the preceding autumn. During that September a party from Lawrence, Kansas, had staked off a place they called Montana City, but some of them, unhappy with the location, moved closer to the mouth of Cherry Creek. Here they laid out St. Charles and, leaving one man behind to guard the claim, they returned home to get a charter and to advertise the new municipality. Upon their return they were surprised to find another group of Kansans, led by General William Larimer, busily platting a town on the very spot where they had located theirs. Since the general showed no disposition to move, but offered to share the site, the founders of St. Charles shrugged off their disappointment and joined up. Larimer had been foresighted enough to bring along a judge, a sheriff, and some commissioners, all appointed by Governor James W. Denver of Kansas Territory, who thought that Arapahoe County, in the far western portion of his domain, ought to have some kind of government. Thus armed with a ready-made officialdom, the founders thanked the governor by naming the place after him, and they settled down to create a new city in the wilderness.

They were not alone. About the time the St. Charles group had marked off its site, some other recent arrivals looked at the lone cabin of Dr. Levi J. Russell and concluded that its location, on the west bank of Cherry Creek, would be a good place to start a town. Quickly completing the necessary paper work, they announced that Auraria, named after Russell's hometown in Georgia, was in business. By the time Larimer and his municipal architects appeared on the scene, Auraria could boast that it was a thriving little burg of some fifty houses. This, and not the Larimer effort, is regarded as the origin of modern Denver.[2]

If the tired young men who straggled into these villages were disappointed at their unfinished appearance, at least they could not complain about the lack of optimism among the founding fathers. Rows of partially completed log houses suggested that speculators had been busy preparing for the spring rush that was sure to follow when the word got out about gold in the mountains. Those who had moved into completed cabins were out of the weather, but they experienced very few creature comforts in these crude dwellings that rarely had board floors, doors, or glass windows. In an effort to simulate some of the amenities of traditional home life one housewife sewed together some cornsacks that represented a carpet laid over the hard, dirt floor. She covered the log walls with sheets and tablecloths in an effort to create the illusion of more sophisticated surroundings. Few chairs were in evidence; stools, tables, and pole bedsteads that recalled frontier conditions a century earlier supplied the basic furniture. Rough boxes served as bureaus and cupboards. Reminiscent of Daniel Boone's time were fireplaces made of poles and plastered over with mud to fireproof them. Only an occasional roof had shingles, for the nearest sawmill was forty miles away; most were made of poles covered with earth and lined underneath with gauze to catch the falling dirt.[3]

Public accommodations were only slightly more sophisticated. The leading hotel was no more than a glorified log cabin whose main floor, most of which was occupied by a saloon, was bare earth that had to be sprinkled periodically to keep down the dust. In grim humor Horace Greeley referred to it as the Astor House of the gold region where every guest was allowed as good a bed as his blankets would make. The rates were the same as those of the more famous eastern accommodations; the bar prices were higher. Whiskey cost twenty-five cents a drink, and for that sum the customer could buy alcohol colored and labeled to satisfy his tastes.[4]

While western optimism was almost irrepressible, by the early summer of 1859 some of the realists in the Auraria-Denver business community had begun to entertain unspoken doubts. Faced with dwindling mercantile activity, a shortage of cash, falling real estate prices, and a population exodus, the promoters who had staked everything on the validity of gold rumors tried to reassure each other that all was well. They rationalized that slack times were not a result of barren hills to the west; on the contrary, they were due to the recent strikes along Clear Creek, which momentarily had depopulated the supply towns, a situation that would right itself when the influence of the new gold strikes was felt in the East. Another aberration in local price structure was explained plausibly by the fact that a number of the recently departed had brought enough supplies to last eight or ten months and, upon leaving, had resold them for what they would bring, thus depressing prices and alarming the storekeepers whose shelves were loaded with costly goods.[5]

Merchandise dumped on the market by go-backers produced a dislocation that promised to be temporary; it was the bad news these returners spread around the East that worried mining-camp boosters. A general slackening of the westward rush would do much harm to the economy. The fact that twenty thousand gold hunters still were digging did not seem to impress eastern critics. Inexplicably they tended to listen to the hundreds who turned up daily at the river towns, loud in their complaints. As the residents of Auraria-Denver watched between fifty and a hundred wagons leave each day, they sarcastically called the movement the "second stampede," and jeered at those of little faith. But in their more sober moments those who stayed on knew that sooner or later they were going to need some good news to counter the bad, or matters would become much more serious.[6]

After a few weeks the strikes made along Clear Creek by Gregory and others began to have their effect upon Auraria-Denver, and by August things looked better. More money circulated, businesses sprang back into life as fresh stocks appeared on shelves, and the building boom resumed, this time with sawed lumber. Other indicators of prosperity were seen in the construction of hotels, mercantile establishments, and warehouses. The appearance of eastern capital in increasing amounts strengthened morale and enlivened the economic scene.[7] Clearly, a second big wave of Fifty-Niners was sweeping westward, and this brought joy to the commercial circles of Auraria-Denver. Although rents and real estate prices went up in anticipation of a new boom, prices of staples and other household goods tended to stabilize and even to drop because the travel season permitted unrestricted commerce on the prairies. Cold weather and winter storms always shortened supplies and raised prices. But now, in the late summer, coffee that had sold for a dollar a pound in May was down to twenty-five cents, and flour had dropped from as much as twenty-five dollars per hundred pounds to fourteen, with "Mexican" flour bringing only ten. Bacon had receded in price from fifty or sixty cents a pound to about half that amount, sugar dropped from fifty to twenty cents a pound, tobacco stocks were so abundant as to be almost unsalable, and the salt supply was enormous. It was a far cry from the "old days" of 1858 when "Uncle Dick" Wootton had rolled into town, headed for a trading session with the Arapahoes and Cheyennes, only to have the hungry miners literally rip the bags of flour and sugar out of his wagons and thrust money into his startled hands.[8]

Because of transportation difficulties occasioned by winter storms on the plains, a slackness of water in the streams, and a certain amount of cold weather, the winter months necessarily were slow in the mining country. The merchants of Auraria-Denver understood this, but, as autumn deepened in 1859, the morale of those who had settled in remained surprisingly high. Bolstering their innate optimism was the knowledge that favorable reports about the presence of gold in the Rockies now circulated in the eastern press. Papers in that part of the country regularly referred to the "re-establishment of the Kansas mines" and they used fewer qualifying phrases when reporting the amounts of "dust" arriving at the Missouri River towns.[9]

Evidence of faith in the future was to be found along the streets of the business districts as commercial construction proceeded apace. Late in the summer of 1859 building sites began to be in greater demand and lots that had declined in price to as little as twenty dollars each brought as much as three hundred. With an eye cast upon the growing possibilities in the field of entertainment, additional facilities were commenced. "We are putting up a building for a restaurant and concert hall which will cost some

$2,000 and will pay, when completed, $50 a day," wrote one entrepreneur. Smaller buildings that cost between three and five hundred dollars to erect rented for fifty and sixty a month, payable in advance.[10]

By the early months of 1860 the twin cities had twelve wholesale houses, twenty-seven retail outlets, four lumber yards, two livery stables, and an express office. A large transient population was served by eight hotels, seven boarding houses, twenty-three bars, four billiard parlors, four tenpin alleys, and two theaters. The best hotels were the Vasquez House and the Jefferson House, both of Auraria, and the Broadwell, opened in Denver early in 1860. The construction of a business building by R. R. Bradford and Company elicited considerable comment because, as Denver's first skyscraper, it soared three stories in height, suggesting that land was getting valuable already in the Queen City.[11]

While such activity during the winter months kept the residents of the town busy and was a heartening economic indicator, such demands upon available supplies tended to drive up prices again. For example, shingle nails were very scarce and their price mounted daily. The cost of ordinary household and personal necessities also rose as winter tightened its vise upon the wagon trains. Food, clothing, fuel, and candles all demanded more money. The few wives who spent that first winter along Cherry Creek complained constantly about prices of dry goods. When candles hit seventy-five cents a pound the ladies voiced bitter complaints. One of the storekeepers, in trying to fend off one of the verbal assaults, explained the candles were high because the Indians were attacking the plains freighters. Drawing herself up in a stance of utter disdain the angry housewife leveled him with the remark: "What! Are they now fighting by candle light!"[12]

As the builders busied themselves that winter, and housewives quarreled with the merchants over prices, the thinkers and planners gathered around stoves, chewed tobacco, and exchanged some heady ideas. One of the founding fathers, General Larimer, observed that with lumber selling at seventy-five dollars a thousand board feet that product could be shipped by rail to Missouri at a great profit. The more conservative of his listeners thought the idea of a yearling city constructing such a rail line somewhat impractical, but the others ignored such doubts and their eyes gleamed at the very mention of steam and rails. They thought the title "Rocky Mountain Railroad" had a nice ring to it, and they saw no reason why a company by that name should not start laying rails toward the Missouri River at any moment. Carried away by the excitement of such ideas, they offered R. R. Bradford the presidency of the imaginary enterprise. An obvious alternative to such an undertaking was the prospect of an eastern railroad reaching Denver. It was generally supposed that if this happened Denver would be one of its major stops. While the latter appeared to be more probable than a Denver-built line, neither of these dreams came true; the first transcontinental railway completely bypassed Colorado.[13]

There were other and more attainable means of communication with the outside world. Enthusiasts who dreamed of railroads also anticipated the coming of telegraph service by means of which they could "talk" to eastern cities in search of news or business information. For this the wait was shorter; by 1861 a cross-country line passed just north of Colorado, and two years later branch service from Julesburg made the desired connection with Denver.

Thus the occupants of that isolated little outpost of civilization known as Auraria-Denver, a community so undecided as to its future that it had two names, spent the winter of 1859–60 laying mental foundations for future greatness. The usual residents were joined by a number of miners who closed down their mountain operations in anticipation of heavy snows and elected to spend the "cold" months in the city. But the weather held and a good many of them went back to work, hampered only by low water in the streams. There was so little snow that attempts at sledding had to be abandoned. The days were beautiful and cloudless, so warm that overcoats were unnecessary. Surprised, the newcomers wrote glowing letters about the Neapolitan climate of this wonderful place; they predicted that its exhilarating atmosphere would attract many people to the Mountain West.

Expressions of pleasure with Colorado's climate, the quality of its people, and the state's great potential were a characteristic that developed at a very early date. There is much evidence among the letters of the Fifty-Niners that many of them came west with the intention to remain and to make their homes in the new country. Thus committed, their backs turned upon old associations, they were quick to proclaim their loyalty to the infant settlements along the Rockies. "There is no use talking, but verily, Denver City is now a great place and a great institution in business and in social respects," wrote one of them late in 1859. In the best frontier tradition, he explained that old things were done away with in this virgin country "and now behold all things are novel and new." This was far from true, but it was indicative of an attitude of civic pride and of great anticipations. This particular booster promised those who might go west when the grass grew green along travel routes that their efforts would be well rewarded, for on the far side of the old American desert lay a land that was rich in agricultural and mineral wealth, not to mention commercial opportunities. He predicted that when capital and machinery were combined with the skill and energy that so characterized the Yankees, wonderful things would flow from this recently discovered land of plenty.[14]

For those who had opted for a fresh start and a new life, Colorado indeed was a place with a future. During the spring of 1860 one young man who was about to complete his first year of residence there calculated that after he paid his bills and totaled his financial resources he was just forty-seven dollars to the good. However, he said, he had four or five town lots and he expected that they would make money for him because Denver was bound to grow. His brother, who was somewhat taken aback by the roughness of the town, expressed similar faith. He explained that crudity was common in new communities but that he felt time would sift out some of the less desirable occupants of the place.[15] This concern, expressed in a private letter, represented a minor variation of the typical assertion that while there were a few shiftless people on any frontier, Colorado was particularly fortunate in having skimmed the cream of the westering emigrants. Before the historic gold rush year of 1859 was out, readers of midwestern newspapers learned that in Denver "we have a hundred per cent, and I might perhaps have said five hundred per cent, more educated, enterprising businessmen of all departments, more intelligent and refined city men and women, and more of the essential elements of success for a sound and social state of things . . . than any other municipal corporation within the scope of our knowledge and observation anywhere."[16]

In praising the high types who came to do business in Denver, one of the Fifty-Niners added that the place also had a number of doctors, lawyers, and sporting gentlemen, a group he lumped together.[17] The territory's first census did not indicate the number of sporting gentlemen who graced Denver's budding professional society, but it did list the doctors and lawyers, showing 116 of the former and 89 of the latter. Doctors of the Denver-Auraria area met in June 1860 and formed the Jefferson Medical Society, with

Dr. W. M. Belt as president. It blossomed only briefly, died, was revived in 1864 as the Denver Medical Association, disappeared again, and was reorganized once more in 1871 as a permanent body.[18]

The "educated, enterprising" businessmen of whom the enthusiastic newspaper correspondent spoke were principally white, Anglo-Saxon, Protestant Americans who had pulled up stakes from successful enterprises in more settled parts of the country to take advantage of the possibilities usually found in new areas, particularly in a mining country. As a rule they were possessed of some education and had made enough money to move their families and businesses westward without much sacrifice; they settled down in their new community with self-assurance. They dominated Denver's commercial life during the day and the upper levels of its social activity after hours, assuming their role as the city's "first families" in the manner born.

Interspersed among the more prominent businessmen of America's newest boom town were lesser lights about whom very little has been written. One such group was a little band of Jewish merchants who had come west quietly with the Fifty-Niners to take their places among other pioneer tradesmen. Anti-Semitism was not noticeably strong during these years in either the States or Colorado, and these newcomers moved about easily in local business and professional circles, feeling little or no prejudice from the majority. They discovered that in this extremely young community men were too preoccupied with developing the land to have time for petty persecutions, and as a consequence it was not difficult for them to find an unobstrusive but secure niche in community life.

During the early sixties the territory's Jewish population was so small that it was barely discernible, and even as Colorado boomed in the coming years this minority grew very slowly.[19] A few years later a visiting rabbi commented that the Denver congregation to which he spoke had only about thirty members; when he appeared before what he termed a "slim audience" of his coreligionists he was embarrassed to find that the presence of the governor and a "number of Christian clergymen" made the Jewish delegation appear even smaller.[20] But perhaps that was the secret of the Jews' success; few in number, they interfered with no one, and they came to have what the *Rocky Mountain News* called a "high place" in the community, and acceptance in "the best metropolitan society."[21] While the latter statement was somewhat overdrawn, it contained some truth.

The occasional blacks, many of them former slaves, who turned up in Denver and in some of the mining camps also found early acceptance among the gold-rush businessmen. Like the Jews, they constituted too small a group even to be recognized as a minority; since they had no real voice for protest, they went almost unnoticed in the region's daily life. Under "free colored" the 1860 census listed only 46 blacks, and the "Gilpin census" of the following year could produce no more than 89. By 1870 the figure jumped to 456, representing a sharp percentage increase, but then the ratio began to widen; by 1880 Colorado would have only about twenty-five hundred blacks out of a total population approximating two hundred thousand. That relative decline was to continue. By 1900, there would be about eighty-five hundred blacks among nearly a million Coloradans.

During the early years a good part of the black population performed menial tasks, as it did in other parts of the nation, but apparently more of its members participated in management than was the case in more settled regions. Ed Sanderlin's Larimer Street barbershop prospered from the start. Barney Ford, a runaway slave, became a well-known hotel keeper, and as early as 1859 a newspaper correspondent reported that Denver's Eldorado saloon was managed or owned by J. G. Sims, described as a "colored gentleman, and wealthy, from Cincinnati." A few years later Henry O. Wagoner operated a tavern on Blake Street. More common were boardinghouses operated by blacks, one of which was run by a man who earlier had been a cook on one of the Missouri River steamboats.[22]

As a group the blacks kept largely to themselves, coming to notice in local newspapers only upon some special occasion or perhaps because of some personal difficulty that editors regarded as newsworthy. The anniversary of the termination of slavery in the West Indies was celebrated for symbolic reasons each August, as it was in other parts of the nation, and it provided a special opportunity for social contact among Colorado's handful of black people. In 1864, for example, the celebration was attended not only by those living in Denver but also by some who came down from neighboring mountain towns to join their friends for the day. William J. Hardin, a Kentucky mulatto who was to become well known as one of Denver's more capable orators, held forth at a local theater. The *News* praised his performance and reported that it was delivered with "much grace and admirable gestures." Editor Byers wrote that he had never heard a "more ready or well read colored speaker," and he thought the ideas and arguments set forth were presented cogently and with force. The community had another opportunity to hear Hardin the following spring when blacks gathered to mourn President Lincoln's assassination. At that time the *News,* noting that several black-operated barbershops were closed out of respect for the late president, expressed the opinion that "the colored citizens of this place are about as patriotic as any class of people in the country."[23]

Like the white population in youthful, tumultuous Colorado, blacks occasionally became involved in violence. Green Terrill, a cook for the Wheeler survey party, recalled a wild night in a Denver gambling den when the lights went out and tables, chairs, and glasses flew in the dark. Terrill was hit in the neck by an airborne stool. The next day one of the participants carried around a man's hand as a memento of the battle, but no one arrested him.[24] When black killed black in a shooting scrape the matter usually was dismissed in the manner of the day as "argument settled." Businessman Libeus Barney described one affair in Denver in which the gun of the loser misfired and a coroner's jury quickly absolved the other duelist of any murder charges.[25] Jim Beckwourth's shooting of Bill Payne in 1864 not only was excused by the *News* but was applauded, for Payne was considered to be a dangerous character, having shot down another member of his race in Denver a few years earlier.[26]

Meanwhile, as the existence of substantial amounts of gold in the Colorado mountains came to be an accepted fact in the East, and the somewhat slower but steady flow of arriving miners gave reassurances that places such as Denver would not be ghost towns, those who now were regarded as the earliest settlers continued to improve their positions. Businessmen, including the Jewish merchant class and the few black entrepreneurs, all boosted their newly adopted town and lost no opportunity to tell the world of its exciting possibilities. Growth, of course, was not only a time-honored American measurement of progress, but in the West it stood out as prime evidence that more and more people were making the intelligent choice of a new place in which to live and to do business. Population figures were among the traditional means of showing growth, but so were various business and civic improvements, particularly those that appeared to indicate permanence.

One of the ancient measurements by which a westering people sought to indicate their progressiveness, not to mention the probable longevity of their towns, was the amount of brick used in construction. Boosters invariably stressed this to make a favorable comparison with older American cities. Therefore it was with pride that Denverites wrote of their brick factory, which was running full blast by the spring of 1860, its management promising to produce three million bricks that would sell at eight dollars a thousand. Beyond the desire to copy eastern architecture, the ever-present danger of fire in the mining camps and supply towns encouraged the use of noninflammable materials. When Denver had its first major fire, in the spring of 1860, the need for such construction was reaffirmed in the minds of all. The livery stable of Summers and Dorsett was lost in that conflagration, but the Fashion Saloon was saved by the near frantic efforts of loyal patrons whose bucket brigade drenched the building with water.[27]

Of particular pride to Denver businessmen was the establishment of a private mint in their city in the spring of 1860. The necessity for it arose out of the fact that, except for specie and gold dust, St. Louis currency was the principal medium of exchange. Even dust was hard to come by, because the miners would not part with it at current prices ranging between sixteen and eighteen dollars an ounce and they did not want to pay the 5 percent charge to have it sent to the States. Perhaps as much as $250,000 worth of dust was held back by the miners at this time. Noting the shortage of money in the new country and the great risk of transporting gold dust and coin to and from the mining country, the Leavenworth banking firm of Clark, Gruber and Company established a mint in Denver. From a two-story building at Market and Sixteenth streets came new ten- and twenty-dollar gold pieces marked "Pike's Peak" on one side and "Clark, Gruber and Company" on the other. The first coins, made of pure gold and worth more than corresponding coins from the U.S. Mint, were too soft and had to be replaced with products that contained a hardening material. There being no federal law to prohibit such manufacture, the firm proceeded, turning out some three million dollars' worth in the first two years of operation. So popular was the institution that during the first year a branch was established in Central City. When, in 1863, the federal government purchased the Denver plant, there were no objections because it was assumed that the new operator would continue to produce coins. However, that would not occur until 1906. The mint confined itself to the melting, assaying, and purchasing of gold in exchange for drafts on the U.S. Treasury. Gruber left the bank and in the spring of 1865 the Clarks reorganized their business as the First National Bank of Denver.[28]

During the building boom that the gold rush generated, competition between Denver and Auraria grew so spirited that it threatened to become destructive. The champions of the rival towns did battle for their chosen causes, and also, as the contest heated up, began to cast apprehensive glances over their respective shoulders at a new and rising community nearby that was becoming a real threat. It was a little town called Golden, named for the promise it held, said some; others thought it honored one of the founding fathers, Tom Golden. Understanding the incidence of municipal mortality, the men from Cherry Creek thought they had better join forces to turn back this dangerous rival. During the autumn of 1859 several such efforts were made, but neither of the high-spirited communities was willing to yield to anything. It took an act of the legislative assembly of Jefferson Territory, an organization that really represented a ghost government, to tie the knot. In a moonlight ceremony at the Larimer Street bridge on April 5, 1860, the pair united under the name of Denver. Auraria settled for the title of Denver City, West Division, a cumbersome expression that was lost in the shuffle of community affairs. Since the sponsor, the Territory of Jefferson, soon passed into oblivion, Denver again was incorporated, this time in November 1861.[29]

For the resolute, those who had made their commitment to Denver and its outlying territory, the summer of 1860 was mildly encouraging, enough so that they took hope from it. Perhaps an average of two hundred people arrived daily, only about twenty-five of whom turned around and headed for home. While merchants welcomed the fresh arrivals, they were disappointed that they were not freer with their money. The new transients camped outside of town, ate their own supplies, failed to patronize the city's fine hotels, restaurants, or even the bars, and did not act at all as recklessly as had the Fifty-Niners. "If they stop at a saloon it is only to get a glass of water," grumbled one disappointed businessman who complained that they even brought along their own whiskey. However, he admitted, a few of them left their nearby camps in the evening and patronized the gaming tables. Unfortunately they proved to be far from big spenders. This slackening of pace caused some worry among those who offered a variety of goods and services, but, as one of them said, dull times in the groggeries meant a proportional decrease of "midday rioting and midnight carousals."[30]

So, as Denver watched and waited during that cautious summer of 1860, its boosters continued to place their faith in the future, arguing that when eastbound gold shipments reached sufficiently impressive proportions the nation's capitalists would produce the necessary investment money. It worried them that a certain amount of bad word still was being spread around the East where those moneyed men lived, and they did what they could by printing all manner of encouraging reports in their stripling newspapers. In later years, as some of the old pioneers recalled the young Cherry Creek communities, they confessed that in the light of subsequent progress these places looked decidedly primitive, but for those who lived in Denver and its now silent partner, Auraria, in those beginning years there were no such admissions.[31] To them Denver was young, but she was still a queen, and they proposed that she should reign over the entire commercial territory that reached out for hundreds of miles in all directions.

Denver did not become famous as a mining town, despite what early reports about it led hopeful prospectors to believe. It was a wholesaling center and as such it would be known, then and later. Although it did not always represent the view of those who had gone into the mountains to dig for gold, it was and it continued to be an economic barometer; it gave off readings of the degree of success or failure experienced in the recesses of the Rockies. The recordings of 1860 did not tilt sharply in the direction of unheard of riches; neither did they suggest that Pike's Peak was a hoax, for enough gold had passed through the place to deny that. What the barometer said was that after some cloudy financial weather those who waited around could expect conditions to be fair and warmer. A number of those who had made the arduous trip across the plains decided that, even if the country did not turn out to be a new California, at least it was one that showed promise. Curious, they settled down to await developments.

# 3

# Seeds of a New Society

The men and women who chose to settle in Denver at first thought that if the rush continued as it had progressed during 1859 the place would be a thriving metropolis of twenty thousand within another year. They were amazed not only by the city's rapid growth but also by the multiplicity and refinement of its facilities, usually associated only with older communities. When their hopes of continued dramatic expansion proved too optimistic, those who remained took the view that slow and steady growth was, after all, a much healthier state of affairs and that quality, not quantity, was the true measure of any community.

All along the mountain front, and into the recesses of the Rockies themselves, replicas of the Denver-Auraria settlement blossomed with such rapidity that people in the States had difficulty keeping track of the names. The term "Pike's Peak" still was used to designate a large patch of territory in the general neighborhood of that lofty mountain, but as the days passed the little towns that sprang up gave a more precise identity to geographical locations and the mapmakers were hard at work.[1] Out of this gathering of strangers and their responses to each other, a new society emerged, molded by circumstances and the accident of metallic discovery in a remote part of the Louisiana Purchase. Before long the newcomers began to show a group awareness and a common desire to upgrade the mix of people one day to be called Coloradans.

Not many of those who rushed westward in the search for gold during 1859 had residency in the Rockies on their minds. But, for various reasons, some of those who made the trip for the sake of adventure or because they had nothing more important to do at home found the mountain country attractive and stayed on. A few admitted that they settled down simply because they were too broke to get back home.[2] Some had even more convincing reasons for staying. One bit of Colorado folklore concerns a Dutchman who had committed a serious infraction of the frontier's rather informal laws and was about to be hanged. As the noose was being prepared, he was asked the traditional question as to any last words. With eloquent brevity he outlined his recent history and future expectations: "I come out mit de spring to stay mit de summer and go back mit de fall, but now I t'ink I vill stay all de vile." He was hanged, buried, and certified as one of Colorado's permanent settlers.[3]

Some of those who joined the gold rush were not miners but business or professional men who thought there were greater opportunities to get ahead in a new community than had existed at home. These pioneers, in particular, formed a class that hoped to settle down, and therefore they tried to provide their new lives not only with the comforts but with the cultural trappings of the old. The daughter of an Ohio attorney who settled in one of the mining towns along Clear Creek admitted that a great many of the newcomers neglected to make any effort at "fixing up" on the theory that they would not be around long enough to make the effort worthwhile. Her father thought otherwise. The family brought along all its furniture, including a piano, and as a result the home was both comfortable and attractive. The mother's ability to play and to sing well was welcomed by their neighbors, especially the lonesome miners who missed social activity and music.[4]

The avidity with which Fifty-Niners—a great many of whom were young, unmarried men—seized any opportunity to share in the family life of the few who had established homes in the new country emphasized the maleness of the mining frontier and the degree to which its residents missed the presence of the opposite sex. Whether the women were married or single, old or young, the miners sought their company, for a number of these young men had come directly from home, leaving behind sisters and mothers, not to mention sweethearts, and to them the few women Colorado possessed at the time were treasured imports. The exact ratio of men to women in the 1859 excitement cannot be determined, but in 1860 the census taker found approximately thirty-three thousand men and sixteen hundred women in the area. The proportion was to change radically during the next ten years; by 1870 there would be roughly twenty-five thousand men and fifteen thousand women. That ratio would stay about the same until around 1900, and after that date the figures would approach a balance until 1960, when there would be more women than men in the state.

The predominance of males among the very earliest prospectors attracted prostitutes, but very few other women. Augusta Tabor, who reached Denver in June 1859, said she was the eleventh white woman to arrive; presumably she did not count the professionals.[5] When she and her husband, Horace, moved down to Colorado City, she was given several town lots in honor of being the town's first woman, and when they moved to California Gulch appreciative miners built the Tabors a cabin for the same reason. Skirts did not long remain a novelty at California Gulch. During the next year one of the residents complained that the demand for the "frail sisterhood," to use his term, was more than equaled by the supply.

Not unexpectedly the "sisterhood" was a part of the early Denver scene. "There are but few ladies here," remarked Libeus Barney, "yet there are many females of questionable morality about town, some in bloomer costume and some in gentleman's attire throughout, while squaws are more than plenty."[6] A foreign traveler made a similar comment, remarking that "these lusty fellows" took very freely to the charms of "the Negresses and squaws." Neither report is accurate. Some Arapahoe and Ute women undoubtedly consorted with the miners; so, perhaps, did occasional black women, but such relations by the latter must have been extremely limited, for the census of 1860 showed a total of nine "free, colored, females."[7]

Unfair also was Barney's insinuation that to be classified as a lady one had to look and act the part. For example, no one ever tried to take that title from Julia Archibald Holmes just because she wore bloomers. As the first woman to climb Pike's Peak she described the outfit as both comfortable and practical.[8] Those who affected male attire were not necessarily sexually loose. Elsa Jane Forest, commonly called "Charley," was one of these. When she gulled an eastern reporter with a tearful story of her origins as a southern belle, her early and respectable widowhood, and the necessity of dressing as a man to provide protection against the advances of neighborhood brutes, the *News* erupted in protest. Byers explained that anyone who had witnessed the notorious Charley's smoking, drinking, swearing, and consorting with village loafers soon would see through this thin story.[9] Having made this inventory of

Charley's weaknesses, Byers jumped easily to the conclusion that she was doling out favors to her friends. Women whose clothing surprised the men were not uncommon in the camps. When Daniel Conner passed through Jefferson in the spring of 1862 he came upon "the ugliest woman I ever saw, dressed in a man's clothing, including the plug hat, and herding sheep for some ranchmen."[10] Perhaps, as Charley said, male attire did offer some protection; Conner showed no desire to linger with the shepherdess.

The other "females of questionable morality" to whom Barney referred dressed like ladies but did not act like them. They carried on operations in both "the dance halls and the cribs," said one of their male observers. "Sunny Sadie, Redstocking, and the Colonel's Daughter, to give them the names they were best known by, were to be found in the Progressive and the Criterion." Reassuring his readers, as men invariably do, that these were not his kind of women, the commentator guessed that possibly there were only about three dozen genuine ladies in town.[11]

For lonely miners who did not know the few young ladies in Denver and preferred not to avail themselves of the town's commercialized sex, there were occasional, if rare, opportunities elsewhere. The manager of the Apollo Theater made this discovery one evening as he brushed the floor around the box office in search of gold dust that might have fallen as patrons paid their admissions. Among the sweepings was a tightly folded note whose contents revealed yet another facet of Denver social life after dark. "Dearest Willie," read the billet-doux, "My husband started for the [South] Park yesterday and, if agreeable, please call around ten o'clock this evening. Yours anxiously, Nelly. P.S. Knock at the back door three times. N."[12]

Because of the mining frontier's urban nature there was a great desire for socialization, particularly where it involved the women. By the autumn of 1859 newspaper correspondents were referring to the community's many dances and parties in great detail. One of them wrote of an evening at the Jefferson House in Auraria, remarking that the supper was as fine as one that could have been served in any of the older cities. In attendance were about seventy-five political figures and businessmen, who were described as "good looking, well dressed fellows." The ladies, about thirty in number, were said to be "just as richly got up as you could see then at a fashionable party in St. Louis or Baltimore." Some of the women worked pretty hard at being ladies, several of them flouncing out of the ballroom when actresses from the local theaters turned up, ready to dance.[13] At a very early date Denver society had its caste system.

Perhaps unconsciously the founding fathers of Auraria and Denver used women to measure community progress. One of them, noting the growing number of families and the appearance of a handful of single women, concluded that the community was beginning to "become settled." It seemed to be a matter of civic pride that the women were fitted out in styles that compared favorably with those of the East. When the demands for fashion could not be met, male ingenuity was put to work so that the women would not be denied such benefits. "Hooped skirts are generally sought after by the lady population here," explained a correspondent to a St. Louis paper, "and there being none of the article imported by our merchants yet, necessity under the circumstances has invented a most popular patent-right hooped skirt constructed of buck-elk raw hide!"

Women were so rare that the men viewed them as some sort of special "nuggets," rare finds to be treasured, admired, and viewed with awe. "I tell you, sir," remarked one man after he had been in a remote mining camp for a while, "when I first came down from the gulches into Denver, I would have given a ten-dollar piece to have seen the skirt of a servant-girl a mile off."[14] Another young miner, after attending a ball at the Criterion, on Larimer Street, confessed that he was deeply affected after having watched "these Denver City adorables" in action. Hungrily he took mental inventory of "their dainty mouths, their delicately arched brows, their clouds of silken curls and eyes," all of which caused him to "dream of intangible visions of love and happiness in the future. . . ."[15]

During the summer of 1859 men looking for inexpensive amusement conducted a mock legislature in the evenings, using the rooms used by the actual legislators during the day, and they vied with each other in introducing bills that were humorous, but that invariably suggested the desires of the male community. For example, House Bill No. 323 provided for chartering the Leavenworth City, St. Joseph, and Pike's Peak double-track railroad, with branches to Taos to accommodate the whiskey trade, and to Salt Lake City to import a supply of women. As an indication of which was the most pressing need, a separate resolution was passed authorizing the presiding officer of the Third House, as the group called itself, to negotiate with the governor of Massachusetts for the delivery of approximately a thousand schoolma'ams for the purpose of teaching the population of the territory. The measure was immediately amended to strike the word "teaching" and to insert "marrying," after which it passed unanimously.[16]

A more practical means of attracting unattached women was the subtle advertising campaign carried on by local newspapers. In Colorado, as well as in other western communities, accounts of how lone women were snapped up in the marriage market appeared constantly. Before the year 1859 was out a correspondent at Denver wrote that marriages in the region were becoming quite common. To support his contention he showed that three sisters, all of whom had arrived in an unmarried condition, now enjoyed the happiness and benefits of married life. The eastern United States was regarded as the great source of single women. Aside from the fact that women did not have career opportunities that would be available to them at a later date, the recent Civil War had taken a great toll of men. In the spring of 1866 a New York newspaper complained that the great excess of women meant that their difficulties in finding respectable employment were greater than in other parts of the nation where the situation already was unsatisfactory. Byers noticed the article and suggested the formation of a female emigration society, such as the one earlier originated in Washington Territory, through which women might find employment and perhaps marriage in the territories.[17]

There was need for such labor in Colorado. Wives had a difficult time finding help to maintain their households and to assist in entertainment. "We go to rich dinners and bountiful teas at the homes of distinguished and wealthy citizens, and sit and eat without the company of the hostess or any other ladies," wrote one visitor in 1865. "She and her friends are busy in the kitchen, and come out only to stand behind our chairs, and change the plates and pass the viands." He felt uncomfortable at being entertained in this manner but he confessed that it was a necessity, for help was unavailable and when it could be found the most ordinary kind of female labor brought two dollars a day and board in the mining country.[18]

There were those who thought Colorado needed women for purposes of beautification; others sought them as a source of domestic labor; but there existed a school that regarded their absence as a downright health hazard. Ovando Hollister, for example, complained that there were too many young men "vegetating in shabby hotels and loose-jointed cabins like cellar onions in winter, growing gray between the memories of the past and the hopes of the future, wasting the present." He thought this detrimental to health, morals, and the general welfare of the community. He balked, however, at going along with Byers, who wanted to bring women westward by the carload, for he thought it would make Colorado the butt of coarse wit in other parts of the nation. The territory's young men must not, he warned, make eastern raids in the manner of Romans on the Sabine women; nor could these same women be expected to scour the scattered western settlements in search of mates. His solution to the problem was to encourage resident women to invite female relatives for extended visits so that the local boys would have a better chance. This way the girls would not have to leap into matrimony so suddenly and they could avoid the problem of "keeping young company at fifteen, married at sixteen, and weighed down with the cares of maternity at seventeen, which is not uncommon in Colorado."[19]

Life in the golden West did not appeal to some of the women who made the move. In the spring of 1861 one of them, who had crossed the plains in a covered wagon, noted that over a hundred women had started on the return trip to the States in the previous week; she advised others who might be thinking of coming that they would be better off in the poorhouse. To make matters worse, there were no members of her own sex to whom she could go for sympathy. "I have not spoken to a woman since I came to the mountains," she wrote.[20] Women certainly accepted the notion than hundreds of male admirers thirsted for a look at them, regardless of their age or condition, but less flattering was the demand by males that they prepare food in the manner of their dear old mothers back home. One young miner from Russell Gulch maintained that a year of cooking his own meals was more than enough to satisfy any man and that as it steadily eroded his digestive equipment the desire to send for his wife grew by leaps and bounds. For men not fortunate enough to possess a wife, he said, the alternative was to board with someone so endowed.[21] H. A. W. Tabor was a man who fitted the latter description, and his wife Augusta was drafted as cook. As the couple moved from camp to camp in the Rockies, Augusta invariably found herself tied to the stove. "There were so many men who did not cook, and did not like men's cooking and would insist upon boarding where there was a woman," she wrote. In looking back some years later, Augusta concluded that in those early days the women did more than the men. In addition to preparing meals, they nursed the sick and wounded miners. "I have had so many unfortunate men shot by accident, brought to my cabin to take care of," she recalled. As if this were not enough, Augusta was installed in yet another role; when her husband traveled to Denver with considerable amounts of gold he took his wife along as a precaution against bandits. "I have carried gold on my person many a time," she admitted. "He would buy all the gold that he could and we would carry it down ourselves rather than trust the express, because our express was often robbed."[22] Horace assumed, correctly, that a lady would not be subjected to a personal search by road agents.

Some of the women in the mining camps elected not to spend their days cooking for hungry males. In 1862 Daniel Conner and his fellow miners moved to a new camp named Parkville, located about five miles east of Breckenridge, where they witnessed an example of such independence. In accounting for the town's rapid rise and the acquisition of such entertainment centers as a theater and several billiard halls, he remarked that "an old lady came into the gulch and set up the first 'deadfall' [saloon] in connection with a hotel." Lady bar-owners were not common in remote camps, and this one brought with her an even greater novelty: a young, unmarried daughter, the first of her species in Parkville. Conner explained that they called the girl "Sis" and that men came from miles around just to look at her. Before long more women reached the new town and "Sis" no longer was a major attraction.[23]

Whether in the saloons, where female singers often performed, in the music halls, or at the more formal theaters, men went to see women. If he was fortunate, a man escorted one of the ladies of the community to theatrical performances. Ballrooms, of course, were places where women could be seen and, for the lucky few, joined in the dance. Both theaters and ballrooms were popular in the mining towns.

Entertainment varied in price and quality in early Denver, a town that was said to be decidedly fast. Along the streets stood gaudily decorated bars from which came the sound of tinny but toe-tapping music. The interiors were filled with miners who crowded around the gaming tables, anxious to try their hands at some evening prospecting. One of the better known bars was a place called Denver Hall, built by Charles Blake in the winter of 1858–59 as a combination saloon and gambling establishment. It was, said one disillusioned patron, "the king hell-hole of the consolidated city." Into this palace of pleasure, measuring 50 by 200 feet and supplied with the best music and the best liquor in the Mountain West, some three to five hundred men crowded nightly—on weekends even more—waiting for a chance to get rid of their earnings at one of the twenty-two gaming tables. A variety of opportunities for investment awaited the visitor, who could play at rouge et noir, Spanish monte, French monte, over and under seven, chuck-a-luck, high dice, bluff, roulette, and other games of chance. Gambling was open, and it operated at full blast.[24]

Another type of gambling establishment, where light entertainment also could be found, was the music hall. Denver's Cibola Hall, owned by a former Missouri River pilot named James Reid, was one of the best-known music halls. Here, at fifty cents a seat, the Cibola Minstrels drew audiences of between two and four hundred each night. During slack periods, or between engagements by better known entertainers, the male audience had to settle for the rather mechanical tinkle of music, to which accompaniment a female singer offered indifferent renditions of popular tunes. Bar girls, wearing fixed smiles and nursing tired feet, would dance with the customers for money or drinks. That they had other talents was evidenced by the reputation Cibola Hall gained as a "brothel dance-hall."[25]

Community leaders, anxious to show that culture had reached the foot of the Rockies, tended to play down the gaudier attractions in favor of offerings on the legitimate stage. Aside from providing some tone for the new society, they hoped, uplifting influences would be felt among young men who might otherwise be attracted by bawdier and more suggestive performances. In short, it was better that youth attend plays and operas than frequent bars where hard liquor and easy women were available.

In most mining communities the theater arrived with the first prospectors. In the case of the Pike's Peak rush one of the earliest of the thespian entrepreneurs was Colonel Charles R. Thorne, who in 1858 had retired as manager of Chicago's Metropolitan Hall Theater and, joined by his three sons, had moved to Leavenworth, where they came to know General Larimer. Late in September the colonel and his company pulled into Denver behind dusty oxteams and set up a stage at one end of Apollo Hall. Within a few days they offered the miners their version of a play appropriately entitled *Cross of Gold.* To indicate that genteel society had reached Denver, the Apollo's newspaper advertisement read: "Front seats reserved for ladies." Tickets were available at a dollar and a half. The drama critic of the *News* praised the performance and, as a historical footnote, added the comment that it had been almost exactly a year since the first shanty had been thrown together in this now-bustling city. The Apollo's manager also was pleased, and as he totted up the four hundred dollars taken at the door, he observed that the turnout spoke well for "the patronage if not for the appreciation of art in this semi-barbarous region."[26]

As always the artists had a burden to bear, for no matter how far they penetrated the wilderness they could not escape the presence of critics. One critic referred to the arrival of Thorne's "Thespian chariots" and of the colonel's "attempts at the introduction of drama and ballet in the gold regions," efforts, he said, that were of doubtful merit.[27] Despite this and other published criticisms, performances continued throughout the winter with moderate success. A. B. Steinberger, recently of Omaha, who may have been Colorado's first playwright, offered his work *Skatara, of the Mountain Chieftain,* a drama in four acts, at the Apollo in December 1859.[28] No mention was made of its fate at the hands of the critics.

Despite heavy competition from music halls and some discouraging setbacks to the sponsors of thespian art in the mining country, the Denver-Auraria stage continued to offer culturally uplifting productions. Late in 1860 the *News,* bursting with civic pride, asserted that a recent musical evening at Broadwell Hall was the "most brilliant affair in the history of Denver." The editor was pleased to report that a "larger number of ladies and gentlemen than we have ever seen convened in this city" made up the audience, a gathering that reminded him of fashionable concert occasions in eastern cities. Duets and solos by several women, a male choir, and solos by a guitarist and a violinist were offered to this discriminating audience.[29] When the People's Theater opened in 1861, similar praise flowed from the *News.*[30]

Apparently there was some backsliding in this exemplary conduct on the part of the audience, for when Denver's new Platte Valley Theater presented *Richard the Third* on its opening night the reporter felt constrained to admit that much noise and disturbance in the cheaper seats marred the production. "The conduct and language of a few rowdies in the gallery was most shameful," he wrote, promising that in the future policemen would be on hand to prevent any deflowering of Denver's budding cultural garden.[31] Audience conduct was little better in some of the neighboring towns. When the well-known actor and entrepreneur John ("Jack") Langrishe and Michael J. Dougherty offered a stage production to the theatergoers of Central City in 1861, the hall was crowded to capacity. The play, *Nick of the Woods,* went off well enough, except for the interruption of a few boisterous members of the audience who offered unsolicited jokes of their own and in general made nuisances of themselves. Probably this was taken in stride by Dougherty, who never refused a drink and usually was well insulated from extraneous interruptions. He died at Central City in 1865, presumably of acute alcoholism.

Despite its early success in Colorado the legitimate theater began to experience difficulty in filling the seats. By the spring of 1869 editor Byers of the *News,* who was an ardent supporter of the theater, noted that while the closing performances of the season were well attended and while Denver owed much to Jack Langrishe, stage productions, in general, were attracting increasingly smaller audiences. Perhaps, he suggested, it was due merely to the general business stagnation.[32] Another explanation was the competition offered by gayer evening performances at such music halls as The Cricket. Byers warred constantly on these places of all-night entertainment that were the forerunners of the city's nightclubs, and he lost no opportunity to publicize any trouble that occurred on their premises. Cricket Hall, to use its more formal title, was built during the late 1860s, and it quickly gained an unsavory reputation.[33]

In a heavily male society only a certain amount of refined entertainment would sell, and in time even the "leg art" offered in more informal establishments lost some of its fascination. Soon the miners and their friends turned to sporting events. As early as the spring of 1862 baseball teams were playing at Denver. The competition was carried on somewhat haltingly, since only a few members of the teams ever had played before. So they read the rules and took the field, a local sports reporter commenting that it would take a few more meetings to enable them to become proficient at the game. Apparently these were not pitchers' duels, for on this occasion the *News* reported a score of eighteen to twenty-eight, the runs being referred to as "tallies."[34]

In that same sporting year of 1862, racing attracted crowds at Denver. But as it did in theaters, the rowdy element left its mark upon the event. At one performance, in which horse, pony, and foot racing were featured, an argument took place as to who was the winner of one of the footraces and, amidst charges of "fix," a general free-for-all erupted in which revolvers and knives made their appearance. That autumn the advent of formal horse racing brought out both spectators and greenbacks in considerable numbers, and the contests were so orderly that it was a matter of note in the press that no fighting occurred.[35] For those who enjoyed fisticuffs, but only as a spectator sport, Denver offered its ring attractions. On a windy spring day in 1863 a highly publicized prizefight was staged near Parkin's ranch just outside the city. For a purse of $250 William McDonough and James Raffles entertained a large crowd of sports enthusiasts, McDonough taking the money with an eleventh-round knockout.[36]

Another source of light entertainment was the annual territorial fair, where band music, variety acts, and racing amused those who were tired of looking at agricultural exhibits. Before the end of the sixties Denverites also had an opportunity to attend performances at a traveling circus. When Dan Castello brought his troupe to town a sellout crowd enthusiastically applauded the gaily outfitted artists who displayed their acts.[37]

Almost from the outset the efforts of Coloradans to reproduce American society as they knew it—but, they hoped, with some of its more undesirable aspects omitted—were evident to newcomers or visitors who examined the young community. As in other parts of the nation, particularly in the newer western communities, the presence of any representation of the national culture, whether it was the construction of an opera house or the visit of a traveling circus, attracted wide attention in the mining country. In a day when the only communication medium was the printed word, those who wanted to make known the presence of cultural opportunities or to publicize any of the new institutions necessarily turned to the newspapers. These information outlets, often small and marginal in their operations, loomed large in the mining camps and the supply cities, their editors serving as constant propagandists for community growth and refinement. The little weeklies and dailies were the mouthpieces, the promoters, and the most loyal supporters of the young towns. Although frequently they constituted no more than a secondhand press in a dingy, rented building with a printer-turned-editor, the newspapers must be regarded as important frontier Colorado cultural institutions.

Among the first of the journalists to reach the Pike's Peak country were William N. Byers, who founded the *Rocky Mountain News* in April 1859, and John L. Merrick, whose *Cherry Creek Pioneer* briefly challenged the *News*. Within a few months Thomas Gibson, who had come west with Byers, began the *Rocky Mountain Gold Reporter and Mountain City Herald* at Mountain City, a "suburb" of Central City. It was followed shortly by the appearance of *The Western Mountaineer* of Golden. The owner of this paper, George West, shortly took leave to participate in the Civil War, after which he returned to Golden in 1866 and started the *Colorado Transcript*.[38] In the autumn of 1860, H. S. Millet began issuing the *Canon City Times* with cast-off equipment earlier used by several other newspapers that had made brief appearances in the territory. Due to the shifting of western routes occasioned by the Civil War, Canon City did not flourish in the manner its founders had anticipated; as its population dwindled, so did the prospects for its newspaper. In the autumn of 1861 Millet gave up his journalistic efforts and left for the States. Anson Rudd, who became a longtime resident of Canon City, later recalled the paper's demise and explained that "whiskey got away with it." This left southern Colorado without a newspaper until Dr. Michael Beshoar's *Colorado Chieftain*, founded at Pueblo in 1868, filled the gap. Although Beshoar soon sold his interest, the new editor, J. J. Lambert, edited it continuously for the remainder of the nineteenth century and made it one of the state's finest newspapers.[39]

Beyond Denver to the northwest lay a number of little towns, a great many of which had newspapers, although in some instances the lifespan of such publications was brief. Reading matter was in such great demand at Boulder that some exuberant residents engaged in piracy to acquire a newspaper. The *Bulletin*, published at nearby Valmont, was hijacked one spring night in 1867 and hauled off to Boulder, handpress, type, and all, where it reappeared as the *Boulder Valley News*. It was succeeded by the *Pioneer*, a newspaper that elected not to go along with the mainstream of the town's thinking and, as a result, was forced out of existence.[40]

The demise of the *Pioneer* suggests that, rather than being opinion molders, newspapers were obliged to respond to local pressures. If they were not particularly creative, editors certainly were willing associates of the business and professional classes who sought to lead the little towns, and they gave freely of their time and talent in support of local projects. It was a constant source of irritation to them that the residents did not always respond financially by subscribing to their journals and, even worse, displayed a chronic disinterest in paying for past services. Columns of early Colorado small-town papers are spiced with invective directed at laggardly patrons of the printed word although at the same time these deadbeats collectively were held up to the outside world as the highest type of humanity, whom the community indeed was fortunate to have as members. Constantly frustrated, the editors often drank too much, went broke, and sought out some new, more promising paragon of civic rectitude to praise; then, perhaps, they repeated the process. In the manner of pick and pan miners they floated from camp to camp, prospecting in print, but never really expecting the big bonanza.

As voices of public opinion in the new country the newspapers reflected a general desire to tell the world not only of the great mineral finds in the Rockies but also of the discovery of a place where climate, a refreshingly new society, and unlimited economic opportunities promised an ideal life in a land unsullied by man's carelessness or improvidence. Here, said men on the streets, was the time and the place to install some of the traditional American institutions in this virgin land and to plant the seeds for as near an ideal society as mortals could expect.

# 4

# Old Institutions in a New Country

A federal judge who came west on assignment during the 1860s commented that, in general, "the New Englander is not a pioneer: he follows the frontiersman just about the time the church and school house catch up."[1] In many ways his comment applies to those who became community leaders in Colorado and whose descendants perpetuated their ideals. These were business and professional men who settled in the new towns and provided services for miners, stockmen, and farmers. As a rule they were not frontier types, but rather townsmen from older parts of the country who sought to upgrade and to transport westward some of the elements of civilization they had grown up with and accepted as being desirable.

In addition to the daily tasks in their shops, stores, and offices, they participated in politics, supported their local editors, and urged each other to become active in municipal and statewide politics. As a group they endorsed local projects such as the building of schoolhouses, reading rooms, churches, and other municipal improvements. From time to time they were accused of engaging in these good works because they hoped to develop a reputation for Colorado that would make it attractive to settlers, and hence to prospective customers. This they did not deny, but they held that if these cultural refinements made the place a better one in which to live one hardly could question their motives.

Inherent in the concept of providing cultural facilities and promoting what the nation's founding fathers had referred to as domestic tranquillity was the notion of social guidance and control.

This goal could be approached through general movements as well as by the establishment of traditional institutions long believed to be important in the development of a stable society. Among the latter, schools and churches were recognized as being necessities if raw, unsettled portions of the frontier were to be domesticated and made to look like other portions of America. Consequently these were among the first agencies of moral and intellectual improvement to be found among the Fifty-Niners.

During the entire westward movement frontiersmen had brought along their religion as a part of the cultural baggage deemed important in the move to a new and untried land. The outward evidence of this inclusion was not always visible; godlessness appeared to dominate the life of incipient western settlements, whether they were end-of-track construction camps, cattle-shipping points, or mining towns. The momentary wildness of such places gave rise to the saying that there was no Sunday west of Junction City and no God west of Salina. Frequently Dodge City was mentioned as the westernmost outpost of God's domain. That appeared to leave Colorado beyond redemption.

If the territory was not quite irredeemable, nonreligious activities offered much competition to worship on the Lord's day. "Sunday is very generally observed by the miners," wrote one prospector. "No work is done, except patching up, tinkering around the cabin, doing their trading, retorting quick silver etc. The saloons, groceries, gambling halls, etc. are always in full blast on Sundays and there is generally more gambling, drinking and fighting then than on any other day." However, at his little camp there were services of some kind each Sunday night. Sometimes it was more a lecture than a sermon, but "preaching is held regularly" in the mining country, he wrote, usually in theaters, occasionally in a miner's cabin.[2]

Colorado was far from godless either before or after the "Anglo" invasion of 1859. It became predominantly Protestant in these early mineral years, as the great waves of prospectors and settlers quickly diluted the Catholicism of the Mexican Americans who had drifted northward from New Mexico. Rather than merely filling a religious vacuum, the Protestants were militant "anti-Romanists" who sought not only to serve the needs of the miners but also to rescue them from any possible infection of "Papism." One example of the fervor with which the Protestant crusaders moved into Colorado was the penetration of the "Blue Banner" Presbyterians who marched as avenging troops against Mormons, Catholics, and others regarded as species of infidels. These "Christian soldiers" talked in terms of fighting battles, occupying strategic points, posting pickets, establishing outposts, and the like; their military vocabulary bespoke an active, well-organized group bent upon achieving a cherished goal.[3]

Churchmen who came west with the gold seekers sought to implant something of the religion they had known in the East rather than embark upon innovative programs. While they recognized that the West was new and rough around the edges, they did not think its people irreligious. Congregationalist minister William Crawford of Massachusetts, who roamed the mountain front during the sixties, was not discouraged by what he saw. "Perhaps there are some who think our society is so rude and wicked that there is no living here in comfort," he wrote from Central City. "Wicked enough, rough enough it is, but not wholly so. In few places will one meet with more well-informed and cultivated people, or with pleasanter families. Our people demand and can appreciate good preaching." The Reverend Crawford's praise of Coloradans did not mean he saw no possibilities for conversions. He told his superiors in the East that funds would have to be forthcoming to support workers in the religious field, for in the bustling mining communities "the money is not in the hands of Christians, and we cannot get it from others." He admitted further that in this new society "the excitement is unfavorable to the progress of spiritual religion. Those who live in the quiet towns of New England do not know what we have to contend with."[4] Nevertheless this earnest Congregationalist did not think that he was among heathens or atheists.

Other Protestant crusaders found frontier conditions equally challenging. In the swirl and confusion of the mineral rush, sometimes it was difficult for the men of God to get a hearing, but in the contest for audiences the Methodists ranked high. Of the seventeen branches of Methodism, five eventually came to Colorado, and of this group the Methodist Episcopal church was the most significant. Among the early names those of H. W. Goode and Jacob Adriance stand out. They reached Denver-Auraria in June of 1859 as part of the first big group of prospectors, and they began their pastoral duties at once. As one pioneer later wrote, these early preachers had much to contend with in attracting the attention of the miners, and before long they realized that the best way to get a crowd was to "sing it up." In addition to the "sing along" services, they offered prayers in tents, in saloons, in gambling halls, and even on the open streets. Whatever the site, preaching was demanding work. One of the Reverend George W. Fisher's listeners thought the preacher was given a very discouraging reception. But when he heard Fisher hold forth at Gregory Diggings and realized that the audience of some twenty miners had been drawn away from a nearby saloon and faro bank, he admitted that such religious prospecting produced surprising results from what appeared to be religious bedrock.[5]

Another miner praised both Fisher and Jacob Adriance, both of whom, he said, had done more good and had made greater sacrifices than "half a dozen of your advertised D.D.'s in their cushioned pulpits and stained glass windows of the East!"[6] This comment points to the great success of the pioneer preachers. While the miners did not always profess a need for religious succor, they had to admire the fortitude with which the rustic-appearing men of God went about their work in that new and untried country. So they listened.

By 1860 the Methodist Episcopal church had established a Rocky Mountain mission, headed by John M. Chivington, who was to become a widely known and highly controversial personality in Colorado; within that mission four subdistricts served the more important mining towns. By 1864 the energetic Methodists had established Colorado Seminary, the forerunner of the University of Denver.[7] In smaller communities they sought to establish themselves by the construction of churches, the outward evidences that organized religion had come to stay. Sometimes they were surprised at the friendly reception given in remote places. For example, when Bishop Chivington dispatched one of his subordinates to the mining camp of Hamilton with orders to seek out some souls, it was thought that the harvest might be meager, but to the minister's surprise he found in that raw mining camp not only the personnel for a congregation but also the desire among his followers to construct a log church. Within a matter of days a primitive structure dedicated to the Methodist Episcopal branch of religion was commenced high in the Rockies.[8]

The missionary zeal of the Methodists rivaled that of the Presbyterians. In later years, when one of them conducted revival meetings in the North Fork country of western Colorado, the degree of emotional intoxication felt by his listeners sometimes reached stratospheric levels. On one historic occasion a German-Russian participant not only prayed for the forgiveness of his own sins but in an outburst of religious fervor requested that an infamous neighborhood horse thief, cattle rustler, and drunkard receive celestial consideration. "Oh, God," he entreated, "come down and save dis miserable sinner. But don't send your son Yesus, for dis is no boy's yob."[9] The circuit riders could have told him that neither was theirs a "boy's yob." It was demanding, sometimes dangerous work, in a raw country.

The Protestant Episcopal church generally fell far behind others who were engaged in missionary fieldwork across the West, but its representatives came early to Colorado and stayed late. In January 1860, Father John Kehler preached a sermon along the banks of Cherry Creek and came up with $8.85 in the ecclesiastical pan.[10] A few weeks later he conducted services indoors, this time at the Apollo Theater on Larimer Street, but even then the sounds of the mining frontier were not far away. The theater was located above a saloon and billiard hall, and as Kehler spoke of heavenly matters, the nether regions emitted temporal echoes of clicking ivory balls and beer glasses. In time religious services were offered more private quarters, but the little churches that emerged were tiny dots in a vast and undeveloped land. When William H. Moore founded the Church of St. John's in the Wilderness he made the comment that his creation was seven hundred miles from the nearest church. However, reinforcements were not far away, and soon some important Episcopal figures began to turn up in Colorado. During that same year Bishop Joseph C. Talbot accepted a field assignment that took him to Central City and a few years later Bishop George M. Randall arrived as missionary bishop. It was under Randall's guidance that Episcopalians carried out the work for which they were so well known in the West: the founding of schools, an example of which was Matthews Hall, a theological seminary established at Golden.[11] The bishop was also instrumental in building the first church at Pueblo, St. Peter's Episcopal Church, which opened there in 1869.[12]

Although Catholic missionaries became famous among the western Indians, they were not otherwise very active on the frontier. Like the Protestant Episcopal church, the Roman Catholic church was not nearly so aggressive in Colorado as were some of the more militant Protestant groups. It may be said that the Catholics arrived early—the first church in Colorado, Our Lady of

Guadalupe, was founded at Conejos in 1858—but in the field they offered little competition to the fierce missionary zeal of the "Blue Banner" legions. Father Joseph P. Machebeuf, who accompanied the famed Bishop Jean Baptiste Lamy to New Mexico, stands out as a leading Catholic figure on the Colorado scene. When he and Father John B. Raverdy arrived in Denver in the autumn of 1860 they found but two hundred Catholics in a population of some three thousand; nevertheless, they set to work building a church. It was a small beginning, but by the middle of the twentieth century the Catholics were easily the largest religious denomination in the state.[13]

While ordinary Fifty-Niners gladly accepted the volunteer services of their chaplains, leaders of the embryonic civic establishment encouraged the construction of church buildings, which, they felt, would be far more suggestive of a permanent settlement. Equally important in their eyes was the need for a building that symbolized education. Schools and churches, often housed in the same building in new communities, had become traditional symbols of Anglo-Saxon claims staked out in the wilderness. As early as August 1859, the newly founded *Rocky Mountain News* complained that the prospective Queen City of the Plains had neither of these facilities. Although the city fathers did not respond by immediately erecting a little red schoolhouse, by early autumn classes were under way at the little settlement on the banks of Cherry Creek.

Education came to Colorado in a manner colorful enough to please even the most adventurous miners. It was brought by O. J. Goldrick, a dapper little Irishman who drove into town wielding a long bull-whackers' whip over a team of weary oxen. Impeccably dressed in broadcloth, a "boiled" shirt, a shiny silk hat, and kid gloves to protect his slender hands from the burning sun, he was reputed to have exhibited his erudition by roundly cursing the lumbering beasts in Latin. Perhaps no entrance ever generated so much comment or attracted so much attention as that of "the Professor" who at once became one of the territory's "characters."[14]

By October the new schoolmaster was teaching some fifteen young scholars, two or three of whom were part Indian, three or four more what Goldrick described as "Mexican half-breeds," and most of the remainder Missourians. Their parents or guardians paid three dollars a head per month "and no questions asked." In the time-honored tradition of teaching, the educator carried on some moonlighting to make ends meet; by serving as a correspondent to eastern newspapers Goldrick earned another twenty dollars a week. At first he taught his classes in a crude log cabin, the flat roof of which funneled rain and snow on the occupants, but by November a larger place was provided. By the next year, primary education in Denver had progressed to a point where still more comfortable quarters were rented, and the "Professor" was obliged to hire a young lady to assist him in his work. The year 1860 also saw the establishment of a second school in Denver.[15]

The desire of the *News* for Colorado to have a permanent building devoted exclusively to education was not satisfied until 1860 when Abner R. Brown began teaching at Boulder. This educator had come to mine gold, but when he passed through the little supply town in the spring of 1860 he wondered at the number of children he saw and, upon inquiry, learned that there were about forty prospective students. It was enough. He left his fellow gold hunters and announced his intention to commence instruction. With the help of local families he put together a frame and shingle building, fashioned benches and desks from cheap pine boards, and constructed a stove from scrap iron retrieved from an abandoned mine. At a cost of about twelve hundred dollars, Colorado's first school building was ready for occupancy by winter. When schoolmaster Brown was not holding forth over his charges, the structure was used as both a church and a meeting hall.[16]

Meanwhile, primary education expanded in Denver. Since there were no tax supported schools in the Territory until 1862, the earliest organizations were sponsored privately. There were four such institutions in Denver in 1861. A private school opened in 1860 at Golden, where a handful of students were taught, and two years later one was opened at Pueblo. During this period residents of Nevada City donated lots for the construction of a school building and collectors made the rounds soliciting donations for the enterprise.

Without doubt Colorado's earliest effort to provide adult education came with the opening of a night school in Denver late in 1859, when one of the clerks from the legislature, a Spaniard by birth, offered instruction in both Spanish and French, both of which were spoken in local business firms.[17]

By the mid 1860s primary instruction had gained a foothold in Colorado, but secondary education apparently was not considered to be of equal importance. Not until 1874, when East High was opened in Denver, did the territory have a high school. During the sixties the *News* complained that Denver, a progressive city of four thousand, had not done right by its youngsters because it had not supplied them with sufficient educational facilities. In the autumn of 1866, when the editor visited the school directed by D. B. Hatch, he said that about a hundred and fifty students were crowded into two rooms. He called such facilities a disgrace and dishonor to the city.[18]

Hatch had other complaints. One of his students later recalled that the principal objected to the presence of black students and resigned in protest to open a private institution that drew off a number of pupils whose parents objected to integration.[19] The question was publicly aired at this time, the *News* taking the view that there should be equal but separate facilities for both races. Byers expressed the current Denver attitude toward blacks: "We do not propose to eat, drink or sleep with one, and neither do we believe it right that our children should receive their education in Negro classes." His proposed solution was separate schools, with each group contributing proportionally to its own institutions. Considering the size of Colorado's black community at this time, such schools for blacks would have received practically no funding.[20]

The school integration question that aroused "Professor" Hatch and editor Byers in 1866 was not new to Colorado. Two years earlier the black residents of Central City had complained because they were being taxed for school purposes yet their children were barred from the public schools. After they petitioned the General Assembly without success, the parents engaged legal counsel and demanded entrance into the public system. They received it in 1869; meantime, a separate school accommodated the twelve local black children who were excluded from the all-white educational system.[21]

During this period the press gave strong support to education, both public and private, arguing that it had an important bearing upon the future of both the territory and the entire West. The *News* called common schools "the ground work of our society" and suggested that taxpayers offer more money and less complaint in support of this worthy cause.[22] That paper's notion of high quality was the employment of men only, as administrators, who would hire "none but capable teachers"—presumably women—to instruct the young. The ladies so engaged were expected to be more than capable; their conduct had to be far beyond reproach. When it was discovered later that one Denver teacher was in the habit of sending out a pupil at recess for fifteen cents worth of beer as a bracer, this breach of morality made the local papers. A sympathetic editor defended her, arguing that anyone cooped up with a roomful of unruly children for seven or eight hours a day had more than earned a mild stimulant and that a tot of beer was in the same league as a cup of tea.[23]

In addition to being teetotalers, school teachers were expected to demonstrate their professional expertise by passing written examinations that were held periodically; only those who passed would be issued licenses to practice. Apparently authorities felt that they could set high standards almost from the beginning of Colorado's educational history, for among the earliest arrivals were a number of men and women who were qualified to teach. During the 1860s Byers of the *News* remarked that the territory had more than enough women to conduct primary schools and lamented the fact that such a surplus existed at a time when domestics were in short supply. He classified the latter group as "laboring women," setting them apart from those who merely could teach.[24] On the frontier practical talents held a high priority.

Despite the establishment of public schools, private schools continued to be opened in the young Territory after 1862. When a girls' school named Wolfe Hall commenced operations in Denver during 1868 the *News* called it a new argument in behalf of Colorado's developing civilization. The next year Jarvis Hall, a school for boys, opened at Golden; later, when it closed, the building was used as a State Industrial School for boys.[25]

During these years public schools were opened in other parts of the state; Pueblo, Trinidad, Colorado City, Central City, Black Hawk, and Nevada all established school districts. Some of the classes were held in improvised quarters; a former saloon was used at Central City, and an abandoned billiard parlor housed the students at Black Hawk. By the time of statehood Colorado would have over 20,000 young people, a high percentage of whom would be enrolled in the schools. Although the residents were anxious to provide their children with these facilities, and the administrators and teachers entered their duties with enthusiasm, efforts to improve the minds of young scholars occasionally met with discouraging reverses. For example, although the first public school at San Luis opened in 1866, not until the spring of 1919 could the institution boast its first eighth-grade graduate.[26]

Colorado's pioneers, both young and old, desired to read and to know. Treasured books often were among their transported possessions; and it was not at all unusual to find in a prospector's or settler's cabin well-thumbed copies of the works of Scott, Thackeray, or Dickens. Letters and diaries of these frontiersmen constantly refer to the desire for reading material and the longing for information from home. "If we only had a good library of books to draw from we could pass the winter quite pleasantly," wrote one young prospector who had left his studies to join the gold rush.[27] Unable to get hold of any books, he settled for out-of-date eastern newspapers at twenty-five cents a copy or read the scanty national news published in local papers.

He was not alone in his hunger for the printed word. In the early spring of 1860 a group of merchants and professional men founded a library and reading room association in Denver-Auraria. With great enthusiasm they elected officers, appointed a selection and purchasing committee, and awarded honorary memberships to important molders of local opinion such as ministers and newspaper editors. Unhappily, other forms of entertainment such as gambling and the parlor houses diverted the attention of potential readers, and within a short time the whole project collapsed.[28] Some members simply failed to pay their monthly dues of fifty cents; one member, John Shear, was hung for horse thievery.

Ostensibly, library associations were organized for the purpose of intellectual and cultural elevation, as well as to fill a need for leisure-time reading, but there were indications that the desire to exercise social control lingered in the minds of community leaders. Running through newspaper editorials of Colorado towns for these years is the theme that such institutions would offer alternatives to barrooms and bawdyhouses and that if given the opportunity young men would frequent the more respectable places. The *Rocky Mountain News* was particularly active in this campaign. On one occasion it suggested that funds accrued from municipal fines be earmarked for construction of a public library, one of whose purposes would be to keep the city's youth off the streets. Consequently, the use of reading rooms for other kinds of recreation and entertainment was stressed by those who sought ways of redirecting the recreational time of young people.

When the various institutions failed in their efforts to set good examples and to provide uplifting influences, other instruments of control traditionally employed by society had to be brought into use. Law and order were regarded not only as necessities in new communities but as attributes that would attract desirable settlers. The institutions that carried out the dictates of the law were less popular, but it was generally agreed that they were a public necessity.

Fortunately lawlessness, so popular a subject among those who have written about early days in the mining camps, made only a brief appearance in Colorado. There were the usual disputes over the comparative merits of poker hands, over women, and between claimants for land, not a few of which resulted in personal violence, but conditions did not call for extensive vigilante action such as that witnessed earlier in California or later in Montana.

For a brief period during the first days of the gold rush, local vigilance committees were obliged to take the law into their own hands on occasion. In the case of Edgar Vanover of Golden, preventive justice was employed. He was hung after a citizens' committee decided that he was lethally dangerous when drinking and that such an action on the committee's part would tend to upgrade the local level of law and order.[29] Witnesses were impressed by how orderly these public hangings were; somehow the solemn deliberation with which the act was performed made it seem more legal. As a rule these spectators concluded that they never wanted to see anything of the kind again, so dreadful was the scene, but on the other hand it often left them with the feeling that they had observed a necessary step in the judicial development of a new country.

Hangings and lynchings caused comment, even in rough mining camps. Those who spent their days in the camps of Colorado, working, socializing, and passing their time in a normal fashion, usually reported that there were few disturbances in their respective neighborhoods. In most of the mining towns there was little serious crime. In Central City, neighborhood crime was so minimal, and punishment of transgressors so severe, that people went to sleep at night in unlocked cabins with bags of gold dust under their pillows. The early establishment of miners' courts and the arrival of federal judges by 1861 meant that in many of the Colorado camps there was almost no "Wild West" period. In some camps the carrying of firearms was prohibited from the very beginning, and about the only need for law officers was to control the effects of public drunkenness on Sundays and holidays.[30]

In the spring of 1861 President Lincoln nominated three judges for Colorado Territory: Benjamin F. Hall, E. Newton Pettis, and Charles Lee Armour. Governor Gilpin then established three judicial districts and assigned Hall to Denver, Pettis to Central City, and Armour to Canon City. By July the system was functioning; courts opened, marshals began their duties, and attorneys were examined to determine their qualifications to practice law in the territory. Law had come to Colorado and everyone was happy; Byers of the *News* praised Justice Hall for the promptness with which he had entered upon his duties.[31]

Despite public pleasure at the establishment of formal law enforcement, some problems were to be expected in the early operation of new machinery. Justice Pettis lasted only a month before leaving for home, and during his stay he failed to try a single case. Justice Armour, who was transferred to Central City, irritated one of the local attorneys to the extent that the offended lawyer posted a large handbill publicly labeling Armour a coward and a liar. The justice became so unpopular that the General Assembly tried to "sagebrush" him, that is, to assign him to a remote post, in this case Conejos and Costilla counties in southern Colorado. Armour refused to accept his exile; instead he remained in the territory, passing his time smoking expensive cigars, drinking toddies, and drawing a salary until his term expired. Irascible on the bench and unpredictable in his everyday conduct, Armour tyrannized those who came before his court. Meantime editor Byers, angry at Hall for his remarks about the "rebel" propensities of Coloradans during the Civil War, endorsed the accusations of a journalist who described the justice as a "vain, bloated, egotistical, self-complacent, bombastic, ignorant old ass."[32] In August 1863, Hall returned to Auburn, New York, to resume his law practice.

After a somewhat tumultuous start, the Colorado judicial system began to function more smoothly, and, with the appointment of such men as Moses Hallett as chief justice, a new era was launched. The rough-and-ready manner in which the bench was managed has been a source of much amusement to writers of early Colorado history. These accounts make enjoyable reading, but more discriminating historians have looked beyond the label of judicial carpetbaggers and have awarded a fairly high grade to the efforts of these pioneer jurists.[33]

A necessary complement to the court system was a facility for housing those sentenced to imprisonment for their transgressions. The mining camps provided crude jails at an early date, the relics of which are tourist attractions today; the little wooden shed with barred windows at Creede is but one example. As cities and counties emerged they provided such accommodations as a natural requirement for any respectable, law-abiding community. Also needed was a satisfactory penitentiary for lawbreakers who were given extended time behind bars. Its necessity was quickly recognized by those who saw it as another instrument of control in a growing society that promised to become more complex as time passed.

As early as 1862 the territory's second governor, John Evans, asked Congress for money with which to establish such an institution. Congressional response was slow, but after a five-year wait Coloradans learned that $40,000 had been appropriated for the purpose. Further delay was encountered when a political fight broke out as to where the building should be erected, but this was resolved by compromise and southern Colorado was promised that Canon City was to be the site. Legend has it that the town had a choice of state institutions, being offered either the university or penitentiary, and that it chose the latter. Although this story continues to delight members of the university at Boulder, there appears to be no historical evidence to support it. Canon City not only acquired the penitentiary but also supplied the first warden, Anson Rudd. Under his direction the establishment "opened for business" in June 1871.

The military had been present on the frontier since the earliest days of the nation. Although its role in western communities was intended to be protection of the white population against Indian incursions, that threat faded quite early in Colorado, and the troops spent most of their time doing garrison duty. The contemporary view of the western soldier was that of a poorly educated, ambitionless man, content to while away his life at some lonely western outpost for a few dollars a month and an occasional chance to brawl in nearby saloons and brothels while the officers drank themselves to death in their own quarters. But there is another side to the story. The western forts frequently represented outposts of civilization where at least some of the personnel carried on normal family life despite crude physical conditions. The post chaplain, the doctor, and the officers in general contributed considerably to the society in which they moved, whether it was a remote station or near a settled area where they could circulate with their civilian neighbors, make friends with them, and share their social lives. In Colorado these men, many of whom were intelligent and of a cultivated background, passed their days watching a new community grow.

During the Civil War and the years that followed, at a time when Colorado was experiencing a rapid occupation by farmers, ranchers, miners, and others who wanted to develop its many resources, the military establishments not only attempted to ensure peace but also acted as stopping points for travelers and as centers of communication in undeveloped portions of the territory. Fort Massachusetts, established in 1852 in the lower San Luis Valley, was the first American army post in what was to become Colorado. Six years later it was moved a few miles to the south and renamed Fort Garland.[34] It protected the small Mexican-American settlements that edged northward out of New Mexico and offered hospitality to passersby, who long remembered the warmth of their welcome, the pleasant strains of an excellent little band, and the colorful uniforms and other trappings about the place that reminded them of home. From the sutler's store, travelers could obtain anything from Wiltshire hams to stationery or cosmetics. At night, when burning piñon logs gave off a pleasantly pungent fragrance, sometimes the post surgeon or the commandant led group singing; those for whom this had no interest played cards or read. Visitors found life at the fort interesting and even exciting, but the men who were stationed there frequently regarded it as boring and lonely; an occasional stranger bearing news from home was one of the few reliefs from this silent monotony.[35] The forts, then, sentinels at the western edge of the Great American Desert, did not attract attention in the mining rush, but their stabilizing presence was an element in Colorado's infant society whose contributions often have been overlooked.

Having attempted to furnish their communities with long-accepted, basic institutions, the founders resolved that, if at all possible, they would stay in Colorado. They were aware that mining, especially placer mining, was of a transitory nature, and that even if quartz mining could be developed to a point of profitability the future of that industry was too uncertain a base upon which to build a permanent society. But they reflected upon the California experience, telling themselves that frequently mining fostered other elements of the economy; perhaps, if they were able to weather the early years of uncertainty, Colorado would become a desirable place to live and one whose residents could prosper. Having laid out their basic plan for the future, they tried to look ahead to a time when the gamble they were making would prove correct.

PART TWO

# The Age of Acquisition

# 5

# The Uncertain Years

The miners had penetrated the unsettled West far enough to find themselves isolated from the States. Those who wanted to get rich and go home were not concerned about this temporary separation, but the men and women who regarded the mountain country as their new home wanted it to develop and were anxious to establish both physical and political connections with the East.

Efforts to gain permanent roots came at a difficult time in national history. The Territory of Colorado was created on February 28, 1861, on the eve of the Civil War, and its first governor, William Gilpin, did not arrive until some six weeks after the outbreak of that conflict. Although the nation was far too busy with other matters to pay much attention to the stripling community at the base of the Rockies, the action of Congress was a step forward so far as the Coloradans were concerned; now they knew at least under which jurisdiction they lived. Prior to that time the miners working south of the fortieth parallel resided in the western end of Kansas and those north of that line were in Nebraska. Prospectors who ventured beyond the Continental Divide found themselves in Utah, while farmers in much of the San Luis Valley were residents of Taos County, New Mexico. Thus Gilpin, the executive head of a territory made up of scraps from other political entities, began his duties in the midst of the greatest internal disturbance the American people ever had experienced. It was difficult for his voice to be heard in Washington, D.C.

The drive for territorial status had commenced almost as soon as the first prospecting parties reached Cherry Creek. As early as the autumn of 1858 residents of Auraria had sent Hiram J. Graham as a delegate to Washington, D.C., with a request for recognition. Congress could offer only the suggestion of a number of names for the proposed territory, among them Colona, Jefferson, Osage, and Idaho. When the rush of 1859 swelled the population of the mining country, there came the usual demand for statehood. Continued silence from Washington elicited the normal and expected frontier response—the establishment of an independent state or territorial government. It came at a poor time; the "go-backer" movement of 1859 shrank the population and made the matter of political organization even more questionable. Stubbornly the constitution makers went ahead, determined to create the State of Jefferson, only to have their work rejected by local voters in September 1859. As an alternative the electorate opted for territorial status once again, but since it did not have the sanction of federal authority the rump government of Jefferson Territory languished until the spring of 1861, when congressional action created Colorado.[1]

The first sanctioned General Assembly met at Denver in September 1861 and decided that the territorial capital should be at Colorado City, but when the legislators assembled there in the following year they found living conditions so unsatisfactory that they moved once more, this time to Golden. After alternating back and forth between that place and Denver for several sessions, the lawmakers finally decided that Denver was the proper place for a capital city, and in 1867 the final move was made. The peregrinations of the capital were suggestive of the turmoil, the uncertainty, the transitory nature of the newly created government at the foot of the Rockies. As one disgusted miner put it, "Politics in this country are much like the whiskey; plenty, and most villainously mixed."[2]

As if frontier conditions themselves were not tumultuous enough, Governor Gilpin found himself as the Republican-appointed administrator of a territory in which a third of the population openly supported the Confederacy and three-fifths of the voters were Democrats. Only a month before his arrival southern sympathizers had hoisted a crudely made "rag of treason," as Union sympathizers derisively called the stars and bars, over the mercantile establishment of Wallingford and Murphy on Larimer Street. Samuel M. Logan, who later was a captain in the Colorado Volunteers, took a calculated risk and removed it. No one tried to stop him, but his action did not suppress the occasional display of smaller versions of the emblem around the town during the weeks to come.

Although the new chief executive was endowed with the title of commander in chief of the local armed forces, he had no soldiers. The erstwhile Territory of Jefferson had sponsored the formation of two straggling companies known as the Jefferson Rangers and the Denver Guards, now disbanded. A few federal troops were stationed at such places as Fort Garland, in the San Luis Valley, and Fort Wise, far down the Arkansas River, but neither of these places was close enough to Denver to be useful. Taking his courage in hand, the governor appointed his own military staff, bought all the shotguns, rifles, and ammunition he could lay hands on, organized the First Regiment of Volunteers, and began arresting southern sympathizers.[3] Being a man of action, Gilpin did not take the time to request or to receive the federal government's consent for his organizational efforts, an oversight that later was to cause him a good deal of trouble. Blithely he issued "Gilpin drafts," to cover any necessary expenses, and it was the U.S. Treasury's unwillingness to honor them that led to his removal from office.

In the spring of 1862 an invading force of Confederates crossed into New Mexico from Texas and began an ascent of the Rio Grande Valley that pointed directly at the gold fields of Colorado. The federal army responded by dispatching troops to head off the invasion, and when they failed to stop the oncoming Confederates a call for help was sent to Denver. "Gilpin's Pet Lambs," as the Volunteers were dubbed, at once set off for New Mexico, much to the relief of Denverites, who were tired of having their goods confiscated and their nights made sleepless by continuous celebrations of these turbulent "chicken thieves" who were said to be "a disgrace to themselves and the country."[4]

The story of the Pet Lambs' descent upon New Mexico to engage the invaders has often been told in Colorado. Commanded by Colonel John P. Slough and Major John M. Chivington, who recently had been the presiding elder of the Methodist Episcopal Church in the Rocky Mountains, they met the Confederates—mainly Texans—at Glorieta Pass, not far from Santa Fe, and in a bold encircling maneuver carried out by the "fighting parson" they destroyed the enemy's supply train and precipitated a retreat that continued until the intruders crossed back into their native state. Colorado pioneers dubbed the victory the "Gettysburg of the West" and stoutly maintained that because these gold-hungry troops were turned away, and Colorado was saved for the Union, a victory of great importance to the outcome of the Civil War had taken place.[5] Some of their contemporaries took the cynical view that it meant merely the return of the chicken thieves to the Denver circuit sooner than they had anticipated. Denver merchants, who were ready to paper their walls with worthless "Gilpin Drafts," were even less happy about the turn of military events in the territory. Eventually the government honored $375,000 worth of the drafts it never had recognized, but this meant that some of the original holders took a considerable loss, having sold their drafts for a fraction of face value. William Byers later commented that there was a good deal of robbery in the final settlement of the matter. Despite the fact that the great victory at Glorieta Pass was believed to have vindicated Gilpin, he was finished politically. In the spring of 1862 he was removed from office.

The turmoil in which Gilpin had involved himself was due, in part, to his own willingness to take what he regarded as emergency action and to assume responsibility for it. But the political and economic climate of Colorado during those days contributed heavily to the problem. Mining was in the doldrums, and merchants suffered as a result. When the call came to display one's patriotism at a considerable distance from the Civil War's battlefront, hordes of idle miners saw this as an opportunity to be grubstaked and to fill some idle hours with excitement. Patriotic merchants responded with equal alacrity, disposing of overstocked goods to the local military establishment at boom prices. The construction of Camp Weld, named in honor of Territorial Secretary Lewis Weld, accounted for part of the funds expended. Complete with mess hall, guardhouse, hospital, living quarters, and a regimental headquarters, the project consumed over eight hundred thousand feet of lumber and thirty thousand bricks. Arms, horses, food, and clothing supplies accounted for more thousands of dollars expended. Denver's moribund business community momentarily sprang into life and prices rose from this supposed injection of federal money.[6] Then came the day of reckoning, the inability to collect the full amount of the drafts.

The preoccupation of Americans with the Civil War tended to disrupt the more normal development of western territories, and this caused concern to those who hoped for Colorado's permanency. In one respect the war may have accelerated the westward movement, in that a good many young men elected to leave the East in preference to service in either of the armies then at war, but it was not the floating male to whom the founding fathers of Colorado looked for future community stability. In addition to the wartime disruption of communication with the East came the unsettling news that a new and exciting gold strike had been made in Montana. As word of it spread, the promoters of Colorado found their task of advertising the central Rockies to be much more difficult, particularly when word also was being passed that the Fifty-Niner diggings were pretty well panned out. As early as 1863, gloom began to settle among the merchants, particularly those of the big supply town, Denver.

Although it was remote, Montana was rich, and the placer strikes at such places as Bannack, Alder Gulch, and Last Chance Gulch were so spectacular that they became the center of conversation in mining circles. As the residents of Denver saw the city's population decline to about two thousand, and disconsolately watched local miners pack up and head for Montana, there was concern that another ghost town was in the making. Cornered, they fought back, and through the mouthpiece of the *Rocky Mountain News* they carried on a desperate propaganda campaign. Good news from Montana was played down or at least blemished by some dark allusion intended to leave readers in doubt about the new Eldorado. Stories about the north country's arctic climate, the unparalleled ferocity of its Indians, its outrageously high prices, and its almost inaccessible remoteness found their way into the columns of the *News* all during the spring of 1863. Any hint that things were not going swimmingly in Montana was seized upon and rushed into print for Colorado readers. Accompanying such items were dire warnings from editor Byers that those who chose to abandon Colorado in favor of the new mining country would bitterly regret their rashness.[7]

When such earnest warnings did not seem to have the desired effect, and it was admitted that at least 500 miners had departed Denver for Montana by April 1863, Byers concluded that although some good men had decamped, so had a number of less desirable occupants of Colorado's pristine soil. "Idlers, loafers and bummers have been infected with the . . . fever as violently as any other class, and we see no reason yet to mourn over the consequences of the epidemic," was his rationalization. He predicted that a healthy purge would be followed by an influx of respectable immigrants from the East, and he concluded that the gold reports in Montana really would benefit Colorado by drawing off some of its social scum.[8] The pioneer editor, in his remote post in the distant Rockies, would have been pleased to know that within a few years a widely known American would make a similar suggestion. Bayard Taylor, the traveler, author, and diplomat, visited Colorado in the mid sixties, and he praised the refinement of its residents. Where had the rough element gone? He concluded that "Montana has acted as a social strainer to Colorado; or, rather, as the miner's pan, shaking out a vast deal of dirt and leaving the gold behind."[9] This was the argument that Byers used, forgetting that a mere four years earlier Mississippi Valley newspapers had said the same thing about a faraway and unproved country known as the Pike's Peak region. Despite the fact that antelope still could be hunted within Denver's city limits, the editor apparently did not see any irony in making invidious comparisons between the two Rocky Mountain mining communities.

It was not only Montana that was draining off the placer miners; so was the country west of Denver and the supply towns that dotted the mountain front. However, this could not be a matter of open complaint like the hegira to Montana, for Colorado commercial circles hoped to benefit from any movement into their own backcountry. The pick and pan miners, as always, were a mobile crowd; when a place they were investigating did not live up to their expectations, or they heard of rich diggings somewhere beyond, they moved. This was the story of Colorado mining from the beginning, and as the miners penetrated the canyons that opened onto the plains and worked their way deeper into the mountains, they left behind a trail of temporary camps.

The first miners had worked Boulder Creek and its tributaries, creating a few little settlements, the most important of which was Gold Hill. Up Clear Creek, beyond Golden, lay a cluster of towns, among them Black Hawk, Mountain City, Nevadaville (also called Nevada and Nevada City), and, of course, Central City, whose fame became widespread and lasting. By the late summer of 1859 the discovery of placer diggings in South Park had pushed the Colorado mining frontier even deeper into the mountains, and when some of the prospectors moved into Middle Park and began to take gold from the upper Blue River country it meant that they had crossed the divide and were working in waters that drained into the Pacific. Some of them ranged even farther, north into the Medicine Bow Mountains of modern Wyoming where, it was rumored, rich deposits of gold lay waiting. Reports of a strike in the summer of 1860 in the San Juan Mountains, then a part of Utah, drew off more miners. Others talked of Arizona and even of Sonora, Mexico, where there were rumors of gold, presumably passed over by the Spanish. Those who stayed on in South Park kept alive such names as Buckskin Joe, Montgomery, Jefferson, Fairplay, Tarryall, Hamilton, California Gulch, and other, nameless, newly discovered bonanzas that still held out a promise.[10]

But the promise was fading. Travelers who passed through South Park as early as the summer of 1860 reported that although a few claims had proved to be rich, many were not, and that generally speaking the new gold fields had been a disappointment. A resident of Hamilton admitted that there were two or three stampedes away from his town during the summer of 1860, as new finds were reported in other areas. More often than not the rumors that siphoned off these people proved to be false, but by the time this was realized the damage was done and the miners who had left for better things did not come back.[11] This was a great disappointment to the Denver merchants who had followed the miners into South Park, establishing branch stores, hoping to keep in touch with the itinerant prospectors.

Merchants from the supply towns often had more at stake than the money it cost them to branch out in the camps of South Park. A lot of them had subscribed to the building of roads that led into those mountains. A good many of the roads were built by toll companies, whose proprietors saw an opportunity to cash in on the gold rush, but since these projects often were financed by bankers in Denver and other commercial towns, local businessmen were deeply interested in them. Colorado City, for example, was quite excited about South Park, and its leading men gladly joined efforts to connect their town with the rich new camps. Never ones to think small, they foresaw the development of a road from Colorado City across South Park and on to Salt Lake City, a thoroughfare that would force the abandonment of the old Laramie and Fort Bridger route to the north. Already Coloradans were thinking of a passage across the central Rockies.[12] This was the optimism of their day and of their kind, or perhaps it was a means of shutting out the realities of life that bespoke a dissolving economy in a once-promising place called Pike's Peak.

The feeling of insecurity generated by the effects of the Civil War, the exodus to the Montana mines, and the decline of mining in South Park was further increased by nervousness over the growing hostility of the Plains Indian tribes. Although thousands of miners had made their way to Colorado without interference from the natives, there was a conviction among the settlers that serious trouble was bound to occur. For some years the eventual fate of the Indians had been predicted, both by the tribesmen and by the westward-pushing whites, and it was generally agreed that the days of the natives were numbered. Only a few years before the gold rush, a London newspaper had announced that the Indians' death warrants were signed and that there was little hope for them. "Go which way they may," said the paper, "the land is occupied; and to remain is only to be embroiled in deadly feuds—to be shot down without hesitation and with very little remorse.[13]

Although history would bear out the prediction, there was surprisingly little difficulty between the races during the early years of settlement. Occasionally stragglers from wagon trains were picked off, a practice that was to continue for the next two decades, but for the moment there were no "Indian wars," as the conflicts later came to be called.[14] Rather than hatred for the natives, the whites simply showed contempt and sometimes amusement. Horace Greeley, whose newspaper regarded itself as being humanitarian, called the Arapahoes "squalid and conceited, proud and worthless, lazy and lousy," and he predicted that "they will strut out or drink out their miserable existence, and at length afford the world a sensible relief by dying out of it."[15] His fellow journalist Henry Villard agreed that extinction probably would occur, but he passed this off as one of the "inevitable contingencies of human progress," one that in the end would be beneficial to all.[16] Those who were not given to such profundities regarded the begging tribesmen as nuisances who sometimes were quaint. Members of one westbound party were delighted when one of the visiting Indians professed to have fallen in love with the wife of one of the men and with great dignity offered to buy her. Meanwhile, the Indian women examined the dresses of their white counterparts with as much thoroughness as possible and showed considerable puzzlement over the hoopskirts, then in vogue.[17] The Indians themselves watched the gold rush with amazement. George Bent, a southern Cheyenne half blood, said his people viewed the great movement with a mixture of wonderment and concern, but when they found miners lost and hungry on the plains they offered food and shelter. "They did not understand this rush of white men and thought the whites were crazy," he remarked.[18] The Indians' concern over the white infiltration grew as it became obvious that this was no temporary development. As soon as a foothold was secured along the mountain front, white delegations to Washington asked that the Cheyennes and Arapahoes, among others, be required to settle down on a reservation and commence farming. By the Fort Wise Treaty of 1861, their wish was granted, and these two tribes ceded their lands east of the mountains, after which they settled on a small reservation along the Arkansas River.[19]

For a couple of years after the Fort Wise Treaty there was no real trouble with the Indians on Colorado's plains. Whites around Denver continued to regard them as a higher form of animal life, but not as any great threat to the populace. "They are about as wild by nature as any other animal found roaming through the forest and jungle," commented Uncle Dick Wootton. "They have never recognized any law but the law of force and the difference between a 'wild Indian' and a 'civilized Indian' is about the difference between the tiger at large, and the tiger in a cage."[20] The difficulty came when the "animals" did not want to remain in the cage; the Cheyennes, for example, refused to recognize the Fort Wise Treaty on the ground that it had been signed by only a handful of tribesmen without consent of the tribe, and they objected to being cooped up on a small reservation.

In the early days of white settlement along the mountain front there was little disposition to make war upon the Indians. Anyone who suggested violence was advised to keep still and to refrain from rocking the economic boat. In the spring of 1861 the *News* strongly advised against involvements with any of the tribes, for, as Byers candidly remarked, once news of any such warfare got back to the Missouri River towns, westward emigration would cease at once. All during the following year that newspaper held to its policy of restraint, advocating a "feed them rather than fight them" course of conduct, but by 1863, as the Arapahoes and Cheyennes grew more restless, the editorial peace policy began to fade. By then the raiders of the plains had become the "detested snakes" against whom a war of extermination was the only answer. In the late summer of 1864 the *News* was asking, "Shall we not go for them, their lodges, squaws and all?"[21] A spokesman for the impatient whites answered, "They need killing."[22] Although a great many residents were not excited by such emotionalism, enough of them were ready for action that the notorious Sand Creek affair had become inevitable.

Briefly, Black Kettle and his southern Cheyennes were encamped along Sand Creek, near Fort Lyon (formerly Fort Wise), in southeastern Colorado, in the belief that they would be protected by federal troops. Joining them were Left Hand and his Arapahoe band; together they composed a group of six or seven hundred Indians. Meanwhile General S. R. Curtis, who commanded the military district, announced, "I want no peace until the Indians have suffered more." Colonel John M. Chivington, of Apache Canyon fame, now in charge of some 100-day volunteers authorized by the War Department and several companies of the First Colorado Regiment, heard the message. At the head of approximately a thousand troops he headed for the encamped Indians, hoping for surprise and an easy victory. He was not disappointed.

One day late in November 1864, Chivington and his part-time soldiers crept up on the Indian camp and at dawn they attacked, killing men, women, and children as Black Kettle vainly hoisted the American flag to signify his peaceful intentions. George Bent, the son of trader William Bent, was an unwilling eyewitness to the slaughter. "Most of us who were hiding in the pit had been wounded before we could reach this shelter," he said later, "and there we lay all that bitter cold day from early in the morning until almost dark with the soldiers all around us, keeping up a heavy fire most of the time. If they had been real soldiers they would have come in and finished it; but they were nothing but a mob, and anxious as they were to kill they did not dare to come in close." But the temporary troopers managed to do away with a considerable number of "the enemy." Chivington followed the usual practice of exaggeration when announcing casualties, asserting that between 400 and 500 of these undesirables had met a just end, but George Bent set the figure at 163 dead, 110 of whom were women and children. Chivington had achieved his surprise victory, and cheaply; 9 of his men were killed. All that remained was a conquerors' welcome in Denver and the delivery of a few Indian children there so that they might be displayed at a carnival. Scalps of some of the Indian dead were brought back and strung across a theater stage by a long rope that all might see more trophies of war.

The aftermath was less enjoyable. Although the *Rocky Mountain News* called the Indians at Sand Creek "murderers," and the

General Assembly passed a resolution praising Chivington, a congressional investigating committee took a different view of things. Its members called the deeds performed by the colonel and his men "such . . . as never before disgraced the acts of men claiming to be civilized" and criticized the officers for carrying out a "carefully plotted massacre" that dishonored the uniform of United States soldiers. As late as 1913 historian Jerome Smiley defended the action and said the committee's conclusions were "widely at variance with the prevailing views and sentiments of the Colorado people and those of their Assembly."[23] Such views, said a visitor, could be summed up as "We did our duty then, if ever, to ourselves, to humanity, to our country, to our God." Chivington, he added, was a leading citizen and a highly respected member of the Colorado community.[24]

Contemporaries could praise the errant cleric all they wanted to, but no matter how it was viewed, Sand Creek was a mistake. Apart from any humanitarian considerations, it failed to produce the results Coloradans expected of it, namely humbling the Indians and by this example bringing peace to the plains country. On the contrary, when word of the outrage spread among the Indians, a period of guerrilla warfare ensued that disrupted travel until the era of the railroad. The opening guns of this new phase of plains warfare were heard soon after Reverend Chivington had completed his work among the Southern Cheyennes. Less than two months later a few of his veterans, bound for the East, were apprehended by a band of these Indians who carried out swift retribution. Upon going through the dead men's effects, the Indians came upon some scalps that were being taken east as trophies, a grisly reminder that white men also fought with savagery. The Indians were enraged by these mementos from Sand Creek.

Very shortly thereafter Julesburg was attacked and plundered, stage and freight routes were cut, and frightened householders called loudly for protection. Almost any alarm caused a panic among the settlers. Mollie Sanford, a settler's wife, recorded one such instance when she and her neighbors gathered up the children and made for Denver as fast as they could. Before they reached safety there was a volley of shots. "I dropped to my knees, expecting my time had come at last, when just ahead of us passed a band of loose mules that had stampeded," she wrote. Mollie and the children made it to a brick building that was so crowded she nearly suffocated, but finally the all clear was sounded; the Indian "attack" had been a false alarm. "It all came from some old people living out a few miles, imagining some Mexican cattle drivers to be Indians," Mollie explained, "and in their fright running two miles to the stage station, where the alarm was sent to the Governor."[25] This and similar scares kept residents all along the mountain front in a condition of perpetual apprehension. As flour went to fifty dollars a barrel in Denver and the prospect of a siege loomed large in their minds, loud complaints reached congressional offices at Washington. That brought out the federal troops, whose efforts reopened lines of travel but did not end the sporadic raiding. By October 1867, the Arapahoes and Southern Cheyennes agreed to exchange their reservation in Colorado for one in Indian Territory (present Oklahoma).

Before terms of the treaty could be carried out these Indians, along with some other hostile bands, went on another raiding spree in eastern Colorado. Once more Coloradans called loudly for help and were given permission to raise volunteers for the emergency, but nothing was said about who was to pay for their services. Remembering the "Gilpin draft" debacle, territorial officials wisely avoided this approach to their problem. Nevertheless, by August 1868 another "war" was under way, much to the embarrassment of community leaders, who had spent a good deal of time and effort trying to show the general public how civilized the place had become. Even worse, vice-presidential candidate Schuyler Colfax was vacationing in the mountains as a guest of Governor Alexander C. Hunt. For a time it appeared that Colfax might have to take up residency in Colorado, being unable to get back home.[26] Before matters calmed down again federal troops frantically hunted the raiders, fought the battle of Beecher's Island on the middle fork of the Republican River, and finally succeeded in stamping out the brush fire of Indian rebellion. The culmination of this phase of plains warfare came at the Washita battle in Indian Territory where General George Custer struck an encampment of Southern Plains Indians and killed over a hundred of them, including Black Kettle, who had escaped from the trap at Sand Creek.[27]

With the restoration of peace and the safe return of Schuyler Colfax to the East (not to mention that of two other prominent eastern political figures who were vacationing in the central Rockies that year), Coloradans again could talk about the absence of frontier problems in their territory and the great promise such a condition held for investors, farmers, laborers, and tourists. But they knew that it was only talk and that only a limited number of easterners would listen to it unless the region was made more easily accessible.

The movers and the doers of the young mining community, particularly the aggressive businessmen of Denver, thoroughly understood that if Colorado's budding settlements expected to have more than a speaking acquaintance with the rest of the nation, they would need much better communication with it. Tourists or health seekers, who might want to sample the already famous mountain climate, were not going to sacrifice their bodies to the punishment dealt out by stagecoaches. Those settlers who intended to raise beef, sheep, grain, potatoes, and other agricultural products whose weight and bulk was great in relation to value could not prosper without a cheaper and more efficient means of moving their products. The miners earlier had been able to cope with high transportation costs because of the valuable nature of the extraction, but those days were fading. Only if heavy reduction machinery could be brought in, and relatively cheaply, would they be able to mine at a profit. Clearly, the only hope was the railroad, and fortunately such a line, chartered in 1862, was under construction west of Omaha by 1865.

Those first rails, feeling their way tentatively across the prairie sod, were regarded as a godsend to Colorado, for they began their westward advance at a time when the territory was approaching the nadir of its hopes for survival, let alone future growth. Rail service, once achieved, promised to serve as an economic lifeline, and as the tracklayers advanced westward the eyes and ears of Coloradans focused upon their every move. The sound of driven spikes echoed a message of hope, one that said help was on its way. Practical men studied plains transportation costs for the three years prior to 1866 and calculated that, at ten cents a pound, the freight bills to the federal government and to the people of the territory amounted to over ten million dollars. This figure, they believed, would show a dramatic decline once rails reached the mountains. Already, said one mining entrepreneur, the Union Pacific's advance across Nebraska had shortened wagon haulage enough to reduce freight costs by 50 percent. Governor Alexander Cummings thought such a speculation not unreasonable; he remarked that the number of arriving settlers had increased during that travel season.[28] While Coloradans expected great things from rail service, they were equally sure that any railroad serving them would find an enormous source of traffic from the rich mining country.

For no particular reason, except that railroads in the eastern United States traditionally had run from town to town, Denverites appeared to think that the Union Pacific Railroad intended to include their city on its route. The news that the builders of this road had no desire to wrestle with the dizzying heights of the Colorado Rockies, preferring the relatively flat land that followed the old California trail, came as a great shock to residents of the Queen City. The wounds to their pride momentarily were salved by the belief that W. A. H. Loveland's Colorado Central Railroad Company would make a connection to the main line, but when it was discovered that the road was to be built directly to Golden, with a branch line to Denver, dwellers along Cherry Creek broke off all negotiations with Loveland and cast their hopes in yet another direction. It was now 1866, and by then a line running out of Kansas City, called the Union Pacific, Eastern Division (U.P.E.D.), had abandoned its earlier plan to angle northwestward to a connection with the U.P. in favor of heading directly across Kansas toward Denver. The joy of this news evaporated when it was discovered that the U.P.E.D., soon to be known by the more interesting name of Kansas Pacific, wanted two million dollars from Denver in return for rail service. Disappointed at every turn, and smarting under the remark being passed around in Cheyenne that "Denver was too dead to bury," Denverites could see but one answer: Denver must build its own connection with the Union Pacific. Accordingly in the autumn of 1867 the Denver Pacific Railroad Company was incorporated.

Led by such well-known and enterprising businessmen as former governor John Evans, banker David H. Moffat, and Bela M. Hughes, the company overcame some very difficult problems and built the 107-mile line that connected Denver to the main road. Evans, who arrived in Colorado in 1862 as an appointee of President Lincoln, was not the typical office seeker who earned a sinecure in one of the territories through favor and then returned to the East when his tenure ended. Rather, he stayed on, as did his son, grandson, and great-grandson, to establish one of Colorado's oldest leading families. Their interest in railroads continued for a century. Moffat, a New Yorker, worked his way west as a young bank clerk, making stops in Iowa, Missouri, and Nebraska along the way. In the spring of 1860 he arrived in Denver, where he ran a stationery store and was assistant postmaster and a telegraph company agent. In 1867 he went back into banking, this time in Denver's First National Bank, and it was here that he was to make his fortune and his name in Colorado. Bela M. Hughes also was interested in transportation, having been involved in the Holladay Overland Mail and Express Company. During 1867, when the Denver Pacific was founded, he became its first president. Late in June 1870, the arrival of the locomotive *David H. Moffat* signified the long-awaited opening of the railroad, and along the track leading to Cheyenne lay the town of Evans, named in honor of one of the Denver Pacific's founders, who now was its president.[29]

In the minds of Colorado's builders the physical connection with other parts of the country provided by railroads did not solve all the problems of isolation. Coloradans cherished a strong desire to achieve statehood, part of it based upon pride, but much of it predicated on the theory that by controlling their own destiny they could achieve a solid prosperity more quickly and surely. Since territorial governors and judges were federally appointed, the newer settlements had to take what was sent to them by Washington, D.C., and frequently they complained that they were receiving less political talent than they deserved. John Evans had been satisfactory enough, for he had worked hand in glove with local businessmen to make Colorado prosper, but the actions of his successor, Alexander Cummings, who was appointed in the autumn of 1865, convinced some of the local leaders that continued territorial status would have a smothering effect upon their efforts at growth. The *Rocky Mountain News* carried on a campaign of vilification against the new governor and argued vehemently in favor of statehood. However, when a constitution was proposed in 1864, the voters turned it down; a similar move was successful in the following year, but only by a narrow margin and that because in certain wards more votes were cast than there were qualified residents.[30]

Despite the decidedly marginal assent by the voters, the statehood advocates bent all their efforts in the direction of making the change, foremost among them Samuel H. Elbert, the territorial secretary who also was John Evans's son-in-law. Both Evans and Jerome B. Chaffee, who were "elected" as senators for the nonexistent state, worked hard for the cause, but they were opposed by Henry M. Teller, who had been defeated by Chaffee and was unwilling to settle for a seat in the House of Representatives. To further confuse the local picture, Governor Cummings, whose job was at stake, did all he could to halt the movement. He told Secretary of State William Seward not only that the whole Colorado campaign was of dubious merit, but that the proposed constitution denied Negroes the franchise. Mention of such a restriction at this point in the Reconstruction era was bound to cause a commotion among Radical Republicans; it was the most damaging blow Cummings could have delivered.

Encouraged by the governor's support of their cause, Colorado's small black community joined the battle. William Hardin, Denver's leading black spokesman, presented a petition to Congress in which the absence of a suffrage provision for his people in the proposed document was challenged. This deeply offended Byers of the *News,* who scolded local blacks, asking if they understood how much the Republican Party had done for their race, and he accused Hardin's group of "an act of treachery and ingratitude rarely exceeded." He chided them for their impatience, for their unwillingness to await the results of education, and for their vanity in desiring national attention at the risk of creating more problems at home. Hardin, who earlier had received much praise from Byers, now was conceded to be a man of more than ordinary capacity principally because of the great amount of Anglo-Saxon blood that coursed through his veins.[31]

As expected, congressional Radical Republicans attacked the Colorado statehood proposal with both vigor and venom. Senator Benjamin F. ("Bluff Ben") Wade, of Ohio, who once had challenged any and all southerners to a duel with squirrel rifles at thirty paces, charged that the action merely would create another rotten borough, Colorado having so small a population. Senator Charles Sumner, of Massachusetts, long a proponent of the black cause, agreed that the mountain community, with a population of twenty-five or thirty thousand and falling, had no business asking for a position of equality with the other states. In fact, he doubted that it ought even to be a territory. Nor did he see any hope for improvement. "It has shrunk inconceivably and beyond all precedent," said Sumner. "I believe there is no other instance in our history where a Territory has gone backwards. Always before population has increased. It is the rule of this country, it is the tendency of our people." His explanation of Colorado's failure was that it straddled the Rockies "like Italy parted by the Apennines" and had few commercial centers and scanty resources, all of which caused immigrants to go farther west in search of a better land. He thought this forlorn territory had only a floating population, one that would seek out such attractive places as Montana, Idaho, or Oregon. To document his "scanty resources" remark, Sumner charged that already Colorado's agricultural resources had begun to fail, and so far as mining was concerned its failure had been demonstrated for the past several years. Now, he concluded, this small and unsuccessful place was asking admission to equality as a state in the Union with a constitution that "tramples on human rights."

Having attacked Colorado's reputation, the senator next questioned the veracity of Evans and Chaffee, alleging that a pamphlet entitled *Colorado* and bearing their signatures contained very few candid statements. He even criticized Evans in the matter of Sand Creek, accusing the then-governor of knowing that the massacred Indians had been friendly.[32]

In defense of the Colorado delegation other senators argued that denial of Negro suffrage historically had been no reason for the rejection of statehood applications; as recently as 1864, in fact, Nevada had been admitted to the Union with a constitution that provided for white male suffrage only. The measure found sufficient support to pass both houses of Congress, only to encounter the opposition of President Andrew Johnson. Johnson held out one hope to Evans and Chaffee: he offered to sign the statehood bill if the two senators-elect would support him in his fight with Congress. When the men turned down the deal, Johnson vetoed the bill in May 1866. He argued that Colorado's population was too small and that the 1864 vote indicated a lack of interest in statehood among the people. There was a surprisingly mild reaction to this in Colorado. While residents were not pleased by attacks like Sumner's, neither were they anxious for statehood. Historian Jerome Smiley thought that half, or perhaps two-thirds, of them welcomed the failure.[33]

Faced by hostility in Washington and indifference at home, statehood forces continued their struggle. During the winter of 1867–68 another effort was made by Evans and Chaffee, with Teller fighting them tooth and nail. Again they might have triumphed had they been willing to make a deal with Republican Radicals. Nebraska showed such a willingness and was admitted in 1867, after which it cast two votes against Johnson in the impeachment proceedings. But Evans and Chaffee would not pay the price, and consequently Johnson's expected veto was not overriden by the Senate. Back in Colorado, meanwhile, Republicans were badly split by the Chaffee-Teller fight, which finally was patched up; ultimately both men served in the Senate.[34]

Supporters of the statehood movement laid much of the blame for its failure at the door of the local blacks, an attitude that did little to soothe race relations. However, Byers grudgingly admitted that since an enlarged franchise was the order of the day in post–Civil War America, Colorado probably would have to pay this price to achieve statehood; in any event, he thought, escape from federal rule would be a fair exchange for yielding on this question. The editor did not have to wait for such a trade-off, because in the spring of 1867 Congress provided for black voting rights in the territories, and by the time statehood was achieved, less than a decade later, federal amendments to the constitution had settled the question of American Negro suffrage.[35]

It is easy now, as it was then, to argue that in its quest for statehood Colorado was the victim of Reconstruction politics, but in truth there was some substance to the criticisms Sumner leveled against the territory. From Denver to the mountain towns there was concern about the decline of population, the stagnation of business, and the inactivity in the mines. To top it off, Denver was ravaged by fire in the spring of 1863 and was nearly washed away by a flood in Cherry Creek a year later. Brave thoughts continued to appear in the newspapers, optimistic words about the great future of mining once a few problems of ore reduction were solved, and about boundless opportunities for those who wanted to till Colorado's rich soil, but it was becoming an increasingly hard line to peddle.[36] By 1865 Sam Bowles, the wandering Massachusetts newspaperman, admitted that pick and pan mining in Colorado was about finished and that all mining had been dull for more than a year. He blamed high labor costs, currency inflation, the Civil War, and Indian problems on the plains. Bowles gave population figures that agreed with those of Sumner—twenty-five or thirty thousand—and he admitted that Colorado had lost between five and ten thousand since 1860. The visitor echoed a locally popular viewpoint when he tried to justify this development by saying that it was the adventurers who had departed and that the substantial men who had remained to make their homes in Colorado would build the future. In another familiar vein the editor criticized the caliber of officials sent out by Washington to govern the territory. The failure of the statehood movement of 1864, he thought, was due to the unpopularity of the men who had promoted it. Presumably they would become more acceptable in the future, for Bowles thought statehood was not far off.[37]

These and other optimistic observations made good reading in Colorado, but much such prose was the result of rationalization. Perhaps an eastern visitor hewed a little closer to the truth when, in 1867, he referred to the territory as being "thus far the land of disappointment to the East." He said he wanted to go out there to determine if there really was such a country and, if it did exist, to discover whether there were any mines there "as in the East both were being seriously doubted."[38] Another traveler who visited Colorado about this time said that the boom had collapsed, and, although things were expected to get better, he felt that the future of the place was quite uncertain. He entitled his article "The Disappointed Sister."[39]

Things did get better sometime between 1866 and 1868, a period Sam Bowles called the "kernel years" of Colorado. As early as 1866 some observers believed that Denver had "turned around" and had begun to lift itself out of the doldrums. Three hundred new buildings went up that year, and the population stood at around four thousand, a figure that did not take into account a large number of transients. During the next year a board of trade was organized, and one of its first efforts was a campaign to secure a rail connection for the city.[40] During this period the *Rocky Mountain News* called more loudly than ever for a population that would develop territorial resources. It solicited men who would till the soil and dig for minerals, but who also would remain in Colorado, as opposed to striking it rich and then decamping in favor of more sophisticated social climes. In the spring of 1866 the *News,* watching the arrival of white-topped wagons bearing families and their possessions, felt a surge of optimism, of hope that the bleached canvas signified the coming of permanent settlers.[41]

When Bowles returned to Colorado in 1868 he confessed that mineral output had not lived up to the optimistic expectations he had expressed on his last visit. In the interim mines had been abandoned, mills had shut down, and eastern capital had indicated a weariness of waiting for returns. The stagnation had produced a retrenchment; quartz miners retreated to operations that were demonstrably remunerative, and placer miners worked much more discriminatingly. However, the discovery of silver mines at Georgetown had restored hope. By now, said Bowles, Georgetown had a population of three thousand and the best hotel in the territory, the Hotel de Paris. Central City had lost some population, but in the fall of 1868 he found all its stamp mills in operation and was told that much more effective means of reduction had been discovered so that business there again was in a healthy condition. Colorado appeared at last to have settled upon a firm foundation, a development the visitor found encouraging.

Denver, always the economic barometer, indicated that business activity was on the rise by 1868. Bowles thought the city had passed what he called its fickle days, when gamblers reigned and tumult was the order of the day, and had become a properous-looking place with long lines of brick stores flanking the downtown streets. Irrigation had produced flowers, fruits, and vegetables in the formerly arid residential section. He believed the town was succeeding because of its central location, which allowed it to command trade from all directions. It was, he said, Colorado's social, political, and commercial capital; it had a great future before it, one that would be doubly assured with the arrival of the railroad.[42]

There were other explanations for Denver's recovery. General James F. Rusling, who stopped there in 1866, also foresaw the benefits of a railroad, but he did not agree that the city's location was of primary importance. He regarded the selection of its site as a geographical blunder, since much of the business had moved westward into the mining country. However, he explained, since gold first had been discovered where it stood, the place had got a start, and its occupants had been aggressive enough to keep it going where other hamlets had withered and died. "The sharpest and shrewdest men in Colorado we found all settled here," said Rusling. "All capital centered here. And Denver brains and Denver capital, it was plain to see, ruled and controlled our whole Rocky Mountain region, north to Dakotah and south to New Mexico."[43] It was a good argument, as later developments would suggest, but it was a hard one for rival cities to accept without admitting their own commercial inabilities or their innovative deficiencies.

Coloradans, of course, agreed that by the late 1860s there were signs of better days ahead, but this assertion was not unusual; they always thought that. As a matter of fact, change was in the air. General Rusling's suspicion that Denver was on its way toward growth and prosperity was correct. Meantime, other cities clearly had fallen short of earlier expectations, and, even this early, some were classified as ghost towns. The general shook his head in dismay when he saw Colorado City, once a thriving little town whose backers had entertained high hopes for its future. Now corner lots were for sale dirt cheap, and there were "plenty of empty shanties, but scarcely any population; and what it had, were the sleepiest-looking Coloradans we had seen anywhere. The 'hotel' or tavern, was dirty; the people, idle and listless and the 'City,' as a whole, evidently was declining rapidly to the status of Goldsmith's Deserted Village."[44]

The decline of once-booming mining camps was the rule, not the exception, during these years. As Sam Bowles and his party moved through South Park during his 1868 visit, they saw deserted cabins, doorless and windowless, now rotting monuments to a faded mineral frontier. Tarryall, where thousands of miners had probed the earth only a few years earlier, now sported only a handful of mud-patched cabins whose chimney smoke drifted lazily over a nearly deserted landscape. Hamilton, once a center of vice and gaiety, now stood silent. Only a handful of men and three or four women presided over some fifty empty pine cabins and a moribund log hotel. Municipal rigor mortis also gripped Montgomery where, by 1868, only a single house among more than a hundred showed any sign of life. There an old-timer who looked at the recent past as if it were years ago moaned, "Why, we had several stores, three or four hotels, more than that number of saloons—we had livery stables, gambling houses in plenty with music, *maisons de plaisir,* theater, and all the modern improvements."[45] And down the road, only about five miles away, were the ruins of Buckskin Joe, another camp that had died quietly. Here stood roofless houses, grass-covered hearthstones, empty fruit cans, faded sardine boxes, rusted prospecting pans, and some old broken shovels.[46] Colorado's first ghost towns, which would fascinate so many people a few generations later, had made their appearance.

The emergence of the ghost towns suggested that Colorado's economy was changing and that its initial developmental phase had been concluded. Under the assumption that abandoned placer camps meant only change, not impoverishment for the territory, community builders went ahead with their plans and their dreams. Sam Bowles, always a friend and booster, took hope from the apparent upturn of the late sixties and announced that Colorado was the West's Pennsylvania; that is, if William Penn's creation had become the keystone of the Atlantic states, then Colorado was "the keystone in the grand continental formation. She holds the backbone, the stiffening of the Republic . . . and may well call her mountains the Sierra Madre, the Mother Mountains of the Continent."[47]

Much had happened to the territory during its infant years. Before it had reached its teens the place had soared to spectacular heights, had fallen from financial grace, and was out to make its second fortune. Although its founders were not all reckless gamblers, nevertheless they knew that their undertaking was fraught with all kinds of financial perils and that, above all, it would require a considerable amount of faith to stay with the game and see it to the end. On the realistic side they told themselves that the young economy had undergone a severe shaking but that perhaps this had separated the chaff from the grain and was all for the best. They looked for more mundane sources of income--agriculture for example—and watched the development of local and regional railroads, convinced that with these basics their growth would be solid if not spectacular. The boosters admitted that to some extent the region might be called the "land of disappointment" by those with an eastern point of view, but with typical western optimism they took the position that all this was past and that a new day was coming. Therefore it was with a great sense of anticipation and a firm resolve to make the most of available opportunities that they looked forward to the years immediately ahead.

# 6

# The "Selling" of Colorado

As Coloradans faced the second decade of their efforts to gain a foothold in the Rockies they were obliged to consider the possibility that the placer miners had picked the place clean and had moved on to richer diggings, leaving behind a trail of ghost towns. All during the 1860s evidence of this awful truth appeared to be increasing, and those who had bet their all on the future of Colorado could either desert or stand and fight. A good many people had no real choice, since to abandon one's investment was to invite financial ruin. It occurred to some that if the place had been promoted into existence once, by Missouri River town merchants, perhaps it was possible to do it again. A group of battle-hardened businessmen and community leaders therefore commenced a spirited advertising campaign that was to continue for a century.

A time-honored frontier method of promoting one's community was to sing its praises before all visitors and to display its virtues in the columns of local newspapers. The Fifty-Niners utilized this method from the outset, and visiting eastern journalists felt the full blast of their propaganda campaign. Another approach was to invade the East itself. Perhaps the first of the eastern campaigns came in 1863 when Edward Bliss left his position with the *Rocky Mountain News* and established an emigrant agency in New York City. William Byers, who was one of the territory's early and great champions, endorsed the work of his former colleague and suggested that mining companies in need of labor should consult with the new agency. He described New York as a great focal point of converging lines of immigration from Europe, a funnel through which a great labor potential flowed. Bliss put to use his recently acquired knowledge about Colorado and through the columns of the metropolitan press he announced that between three and five dollars a day could be earned in the mines and that everything necessary for the comfortable subsistence of a large population was available in the new communities. He thought that there was both room and demand for a hundred thousand more people in the territory.[1]

The promotional activities of mining entrepreneurs were not confined to this country. Robert O. Old, an Englishman who had come west in 1860, had been very successful as a miner at Georgetown. In 1868 he established the British and Colorado Mining Bureau in that prosperous town, with a branch office in London. At the London office, situated right behind the Bank of England, were displayed over five hundred Colorado ore specimens, plus a large selection of books, photographs, and maps that described the new California in detail. In addition to its promotional activities the bureau served as an agent for those who wanted to send ores to Great Britain for smelting, and, indeed, some ores were shipped this great distance at a profit. Old also encouraged British investment in Colorado, and the Denver Board of Trade, attracted by such activities, promised to donate land to those who would put such money into local smelters.[2]

In the search for favorable publicity no stone was left unturned. Among the efforts of the businessmen to attract attention to the mines was the appointment of a commissioner to represent the brash young territory at the 1867 Paris exposition. J. P. Whitney, a Boston financier interested in western mining, volunteered to take a batch of ore samples to France so that all might see the richness of Colorado's deposits. While he was there Whitney met and became friends with Louis Simonin, a well-traveled French mining engineer who taught at the Ecole Centrale d'Architecture in Paris and whose writings were widely read. Here was a man of international reputation, one whose endorsement might mean a great deal to Colorado in the form of European investments. "Mr. Whitney proposed, as if it were the most natural thing in the world, that I come to visit his mines," said Simonin, who quickly accepted the offer. By early October the Frenchman was viewing the

Miners had little time for architectural achievements or home maintenance. Anything that would keep out the weather—and some cabins failed this test—would suffice on a placer mining frontier where residence was often a temporary affair. *Denver Public Library, Western History Department*

Mining often tore up the countryside for miles. These old sluices illustrate both placer mining methods and the damage done to the land. *Western History Collection, University of Colorado Libraries*

This old prospector, dressed in his Sunday best, is demonstrating the use of the gold pan. *Western History Collection, University of Colorado Libraries*

The miners were fond of musical entertainment, and in some camps they organized their own bands. Here is, Colorado's first brass band, Blackhawk, 1862. *Denver Public Library, Western History Department*

A wagon train, out of Leavenworth, Kansas, in downtown Denver, 1868, on Market Street (then called Holliday) between present 15th and 16th streets. *Library, The State Historical Society of Colorado*

Planter's House was a familiar name to those who stayed at hotels across the West and the Midwest. The Denver Planter's House (corner of 16th and Blake streets) also housed the ticket office for the Overland Stage in the 1860s. *Library, The State Historical Society of Colorado*

Denver in the 1860s, corner of 15th and Blake. The city fathers were proud of the brick buildings downtown, a sure sign of permanence—as well as protection against fire. *Denver Public Library, Western History Department*

Downtown Denver still was somewhat undeveloped in the 1870s, but it was on its way. The old frame Broadwell House stood in contrast to a neighboring three-story brick "skyscraper," an ancestor of the city's later tall buildings. *Denver Public Library, Western History Department*

Ute horsemen crossing the Los Pinos River. *Denver Public Library, Western History Department*

For the "noble red men," as the American Indians frequently were called, life was far from romantic, particularly on ration day at the agencies. Here some of the original Americans gather at a Ute agency in Colorado. *Denver Public Library, Western History Department*

When the Utes departed the North Park area, in what is now the Routt National Forest, they left behind some of the crude brush and pole tepees in which they had lived. *Denver Public Library, Western History Department*

Officers' quarters at Fort Garland, in the San Luis Valley—a welcome sight to travelers, both military and civilian, who passed that way during the early days of the fort's history. *Denver Public Library, Western History Department*

Crosstown traffic at Denver's Larimer and 16th streets during the 1880s was hectic—and muddy. *Denver Public Library, Western History Department*

The "skyline" of Denver, looking east, in the 1870s. Wolfe Hall looms on the horizon. *Library, The State Historical Society of Colorado*

Just as modern travelers often find airline ticket offices located in their hotels, guests at Denver's Albany Hotel could buy passage on the Denver and Rio Grande, the Missouri Pacific, and other railroads at this convenient location. *Library, The State Historical Society of Colorado*

The arrival of rail service was always an occasion for celebration. Townspeople invariably —and often incorrectly—assumed that freight rates would plummet. Those who welcomed the first train into Aspen, October 27, 1887, cheered the Rio Grande; later they complained bitterly about its rates. *Denver Public Library, Western History Department*

The Denver and Rio Grande's narrow gauge, running up Animas Canyon to Silverton, provided passengers with some breathtaking moments and a sample of the spectacular engineering achievements of Rocky Mountain railroad builders. The same view is available today, and thousands of tourists take advantage of it every summer. *Denver Public Library, Western History Department*

Downtown Aspen offered residents "the Ride" in early mining days, a modern transit facility that indicated how progressive a new western town could be, and one that brought shoppers into contact with eager merchants. *Denver Public Library, Western History Department*

In later years Aspen made a great effort to look "quaint." Here's how it got that way—during the mineral days. *Denver Public Library, Western History Department*

The junction of Casey and Lawrence streets in Central City illustrated the hilly nature of many of the mining towns. *Denver Public Library, Western History Department*

Mountain freighting was slow and expensive. This wagonload of coal, moved by six horses and a driver, mounted rapidly in value as it moved toward its destination. *University of Colorado Museum*

This victorian home in Lake City, as it appeared in 1974, is representative of the attractive, well-kept dwellings found in a number of Colorado mining towns during the late nineteenth and early twentieth centuries. *Photo by Frederic J. Athearn*

Agricultural colonies were popular in Colorado beginning in 1869 with that of Carl Wulsten. This picture in the March 26, 1870, issue of *Harper's Weekly* showed the group leaving from Chicago and thereby gave the "sell Colorado" program some free advertising.

This little cattle ranch is typical of many hidden away in the valleys of the Colorado Rockies. *Denver Public Library, Western History Department*

Cotopaxi, Colorado, where the unfortunate Jewish colonists made a vain effort to eke out a living tilling the unfriendly soil. *Denver Public Library, Western History Department*

Greeley, Colorado, was somewhat primitive in the early days. The cloth and board shanty in the foreground may have been "home on the range," but some of the settlers, upon seeing such accommodations, wished they had remained in the Midwest. *Denver Public Library, Western History Department*

The chuck wagon was an important part of cowboy life on the range. Here is a group "nooning" near Barela, east of Trinidad. *Denver Public Library, Western History Department*

Parades were patriotic social functions in lonely western towns. Here some residents of Montrose commemorate Washington's birthday, 1888. Beyond lies the stark new land, yet to be developed. *Denver Public Library, Western History Department*

Camping and hunting (note the rifles, center) have been popular in Colorado since the days of Fifty-Nine. Frequently the outings were family affairs, for children and all. *Library, The State Historical Society of Colorado*

The booming camp of Leadville was a man's world. Here, at the Pioneer Club, the men kept their hats on, and the ladies were notable by their absence. *Denver Public Library, Western History Department*

marvels of Denver, "some two thousand five hundred leagues from Paris."

If Whitney hoped that Simonin would spread the good word he was not disappointed. In a work entitled *Le grand-ouest des Etats-Unis* the visitor praised Denver as being well built, attractive, and replete with all the trappings of civilization, including newspapers, schools, and churches. However, he was not impressed by western cooking. "M. Tallyrand was right when he said that in North America he found one dish and thirty-two religions. There are no cooks in this country, but everyone is a little religious," was his comment. He saw hope in the fact that Frederick J. Charpiot had brought French cuisine to the mountains; it could be sampled at Charpiot's Lawrence Street cafe, already known as the "Delmonico's of the West."

Simonin talked enthusiastically about minerals, agricultural products, and even furs that stimulated Colorado's young but thriving commercial life. Amazed at the size of a cabbage he was shown, he was willing to state that mountain-country vegetables were tastier than those of his native land. Gold, he thought, had been the cornerstone, and in eight short years it had furnished a foundation for a happy and prosperous portion of America that now would diversify its efforts and become economically secure. It must have pleased his hosts to read in Simonin's account of his visit that Colorado society was of high quality, mostly American in origin, and that very little social scum had drifted westward to foul it. "I have seen ladies here whom New York or Boston would envy or regret losing," he wrote.[3] This was exactly the kind of publicity both Denver and the rest of Colorado wanted and needed during the gloomy days when it looked so hard for the light at the end of the tunnel.

While it was pleasant to have outsiders praise one's social and cultural accomplishments, what the business community really wanted was men who had money, eastern connections, and qualities of leadership. In a young Civil War general named William Jackson Palmer they found what amounted to their ideal man. He was intelligent, ambitious, and possessed excellent credentials and moneyed friends in the East; best of all, he wanted to make his home in Colorado. That he belonged to the dreamer class of promoters did not bother those who welcomed him, for there was a little of the dreamer in most of the business leaders who had moved west, and in Palmer they acquired a colleague whose idealism did not blind him to practical considerations.

The young easterner, who was to leave a deep mark upon Colorado history, came west as a part of the Kansas Pacific's construction forces. He had a plan for a north-south narrow-gauge railroad that would run along the mountain front, connecting major transcontinental lines that might pass through the region. He called his creation the Denver and Rio Grande Railway, and its first train rolled southward from Denver in the autumn of 1871. The railroad was only part of a larger idea; he wanted cities to be scattered along its route—even if he had to build them himself.

Selling the granted lands of railroads was a common promotional enterprise in the West; after collecting money for the farmsites, the promoters expected to generate traffic from agricultural produce. In the case of the Denver and Rio Grande Railway, there were no granted lands, but only a narrow right-of-way and occasional depot sites; consequently it was all the more important for this railroad to encourage town growth in its territory. One of the first efforts was the Fountain Colony at Colorado Springs. Begun early in 1871, the little city had a hundred and fifty buildings and a population of eight hundred by the end of the year. Nearby Colorado City, whose promoters had struggled so hard to make it benefit from the mining boom, soon was swallowed up by what the *Rocky Mountain News* called a "mammoth enterprise." Once a town of ten thousand, Colorado City had shriveled to a mere three hundred people. Their outcry at the invasion was muffled under what a Denver newspaper called "the footsteps of a new civilization." The editor, who understood the price of progress, offered the unhappy residents of the dying municipality the consolation that "the dead must bury dead, now, as in other days. The mourners must go about their streets bemoaning the new days and the strange ways."[4]

The emergence of a miniature railroad system with impressive steam engines and brightly colored coaches to speed tourists and businessmen to new towns, such as Colorado Springs, made a deep impression upon those who earlier had settled in the territory. But this was only a part of Palmer's plan. He wanted to shape a new society in this virgin West, an almost Utopian ideal that later was reflected to some extent in the social fabric of Colorado Springs.

As he envisaged a network of rails across the central Rockies, Palmer shared his dreams with his future wife. He promised her that five hours a day would be sufficient time to run the business; the remaining hours would be devoted to his mate and to his "family," as he referred to the new company. It would be a happy family, one that would breathe invigorating air, enjoy priceless scenery, and live the good life. The workingmen and their dependents would be cared for and uplifted by their corporate godfather, who would protect them and provide them with schools, bathhouses, libraries, lectures, and all the things that would contribute to a healthy physical and intellectual existence. In this idyllic society such troubles as strikes or labor discontent would be unknown because there would be no difference between capital and labor. By investing their savings in the road, the workingmen would become capitalists, and therefore they would share the responsibilities of management. Thus, by creating a trinity of capital, labor, and rich western resources, the former army officer dreamed of originating a new economic and social structure that minimized a good many of what he called the "vexed social problems" of that day.[5]

The average western businessman, less interested in current social problems than was Palmer, wanted growth and prosperity, two conditions that appeared to go hand in hand. The great advertising campaign had been carried on largely by such private enterprises as newspapers, business organizations, and railroads, but in 1872 Colorado made its official plunge into the game of soliciting immigrants when the General Assembly created a Board of Immigration.[6] The announced purpose of the board was to advertise the territory's resources and their availability to the general public, but underlying this was the desire of civic leaders to achieve statehood, to increase the tax base, to provide new sources of business for the commercial class, and to acquire more farmers whose efforts would make mining centers less dependent upon the importation of foodstuffs. Another service of the board was the establishment of an information center to answer inquiries about the territory received daily in the governor's office and by various newspapers. Perhaps less important, but not to be ignored, was the motive of competition; almost every other western state or territory had a similar organization, and the bidding for immigrants to settle both private and public lands often reached dizzying proportions.

The first step was to collect the information to be disseminated.

The board turned to the respective county commissioners, asking them to appoint corresponding secretaries who would provide ammunition for the forthcoming campaign. It goes without saying that the response was of varying quality. But by the application of western optimism and some selective editing, the most favorable "facts" were selected and entered into a pamphlet that described the glories of Colorado in the most florid terms. Early historians, among them onetime Secretary Frank Hall, condemned the effort as having been worse than none at all, for the literature left the impression that all avenues of endeavor were open and waiting for practically anyone who wanted to come west. Taking the advice literally, a great number of people exhausted their savings to reach the mountain Mecca, only to discover once again, as had many of the Fifty-Niners, that easy pickings were not to be had. Unable to find work, or failing to locate upon fertile land, a good many joined another "go-backer" retreat, shouting their denunciations. Frank Hall concluded that the effort to generate a tide of immigration in the direction of the territory had backfired, and that only the great discoveries at Leadville toward the end of the decade countered the unsavory reputation Colorado had acquired.[7]

The 1874 legislature did not respond to requests for continuation of the board's services, and its functions lapsed until 1889, when a new agency was created. This one lasted for ten years and was superseded in 1909 by yet another organization, whose members distributed Colorado products at agricultural exhibitions in the East and assisted in promoting the "Western Governors" tour of the East where specially designed cars displayed western products.[8]

Although the promoters of Colorado played down the lack of rainfall, frequently denied that the Great American Desert extended so far west, and emphasized the possibilities of irrigation when addressing themselves to prospective settlers, there was one area of the "sell Colorado" program where the lack of humidity was an asset: the field of health and tourism. The Rockies widen in Colorado, dividing into several ranges with high mountain parks between, providing an area, more than half the width of the state, whose high, dry climate earned it the title "The Switzerland of America."[9]

Colorado acquired its reputation as a climate capital very soon after the arrival of first settlers. A decade after the Fifty-Niners marveled at the clean mountain air, a traveler wrote in jest that this was an ideal place for anyone having but one lung. A large number of people who were actually little better off than this headed for the Colorado mountains, hopeful of a few more years of life, if not a cure. A good many of them survived, made their contribution to the state, and sometimes became prominently known. Others died. One of these was John Henry "Doc" Holliday, who expected to die in his bed despite the reckless and dangerous career he had pursued. He did—of tuberculosis, at Glenwood Springs, in November 1887. He was thirty-five years old.[10]

But Doc Holliday was beyond redemption; even Colorado's climate was unable to perform its wonders for him. Happier stories were told about those who lived, who were so healthy they appeared to be indestructible. Applicable to Colorado was the western claim that out in this country it took twice as much killing to finish off a man and that horse thieves had to dangle five minutes longer than in a less salubrious climate, just to be sure the job was finished. A visitor to Colorado asserted that it was almost impossible to get sick there. As proof he quoted a friend who explained, "I once knew a man who tried to make himself ill in order to get off serving on a jury. He ate nothing but fat pork and drank nothing but lemonade for a week, but he couldn't do it, sir. The air that you breathe in Colorado enables you to avoid anything."[11] It was even harder to die. P. T. Barnum, professing to be amazed at the wonders wrought by the mountain climate, remarked, "Two-thirds of them came here to die *and they can't do it!* This wonderful air brings them back from the verge of the tomb." But even Barnum was topped by the tale of one traveler who wrote, "I was told that in some sections [of Colorado] it was so healthy that a man had to be killed to start a burying ground."[12]

The early arrivals may have benefited greatly from the clean air, but they still needed medical advice. Living in rude shanties, sleeping on the ground, and cooking over open fires, the miners were surrounded by dirt all the time. The kind of food these bachelors ate and the way they prepared it called for iron constitutions, and even those possessed of superior digestive equipment fell victim to occasional intestinal insurrections. Their fare of pancakes, fried bacon, soda bread or corn cake, stewed dried apples, and viciously strong coffee varied little from day to day. "I believe I make more practicing medicine than in mining," wrote one westering medic. "I make no prescription for less than $5 and if I give medicine from $8 to $10." A doctor from Ohio said that by prescribing to sick miners he was averaging twenty-five dollars a day and never less than ten.[13] Travelers noted the absence of ague, fever, and ailments common in the Midwest, and they minimized the digestive battles being carried on by the male population as being part of the price paid in winning the West. The anticipated arrival of women promised dietetic relief, among other things.

Stories of the bracing air and freer breathing made their impact upon eastern readers. As the word spread, more and more invalids headed for Colorado to inhale its ozone and to try its mineral or hot springs. Before long any number of "living examples" could testify to the marvelous recuperative powers of the Colorado climate. One young man came west by wagon so ill with consumption that boards to make his coffin were brought along; he lived to be eighty-six. From the earliest years it was not an unusual sight to see tuberculars moving around the region in covered wagons, resting on feather beds as they gasped for the rarified air and gazed at the mountain scenery. One who made a remarkable recovery was James John Hagerman, a rich consumptive who left Michigan to gain health and more wealth in Colorado as a mining and railroad entrepreneur. He lived in Colorado Springs, as did Helen Hunt Jackson, who also came west as an invalid and later became internationally known for her books about the Indian problem, *A Century of Dishonor* and *Ramona.*

One traveler claimed that nine-tenths of the population were cured invalids. He exaggerated, but still the percentage was much higher than anywhere else in the West. By the late seventies, said one observer, thousands of invalids made Denver a winter resort. He regarded it as a place that combined the comforts of civilization afforded by hotels, stores, and society with the crisp high-altitude air.[14] So many victims of pulmonary ailments were attracted by this kind of publicity that before the end of the century a fifth of Denver's population was believed to have come from the group then known as the "one-lung army."[15] Contemporary claims that during these years fully one-third of the state's population comprised health seekers have been supported by a modern scholar.[16]

Promoters of Colorado made sure that the news of Colorado's "champagne air" reached the ailing, particularly those possessed of financial means. Through prose and poetry local publications praised the mountain atmosphere in extravagant superlatives. One verse, entitled "Colorado Sunshine," announced:

> Sunshine for the pale and palsied,
>   Sunshine for the chilled and weak,
> Giving pallid lips the rubies
>   And the rose to Pallor's cheek.
> Praise God for the floods of sunshine,
>   Free as e'en the mountain air!
> This is Colorado's glory,
>   Poured like rivers everywhere.

Readers were left with the impression that a few whiffs of this remarkable commodity would supercharge the weakest invalid and prompt him to tear up his will.

Editor Byers of the *Rocky Mountain News*, who seems to have explored almost every avenue of promotion, looked into the possibilities of health spas and tourist attractions. Foreseeing this untapped potential, he gained control of some medicinal springs in Middle Park, once used by the Ute Indians, after which he staked out the town of Hot Sulphur Springs, erected a bathhouse, and began selling baths to passersby at seventy-five cents a dip. Although it was said to show promise as a resort by the end of the seventies, it failed to develop to the degree Byers had hoped.[17] The railroad of which he dreamed would not pass that way during his lifetime.

But railroads served other health resorts in Colorado and through their advertising made such places nationally known. Colorado Springs received a good deal of publicity from General Palmer's Denver and Rio Grande Company, as well as from Dr. Samuel E. Solly, who, after recovering his own health there, promoted the place with great vigor. Nearby Manitou Springs, of Indian fame, vied with the city of Colorado Springs for the title "Saratoga of the West." One of Solly's pamphlets, published in 1875, ascribed to the waters of Manitou marvelous restorative powers that gave new hope to those afflicted by a variety of ailments including dyspepsia and flatulence. The doctor's literary effort, termed a "medical masterpiece," attracted wide attention and loosened many a purse string.[18] By 1880 the flood of visitors to the Colorado Springs area reached an annual figure of thirty thousand; within a decade it would reach two hundred thousand. General Palmer's railroad, well aware of the potential in health-seeking tourists, issued a booklet in 1881 entitled *Health, Wealth, and Pleasure in Colorado and New Mexico.* Thousands of copies were distributed.

While Dr. Solly may have left the impression that Manitou was the source of all healing, other mineral and soda springs across the state were being patronized by the late seventies, and as railroad service increased so did their popularity. Idaho Springs, Morrison Springs, and Pagosa Springs were names familiar to invalids in search of relief. More baths were to be found in both Middle Park and South Park. By 1880 health seekers could go by rail to the Mount Princeton Hot Springs, where a hotel was opened a few years later.[19]

Although the ailing provided great prospects for the purveyors of Colorado's advantages, the healthy, whose financial competence allowed them to travel, were not to be overlooked. While Dr. Solly was making a literary name for himself, General Palmer's Colorado Springs Company fired off a couple of broadsides designed to entice prospective members who were of good moral character, of strict temperance habits, and who had money. *Our New Saratoga: Colorado Springs and La Font* and *Villa La Font: The Fountain Colony* made fascinating reading for those of some means who were inclined to go west in style. Carefully the company "checker-boarded" its lots, offering alternate "villa sites" for sale and keeping the remainder for itself in anticipation of a certain rise in land values as the adjacent property was sold. With this in mind, Palmer and some of his English associates went after the well-to-do classes of England, hoping to attract people of gentle breeding to come "notwithstanding the . . . remoteness and rather wild repute of this frontier," to quote a local newspaper.[20] At the foot of Pike's Peak the promoters measured off Colorado Springs, which a visiting Englishman described as a "very high-toned sort of new town," one that was run by a "very tony company on teetotal lines."[21] The response to their efforts was so great that Colorado Springs became known as "Li'l Lunnon." It was said to be a fine place to live because so few Irish polluted its refined atmosphere.

So attractive was this future "Newport in the Rockies" that from the outset inquiries poured in from all over the Eastern Seaboard, as well as from Europe. In 1872 the town company's secretary answered nearly four thousand inquiries, and during a single month that summer more than fifteen hundred visitors arrived. Within six years that figure would multiply by ten. Meantime, a brochure telling of the benefits of the winter climate drew nearly eight hundred visitors during the 1873–74 season, most of them invalids. The resort's popularity was explained by a Denver newspaper. These travelers, it reported, were tired of the "enervating influence" of more famous eastern watering places; instead, they sought a simpler life in the quiet villages of the Rocky Mountains. However, cautioned the Colorado journalist, if the "gay butterflies" who were used to displaying their wings at such places as Saratoga imagined that they would find the simplicity of a wilderness at Colorado Springs they were in for a surprise, for this was a town where one was expected to dress rather better than in London and "always to have plenty of time to do nothing in."[22]

Tourists who stopped at Colorado Springs, then and later, came with the idea that they were going to spend money, a notion which local merchants enthusiastically endorsed. But early on there were those who warned against abusing the geese that were laying golden eggs. Alarmed by complaints echoing from the resort city as tourists paid their hotel bills, a Denver paper warned innkeepers not to emulate their eastern counterparts by overcharging visitors. "Be satisfied with a moderate share of the tourist's spare cash assured that he will give you another chance to pluck him . . . and he will be sure to bring or send others from whom an egg or two can be taken," advised a Denver newspaper.[23]

In 1874 a Greeley newspaper disapprovingly watched the Colorado Springs boom, noting that as many as four hundred carpenters were at work building houses for well-to-do newcomers, and it remarked that the majority of those living in General Palmer's new paradise were said to be so wealthy as to be able to live on the interest of their money. The egalitarian editor complained that "while the people of Greeley are engaged in creating wealth the people of Colorado Springs are spending it."[24]

The more thoughtful citizens of Colorado Springs realized what was happening to their town as a result of superpromotion. A local editor admitted that Palmer's railroad and his colonizing zeal had enticed people to Colorado "who are really better off out of it, people who would stay at home if there were only the prospect of an ordinary settler's life before them. . . ."[25] But such cautious fears that the promoters were guilty of overkill did not slow the program. The Denver and Rio Grande Railway offered attractive excursion rates from Denver to Colorado Springs so that both public and press might watch the growth of the West's great tourist attraction and health spa. "Inspired" articles, written by western editors and by literate visitors, were sent to eastern newspapers by the bale, intended for the eyes of footloose Americans who might be moved to take a train bound for the golden West. Meanwhile, J. E. Liller, editor of *Out West* (later to be the Colorado Springs *Weekly Gazette*), devoted a good deal of space to praise of the Pike's Peak region, offering travel tips as well as social notes of interest to the tourists already in town, and foreign items for the growing number of visitors from abroad. In the manner of the day out-of-state newspapers tended to snip items from Liller's journal to fill empty spaces in their columns, and the fame of Colorado Springs continued to grow.[26]

Occasionally the enthusiasm of the salesmen led to some misunderstanding. Rose Kingsley, daughter of the English author Charles Kingsley, wrote that one immigrant family severely questioned the credibility of promotional literature when its members finally viewed the city of their dreams. They expected Colorado Springs to be a large town, with rich farming lands already plowed and fenced awaiting their occupancy, but they ended up in a shanty with no bedding or household necessities. "Never will I persuade people to emigrate after seeing these arrive," said Miss Kingsley. "Finding what it is in reality, they turn around and accuse those who have advised them to leave the struggle for existence in the old country of sending them to their death and ruin in the new."[27]

Some of Miss Kingsley's countrymen who listened to the blandishments of western promoters carried back the advice to hopeful emigrants that they should be careful about listening to American land salesmen. Even the more realistic of prospective buyers here, those who would not expect to find farms fenced and waiting for the plow, had heard so much about Colorado's climate that they came to anticipate something special in that respect. The high degree of such expectations may have accounted for the pique of one young Englishman who arrived at Colorado Springs during one of Colorado's famous March snowstorms. Stepping from the Denver and Rio Grande Railway car into a blast of arctic air, he asked: "And his this the Hitalian climate of Hamerica?!!"[28]

While Colorado could not control its weather—a favorite saying was "If you don't like the weather here wait a minute"—the fact that the Englishman at Colorado Springs emerged from a warm railroad car that March day was significant. Such service was

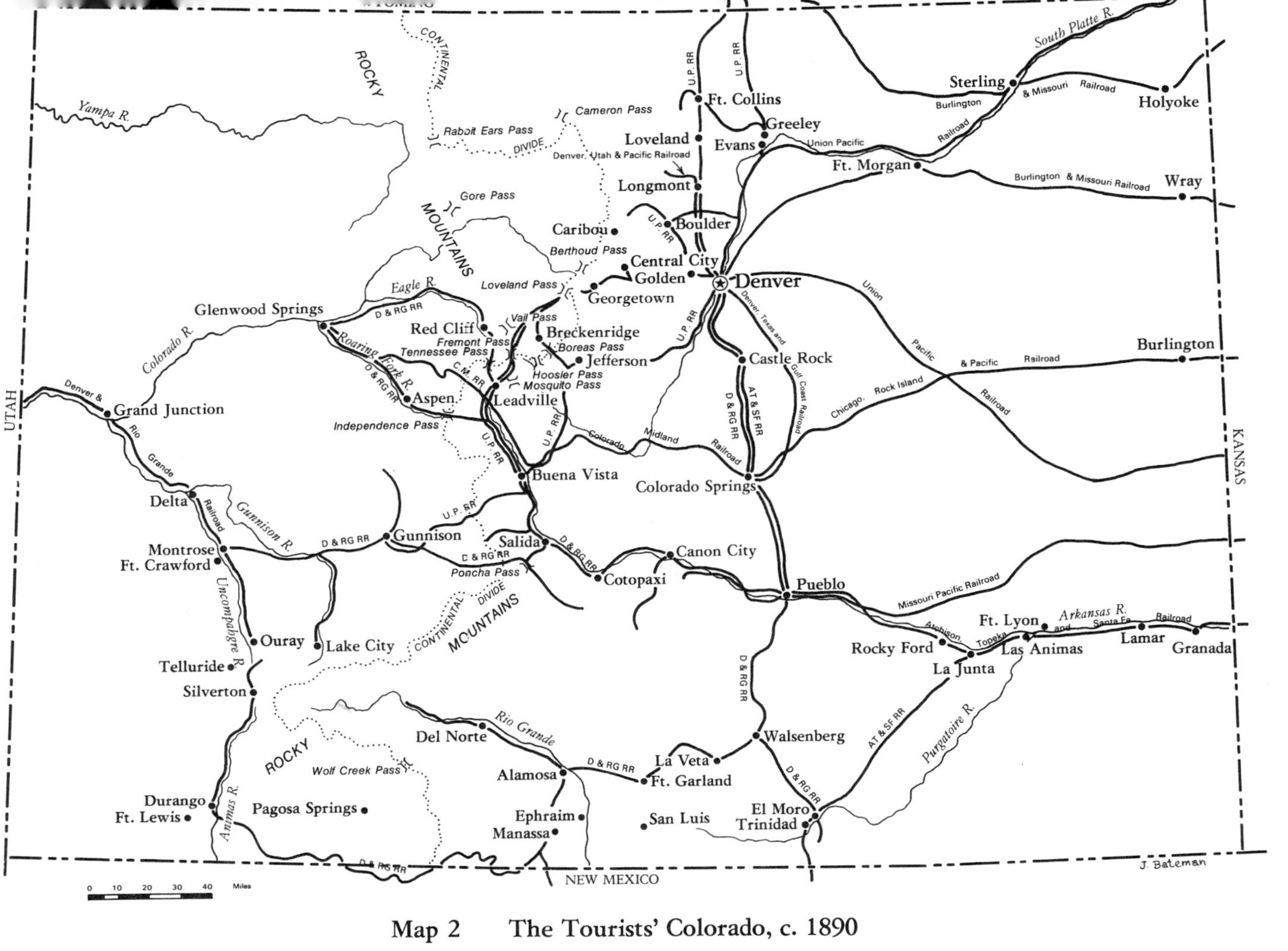


Map 2 The Tourists' Colorado, c. 1890

available only a little more than a decade after the Fifty-Niners had slogged their way westward over a man-killing desert, and this development considerably shortened the pioneer or "Wild West" era of Colorado's history. When Jerome Smiley wrote his history of the state in 1913, he stated categorically that the coming of the railroad in 1870 "terminated the pioneer period."[29] What he meant was that the railroad made possible the transition from the random, aimless type of settlement characterized by the movements of the placer miners to a more organized method. The coming of the roads also shortened travel distances and put within reach of all, from invalid to infant to unescorted maiden, a scenic grandeur consistently compared to that of the Swiss Alps. Above all, promoters of Colorado stressed its easy access, and they would continue to do so in the age of the automobile and the airplane.

It was natural enough for the Englishman in search of the "Hitalian climate" to get off the train at Colorado Springs, for that was one of the places in Colorado easily reached by rail, but there were other, if lesser known, locations that offered good to excellent accommodations. The Hotel de Paris, at Georgetown, was in operation early, and within a few years that mining town would have rail service. Boulder and Fort Collins offered the amenities of civilized society, as did Central City, and even rip-roaring Leadville prided itself on the advanced state of its services, not all of which were there to please the lusty male population at work in the mines.

The increase in tourism was just one of the many benefits Colorado derived from the coming of the railroads, but its importance was not lost upon those who worked so hard to build the state. Visitors might come out of mere curiosity, for relaxation, or for reasons of health, but whatever their motive a good many of them were people of means, and when they passed this way enterprising salesmen invariably showed them an amazing number of rewarding avenues for their investment money.

Newspapers, chambers of commerce, and railroads all joined in the campaign to promote tourism. Beginning in the seventies, railroads advertised steadily; as early as 1872, they began to offer excursions for politically and financially important people. The number of inquiries made by businessmen and others was reflected in the establishment of the Denver Board of Immigration in 1872, and in the easy availability of the *Handbook of Colorado,* a directory of routes, distances, and other statistical information published at Denver.[30] Another favorite piece of reading, found in the pockets of many a traveler, was George A. Crofutt's *Grip-Sack Guide of Colorado* (1881), a little handbook containing detailed descriptions of the state's points of interest, some of their history, and mileage tables. Photographer William Jackson's souvenir views of Colorado scenery added yet another dimension to the program of "sell Colorado."

At an early date Palmer's narrow-gauge Denver and Rio Grande Railway began to promote tours by which visitors might see the American Alps comfortably and safely. One of these, the five-day "Round the Circle" excursion, featured that part of the route completed during the seventies, and it was the beginning of a whole series of similar trips by which anyone might explore the Rockies. Privately managed "package tours," so popular with travel agencies at a later date, also were available. The Raymond tour, for example, featured the rental of an entire railroad car from which viewers could enjoy the scenery in a luxurious and leisurely manner. During the 1880s Ernest Ingersoll rented a car for himself and his party and cruised the Rockies behind trains and on schedules of his choosing.

By every means at hand, promoters tried to advertise Colorado's resources and beauties to potential settlers and investors. Newspapers kept up a drumfire of publicity, trying to attract national and international attention to this land of promise. By and large their efforts were successful, certainly more so than similar efforts in neighboring territories, but there remained one final major task for the publicists: to convince fellow residents that if Colorado hoped to grow and to prosper even more, it ought to be a state.

While the residents were appreciative of the high-pressure efforts of business and political leaders to siphon off eastern population and money, many of them did not see how statehood would further this program. The pro-state faction had suffered several reverses in the mid sixties, but it never had abandoned its campaign. As population grew in the early seventies and as prosperity appeared to be returning despite the panic year of 1873, the group felt that the time had come to renew its efforts. In addition to the positive factors of better times and a growing population, certain negative conditions appeared to demand some kind of political change, the most irritating of which were the political battles of the territory's management and continued complaints about the type of officials being sent out by Washington. Governor Edward M. McCook, appointed in 1869, generated even more complaint than had Governor Cummings. Constant rumors of fraud and embezzlement, particularly in connection with Ute Indians, kept McCook's critics busy; finally President Grant had to recall his old comrade-in-arms. It was when Grant foolishly and stubbornly tried to send him back to Colorado that the political pot really boiled. The complaints became so loud that McCook, who had been confirmed by a single vote, resigned, and John L. Routt, of Illinois, became the last territorial governor.[31]

By 1875 the national Republican party felt a need for Colorado's electoral votes as its leaders realized that the contest of 1876 was going to be close. They were right; Colorado's three Republican votes gave Rutherford B. Hayes the narrow margin that sent his candidacy to the electoral commission in disputed election. As a result of this search for political insurance, Congress voted for and President Grant approved a proposal for Colorado statehood. In turn, Governor Routt called for the election of delegates to a constitutional convention to be held in late October 1875. Those who were chosen met at Denver that December to draft a constitution. After approximately three months of effort, and despite some absenteeism and the advanced state of inebriation that caused one delegate to fall out of his chair, the assignment was carried out.[32] The next step was to submit the document to the voters for their approval, and it was here that the proponents of statehood were obliged to turn out in force to convince the populace that statehood would be of general benefit to Coloradans. Anticipating a hot contest for ratification, the makers of the constitution worked hard to frame a government that would be inexpensive to operate. For years the expected high cost of state government had been used as a leading argument against abandoning territorial status. Pro-statehood newspapers set forth elaborate arguments in which they tried to show that although the change would cost a little more, the difference quickly would be made up by more immigration and increased railroad construction, both of which would provide a larger tax base.[33]

Some of the newspapers found themselves in a dilemma. For example, the Colorado Springs *Gazette* opposed statehood, but when eastern journals also came out against statehood, advancing the old argument that Colorado did not have sufficient population and that it would become just another rotten borough, like Nevada, the *Gazette* was put on the defensive. The crowning insult was the assertion that Colorado was no more civilized than New Mexico, a place where the entire "American" population, except for soldiers, transient miners, and hangers-on, could sit in the shade of a good-sized apple tree. Since Coloradans tended to lump the native New Mexicans and the Indians together as a primitive, uncivilized group of subhumans, charges such as this struck hard at their pride. The *Gazette* tried to work its way out of the dilemma by admitting that although the mountain community was small and not yet ready for statehood, it was bound to grow.[34] Openly opposed was the Golden *Colorado Transcript,* whose editor flatly rejected the proposition on the ground that Colorado's population was too small, that its resources as yet were unproved, and that the burden of taxation would be too heavy. For almost these same words, a decade earlier, Senator Sumner had been roundly castigated in the central Rockies. Nor was there much enthusiasm from Pueblo, one of its papers remarking that Coloradans simply could not afford the luxury of statehood.[35]

Part of the opposition came from the Catholics, who objected to a clause in the proposed constitution that prohibited the use of public funds for the support of churches or church schools. Bishop Joseph Machebeuf, a powerful figure in a growing Catholic population, protested against any such restrictions, arguing that the matter should be left for legislative consideration at some later date. The bishop's stand prompted a Denver paper to lament the fact that he had entered the political arena. His action further antagonized a large group of Protestants who harbored chronic concerns about the long arm of the Papacy. Before the constitutional convention concluded its business, forty-five petitions were received on the school issue, most of them opposed to such a use of appropriations. The authors of the constitution, who were predominantly Protestant, reasserted the old notion of a division between church and state and included a proviso that denied public funds to any church or sectarian society.

The religious issue pervaded a good many of the discussions, not only among the constitution writers but also in the press and public forums. There was a spirited discussion at the convention as to whether or not the Supreme Being ought to be mentioned in the forthcoming document. Although no such mention had been made in the national constitution or in most of the state constitutions before 1860, in recent years constitution makers had responded to the greater emphasis upon religious orthodoxy by making such an inclusion. In Colorado's case the statehood architects responded to public pressure and, with only four dissenting votes, acceded to the demand.

Another matter relating to churches, but one that perhaps was more economic and political than religious, was the question of taxing church property. The matter was much in the public mind in 1875, for that year President Grant had stated in his annual message to Congress that the value of such holdings across the nation amounted to about eighty-three million dollars. Coloradans appeared to feel that the Catholic church, whose "management" was foreign based, posed the biggest threat as a religious property owner. They looked southward and saw a large Spanish-speaking population that was heavily Catholic; those who feared this "solid South" pressed hard for complete ecclestiastical taxation. Some of the extremists argued that the new state ought not have chaplains in public institutions, Bible reading in public schools, officially sanctioned religious holidays—not even an official Thanksgiving Day—or laws that enforced the Sabbath, such as Sunday closings. Frightened businessmen pointed out that an anti-Christ state such as these people envisaged surely would drive away capital and bring on a financial drought. The Colorado community, in general, shared this concern, for it had a deep-seated desire to make a good impression on prospective settlers in the rest of the nation. Therefore moderation prevailed on this question; churches and church-related property, including schools and cemeteries, were to be exempt from taxation.

After a heated campaign the issue was put before the voters on July 1, 1876, and in a total vote of just twenty thousand the proposition won by a ratio of approximately three to one. There had been an expectation of strong opposition from the southern counties, where the Spanish-speaking population had shown little enthusiasm for the proposal. Not only were they predominantly Catholic, and therefore resentful of the obvious prejudice against their religion among the delegates, but also they viewed the new government as one that would perpetuate their minority role in future affairs. Yet when the vote was taken only four southern counties rejected the document; it passed in all the remaining counties. The Denver vote was overwhelmingly in favor, only sixty out of more than fifty-six hundred voters casting negative votes.[36] Accordingly, on August 1, 1876, President Grant issued the necessary proclamation and Colorado entered the Union. R. W. Woodbury, owner of the *Denver Times,* was given credit for suggesting the nickname "the Centennial State," in recognition of the nation's hundredth anniversary.[37] Political parties met quickly and made their nominations for the upcoming election. The Republicans chose Territorial Governor John L. Routt for the gubernatorial post, and, in deference to southern Colorado's recent cooperation, they picked the well-known Lafayette Head of the San Luis Valley for the position of lieutenant governor. Jerome B. Chaffee and Henry M. Teller, who had battled so long over the question of statehood, became the two newest United States Senators.

Having sold Coloradans on the idea of statehood, the promoters returned to the task of convincing outsiders of the new state's great future. By the end of the seventies publicist Frank Fossett could write that Colorado was the most prosperous part of the West because the state's varied and extensive resources, which were being "developed and taken advantage of by an enterprising and intelligent population." The newly created Centennial State, he said, was attracting more attention than any other section of the country, not only among the moneyed men but also from the masses. The tide of emigration that once more washed against the Rockies confirmed his belief that Colorado was a place of superior prospects for labor and capital.

# 7

# The Agricultural Towns

The early promoters of Colorado tended to overplay its mineral wealth. Whenever mining experienced a decline, particularly during the 1860s, it became necessary to laud other qualities; hence the efforts to attract tourists and invalids by advertising the climate and to attract farmers. Agriculture, of course, had been the traditional occupation of westering frontiersmen, but in Colorado the glitter of gold momentarily diverted the attention of more than one migrating farm boy. As if that were not enough, the "Great American Desert" syndrome had fixed itself in the minds of midwestern farmers so thoroughly that they were convinced there was no hope for agriculture in this great, barren land.

Among the famous doubters was Horace Greeley, who not only dismissed the feasibility of agriculture in the region but said that aridity would prevent it from becoming even a stock-raising country. He was sure that settlers would be few and far between for many generations and that only prairie dogs and rattlesnakes could exist in the desert. Greeley was but one of many skeptics; the literature of his day is filled with similar forebodings. Yet among the Fifty-Niners many a man suppressed a desire to till the soil; many of them had grown up on farms, and the temptation to grow something was irresistible to them.[1]

As early as 1854 "Uncle Dick" Wootton had engaged in what he termed "farming after the eastern fashion" by irrigating lands along the Huerfano River. A producer of corn, wheat, and all kinds of vegetables, he regarded himself as the pioneer Anglo farmer of Colorado; at this time Spanish-American farmers worked lands in the San Luis Valley that they had gained under old Mexican land grants.[2] A few years later the Fifty-Niners talked about William Kroenig, who had a five-hundred-acre farm along the Huerfano on which he successfully raised cereals. Not only had he built a flour mill but, in anticipation of an urban, heavily male market, he was then erecting a brewery. Just outside the little mining town of Golden, an Indianan named David N. Wall began to grow vegetables along Clear Creek, convinced that he could sell his produce to miners at a good profit.[3] Some of the miners in the Boulder vicinity noticed considerable verdure along their ditches, and a few of them began to experiment with a variety of vegetable crops.

When those who dabbled in agriculture along the mountain front began to show results, and hence presumably to contradict the "desert" concept, others joined in the effort. Irving Howbert, who lived to be one of Colorado's better-known pioneers, arrived in 1861 with his minister father; after a brief stay in the mining camps they moved to a farm near Colorado City. He later wrote that agricultural attempts near Pike's Peak were so successful that by 1862 a flour mill was erected at Colorado City; a second was built a year or two later, followed by a third farther up Fountain Creek. In Howbert's view agriculture temporarily kept Colorado City from dropping out of existence.[4]

Although agriculture showed growth during the sixties, Coloradans hoped mainly for self-sufficiency, as opposed to the development of commercial agriculture as a principal industry. As early as 1861 there was evidence that this modest goal was a possibility. That spring Gus Wildman told his father that a good deal of river bottomland was being broken for farming purposes and that it raised "the most splendid vegetables." A few months later, at harvest time, he said that so much had been raised during the summer that the cost of living was about a third cheaper than when he arrived. Flour was down to twelve dollars a barrel, and potatoes could be had for three dollars a bushel. The favorable price level continued; by 1865, the price of staples in Colorado was a third or a half of that being asked in the Montana mining camps.[5]

Colorado agriculture in the 1860s posed some problems for the prospective homesteader. Although land was available under the Homestead Act of 1862, and although the mining camps provided a market for foodstuffs, other difficulties made prospective homesteaders think twice before pulling up stakes and heading west.

Until the late spring of 1865 the Civil War siphoned off thousands of young farm boys who otherwise would have been raising crops. This, in turn, put a premium on farm labor and raised farm prices in the North, offering an additional reason for staying at home rather than emigrating to the West. Once the war had ended, the agricultural frontier resumed its westward advance, but twenty years would pass before it edged into eastern Colorado as a part of continuous and contiguous movement. In the meantime, the average individual farmer who migrated to Colorado had to consider the great distance to be crossed, the Indian barrier, and the expense of maintenance until the first crops came in.

Nevertheless, by the late sixties Colorado agriculture beckoned. During November 1867, the Union Pacific Railroad reached Cheyenne, only a little over a hundred miles from Denver. Within another three years Colorado would be connected to the East by two railroads, making it possible for farm families to come west with relative speed, comfort, and safety. Even for those who chose to use the traditional wagon transportation—and many still did—the journey was easier, for the Indian threat no longer was serious along main travel routes. Furthermore, the latter years of the sixties showed an upturn in gold production and hence the prospect of a steady local market for farm produce in the foreseeable future. Of great interest to hopeful settlers was the claim that Colorado's production of grain, vegetables, dairy products, and hay for the year 1869 was valued at about three and a half million dollars, or nearly as much as the mineral income for that year. If the Great American Desert theory still lingered in the minds of those who thought about western farming, here was an alternative: to cross the desert by rail and to take advantage of Colorado's climate, soil, water, and agricultural market.

Publicists such as Sam Bowles did much to help many a restless midwestern farmer make his final decision about moving to Colorado. The journalist, who had written about the place after his 1865 visit, returned in 1868 and professed absolute amazement at the agricultural advances that had taken place in his absence. Almost miraculously the territory appeared to have become self-supporting. While this was not true—as late as the mid 1870s the territory would spend $1.3 million to buy vegetables, poultry, and dairy products from outside sources—nevertheless he was on the right track; production had increased. By 1868 Colorado was able to sell some of its agricultural surpluses to the Montana mining camps, to regional army posts, and to contractors building the Union Pacific Railroad. Bowles estimated that a million bushels of corn, half that amount of wheat, and large quantities of other grains had been raised during the previous growing season. Some fifty thousand head of cattle and almost twice that number of sheep were available to buyers. Mining had attracted this easterner at first, but now he was intrigued by the possibilities of agriculture in the new country. He predicted that it was and would be Colorado's dominant interest, and he called it the basis of wealth, power, and morality, and the conservative element of all national, political, and social growth.[6]

Anxious for factual material to support agricultural claims being made to prospective settlers, editor Byers of the *Rocky Mountain News* sent reporter William R. Thomas out to examine the countryside. It was the spring of 1868, just before Byers was to begin his association with the National Land Company and a time when he was actively supporting Colorado agriculture. Thomas first visited the upper Platte Valley, above Denver, where he saw the land in transition. The log cabins of the Fifty-Niners still stood, but interspersed among them were the neatly kept farmhouses, surrounded by fruit and shade trees and occupied by families who had determined to make their homes in Colorado. Thomas stressed this notion of permanency in his report, hoping that readers who were nervous about the economic instability of the territory would take comfort from it. He praised Bear Creek Valley for its beautiful farms but expressed disappointment that Cherry Creek Valley was so sparsely settled. He blamed it on the mercurial nature of Cherry Creek, which could not be depended upon to furnish a steady supply of irrigation water.[7]

To the south, in the valleys around Pueblo, Thomas found a thriving agricultural community. He visited over eighty farms in the Fountain Valley where corn was the main crop, but where wheat, barley, oats, and other grains also were being grown. Along the Charles River lay a splendid livestock range. Westward, in the area of Beaver Creek, and particularly around Hardscrabble, where one of Colorado's very early settlements had been founded, were more irrigated crops of corn and wheat. The investigator was somewhat disappointed in the lower Arkansas Valley, east of Pueblo; as yet not much land was under cultivation, a situation he attributed to a lack of market for produce.[8] In a few years the arrival of rail service would alter this situation.

In the Huerfano Valley the reporter witnessed a mixture of Spanish-American and Anglo farmers. The former, he said, were content to rent their land for a lifetime, or so long as it provided a house and sufficient food, but the Anglos were more restless and would rent only until able to buy the land. In the manner of the day, Thomas praised the Anglo farmers and ranchers. He referred to them as "Americans" and remarked that landowners preferred them over the Spanish Americans because they were much more industrious and required less direction once they had taken up their tasks.[9]

The mission upon which Byers sent his employee was reflective of the editor's deep interest in Colorado's agricultural future. Since his first days in Colorado the former Ohio farm boy had used a lot of ink promoting the idea of an agricultural society and an annual fair.[10] During the decade of the sixties he saw both ambitions fulfilled, the society being organized in 1863 and the first fair held three years later.

Realizing that as early as the mid sixties one could find abandoned camps in the placer country, Byers and his business acquaintances looked to agriculture as a stabilizing influence in the economy. The question that puzzled them most was how to attract the desired settlers. The availability of railroad transportation had removed one major barrier, but it did not solve the problem of Colorado's remoteness or the lingering doubt in the minds of many as to the arability of the territory's soil. Publicists and promoters—Byers was both—had done their best, but more incentives were necessary. Midwestern farmers might be persuaded to move, but many of them were reasonably comfortable and only if the change could be made easily and securely would they pull up stakes; there were few Daniel Boones among these latter-day frontiersmen. The planners of Colorado's future agricultural community concluded that group settlement was the answer.

Traditionally American farmers had edged westward as individuals or in small, loosely formed groups organized only for the journey at hand. On occasion there had been joint settlement efforts, such as the socialistic cooperative organizations commenced in the Midwest during the 1820s and the Mormon experiment in Utah, but, in the main, the individualistic American agrarians did not choose to give up their personal independence as a price of gaining the advantages of cooperation. Despite this general attitude, settlement in groups known as colonies was not unusual, and most western states saw at least a few such units develop. In Colorado, the practice became quite common.

Even though Colorado had telegraph and railroad service to the East rather early, many of its settlers felt a sense of isolation and hence a desire to live together for protection and for social intercourse in the manner of the mining camps of the nearby mountains. Besides giving the newcomer a sense of "instant community," cooperation was practical for those who wanted to farm by irrigation. To conduct water onto the land was both expensive and time-consuming; few individual farmers could afford it.

Territorial Colorado's first "Anglo" colony was organized at Chicago, in 1869, by a Prussian named Carl Wulsten, a Civil War veteran who worked for a German-American newspaper after the war. In the belief that a cooperative effort would be more successful as well as cheaper for the individual, Wulsten proposed that his German Colonization Company sell memberships at $250 each. For this amount of money the member would be given his transportation, land, provisions, tools, stock, seed, and housing. The promoter admitted that it cost more than that to move a family of four to the West and to maintain it until the first crop came in, but he thought the cooperative nature of the venture could cut expenses to the figure he suggested. In November 1869, he and two others came to Colorado in search of the proper location for a colony. They were attracted to the Wet Mountain Valley, south of Canon City, because of the abundance of water, the excellent grazing lands, and the fact that earlier settlers there had raised both wheat and oats. These virtues, plus the mountain scenery that moved Wulsten to compare it with Switzerland, convinced the Germans that, in Brigham Young's words, this was the place.[11]

In the early spring of 1870 some three hundred German-American men, women, and children left Chicago by railroad. In the manner of later settlers who used this means of travel, they took along household furnishings, seeds, implements, and even livestock. This group also carried the machinery for a gristmill, a sawmill, and a sash and door factory. Since the Kansas Pacific Railway, by which they crossed Kansas, as yet was uncompleted, the group had to travel beyond Fort Wallace by wagon. Wulsten appealed to Vice-President Schuyler Colfax for help in moving his people beyond the railhead and that charming gentleman, known as "Smiling Schuyler" to both friends and enemies, used his influence to get army wagons, guarded by soldiers, to carry out the assignment. By way of thanks the colonists named their chief town Colfax.[12] The favor angered the Pueblo *Chieftain*'s proprietor, Sam McBride, who thought the romance of pioneering indeed had evaporated from the westward movement when such mollycoddling was used to attract newcomers.[13] His printed criticisms led to further animosities that climaxed in Pueblo one April morning when McBride put a shot through Wulsten's upper forearm. The wounded man recovered and the editor was not prosecuted, but the affair did not make life any easier for the newly settled colonists.[14]

The colony's activity dates from March 1870, when its members began to plant crops, construct permanent homes, and build roads and bridges in the valley. A thirty-acre communal garden was planted, and the town of Colfax was laid off a few miles south of Silver Cliff, each of the members being entitled to a lot. Witnesses to the group effort praised the rapidity with which the settlement was being perfected, and commented favorably upon the introduction of thrifty German farmers into the Colorado economy. But before long, murmurs of dissatisfaction were heard from the new Utopia nestled between the Wet Mountains and the Sangre de Cristo Range.

Part of the problem lay in land ownership. Originally Wulsten had asked the federal government for a grant of 40,000 acres to be parceled out to members in quarter sections. Under the Homestead Act individual applicants were entitled to this, but because the colony was to be of a cooperative nature, its officers preferred to maintain a measure of control. Wulsten also pointed out that compactness would offer protection against attack, although by this time the Indian threat in the Wet Mountain Valley was almost nonexistent. Unwilling to wait for congressional approval of the request before leaving Chicago, the group moved to Colorado and occupied the land as squatters, hoping for governmental sanction of its actions. In the summer of 1870 Wulsten went back to Washington, D.C., to find out what was causing the delay over the land grant. By the time he returned, the problem had been "solved"; the colony was on the verge of breaking up.

In addition to the friction over land tenure, the prospect of a lean winter due to a bad crop and the irritations inherent in communal living shook the confidence of the colonists. In Colorado's only true cooperative colony, where labor and capital were merged for the benefit of all, there was a good deal of grumbling over the fact that everyone—the ambitious and the drones, the thrifty and the profligate—seemed to receive the same returns for their efforts. "There was too much *Kommunismus,*" explained one of the group. As early as the summer of 1870 some of the dissatisfied began to drift away to Denver, Pueblo, Canon City, and other towns. A few stayed on and survived the winter, thanks to donations from Denver businessmen. With the coming of spring there was a general exodus. Only a few of the original group homesteaded and lived out their lives in the valley, where their descendants are to be found today.[15]

Wulsten's colony was not Colorado's first group effort; that honor goes to José María Jácquez and his New Mexican followers, who founded the Guadalupe Colony in the southern San Luis Valley in 1854,[16] but the German Colonization Company was the beginning of Anglo colony settlements in politically organized Colorado. Next came the Union Colony, which founded Greeley; its success inspired a good many later efforts to emulate it. Unlike the Wet Mountain Valley effort, the settlement at Greeley was only semi-cooperative. This, in part, accounted for its success, although location and leadership certainly were important factors.

The Union Colony had its origins in the mind of Nathan C. Meeker, the agricultural editor of the New York *Tribune,* who visited Colorado in 1869 and came away convinced that there were attractive homesites and sources of water along the eastern slope of the Rockies. Horace Greeley, the renowned editor of that newspaper, approved the idea and lent both his name and the prestige of his journal to it. Late that same year, in New York City, the colony was organized and given its name. With Meeker as its president, General Robert A. Cameron as vice-president, and Horace Greeley as treasurer, the new organization announced that anyone of good character who was a temperance advocate and had $5.00 could be initiated; another $150.00 paid the dues. In return the member was entitled to a piece of farmland from five to eighty acres in size depending upon the distance from town, and the right to buy a town lot at $25.00 or $50.00. Early in 1870 the three officers went out to Colorado and decided that the land near Evans, then the temporary terminus of the Denver Pacific Railway, was the proper place to settle. Well watered and with rail service, the Cache la Poudre Valley promised success to hopeful farmers.[17]

If the inspecting committee members entertained any doubts as to where to locate, their minds were set at rest by one of Colorado's leading salesmen. William N. Byers, pioneer journalist and perhaps the territory's greatest booster was, among other things, local manager of the National Land Company. That company, in turn, was the agent of the Denver Pacific Railway, whose officers were anxious to sell the road's granted lands. Denverites, who had voted a half million dollars' worth of bonds to support that railroad, also were hopeful that the lands would be sold. Therefore, it is not surprising that some remarkably favorable stories about the colony at Greeley appeared in the *Rocky Mountain News.*[18]

Colony officers bought approximately twelve thousand acres of land, most of it from the railroad and the remainder from private sources, after which they persuaded individual members to file on some sixty thousand acres of public land that surrounded the settlement site "to prevent uncongenial neighbors." Some five hundred people who wanted to follow Greeley's historic advice to "Go West" joined this organization endorsed by the famous man. Early in May 1870, the first contingent of about fifty families arrived by rail, ready to make new homes along the mountain front. They were not ordinary immigrants, wrote Frank Hall, one of the state's early historians, but "chiefly intelligent, well-to-do people, resolved to take up the work assigned them in the redemption of the wilderness. . . ."[19]

Unlike the slower accretion of buildings that characterized the growth of most western towns, the agricultural town of Greeley, as well as others that resembled it, sprang into life with a speed that was reminiscent of the mining-boom camps. So rapid was its establishment that the first arrivals lived in tents. Meanwhile, whole buildings were moved from nearby towns where the boom had crested. One structure, recently part of Cheyenne, quickly was dubbed the "Hotel de Comfort"; others came from neighboring Evans, a place that threatened to become a ghost town now that it no longer was a railhead. Before Greeley was two months old, it could boast 130 buildings. By the spring of 1871 it was incorporated, at which time its newly elected officers took over most of the duties earlier performed by colony officers, who now turned their attention to the development of the organization's farmland.

Coloradans, who thought that the future success of their territory lay in the accretion of population, were pleased both by the numbers and the quality of this latest group of colonists. Most colony charters mentioned the fact that applicants should be of high moral character, but in the Union Colony efforts were made to ensure this condition by a prohibition of alcoholic beverages, a rule that was enforced to the point of violence. When an attempt was made even to establish a billiard parlor, the guardians of moral rectitude blocked it. Those who were willing to settle for a vicarious view of life's seamier side could witness the production *Ten Nights in a Bar-Room,* a reminder by the local dramatic association that paradise indeed could be lost.[20]

If the occupants of the colony were sworn enemies of Demon Rum, they also were heavily Protestant, Republican, and Anglo-Saxon. David Boyd, an early historian of the settlement, said that Catholics had given the town a wide berth, explaining that "Catholicism, at least Irish-Catholicism, and whiskey go in harmony together." The racial homogeneity of the place was somewhat harder to account for. Considering the white, Anglo-Saxon, and Protestant nature of the colony's makeup, he could understand the absence of Catholics, but since a heavy proportion of the early members were Republicans and former Abolitionists he thought the acceptance of blacks would have been a foregone conclusion. But such was not the case. "For a number of years not one was to be seen here," he wrote later, "and now they could be counted on the fingers of one hand. Even our barber shops are all run by white men. The writer is not aware of a single piece of real estate in either the town or colony being owned by a Negro."[21]

Although the Union Colony generally was a success, it shared the difficulty of its sister colonies in the earliest days. Some of the settlers came west with the notion that farming here could be carried on without any difficulty, stayed around only long enough to discover it was not true, and then went home to spread the bad word. It was reminiscent of the days of 1859, when the go-backers failed to find their imagined bonanza on the first try. One of the Union Colony's early critics was an Illinois newspaper editor named George A. Hobbs, who beat a hasty retreat from Colorado, loudly warning prospective settlers that Greeley, Colorado, was "the last place on the face of this terrestial ball that any human being should contemplate to remove to. . . ." It was, he charged, "a delusion, a snare, a cheat, a swindle, . . . a graveyard in which are buried heaps of bright hopes and joyous anticipations." Hobbs complained about the lack of irrigation water, and he was not alone. Some of the colonists, who had read glowing accounts about the availability of that precious commodity in the *Star of Empire,* a magazine published by the National Land Company, were disappointed to learn that their membership money did not include canal rights. Without water, Hobbs concluded, Greeley was just another outlying piece of the Great American Desert, located "on a barren, sandy plain . . . midway between a poverty stricken ranch and a prairie-dog village and . . . bounded chiefly by prickly pears."[22] Colony officers undertook the construction of irrigation ditches, but it was an expensive matter and they found it necessary to charge the unhappy landholders for this service. More complaints were heard when the officers attempted to raise membership fees.

Early settlers at Greeley later admitted that in the beginning life at the colony was not without its problems. One of them recalled that when a newcomer stepped from the railroad train those who struggled with the land would comment, "Here comes another victim." Although there was periodic grumbling, and the colony officers were subjected to considerable abuse, the settlement at Greeley fared quite well.[23]

The importation of immigrant groups and consequent block sales of land, such as that to the Union Colony, moved William Byers to suggest other such projects. In the autumn of 1870 he wrote to C. N. Pratt of the National Land Company at Chicago, describing six possible sites within the land grant of the Denver Pacific Railway. The response was favorable, and in November the Chicago-Colorado Colony was founded. Its officers were Robert Collyer, a Unitarian minister, president; Sidney H. Gay of the Chicago *Tribune,* vice-president; and Colonel C. N. Pratt, secretary. The same $155.00 initiation-membership fee was set for the new colony, and for that money members were to be given the same land allotments as were spelled out in the earlier Union Colony constitution. A campaign for members was commenced and by May 1871 some 390 had joined, nearly half of whom were from Illinois. Massachusetts, with 36 names, contributed the highest number from any eastern state.

As the organizational moves were made, a committee went out to Colorado and selected a site in the Boulder Valley, slightly north of the village of Burlington, naming it Longmont in honor of Long's Peak, which towered in the background. Burlington, a little agricultural town of 250 inhabitants, and a place that hoped to be the home of the University of Colorado, had no notion that the invaders from Chicago would create a monster that would gobble up their entire village. The founders of Longmont bought 23,000 acres of land from the National Land Company and another 30,000 from the federal government, the entire tract to be set aside for colony members. Another 2,000 acres came from private donations. By April nearly a hundred persons had arrived and were living in temporary shelters; homes would be built after the urgent matter of crop planting was attended to. Although group activities included the distribution of land, the laying out of the town, and the construction of irrigation ditches, this was not a cooperative-type colony. Individuals worked their own acreages, and, after 1873, when the town was incorporated, city officials took over political matters as in the case of Greeley, while colony officials continued to interest themselves in land distribution.[24]

Like the Union Colony, the new effort at Longmont grew rapidly, reaching a population of 415 colonists by early June 1871. Although it was well located, with an adequate water supply and excellent railroad service, there were problems in the early days, just as there had been at Greeley. Some of the colonists had difficulties over their land titles; frequently the ditching was inadequate; and in 1871 grasshoppers came in clouds, devouring the young crops. David Boyd, the acerbic historian of the Union Colony, found his own reasons for the new settlement's difficulties. According to Longmont's constitution, it was a temperance town, but Boyd was quick to point out that on this score there was a great deal of backsliding. Without a "great principle to rally around," such as the battle against Demon Rum, it appeared clear to him that such people were bound to fail. However, he thought that the farmers around Longmont had prospered more than those of the Greeley area because they chose to live on their farms, as opposed to taking up residence in the colony town.[25]

In 1870, about the time the Chicago Colony at Longmont was being organized, another group settled on adjoining homesteads a few miles west of Burlington. More of a joint endeavor than a formally organized colony, the little settlement was made up of immigrants from the parish of Ryssby, in Smaland Province, Sweden. Together they began to construct an irrigation ditch, known in modern times as the "Swede ditch," to conduct water from the South St. Vrain River eight miles away. That first winter, as yet without irrigation water and suffering from a very light harvest, the group was faced by hunger. A number of the men went to work in the mines at Black Hawk, while others cut timber in the mountains, and the women stayed home, nursing sick children.

Their hopes for a better crop were realized the next year and, encouraged by this success, others from Ryssby migrated and joined the Colorado group. By 1873 there were fourteen families in the settlement. In 1875 a log schoolhouse was constructed; it also provided a meeting place for Sunday church services. Construction of the stone church, so well known to Boulder county residents today, was commenced in 1881. The Ryssby Settlement, as it came to be known, provided the close integration and social intercourse for its people intended in the colony ideal.[26]

Inspired by the interest in colonies shown by midwesterners, yet another project was undertaken in Illinois late in 1870. Reverend Andrew C. Todd, who lived in a little village in the southern part of the state, had been impressed by the possibilities of colonization in Colorado while visiting there during the summer. Byers, with whom he had met and talked, told the minister a good deal about the National Land Company's fertile acres and the ease with which they might be acquired. At first called the Western Colony, the name was changed to St. Louis–Western Colony when its headquarters were moved to St. Louis, where the advantages of a large city could be put to use in recruiting settlers. Again, as in the other two agricultural colonies, a modest amount of money was asked of each member, in return for which plots of land were allotted. The site of the colony was adjacent to Evans, the onetime railroad terminus, located four miles south of Greeley.

The colony company bought 1,600 acres of land for $12,000, and by the summer of 1871 Evans was said to have acquired nearly six hundred colony residents. Unlike Greeley the St. Louis–Western Colony was "open" with regard to saloons and pool halls. David Boyd dourly predicted that King Alcohol soon would prove to be a tyrant and that the place would suffer from his influence. Andrew C. Todd, the founder, spent nearly twenty years at the colony, and when he left, he inferentially agreed with this prediction, commenting that the Devil had a mortgage on the town and it appeared he would soon foreclose it. While Evans did not wither under the influence of the devastating moral climate attributed to it by the critics, it did not grow as rapidly as Greeley, much to the pleasure of Colorado's "cold-water" army of temperance advocates.

Several reasons have been advanced for the difference in the development of these neighboring colonies. One explanation for the relative failure of Evans was the tendency of its members to live in town as "suitcase farmers" and thus neglect their farms. The Reverend Todd was one of the accused. Other arguments held that the land around Greeley was better, a contention hard to justify, and that the Union Colony's residents simply were more sober and industrious. Perhaps. A better answer to the question is that the two towns were so near each other that only one could thrive as a supply center for the surrounding agricultural community; in this case, it was Greeley.[27]

Down the South Platte River some twenty-seven miles, near the present town of Masters, another "colony" by the name of Green City cropped up in 1871. Formally known as the Southwestern Colony, and promoted by Colonel David S. Green of Memphis, Tennessee, it was organized purely for purposes of land speculation. For $100.00 each, members were promised aid in securing free government land, a town lot, and a share in the jointly held colony farm. There were no promises of irrigation. Green and his associates simply filed on a section of government land for a townsite at a cost of $1.25 an acre, subdivided it into lots each having twenty-five front feet, and promised a number of benefits to buyers who, by virtue of their purchase, had become members of the "colony." It was estimated that the promoters realized around $60,000 through sales made to purchasers who had little idea what they had bought. Highly colored literature, the hallmark of land speculators, gave a vivid description of the marvelous things that awaited the lucky buyers of property in Green City. One circular was said to have hinted that the city was destined to become a great entrepôt of trade; a poster showed a steamboat tied up at the busy wharf on the South Platte River. But neither riverboat nor rail reached Colorado's unborn port of call. The uninitiated, who had fallen for yet another western land scheme, soon drifted away, and those who remained, not wishing to be reminded that the name of the founder was the only thing about the place that was green, changed the name to Corona.[28]

During the years 1869–71 the agricultural colony fever seemed to be infectious. In addition to those already mentioned, there were other less newsworthy efforts. Perhaps it was significant that one of these should be headed by Green Russell, of 1859 gold rush fame, for it was said often, and frequently it was true, that many of the early miners found their gold in other forms of western economic enterprise. In the spring of 1870 a Denver paper mentioned that Russell was back, this time leading a hundred and fifty settlers from

Georgia and North Carolina who intended to farm along the upper Huerfano River. Although they employed the name "Georgia Colony," this was no more than a group movement westward; upon arrival members of the party took up land individually.[29]

Another settlement made in the spring of 1871 was located at Platteville, where several thousand acres of railroad land were purchased from the National Land Company. Lying some thirty-five miles north of Denver, along the east bank of the South Platte, it took advantage of rich, well-watered acres at the foot of the Rocky Mountains. Once again, this was a development project, undertaken for the purpose of selling granted railroad lands, and it was a colony in name only. As in other similar projects, town lots were awarded as a part of membership and farm sites were parceled out; membership fees did not pay for any irrigation. Platteville was yet another project in which William Byers interested himself.[30]

Encouraged by the success of the Greeley Colony, General Robert Cameron, who meantime had lent his talents to the formation of the Fountain Colony, decided to try his hand at yet another project. When, in 1872, the army decided to abandon the Camp Collins military reservation near La Porte he proposed the establishment of a town company to be known as the Fort Collins Agricultural Colony. Following the formula used earlier, both farming and city tracts were made available by the payment of fees ranging from $50 to $250. Within a year an "instant" town was functioning, an irrigation ditch was under construction, and a place that soon was to become an important municipality was on the map.[31]

In addition to those colonies already mentioned, there were a number of less publicized efforts by groups from Kentucky, Ohio, Pennsylvania, Iowa, Illinois, Wisconsin, and Tennessee, most of which were modeled after the efforts at Greeley, Evans, Longmont, and other places where land companies sponsored settlement. By the latter part of the decade, however, the agricultural colony method grew more popular throughout the West and began to plant some of its converts in the San Luis Valley.

The selection of southern Colorado as a site for Mormon settlement was more or less an accident. A young missionary named John Morgan, who had been making conversions in Alabama and Georgia in the post–Civil War period, wrote to Brigham Young in the summer of 1877, telling him that some of his newfound flock wanted to migrate to the West. Young replied that, indeed, Zion was growing, and he suggested New Mexico and West Texas as possible sites for a colony. He had no preference as to location, but he said that it should be healthy and it should have an abundant and easily utilized water supply for purposes of irrigation. He added that if the place chosen was near any of the Indian tribes, so much the better, for it would give the Mormons a further chance to wield their good influence over the natives. Shortly Morgan advised church authorities at Salt Lake City that he intended to accompany his converts to the terminus of the Denver and Rio Grande Railway, at Fort Garland, Colorado, and from there he would take them by wagon into New Mexico. At the time of writing he had not decided upon a final location.[32]

The group of seventy-two men, women, and children arrived at Pueblo on a cold November evening in 1877, tired and dirty after a long train ride from Alabama. They were given temporary housing in the old Thespian Theater until barracks could be erected on an island in the Arkansas River. Within days a rude structure, roofed over with building paper, 100 by 15 feet, was ready for occupancy. At each end was a small room that served as a communal kitchen and dining room for half of the occupants. Tiny living quarters were walled off for the ten families present; single men bunked together and even on temporary beds set up in the kitchen.[33] During the winter the men did odd jobs around Pueblo, picking up enough money to get the group through the cold months. Some of them made $1.50 to $2.00 a day cutting ties; others worked at their respective trades of blacksmith, carpenter, bricklayer, and the like. Any money they earned was turned over to the company's treasurer to be applied to the group's subsistence.

During December, Morgan visited Salt Lake City, fully intending to return for his charges and escort them to New Mexico, but church authorities decided to reassign him to the South, where he had been successful with conversions. John Taylor, who had succeeded to the church presidency after Brigham Young's death in 1877, now selected James Z. Stewart to lead the converts to their new home. The young man agreed to go, but he pointed out that he had no money. The president swept aside such a minor detail with the comment "Brother Stewart, the Lord will open up the way." Resolutely the missionary borrowed sixty dollars and set off for Pueblo.[34]

As it developed, Stewart was not obliged to lead his flock into the wilderness on his own. John Morgan already had made some arrangements that would simplify matters, at least insofar as decision making was concerned. A conference with Alexander Cameron Hunt, a former Colorado territorial governor now deeply interested in the settlement policies of the Denver and Rio Grande Railway, revealed that lands were available in the southern end of the San Luis Valley. Satisfied that the land, owned by the state of Colorado, could be purchased at a reasonable figure, that the railroad intended to serve the area, and that Mormons in need of money would be welcome on railroad construction crews, Morgan had agreed to settle the group at the suggested location. James Stewart was given the signal to start the Pueblo group for their own promised land.

Taking three of the converts with him, Stewart boarded a train for Fort Garland, after which the men moved southward on foot. Slogging along through rain, snow, and mud they reached the Conejos area in late March. Here they found themselves nearly seven thousand feet above sea level, in a well-watered country, but one that would have a relatively short growing season because of the cold. Stewart foresaw no difficulty in settling at least a hundred families there; the river bottomland was rich, and even the gravelly benchland was producing something for the local Mexican-American farmers.

The area was remote, with little prospect of any land rush to it, so local landowners were willing to sell cheaply. The missionary bought 120 acres and a good house for thirty-five dollars from one of them. When he admitted he had no money, the seller took his note. Later President Taylor, who had said the Lord could do these things, paid off the obligation. Meanwhile, encouraged by the ease with which property could be acquired, Stewart purchased another farm for fifty dollars. Again using his newfound credit, he acquired a yoke of oxen and a plow; then he turned to his benefactors and borrowed a wagon from them. These matters settled, the agricultural prospector left his traveling companions behind and returned to Pueblo to get the others.[35] In mid May 1878, the Pueblo contingent was loaded onto Denver and Rio Grande cars after the railroad agreed to cut the fare to Fort Garland from ten dollars to one dollar each and to carry baggage free. At the end of the track the families hired Mexican-American drivers and wagons to take them to lands purchased by Stewart. It was a new world for the southerners, who now had to adjust to a strange climate and different crops.

In the early autumn, Mormon church authorities decided to strengthen the toehold in southern Colorado by sending in Elder Hans Jensen with a few Utah families. Writing from Conejos, Jensen said they had been called by the proper authorities to leave their homes and to take a mission in the San Luis Valley. He found the southern contingent "feeling well in the gospel . . . and rather low in circumstances." The weather was cold and food supplies ran low, but President John Taylor sent forty-five dollars at Christmastime with which they bought twenty sacks of flour. The gift was much appreciated, and apparently Taylor got his money's worth, for Jensen said that with full stomachs "we have now a lively and good time in spreading the word of truth." That the religious campaign was bearing fruit was seen in the announcement that Brother Salvador Chávez had signed on with the Saints.

Mormon recruitment among the Mexican Americans did not find favor with the local Catholic priest. When Jensen and several of his friends visited the padre "he called us thieves, liars, whoremongers. . . . Then he turned against us, as a crazy man, and called for help to throw us out, although we went quiet and peaceably." On the other hand, local Presbyterian churchmen got on well with the Mormons, attended their meetings, and met frequently with the newcomers. One of the ministers became very friendly with the group. "He has considerable faith in the work of God, and preaches half 'Mormonism' already," wrote Jensen in triumph.[36]

In the spring of 1879 John Morgan, who had returned to his mission in the South, sent in 60 more converts, and in November he added another 110, making a total of around 400 for the year. He planned to bring in even more during 1880, but illness among the immigrants reduced that figure. Meanwhile, Hans Jensen and his Conejos group located and surveyed a prospective townsite they named Manassa.[37] Adjacent to the town were ten-acre parcels of farming and meadow land that were to be portioned out to the residents on the same plan as the "Big Field" near Salt Lake City. The Mormon pattern, reminiscent of settlement in colonial New England, was to be carried out in Colorado. Two missionaries working in Virginia contributed 80 converts to the San Luis Valley settlements during these months, and one of them predicted that sometime in the future Manassa would become well known. He did not know it at the time, but the town was to gain its real fame from a pair of the settlers he sent west that spring. John Dempsey and his wife produced a son who rose to international fame in the boxing world as the "Manassa Mauler."[38]

Three and a half miles north of Manassa the Mormons established another town and named it Ephraim. The biblical names of the two little cities honored two sons of Joseph, who was sold into Egypt. High hopes were held out for Ephraim, a place that was expected to overshadow Manassa and similar towns later to be founded. Hans Jensen thought the land around Ephraim would support more than a hundred families, but experience proved otherwise and the place was vacated a few years later.[39] By 1881 some of those who had settled at Manassa were attracted by the land around La Jara, and a number of them set up temporary quarters on a site that became Richfield. Sanford was next laid out, a few miles north of Ephraim. It was attractive enough to siphon off some of the Richfield and Ephraim settlers during the next few years, and, along with Manassa, it survived.[40]

With their roots planted in the San Luis Valley the Saints now were ready to create other towns, acquire farmland, and accept more settlers. To encourage additional immigration from Utah, Jensen sent the *Deseret News* a description of Colorado's opportunities and advantages. He said the federal government had set aside a hundred thousand acres of land in the state for school purposes, and about a fifth of the total was situated in Conejos County. It would be sold for $1.25 an acre, the going government price of land, the state to be the beneficiary. Colorado governmental officials, he added, looked favorably upon Mormons. Meantime, the church was financing the purchase of seeds, implements, and stock. At that time the Denver and Rio Grande Railway was only twenty miles away, and when it passed down the valley it would run within two or three miles of the new settlement. Since Colorado was an important mining state, Jensen assured Utah readers that there would be a ready market for foodstuffs raised in the valley.[41]

The new colonies met with hardships not unknown to such ventures. The southerners, unused to severe winters, experienced considerable suffering. Added to the general discomfort was sickness, so common on the frontier, but colony leaders rationalized both these problems, assuring their flocks that it was just a matter of getting used to the new climate. Some of the Mississippians were doubtful that they would ever accommodate themselves to a thermometer that read twenty-six degrees below zero, as it did one day in 1880, but they told each other that Mormons often had to settle where no one else would live. As people of strong faith, these settlers resolved to stick it out, even as they watched some of their neighbors pull up stakes and go home, and they resolved to make yet another desert bloom. It was the moral climate that troubled some of the immigrants from the Deep South, who could not get used to the outspoken language of these western Mormons. Their rigid fundamentalist background made them recoil when they heard people who called themselves saints use the words *damn* and *hell* with great regularity. It was explained that even people who called themselves saints were not always perfect, but this did not satisfy the southerners, who tended to take religious matters quite literally and objected to profanity in the kingdom of heaven.[42]

The heavy immigration made necessary some kind of temporary employment for the newcomers as they prepared their lands and awaited their first crops. Fortunately the revival of railroad building during the early eighties required a good deal of labor, and, as they had been in the construction of the Union Pacific into Utah, now in Colorado young Mormon boys were put to work on Denver and Rio Grande construction crews. They were able to earn between $3.50 and $4.00 a day, a sum that meant a great deal to struggling farm families trying to get a fresh start in the West. So great was the demand for construction crews that labor contractors began to solicit workers in Utah, agreeing to transport them to southern Colorado for $10.00 a head. The Church of the Latter-Day Saints cautiously agreed to a limited amount of such emigration from Utah but insisted that it maintain control of any such movements.[43]

Perhaps it was because the Mormon farm families and the single, male railroad workers came in groups directed and often financed by the church that they succeeded where others frequently failed. Another factor worked in their favor, however, and must be included in their success story: the friendship offered to them by the Mexican-American residents of the San Luis Valley. The warmth with which James Stewart's first group was received did not cool as succeeding contingents of Mormons arrived and prepared to farm. John Morgan, who continued his earlier work with this immigration, made references to "our Mexican friends," and remarked that in many instances the locals had offered their farms for rent and had supplied seeds, teams, houses, and even the loan of milk cows. He made an important point when he explained that "thus the way is opened up for the people who come unprepared to purchase and to do farming immediately. . . ." This applied particularly to the southern converts, most of whom were without money, draft animals, or farm machinery. Thus the Mexican-American population and the newcomers mixed easily in economic, social, and even religious matters. Catholicism surrendered some of its Spanish-speaking flock to the Mormons; some years later, one of the Saints could state that Samuel Trujillo "was the first Latter-day Saint child born in the San Luis Valley."[44]

Coloradans accepted the Mormon immigration because it touched a part of the state that had shown no particular agricultural promise to date and therefore was coveted by no one, because the Denver and Rio Grande Railway wanted to populate the area it served, and because the Mormons showed little interest in politics. Even when they threatened to control Conejos County politically there was no great concern because it did not appear that their votes would alter the general voting patterns of that part of the state. Southern Colorado was Democratic, and the Mormons who came from the South tended to favor that ticket. There was little disposition on the part of those who came over from Utah to vote Republican, because that party had shown nothing but antagonism toward the Mormons on the polygamy question. As the years passed it became even more clear that these people had come to Colorado to farm and not to agitate for any political change.[45]

It took the Mormons about a decade to establish themselves firmly in the San Luis Valley. By the end of that period they controlled about forty thousand acres of farmland, several thousand of which were irrigated by a series of ditches and canals. About a half-dozen small towns were located at strategic points and were under the traditional control of the church. Meantime, the settlers indeed had made another agricultural desert flower, for until they came relatively few farmers had undertaken to till the gravelly soil in that high, cold country.

The Mormon settlements in the San Luis Valley, commenced in the latter part of the seventies, characterized a decade of agricultural colony effort in Colorado, a conscious program of promotion that brought a great many settlers into the young state. The notion that group settlement would rapidly increase population proved true almost from the beginning, for as early as the summer of 1871 a Denver newspaper asserted that at least three thousand people already had responded to the call. Others, attracted by colony advertising, had elected to come on their own and to settle near the new towns, or in some other equally desirable neighborhood, and they represented a spin-off from the major group movements. With the addition of these individual settlers it was estimated that within the first year Colorado's population had increased by around five thousand, and for a mining country to which the decade of the sixties had not been kind, this infusion of new blood was significant. Farmers and their little villages were not as flamboyant as the high-flying miners and their colorful communities, but the tillers of the soil had the virtue of permanence, once they had put down their roots, and it was to this type of settlement that Colorado leaders had looked when arguing the case for statehood, or when trying to bolster the local economy through diversification. In the eyes of many a booster the prosaic agrarians were long-term investments against the failure of a western dream.

# 8

# New Frontiers

For the greater part of the two decades that followed the gold strike of 1859, Colorado's precious metals industry stood in question. The doldrums of the late 1860s continued well into the 1870s, and it was not until the "big one" came in at Leadville toward the end of the period, to be followed by other strikes, that doubts as to the state's mineral wealth finally were set at rest. During the intervening years, business and political leaders anxiously sought other means of income, such as tourism and agriculture. But even as they explored these possibilities they never abandoned hope that yet more treasures were to be found deeper in the mountains.

To make the continuing search of Colorado's mountains more productive there was a burning need for additional topographic knowledge. Surveyor Ferdinand V. Hayden remarked that Colorado offered a particularly fruitful place for his profession because of the probability of great expansion in the Central Rockies in the 1870s. He wanted to examine the geological formations, the flora and the fauna, the topography, and even the spectacular scenery of the region. His photographer, William H. Jackson, was particularly interested in the last of these. Hayden and his crews spent four seasons in Colorado between 1873 and 1876; the result of their ambitious project was an atlas officially known as the *Geological and Geographical Atlas of Colorado and Portions of Adjacent Territory*. Railroad builders, mining investors, and land developers instantly seized upon the publication.[1] It was of particular interest also to historians because it brought the prehistoric remnants of

Mesa Verde to the public's attention for the first time, although not for another decade would the rich find of artifacts in the Cliff Palace be made.[2] For the moment, ancient ruins did not hold any fascination for the aggressive promoters of Colorado, who were interested in economic development first and culture later.

Even as Hayden and his men sighted through their transits and Jackson took his photographs, seasoned prospectors probed likely spots in western Colorado, looking for new bonanzas. When they found something promising, a new town was certain to appear almost overnight, as was shown once more by the example of Lake City. During the winter of 1874–75 two brothers who were working on a toll road from Lake San Cristobal to Silverton came across some promising ore. Loading all they could onto a wagon, they dragged their find through the snow to a smelter, where they were rewarded with $18,000 for their efforts. Very soon thereafter Enos Hotchkiss located his Golden Fleece mine, the product of which quickly changed struggling Lake City from a small cluster of cabins into a roaring mining camp of five thousand. A visitor to the new mining camp measured its development by the fact that in a very short time it had twenty-eight saloons and the dance halls and sporting houses were running at capacity.[3]

During the time that Colorado's western slope was undergoing an examination by surveyors and prospectors another kind of inquiry was being conducted, namely, an examination of possibilities for technical improvement in the reduction of ore. This was done in order to reduce the declining grades of known deposits more cheaply and to prepare for a more thorough exploitation of future finds. The search for technical help led to Nathaniel P. Hill, a Brown University chemistry professor who, along with metallurgists Hermann Beeger and Richard Pearce, had achieved considerable technological success in refining precious ore. Backed by eastern money and utilizing the latest scientific methods, Hill's Boston and Colorado Smelter at Black Hawk pointed the way for the mining community in general. Ultimate success, however, was to be a slow process; meantime, gold production tended to taper off. As it would again, silver offered some help, and by 1874 the value of its output would surpass that of gold.[4] This did not mean that the gold miners had given up in Colorado; rather, it meant that they now pursued all avenues, ranging from technical improvements to the encouragement of rail service, while hoping that in the course of time another big bonanza would be found. Their trust in the hidden mineral wealth of Colorado was justified within a few years, for by 1877 the spectacular Leadville mines made international news.

What became known across America as the "Leadville excitement" was proof that, once abandoned, a mineral site should not necessarily be written off. In this case an old mining camp lay dormant for well over a decade before it was rediscovered. It had come to attention first in the spring of 1860 as a part of the mad search that was carried out in the South Park country at that time. Some members of the small army of prospectors in the region worked the gulches near Mount Elbert and Mount Massive, and, as frequently happened in the game of mineral roulette, one of them, a Georgian named Abe Lee, came up with an exceptionally rich pan of gold flakes. "By God! I got Californy here in the bottom of this here pan!" he shouted, and so the place was named California Gulch.

A series of little camps blossomed along the gulch. The most important was Oro City, which for a time was *the* gold-mining site in Colorado. Wolfe Londoner, a young Jewish merchant who was there in the summer of 1861, said that as many as ten thousand people swarmed around the placer-mining locations, many of them living in tents, others in their wagons, and the gamblers set up wayside tables to provide "drive-in gambling" for the passersby.[5] Then the place faded, suffering the economic anemia that attacked so many of these placer camps, and perhaps as few as four hundred diehards stayed on—hoping. By 1870 all of Lake County had only around five hundred residents, and in the middle of that decade, from the district where individual miners once panned as much as a hundred dollars a day each, only about twenty thousand dollars in gold was retrieved in an entire year.

In 1873 a prospector named William H. ("Uncle Billy") Stevens, who earlier had worked California Gulch, returned to his old haunts and this time he suspected the presence of silver. The following spring he and a metallurgist found a place a mile or so above the future site of Leadville where the silver-bearing lead carbonate promised to yield as much as forty ounces of silver per ton. They kept their secret and late in 1875 they hired some workmen to extract what they described as lead ore—but, as usual, the truth emerged. By 1877 Colorado witnessed another mineral rush and the word *Leadville* was on the lips of miners and financiers all the way to London. Nearly twenty years had passed, but it was

1859 all over again; once more, cautious eastern newspapers warned local readers not to leave hearth and home for the mere rumor of riches in Colorado. As before, thousands ignored such advice and raced westward.[6]

The sensational growth of Leadville, its fabulous mines, and its colorful characters—who sometimes made only brief names for themselves but in other cases went on to become well-known Coloradans—is a story often repeated in recounting the state's history. Leadville stands high in the list of rip-roaring camps where money and liquor flowed freely and sin was a twenty-four-hour-a-day proposition. When actor Eddie Foy played there in the fall of 1878, the town was growing so fast that he was unable to find a place to live and was obliged to sleep on an old straw tick backstage. As he viewed the nonstop commotion on the streets, watched men bet anywhere from five cents in a chuck-a-luck game to five thousand dollars on a poker hand, and witnessed the violence of a male society, he looked back upon Dodge City, where he had played his last engagement, and decided that Leadville made the Kansas cowtown look like a Sunday school. When he returned to Leadville the next season, Foy said it was overrun with "Seventy-Niners," as they called themselves, and everything had grown miraculously, including the high state of lawlessness and disorder. It was here that he saw his first lynching.[7]

Leadville was a boomtown that could boast of nearly fifteen thousand residents by 1880 and claim to be Colorado's second city at the ripe old age of two years. It was here that James B. Grant, a young metallurgist, built a smelter the great success of which led to the construction of a much larger one at Denver, and both of which brought him fame and fortune. By 1883 he was governor of Colorado. Similarly, H. A. W. Tabor grubstaked some lucky miners and ended up with so much money he could afford to dispense with the services of the faithful Augusta and marry "Baby Doe" McCourt. Politically, he made it up the ladder to become mayor of Leadville, then lieutenant governor, and do a brief stint as U.S. senator, but it is not in the realm of politics that he is remembered today. One of Tabor's attorneys was Charles S. Thomas; he became governor and finally U.S. senator. Marshall Field, better known as a Chicago merchant, put $500 into Tabor's hands and got back $700,000 from the mining investment. Another merchant was David May, whose great chain of department stores originated at Leadville. David H. Moffat, to become so well known in banking and railroad circles, took a sizable amount of money out of the "carbonate camp," as did Meyer Guggenheim, whose American Smelting & Refining Company originated there. The roster of Leadvillites whose names loom large in Colorado history is long, but most of them took their fortunes elsewhere or spent the money upon themselves for purposes of self-adornment and sometimes to satisfy political ambitions. Very few displayed philanthropic tendencies, the Guggenheims and a few others excepted, so far as the state and its people were concerned.

Always anxious to show that they were progressive, the mining towns eagerly sought to acquire the most modern of conveniences, one of which was the newly developed telephone. Leadville's service commenced in the autumn of 1878 when the Western Union Company brought a line over Mosquito Pass from Alma to provide men with the latest silver-market information. During the following year connections were made with several smelters in the area, further facilitating the business of mining and smelting in the Leadville region. By 1880 the little exchange in that city did a forty thousand dollar business, a statistic that was a matter of pride among residents of that mining camp. Male operators were employed because the telephone facilities were used by rough-and-ready establishments in which the language used was not considered proper for the ears of young ladies.[8]

Other developments in the town's early history suggested that although the place had such modern facilities as the telephone, it lagged in the development of certain municipal services. The Harrison Hook and Ladder Company, one of several volunteer fire departments organized to protect the city's fragile wooden structures, was a case in point. So long as the group gave dinners and dances and raised funds for the worthy cause of fire fighting, things went well enough, but in the case of a serious fire the amateur nature of the organization became apparent. Upon one occasion this deficiency generated a civic dispute of such serious proportions that major changes in the city's policy followed. In April 1882, a fire devastated approximately a block of the business community and caused an estimated five hundred thousand dollars' worth of damage. Local firefighters lodged a bitter complaint against one of the aldermen for officious interference at the scene of the blaze. It was alleged not only that he had referred to the firemen as "drunken sons of bitches," but that he had knocked down and kicked one of them.

Upon investigation the city council discovered that at least part of the alderman's allegations were true: the hook and ladder boys indeed were drunk. After the alderman had ordered the arrest of one of them, the others "raised spanners and other weapons in a threatening attitude" toward him, and it was at this point that he punched the fireman, but did not kick him. It saddened council members to relate further that the alderman simply was endeavoring to dissuade a group of intoxicated firemen from gutting and robbing the saloon of William Roberts on Chestnut Street, and trying to prevail on them to return to their duty at the fire. Equally lamentable was the fact that "said intoxicated firemen did steal and take by force from said Roberts 600 cigars, and a lot of liquor and beer." As a result of the investigation the councilmen concluded that Leadville no longer could accept the donated efforts of volunteer fire companies. Therefore it created a paid fire department whose efforts, it hoped, could be confined to the sober extinguishment of fires without the looting of local business establishments and unnecessary destruction of property.[9]

In the search by Leadville's young men for recreational activities that did not threaten the town's existence, they formed clubs whose function was strictly social. One of them was the Benevolent and Protective Order of Elks, brought to Leadville by the English actor Charles Vivian during a theatrical engagement there in the winter of 1879–80. Earlier he had belonged to a group of London actors who called themselves the Jolly Corks, and after he reached New York, in the late sixties, he had organized a similar club in that city. Before long the group had changed its name to the Elks. As branches grew, it became an internationally known fraternal order. Colorado mining towns, with heavy male populations, took to the organization with alacrity.[10]

Thus did another "instant" mineral city spring up, prosper, brawl, and struggle mightily for overnight maturity and civic calm. Stories about the colorful thousands who bulged its crowded facilities and tales of the antics of boom camp society made colorful reading in eastern climes, but so did tales of incredible riches that had come to ordinary men and made them gentlemen overnight. The inevitable result, a search for more Leadvilles, drew men from the remotest parts of America, men who took new hope that El Dorado was not dead, but only sleeping somewhere in the Rockies. As one historian later expressed it, Leadville "was only an ornate vestibule to a great mineral kingdom beyond."[11]

Into this potential kingdom poured a small army of prospectors, some of them making discoveries at Robinson and Kokomo, a few miles north of Leadville, while others reexamined the Blue River country and sampled ores along the Eagle River. The silver camp of Redcliff was established in 1879 as a result of this latter probe. That same year Pitkin, Tin Cup, Virginia, Irwin, and Gothic gave the Gunnison country new fame. The Sylvanite mine, at Gothic, produced another "bonanza king" overnight. Obediah B. Sands, the already wealthy owner of the Sands Hotel in Chicago, had come west for his health, and, in the manner of Horace Tabor, he grubstaked some miners in return for half of anything they might find. They hit it big, and the ailing Mr. Sands became considerably richer.[12] Another highly profitable result of the mineral search that followed Leadville's success was the discovery in 1879 of rich deposits along the Roaring Fork of the Colorado, leading to the establishment of Aspen.

These important mineral strikes attracted hordes of miners whose need for housing, food, and supplies quickly created a transportation problem in some very rugged country. Pack animals, mule trains, and wagons were called into service, but by the eighties the possibilities of rail service offered mining camps a cherished connection with the outside world. In the first years of Colorado railroading, the decade that followed the arrival of the "transcontinentals," mountain traffic had been pretty well cornered by the Colorado Central—it entered the "Little Kingdom" of Gilpin County in 1872—and by the narrow-gauge Denver and Rio Grande Railway, whose tracks threaded their way westward over La Veta Pass during the mid seventies. General Palmer chose the La Veta Pass route for two reasons: the Atchison, Topeka, & Santa Fe had "cut him off at the pass" when he tried New Mexico by way of Raton; at the same time he was aware of the mineral potential of the San Juan country in southwestern Colorado. When the surprising Leadville boom took place, the general at once sent a brigade of tracklayers through the keyhole today called the Royal Gorge and up the Arkansas River toward the new mines of Midas. Along the way he had to fight the A.T. & S.F. in the so-called Royal Gorge War, an affair that was carried on more in the courtroom than on the battlefield. Meantime his road also had traversed the southern reaches of Colorado, where the new town of Durango sprang up, had crossed Marshall Pass, using Otto Mears's old toll road to reach Gunnison, and was on its way through western Colorado toward

Salt Lake City. By 1883 Palmer's road was used for trading with the Mormons. Meanwhile, the eighties saw the little D. & R. G. fan out in a crazy-quilt manner, probing the valleys and scaling impossible heights, in search of new mining camps to serve. It was jokingly remarked that if a farmer had a wagonload of pumpkins on the other side of the mountain, the redoubtable General Palmer would throw a railroad line across it to pick them up.[13]

The Panic of 1873 had left its mark on Colorado, just as it had upon other regions and other segments of the economy, but in a period of growth this western community had suffered only a slowing of its development, as opposed to the stagnation felt in more settled parts of America. Now, in the eighties, money again was available, and with new mining camps calling for transportation, Colorado's golden age of railroad building ensued. Suddenly there was a new kind of boomtown: the railroad town. Helen Hunt Jackson spoke of it as she passed through Garland City in 1877, noting with some amazement that over a hundred houses stood where twelve days earlier the land had been bare. Four sawmills were at work night and day, trying to keep up with demand. As the author ate lunch at a partially completed hotel, the proprietor explained that he had disassembled the place only a week earlier, at Wagon Creek, and that he was reassembling it at the new railhead right over the customers' heads. "Beds were piled on the floor, one wall consisted of propped up doors, the rooms were separated only by sheets," explained the startled lady from Colorado Springs.[14]

If prospectors and financiers fought each other for the riches of the Colorado mountains, so did the rail lines. Even as Palmer's D. & R. G. was engaged in a running battle with the Santa Fe Company, he had to compete with the Denver, South Park and Pacific, whose owners—first John Evans and then the Union Pacific Railroad—challenged him for the Leadville traffic and raced him for Gunnison. When the D. & R. G. headed for Aspen during the late eighties, it was the same old story. This time the opponent was James John Hagerman's Colorado Midland road, but again the D. & R. G. won, even though the costs were fearfully high.[15] Aspen was grateful and praised the D. & R. G. for its efforts; so was Grand Junction, when Palmer's road reached that isolated place in western Colorado. A Grand Junction newspaper emotionally referred to the railroad's tracklaying crews as "our army of relief—of rescue." It also predicted that the road would bring thousands of people to populate the valley, not to mention all the conveniences and comforts that were enjoyed by the people of older Colorado cities.[16]

If the mineral rush into the deeper recesses of the Rockies, and westward across Colorado, had scoured the land and then abandoned it in favor of some more promising place, time and nature's healing would have covered the scars on the land. In that case the Indians, mainly the Uncompahgre and White River Utes, might have survived the onset of "civilization" a little longer. But this was no placer-mining frontier; instead, it was one that sent those in search of both silver and gold deeper into the earth. It required capital, machinery, a labor force, and transportation; thus it was less transitory than pick and pan mining. Furthermore, the advance of the railroad and the development of towns required a more permanent type of settlement if either of these institutions was to live and prosper. That, in turn, meant economic diversification and the coming of farmers and ranchers. Inevitably it was the appearance of these groups that spelled the end of Indian tenure in any part of the West.

In the frontier tradition, Coloradans assumed an attitude of indifference toward the Indians until the natives caused trouble or until their country became desirable for white occupation. In the case of the Utes there was little difficulty so long as those Indians lived and hunted on the western slopes of the Rockies and there was no immediate desire for their lands. A growing impatience with them developed as the western part of the state showed evidence of containing mineral and agricultural sites of value. When a large section of southwestern Colorado was set aside as a Ute reservation in 1868, the *Rocky Mountain News* had asked that good faith be kept with these Indians because of their past record of peaceful actions.[17] Treaty provisions stated that this land belonged to the Utes forever, except that railroads and highways might have rights-of-way through it, a stipulation that not only was contradictory but was bound to cause trouble.

It was not long, however, before "forever" was a forgotten word and about the best the miners could do in the way of recognizing these Indians was to name one of their mining towns—Ouray—after a local chief. But that was the end of their concessions; what the whites wanted was a revision of the 1868 treaty that would allow them to search for ore in southwest Colorado. Very shortly they would have their wish. By 1872 a commission was appointed to commence negotiations, and, even though the Utes balked, their resistance was short-lived. In 1873 the Indians ceded the San Juan Mountain section of their reservation, a piece of land about sixty-five by ninety miles in size. That satisfied the miners, for the time being.

Although the next confrontation with the Utes did not grow out of such specific origins as in the case of the San Juan country, its results pleased both miner and ranchman. The "Meeker affair," in which agent Nathan Meeker, of earlier Union Colony fame, was killed by Indians at the White River Agency, generated what has been called the "Ute War" of 1879. The immediate outcome of this episode was a new treaty, in 1880, one in which the Utes lost all their Colorado lands except a narrow strip in the southwestern corner of the State. To insure permanence of the treaty, Fort Crawford, named for Captain Emmet Crawford, was established a few miles south of where the town of Montrose would be built. With these matters set at rest, miners now could explore the countryside at will and settlers could build their cabins without fear of the "Indian menace," as it was then called. When Congress declared six million acres of former Ute lands open to public settlement in 1882, a Denver paper called it the most important piece of Colorado legislation to be introduced in several years. Now, said the newspaper, men and money would flow in very rapidly, and an area larger than Massachusetts and Connecticut combined would be put to use by industrious settlers.[18]

Publicists of the day hailed western Colorado as a place of great promise, an area once sealed off by a mountain barrier that held great rewards for both mining and pastoral endeavors. Parks and fertile valleys such as those found in the Gunnison country, where lately some twenty thousand tons of hay had been raised, were set forth as new frontiers that would provide homes for thousands of Americans. While such national publicity pleased Coloradans, it was not required reading for them; they had looked beyond the crest of the Rockies for some time and had wondered about the possibilities held by that unknown land. But once the Utes were on their way, and even before Congress opened the land for purchase, the westward rush had resumed.[19]

Into the fertile valleys poured the homesteaders, searching out farmsites, hastily erecting shelters, and planting their first crops. Although the legislation that opened the land to settlement prohibited homesteading on the reservation lands, tracts were for sale at the standard government price of $1.25 an acre, a very low figure for irrigable lands. The valley of the Uncompahgre offered about two hundred thousand acres of arable soil, and, as it was seized by the eager farmers, the little town of Delta sprang up at the mouth of the valley to supply their needs. The Grand Valley had even more land ready for the plow, as much as two hundred fifty thousand acres, and with water for irrigation available from the Grand River, highly intensive agriculture could be pursued. The supply town of Grand Junction, laid out near the union of the Grand (Colorado) and Gunnison rivers, quickly announced itself as the commercial center of the new agricultural frontier.[20] A third important agricultural town was Montrose. Its name was taken from a Walter Scott novel, *A Legend of Montrose,* said to have been suggested by Joseph Selig, one of the town's founders and a member of Colorado's Jewish community. The arrival of the D. & R. G. in the spring of 1882 assured the town's role as a distributing point for its region. At first a raggle-taggle sprawl of log shanties, the place shortly took on the appearance of a neatly laid-out town with wide streets and frame houses. Otto Mears put up six thousand dollars to build a hotel, businessmen commenced construction of substantial stores, and fourteen saloon owners took out licenses to operate. Gambling establishments opened their doors to cowboys, muleskinners, and floaters, who soon made the place so lively that the first mayor left town when the shooting began to erupt.

Meanwhile, cities began to appear in the southwestern corner of the state. Durango, a child of the D. & R. G. Railway that came into existence during 1880, literally blotted from the map the nearby town of Animas City, whose civic leaders had not jumped onto the railroad bandwagon quickly enough. Just a few years earlier, nearby Silverton and Ouray had blossomed as mining camps, providing part of the incentive that drew General Palmer and his little narrow-gauge railroad into that region. As was the case with other portions of western Colorado, the coming of rail service, induced by mineral wealth, tended to encourage farming and grazing. Hardly had the Utes moved their lodges before one of the Mormons notified the brethren that here was a place with a mild climate and rich soil, a new country where vegetables and high-quality fruit could be grown. During the spring of 1880 about seventy Mormon familes responded to the call.[21] A few years later, when an army doctor from Fort Lewis visited the little town of Mancos, he found a prosperous community of Mormon families whose cooperative store was stocked with everything a community might need.[22]

Fruit raising, to become an important element in the western slope's development, achieved an early start. During the winter of 1881–82 a group of settlers fought their way through snow to reach the North Fork section of the newly opened country. Sam Wade brought along some young fruit trees, a cargo so precious that fires were kept going each night to prevent them from freezing. He planted them near the site of modern Paonia. Enos Hotchkiss, locally famous for his Golden Fleece mine at Lake City, now joined the land rush, and he, too, set out a few fruit trees that spring. So readily did the seedlings take to the soil along the North Fork that Wade, Hotchkiss, and others sent for more the following year. By 1885 western Colorado was well along the road to renown for its excellent fruit.[23] Among the new little towns that popped up was one named Hotchkiss. Perhaps it foretold a transition in the state's economy, for its namesake, so widely known in mining circles, was honored not for his wealth in minerals but for his interest in the soil.

In a sense, the settlement of the lands opened by the Ute removal saw several stages of frontier development telescoped into a period of a very few years. Cattlemen, sheepmen, farmers, and fruit growers all swarmed onto the land together. Almost at once the railroad came, altering the usual pattern of evolution by providing a very early connection with the rest of Colorado, Utah, and the nation itself. Rapid urban growth, considered to be a characteristic of the mining frontier, appeared very quickly in the valleys that were opened to agricultural settlement in 1882, and with it came schools, churches, libraries, and other cultural attributes generally associated with civilized life. All these refinements came to the rest of the West in due course, but in the surrendered Ute Reservation lands the process took only about five years.

During the years that surveyors, miners, stockmen, and farmers pushed their way into the valleys of western Colorado, the agricultural advance eastward toward the arid high-plains country picked up momentum. The possibilities of irrigation from water flowing out of the mountains had been obvious to the early settlers along the east slopes of the Rockies, and they had exploited those possibilities at a very early date. The question that remained was, How far out in the flat country could irrigated farming be carried on profitably? To discover the answer it was necessary to experiment, and in the case of irrigation this was expensive, far more so than with dry farming. During the seventies a number of cooperative communities had been developed in which the costs of getting water on the land were shared. In the following decade private corporations began to construct canals, and this meant that—as in mining, stock raising, railroad building, and manufacturing—large amounts of outside capital came to Colorado. Welcomed at the time, the invasion by "foreign" money—meaning money from almost any place east of the Mississippi—later would generate much criticism and unrest among Coloradans.

Thus, by the eighties, two major barriers to an eastward expansion in Colorado had been severely diminished: the lack of capital and the need for rail transportation. The availability of investment money was indicated not only by the appearance of privately financed irrigation companies but also by the great outburst of railroad building that affected eastern Colorado. The Union Pacific's Julesburg branch, completed in 1881, angled across the northeastern part of the state; it served the South Platte Valley, where ranching and irrigated farming were becoming important. During the following year the Burlington passed that way, en route to Denver. Later in the decade two more lines entered the state, the Missouri Pacific reaching Pueblo in 1887, the Chicago, Rock Island and Pacific reaching Colorado Springs a year later. The rapid development of Colorado's mineral kingdom and the growing proof of its agricultural capacities generated among the various roads what one historian has called the "fight for the eastern Colorado gateways." Despite the formidable mountain barrier that had turned away the Union Pacific in the 1860s, there now was a great desire among railroads to tap the central Rockies, particularly Colorado, the richest and most promising of the mountain communities.[24]

With the building of the Larimer and Weld Canal, the Loveland and Greeley Canal, and the High Line Canal in the 1880s, all backed by English money, the era of corporate canal construction was under way. The North Poudre Canal, also built during these years, was financed by a subsidiary of the Travelers Insurance Company. These projects, some of which reached out eastward for nearly a hundred miles, acted as probes for farmers who moved gingerly toward the fabled "desert" country. In northern Colorado the canal diggers worked their way along the valley of the South

Platte, and before the end of the eighties the Fort Morgan and Bijou canals were built. At the same time corporate efforts to bring water to the land progressed in the Arkansas Valley and by 1884 the state's longest project, the Fort Lyon Canal, was under construction; when finished it irrigated some 120,000 acres. Serving the Rocky Ford, Fort Amity, and Pueblo neighborhoods were smaller systems, most of which were built late in this period. Corporate effort came to the San Luis Valley during this same "canal" decade, in this instance promoted by the well-known developer T. C. Henry, who represented the Travelers Insurance Company. He was instrumental in creating the Rio Grande Canal, near Del Norte, a waterway that served as many acres as did the big Fort Lyon Canal.[25] Thus the agricultural frontier invaded the eastern portion of the state, but it also penetrated the large mountain parks and valleys of the Colorado Rockies.

During the latter years of the nineteenth century Colorado continually made national and international news because of the succession of gold and silver strikes that appeared to occur there with unfailing regularity. These events spawned new, brawling mining towns whose colorful characters provided good copy for visiting journalists; consequently, it was not difficult then, nor is it now, to get the impression that these strikes were the leading events of the period. Despite the fact that Colorado's mineral industries would last longer than those of most other western states, and that they sparked a good deal of development in the field of transportation, it is still true that it was the farmers and stockmen who filled in population vacuums and established a more stable, lasting society.

Even as the corporate world sought to exploit agricultural possibilities by supplying ditch water to farmers who wanted to practice intensive agriculture, a group of "drylanders" tried to show that the Colorado desert was as productive as the Nebraska and Kansas deserts. By the early eighties the westward-moving agricultural frontier had pushed across the plains into the farthest reaches of Kansas and Nebraska, and now eastern Colorado became their objective. Many of the homesteaders who edged forward in this wave of the invasion were midwesterners who tried to apply agricultural methods used in more humid regions. Lacking the proper amount of capital reserve, and ignorant of methods later to be utilized in dryland farming, they failed. Over a half-century later one of them recalled his efforts to employ traditional cultivation. "As time went on I tried to raise ear corn like in old Illinois, but the fates were against me most of the time, as the hot winds of earing time blasted the tassel into a nubbin," was his doleful remembrance. To keep from starving he taught school part of the year.[26]

The prairie sod, torn up for cropping purposes, now reverted to its natural state, and lonely houses, representing the hopes of a lifetime, withered in the sun and abrasive winds. The shock troops made another attempt in the early nineties, but a financial panic and more body blows by the undiscriminating harshness of a semiarid climate sent these volunteers reeling back upon the redoubts of humid America. Further suggestions that new weapons would have to be utilized in this war brought scornful rejoinders from the traditionally conservative brotherhood of farmers, and not until dry farming was proved to be the only method by which nonirrigable lands could be made to produce were they finally convinced.[27] Reluctantly they took up soil tillage for purposes of conserving water—sourly known as "horse-leg irrigation"—and in wet years they found success. Then came dry cycles in the twentieth century, and more abandoned farms gave grim evidence that the Great American Desert had not been tamed.

Despite the bad name given the high plains by the drought years, Colorado's reputation as an agricultural state did not suffer as much as did some of its neighbors'. The success of irrigation in more favored sections of the state preserved its record as a producer. The spirited propaganda campaign carried out by promoters also tended to gloss over some of the problems dryland farmers were having in the eastern sections of the state. As a result of these factors, plus favorable news emanating from other sectors of its economy, Colorado compared most favorably to other western states when the talk turned to soil cultivation. Wyoming was dismissed as a "state where the bare mention of agriculture raises a laugh of derision," and the bleak region west of Salt Lake City was described as offering "larger and more favourable opportunities for successful starvation than any other section of America."[28] As yet, Montana had not made its name as a producer of cereals, and its struggling farmers were viewed as unwelcome poachers by the cattlemen who dominated that sprawling pastureland.

Colorado, on the other hand, had early established itself as a cattle- and sheep-raising country, but one that was not limited to this means of utilizing the land. The state possessed one of the best grazing regions of the world, publicist Frank Fossett assured his readers in 1879. Praising its beef as being far superior to that of Texas, he gave a figure of three and a half million dollars as the annual return from this industry. The sheep industry had shown even greater strides, increasing from twenty thousand to over two million amimals in the previous decade. Fossett estimated the income from wool and mutton at well over two million dollars. Granted that the eastern ranges were filling up rapidly, the author said that the state's western slope soon would be opened, making room in the rich valleys for more thousands of farmers and stock raisers.[29]

The day of the open range, a phase of western history much written about and highly romanticized, passed quickly in Colorado. The Fifty-Niners had seen possibilities in the high-country grasslands and frequently they noted that work oxen emerged from some rather rigorous winters looking fat and sleek.[30] Early on, some of those who had come to mine gold saw some alternatives and they turned to cattle. One of them, John Wesley Iliff, to become renowned as a "cattle king," had come to Denver in 1859 and ran a grocery store there. In 1861 he sold out and bought a small herd that he grazed along Crow Creek and the South Platte. When Oliver Loving and Charles Goodnight drove a herd of cattle from Texas to Colorado in 1866, Iliff had enough money to buy nearly eight hundred of them. During the following summer he began to furnish beef to the Union Pacific construction crews then working toward Cheyenne. By the seventies he owned about fifteen thousand acres of land, which meant that in open range country he controlled a good deal more, and he ran about thirty-five thousand head of cattle. Even when he lost some of his herds due to bad weather, as he did during the winter of 1871–72, profits were large enough to make up for the loss. In Colorado's growing economy Iliff became successful, rich, and "titled" as a cattle king. In the late eighties a town was named for him. Later, his widow married a Methodist bishop, and in honor of her former husband, whose first two names were appropriate for the purpose, she endowed the John Wesley Iliff School of Theology that later became part of the University of Denver.[31]

Another young man who had responded to the gold excitement of 1859 was Jared L. Brush, who tried his hand at placer mining in Russell Gulch, worked in other camps for two more years, and in

1862 gave up the quest in favor of ranching. The cattle boom proved to be more remunerative for him than mining, and it was here that he made not only his fortune but a name that took him to the lieutenant-governorship of the state. He, too, was honored by having a town named for him, indicating that one did not have to be a mining entrepreneur or railroad financier to find a place on the map of Colorado.[32]

In the beginning a man could start a cattle ranch with a reasonably small stake, but as time passed and stock growing became a big business, it grew more expensive to establish what the cattlemen called a "spread." Much of the early financing came from eastern and foreign investors who believed that the new boom in beef was a profitable place to invest their money, but even for them the rapidly inflating cost of starting one's own ranch soon began to pose some problems. By the early eighties the Earl of Airlie was telling his countrymen that these undertakings required "a fair amount" of capital. In Colorado most of the good ranches already were in the hands of a few owners, watering holes had been fenced off, and the day of the open range had begun to disappear. When that happened, the big operators, who had grazed their cattle on the federal domain, had to yield to smaller, independent ranchers who had staked their claim to some of the government land.[33]

Individual ranchers made their power felt through associations and organizations, the first of which was the Colorado Stock Growers' Association, founded in 1867 as a response to the great influx of cattle into Colorado that was part of the post–Civil War livestock boom on the high plains. As happens in any industry that develops with unusual rapidity, certain irregular practices that needed correction tended to spring up. In the range-cattle industry, many areas required supervision, one of which was the informal use of the branding iron, by which some impoverished cowboys attempted to acquire a large spread and the title of "King." Rustling, as it was called by those who lost cattle to these enterprising herdsmen, was an infraction of the rules that an association could help to control, if not eliminate. Other forms of cooperation included the return of strays to their owners, the joint hiring of detectives to uncover thefts, or the employment of watchers at the big stockyards who might uncover the attempted sale of stolen livestock. Dave Cook, one of the West's famous lawmen and detectives, worked for the Colorado Stock Growers'

Association.[34] The need for such services increased sharply after the coming of the railroad in 1870, when cattle began to be stolen by the carload.

The crowding of the Colorado range during the late seventies, and early experience with bad winters such as that of 1871–72, made thoughtful stockmen turn to better methods and more efficient organization, both on their own ranches and among themselves as a group. In the field they cooperated, arranging for roundups, carefully recording brands, reporting violations of stock laws, and blackballing employees caught "mavericking," that is, adopting animals not belonging to them.[35] In politics and government they made their presence felt at legislative meetings, where they lobbied for the amendment of laws found to be inefficient or for legislation that sought to alleviate new problems. As boom days of the cattle drives filled Colorado's eastern ranges, ranching in that area stabilized. Meanwhile, a local expansion took place in the western portion of the state as the region was opened to ranchers and stockmen. Ranchmen, who had despised barbed wire in the open-range days, now began to fence not only their own land but such portions of the public domain as they dared. The spread of farmers across eastern Colorado, a particularly heavy movement during the eighties, considerably reduced the latter practice. The formation of the National Live Stock Association at Denver in 1897, and the organization's resolution that urged leasing of public lands, was a belated recognition that the open range was gone.[36]

Ranch life in Colorado, typical of cattle raising on the high plains, was routine and unexciting, as the son of an eastern college president discovered when he came out to the state in 1878 and spent some time on a ranch near Hugo. His diary reflected the monotony of day-to-day living, with much reference to the weather and other mundane matters. The ranch itself, he said, consisted of a shanty, dug into the side of a hill, a barn and corral, all made of rough, unpainted lumber, and some dreary acres that straddled a meandering creek. About the only excitement he witnessed was the cattle drive into Hugo, after which a few of the hired hands lingered on at a local bar, "two of whom inspired by bad whiskey gave us some circus performances, and spurred their horses up onto the hotel piazza causing a lively scattering among the fellows sitting there." The only other event worthy of note that summer occurred when one cowboy hit another over the head with a piece of wood and killed him.[37]

From time to time there were human interest stories to be found in the lives of the cattlemen and their families, amusing vignettes of rural life that told more of daily living than they did of saloon gunfire or other antics performed by bored cowboys. Harry Cornwall, who ran cattle along Ohio Creek, north of Gunnison, raised hay for sale and kept a small herd on his five-hundred-acre ranch. He was much amused by his neighbors, a German family named Bohm, whose habits and attitudes were a constant source of entertainment. On one occasion he made an offhanded inquiry of Bohm as to how things were going. "Bad, Harry, bad," was the worried reply. "My black mare lost her colt, my best milch cow lost her calf, and my wife lost her baby. No luck at all with livestock this year." But it was Mrs. Bohm who really delighted Cornwall. Like many ranch women she used old flour sacks to make skirts, blouses, and sometimes underskirts. Across the generous bosom of this plump housewife was emblazoned the slogan "Pride of the Family," and on the rear of her skirt was another, reading "Rough and Ready," these being two of the favorite brands of flour of that day.[38]

In mining, railroad construction, cattle ranching, farming, and most aspects of business, the decade of the 1880s was a time of expansion and the development of new frontiers. The years that immediately preceded the new boom era represented a period when Colorado established its institutions, achieved statehood, and prepared itself for a prosperity the boosters said lay just around the corner. Frequently the optimists have been wrong, but in this case they were not. By the end of the seventies the new state had nearly two hundred thousand people, and in the following decade its promoters pressed into undeveloped parts of the state so assiduously that the population more than doubled. On the theory that growth meant progress and prosperity, they felt that their faith in the community that straddled the central Rockies had been well placed. Political and business leaders looked ahead, and talked of more growth, but many of them also gave some thought to means by which their growing society could be improved and perfected. To do this they were obliged to think in terms of reforms, of planing and sanding the structure they had fitted together, and of the best way to ensure that the gains they had made would be meaningful to coming generations.

PART THREE

# In Search of Maturity

# 9

# The Thrust of a Developing Culture

The quarter-century that followed the arrival of railroads, the achievement of statehood, and a rapid physical expansion saw Coloradans make a conscious effort to nurture the young society they had founded in the early 1860s. They were conscious of their material gains, as were all Americans of that era, but perhaps they were even more sensitive than the others to the importance of providing the community with a healthy intellectual climate. Some, of course, regarded the addition of cultural trappings as an embellishment of the general business and commercial structure, an attitude that would persist well into the next century, but there were those who believed that such things were important in themselves and that it was not necessary to gauge the benefits to be derived in any material sense. The latter group represented elements of the earlier arrivals who had tried to plan for the future in the belief that if the new society were properly shaped some of the reforms easterners had begun to call for would not be necessary in the central Rockies.

The notion of social guidance through moral and intellectual leadership was more than a generality accepted by the public as an undeniable community benefit. Specific groups made their appeal to the minds of Coloradans by means of well-organized campaigns designed to rescue errant souls from the temptations of sin by means of the printed word. One of these was the Women's Christian Temperance Union, whose leadership established reading rooms where temperance literature and nonintoxicating refreshments were available. The reading room at Ouray came into being when one of its male residents admitted to a WCTU organizer that the only place in town where a man could find a place to sit down and relax was in a saloon. The organization provided similar facilities in a number of Colorado cities, including Denver, Pueblo, and Boulder.[1] Apparently the search for peace and quiet was not always an easy one, for in May of 1882 the Boulder WCTU chapter found it necessary to move its newly established reading room to a location free from "molestation." Despite the change, the project floundered until 1886, when it closed.

Another organization interested in providing facilities for intellectual improvement was the YMCA. That group's Denver reading room dated from 1867, and, although constantly threatened by insolvency, it provided a place of contemplation and reading in the capital city for over twenty years. Similar YMCA reading rooms were established in Boulder and Colorado Springs and made available newspapers from various places in the United States as well as other printed matter.

More specific efforts to influence individuals were seen in the attraction libraries had for particular groups or industries. The Miners' and Mechanics' Institute, developed at Central City in the mid sixties, was intended to provide a suitable distraction from competing activities that might be detrimental to the employee. Similarly, the Denver and Rio Grande's Burnham Library at Denver was established during the eighties to attract the company's shop employees. Here, again, management hoped to keep workingmen off the streets and out of seamier places of recreation. Additionally, by a careful selection of books it had the opportunity to indoctrinate readers with knowledge that bespoke management's problems, if not its high ideals. The Knights of Labor's library, established in Denver about this time, also saw the possibilities of offering concepts that explained the position of that organization.

The various religious groups used reading rooms to further their programs, hoping to attract wider attendance at Sunday services. In addition to the St. Patrick's Benevolent Society library, the rooms of which were open to the public, the Young Men's Catholic Club and the Catholic Library Association, both of Denver, solicited money for this purpose. The Protestants lost no time in competing and as early as 1866 there were a dozen such reading rooms in Colorado.

Those who worked in public institutions also sought the benefits of reading material, the firemen's libraries being the most common.

During the seventies, armories for military organizations, such as the Governor's Guard, were provided with library facilities where newspapers or military journals were available to the membership.

Beyond the motive of social control lay the sometimes thinly disguised intent to promote cultural activities for the purpose of civic prestige. In other words, the announced desire to display some of life's refinements reflected the more subtle aspects of boosterism. The *Rocky Mountain News* revealed such thinking as early as 1872 when it pronounced a library a necessary adjunct to a civilized community and predicted that such a facility would be a credit and an honor to the city. The *Daily Camera,* spokesman for the university town of Boulder, became quite angry when local businessmen did not show proper enthusiasm for a library project. It distressed the editor to think that in the Athens of Colorado lived men of such limited vision that they would not support a cause unless it promised personal, material gain. The board of trade was scolded roundly for its lack of vision and for its inability to understand the ultimate material benefits of cultural endeavors.[2] Later efforts by the Boulder merchants indicated that they were educable, for upon a number of occasions in the years to come they were to use the presence of the state university as a lure in a number of financial fishing expeditions.

Prior to the existence of the now commonly accepted free public libraries, people in search of reading material frequently turned to private, subscription-type reading rooms, sometimes referred to as mercantile libraries. The short-lived Denver and Auraria Library and Reading Room Association represented this type of endeavor, as did its successor, the Denver Library Association, which began service in 1872. It, too, failed and was succeeded by yet another private association, which, in turn, gave up the ghost in 1878 and donated its books to the East Denver High School library. This collection ultimately became the Denver Public Library, today a widely known and highly respected institution. Despite repeated collapses in efforts to maintain privately supported reading rooms, the Mercantile Library opened in Denver in the autumn of 1886. In terms of its holdings or the people it served this type of service, widely used in other parts of the nation during these years, was not as restricted as the name might suggest. Upon payment of a fee the general public was invited to use its rather broad-ranging collections. The quasi-public type of library was found in a number of Colorado communities.

The coming of publicly supported libraries, particularly the Carnegie library movement that came on so strong in the early years of the twentieth century, supplanted the rather irregular efforts of groups or individuals to serve the literary needs of the state. In the Carnegie program, communities were awarded library buildings if the local government agreed to tax support equal to one-tenth of the structure's cost. Thirty-five buildings went up in Colorado as a result of the offer, nine of them in Denver, and the others scattered across the state, providing the reading public with long-sought-after facilities that the private sector had tried to supply.

Public reference libraries, such as the State Library and the Supreme Court Library, had existed since very early territorial days. The State Historical and Natural History Society, established in 1879, also collected books and documents relating to the state's history, and these were available to the public. Despite the best efforts, public and private, Colorado has not done particularly well in this area. As late as 1948 Malcolm G. Wyer of the Denver Public Library could write that perhaps 350,000 of the state's residents were without any library service and that in twelve counties there were no free public libraries.[3]

Those who came early to Colorado displayed a considerable interest in the printed word. Fifty-Niner diaries include countless comments about the great desire for reading material of any kind. One tends to think of the typical pioneer as being a fine physical specimen, out west to wrest the land from the natives and to apply his brawn to the thorny problems of the untamed land, yet a man whose acquaintanceship with books and learning was of necessity limited. This was far from the case, however; of the thousands of young men who were attracted to the mines and related industries, a great many had achieved an educational level beyond that of the traditional frontiersman. Among them, too, were a number of professional men who brought along their families and desired something of the cultural facilities they had known at home. Their interest in education, as evinced by the early establishment of both private and public schools, quickly led to a desire for institutions of higher education for the young. Colorado was far removed from many of the older colleges, and transportation was both a time-consuming and an expensive affair. Additionally, it was a matter of civic pride among young territories to show the world that they had such establishments of their own; it was regarded as a sign of both advancement and of permanency to be able to point to their existence.

The growing number of pupils in elementary and secondary schools tended to put pressure upon territories and states to provide a means of higher education, but Coloradans did not wait until natural increase required such facilities; rather, they brought such plans with them in the days of Fifty-Nine. Technically speaking the University of Colorado, at Boulder, was the first such institution, since it was incorporated by an act of the legislature in October 1861, but it was not until 1877 that its doors opened to students.[4] Meanwhile, in 1864, the General Assembly chartered a collegiate-level school, founded by the Methodists, and called Colorado Seminary. Even before the charter it was referred to as the University of Denver, as it would be later. Governor John Evans donated four lots across the street from his home as a campus, and in November 1864 some fifty students commenced their studies. The *News* praised the seminary, and said that its steady growth suggested to Coloradans the folly of sending their children east for higher education. In 1867 the editor said Colorado had but one seminary and he urged residents to patronize it; he hoped it soon would be crowded with young people from all over the territory.[5] It was not. The school closed down that very year, a bankrupt enterprise, and for the next sixteen years it had what historian Wilbur Fisk Stone discreetly called "a more or less uncertain life." In short, it went into educational hibernation to emerge, in 1880, as the University of Denver. John Evans, who had not abandoned the project, was chairman of the new board of trustees.[6] Despite the operational lapse, the Colorado Supreme Court, in a case involving tax litigation, later could refer to the university as "the pioneer school of higher learning in this state."[7]

During the years that Methodist efforts at higher education in Denver sputtered and almost died, there were efforts at Colorado Springs to put that new city on the academic map. Colorado College had its origins in a grant of land made by General Palmer and the founding fathers of Colorado Springs. The doors that opened to the first eighteen students in 1874 were in a downtown rented building. The Congregationalists, who commenced this "outpost of Boston," encountered problems similar to those that plagued the Methodists at Denver: constant financial adversities. Even though the college moved into its own building by 1880, and President Edward P. Tenney was able to borrow $100,000 from his friends in Boston, keeping the place afloat remained a daily problem. However, by 1900 the school had about four hundred students, and several well-equipped buildings. While this did not mean that its problems—or those of any privately endowed college—were at an end, there was evidence that the New England transplant had passed its period of probable rejection and it was recognized, as it is today, for its academic excellence.[8]

The Catholics, whose efforts at missionary work and education in the West had been so important, did not overlook the possibilities of establishing schools in fast-growing Colorado. As early as 1864 they founded St. Mary's Academy at Denver, a later outgrowth of which was Loretto Heights College for women. During the eighties Bishop Machebeuf asked the Jesuits to open an institution at Morrison, and Sacred Heart College was the result. The Jesuits also had a college at Las Vegas, New Mexico, opened in 1877, but after a decade neither this institution nor the one at Morrison seemed well situated, so a new location was chosen in north Denver. In 1921 the name was changed to Regis College. During this period another church-oriented effort was commenced by the Baptists, who established Colorado Women's College. The cornerstone was laid in 1890, and in 1909 the small institution was opened as a senior college.

It has been asserted that denominational colleges were a negative response to western conditions and that their founders were engaged in a form of missionary effort.[9] Denominational schools in Colorado generally fit this description, but it should be added that community leaders who initiated and supported such endeavors anticipated certain practical benefits to be derived in future growth. Both John Evans, at Denver, and General Palmer, at Colorado Springs, may be called benefactors, and their efforts in this area were not confined to education. Both had in mind what kind of city they wanted to build, and, among other cultural attributes, education took an important place. Palmer's motivation was, in part, a reaction to western conditions in that he did not want Colorado Springs to be dominated by, or even inhabited by, the kind of people who frequently gave booming western railroad towns an unsavory name. From the outset the founders of Colorado Springs were determined that it would be not only the social but also the cultural center of the state. In this respect their efforts in the direction of higher education simply were in line with the master plan.

In its infant years Colorado was too poor, in terms of its ability to collect taxes, to finance collegiate education. Moreover, the founding fathers, busy with the matter of economic survival, regarded such an expenditure as one that could wait for a more stabilized financial condition. For the time being, no sense of mission permeated the minds of those who were trying to establish a new mountain commonwealth. Only when the matter of statehood became a probability did this part of the western dream take on importance.

Therefore efforts at publicly supported higher education languished, and not until the "soaring seventies," when all of Colorado began to prosper, were there any tangible results of earlier legislative acts. In Boulder, David Nichols and A. J. Macky kept alive hopes for some tangible evidence of a university by reminding businessmen constantly that its existence would aid in the town's growth. Merchants listened with interest but took no further action, not even attending some of the planning sessions designed to further the cause. A split in the Boulder County legislative delegation developed when a member from Burlington, a place later to be swallowed up by Longmont, wanted the institution in his town for reasons of potential municipal growth. The matter drifted into a running fight between the communities, Boulder arguing weakly that it had first thought of the idea and that it was closer to stone quarries from which building materials were procured. The squabble moved some Boulder residents to donate twenty acres of land in 1870 as a gesture of goodwill and "earnest money," but since no funds were available for building the situation reverted to talk but no action. By 1872 the *Rocky Mountain News* was lamenting the fact that Coloradans appeared to have no interest in founding a state university. Once more stirred into action, Boulder city fathers selected a new site, south of town, and accepted a little over fifty acres as a gift from three townsmen. Efforts to persuade the General Assembly to provide construction money again failed, but the matter would not die, and in 1874 an appropriation of $15,000 was made for this purpose. When statehood was achieved in 1876, the university received seventy-two sections of land as a federal grant, at which time it was made a state institution. In the autumn of 1877 classes commenced at the new school as forty-four students attended classes taught by President Joseph A. Sewall and his staff of one—Justin E. Dow.[10]

Colorado Agricultural College, later to be called Colorado State

University, had its legal beginnings in 1870, but, as at Boulder, matters at Fort Collins languished even though public-spirited residents donated land upon which to build. However, some ninety thousand acres of federal land had been set aside for the school even before 1870, and when statehood was achieved the constitution brought the college into existence. The first session of the new state legislature created an "agricultural college tax" to support the school, which, by the autumn of 1879, commenced operations with twenty students in attendance. By 1900 the student body numbered almost three hundred fifty and the school had become a well-established part of Colorado's system of higher education.[11]

The Colorado School of Mines, at Golden, grew out of Bishop Randall's Jarvis Hall, mentioned earlier. In 1871 the General Assembly appropriated money for a school of mining, and, when the Episcopalians assigned their interest in Jarvis Hall to the state three years later, the Colorado School of Mines came into being at that location.[12]

The founding of colleges as a means of both enhancing local prestige and improving the financial position of those engaged in real estate was not lost upon other Colorado cities. A State Normal School, at Greeley, was approved in 1889 and public-spirited residents quickly came forward with forty acres of campus land as well as with money to help erect the first building. By the autumn of 1890 the establishment was functioning, with ninety-six students in attendance. Later the institution became known as Colorado State Teachers College, and in 1931 it was changed to Colorado State College of Education. Today it has graduated to the title University of Northern Colorado.

The city fathers at Gunnison also saw the desirability of having an institution of higher learning in their town; again, the usual forty acres was forthcoming for the purpose. In 1901 the General Assembly appropriated money for the planting of trees and for improving the site, but there the matter rested for another decade. A $50,000 appropriation by the state made things move once more, and in 1911 the State Normal School at Gunnison, later to be known as Western State College, was opened. At first it offered only a two-year curriculum, but by 1920 this was enlarged to a regular four-year course.[13]

In the field of higher education, the West, including Colorado, has tended to import its purveyors of knowledge from eastern institutions of higher learning. At first this was necessary; there were no homegrown products. When Colorado College began, it was a matter of local pride that the president and his staff of six professors all were graduates of New England colleges, except for the professor of metallurgy, who did his work at Columbia. These credentials were advertised to show that the West had bought only the best. As the years passed, other regional schools did their shopping in that same exclusive market in the belief that they were setting high standards against which rivals must measure their own progress. It was another example of the self-consciousness of a new and as yet somewhat uncertain society.

Having imported their intellectual stewards, they took pride in them, not because they understood what they were trying to do or say, but because often they were more expensive and therefore presumably more distinguished than those who ministered to the educational wants of other peoples' children. Those who taught specific subjects such as engineering, mathematics, chemistry, or business were regarded as practical acquisitions on the ground that something concrete and useful would result from their efforts, something that would advance the community. In this respect higher education was given a special western flavor. Such fields as classics, philosophy, or even history were harder to explain to taxpayers because the results of such study seemed to be harder to apply. But since such trappings were believed to be a part of the entire package, any objections to the inclusion of such abstruse information were shrugged off on the ground that it might provide some long-run if indefinable benefit.[14]

Yet another form of cultural-educational uplift frequently found in young, aspiring communities was the legitimate theater. Denver and the mining camps that fanned out from it across Colorado had offered theatrical productions from the days of Fifty-Nine, some of them "light" and a few of them "heavy." To the unhappiness of community leaders who wanted to bring a high form of culture to the mountains, the lighter side of the stage tended to be favored by miners, who were independent in the way they spent their money. The serious theater in Denver struggled through the 1860s, gradually giving way to more frivolous entertainment and beer-hall variety shows. During the next decade efforts were made to provide the city with an opera house, but when no suitable financial backing could be found the project collapsed. But William Byers of the *News* would not give up easily, and he kept up a drumfire of publicity in his journal, constantly reminding readers of the city's need for a really fine theater. Finally, a group of businessmen who belonged to the Governor's Guards, a forerunner of the National Guard, put up enough money to build a Governor's Guards Hall, but when it opened for business in 1873 only a local dramatic association used its facilities. To the disappointment of Denverites a good many of the traveling companies it had hoped to host failed to put the Queen City on their itineraries.

Nor did they go to Central City. Anxious to provide facilities that would attract outside talent, residents of that mining town determined to build a suitable opera house, which they did, and it was opened in the spring of 1878. Almost a century later it still functions, providing summer tourists with attractive offerings that draw steady crowds. Not to be outdone by Central City, civic leaders of Leadville urged construction of an opera house; their appeals were answered by millionaire H. A. W. Tabor, and the establishment opened in the autumn of 1879. The stars employed by Jack Langrishe provided the first season's entertainment. Two years later Tabor's munificence provided the Tabor Grand Opera House for Denver.[15]

As Colorado Springs watched the construction of theaters in rival cities, its residents became even more restive over the lack of such facilities in their town. During the first decade of its existence there was no theater building in General Palmer's town; plays and musical attractions were given in a hall that offered only limited seating and a makeshift stage. Having made some money in Leadville mining, Irving Howbert and two of his friends decided to build an opera house on some lots they owned. By the spring of 1881 the structure was ready, and in April the opening performances were given in a theater Howbert claimed was the most completely equipped in the state.[16] It was a fine building, indeed, but according to one critic it far outclassed the artists, who never were more than second-rate. The author of this unkind comment expressed the conviction that perhaps the loyal patrons who turned up for such mediocre performances eventually would entice some of the brighter theatrical stars as they passed across Colorado en route to more rewarding places.[17]

Despite the gloom Byers had shown, and the occasional disappointments suffered by Coloradans when traveling stage productions passed them by in favor of better barnstorming in some of the newer Rocky Mountain mining camps, opera and other dramatic productions continued to attract a small but steady patronage.

Statehood, a more solid economic base, and steady growth meant that such attactions would be attended by a growing class of men and women who had both time and money for such events.

Providing higher education for those who chose to stay at home to receive it, supplying the populace with opportunities to become informed through reading in free libraries, and offering cultural salvation at the local opera house were only a few of the efforts made to uplift Coloradans. The drive to control the use of alcohol was yet another variation of the attempt to mold a society free from the downgrading influences increasingly felt in the growing metropolitan areas of the East. In Colorado the temperance movement was not so much an effort to reform the victims of alcoholism as it was to develop a nonpolluted social atmosphere that would make it unnecessary to stamp out the evil at some later date. Thus the young state's temperance movement had early origins and a vigorous life that saw prohibition laws enacted even before the passage of similar national legislation.[18]

As Colorado society began to take firmer roots during the latter part of the nineteenth century, its attraction to temperance grew stronger. During these years a large proportion of its settlers came from the Northeast and the Ohio Valley, particularly from New York, Ohio, Indiana, and Illinois, sections where such movements were strong. From time to time spectacular mineral strikes would spawn a new Leadville, a Cripple Creek, or a Creede, places where night never fell and vice worked a twenty-four-hour shift, but these municipal eruptions were not representative of Colorado's developing social fabric. They blinded observers to the existence of farming and ranching towns, whose residents and outlying customers showed disapproval of saloons, or such a place as Monte Vista, where they were banned at an early date.

Colorado's experience differed from that of some other western states in that it spawned more colony towns than most of its neighbors. While some of these towns were out-and-out "dry" communities, so designed at the outset and sternly maintained as such, others exercised less stringent moral policing. In the latter places social control was achieved without the near-vigilante violence that led to saloon burnings at Greeley and Longmont. In these nominally dry towns there was a certain amount of tolerance and some winked-at bootlegging. For example, Sterling was supposed to be a temperance town, and every lot sold there carried a proviso that if liquor were sold on the premises the property would revert to its former owner, but that failed to stop a certain amount of seepage. R. E. Arnett, who lived there during the eighties, recalled that the local druggist sold whiskey regularly and just as regularly would be arrested and fined some three hundred dollars. Then he would continue his sideline, having paid for what he thought was a very cheap license. Neighborhood cowboys kept the druggist busy and provided the sleepy little agricultural town of some two hundred fifty souls with occasional bits of excitement.

Whether in temperance towns or in places that were slightly damp, the desire to dry up liquor outlets simply reflected a general attitude prevalent throughout the state's agricultural communities. Often these farming towns resented the licentiousness and the tinsel atmosphere of the mining towns, of which they were slightly jealous. By holding up the mining camps as villains the agrarian communities could sniff with self-righteousness and renew their determination to stamp out sin in the new Eden. It was in such towns that the militant Women's Christian Temperance Union found its most loyal followers. Of political consequence were a resolution of the Colorado Grange in 1875 to deny endorsement to intemperate candidates and that organization's support by 1890 of both state and national prohibition.

Colorado's excellent transportation system, developed because of its mineral riches, made it one of the easiest of the Rocky Mountain states to reach and to cover by rail. With such accessibility it was easy to import nationally known reformers, men and women who attracted large audiences. Among the listeners often were people who had brought their pulmonary ailments—and their money—westward, many of them professional men or newcomers possessed of background and education. Probably none other of the plains and mountain states had so many of this class, and while they were not universally opposed to the use of liquor, frequently they were interested in socially beneficial programs. With time and money to engage in such activities they offered their hospitality to eastern reformers who chose to visit Colorado.

Toward the end of the nineteenth century, as the "new" immigration made its presence felt in the United States, a growing number of southern Europeans found their way into Colorado's labor force. They worked in the coal mines, or in other urban areas, and lived in company towns or in the early urban sprawl created by the extractive industries. Crime and political corruption frequently accompanied such developments. The battle against saloons was part of the campaign against political and social pollution, for such places were considered incubators of the diseases that attacked the body politic. When violence flared in the coalfields, reformers lost no time in arguing that the miners would be happier and healthier without the debilitating effects of liquor.

Temperance advocates drew large audiences in agricultural areas, and they were wont to concentrate their efforts at salvation among the industrial workers. Nevertheless the leaders of the movement took the position that this was not a class movement, but rather a continuing cultural campaign to upgrade society. Those who were somewhat less optimistic hoped at least to prevent retrogression of the societal gains they had eked out over the years. The answer to these desires came with the passage of a constitutional amendment in 1914 that, by January 1, 1916, ended the legal sale of alcoholic beverages in Colorado.[19]

The battle against Demon Rum was indeed a hard one in a heavily male mining-camp society, and the fact that it was won was due, in part, to the gradual decline of that group and the increase of farm families. Although mining men might resent efforts to close down their social centers—the saloons—they did not oppose so vigorously efforts to give women the vote. Since women were a decided minority in the camps, the men not only deferred to them but did not see in them any political threat. As early as 1866 the *Rocky Mountain News* had lamented the political plight of women (particularly those in the East, where conditions always were thought to be worse than in the more enlightened West), and it expressed the view that surely this group of underprivileged Americans ought to have the ballot before it was granted to Negroes. The editorial was written at a time when the question of black suffrage was very much before the American people and at a moment when editor Byers was highly annoyed at Colorado blacks for rocking the statehood boat by making an issue over their lack of the franchise.[20] Former governor John Evans agreed with Byers that the ladies should come first, and he made an effort to stir up interest in the question of woman suffrage, but it was a difficult crusade to carry out in a nearly all-male society.

Byers kept the idea alive in the *News*, arguing that sex was no barrier to voting, to holding office, or even to bearing arms, but the electorate saw no need for women to do any of these things, and this particular campaign for human rights in Colorado languished until 1870. In that year Governor Edward M. McCook called the matter to the attention of the territorial General Assembly, but since he was not in great favor with the residents his sponsorship was of little value. Nevertheless, the matter came before the legislators, and it was debated at great length before being turned down. As always the lawmakers expressed great admiration for women, and they offered any number of gallant statements about them, but the men saw no reason why members of the opposite sex should be distracted from their demanding roles as homemakers and mothers. Even Byers of the *News* appeared to have lost some of his enthusiasm for the cause. Earlier he had warned the women that while their cause was just they ought not "start off by abusing everybody who does not at once accept their faith." Now, he inferred, they had done just that and worse; they had accepted support from unpopular Governor McCook and his activist wife. Mrs. McCook was particularly bitter over the fact that some of the local women had not entered the fray with the enthusiasm she felt they should have mustered.[21] It was a time of frustration, all around.

The matter was not dead, however, even though Byers had so pronounced it. The fires were quenched, but the embers smoldered on, and during the next few years an occasional woman turned up at minor elections, demanding and frequently receiving a ballot. In 1874 the U.S. Supreme Court held that the national Constitution neither granted nor denied suffrage to women and that it was up to individual states to decide this franchise issue. Very shortly after this event Coloradans went to work forging a constitution of their own, and when that happened the political architects heard a great deal from women about the desirability of having the state come into existence unsullied by any prejudice against them. During the debates that took place in the constitutional convention, suffrage advocates flooded the proceedings with requests for the vote, most of which were politely set aside. "Here on the table are petitions of hundreds of women to be allowed to vote," said one supporter of the cause, "and we coolly fling the request aside as though it came from the Cheyenne Indians. . . ."[22]

Granting the ballot to "savages" was, of course, regarded as being beyond the thinking of civilized men; but even to go so far as to give it to women was not without political risks. Strategists warned that to do so might jeopardize the chances for approval of the constitution when it came before the all-male electorate. These western statesmen were not entirely devoid of feeling, however, and they tossed the ladies a crumb by agreeing that they could vote at school elections and could hold elective school offices. As a further concession they suggested that the next legislative session take up the matter and place it before the voters. Any and all subsequent legislatures were given permission to take the same steps if by then woman suffrage had not been granted.

The women at once took up the offer and urged legislators who met during the winter of 1876–77 to give them the ballot. They were stoutly opposed by Father Joseph P. Machebeuf, who was to become the first Catholic bishop of Denver, and by a Presbyterian minister who aired his views on the matter from the pulpit each Sunday. Opposition came also from some of the state's major papers, the Pueblo *Chieftain* being one example, but some of the mining-camp journals supported the movement. The women brought out some of their big guns, offering the voters a chance to hear such nationally known figures as Lucy Stone and Susan B. Anthony. But all in vain; the proposal lost heavily, by more than two to one. With the chant "Goodbye to the female tramps of Boston," the *Chieftain* congratulated Coloradans for having withstood pressures from outside the state, particularly from Massachusetts. Only in Boulder County were the voters willing to admit women to that private club known as "franchise." A paper in that city blamed the defeat on the "Mexicans" who dominated the state's solid South.[23]

The defeat of 1877 so discouraged the crusaders for equal suffrage that for over a decade and a half the battle was dormant. In the interim there was some desultory firing from the rejected group, but the main thrust of the attack seemed to have lost its vigor. During the eighties, Mrs. C. M. Churchill kept the guns clean by means of an occasional blast from her paper the *Queen Bee,* a journal that claimed to be the only one in the state advocating woman suffrage. Although the editor was greatly concerned about the right of her sex to vote, she did not neglect other civic problems such as temperance, the fight against dance halls, the great Catholic threat, inefficient garbage collection, the evils of tobacco, and H. A. W. Tabor, who had abandoned Augusta in favor of Baby Doe. Despite bitter complaints from the ladies it was not until 1893 and the coming of the Populists that Colorado women achieved their long-sought goal.

In that year a legislator from Montrose introduced into the

General Assembly a bill asking that the voters be given a chance to speak on the question of woman suffrage. His Populist colleagues, aided by a few Republicans, overrode the opposition, and Populist governor Davis H. Waite signed a measure that was approved by the voters that autumn. This put Colorado in the record books as being the first state where women were granted voting privileges by the male electorate, the more famous Wyoming decision of 1869 having been rendered by the territorial legislature. Then the women of Colorado displayed their ingratitude by helping to unseat Governor Waite in the following year, an act he declared to be the work of conservatives who callously used the ignorance of these new voters to do their dirty work. Upon reflection the ex-governor decided that, in addition to denying the state the benefits of Populism, the presence of female voters, many of whom were Catholics, had advanced the cause of Papism in Colorado.[24] He was sorry he had doffed his political cap to the ladies.

The Populists should not get more credit for enlarging the suffrage than they deserve. Other factors entered the picture, among them the general discontent with economic and political conditions that plagued the state. A Denver newspaper suggested that in the panic year, when the idol of silver had been smashed, both the world and the nation had commenced to look upon Colorado with doubt, if not some disdain. The editor somehow convinced himself that such bold political action as the granting of woman suffrage would "fling down the gauntlet to all prejudice and opposition."[25] The implication was that women would vote for free silver. Perhaps another boost for the cause of suffrage was its open opposition by the state's liquor dealers, a group that was coming increasingly under fire, particularly in some of the smaller communities. There were some who attributed the change to western chivalry, but there was little about the Colorado of 1893, particularly in the larger cities where voting was heavy, that bespoke frontier conditions.[26] Perhaps the best explanation was one made by a Denver newspaper that said the most commonly heard comment favoring the move argued that women ought to vote because "they can't do any worse than men have."[27]

The first election in which women participated produced some interesting side effects. As the appointed day approached, the proprietor of a Colorado millinery shop noticed a sharp acceleration in trade. He said in surprise:

> I wasn't prepared for any rush in the business. In fact, I don't suppose I was much interested in the suffrage question. But all of a sudden I noticed a sharp increase in our sales; then mail orders came in, thick and fast; and finally we had crowds around our bargain counters equal to the week before Easter; and even our imported hats, on the second floor, were going with a rush.
>
> "What's the matter with the women?" said I to the forewoman. "Any W.C.T.U. convention, or public reception, or high church holiday?"
>
> "No, indeed," said she. "Why, don't you know? They're going to vote tomorrow!"[28]

The results of this long-sought reform were variously interpreted. Since women long had dominated activist church groups and had led many a fight for a cleaner moral climate, it was assumed that their vote would help to purge the murky political atmosphere. The *Rocky Mountain News* made this point, suggesting that municipal corruption, so widespread in the nation, might be trimmed back in Colorado by means of this new, sharp pruning knife. In 1895, the editor noted, Denverites would go to the polls three times to decide various issues, and he predicted that the outcome of these elections would depend upon votes cast by women.

Five years after Colorado women had gained the right to vote, the General Assembly declared that the change had resulted in a better selection of candidates and cleaner elections, a sentiment that some thought was more a gesture than a description of the reality. When Beatrice Webb and her Fabian Socialist husband, Sidney, passed through Colorado in 1898, she made note of the fact that women here had gained the franchise and she tried to summarize the changes wrought. The new voters, she said, tended to vote along with their husbands. While they had brought no new wisdom into politics, they were quicker than men to condemn open corruption. It was the English visitor's belief that in America the expanded suffrage was justified, since women were as capable politically as men, but she saw them also as voters who were better intentioned and who had a greater desire for information.[29]

Critics among American women were less charitable. When a national magazine sent a woman reporter to Colorado about this time, she concluded that little change had resulted from this progressive legislation. She noted that women's wages were no better than elsewhere, that there were no women on the Denver school board, and that municipal elections appeared to be as corrupt as ever. One explanation for these conditions appeared to be the unwillingness of women to join together in a given cause; rather, as Mrs. Webb had pointed out, they tended to vote with their husbands. Thus, said the unhappy eastern reporter, once the victory had been gained these western women had become politically inert. The first time they had a chance to vote, 94 percent of them registered and 84 percent voted. At the next election only 50 percent turned up at the polls.[30] But, as a prominent Colorado novelist put it, woman suffrage in his state had offered no shortcut to the millennium; rather it had been what he termed "an incident rather than an epoch." While the ballot in the hands of woman had "neither unsexed her nor regenerated the world," he felt sure that it had worked in the direction of improved civic affairs, of greater cleanliness in the streets and parks, and of better conditions in schools and state institutions.[31]

Carefully watching these various cultural and political developments and constantly checking the pulse of the community at large were the newspaper editors and their reporters. They served as watchdogs over public morality, pushed various civic enterprises, and fought with neighboring newspapermen over the relative virtues of their respective towns. As boosters they had no peers, as a puzzled western traveler once concluded when he inquired how a tiny burg through which he was passing could possibly support four newspapers and was told that it took that many to keep up such a city. There was some truth to this; thousands of adjectives were hurled into the air in the hope that they would float eastward and descend in useful places. Westerners believed in advertising.

The early newspapers, as already mentioned, were produced in the crudest of physical surroundings, but as time passed many of them moved into better quarters and frequently took on a prosperous appearance as they grew. As was true on the frontier, generally, the farther one moved into undeveloped territory the more constantly were such crudities in evidence. H. M. Woods, who ran the *Lake City Silver World,* suggested in 1875 that conditions in new communities changed little over the years. His office was a log cabin, built on a sand bed, and the presence of several inches of dust on the floor was the normal state of affairs.

Nor was that the only annoyance. "The roof is of saplings covered with mud and the dirt sifts down upon us in a never ending shower," he wrote.[32]

As Colorado settlement spread out, east and west, the new towns told the rest of the country about their hopes for the future through the columns of their little newspapers. Otto Mears, for example, who became widely known for his association with Indian affairs, merchandising, and particularly toll roads and railroads, is little remembered for his contribution to journalism, yet when he founded the Saguache *Chronicle,* in 1872, it was for the purpose of boosting that little village and the San Luis Valley.[33] Similarly, a decade later, the newly established city of Grand Junction lost no time in putting into operation its publicity organ, a newspaper known simply as the *News.* Edwin Price, who had owned a job-printing shop located above Wolfe Londoner's store in Denver, reached the western slope city in October 1882, and within a matter of days the *News* was in production. Its first copy sold at auction for $25 as a souvenir item, so glad were the townspeople to have a newspaper of their own.[34] During that same year three brothers started the Del Norte *Democrat,* a little four-page paper created to advertise that city as the "Gateway to the San Juan."[35]

The eastern plains of Colorado, settled during the eighties and nineties, acquired their "communicators" during those years. Akron, surveyed by the Lincoln Land Company in 1882, lay almost dormant for three years and then began to grow as agricultural immigration to that area of Colorado picked up. Its newspaper, the *Pioneer Press,* was commenced in the autumn of 1885 by D. W. Irwin, and later it was edited by a journalist with the appropriate name of Horace Greeley Pickett.[36] Southeastern Colorado felt the pressure of the agricultural frontier during these years, and in the mid eighties a land company headed by a member of the Santa Fe Railroad's land department founded a little settlement in the Arkansas Valley and named it after Secretary of the Interior L. Q. C. Lamar. In the autumn of 1886 the *Lamar Leader* began operation and in the following spring the *Lamar Sparks,* edited by a woman, established itself as a rival.[37]

Although the average small-town newspaper was intended to be a disseminator of news, usually local, and a means of exchanging information or perhaps carrying on some civic crusade, there were papers founded with more specific purposes. The weekly *Aspen Union Era* was one of them. It was launched by Davis H. Waite in

1891 to broadcast Populist and other reform ideas. Though its life-span was little over a year, the newspaper brought sufficient fame to its editor to elevate him to the governorship of Colorado in 1892. Beyond that, the *Era* was important as one of the forces that created and developed the Populist Party in Colorado. The state may be said to have "gone radical" but once in its history; Waite personified this development and his newspaper was its daily spokesman and oracle.[38]

Other newspapers were established to advertise the colony towns they represented. *Out West,* founded at Colorado Springs by General Palmer and edited by the Englishman J. E. Liller, is one example. Originated in 1872 as a weekly and supplemented by a monthly magazine in 1873, it was created to advertise and to build up the community. It differed somewhat from other Colorado newspapers in that it printed not only news items but also a good deal of miscellaneous matter such as articles by Rose Kingsley, daughter of the well-known English novelist, Charles Kingsley, as well as letters from Canon Kingsley himself. The *Greeley Tribune,* begun in 1870, and the Longmont *Sentinel,* begun in 1871, are other examples of newspapers originated to promote colonies and to supply the residents with news.[39]

Among the editors of these early Colorado newspapers, William Byers of the *Rocky Mountain News* became the most famous. Well known also was Carlyle Channing "Cad" Davis of the *Leadville Chronicle,* who is remembered for his editorial leadership and for his book *Olden Times in Colorado.*[40] But easily the most interesting of them all was David F. Day, editor of the Ouray *Solid Muldoon.* Somewhat puzzled as to how to describe this complex man, Wilbur Fisk Stone referred to him as "one of the unique characters of Colorado journalism."[41] The humorist of the San Juan, as Day became known, certainly was a character, and from 1879 until he moved the paper to Durango in 1892, the Civil War veteran shot into the air of western Colorado sparks of humor, sarcasm, and acidic denunciation that reached far beyond the borders of the state. Republicans and questionable mining promotions were his chief targets. So enthusiastic was his pursuit of both that at one time he was swarmed over by forty-two libel suits, and, upon occasion, he had to carry out his editorial duties from jail. As one of Colorado's most interesting newspapermen he deserves far more attention from historians than he has received to date. This may be said also of Cy Warman, editor of the Creede *Candle,* who wrote poetry in addition to his editorial functions. One of his poems ended with the lines "It's day all day in the daytime, And there is no night in Creede," which became a widely used quotation among those who later wrote about Colorado.

Denver was the home of Colorado's first newspapers and continued to produce them. The editors supported the city's growth, nagged at those who were thought to be laggardly about community affairs, and constantly stood high in the ranks of local leaders. Professor O. J. Goldrick, discussed earlier as one of Colorado's first educators, also was a journalist; he edited the *Rocky Mountain Herald* during the seventies and eighties. The *Denver Daily Times,* the *Tribune,* the *Democrat,* and the *Republican* originated during these decades and, as was the custom, served as outlets for the views of major political parties.

The *Denver Post* was founded in 1892 and eventually became one of the state's leading newspapers. It began as a Democratic organ. The *Post*'s support of the current leading Democrat, Grover Cleveland, who was very unpopular in Colorado, appears to have been a serious mistake, for the paper suspended operations in the summer of 1893, to be reincorporated in the following year as the *Evening Post.* It struggled during the depression years and in 1895 was purchased by Frederick G. Bonfils and Harry H. Tammen, who displayed a brand of journalism labeled "yellow" by its enemies and "showmanlike" by its friends; in either case, it sold newspapers as they never before had been sold in Colorado.[42]

That Colorado editors and their newspapers participated actively in the development of the state is obvious even from a cursory examination of the past. The editors played an active role in community affairs, associated with and were accepted by both business and professional classes, and served as clearinghouse directors for a multitude of community projects and concerns. On occasion they ran for political offices, serving as governors, members of Congress, members of various state boards and commissions, and in the General Assembly. Except for the brief flurry of Populism the newspapers stayed with the major parties, and one does not have to scan their columns very carefully to tell whether they were Republican or Democratic in sympathy. In the manner of the day, they practiced personal journalism and did not hesitate to call names and risk challenges at arms, but invariably they manned the barricades of local pride with a ferocity that sometimes amazed their readers. They made enemies this way, but they also gained a loyal following and thus they came to wield an influence that looked toward a higher level of community achievement in terms of everyday living.

Almost from the outset Colorado's population could boast of a relatively high incidence of literate men and women, newcomers who were possessed not only of the physical drive so much associated with frontier folk, but also of an intellectual curiosity that bore with it an inherent desire to reproduce a society at least as advanced as that from which they had come. This is not to suggest that they were, indeed, God's chosen people, as some of the pioneers later decided, but rather that the great rush of Fifty-Nine and the successive afterwaves did not wash westward the percentage of society's offscourings frequently associated with earlier movements to unsettled lands. Other mineral developments in the Rockies, such as the gold rush into Montana, produced similar results, but because of its central location, its railroad connections, and a steadily growing economy promoted by an active leadership, Colorado maintained its early momentum better than did Montana. Frontier conditions disappeared more rapidly from Colorado than from many other parts of the West.

# 10

# High Country Society

The efforts of Colorado's leaders to elevate the general intellectual level by fostering education, while at the same time encouraging acquaintance with the printed word through the establishment of libraries, were regarded as a part of the forward-thinking, progressive manner in which ambitious young communities were supposed to operate. In a similar vein, acceptance of women's demands for suffrage and a gradual yielding to programs set forth by temperance advocates were believed to be indications that the state was abreast of or ahead of the times in the field of social legislation.

These measures were largely promoted by a predominantly white, Protestant group that regarded itself as being composed of upper-middle-class, and surely no less than "middle-middle-class," Americans. They were conscious of their status in the new community and of the inferential responsibilities that the role assigned to them. Although outwardly they wore the political clothing of a democratic people, they believed privately that theirs was a kind of aristocracy often recognized, but seldom advertised, among frontier folk. In every aspect of life—and even of death—they thirsted for self-improvement, for cultural uplift. As one of the founders of a cemetery outside Denver's city limits explained it, the final resting place for Colorado's elite must be beautiful, well-groomed, and tasteful, for it was an "outgrowth of the higher civilization and refinement of the age in which we live." To the end, Colorado's leaders were class-conscious.

But there were other groups of Coloradans who, because of an unsatisfactory bloodline or a presumed lack of the sterling qualities demanded of them by the dominant group, stood off to one side and were assigned minor roles in the great work at hand—that of building a right-thinking, progressive home in the West where the deserving would live and prosper.

Black Americans, who were a part of the first great mineral rush to Colorado, were neither petted nor persecuted but rather were accorded a grudging kind of recognition that arose out of necessity: the miners simply were too busy to pay them much attention. Fewer blacks were found in the little agricultural towns than in the mining camps because in the latter places there was more money, less time, and therefore a greater demand for menial labor and personal services. In Denver, the metropolitan center, opportunities for this minority faded as time passed and as that community settled upon its course toward "civilization" and sophistication, a development that saw a tightening of class lines in both economic and social spheres. In the process the blacks found themselves increasingly relegated to the more familiar roles assigned their people—those of unskilled labor—and as early as 1870 it was possible to show that in the Denver labor force they were little better off than were their brothers in such a city as Atlanta. Nor did things improve. The Colorado population explosion of the eighties and nineties was essentially white and hence led to a steady proportional shrinkage of the black segment.

In 1887 the descendant of a slave family, O. T. Jackson, came to Colorado, and for years he watched the shrinking possibilities available to his people. During this period he farmed near Boulder, and later he found a position as a messenger in the governor's office. While employed there he described his hopes for a black colony to Governor John F. Shafroth, who encouraged him, as did a Denver physician of his acquaintance who thought the Greeley area was a likely location for settlement by a group of black farmers. By 1911 Dearfield was founded; sixty black families, led by Jackson, formed the nucleus of a group that would grow to seven hundred persons by 1921. Then the experiment would wither, as was the case with a great many other joint endeavors on the agricultural frontier, and one by one the members of the colony would drift back to the cities, or move to other farming areas, marking the failure of yet another experiment designed to aid a minority people.[1]

But even as the black population found itself gradually

maneuvered into a position of economic, political, and social inferiority, it continued to feel only a passive prejudice by the dominant whites. It was for the Spanish-speaking Americans, invariably and incorrectly referred to simply as "Mexicans," that they reserved their open disdain and active prejudices. Ignoring the fact that Spanish interest in the region north of New Mexico predated the rush of 1859 by more than three hundred years, and that Santa Fe had sent its traders northward along the Rio Grande at a time when English Jamestown was a struggling colony of doubtful longevity, the "Anglos" of Colorado took the position that the Mexican Americans were a naturally inferior people and should be treated as such. The relaxed, easygoing way of life of these people, their apparent lack of aggressiveness in business matters, and certainly their Catholicism grated upon the nerves of transplanted New England Puritans, whose rigid moral, religious, and economic beliefs differed so widely from those of a Latin background.

As the Fifty-Niners had watched those they termed "the Mexicans" mine gold, they had been critical of methods they considered old and therefore "backward." A newspaper correspondent of that day once told his readers, "You have doubtless heard something of the national characteristics of the Mexican people, and have been told that they are prone to indolence, drunkenness, filthiness and gaming. . . ." He explained that they would work for two or three hours each morning, acquiring a few dollars' worth of gold, after which they would "adjourn to camp and there seated upon the ground with their whiskey bottle and cards they will drink and gamble until the last cents worth is gone, and then, rather than go to work again that day, they will sell the last coat from their backs to continue the game." He did not try to justify the gambling and drinking propensities of the Anglos.

While occasional remarks are found in contemporary accounts about the Spanish-speaking miners—"Spanish Bar" near Idaho Springs was a well-known camp in the sixties—most references are to the agricultural pursuits of this element. It was argued that agriculture was possible in Colorado because in the Rio Grande Valley "even the indolent Mexicans" had succeeded in raising crops. Sam Bowles made such a remark on one of his visits to Colorado, asserting that huge crops were being raised there by "ignorant, degraded Mexicans." Agricultural produce was much in demand in the mines, and this market drew a great many farmers out of New Mexico and into Colorado during the early days of mining. As early as 1859 J. M. Francisco, a settler from near Fort Massachusetts in the San Luis Valley, had established trade with the Denver area. "His trains of flour, corn, seed wheat, barley, potatoes, etc., will arrive in a few days," one of the miners reported. Francisco later became a well-known business and political figure in his community.[2]

In the first mineral rush there was little difficulty between the Spanish Americans and the newcomers. The "diggin's" were so predominantly "American" that the various minorities dared not voice complaints very loudly. Since the southern part of the state was primarily grazing and farming country, and not yet thoroughly prospected, the Mexican-American groups had this section pretty much to themselves and for a decade there were no serious signs of trouble. Early in 1868, however, a dispute over the outcome of a wrestling match in Trinidad triggered a miniature war in which three Spanish-speaking participants were killed and five wounded, with one Anglo suffering injuries. Cavalry units were sent in to restore order, and, as the *Rocky Mountain News* put it, "The greater portion of the Mexican population vamoosed on the arrival of our 'Uncle's boys.' " The *News* suggested deeper problems when it commented, "The Mexicans have the idea that they are to be driven out of the country, which is to their minds confirmed by the large emigration to the Mexican mines [in Colorado], and have determined to exterminate the Americans."[3] Matters quieted down with only occasional instances of violence being reported. For example, in 1869 the Pueblo *Chieftain* noted that a Negro named Bob had been attacked "by a party of Mexicans" who beat him severely.[4]

In 1880, E. P. Tenney, president of Colorado College, at Colorado Springs, identified the Spanish-speaking residents of Colorado in his book *Colorado: And Homes in the New West.* He said that in Mexico itself there were perhaps a million people of Spanish descent, some three million of Indian origins, and about four million of a mixed race composed mainly of Spanish and Indian blood "commonly called greasers." The population of New Mexico had about the same proportion, and in southern Colorado, where about thirty thousand "of these people" lived, the ratio remained the same.[5] Despite such delineations, contemporaries rarely made any distinctions as to bloodlines or origins. On the rare occasions when they failed to use the term *Mexican*, they employed that of *greaser.* Both expressions were very common in the literature of the nineteenth century, yet those who talked of "Mexicans" and "greasers" would have denied prejudice as quickly as would a rural southerner employing the word *nigger.* In many respects the so-called Mexicans were assigned a role in Colorado history not dissimilar to that of blacks in the South. When Bowles visited Colorado in 1868 he thought this group represented a quarter of its population, "all in the southern section, and ignorant and debased to a shameful degree." Fortunately, he said, the higher class Anglo-Saxons in the remainder of the territory made up for such a deficiency.[6]

Later visitors continued to look upon Spanish-speaking Coloradans with the same Olympian disdain. One of them remarked that there were "Mexicans, dirty 'greasers' by the score" in the southern part of the territory. He noted that some of the early trappers had married among them and at Pueblo "half a dozen curious products of this frightful amalgamation, murderous-looking little devils they are," stared at him. "How their black, snaky eyes gleam upon me, and how repulsive are their greasy, yellow, brick-dust faces, and coarse, black matted hair! They are thieves and cut-throats 'to the manner born'. . . ."[7]

Another of the passersby was similarly disturbed when he visited Pueblo. He noted that the place was filled with "greasers" who had become citizens by a stroke of the pen, as had the blacks, and he wondered if the Indians and Chinese would be next to gain such an undeserved privilege. In a passage that spoke of the disappearing buffalo and antelope herds on the plains he stated his notions of racial superiority more succinctly. "Useless animals are superseded by those that are necessary to man," he explained, "as useless men, Indians, greasers and Negroes are being swept away by those lords of creation born of the Anglo-Saxon race. It is a high title, but they have assumed it, though all of them do not bear the stamp of nobility." To him these minorities appeared to be members of some strange, invading race who had taken a land that now must be rescued from them. It worried him that Pueblo carried a name that originated with the Spanish-speaking people, but he did not challenge the adoption of "Colorado" to describe a region that once had been known simply as Pike's Peak Country. He thought Pueblo should have a good Anglo-Saxon name such as Smithville or Brownopolis. The critic was happy to report that better days were ahead for the unfortunate town, because it "has been rescued from the hands of its original inhabitants" by the coming of the railroad; with the infusion of new blood, brought in by rail, it promised to take its place as an important Colorado city.[8]

To those who came to live in Colorado, or saw it merely as tourists, the Spanish atmosphere in the southern counties attracted comment. When Irving Howbert and a group were trailing some horse thieves in the summer of 1865, they stopped at Trinidad, where "we had supper at a Mexican hotel, the food being plain but well cooked." He called the place "a typical Mexican town," and since few members of his party ever had been in such a settlement before, many of the things they saw were strange to them. Sam Bowles noticed that "Mexican terms" were much in evidence, even in Denver. He explained that an animal enclosure was called a *corral* and that "a house of turf and mud" was *adobe,* while a farm often was referred to as a *ranch.* Evidences of an earlier heritage were seen in the adherence to methods used by another generation. "We saw Mexicans reaping grain with a knife that resembled the sickle of Palestine, the same as that used by their forefathers," wrote another tourist. "Their plough is especially ancient . . . the crooked stick of the Orient. Their method of grinding is similar."[9]

Members of the invading Anglo-Saxon forces not only dismissed the Spanish-speaking elements, but they appeared anxious to erase evidences of their culture. In the late eighties Ernest Ingersoll, the well-known writer and traveler, looked at the new names on the land, noticed that rivers were named Green, Red, Blue, and Grand, and commented that those of non-English origins usually were mispronounced. He wrote it off as "characteristic of the pig-headed ignorance and conceit which crops out so offensively in all frontier society." When one of the dominant race explained to him that he purposely mispronounced Spanish and Indian names "because he hated Greasers and Redskins and thought it a shame that anything should be named after them," Ingersoll was appalled. While visiting Antonito he saw further evidence of erosion of the Spanish tradition. Not only had the newcomers "Americanized" the place, but the innovations were dull. "In a real Mexican town," he explained, "the church is always an entertaining place to visit, because it is ruinously ancient and strange; but here the large, well-conditioned structure has been roofed, painted and modernized until it is not worth a glance except from the point of comfort and security from decay."[10]

The lack of interest shown in the Anglo-Saxon way of life by the

Spanish-speaking residents of Colorado was a constant irritant to the majority group. William Pabor, journalist and promoter of Colorado's great future, was annoyed by their "careless" agriculture, a characteristic he attributed to natural indolence and their intense dislike of what he viewed as civilization. Helen Hunt Jackson, defender of the Indians, quoted her driver's opinion of the "Mexicans" while on a trip through the Cucharas Valley. "Give a Mexican five cents a day and he'll lie by and do nothing he'll feel so rich. He'll squat on his heels and chew pinon nuts from morning till night." In a similar situation, one of the stagecoach employees remarked to a passenger viewing the Sand Dunes of the San Luis Valley that a few years back six "Mexican" sheepherders and a thousand sheep were buried in a sandstorm. "Pity it was not six sheep and a thousand Mexicans," growled one of the passengers. An eastern visitor gained much the same impression of the harsh Anglo attitude when he described western bullwhackers. They were silent, indefatigable, and even brutal, but, he said, they were patient in difficulty and cooperative with fellow drivers—unless, of course, "the other is a 'greaser.' "[11]

The attitude died very slowly. When Frank Hall wrote his *History of the State of Colorado* in 1889, he made uncomplimentary references to those whose origins were Mexican. He was a typical Anglo-Saxon, a community leader, and a man who had served in high office; in all probability, he would have been both annoyed and hurt if anyone had criticized him for the slight he had given a minority people.[12] Later generations would realize that Hall and his contemporaries were unwilling, or perhaps unable, to understand the basic cultural differences that separated Spanish-speaking Coloradans from the rest. But such attitudes would not change until well after the close of World War II, when an enormous influx of people from other parts of the nation made the discovery that Colorado was a desirable place to live. The newcomers had a lot of strange ideas, among them the notion that bigger was not better and that population growth was not necessarily the answer to all problems. Thus it was easier for them to sympathize with these presumed enemies of progress, who for years had tried to enjoy the place they lived in rather than exploiting it under the guise of development.

In some respects the low regard held by early Coloradans for the American Indians living in and along the central Rockies was similar to that which they had for the Mexican Americans. In both cases it was an attitude of dismissal as opposed to active hatred, except that in the case of the Indians it somehow was easier to rationalize the case for extinction or at least the banishment of a race. Presumably this came from an ingrained conviction that these were inferior beings who were not even Christians. Sam Bowles, the Massachusetts journalist, reached far back into American history when he commented that the whites should stop putting themselves on a par with the Indians because "we know they are not our equals; we know that our right to the soil, as a race capable of its superior improvement is above theirs; and let us act openly and directly our faith." He then quoted an old Puritan premise to document his case: "The earth is the Lord's; it is given by Him to the Saints for its improvement and development; and we are the Saints." These words, he argued, "are the faith and practice of our people; let us hesitate no longer to avow it and act it. Let us say to him [the Indian], you are our ward, our child, the victim of our destiny, ours to displace, ours also to protect. We want your hunting-grounds to dig gold from, to raise grain on and you must 'move on.' " Bowles was pleased when the Utes were moved to a reservation where they could be Christianized while the conquerors looked for gold on their former lands.[13]

Prejudices toward Colorado's other racial minorities have been slight, simply because of the minimal impression some of these people have made upon the majority. Orientals, for example, have played a small part in the state's history. As late as 1900, census figures showed only forty-eight Japanese, a number that grew rapidly after that time but never became large. The Chinese drifted into the mining camps, particularly after the completion of the Pacific Railroad, upon which many of them had worked, but by 1880 there were only some six hundred of them in the state. Because they lived more cheaply and "worked the tailings" in the placer country, they generated resentment among those with whom they competed. A lady traveler who visited Leadville in 1880 was shocked to see a sign that stated simply: "All Chinamen will be shot."[14] Ernest Ingersoll, writing of Leadville, made reference to the exclusion. With some amusement he related that the enforcers of this edict recently had come close to making a serious error when they nearly put an end to "an unfortunate Mexican bull-whacker" whom they thought was an Oriental interloper in disguise. "John Chinaman," as he was universally called in the camps, was ordered out of the mining town of Gothic in 1881, because "his cheap rates proved a serious detriment to the old time washer women and caused them to become very indignant," said the local newspaper. The "Irish washerwomen" had acquired a very strong grip on this sphere of the labor market, and when their domain was threatened their "Americanism" surfaced very easily.[15] Members of this "yellow peril" to labor were chased out of Caribou, Colorado, in the mid seventies, and a Boulder paper praised the right-thinking residents for their action. During these years a South Park coal company replaced some of its Italian miners with Chinese, and there was more trouble.[16]

Violence erupted along Denver's "Hop Alley" in 1880 when rioting, burning, and one killing occurred as a result of the buildup of resentments. Part of the trouble arose from animosities present throughout the state, particularly in the camps, part from the alleged opium dealing and vice in the Alley that offended city leaders, but also to be considered was the national anti-Chinese sentiment that stirred the country during these years.[17] California's discontent, and the subsequent Chinese Exclusion Act of 1882, were reflected in growing, self-conscious Colorado.

The Italians came to Colorado in part because employers were in search of cheap labor. Almost none of them were among the Fifty-Niners—the 1860 census indicated only six—but by the eighties they began to arrive in numbers to work in the mines and smelters and on the railroads. The newcomers found their place on this frontier unenviable, so much so that the Italian consul at Denver openly accused the labor contractors of fraud. A writer who stopped at Denver in 1879 made reference to the "wretched dens" in which the Italian population was obliged to live.[18] Life in the mines or around the fringes of economic life in places such as Denver was grim for these people, but the strength of their old-country heritage and their religion made their days somewhat more tolerable. Angelo Noce began his Italian language newspaper *La Stella* in 1885; although it expired in a few years, others followed, at least two of which survived until the mid twentieth century. Despite conditions that were far from favorable, Italians continued to come to Colorado, and after 1900 they stood high in the rankings of foreign-born arrivals.

During the early years a large percentage of Colorado's foreign born came from northern Europe, as was true in the remainder of the United States. Prior to 1910, England, Ireland, Scotland, Wales, and Germany stood high on the numerical list, and after that time

Italy, Russia, and Mexico dominated. A good many of the English were immigrants bound for farm or ranch; a few of them—and of the Scots—were capitalists in search of investment possibilities. The Welsh and Irish frequently worked in the mines, as did the Cornishmen. By 1890 nearly a sixth of Denver's population was Irish, a figure that represented close to half of that group in the entire state. Such concentration tended to discount the oft-repeated claim by these people of their love of the land, since they chose urban as opposed to rural lives. Another large foreign-born group was Swedish; again, these people tended to settle in towns rather than rural areas. Like the Irish, about half of Colorado's Swedes lived in the Denver area in 1890. In other parts of the West they tended to settle on farms.

Prominent among the immigrant groups that sought out farms were the German Russians, an interesting people who played an important part in the development of Colorado agriculture. These descendants of German colonists who had moved to Russia's Volga Valley in the eighteenth century at the invitation of Catherine the Great began to enter Colorado around 1880. Some of them came by way of Kansas, where crop failures had driven them out. Later in that decade a group of them moved from South Dakota to Burlington, Colorado, and in the ensuing years others joined them. By the early twentieth century a good many of them were farming, principally in sugar beets, around Loveland, LaSalle, Windsor, and down the Platte Valley. Like other pioneers they suffered, frequently living in tents until they could build homes and establish themselves financially. In 1910 eight or nine hundred German Russians lived in Colorado; by 1930 the figure had jumped to nearly fifty thousand, most of whom were engaged in agriculture.[19]

Historians of these industrious people have suggested that as western settlers they were more effective than any other group and that they worked their way to prosperity the most rapidly. Instance after instance has been cited to show how well they did in new and strange circumstances. Their family life showed exceptionally strong patriarchal characteristics; the children, even after marriage, often continued to live and work with their parents as one large family. The birth rate among them was very high, the divorce rate close to nonexistent. As did most western farmers, they lived in their own homes, but among the German Russians the incidence of home ownership in the towns was much higher than the average. In the construction of their houses they tended to copy the style of their European ancestors rather than building in the American design. Church architecture also followed traditional, old-country lines. So did clothing, particularly of the women, who preferred the head scarf to the hat. As new Coloradans they showed earlier residents that they were hardworking, honest, and peaceable. It was the kind of agricultural population the promoters had been looking for.[20]

Another group of immigrants from Russia did not fare so well. During the late 1870s persecution of Jews in that country reached such proportions that a committee of their coreligionists in the United States founded the Hebrew Immigrant Aid Society, an organization that before long had some $300,000 at its disposal, and had begun to receive refugees at New York City. Anxious to settle some of these arrivals in places where they could begin a new life, the committee members cast about for possible locations. One of the responses came from a little place called Cotopaxi, in Colorado.

Located along the Arkansas River between Canon City and Salida, Cotopaxi was given its unusual named by a miner named Henry ("Gold Tom") Thomas because the countryside reminded him of terrain he had prospected in South America and he remembered a volcano there named Cotopaxi. Thomas discovered substantial deposits of silver and zinc in this part of Colorado, but he did not have sufficient funds to develop his mines. This fact interested Emanuel H. Saltiel, a Portuguese Jew who had arrived in Colorado a decade earlier and had acquired both property and money during the intervening years. By profession Saltiel was an engineer and metallurgist. Now, in 1878, he thought he saw a way to acquire a cheap labor force for the mines at Cotopaxi.[21]

Filing on 2,000 acres of government land, Saltiel organized what he termed a town and land company, the ostensible purpose of which was to increase the agricultural yield of the upper Arkansas Valley. At the same time the entrepreneur acquired seven different mining claims. His search for a source of cheap labor was answered when he made contact with Jacob Milstein, a young man who was in the United States to investigate the possibility of emigration for a group of Russian Jews who wanted to free themselves from the Czar's increasingly anti-Semitic policies. Saltiel, the promoter, made glowing promises of furnished houses, barns, implements, draft animals, wagons, seed, and even a year's supply of forage. The entire cost, including transportation, would be less than $10,000 or just under $435 for each family in the proposed group.

The Immigrant Aid Society appropriated the $10,000 Saltiel said was necessary to settle a group of Jews at Cotopaxi, but before proceeding further it sent an investigator named Julius Schwartz to Colorado to examine the soil, climate, potential markets for agricultural products, and the like. He reached his destination, but failed to make any kind of report. Instead, he fell in with Saltiel and became a junior partner. Meantime, the group had arrived in America and was using up HIAS funds for subsistence during the winter of 1881–82. Without a report, but under mounting pressure, the society decided to take a chance and to send on twenty families. They reached Cotopaxi in May 1882.

The welcoming committee did not exude western hospitality. Residents of Cotopaxi who gathered at the Denver and Rio Grande's little depot, curious as to the imminent arrival of the "Jew Colonists," were openly scornful of the strangely clad, frightened newcomers. But, being used to scorn and adversity, members of the group resolutely faced the dry, rocky slopes that overlooked the Arkansas River, determined to dig in for this, the final stand. They had one hope: during the preceding October Saltiel had written to the Aid Society saying that the houses were ready and that adequate barns would be finished shortly. He also described additional equipment he would have on hand for them if funds were sent. They believed Saltiel and were sure that at last they had come home.[22]

What the newcomers saw was heartbreaking, to say the least. Not twenty, but merely twelve boxlike shanties measuring some eight feet square and only six feet high, with flat roofs, and without furniture, doors, windows, or even chimneys, were their new homes in the West. Only four of the shacks had stoves for heating or cooking. Nor did the land, described in such effusive terms by Saltiel, prove to be any more encouraging. Devoid of fencing, wells, or roads, these parched acres were rough and barren, relieved of their monotony only by occasional patches of hardy mountain grass and scrubby-looking little pines. A few discouraged cattle nibbled at what little foliage struggled for existence. Even marginal farming, it appeared, would require some kind of miracle. In the finest tradition of land developers, Saltiel explained that missing items, such as window frames, furniture, equipment, and lumber were temporarily delayed and that this small oversight would be rectified in no time at all. Having offered his explanation, he vanished on an extended business trip, leaving the immigrants to shift more or less for themselves. As it turned out their only real friend was the errant investigator, Julius Schwartz, who was sympathetic to the colonists. He joined them in their religious activities and became secretary to their congregation.

Meanwhile, Saltiel returned from his trip and refused to talk further about any of his obligations. The local store, of which he was half owner, informed the settlers that no more credit would be extended. On top of this came the failure of the potato crop due to an early frost. Only one farmer averted total failure. He sowed fourteen bags of potatoes and harvested fifteen bags, the quality of which was poorer than what he had planted.[23] As winter deepened, the settlers, faced by both hunger and cold, had to make some move for survival and the one they chose was exactly what Saltiel had in mind: they went to work in his mines at $1.50 a day. But even these wages, lower than the usual rate, were further reduced when Saltiel issued store orders rather than cash and obliged them to pay the high prices his store set for its captive customers. Fortunately a savior appeared on the scene. The Denver and Rio Grande Railway, then expanding westward into the mining camps, was in need of laborers and it offered these people $3.00 a day, in cash, as construction workers. By this means the sixty-three members of the colony survived the first winter.

The second year at Cotopaxi was not encouraging. A late spring blizzard, quite common in Colorado, severely stunted the young crop, with the result that the yield was no better than that of the previous year. Some of the families gave up the effort and moved on. By the time the third crop was planted, in 1884, only six families remained. Again, a later spring storm severely damaged the crop. It was too much. In June 1884 the colony was broken up and the remnants of it scattered throughout Colorado. In general those who had come as farmers and had failed as farmers, tended to drift into the towns, went into business, and frequently formed the nucleus of Jewish communities in these small places. A few found more arable land and farmed, some went into the cattle business, and one or two of the families left the state. For all of them it was their last venture into cooperative enterprise.

Beyond doubt Cotopaxi was destined to failure from the outset, if one takes into account the problems faced by the average colony settlement in Colorado, but this one was burdened by additional handicaps not found in most other efforts: poor farming land and a dishonest promoter. Failure did not come from any lack of determination, unwillingness to sacrifice, or disinclination to work long, backbreaking hours. It was there, at Cotopaxi, waiting for the newcomers the day they arrived. Perhaps the Cotopaxi story tells more about the lengths to which Colorado's mining magnates would go to find a source of cheap labor than it does about agricultural colonies in the state. In any event, those who came and tried to farm discovered that there was a limit to the extent of the West's agricultural possibilities and that they had been thrust into an area where failure in that particular endeavor was guaranteed.

Aside from the ethnic groups that played minor roles in Colorado's rapidly developing society, the number of women was steadily growing. After the first boom had passed and the territory settled down to a more normal kind of expansion, the feminine flotsam that was a part of most boom societies stepped aside in favor of wives, sisters, or daughters of the men who mined, farmed, or traded in the communities. While these women are, by and large, an unsung group of pioneers, they did their part, alongside their men. Helen Hunt Jackson saw some of them when she passed through the mining camp of Schofield in the early eighties.

"I've no patience with this boom business," complained one of the women with whom she talked. "It's the ruination of this country. It just spoils everything. There isn't a decent house in the town, and there won't never be!" She was right. Poor transportation facilities and low-grade ores spelled an end to that hopeful metropolis within two or three years, just as it would in hundreds of other camps. The author from Colorado Springs elaborated on the situation in which she found these mining-camp women, characterizing them as "fierce and restless, like the men." As she saw it, they had little incentive to improve their living conditions, not because of any inherent slovenliness, but because there was so little hope that they would be there any length of time. Meanwhile, she said, "They stand in their doorways, idling, wondering, waiting, gossiping, and quarreling."[24]

While wives made up a large part of the feminine population, especially as the nineteenth century drew to a close, a number of women, not infrequently widows, came west and worked in the camps as teachers, waitresses, and laundresses. On rare occasions one of these women made a lucky strike. Mrs. Sallie Ray, a young

Provisions for both man and beast had to be brought in to the gold camps, as this hay wagon at Idaho Springs suggests. *Denver Public Library, Western History Department*

The miners' lives were primitive and recreation limited. A game of cards after dinner helped to while away the time. *Denver Public Library, Western History Department*

Air pollution came early to the mining towns. Here a pall of smoke hangs over Leadville; Mount Massive, in the background, towers over the town (c. 1900). *Denver Public Library, Western History Department*

Mining towns competed vigorously with one another to display civic pride. One proof of a community's cultural status was the possession of an opera house. The Leadville opera house resulted from the munificence of the wealthy H. A. W. Tabor. *Denver Public Library, Western History Department*

By the 1880s the Denver skyline was looking modern—note smog, upper center. Multistoried brick buildings predominated. *Library, The State Historical Society of Colorado*

The Albany Hotel, opened in July 1885, became one of Denver's leading attractions. Its modern facilities were a matter of great civic pride. *Library, The State Historical Society of Colorado*

The interior of the Albany Hotel was similar to that of the Brown Palace. The balconied lobby was a great attraction. *Library, The State Historical Society of Colorado*

The Albany Hotel offered many delights, including music by a four-piece all-girl orchestra (c. 1907). *Library, The State Historical Society of Colorado*

This advertisement, from the Rocky Mountain Official Railway Guide for September 1897, indicates that the Albany Hotel offered facilities as modern as those in other parts of the nation. *Library, The State Historical Society of Colorado*

DELMONICO OF WEST,

Denver, Col. 187

M

To Charpiot's Hotel & Restaurant, DR.

JEROME S. RICHE, Proprietor.

LARIMER STREET.

| | |
|---|---|
| 4 Fish | 1.60 |
| 4 Chops | 1.20 |
| 4 Duck | 2.00 |
| 4 Peas | 1.20 |
| Cheese &c | 1.00 |
| | 7.00 |

P.d JSR.
Mr. Dudley

Those who ate at Charpiot's probably complained about the high prices, but they knew they had been to "the Delmonico's of the West." *Library, The State Historical Society of Colorado*

If you were the bellman in Denver's Hotel Metropole during the early 1880s and had been called to room 725 by Mr. J. M. Smith, this is the overfurnished scene that would have greeted you. *Library, The State Historical Society of Colorado*

Hiking and riding early became popular Colorado recreations. And just as early the natives learned to capitalize on their resources, as the "toll trail" sign in the background indicates. *Denver Public Library, Western History Department*

Railroad tours became popular during the 1880s. The hanging bridge in the Royal Gorge was a hit with tourists from the beginning. *Library, The State Historical Society of Colorado*

The Manitou and Pike's Peak Cog Railroad, opened in 1891, attracted throngs of visitors. *Denver Public Library, Western History Department*

The air was thin, but the view was long when one topped 14,147-foot Pike's Peak by cog railroad. *Denver Public Library, Western History Department*

Railroading in the Rockies produced some spectacular engineering feats, one of the most popular—then and later—being the famed Georgetown Loop. *Denver Public Library, Western History Department*

Boulder Canyon was one of the many "gateways" to deeper recesses in the Rockies. These buggies are carrying tourists, c. 1900. *University of Colorado Museum*

Early tourists "roughing it" at lawn tennis, Elkhorn Hotel, Estes Park. *Denver Public Library, Western History Department*

The warm pool and commodious bathhouse at Glenwood Springs were a great attraction to Coloradans about the turn of the century. *Denver Public Library, Western History Department*

The battle against Demon Rum was a serious matter, as we can see from the stern faces of these members of the Women's Christian Temperance Union. *Denver Public Library, Western History Department*

A typical one-room log schoolhouse of the 1890s, with faculty and students. Summit County. *Denver Public Library, Western History Department*

The Reverend George M. Darley was a religious frontiersman who carried the "Blue Banner" of Presbyterianism westward in a militant fashion. In 1876 he helped to construct this church in Lake City with his own hands. *Photo by Frederic J. Athearn*

Churches were important indicators of cultural advancement, particularly when they were built of brick. Greeley was especially proud of its Trinity Church. *Library, The State Historical Society of Colorado*

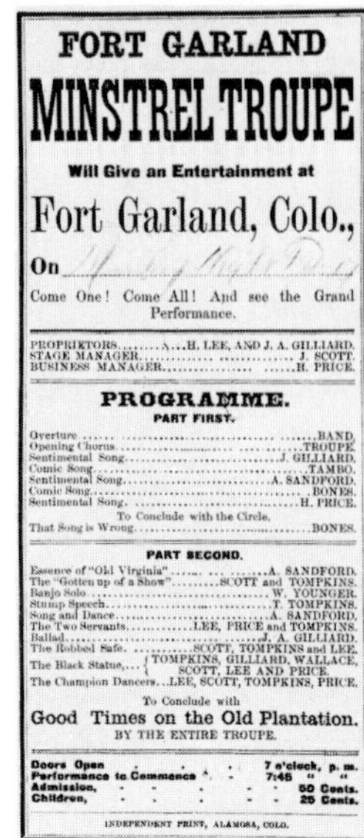

FORT GARLAND

MINSTREL TROUPE

Will Give an Entertainment at

Fort Garland, Colo.,

On [illegible]

Come One! Come All! And see the Grand Performance.

PROPRIETORS.........A...H. LEE, AND J. A. GILLIARD.
STAGE MANAGER............................J. SCOTT.
BUSINESS MANAGER.........................H. PRICE.

PROGRAMME.

PART FIRST.

Overture........................................BAND.
Opening Chorus.................................TROUPE.
Sentimental Song...........................J. GILLIARD.
Comic Song......................................TAMBO.
Sentimental Song..........................A. SANDFORD.
Comic Song......................................BONES.
Sentimental Song..............................H. PRICE.

To Conclude with the Circle.

That Song is Wrong.............................BONES.

PART SECOND.

Essence of "Old Virginia"..................A. SANDFORD.
The "Gotten up of a Show".........SCOTT and TOMPKINS.
Banjo Solo.................................W. YOUNGER.
Stump Speech..............................T. TOMPKINS.
Song and Dance............................A. SANDFORD.
The Two Servants..............LEE, PRICE and TOMPKINS.
Ballad.................................J. A. GILLIARD.
The Robbed Safe.............SCOTT, TOMPKINS and LEE.
The Black Statue,...{ TOMPKINS, GILLIARD, WALLACE, SCOTT, LEE AND PRICE.
The Champion Dancers...LEE, SCOTT, TOMPKINS, PRICE.

To Conclude with

Good Times on the Old Plantation.

BY THE ENTIRE TROUPE.

Doors Open . . . . 7 o'clock, p. m.
Performance to Commence . . 7:45 " "
Admission, . . . . . 50 Cents.
Children, . . . . . 25 Cents.

INDEPENDENT PRINT, ALAMOSA, COLO.

Both music and photography were very popular in the Colorado Rockies. This portrait of the American Quartet and Mandolin Club was taken outside the studio of "Rocky Mountain Joe" Sturtevant, a well-known Boulder photographer. *University of Colorado Museum*

Minstrel troupes were popular both in the mining camps and at military posts, where local residents joined the soldiers in the audience. *Denver Public Library, Western History Department*

The Montrose lodge of the Woodmen of the World, with ladies' auxiliary, display their prize for log rolling. *Denver Public Library, Western History Department*

Coloradans participated in the bicycling craze that spread over America during the 1890s. Some of these Colorado Springs cyclers ride the "Penny Farthing" model. *Denver Public Library, Western History Department*

The Silver Plume baseball team, champions of Clear Creek and Gilpin counties, 1899. *Denver Public Library, Western History Department*

Coloradans were proud of the rapidity with which their new communities became civilized; this lynching at Greeley, however, occurred as late as January 4, 1888. *Denver Public Library, Western History Department*

The orphanage at Fort Amity housed a number of children brought in from the East to enjoy Colorado's healthy climate and to work in the colony's cantaloupe fields. *Library, The State Historical Society of Colorado*

General Irving Hale and his staff celebrating their return from the Spanish American War. *Denver Public Library, Western History Department*

In general, Chinese were not welcomed in placer mining camps. Later, however, hard-rock mining companies and coal companies employed them, in spite of loud objections to the practice. This group worked at Idaho Springs. *Denver Public Library, Western History Department*

Labor violence flared in Colorado in 1903. The establishment called for troops, and the state responded. Here is a Gatling gun trained on the approach to the depot at Cripple Creek. *Denver Public Library, Western History Department*

Feeding the troops brought in to quell the Cripple Creek strike, 1903. *Denver Public Library, Western History Department*

Irish widow known as the Leadville washerwoman, turned the profits of her labor into real estate holdings at a time when that fabulous camp was getting its start. As early as 1879, said a traveler, she had rented out her property and had retired to Denver in the manner of the mineral kings. Here she was living a life of ease on a $30,000 annual income.[25] Other women chose to go directly into the field, in competition with the male prospectors. Ellen E. Jack, known as Captain Jack, worked the countryside around Gunnison in the 1870s. Armed with the usual pick and shovel, a blanket, and some food, she probed remote areas until she found what she wanted. Before long she was half owner in the Black Queen mine. Although she could ride, shoot, and rough it, she was not a masculine female of the Calamity Jane type. She liked jewelry and carried hers in a chamois bag suspended from the neck; she felt the romance of the country through which she traveled and tried to write poetry about it; later she expressed her feelings in an autobiography called *Fate of a Fairy*.[26] A good many of the women lived less noteworthy lives, simply adjusting to frontier conditions as a matter of course, unaware that they were possessed of any special fortitude. Two young women who lived in South Park with their brother during the 1870s were part of this group. When a visitor asked them if the presence of Indians did not worry them one of them said, "They try to scare us some times. They tell us 'Bime-by Utes get all this country—then you my squaw,' but we don't scare worth a cent."[27] A widely read woman author found Colorado's women "on mountain or plain, in town or ranch, singularly courageous and cheery. . . ." She thought this was due mainly to their excellent health, and the absence of ague and fever that dragged down women in more humid regions.[28]

Max Clark, who was a member of Greeley's Union Colony, remembered the pioneer women somewhat differently. As he saw it, men adjusted to frontier conditions; whether they lived in a rude mountain cabin or in a prairie dugout they settled in and called the place home. "But with the women it is different. To a majority of women a little sea of fair weather is better than the opportunities of the great ocean with its possible storms. In every change she naturally fears the worst rather than hopes for the best. . . ." Nevertheless they followed their men westward to an uncertain future. He admitted that the more optimistic men sometimes were disappointed, but they seemed to shrug off adversity more easily than did women. Still, he concluded, it was better that the women came with the men, for if the wife waited behind until the man had established himself before sending for her, it was hard on both parties.[29] Once established in their new western homes most women made the best of their lot and contributed more than their share to family life. One Coloradan later recalled his upbringing in the northwestern part of the state, and the conditions under which his mother lived. "When we had the dirt roof and it rained and leaked thru she would stand over the cook stove with an umbrella and cook meals with a smile."[30]

Men recognized the fact that western women were thrust into crude living conditions, that by nature they missed having many of the finer things of life that as yet were not available in frontier communities, and that the cultural vacuum of a new country perhaps was harder on them than it was upon the men. Western boys grew up unconsciously knowing that members of the opposite sex were to be treated with respect; as a rule they did not come by this information through lectures from their fathers or from other men but simply by observation of their elders. Courtesy toward women, sometimes to a degree that made men appear uncomfortable, was characteristic of frontier society.

When Mary Blake visited Colorado in the early eighties, she saw this exaggerated, self-conscious courtesy at work. "The men were invariably polite, and well-behaved to a degree that struck one in sharp contrast to their uncared-for appearance," she wrote of her visit. "We never stepped into an elevator in any house [hotel], from the time of leaving Chicago, without having every hat lifted until we left it again. A group of rough, unkempt miners would step into the mud on a bad crossing, in order that your feet might pass dry-shod; and the moment they were addressed by a woman, their pipes were taken from the mouth."[31]

While it was generally agreed that women were a civilizing influence, that their work in education, law, order, and good morals was of great importance to a growing community, and that always they must be treated with respect, now and then members of a male society showed their annoyance at critical members of the fair sex. The story of the stage driver on the Gunnison–Lake City run and the lady "dude" is remembered on Colorado's western slope. As the coach lurched along toward Lake City one day during the eighties, one of the women passengers waxed eloquent on the gorgeous scenery along the route. "It is beautiful, I suppose," a lady from the prairies grudgingly admitted, "but I'd rather see an

Iowa corn field." At this remark the driver, who stuttered, spat contemptuously at the dusty road and grimly remarked, "So-so-so-so would a hog."[32] Even in that early day "flatlanders" took their chances when criticizing Colorado's highly prized scenery.

The people who settled in the central Rockies and became known as Coloradans represented not only a cross section of the national distribution, particularly that of the North and Northeast, but also the nature of settlement in the northern reaches of the trans-Missouri West. The Fifty-Niners and their descendants continued to provide social and political leadership for the community as the years passed. In time various ethnic groups came west to serve as laborers in mining or industry, to take up farms, or to follow ancient trades in the new towns, but while their presence flavored the growing population, it did little to alter the main lines of development set at an early date by the firstcomers.

Mineral extraction influenced the lives of all Colorado's residents, directly or indirectly, for a long time. This was also the case in other western mining states, but in Colorado the economy became sufficiently diversified to prevent domination by any single industry. For example, Colorado never was essentially a cattleman's domain, such as Wyoming, or a state that depended largely upon agriculture, as did some of the high plains states. Also, there was social diversity. The Spanish-speaking population, living primarily in the southern counties, tapered off sharply as one moved northward, to form a cultural bridge between the Southwest and predominantly Anglo-Saxon Wyoming. Nor was Colorado swayed by the influence of any particular religious sect, such as that experienced by Utah, where the nagging question of polygamy impeded statehood for years. Rather, it tended to follow mainstream America, even to its prejudices, and to maintain a cautiously conservative course that kept it well in the middle of the road, always hopeful that such conduct would pay handsome dividends through a slow but steady growth. As they did all over the United States, the minorities had a place in society, but it was a relatively fixed position in which the membership was not disturbed by the ruling class unless it began to make demands or got in the way of "progress." The one exceptional minority was the women, who, because of their relatively small numbers, were regarded highly in a predominantly male society that tended to defer to them even in their politically oriented demands.

By the 1890s Colorado society had settled into a fairly fixed position, one that was not to change for some decades to come, and those who had molded and nurtured it felt that theirs was an accomplishment of significant proportions. The architects of the new society looked forward to the closing years of the century, certain that prosperity and the good life would be the reward of men and women who had come West to start over, to grow up with the country.

# 11

# The Not-So-Gay Nineties

The quickening hopes of the seventies had been realized in the bright booming eighties, but as that happy decade receded into the distance Colorado entered another of its slack periods, and once more there was gloom among the boosters. The final decade of the nineteenth century started off well enough; although silver prices were in a decline, a new mining town called Creede, one that would yield almost five million ounces of silver metal in 1892, suggested that offsetting factors were at hand to save the situation. Meanwhile, manufacturing showed signs of growth, with woolen, cotton, and paper mills making their appearance in Denver. The Colorado Coal & Iron Company, incorporated at Pueblo over a decade earlier, merged with the Colorado Fuel Company in 1892 to become the Colorado Fuel & Iron Company, the state's largest single industrial corporation. Commercial progress was reflected in a crop of new architectural triumphs such as Denver's Brown Palace Hotel and the new Equitable Building, the latter built at a cost of $1.5 million. Both of these structures were finished during 1892. A new and elegant state capitol building was under construction at this time; it would be opened in 1894, and would cost $3 million, or three times the original estimate.[1] The 1890s also saw a sharp increase in urban population, due to prosperous days for business, but perhaps half the thriving cities made their gains from the growth of agriculture. Then came the panic of 1893, a sharp financial recession that was to affect Colorado much more than the national downturn experienced two decades earlier.

Part of the problem arose from the falling price of silver, a decline so precipitous that even the discovery of new, fabulously rich mines could not offset the imbalance. One by one major nations had gone to the gold standard, with the result that the silver content of the American dollar fell in value from $1.02 in 1873 to 48¢ by 1900. Unfortunately for the western silver states, the coinage of silver dollars had been discontinued in 1873, an event that caused no complaint at the time but became very serious as the price of the metal plummeted. Efforts to bolster the price of silver through legislation proved to be palliatives, not cures, and when the mints of India closed in June of 1893 the consequences staggered an already weakened silver-mining community in the Rockies. Bitterly complaining about the British Indian Council's action, the *Rocky Mountain News* charged that "it was England's last card against silver and her final effort to fasten the curse of her ruthless financial policy on the world. . . ."[2] Coupled with the current national financial panic, the "Silver State" had suffered another sharp blow, and charges by a leading newspaper that foreign influences were at the bottom of the trouble provided an old and familiar scapegoat.

By July of 1893 the state's banks began to suffer, and in a three-day period twelve of them in Denver alone closed their doors; only a few reopened later. Business firms suffered from this financial drought, a large number of them going down with the banks. In turn, unemployment mounted as both miners and merchants retrenched. By the end of the summer a small army of unemployed men camped in Denver, where they lived in tents and ate handouts. Thousands of others simply left Colorado for the East. So great was the rush that freight trains were commandeered by penniless men who took part in the desperate flight away from the mountains. The scenes were reminiscent of the "go-back" movement of 1859.[3]

Colorado had suffered reverses before, but each time rich new mineral strikes providentially had come to the rescue of the ailing economy. During the dark days that followed the plunge of 1893 a place called Cripple Creek offered hope. For over three decades prospectors had milled around Pike's Peak, but it remained for a cowboy named Bob Womack to discover gold on the southwest side of this famed mountain early in 1891. After a modest start, gold production in the new diggings grew steadily until the figure stood at $18 million annually by 1900 and averaged $15 million a year for the next decade. While this did not solve Colorado's economic problems and did not compensate for the enormous losses suffered by the silver miners, the recovery of that much gold each year from a single camp certainly lessened the blow.

One of the principal influences of the Cripple Creek strike was the renewed stimulus it gave to the state's mining industry. During a four-year period after 1893, more than three hundred new mining companies were organized, their average capitalization being $1 million each. As had happened after the Leadville strike, once more an intensified search for more gold ensued. Such intensive exploration was bound to bring results in a region already well known for its deposits; by 1902 Colorado's mineral output amounted to some $3 million a month. Now and then there was a bonus, such as that found at Ouray in 1896 by Thomas F. Walsh. The discovery of ore that yielded $1,600 a ton in gold brought the promoter $2.5 million, after which he sold his claims for another $5 million. The gold mining resurgence somewhat eased the problems of financial panic, drought on eastern plains, sagging silver prices, and the political pains of populism.

New gold strikes, by now a familiar panacea in times of trouble, may have soothed some of the economy's wounds, but there were some long-standing difficulties in certain sectors that would not be set at rest by such developments. Despite periodic outbursts of prosperity resulting from mineral booms, labor, both in and out of the mining industry, had not benefited proportionally. As in the rest of the nation, the response of the established order to labor's demands was one of paternalistic toleration interspersed with occasional instances of rather harsh repression when the workers were thought to be getting out of hand. These incidents have become widely publicized in historical works as the most deplorable examples of political reaction to labor's demands, but, as is always the case with examples, they do not tell the whole story. The extent of Colorado's industrialization as compared to that of its neighbors, and its overall labor relations record, should be taken into account. So should the ideologies, background, and beliefs of those who settled the state and shepherded its economic development through the years. Their attitudes go far toward explaining why things happened the way they did.

In the beginning common laborers were in much demand, both in the mines and in the rapidly growing supply towns that served the mining country. This situation generally obtained until the Panic of 1873, when a number of the eastern-owned mines closed down, throwing a great many workers onto the labor market. The unemployed of that day simply moved on to other mining areas of the West or found what employment they could; it rarely occurred to them to protest or to demonstrate. A coal strike at Erie in 1871 was an exception to this rule, and even here the dissidents were quickly put down as management arranged for the arrest of the ringleaders and the replacement of mutinous workers by strike-breakers. Except for a few scattered incidents during the remainder of that decade, the Colorado labor scene remained peaceful until the Leadville strike of 1880.

By the eighties the nature of mining had undergone some changes that were to affect that industry and the politics of Colorado. For the first two decades of search and recovery in Colorado, the possibility of operating under the much-cherished American ideal of individual enterprise had held some promise. During this period the mining frontier retained its mobility, and so long as there was movement there was hope of finding new placer mining sites or quartz deposits rich enough for extraction by individual miners. As the mining frontier in Colorado tended to stabilize, and as outside capital arrived in quantity to finance the increasingly complicated and expensive extraction, the role of the miner changed. Instead of the independent prospector with pick, pan, and burro combing the hills for "color," a more traditional type of miner appeared, a man who worked underground a specified time for a fixed amount of money, much in the manner of those who had mined for centuries in other parts of the world.

This highly institutionalized subsurface laboring force presented a new picture in Colorado. By now a good many of the American miners had departed in search of new bonanzas, and they were replaced by the foreign born, a great many of whom were imported in wholesale lots to work the mines.[4] Not infrequently these men had worked as miners in the East or abroad, and they were familiar with labor organizations, the leaders of which demanded job security, a living wage, and reasonable working conditions for their members. In a five-year period during the early eighties, there were 109 strikes in Colorado, 46 of which were by miners, a majority of whom worked in the coal industry. Among the metal miners the most publicized strike during these years was called at Leadville in 1880, and although the workers asked for better pay and an eight-hour day and lodged certain complaints against management —all standard demands for that period—none of the principal aims were realized by the time the workers agreed to return to the jobs.[5] The introduction of the militia, ordered to Leadville by Governor Frederick Pitkin, indicated that industrialization had come to Colorado, eastern style, and that the armed forces of the establishment were available to management as they were in such places as the mines of Pennsylvania.

Despite the increase in unionism and the growing number of strikes in the early eighties, labor's protests appeared to be largely ineffective. Most of the walkouts prior to the middle of that decade were executed precipitously; grievances would come to a head, the men would indicate a growing restlessness, and then some controversial event would trigger action. In very few cases were the strikes preplanned actions ordered by labor organizations. The Union Pacific strike at Denver in the spring of 1884 typified the spontaneous kind of action or sudden flareup that occurred when the men were told of a reduction in wages. Although the railroad quickly restored the previous $2.25-a-day wage scale, the end result was not entirely favorable to labor, for a good many of the participants felt that if they had gained their desired end so easily there was no real reason to organize. This successful strike, one of very few during these years, probably did more harm than good to the cause of unionization. Management applied the stick as well as the carrot. While yielding quickly in some instances, employers often used threats of violence to intimidate potential strikers. Pinkerton detectives were brought in to frighten labor leaders, and to augment such threats the state military was called upon. It was such a combination of forces that largely accounted for the failure of the labor revolt at Leadville in 1880.

More beneficial to Colorado laborers than strikes was the union movement itself. While it had an early start, a typographers' organization having existed in Denver as early as 1860, unionism grew slowly in the state. In this it paralleled the national trend. By the early eighties there were only about a dozen unions in Colorado, a figure that jumped to 34 by 1884 and to 112 only four years later. In part the increase simply reflected the national labor movement's growth during these years; also the strikes, particularly when they were long and bitter, tended to make men think about the long-range advantages of pooling their efforts. To mention a national influence is not to say that it was pervasive; rather, it might be termed suggestive. From the beginning, Colorado organizations tended to grow out of specific needs, and even in the day of growing acceptance of organized labor, local influences continued to play the dominating role.

As was true nationally, there were several types of Colorado unions. The trade unions represented carpenters, painters, plumbers, bricklayers, stonecutters, brewers, and other workers normally found in the larger cities. The railroad brotherhoods, another organized group, were numerous in a western state with more railroad companies than any of its neighbors. Still another group, the Knights of Labor, indicated the presence of a national organization in the state.

Also following national patterns were Colorado labor's early and unsuccessful efforts to gain its ends through political action. The espousal of third parties failed to bring desired results, and Colorado labor leaders finally turned to playing one of the major political parties against the other in search of support. There was no other choice. Every time labor leaders tried to get together a "workingman's ticket," even at the municipal level, a discouragingly small number of workingmen voted for it. Part of the reason for this was that a good many workers in Colorado believed, or were led to believe, that their conditions were better than those in other parts of the country. A journalist who viewed conditions in the mines in 1881 declared that as a class Colorado miners probably enjoyed better conditions and greater prosperity than any other laboring men in the West. "Their employment is regular and remunerative," he wrote, noting that "the work in the shafts and galleries below ground causes them no inconvenience, and they allow themselves some of the luxuries of life."[6]

The Colorado press appreciated talk such as this. The establishment, as was the case elsewhere, wanted to minimize labor discontent, and through friendly newspaper outlets it took the line that Colorado labor was particularly fortunate to live and to work in the mile-high country. When radical organizations began to make their appearance during the early eighties, papers such as Denver's *Tribune-Republican* advised local workingmen to stick with homegrown unions and to stay away from anything tainted by internationalism. Irving Howbert's reaction to the Cripple Creek strike of 1894 illustrated the businessman's response to labor violence. The strikers took possession of the camp, "refused to recognize the legally constituted authorities, and by their actions brought about a condition of anarchy that continued for a number of months," he complained.[7]

Although serious strikes made more conservative members of the community recoil, they listened—and they thought about the situation. Politicians began to pay more attention to labor's problems, as did the press, and they tried to make the workers feel that in this great new country each man's grievance would receive a hearing. Encouraged, labor asked not only for more money, the normal cause of strikes in Colorado in earlier years, but increasingly for better working conditions and shorter hours. Mine and mill owners resisted demands for an eight-hour day and were supported by both farmers and businessmen, many of whom still regarded labor as something to be purchased without negotiation. Until the day of populism, labor had few friends in Colorado, but with the emergence of that political force and the consequent election to the governorship in 1892 of Davis H. Waite, a labor sympathizer, the long-desired curtailment of work hours appeared to be a realizable goal. By 1895 such a law was on the books, but immediately mine and mill owners cried "Unconstitutional!" and the matter went to court. The Colorado Supreme Court decided that the measure violated the right of parties to make their own contracts and that it was contrary to the state constitution because it was class legislation. Another legislative effort, in 1897, also failed, but proponents took hope from a Utah case where both the state and later the U.S. Supreme Court upheld an eight-hour law. In 1899 Colorado supporters once more pushed a bill through the General Assembly, this time a replica of the Utah law, and it was signed by the governor. Then the reformers sat back to see what management would do.

The answer was not long in coming. Coal mine owners quickly notified their employees that henceforth they would be paid by the hour and that anyone who volunteered to work more than eight hours would be permitted to do so, at the hourly rate. In an elaborate effort to comply with the law, management assured labor that no one would be penalized for failing to work longer than the legal limit and that unwillingness to volunteer for longer hours would not be justification for discharge. Employees of the Colorado Fuel and Iron Company meekly complied and reported for work, but at Durango and Denver smelters they struck.

Meanwhile the matter again went to court, and in the summer of 1899 the Colorado Supreme Court decided that the eight-hour law was unconstitutional on the ground that the legislature had no power to limit the number of hours per day a man chose to work.

Labor reacted by pushing for a constitutional amendment, but the one that was enacted merely permitted the legislature to pass an eight-hour law. Squabbles among the lawmakers led to further delays, and, in their frustration, miners engaged in a series of strikes that involved violence. Lengthy walkouts hurt the workers financially, antagonized the public, and failed to achieve the desired end. Not until 1911 was a new law passed that appeared to answer labor's ancient demands. Once more management fought back, challenging the law while proposing new measures by means of the initiative. After a confusing ballot, in which voters did not appear to understand the question, the matter once more went to the state supreme court. The judges suggested that the General Assembly erase much of the previous legislation and start over again, which it did, in 1913, and with that the twenty-year struggle for an eight-hour day in the mines, mills, and smelters ended.[8]

The fight for the eight-hour day symbolized a period of transition in Colorado labor history, for it was during the years that the struggle took place that labor's militancy increased. The Cripple Creek work stoppage of 1894 saw some twelve hundred men deputized by the sheriff, after which they were armed and presumably financed by the mine owners. National Guard units had to be dispatched to prevent open warfare. In 1896 trouble broke out again at Leadville, stirred this time by the newly organized Western Federation of Miners, and once more industrial warfare erupted, necessitating the calling of the establishment's enforcers —the National Guard. Three years later there was trouble at Lake City, and in 1901 Telluride witnessed disorder, to be followed by more unrest at Cripple Creek in 1903.[9] Most of these conflicts had developed in the metal mining industry, but now it was the coal miners' turn; in 1903 a strike was called by the United Mine Workers against the Colorado coal operators. Difficulties were settled quickly in the northern fields, but in the southern part of the state violence erupted and once more the governor had to dispatch the Guardsmen.

A brief period of peace ensued, but in 1910 another strike occurred. It smoldered until 1913, when renewed violence resulted in the calling out of troops. It was at Ludlow, a coal mining camp between Trinidad and Walsenburg, that Colorado's most publicized industrial warfare took place. In April 1914, clashes between the workers and the young National Guard recruits developed into a small battle, the casualties of which included women and children. The "Ludlow Massacre," a major scandal, drew the attention of the entire country to Colorado's labor strife and left upon the state a stain that has not faded with the passage of time. About the only positive thing to come out of the violence was the willingness of the Rockefeller interests to improve conditions in the Colorado Fuel and Iron Company and its subsidiary coal-producing companies. Better conditions for workers and a new period of labor-management peace were bought with blood as Colorado took its place alongside some of the eastern states where workers died in similar causes.[10]

Associated with management's mounting suspicion of labor—a sentiment shared by a surprisingly large number of nonmanagement individuals—was an increasing hostility to the foreign born. It was nothing new; the Know Nothing era of midcentury had made life difficult for immigrants, but now the frequency with which foreign-born persons turned up in radical labor movements helped many a doubter to reach the conclusion that such people were un-American. Historically, when fear and apprehension have begun to cloud men's minds, organizations to which they could take their concerns inevitably have arisen. In this case the organization was the American Protective Association, which became so powerful in Colorado that by the spring of 1892 it had captured the state's Republican Party.

The A.P.A. was nationalistic, patriotic, and sufficiently anti-Catholic to satisfy American white, Anglo-Saxon Protestants in whose minds lingered a dread fear of papal influence. The organization was new, having been founded in Iowa in 1887; and although it professed to be open to all creeds and advertised a democratic initiation fee of one dollar, the group was used as a weapon against immigrants, especially immigrant labor. At the time it rose to prominence in Colorado there were a number of foreign-born workers in the state, particularly at such places as Cripple Creek, and Colorado conservatives regarded these people as a threat to peace and quiet. Denver became a center of A.P.A. activity; by 1894 it was believed that membership in that city amounted to as much as ten thousand, a figure that included several Negro "locals," or councils, as they were called. The group was active politically and it took part of the credit for the defeat of Governor Waite in 1894, a claim that was somewhat exaggerated. However, during the term of Albert McIntire, who succeeded Waite, no Catholic held a major appointive office. The victory over papism and the threat of subversion from foreigners, however, was short-lived. Within two years, by 1896, silver became the big issue in the state and so occupied the minds of the voters and patriots that they found little time for hatred. Almost overnight the A.P.A. was forgotten in Colorado, but its seeds would lie dormant, to emerge again at a later date when passions against various "undesirables" once more would be in evidence.[11]

Growing animosities between labor and management, coupled with the suspicions of the foreign born and Catholics, were symptomatic of deep class conflicts that surfaced in the nineties, carried over into the next decade, and reflected a general uneasiness in American life. The nation at large experienced a growing restlessness in the post–Civil War years, and there were frequent calls for a turn away from the path of materialism toward things of the mind and spirit. The progressive movement was at hand, and Colorado would feel its influences.

Those who sought such change, and who welcomed any evidences of philanthropy in a day when such ideals appeared to be out of vogue, must have been attracted to an experiment carried out in eastern Colorado during the closing years of the nineteenth century. Here, at the western edge of the Great American Desert, the Salvation Army proposed to plant a settlement reminiscent of James Oglethorpe's earlier efforts in Georgia. The idea grew out of a desire to remove some of the chronically poor from the cities, to place this potential labor on the land, and thereby to realize a long-cherished dream of the Salvation Army's founding father, General William Booth. The plan was set in motion when the general's son-in-law, Commander Booth Tucker, head of the army's American branch, authorized the establishment of three such colonies, in California, Colorado, and Ohio, respectively.

Such a proposal had wide appeal to critics of society who were shouting their condemnation of unsavory conditions in the large cities; any suggestion that some of the slum residents might enjoy an opportunity for rehabilitation had their endorsement. Here, it appeared, was an unusual opportunity for the unfortunates to surmount the practical difficulties of penury that had condemned them to life sentences in the ghettoes. The Salvation Army could not empty the slums, but it could make a beginning by offering a way out for some of their occupants. The selectees were advanced money for transportation, food, clothing, housing, livestock, and land, with the expectation that the debt would be paid over a period of years at modest interest.[12]

The Colorado project, known as Fort Amity after the vendor, the Amity Land and Irrigation Company of New York City, was located along the Arkansas River twelve miles from the Kansas state line. There, on approximately eighteen hundred acres of bottomland, Commander Booth Tucker hoped to "put the waste labour on the waste land by means of the waste capital and thus convert this trinity of waste into a unity of production." For this bare and unimproved land, the Salvation Army paid the high price of $20 and $27.50 per acre in separate transactions. Although it resold the land to the settlers, on time, at $30 to $40 an acre, the organization invested heavily in improvements, and ended up losing $60,000 to $70,000.[13]

The first group of colonists, who came mainly from Illinois and Iowa, arrived in mid April 1898. Of the thirty families, about half were from Chicago, where the rolls of the poor had been gleaned for respectable but impoverished candidates worthy of aid. Although some of this group had lived on farms earlier, all of them were city dwellers and had been so for some time; other heads of families had no agricultural experience at all. In the traditional manner of frontiersmen, they set about planting at once; by fall, they had grown eighty acres of cantaloupes. Then the testing period began: an early frost killed the entire crop. However, the Salvation Army stood behind its colonists and borrowed money at 6 percent, a figure then regarded as excessively high. It hired the men at two dollars a day to erect fences, dig irrigation ditches, and build houses; it also bought livestock from Chicago and Kansas City stockyards and parceled out the animals by lot.

While some colonists moved away, and others lagged in their payments to the army, there were those who honored their obligations and made a success of the farming venture in the West. In April 1902, just a few years after the colony was founded, the first member paid his entire debt of $900. He had come with only a team of horses and a few household possessions; now he owned twenty acres of land, a stone house, livestock, and poultry, without any encumbrances.[14] Some of the others, who had borrowed larger amounts, still owed money, but Fort Amity records indicated that they were paying off the indebtedness with regular installments.

As was customary with the colonies, the town became the center of affairs. By 1905 Amity had a population of 350, and was served by the usual stores, lumberyards, a hotel, a bank, and other businesses. There were no saloons. Also, Amity had an orphanage, built by the Salvation Army at a cost of $20,000; later the building was used as a sanatorium for consumptives. The orphanage, known as the Cherry Tree Home, was populated by street waifs who had been maintained by the Salvation Army's home in New Jersey, a place that was abandoned in favor of the Colorado location. The principal reason for the move was the theory that the children could be put to work in the sugar beet and cantaloupe fields, where they would do useful work while learning the art of farming. Colorado's climate, by then recognized internationally as healthful, was another consideration in locating the children at Fort Amity.[15]

The smallness of the farms—made possible by intensive agriculture with the aid of irrigation—meant a more compact community. This, in turn, made possible a greater social intercourse than was common in dryland farming areas of the West and thus made the town, normally a center of activities in farm communities, even more significant because of its easy availability. A contemporary writer praised the system at Fort Amity, calling it one that was highly regarded throughout the area. The town, he added, rapidly was becoming the intellectual, moral, and religious center of the neighboring countryside, a place where advanced and scientific methods of agriculture were attracting wide attention. Lest the experiment be confused with communistic enterprise, the writer hastened to explain that while it was cooperative in nature, each member of the community was an independent landowner.[16] Nor was the Salvation Army trying to impose any religious or moral system upon the settlers; it offered them various social and intellectual outlets but did not make any overt attempt to persuade them to join up. Unlike the Mormon settlements in southern Colorado, this was not a religious colony but a philanthropic one founded by an organization with religious overtones.

For a few years the experiment at Amity appeared to be highly successful as the farmers prospered and that little patch of the Great American Desert bloomed. Then water seepage began to spread alkaline deposits; orchards died, crops failed, and even some of the heavier buildings began to settle. Frantic drainage efforts were instituted, but they proved so expensive that the Salvation Army had to abandon its efforts. The children's home was evacuated, its occupants were sent to California, and finally the building itself was razed. Approximately ten years after the colony was founded the abandoned farms were sold to J. S. McMurtry of Holly, Colorado. Successful drainage methods later reclaimed the land and once more sugar beets grew there, but too late to be of assistance to the colonists who had scattered to the winds.[17]

Despite the failure of the Fort Amity experiment the idea of settling the urban poor on some of the world's vacant lands had an international appeal. In the spring of 1905 the British Colonial Office appointed the famed writer H. Rider Haggard as an inspector of the Salvation Army's agricultural settlements in order to learn more about the possibility of placing some of its own poor upon vacant British Empire lands. In his report Haggard admitted that, in general, the Salvation Army's agricultural experiment had failed, at least from a financial standpoint, but he saw merit in the colony idea. He thought that the organization had not charged its members enough for goods and services. The disappointing results obtained along the Arkansas River in Colorado were ascribed to bad luck and the inability of anyone to anticipate the seepage of alkali to the extent that it occurred.

Haggard was not dismayed by the inability of the experiment to prove a theory. In his report to the Colonial Office he expressed his conviction that the future welfare of Great Britain, as well as that of the United States, depended upon whether or not "a fair proportion" of their inhabitants stayed with the land. "Upon that soil men and women grow up in health, and become furnished with those sober and enduring qualities which have made the greatness of our nation in the past, who, if they are relegated to the unwholesome conditions and crowded quarters of vast cities, must dwindle in a body and change in mind," he concluded.[18]

The notion of cooperation, inherent to some degree in most of Colorado's colonies, arose from the belief that it was the most practical way to settle land that required a heavy capital outlay to furnish irrigation water. It was cooperation out of necessity as opposed to an ideal or a desire. Far more idealistic, and even Utopian, was the concept of the Colorado Cooperative Company, founded in Denver early in 1894 by ten men and one woman. The incorporators proposed to establish a community for the homeless where "equality and service rather than greed and competition should be the basis of conduct."[19] The name of the company's little publication, the *Altrurian*, was suggestive of the goal the group set for its membership.

The search for a tract of land that was available and subject to irrigation by means of a single system ended in far western Colorado along the San Miguel River a few miles south of the hamlet of Naturita. By the spring of 1896 a small settlement known as Pinon was established at the mouth of Cottonwood Creek, and here the main irrigation ditch was begun. It took almost a decade of hard work to build the seventeen-mile ditch, but its completion satisfied the membership that cooperative effort had put a theory to work, and with practical results.

As the system began to function the little settlement of Pinon moved nearer the center of things, to Tabaguache Park, and in search for a name for the projected town the innovators, hopeful that they had formed the nucleus of a socialistic community in the West, used a corruption of that word to name the town Nucla. But before long the experiment in Utopian socialism began to crumble as colonists came to prize more and more highly their lands, their tree-shaded homes, and their possessions gained through persistence and hard work. Despite a decline in the popularity of the cooperative method, and a return to the more traditional private ownership and operation of the farms, the big canal, jointly constructed, continued to be owned and used cooperatively. But it was the only remnant of the original dream that began the venture.

Colorado's political leaders were not entirely happy with the establishment of agricultural colonies that smacked of socialism, even that of the Utopian brand, and there must have been some satisfaction expressed privately when the founders of Nucla were obliged to yield to the demands of that much cherished way of life, private enterprise. Yet, the notion that group settlement was a sound way of settling the farmlands of the state persisted, and localities that wanted such acres populated and tilled responded readily to any proposal for mass immigration to their respective communities. Residents of the San Luis Valley, who had watched the Mormons turn sagebrush country into profitable farms, represented such desires.

During the early 1890s agents from both England and Holland visited Colorado to learn if its agricultural lands were as rich as advertised and whether the establishment of yet another colony in that state was appropriate. It was during one of these visits that a representative from the Holland American Land and Immigration Company passed through the San Luis Valley. After considering the soil and the availability of water and railroad service, he sent in a favorable report and his firm bought 15,000 acres of land.[20]

Over two hundred adults and a small army of children arrived at Alamosa late in November 1892. A Denver newspaper, learning that this was but the vanguard of a project involving two thousand Dutch farmers and their families, called it the biggest thing in the way of a colonization scheme ever undertaken in the state. The residents of Alamosa, who expected to benefit from the influx of settlers, gave the newcomers a rousing welcome, a warm meal, and temporary quarters in the local armory.

Shortly the group moved into two large barracks that had been provided in anticipation of their arrival, but these hastily constructed quarters proved to be cold, crowded, and uncomfortable. The only advantage they gained from being forced to sleep up to five in a bed was warmth. The discomfort of the early days was a harbinger of worse things to come, for dissatisfaction with the group's management soon brought charges of inefficiency and even dishonesty by increasingly unhappy members. To add to their misery, scarlet fever and diphtheria broke out among the children, and in the crowded quarters sickness spread rapidly. The intervention of the Denver and Rio Grande Railroad, whose officials provided two railroad cars as isolation wards, helped to prevent an even more serious epidemic. Even so, thirteen children died.

At this juncture the Empire Land and Canal Company offered to locate individual families on various parcels of its land, most of these being within about five miles of Alamosa, to provide housing, and either to rent or to sell the land worked by the immigrants. In the meantime word reached Amsterdam that there was great turmoil in the Colorado colony, a report that resulted in the termination of plans to send any more Hollanders to the San Luis Valley; instead they were rerouted to northeastern Colorado. When representatives of the Holland American Land and Immigration Company reached Alamosa, determined to investigate matters there, they were surprised to find that most of the immigrants had moved onto Empire farmlands, a few miles away from the tract originally selected by the Immigration Company.

Since another effort was to be made, this time in the South Platte River country, those who remained at the Alamosa barracks joined the most recent group of immigrants at a site located near Crook. It was February 1893. A hotel and a company office building were built at Crook, from which point the manager directed affairs and inducted newcomers into the system. However, despite Dutch frugality and hard work, the operation was abandoned by the autumn of 1893, dissatisfaction with the management and financial losses being the reasons given for the failure. A few families moved to Greeley, Brush, and Fort Morgan to take up individual farms, but the bulk of the immigrants went back to Holland. Those who remained in the San Luis Valley also became discouraged, and by the spring of 1903 most of them had abandoned the region where the Mormons had been highly successful.

The Dutch settlers made a colorful addition to the Colorado population, most of them retaining their native costumes of bulging trousers, peaked caps, and wooden shoes for men, and stiffly starched white lace caps, colorful dresses, and aprons for the women. The children attracted even more attention. Scrubbed clean, and politely shy, many of the young boys smoked villainous-looking long black cigars and drank incredible amounts of beer for their size.[21]

About the time the Dutch experiments were floundering, another effort was made along the South Platte River, and it, too, suggested that cooperative enterprise in Colorado's agricultural regions was not always the answer to the difficulties of weak financing and the limitations of individual efforts to farm in the West. In this case it was again a group of Russian Jews, as it had been at Cotopaxi, who tried the colony method. In 1891 B'nai B'rith inquired of its Denver lodge as to the possibility of Colorado absorbing some of these people. T. C. Henry, a well-known western land developer, came forward, interested in selling some of the land he had under contract in the northeastern part of the state. The price was not out of line; he asked only three or four dollars an acre, a figure that closely approximated the amount the Union Pacific Railroad had obtained for its lands in both Nebraska and Kansas. By the spring of 1896 a colony was formed and Louis Fine was chosen to direct it.[22]

In contrast to Cotopaxi, the land around Atwood was rich, the neighbors were friendly, and the livestock, lumber, and supplies promised as Henry's part of the transaction ultimately were forthcoming. Into the colony came an estimated two hundred settlers, some from the eastern United States and a few from as far away as South America. Despite the favorable conditions, unlike those that helped defeat the earlier Jewish colony effort, there was dissatisfaction at Atwood. Part of the difficulty came from the presence of an unusually large number of single men who did not assume the life-style of the families and who were at odds with the others from time to time. Religious dissension added to the difficulties, as some adhered to orthodoxy while others did not. One by one those who were discontented drifted away from the colony, some going to Denver to engage in whatever trade they knew, others returning to the East. The colony struggled on for about ten years until it finally dissolved, the land being sold for taxes.[23] Coming from diverse backgrounds, the colonists had no previous experience in coordinated efforts and found farm community life difficult. Although they were willing to work, most of these people knew little about agriculture or stock raising, and the difficult period of the early nineties, in which there was a financial panic, was an especially hard time to learn a new livelihood.[24]

The emerging humanitarian hopes of the late nineteenth century, evidenced by the desire to humanize working conditions, to reduce exploitation of labor, and to experiment with philanthropic patterns of settlement in such places as Fort Amity, were growing more apparent in other aspects of human relations. A part of this drive was the effort made by an increasingly sophisticated population to ameliorate prison conditions and to "civilize" public hangings, or even to eliminate them.

By the late eighties there were increasingly loud demands that Coloradans abandon the spectacle of public executions, and in his inaugural address of January 1887 Governor Alva Adams asked for such a change, a request that was answered by the General Assembly two years later. As a further means of restricting public viewing of this ceremony the place of execution was shifted from county seats to the state penitentiary. The authorities at the prison protested loudly, arguing that they did not want the Canon City institution to become a slaughterhouse.

The uproar over this effort at enlightened policy gave the advocates of abolishing the death penalty added fuel for their campaign, and in 1893 Governor Davis Waite recommended such legislation in his inaugural address. By 1897 the reformers were successful, but a mere four years later the death penalty was resumed, thanks to efforts of the press and, to some extent, of the clergy. When Governor Charles Thomas, on his last day in office, pardoned Alfred Packer, the notorious "man-eater," proponents of capital punishment made the most of it. Although Packer had served his time quietly, public outcry against turning this convicted cannibal loose on society mounted, and the publicity surrounding his release helped to restore the death penalty.

From time to time conditions at the pententiary provoked public criticism. During most of its history the correctional facility has been involved in state politics; rarely has a Colorado governor avoided difficulty with it. Among the many issues was that of corporal punishment, one of the most primitive of which was "stringing up." In this process a prisoner was handcuffed and suspended by his wrists so that only his toes touched the ground. Chronic back conditions plagued some of the recipients of such treatment for the rest of their lives. Water hosing, in which the blast from a fire hose was played upon the victim's mouth and nose, was another form of torture-punishment. Paddling was commonly applied, and it persisted as late as the mid twentieth century. At that time it once more placed the penitentiary in the glow of publicity. Paddlings, "stringing up," and water torture at Canon City were not publicized disciplinary measures; for the most part, Coloradans had no idea such medieval measures were being employed. Ironically, many of these abuses took place during a period of reform that began in the eighties and has sputtered along ever since.

Those who were distressed by the high incidence of recidivism, or the return of "repeaters" to the penitentiary, sought some means of segregating young first-termers as an alternative to matriculating them in the Canon City "college of crime." In 1889 legislation was passed that established a reformatory, and Buena Vista was selected as its site. The courts were given a choice of institutions for their convicted, the circumstances of the crime and the age of the convict being taken into consideration. The Buena Vista establishment was intended to detain more than juveniles. Those of both sexes under the age of sixteen were sent to the State Industrial School at Golden until a separate school for young girls was established late in the nineteenth century.

Colorado has not been particularly innovative in the establishment and operation of its penal institutions. Such changes as were made—and change invariably is believed by those who institute it to denote progress—usually were responses to eastern advances and to the traditional western desire to keep abreast with that part of the nation. An example of this pattern was the creation of the reformatory at Buena Vista, a situation in which eastern precedents were copied. Liberals hoped that the new institution really would be a reformatory or a correctional facility, but it turned out to be just another prison.[25]

Colorado's leaders always have been anxious to make their part of the nation an attractive, desirable place to live, and their efforts to accomplish this aim have grown out of the best motives. Law, order, and progressive methods of rehabilitating violators of the established codes of conduct have been among the goals of those who sought to build a new western community, but, predictably, the aspirations of the planners have not always met with complete success. Undercurrents of reform have been felt in the state from very early times, and on occasion they have had a controlling influence, but somehow these occasional surges of uplift have given way to the darker side of human nature. Colorado's occasional bursts of progressivism have been marred by periods of retrogression. In the development of social control through legislation, jurisprudence, and penal correction, one sees this tendency showing through the fabric of political idealism.

As the Coloradans experimented with reform and dabbled in various humanitarian enterprises that they felt befitted a maturing people, they drifted along in that decade so frequently referred to as the Gay Nineties, happy in the thought that they had achieved satisfactory progress, but somewhat uncertain as to the course that lay ahead. Being well connected to the rest of the country by rail, and visited by growing numbers of tourists, Coloradans continued to reflect the attitudes of other Americans and to adopt readily their latest social customs and fads. They entered that tennis-playing, picnicking, bicycling decade with enthusiasm, apparently anxious to indicate their participation in the national trends.

Bicycling typified the kind of outdoor activity and the robust life soon to be made so popular by Teddy Roosevelt. Cycling clubs sprang up all over Colorado. Some were founded simply in a quest for exercise, and in addition many of them fielded racing teams to challenge members of other clubs. Each Memorial Day the Associated Cycle Club sponsored a road race of twenty-five miles; a number of similar organizations presented their own contests. In the fall a Labor Day race drew numerous entrants. During the summer of 1896 the Colorado hundred-mile relay was added to a list of events that already included a round-trip race between Denver and Colorado Springs.

As the men vied for new course records, Mrs. A. E. Rinehart of Denver came to the public's attention by cycling 100 miles a day for twenty consecutive days. She also set a new 200-mile racecourse mark at sixteen hours and eighteen minutes, one that stood for a couple of months until an ungallant gentleman cut two minutes from her time. Mrs. Rinehart again made cycling news when she was given one of the ten-mile stretches in the great overland race from San Francisco to New York in the summer of 1896. She was the only woman ever to have been accorded such an honor. With great pride the *Rocky Mountain News* announced that the lady's total mileage for the year 1896 was 17,152 miles, thought to be a record for an amateur.[26]

The search for recreation and amusement was not so apparent in the small towns, where the leisure class necessarily was smaller and workaday demands stood in the forefront, but in places near military posts social events were more in evidence. Colorado's Indian problem having been disposed of early and with little violence, the forts lingered on as an afterglow of frontier development, and as they waited for orders to disband the posts, men and officers stationed at them frequently found boredom to be their principal enemy. Forts Collins, Morgan, and Sedgwick in the north and Forts Reynolds and Lyon in the south had been founded in the sixties; all except Lyon had been abandoned in just a few years. In the western portions of the state, where settlement was slower, the forts came later. Forts Lewis and Crawford functioned primarily during the eighties; Fort Garland, established early in southern Colorado, was abandoned during that decade. Fort Logan, near Denver, the last post to be founded (1887), served as a supply post for troops in the Spanish American War and World War I.[27]

During their brief years of activity, these posts stood as bastions against possible Indian wars and later as garrisons to be called upon in the event of such unexpected hostilities as the Ute uprising of 1879. In some instances the establishments lived such short lives that they did not have an opportunity to influence nearby communities; in other cases they were not near enough to cities to affect them. Forts that were near growing towns, such as Fort Lewis, near Durango, or Fort Crawford, near Montrose, influenced the society of these small communities, which benefited from the presence of the military. In both these situations town and fort originated at about the same time and developed in parallel fashion. Here military representatives and civilians traded in beef, vegetables, milk, eggs, grain, lumber, and other supplies. Services also were supplied by the local communities; in Durango a civilian firm contracted for all the official drayage between that railroad town and the fort twelve miles distant.

Commercial relationships were accompanied by social intercourse between the two groups. Durango's hotels and restaurants attracted officers from Fort Lewis, but they had to limit their visits somewhat, for Durango, like other mining and smelting towns, was an expensive place to visit or to live. Carpenters were paid as much as $120 a month and stonemasons up to $150; army pay did not approach this, particularly that of the privates, who had to get along on a monthly income of $13. Armed with that small amount of money the ordinary soldier could visit one of Durango's twenty-five saloons or negotiate with members of the large corps of sporting women, but faced by mining camp prices it was difficult to get into much trouble even by spending a whole month's pay. Perhaps prices were cheaper at the nearby "hog ranch," about two miles from Fort Lewis, but the attractions were less in that establishment, which locals referred to as a "vile den."[28]

The social traffic between the forts and nearby towns was not one-way. While officers, men, and their wives sought out the shops, hotels, theaters, and other city facilities, townsmen frequently visited the forts for reasons other than business. Fort Lewis had a theater, a dance hall, and, for a short period, two regimental bands. Civilians were invited to post dances where suppers and refreshments such as rum punch were offered the guests. Young officers were welcomed in the homes of residents with young eligible daughters, but, as was true throughout the West, the enlisted man's uniform virtually barred him from acquaintance with respectable girls. Bachelor officers had no trouble in getting dancing partners at post dances; the girls were more than willing to attend. Daytime pleasures at the posts were provided in the form of picnics, baseball games, and horse races, after which attractive suppers were available. Baseball games, in particular, drew civilian and military communities together. In cases where communities near the forts were very small and as yet undeveloped, a further attraction of the post was its doctor and its chaplain, both of whom were generous with their services among civilians in need. In fact, army surgeons were preferred to civilian medical men, so good was their reputation among the residents.

Thus the unsavory reputation the federal army frequently had in western areas was not universal, and in many a community the local garrison was looked to for both economic and social benefits.

Here was an example of a governmental agency, intended as a punitive, or negative, force, rendered idle by lack of activity in its designated realm and, as a result, becoming a part of the peacetime establishment earlier than did the army in other parts of the West where Indian difficulties lingered.

If the soldiers in Colorado were bored with the endless routine of life in quiet western outposts, so were many of the young men who pursued uneventful civilian lives in the villages and on the farms in the region. Not a few of them had grown tired of observing various anniversaries connected with that great war between the states; as they listened to thrice-told tales of valor at Gettysburg or Cold Harbor related by now-aging veterans, the younger generation feared that it was to be denied an opportunity to show its martial talents. In their innocence they entertained beliefs, perhaps subconscious, that the role of the warrior was part of life's assignment, one in which men carried out their responsibilities and earned a dividend of excitement. In such an atmosphere a native jingoism had flowered and its protagonists had gone a long way toward convincing the populace, even the young, that the most dramatic way to prove the greatness of America was by a baptism of fire. A war with almost any opponent in which the United States was certain to be the victor would, in their view, establish the nation's position of primacy in world affairs.

For Coloradans the mixture of feelings, the societal cross-currents, were even more apparent because the flush days of mining had faded and life in sleepy little agricultural towns appeared to be the inevitable successor to the once-roaring camps of the mountains. Even the West itself had surrendered to civic quiet, and that once turbulent land could be examined in safety from railroad cars that crisscrossed its great expanses.

It was this atmosphere that led westerners to view the hostilities in Cuba as an opportunity to acquire stories for their grandchildren. Even before war was declared Governor Albert W. McIntire foresaw the employment of cowboys as cavalrymen in a war against Spain. "Colorado will have absolutely the best cavalry troop in the whole army, barring none," he predicted. "It will be made up of cowboys and range men who are accustomed to being in the saddle day and night and know no fear." General Nelson Miles, who was to play a prominent part in the war, agreed. He called the cowboys the best horsemen in the world.[29]

In anticipation of one last fling before civilization smothered the restlessness of westerners, a variety of would-be defenders of the national honor made their talents available. William E. Scott, an old Negro who had earned his military spurs in the Indian campaigns, offered to raise a troop of black warriors. Bob Middleton, a retired outlaw and cattle rustler, promised the services of 100 of his former colleagues. Not to be outdone in the realm of patriotism, 100 Navajos said they would be ready within twelve hours if someone could locate the necessary guns and horseflesh. A lady from the State Horticultural Society informed the governor that 200 Colorado women were willing to raise a cavalry unit, but the cowgirls were never called up and they had to satisfy themselves with volunteer effort on the home front.

Out of this welter of proposals, two troops of cavalry were accepted from Colorado by Colonel Jay Torrey, who organized a Wyoming cavalry regiment. Idaho, Nevada, and Utah also contributed two troops each, with Wyoming's seven troops completing the force. The cowboy cavalry went to war with much fanfare, but hostilities were over before they could see any action; most of them spent their time fighting off illness in humid southern camps. By October 1898 the cowhands, many of whom were sick, were mustered out of the service. Some forty members of Torrey's regiment had succumbed to the southern climate. As one poet put it:

> With gusto, guns, and horses galore,
> Torrey led his Terrors off to war;
> He marched them up and marched them down,
> But only round the camp and town;
> Never a glimpse of Spanish foe,
> But days, weeks, and months of woe;
> No battles to fight, no laurels to win,
> So, he marched them home again.[30]

The only cowboy cavalrymen from Colorado to see any action were a small group of twenty-five who went ashore with Teddy Roosevelt's Rough Riders. Ironically, when they sailed from Florida they left their horses in the United States.

Most of the Coloradans who saw any fighting in this short war did so in the Philippines. The men of the First Colorado Regiment, 1,000 strong, sailed from San Francisco in mid May 1898 and participated in the attack upon Manila. Much of the remainder of their military activity consisted of garrison duty and struggles with the natives themselves, who fought rather than accept American authority. By mid September the First Colorado Regiment had returned to San Francisco, where it was met by Governor Charles Thomas and a delegation from Denver and then was mustered out of service. If the Colorado troops who had hoped to free Cuba by horseback, and those who ended up thousands of miles away in the Far East, wondered about their contribution to American security, they were not alone among Americans who participated in this unhappy and unsatisfactory foreign war.[31] The enthusiasm and the rampant patriotism with which they had greeted the event now seemed almost lame and superfluous. But other than the initial excitement, the Spanish American war barely touched Colorado. Governor Thomas's biographer gave that international conflict only two lines of print.[32]

As Teddy Roosevelt later remarked, it was not much of a war, but it was the "best war we had." Accepting this frank admission, one must agree nevertheless with a critic of that day who commented that the war represented a major change in the direction of world affairs. While it did not appear to affect Colorado, except for what its outcome might do to the sugar market—an important local industry—the changes that it occasioned in national events sooner or later would visit the mountain West. By chance the war nearly coincided with the coming of a new century, which provided Americans with an opportunity not only to look out upon the world from the viewpoint of a major participant in its concerns, but also to sum up the accomplishments of a century in order better to anticipate another hundred years. Colorado's history was too short for such a summation, but its people were aware of the giant strides they had made in four short decades, and they joined their countrymen in the exercise of commemorating the great calendar change. They were particularly proud of social advances in a state dubbed "Centennial" and it was with anticipation that they looked forward to the immediate future.

PART FOUR

# Colorado in Midpassage

# 12

# A Time of Bounding Hopes

As Colorado entered the twentieth century its people looked ahead with a mixture of hope and apprehension. The average American probably viewed things somewhat more optimistically; business was good, the nation had just completed what Secretary of State John Hay called "a splendid little war" with Spain, and on all sides prosperity and progress appeared to be the watchwords of the day. To a degree Coloradans could share these generalities, but there lurked in the back of their minds the uncertainties arising from the collapse of silver, which had led many people to move to other, less depressed sections of the nation. A Denver editor could reassure his readers that "with bounding hopes and intelligent confidence the people of Colorado greet the dawn of a new century," but he quickly added that since the silver industry had been destroyed by Congress the brilliance of the state's future was somewhat flawed. The most optimistic prediction he could offer was the assurance that these were hardy people, used to adversity, and that their hard work and resolution would overcome all.[1]

All around the world the arrival of a new century generated numerous predictions and comments, both by famous figures and by ordinary people on the street. It was the same in Colorado, where reporters asked men and women of all stations of life what they thought were their community's most pressing needs. In Denver, Governor Charles S. Thomas asked for beautification, particularly the burying of overhead wires, which he thought endangered life and disfigured the city. Others called for cleaner streets, the installation of public cuspidors, a more commodious jail, the addition of fifty policemen to the force, and a civic auditorium where the people might have a forum to discuss their municipal needs. Some asked for better hospitals, particularly to aid indigent consumptives in a city long known for its large "one-lung army." That Denver's rapid growth had generated the kinds of social problems associated with large cities was suggested by one who identified himself simply as "a thief." "Denver needs a hospital for cocaine and morphine fiends," he told reporters. "Every town ought to have a hospital where we can be locked up and cured. I have stolen money to get cocaine and morphine, and others do the same." An admitted drunkard thought the city's saloons should be closed.

Some of the suggestions reflected the influence of a budding progressive movement that was being felt in other parts of the country. When asked what he thought Denver needed, an attorney recommended the public ownership of utilities. The mayor agreed, saying that municipal operation of these facilities would benefit all the people. Concerned about Colorado's youth, a detective sought more attention to juvenile delinquents, a suggestion that anticipated the work of Denver's Judge Ben Lindsey.

A local physician's remark that the capital city needed a rigid enforcement of laws governing the smoke nuisance was typical of a growing dissatisfaction over the deterioration of the city's fabled pure air. "Enough smoke filled the air early this morning to make pedestrians believe they were in St. Louis or Pittsburgh, Pa.," complained the *Denver Post.* "Wherever a lump of it fell a greasy spot remained to remind the victim that the air was unhealthful." The editor was unhappy over the fact that corrective legislation had been enacted three years earlier, only to have the courts throw it out. Now, he said, proprietors who had paid to have their buildings cleaned had to stand by and see them again blackened. The same thing was happening to the clothing of people who ventured outdoors. In a story entitled "The Deadly Cigarette" the newspaper promised that before long additional protection would be offered to the residents' lungs. The Anti-Cigarette League, recently organized at Chicago and already boasting a hundred thousand members, promised to establish a branch in Denver, where the fight to stamp out the "coffin nail" would be launched in Colorado. By the early 1900s air pollution had become an issue in the Centennial state.

Further responses to reporters' questions suggested that at this early date growth problems already had come to Colorado. One irate householder thought that if all the "real estate sharks and land boomers" had been driven out of the city ten years earlier it would be a much nicer place in which to live in this new century. But another of those interviewed inferentially asked the question, A nicer place for whom? He was Judson Singleton, identified as a colored vagrant, and his view was that there ought to be more work in the city for the laboring men.

While his race may or may not have had something to do with his unemployment, Singleton's problem was a reminder that blacks in Colorado still were relegated to menial jobs—if they could find even that kind of work. It was even possible to show that their position had deteriorated steadily since the gold rush days. Coloradans ushered in the new century, one that was supposed to reflect enlightenment and progress, by witnessing the lynching of a sixteen-year-old Negro near Limon. Accused of raping a white girl, he was chained to an iron stake and burned alive, the father of the girl being accorded the honor of lighting the fire.[2] Although black lynchings were extremely rare in the state, this particularly barbaric act was symptomatic of the suppressed violence that lay submerged in an otherwise progressive era. Further evidence that Negroes could expect little from a presumably enlightened Colorado society is seen in the fact that, among twenty-two murders committed in Denver in 1903, only three resulted in convictions, all of them awarded to black defendants.[3]

Nevertheless Coloradans of 1900 were proud of, and a little self-conscious of, their very short history. They had an emerging awareness of social problems, and, like others around the world in that momentous year, they wondered about the future. A poem written by James Barton Adams asked what surprises the new century would "spring":

> Great ships of commerce traversing the air?
> Men upon wings flying 'round here and there?
> People all honest and square in their deals?
> Workingmen riding in automobiles?
> Women in Congress and cabinet hall?
> Fair mistress President over them all?
> Babies of new incubator design?
> Woman the oak and poor man but the vine?

Other questions asked if coming generations would get their heat from "electric contrivances," eat food made of tablets, and reach Mars and "other inhabited stars" by wireless telegraphy.[4]

Beneath all the talk about the triumphs of the past and high hopes for the future lay the feeling that the political machinery, both state and municipal, was in need of repair. Several of the people interviewed by the *Post* spoke vaguely of their desire for "honest politicians" and for a better class of public officials, and of the need to formulate a new city charter that would free the city from state and national political influences.[5] By 1902 Denver's quest for municipal independence was realized with the passage of a constitutional amendment that provided for home rule. Although the organized political parties fought the measure, fearful of losing patronage, they had to admit defeat after a ten-year running battle with the independents. In 1910 a third party, dedicated to reform, triumphed over the major parties in a city election, and before long some important changes were made. Civil service for municipal employees, a long overdue improvement, at last was realized. The commission form of government, increasingly popular across America during these years, was experimented with, only to be abandoned a few years later.

These and other innovations were adopted at the state level, and by 1912 Colorado had the initiative, the referendum, recall for judges and their decisions, and municipal home rule. Also it had established industrial railroad commissions and had passed an eight-hour labor law.[6] During this period increasing complaints about the influence of corporations over elected officials led to legislative efforts to control the spread of that abuse. When a law of 1909 considerably tightened the manner in which campaign donations could be made, Democratic Governor John Shafroth asserted that Colorado was the first state in the union to enact such legislation. "One of the most pronounced evils under the present system of elections has been the undue influence created by corporations financing the campaigns of political parties," he wrote. "Such contributions are often, in moral effect, indirect bribes." Quite accurately he explained that a good many corporations did not want to make such contributions but "did so because they felt that to refuse might make them the subjects of persecution." He thought corporations should welcome the advent of such legislation as a protective measure for themselves. While the governor was unduly optimistic in believing that mere laws could bring a halt to old political practices, his views indicated that public figures such as himself were sensitive to the tenor of the times and to the increasing demands by Coloradans for the laundering of political robes.[7]

While Colorado certainly was influenced by a national trend toward reform, there were other reasons for the expressed desire to clean up government, both at the capital and throughout the state. Denver, in particular, was concerned that political and social problems generated by its very rapid growth threatened to mar its image as an attractive place to visit and perhaps to live. Additionally, newcomers were critical of the established order and were not always impressed by the arguments advanced to justify its existence. Many of them were unaware that in an earlier day, when gloom had descended upon the place because fading mineral prospects in the mountains threatened to create yet another ghost town, a group of aggressive men had fought hard to save their investments and to build the "Queen City of the Plains." Down through the years what was to become known as the Seventeenth Street Crowd maintained firm control of both the economic and the political apparatus of the city. They intermarried, belonged to the same clubs, and continued to run Denver in the manner they thought best for it and for themselves. As one of the local ministers expressed it, "There is truth in the statement that they have made the city, but far more in the statement that the city has made them."[8] By the turn of the century Denver's population was growing rapidly, and recent arrivals sometimes found it difficult to pay proper respect to these descendants of the founding fathers. This attitude, plus the restiveness that swept the nation in the form of the progressive movement, combined to generate a loud outcry for change in both the capital and the state.

During this period of upheaval and change a social experiment was undertaken at the state penitentiary that appealed to many a taxpayer as the constructive kind of reform an ailing society could well use. In 1908 Governor Shafroth, who was anxious to take his place among reformers, appointed a traveling salesman by the name of Thomas J. Tynan as warden at the Canon City institution. To appoint a man who had no previous experience or intellectual interest in criminology might have been a long gamble in other parts of the country, but in the West, where practical ideas historically were highly valued, it seemed perfectly acceptable. Tynan showed that he understood this when he said that the existence of seven hundred idle men and more than a score of idle women "sort of got on my nerves" because it was unbusinesslike and wasteful. In search of projects that would give these men healthy employment and would not interfere with free labor, he put them to work building roads.

A journalist who visited the camps and road crews in 1913 saw nothing that reminded him of southern chain gangs. There were no striped uniforms, no leg irons, no shaved heads or rifle-bearing guards. Using trusties, Tynan put the men out in the manner of any contractor with the promise of heavier meals and reduced sentences. At the time the cost of feeding a dormant convict was estimated at twelve cents a day, a road-worker convict at thirty-six cents; the difference was paid by the county requesting road work. Only at night were there guards, and as a rule only two were used, more as a matter of form than anything else. As of that time, the journalist wrote, there had been only two escapes, one of the men having returned voluntarily.

Another of Tynan's ideas was the convict ranch. Almost as soon as he began his job the warden started to lease neighboring ranches "on shares." In 1912 his men worked seven hundred acres, made a profit of twelve thousand dollars, supplied the penitentiary with all the fresh fruits and vegetables it could use, and, in anticipation of winter, stored a large quantity of food for the men and fodder for livestock. On four ranches "Tynan's boys" raised everything from hogs to sugar beets. Other projects put men to work at construction; with the use of prison labor a new prison hospital was built at a cost of fifteen thousand dollars instead of eighty thousand. The work program was said to have saved the state more than three-fifths of the penitentiary's biennial appropriation, which totaled two hundred and fifty thousand dollars.

Tom Tynan made no claims of revolutionary sociological discoveries. He simply "trusted the trusties" more than had any previous warden. As a result inquiries came to Colorado from all over the world as to the details of his program, one that both he and his associates considered no more complicated than one man putting his faith in another. Tynan's weak lungs had sent him to the Rockies, where he hoped the mountain air would restore his health. Like many another recruit to the "one-lung army," Tynan used his mind and his imagination to make a contribution to his adopted home.[9]

Coloradans were pleased by the changes made at the Canon City institution because they appeared to be constructive. They were proud of their new state and sensitive to any criticism of it or any implication that matters of civic interest were being neglected. In 1906 they had an opportunity to look back upon what they assured themselves was a profitable and progressive past. The occasion was the celebration commemorating the centennial of Lieutenant Zebulon Montgomery Pike's visit to the central Rockies. Amidst the usual pageantry of Indians, cavalry, cowboys, war veterans, and brass bands, an attempt was made to present a panorama of Colorado's progress during that century.

Overlooking the fact that nothing very significant had happened in Colorado during the first half of the nineteenth century, the centennializers illuminated the famous mountain named for the explorer, made much of the fact that invalids now could ascend a peak that Pike had failed to top, merely by stepping into a cograil car, and passed out some of the hundred thousand souvenir medallions produced at the Denver mint. The oratory of the day stressed Pike's inability to foresee the future, especially when he had compared the Great Plains to African deserts, and it dwelled on how the mountain community had grown since the arrival of the Anglo population. Denver, said the boosters, contained nearly three times as many people as had New York City in 1806. And to visit this mountain metropolis one had a choice of five different transcontinental railroads, the tracks of which traversed Pike's famous desert country.[10]

While such celebrations have their Chamber of Commerce overtones, Coloradans were truly curious about their history, and in observing the anniversary of the explorer's accomplishments they experienced not only the exhilaration such displays generate, but also a grasping at roots in search of continuity and guidance. By now they knew they had made great material strides; unconsciously they turned toward less tangible things such as the quality of life in the generously endowed part of the country in which they lived and raised their children.

One example of growing interest in the state's heritage was the culmination in 1906 of a concerted movement to preserve the ruins at Mesa Verde through the establishment of a national park. While other parks in the West, including Colorado, had been set aside for recreational purposes and for the enjoyment of natural beauty, this was the first time one had originated for the additional purpose of preserving ethnological and archaeological artifacts. As a park Mesa Verde was distinctive in another sense: its creation resulted largely from the unrelenting pressure maintained by a group of some two hundred women for approximately a quarter of a century. While the legislation creating the park cannot be classified strictly as a part of the reform movement of the day, nevertheless its timing and the overtones of the demands for its creation are suggestive of the restlessness felt in Colorado during those years, a sometimes indefinable feeling that materialism had overrun its course in this historic place.

The systematic extraction of artifacts during the late nineteenth century, some of which went to Europe and others to eastern museums, began to alarm the state's more concerned residents. At its 1897 annual meeting the Colorado Federation of Women's Clubs appointed a Committee for the Preservation and Restoration of the Cliff and Pueblo Ruins of Colorado, a move that made official the earlier activities of some of the women interested in the project. Through the efforts of the committee the immediate area was mapped, and when it was discovered that part of the area under consideration belonged to the Utes, a lease was secured from the Weeminuche Utes that allowed the association to protect the historic site.

In the spring of 1906 Congress approved an act creating Mesa Verde National Park, but it did not include the ruins lying within the Ute Reservation. Not until 1913 was the additional land set aside. Meanwhile, Coloradans had become increasingly aware of the problem as they watched experts from the Smithsonian Institution make a thorough examination of the site; they better understood the implications of the pot hunting that already had damaged much of the ruins. A small "rush," reminiscent of placer mining days, had taken place near Mancos with the result that the diggers had pretty thoroughly looted the site. Blasting for better diggings had severely damaged part of the ruins, while the burning of beams for firewood had eliminated most of the roofs.[11] "Pottery, mummies, wall pictures, relics of every kind have been made merchandise of by those who visited these ruins only to sack them," complained a lady visitor in 1908. "Not only were the things taken out but walls which hindered the search were ruthlessly torn down so that it is difficult to tell what is the work of time and what that of the iconoclast."[12]

The efforts by Coloradans to preserve the past were evidence of approaching maturity and thoughtfulness. Time passed rapidly in the West, and great material changes left the illusion that the days of Fifty-Nine were ancient history when, in reality, they were only yesterday. But westerners matured early—and often grew old early from the rigorous life they lived—so it was not unnatural that they regarded their young state as being older than it was, and therefore entitled to a history. Or perhaps it was a case of self-conscious youth trying to appear more mature than its years, and seeking this status by copying older segments of national society. In any case, Coloradans understood that they were in midpassage not only between centuries but between eras and that although their life-styles and society affected more established customs, somehow they were different.

When Mrs. Crawford Hill wrote an article about Denver society for an eastern magazine in 1910, she confessed that a discussion of social Denver was almost an impossibility because, in the minds of many easterners, no such place existed. Rather, it was viewed as just another western town where blanketed Indians stood around on street corners and watched occasional herds of buffalo pass by, disturbed only by cowboy gunfire and the antics of unconventional women. Young as the city was, Mrs. Hill maintained, Denver's residents entertained much as did other people, read the same books, had the same literary, musical, and other organizations, and wore conventional American clothing. However, she did not think wealth affected one's social position in Colorado to the degree it did in large eastern communities. Clubs played an important role—the Denver Club being the "oldest and handsomest"—and the place was different in that there was no fixed "social season." The latter characteristic was due to the fact that the residents were not forced to vacate their homes in the summer to avoid heat and humidity; rather, they were inclined to stay at home and to spread their entertainment over the year. Social items in the newspapers tended to be very democratic, columnists moving in and out of homes quite freely, with the result that there was little differentiation between "Mrs. Somebody" and "Mrs. Nobody," both of whom were reported as charming hostesses. That these newspapers accepted people as they were, as opposed to how they would have liked them to be, was to Mrs. Hill the greatest difference between eastern and western society.[13]

Another observer saw Denver as being a genuine cross section of America. "If one is to pick the most American city—the city that represents the thought and spirit of every part of the country—he must point to Denver as the needle points to the pole," wrote

Arthur Chapman. He did not think the city in any way typified the West that was so popular in the American mind. "Let a cowboy, with chaps, spurs, and his rope at his saddle, ride through the streets of Denver, and he will be stared at as if he were in the streets of New York." Nor did Indians hang around the capital city much anymore. To view the native American one had to travel a day and a half by railroad from Denver, to southwestern Colorado, where a few reservation Utes might be seen. Now and then a few Indians were imported when a Wild West show was staged, but when that happened they were as much a curiosity as if they were performing before eastern audiences. "Twenty years ago, or even fifteen," said Chapman, "Denver could have been called western but today it is simply American." In fact, he concluded, Denver was growing so fast and was becoming so "modern" that if it kept up the pace the pollutants that so commonly filled the air of highly urbanized areas threatened to reduce seriously the city's claims to the perfect climate.[14]

Residential Denver was representative of the American scene in the diversity of its living accommodations. Thousands of working-class people lived in small homes laid out in neat but monotonous patterns, while the much smaller number of rich furnished the showplaces. Mrs. Hill, who watched the city's social scene with interest, was fascinated by the architecture of the mining magnates' mansions. She thought Denver compared favorably to any city in America or Europe for the magnificence of its structures and the broad expanses of its avenues. The more elegant homes often were reproductions of French or Italian originals, protected by stone walls or ornate iron fences and surrounded by elaborately terraced gardens. Interspersed among these European copies were colonial brick replicas, complete with white pillars, expansive lawns, and shrubbery.[15]

A short trip by rail to the south brought visitors to another "city of homes" nestled against the base of the Rockies. Colorado Springs, a showplace from the beginning, had undergone continual refinement, even in the 1890s. When Walter Wyckoff returned there in 1908 after an absence of ten years, he found the regularity of the city's plan and the "curious mingling of brick and wood and stone" familiar, but he was surprised at the growth that had taken place. Many of the new homes were of frame construction "painted in a profusion of color that was dazzling as one looked up the vista of an avenue." Some streets were less colorful, but their buildings appeared graceful and built in good taste. What impressed him was the "turf that surrounded even the smallest cottages and spread about great houses like English lawns for faultlessness of quality and of keeping." The well-kept yards were, as he put it, no free gift of nature, for they had to be watered with great regularity to keep them from turning brown. Already Colorado Springs controlled the use of precious water by limiting the hours of sprinkling.

Although "Li'l Lunnon," as the British called it, presented a face that appeared to be clean and tidy, there were those who felt that its social structure had become a little loose in spots. Emily Post, whose name was a household word, made note of this in a book that described her western travels in the early years of the new century. As she watched the transient society of health seekers play, she came to the conclusion that in their effort to "get all the fun out of their enforced extradition" they burned the candle at both ends. Many, she remarked, spent their days with tennis, polo, and driving fast cars when they were not gambling or flirting. They appeared to believe in the injunction to eat, drink, and be merry, but they never mentioned the rest of the line, never talked of death. There were so many of these hard-living invalids at Colorado Springs that she dubbed it "The City of Recklessness." "It is the fastest society on earth!" a scandalized old lady told social arbiter Post. "They just live for excitement, and they don't attend church half as regularly as they go to each other's houses to dance or gamble." The eastern lady's description of the Newport of the Rockies was not one that its founders and subsequent boosters wanted to read. They preferred to think of Colorado Springs as a quiet residential city where people stood around watering their lawns and nodding in a friendly manner to passing tourists.[16]

Visitors who admired Colorado Springs during these prewar years had only to circle around to the western side of Pike's Peak to find a world so different that it appeared to live in an earlier age. Cripple Creek, one of the youngest of the state's big mining boom towns, had changed, but not for the better, when Walter Wyckoff saw it again in 1908. The ten years that had elapsed between visits merely had turned its lustiness into a municipal dowdiness. As the visitor topped the rise and looked down into the valley in which the town crouched he saw the famous camp that still fascinates tourists, but he felt that all the old picturesqueness he had known had faded away. Before him were the results of extraction. "Not a tree had been left standing," he wrote sadly. "Every hillside was clean shaven to its crest, then indented everywhere with gaping prospects, each surrounded by its heaps of debris. The whole region looked as though thirteen-inch guns had been playing upon it from every quarter." He concluded that gold mining in its latter states was as destructive an industry as the mining of coal. In fact, most of the activity was reminiscent of that seen in early industrial cities, for here, too "were power-houses belching black smoke from tall iron chimneys and millions of tons of rejected ore spreading like heaps of culm about them."

Then he turned his eyes upon the city. "In the midst of this desolation stood the town, brick at its core and ugly with an ugliness to match the surrounding ruin, spreading in gaudy wooden cottages that became only more grotesque in color as they climbed the scarred and barren slopes. There were vivid blues and reds and yellows, with shades of pink and lavender interspersed and harrowing tints of green." It translated into "the hideousness of a city built solely on the greed for gold," he wrote. What further depressed him was the realization that in an early day miners had lived in snug little cabins with grass sprouting from their dirt-covered roofs, and a brook flowed through the camp, beyond which one could see trees on the neighboring hills. Now thousands worked underground as in the mines of any highly industrialized country, and they lived in the same cheap gaudiness that characterized those unenvied places.

If Wyckoff was saddened by Cripple Creek, the journalist Julian Street was absolutely scandalized. After wandering up a principal avenue he turned off onto a side street lined with tumbledown, flimsy buildings, some of which were abandoned. Instead of numbers the doors bore various feminine names, and except for an occasional male saunterer, or a woman dressed in a loose, pink wrapper, hurrying across the street, the visitor saw no one. Presently there was action. "From another window a . . . woman with very black hair and eyes and cheeks of light orchid shade, showed her gold teeth in a mirthless, automatic smile, and added the allurement of an ice-cold wink." Now he was oriented; he was in the middle of Cripple Creek's red-light district.[17] When this description of their fair city was placed before a national readership the outraged officials of the fading mining camp promptly changed the name of the red-light district's principal thoroughfare to Julian Street.[18] After the visiting writer offered due apologies, the city fathers restored the original name, Myers Avenue. Today one of the few remnants of that historic street is the Old Homestead parlor house, a museum that recalls the days of Hazel Vernon, Pearl DeVere, Nell McClusky, Laura Evans, Laura Livingston, and the other professionals who made that particular brothel famous for the "class" offered its clientele. The museum's brochure is not far wrong in calling this pleasure palace "one of the greatest gold mines of them all."

While Cripple Creek and the other mining towns ran their red-light districts openly and apparently as a matter of public necessity, places such as Denver began to close down these operations and to drive the trade onto the streets under the assumption that such actions "cleaned up" the town. There had been occasional efforts to eliminate houses of ill fame, but not until the approach of prohibition were the reformers successful. "This time the red lights were dimmed forever," wrote one historian of Denver's demimonde. "The year 1915 saw the tumult and the shouting die, the madames and pimps depart."[19]

The act of "closing down the town," as the phrase has it, indicated that Denver's moral climate was changing, if only superficially. By 1912 the movies were beginning to be regarded as a possible source of temptation to the young, and, as further evidence of changing mores, the city council passed an ordinance regulating these and other places of amusement. It now became unlawful for any person under eighteen not accompanied by a parent or guardian to attend public dance halls after 10 P.M. or for children under sixteen to see a movie or be in any place of public amusement after 7. Dance hall proprietors were obliged to keep written records of the names and addresses of anyone under twenty-one who attended dances; the participants had to record their own names or to be refused admittance to the establishment.[20]

The growing awareness among Coloradans of problems concerning the young during these years has been most widely recognized in the work of Ben B. Lindsey, frequently referred to as the "kid judge." He came from Tennessee in 1880, and seven years later he was admitted to the Colorado bar. By 1901 this small, vigorous man, by then well known to Denverites, became a county judge. Before long the intense jurist, with his bulging forehead, large black mustache, aquiline nose, and expressive eyes, had gained a national reputation, not only for his crusading against vice but also for his work with children. The establishment of a juvenile court at

Denver in 1907 was largely the result of ceaseless pressure exerted by Lindsey for such a facility. Although the judge was so dedicated to his work that he spent his salary on it and lived in near-penury, his enemies were many and powerful.

Within a few years after the establishment of the juvenile court, Lindsey's reputation began to suffer, not for reasons connected with juvenile reform, but because of his extensive, flamboyant crusades in related fields. In 1914 he was described to a visiting reporter as the most hated citizen of Colorado within the state and the most admired outside of it. His work with children was regarded as commendable both at home and abroad, but constant demands for reform in general began to wear on Coloradans' nerves. As one man on the street remarked, there had been "too much hollering about reform," and when one considers the fact that already Denver depended heavily upon the tourist and convention trade for her prosperity it is not surprising that the city fathers were sensitive about the reputation of their stamping ground. By the late 1920s Lindsey had made so many enemies that he was disbarred as an attorney and left Colorado for California. Perhaps the greatest tribute he received was from a utilities executive who, upon being sentenced to jail, roared: "This state has more sunshine and more bastards than any place on earth."[21]

During the years that Judge Lindsey was attracting widespread attention through his work with young people, another, somewhat less spectacular Coloradan indicated a sympathy for that subject. In 1912 a former newspaperman named Edward Keating was elected to Congress. As a Democrat and as the son of Irish immigrant parents, he had shown an early interest in labor, one that shortly found him on the House Labor Committee. Two years later, when the National Child Labor Committee was looking for someone to sponsor its bill in Congress, Keating's name was suggested. After considerable delay the legislative effort to curb child labor was passed by the House and sponsored in the Senate by Robert L. Owen, of Oklahoma. With the aid of President Wilson, who pushed hard for passage, the Senate also agreed, and the bill was signed into law even though Wilson had lingering doubts as to its constitutionality. His suspicions were borne out. The court rejected it; when the law came back before that body in an altered form, it was rejected again. Like many a reformer of that day, Keating was somewhat ahead of his time, but he was vindicated when a similar measure became law in the administration of

Franklin D. Roosevelt. Meantime, Keating's involvement in the problems that faced children in a rapidly industrializing nation indicated that Colorado was capable of showing an interest in social legislation and even of flashes of liberalism.[22]

Associated with the problem of youth was the question of prohibition. For example, early in Judge Lindsey's career he concluded that Denver's saloons brought a good many errant youngsters to his court, not only because of wide open conditions that tended to encourage gambling and prostitution, as well as early drinking, but also because many of the children he worked with came from homes where alcoholism was a problem with the parents. Although the judge later decided that the national prohibition act was a failure and opposed it, in earlier days he fought the open sale of liquor and accepted the support of prohibitionists when running for office.[23]

The struggle for prohibition, a long one in Colorado, culminated in 1916, at which time it became illegal to manufacture or import, except for medicinal or religious purposes, any form of intoxicating liquor. Up to that time the prohibitionists, who had been active from earliest territorial days, had enjoyed little success until 1907, when the legislature passed a local option bill, an action to which twenty municipalities responded by going dry. In 1914 the Women's Christian Temperance Union and the Anti-Saloon League put on a spirited drive that resulted in the termination of liquor sales as of January 1, 1916. However, since the law permitted each household two quarts of hard liquor, six quarts of wine, or twenty-four quarts of beer each month for medicinal purposes, drinkers hardly perished from thirst. In addition, a steady supply of spirituous refreshments was brought in from Cheyenne and other out-of-state sources. In order to reduce the demand for "medicinal" liquids, advocates of prohibition, who went far beyond those who recommended temperance, fought for and gained a "bone dry" law in 1918. Druggists and clergymen now were the sole possessors of legal alcoholic liquids. The war itself aided the bone-dry brigade, whose spokesmen argued that it made no sense to ask people to observe "wheatless" days when so much grain was going to distilleries. Even "wet" Denver, whose voters previously had turned down prohibition with great consistency, went "dry" this time.[24]

As Lindsey, Keating, and others sought to improve the lot of younger people, others joined the campaign to benefit Colorado's upcoming generations. In addition to closing down undesirable hangouts, an effort was made to get boys and girls off the streets and into more attractive recreational areas. Foreseeing the era of cheap transportation by trolley and the new automobile, Denver's city fathers acquired the sites of Lookout Mountain Park, fourteen miles from town, and Genesee Mountain Park, twenty miles distant. But that did not promise much for the thousands of youngsters whose families had no automobiles or money for public transportation. Consequently the City Playground Association organized outings for the children who were in the habit of using the conventional municipal parks and playgrounds. As the program developed and youngsters were taken on camping trips, it was discovered that some of them who had been born in Denver and had lived all their lives within sight of snow-capped mountains never had been out of the city. The fabled Rockies meant absolutely nothing to these young Coloradans.[25]

Although the state's recreational areas had grown steadily more accessible as railroad and interurban transit developed, the early years of the twentieth century saw a wider use of the automobile and an increase in mountain highway mileage. Estes Park, northwest of Denver, had been an attraction ever since the 1860s. The Earl of Dunraven's interest in this beauty spot had helped to publicize it and by the mid seventies it was connected to Longmont by a stage line. The Estes Park Hotel was built in 1877.

In June 1903, a frail tubercular, weighing just over a hundred pounds, whose physicians had sent him west to give him a few more years, made his way to Estes Park. His trip was slightly unusual, for he insisted upon driving a steam-powered automobile he and his brother had invented through the rugged passageway to that mountain village. But Freelan O. Stanley, who already had made a fortune through the development of a new dry-coating process for photographic plates—he and his brother sold this one to Eastman for a million dollars—was a man of vision. He found the climate and the general atmosphere at Estes Park so delightful that he decided to build a hotel there. The resulting Stanley Hotel was the largest in the area. Of course, he designed the place himself, installed an all-electric kitchen, supplied the missing hydro-electric plant to furnish power, and sold the remainder of the generated electricity to the town. To make his notion of a resort hotel even more practical and profitable, he helped to finance a new road through the North St. Vrain Canyon, over which he operated Stanley Steamer Mountain Wagons between the hotel and the railhead at Lyons. By 1926 Stanley, who had failed to succumb to his lung ailment, finally sold the hotel and its adjoining land.[26]

The Estes Park area had another enthusiast, who also became very well known to the American public. His name was Enos Mills. For some time he had been scaling surrounding mountain peaks, among them Long's Peak, which he claimed to be the first to have climbed in winter. In 1909 he suggested that about six hundred square miles of the adjacent region be made into a national park, and four years later Robert B. Marshall of the U.S. Geological Survey was delegated by the secretary of the interior to inspect the area of the proposed reserve. Marshall concluded not only that the project was feasible but that it was highly desirable because the region as a whole was as beautiful as any to be found in the United States, or even the world. Additionally, the area was easily accessible to residents of the state as well as to those from other parts of the nation. Denver was well served by railroads, and even in 1913 Estes Park was regarded as being only three hours from Denver by automobile. At that time some thirty thousand visitors stopped there each season; Marshall predicted that the figure would rise to at least a hundred thousand if it became a national park.[27] Rocky Mountain National Park, a little over four hundred square miles in size, was created in January 1915.

During the last quarter of the nineteenth century, as the railways spread their network across Colorado, tourists found viewing the mountain scenery easy and comfortable, but even though excursion rates made travel costs reasonable, many American families could not afford to make such trips. Conventions, however, were often combined with sight-seeing excursions, and Coloradans worked hard to promote such conventions. For example, the American Bar Association met in Denver in the summer of 1901 and was followed by an enormous gathering of the Grand Army of the Republic that September. Denver had a Convention League that worked hand in glove with a very aggressive Chamber of Commerce; between them, during the summer of 1906, they attracted twenty-five conventions that brought seventy-five thousand conventioneers to Denver. Numbers such as these generated the demand for a convention center and auditorium, which was built during the following year. These visitors, of course, left money behind, and it was hoped as well that this kind of advertising would bring permanent residents to the state, where publicists still worked hard to sell Colorado.[28]

For families or individuals who sought a quiet spot in the mountains where they might spend some leisure time and perhaps do some fishing, there were smaller mountain-front towns. At Boulder, where the Colorado Chautauqua had been established just before the turn of the century, vacationers found a pleasant place to stop. Here one might rent an unfurnished tent for $12.50 or a cottage for $75.00 for the six-week session, the management providing household necessities for a small charge. Boulder also had several good hotels where board could be had for $4.00 to $7.00 a week. In 1911 one visitor called the city a "good-natured cosmopolitan community of about 10,000 inhabitants" who were a hospitable people; even better, he said, the place was not yet a commercialized summer resort.[29]

Tourists who used the newly developed automobile or moved about in hired rigs could reach a number of camping places easily. Along the creeks running through the many canyons that wrinkled the face of the Rockies were cool, attractive sites where wood, water, and solitude were plentiful. Some of these locations had been used for years, but by a relatively limited number of people. As early as the 1870s photographer William H. Jackson made note of the "pleasure seekers" who camped along Clear Creek, a stream Horace Greeley already had described as flowing through a solitude that was "sylvan and perfect." Sam Bowles called these mountains "our Switzerland" and "first cousins of the Alps," an allusion Robert Strahorn repeated in his *To the Rockies and Beyond*, published in 1879.[30]

That Colorado's forests ought to be preserved both for recreational reasons and as a future natural resource was recognized by the framers of the state's constitution. Frederick J. Ebert, a professional forester and a member of one of the standing committees at the convention of 1876, urged a comprehensive forestry program and the creation of a state forest bureau. Although the final constitution fell far short of his desires, two of its sections recognized the need for conservation, and these became the first such safeguards to be included in any of the American state constitutions.[31] Although the new state's response to such pleas was minimal, only fifteen years were to elapse before the federal government began to withdraw forest lands from public entry, and with this movement, commenced in 1891, the drive toward conservation that became so popular in the days of the Progressives was under way.

Withdrawals in Colorado began with the White River Plateau Timber Land Reserve of 1891, followed by 4 more during the following year. After that the state was little affected until the era of Theodore Roosevelt, during whose administration 150 withdrawals were made, 14 of which were in Colorado. By 1944 over thirteen and a half million acres, amounting to approximately one-fifth of the whole state, had been so reserved.[32] At the close of World War I an extension of the forest conservation notion evolved, one later to be known as the "wilderness concept." Arthur H. Carhart, a young landscape architect and war veteran who worked for the U.S. Forest Service at Denver, began to write on the subject in 1919. His survey that year of the Trappers Lake area, in the White River National Forest, led to the notion of complete preservation in the natural state. When President Lyndon Johnson signed the Wilderness Bill on September 3, 1964, a campaign in the conservation battle that had been waged for nearly a half-century in Colorado reached its fruition.[33]

The federal government's "invasion" of Colorado at the turn of the century generated considerable complaint among those who wanted to utilize the land for the state's economic development. The creation of large forest reserves was opposed, for example, by cattlemen, who saw huge quantities of grazing land gobbled up by such moves. Less objectionable was the federal government's entry into reclamation and water usage. In the earlier, privately financed irrigation projects, water was sold like any other commodity, and this practice was acceptable to users under reasonable conditions. During the hard years of the nineties, however, a good many of these irrigation companies went bankrupt, and the feeling grew that although the concept of private enterprise was desirable some of the projects were too complicated and too expensive for any other agency than the federal government itself. In western Colorado, for example, only about half of the potential had been developed by private sources. Here federal funds were used to construct the Uncompahgre Project, by which water was diverted through the Gunnison Tunnel for nearly six miles to bring water from the Gunnison River to the Uncompahgre Valley. By 1909 some eighty thousand acres of land were served. Three years later the Grand Valley Project was commenced; when completed, its water was diverted from near Palisade to farms lying more than sixty miles distant.[34]

Increased irrigation, favorable prices, and a growing out-of-state reputation for Colorado fruit products led to an agricultural boom on the western slope during the early years of the twentieth century. After 1912, however, a sharp decline occurred, owing principally to late spring frosts, outside competition, falling prices, and crop diseases. Times would improve, and the annual peach crop was to make a great name for itself, but the apple business declined steadily in the Grand Valley. During these troublous years Colorado's potato production fell off, especially after the spread of disease, beginning in 1911. Several potato crops along the immediate eastern slope, particularly in Weld County, were almost total failures. Farther out on the plains farmers had twice experienced severe setbacks in their attempts to raise wheat, the most recent being in the 1890s. Experiments with dry farming showed encouraging results, and after 1900 yet another wave of farmers advanced upon these unpredictable lands, to try once more. As it turned out, they came at a fortuitous time. A few wet years, so abnormal in the "desert," combined with a growing demand from Europe due to the war, resulted in a temporary upturn in the fortunes of the farmers.

The outbreak of hostilities in Europe during the summer of 1914 benefited not only a lagging Colorado agricultural economy but gave at least temporary relief to mining. Labor unrest, particularly the unhappy events surrounding the highly publicized Ludlow Massacre near Pueblo that year, suggested that Colorado's extractive industries were in deep trouble, but during the ensuing years the need for coal, steel, and certain other minerals momentarily revitalized them. Understandably the production of gold and silver continued to decline in favor of less glamorous metals, but so did the production of zinc, lead, and copper. On the brighter side, a sharp demand for tungsten and molybdenum, used in steel manufacturing and in alloys, created a small boom.

Ever since 1875 miners around Nederland had been familiar with tungsten, a heavy, dark substance they called "black iron," but it was not until 1900 that they realized it had any great value. Samuel P. Conger, a well-known miner, listened to his partner, who recently had seen some of the ore in Arizona, and concluded that its extraction might be profitable. He leased an abandoned shaft where the substance was known to exist. About the same time

John H. Knight, of nearby Ward, recognized the value of tungsten not only for its use in hardening steel but also because it was used in the increasingly popular electric light bulb, and he began to mine it. In addition to American purchases, the German, Belgian, and French demand increased as European steel manufacturers geared up for war. Prices soared, and by 1916 Colorado was producing about five million dollars' worth of these metals annually, a figure that represented almost the entire American production. The Conger mine was worked under various ownerships for nearly two decades after 1900; it was acquired later by the Vanadium Corporation of America, whose owners closed it down in the postwar market collapse.[35]

Also stimulated by the war was a demand for uranium, whose by-product, vanadium, was valuable in steel manufacturing. As a source of radium it had been used for some time in the making of luminous figures for watches and clocks. The brief uranium boom in Colorado collapsed shortly after the war when large quantities of the ore were found in the Belgian Congo. Much later, when nuclear physicists discovered a new use for uranium, another boom, also brief, took place in the state. These latter-day mining rushes of the early twentieth century also left their names on the land, as places like Uranium, Vanadium, and Uravan appeared on the maps. (The latter name was derived from the first two.)[36]

For three years after the outbreak of war in Europe, Coloradans enjoyed the upturn in their economy occasioned by that international disruption. Then, in 1917, they had to face the more serious problem of participation. When the United States entered the war, Colorado's response was typical in that it provided manpower, took pride in oversubscribing to five different war-bond issues, and vied with other members of the union in its aggressive patriotism.

Colorado provided approximately forty-three thousand men, or about 1 percent of the nation's armed forces. Of these some three hundred were killed and over a thousand suffered wounds. So far as home-front activities were concerned, the state created a local Council of Defense, the functions of which were to protect property and to conserve resources. This was the first of such organizations in the nation. In another "first," the General Assembly was called into special session in July 1917 to provide for such exigencies of war as the cost of raising and maintaining the Colorado National Guard, the necessary policing of the state during the emergency, and any other necessary expenditures.[37]

In their enthusiasm for the war effort Coloradans appeared to be almost overanxious. Their mood of superheated patriotism often went to extremes, and they made life difficult for those of their neighbors whose Teutonic background was temporarily out of favor. Although this was not unusual when compared to similar activities by other Americans, the misguided efforts of individuals and newspapers did little credit to the state as a whole. Nearly 10 percent of Colorado's population was of German or Austrian origin, and almost all of these were U.S. citizens. Although these people made every effort to demonstrate their loyalty and their support of the war effort, nevertheless they were related to the enemy in the public mind and therefore suspect. The editor of Colorado's only German newspaper, the *Denver Colorado Herold,* argued that his countrymen had emigrated in order to avoid German-style militarism.

To no avail. In one small farm community a German-American farm laborer was relieved of his shirt, after which a yellow stripe was painted down his spine. In neighboring Wyoming a similar incident took place because the victim, who was of Russian origin, refused to buy a government war bond. In both states those suspected of lacking patriotism were forced to kiss the flag publicly. In the Colorado incident the accused was threatened by his tormentors, who took him out on a railroad bridge, tied a rope around his neck, and threatened to push him off. In both of these neighboring western states book burning took place, and in Wyoming an editor boasted that since no foreign-language newspaper was printed in his state the place was "clean." Coloradans were warned that a large number of professors at their state university probably were suspect since many of them had studied in Germany. The extent of the hysteria was shown by a book-burning rally sponsored by the university's preparatory school at Boulder; not only were volumes printed in German destroyed but any books written in English that were favorable to the enemy were also consigned to the flames. Coloradans also used the tense situation as a further outlet for their prejudices against Spanish-speaking residents. Rumor had it that agents from Mexico planned to infiltrate the migrant workers in Weld County and get them to return home, where they could be enlisted on Germany's side in the conflict. The implication was that anyone with dark skin and a Spanish accent ought to be watched with great care.

Like all such situations, the patriotic fever had its humorous aspects. For example, a highly patriotic Denver woman became suspicious of several bearded men whose apparently clandestine activities told her that subversion was in the air. Anxious to do her duty and to save the country, she reported them to federal agents, who, armed to the teeth, crashed the hideout of these dangerous plotters. To their embarrassment they uncovered not a nest of spies but a small group of startled Civil War veterans who were planning a Christmas program of remembrance for American soldiers. Less humorous, but equally ridiculous, were assertions that a stock market decline was the responsibility of the awful Hun, who was trying to undermine American confidence in its cherished free enterprise system. Another improbable story had it that the Indians, who showed a great disinterest in the draft, were being infiltrated by German agents, who might well excite them to a fresh uprising and terrible reprisals upon the whites. In this ludicrous vein was the warning issued to householders that they should scrupulously avoid salespeople with Teutonic accents, particularly sellers of soap, a product said to contain poison, and certainly purveyors of court plasters because these innocent-looking items probably had been loaded with tetanus or typhus germs. Public water reservoirs, of course, were closely guarded to avert mass murder by secret agents determined to wipe Colorado off the map.[38]

The people of Colorado spent the war years producing meat, foodstuffs, minerals, and manufactured goods as their contribution to the national effort. After hours some of them searched for spies, reported suspected subversive activities of their neighbors, and listened to each other give patriotic speeches. A few even joined the Nathan Hale Volunteers, a "secret patrol" whose mission was to ferret out suspicious characters and report them to the authorities. These witch-hunters anticipated the existence of such secret groups as the Minute Men who lurked in the mountain shadows a few years later. In the main, however, those who lived in the Centennial state were too preoccupied by the demands of daily living to engage in such extracurricular activities; they spent their energies working in their fields and shops.

As Colorado prepared to enter the post–World War era, its more thoughtful residents realized that the day of mineral bonanzas probably had passed, and that the haste with which farmers had put marginal lands into use during the period of wartime high prices was bound to cause problems if agricultural prices declined.

The recent war had touched them little, except in its demands for resources, and now that this phase had passed the state would have to readjust its economic thinking, as it had been obliged to do in the past, and to prepare for difficult times unless new solutions to old problems could be found.

# 13

# "'Tis a Privilege"

From the days of the Anglo-American invasion of Colorado, its dominant class represented a cross section of American life more thoroughly than was true in any of the other mountain states. Part of the explanation is to be found in an early rail connection with the States that made it easy for mining entrepreneurs, land developers, and travelers to invade the place and to sow some of their ideas. As a result Colorado always has maintained closer social and cultural connections with the East than have its neighbors. It was not unnatural, therefore, that national trends were strongly reflected throughout the state during the years that followed the emotional tumult of World War I.

Part of America's disillusionment with the outcome of the "Great Crusade" in Europe was its conscious preoccupation with material aspects of life and its isolation not only from foreign entanglements but also from intellectual temptations. The liberal humanitarianism of prewar days that had sought so earnestly to stake out a claim for latecomers to the American dream now gave way to a resurgence of an earlier economic elitism. Social legislation appeared to have lost its charm for voters, and legislative innovators who once were hailed as the architects of a new and better society now were regarded as crackpots by some and as outright subversives by others. Those who had felt alarm at the great progress made by liberals before the war had used the cudgels of patriotism with which to chastise them during the war years when national security could be used to justify all retrogressive measures.

In Colorado the "patriots" who had conducted an enthusiastic search during the war for spies, subversives, or anyone who appeared to be anything less than one hundred percent American discovered that the war's conclusion did not necessarily mean that their efforts to purify society no longer were in vogue. While the continuing efforts of these zealots may not have represented the views of the majority in Colorado, the unwillingness of the majority to speak out against the excesses of a few not only lent credence to the program of hate, but appeared to confirm the innate conservatism embedded in the community. It may be argued that Colorado was not alone among the western states in joining the rush to the right during these uncertain years, but there is evidence to show that here the manifestations of the national hysteria were stronger, more blatant than among the state's neighbors.

The great catchall expression that was used by the nation's ultraconservative forces in their efforts to suppress labor organizations, civil liberties groups, and "liberals" in general was the "red menace" or Bolshevism. Their often misguided efforts to save the nation have been characterized as the "blue menace," a force America had reason to be concerned about if such repressive efforts were allowed to run rampant. Growing concern over the emergence of the red danger, as dramatized by Attorney General A. Mitchell Palmer's roundup and deportation of presumed subversives, was reflected in Colorado by a 1919 law that forbade display of the "Red Flag, the emblem of anarchy" in public. Violators were promised a one-to-ten-year sojourn at Canon City.[1]

Westerners who read of the Palmer raids and were told that the nation faced a new danger, this time from Communism, wondered if this suddenly active political virus had reached the Rockies. When a lecture on socialism attracted more than two thousand Denverites in the fall of 1919, that city's *Catholic Register* guessed that the audience contained at least four hundred "open Bolshevists," some of whom had not even mastered the English language. From that premise it was not hard for the editor to conclude that the Russian government had a number of paid agents in Denver.[2] When a federal judge issued an injunction against coal miners who took part in a national walkout, the *Denver Post* called it "a necessary and timely rebuke to the anarchists, to bolshevists and to the foreign labor leaders who have come to this country to destroy it."[3]

Colorado red hunting was widespread at Pueblo that fall because a nationwide steel strike produced economic unrest in a part of the state where a relatively large number of immigrant workers lived. The International Workers of the World, a small but militant labor organization that had staged some spectacular strikes across the country, had a local unit in the steel city. A police raid upon its headquarters that yielded two leaders and a large quantity of radical literature prompted a delegation of concerned citizens to wait upon the governor and to request protective legislation against Bolshevism. Denver's establishment, quickly perceiving the danger posed by militant labor groups, engineered the passage of a local ordinance designed to prevent gatherings that might incite revolution in the capital city. When a favorite meeting place of radicals was closed by police, labor leaders protested, but American Legion representatives reassured the city administration by promising that the old troopers would deal with reds "the way they deserve."[4]

As a nationwide resurgence of nationalism stressed the virtues of Americanism, foreigners, Catholics, and Jews came under increasing pressure. Labor organizations, widely believed to be under the control of radicals—who, in turn, were supposed to be of foreign origin—were marked as "unreliable" in the realm of Americanism. The *Denver Post*'s anxiety to set a good example was so intense that it offered to pay the first month's dues for any employee who qualified for the American Legion, an organization the paper endorsed as one hundred percent American. In its 1920 "Glory Edition," featured each New Year's Day by the *Denver Post*, the Leo Leyden Post No. 1 of the American Legion ran a quarter-page advertisement soliciting membership, explaining that it was a nonpolitical and nonmilitary, but thoroughly American, organization. In welcoming those who loved the stars and stripes it warned against the dangers of Bolshevism. Scattered throughout that entire issue of the *Post* were small blocked-off statements that underscored the clear and present danger: "If you don't want the majority to rule, then go back to Russia." "Are you an American? If not, why did you come here?" "The man with the loudest howl usually has a foreign accent." "America saved the world and Americanism will save America."

In the same edition were more detailed comments, written by prominent Coloradans and intended to purify the minds of the readership. Tully Scott, a justice of the state supreme court, pointed to the immigrant as a source of the problem. "By reason of our generous invitation to the oppressed of all nations, there has come unobserved into our midst the virile seed of both sedition and disloyalty, until now like a cancer, it gravely threatens the whole body politic," he wrote. "It is a vile growth that must be eradicated while there is yet time." The jurist left no doubt as to how this political virus was to be stamped out. He urged that subversive aliens be deported at once, while others, who hid their disloyalties under the cloak of citizenship, were to be punished to the extent of the law. Naturalized citizens of this stripe were to be "denaturalized" and evicted from the country, an action he described as a healthy pruning of diseased limbs.

Justice Scott's warnings were reemphasized by the Right Reverend Irving P. Johnson, the Episcopal bishop of Colorado, who announced that never before had a greater call for a militant church existed and that in this case the identity of the enemy was beyond doubt. It was the duty of the church, he proclaimed, to do battle against all radicals, and its role in freeing America from the danger of Bolshevism was of vital importance. "The temples of America must be the armories of American citizenship," concluded the bishop.[5]

The contest to see who could be the most American was conducted with such enthusiasm that an American Legion post in Denver resorted to retroactive patriotism. Its members recommended that Manassa-born Jack Dempsey be prohibited from fighting in his native state because he had worked in a shipyard, under legitimate deferment, during the recent war. He was, *ex post facto*, a "slacker." The Sons of Colorado, another organization dedicated to warding off subversive influences, promised that persons suspected of bearing such infectious political germs would be turned back at the state line.

It was well that the guardians were at their stations, for in April 1920 a *Denver Post* headline announced that the reds were planning to overthrow the United States government on May Day. The appointed day came and passed uneventfully, but later that summer the *Post* had reason to suspect that its warning had not been entirely in vain. During August labor struck the Denver Tramway Company and rioting broke out in which streetcars were overturned and people died at the hands of professional strikebreakers hired by the company. The *Post* found itself in the midst of battle, its building being invaded and sacked during the disorder.

Although the press blamed all these difficulties on unions and the "serpent tongue . . . of the I.W.W., the Soviet, and the revolutionists," public sentiment recoiled at the violence with which the disturbance had been suppressed. The Catholic bishop of Colorado was applauded when he told a crowd that wages were the first claim against industry. In the opinion of a labor advocate the trouble came from the U.S. Chamber of Commerce's earlier declaration of war upon unions, a struggle into which the Denver company had been drawn when it tried to put into practice the national organization's theories. Not only did men die in the capital city's streets as a result of the conflict, but the action tended to accentuate the red scare in Colorado.[6]

Amidst the shrill voices of suspicion came the calm and reasoned words of George Norlin, president of the University of Colorado, who told his fellow Coloradans that Americanism was not measured by a decibel count of sound and fury but rather in the quiet love of a land one was prepared to defend. The word *Americanism,* he thought, had been bandied about so recklessly that it had lost meaning, yet it was not at all a vague term, but rather one understood by the founding fathers and their successors as encompassing a protest against intolerance, oppression, bigotry, and superstition. To be a good American, he suggested, was to show courage in the midst of panic, to cherish liberty in the midst of its excesses, and to go forward even when progress was in disrepute. Such advice from the shy, slender professor of Greek who directed the institution of learning at Boulder was far too sensible to attract a very wide following in a period of passion and hatred that featured threats of violence to those who would not or could not conform to the white Anglo-Saxon and Protestant pattern formulated by the political and social establishment.[7] It was during this discouraging period of the state's history that the *Denver Post* published Charles Edwin Hewes's poem "There's A Land Where," a little verse that concluded with the words "I'll tell the world, 'Tis a privilege to live in Colorado."[8]

Rioting in the streets, accompanied by bloodshed, was a sad enough commentary upon the place where it was such a privilege to live, but the unrest Colorado experienced in those troublous postwar years was further emphasized by the extent to which these westerners embraced the tenets of the Ku Klux Klan. In an earlier day thoughtful men and women could scoff at adults who paraded around after dark "in their nightshirts," recited their catechisms of hate by the light of fiery crosses, and threatened Negroes, but this was written off as a manifestation of turmoil in the backward South. In the 1920s, however, the new Klan expanded its program of prejudice to include Catholics, Jews, miscellaneous foreign influences, and anyone mildly suspected of lacking American qualities. One would not have thought that these hooded political throwbacks could find an audience in the West, so long believed to be liberal, but the mood of the day was right and white sheets sold like hotcakes. Unhappily the seeds of discontent fell on fertile ground in the Central Rockies, where preparation for it had been made as early as the war years. As one historian of the Klan has said, "The success story of the western Klan was Colorado."[9] Here it took over the state government and threatened not only to wipe out any political and social gains made in the progressive era, but also to place Colorado at the forefront of reactionary segments of western society.

Not surprisingly, supporters of this clandestine group pleaded patriotism and a love of the flag in defense of their position. The first issue of the Klan paper, *The Rocky Mountain American,* published at Boulder January 31, 1925, argued that social unrest was an important public issue and that following the recent war both public and private morality had experienced a breakdown. The editor, William Francis, explained that the Klan's rise to power at this particular time merely represented "the all pervading popular reaction to this moral collapse." Francis asserted that the Klan asked no more than an honest enforcement of the Prohibition amendment, a healthy distrust of dishonest officeholders, and a condemnation of moral laxity in the individual.

The Boulder editor denied that his organization harbored any prejudice against Catholics, Jews, or Negroes. While he lamented the fact that the first two simply had separated themselves from the mainstream of Americanism, he felt that the Negro presented "an absolutely different proposition" because of his natural inferiority to white men. The average Klansman, said Francis, "is a friend of the Negro and wishes to see him advance and prosper, but he recognizes the Negro for what he is, notes the line of demarcation between the white and black races, and unhesitatingly advocates and insists upon the supremacy of the white race." This position, he said, simply recognized the laws of nature and of the commonwealth "which prohibits and brands as a felony in Colorado, any marriage between those of white or Negro blood."

It was in such an atmosphere that the Klan had emerged in

Denver in 1921, and by 1924 it had pretty largely acquired control of Colorado's political apparatus. At first its members had concentrated upon law and order, constantly reminding voters of their heritage and their responsibility to it. In 1923 the group used its power in Denver to unseat the mayor, who had not been friendly to its cause, and to support the candidacy of Ben Stapleton, who denied he was a Klansman. In office, Stapleton appointed a number of the brethren to important offices, and when he was able to withstand a recall election the head of Colorado's Klan took credit for the accomplishment. By 1924, city attorney and Klansman Clarence J. Morley became the organization's choice for the governorship, and with that decision the group expanded to state-level politics.[10] For an organization that had been operative in the state only two years, this was a rather remarkable achievement that told much about the postwar disillusionment and unrest among the people.

Under the leadership of Grand Dragon Dr. John Galen Locke, the self-appointed crusaders against all things presumed to be un-American fastened their grip on the minds of townsmen all across the state. Local patriots, who only recently thought they had saved Colorado from the Kaiser, now hastened to secure it from the perils of Catholicism, Judaism, and any black threats to white supremacy that might appear. The Klan first seized municipal offices. The election of Morley to the governorship on the Republican ticket, and Republican control of both houses of the legislature, promised much for the Klan, whose forces controlled that party. Among other things they wanted to exclude certain aliens from the state, and to enforce the Prohibition amendment to the degree that wines could not be used for sacramental purposes. Another of the Klan's desires was to dismantle a number of state agencies in order to eliminate jobs held by those not sympathetic to their cause, and to create new positions for which the applicants would have to pass rigid tests of Americanism. One of the agencies they wanted to abolish was the State Civil Service Commission.[11]

All that kept the state from passing to Klan management was the opposition by a group of Republican senators who foresaw disaster if the proposed legislation became law. Six of them, allied with fourteen Democratic senators led by William H. ("Billy") Adams, managed to kill these "patriotic" measures. The anti-Klan group showed the extent of its opposition when it pointedly allowed the passage of one harmless administration bill that abolished the

Board of Horseshoe Examiners, an agency that long had outlived its usefulness in the automobile era. Although the Klan-controlled House threatened to stop all proposed measures unless the senators retreated, the deadlock continued until the lower house backed down. Before the session ended the legislators had sidetracked the governor's program and had passed measures necessary for the state to carry on its functions.

Not unexpectedly the state university came under fire during this period. It was accustomed to fending off political attempts at interference, but in the case of the Klan the request was too outrageous even to be considered. When Governor Morley informed President Norlin that the school might have a suitable legislative appropriation provided all Catholics and Jews were dismissed from its staff, the response was a prompt and unequivocal "no." The existence of a millage levy, recently passed by a referendum, provided enough funds to keep the university afloat until the political storm had abated.[12]

Klan influence lingered in the next legislative session, but the group had lost much of its power. The weakening of its influence across the state was evidenced in the next election, when none other than Billy Adams succeeded Clarence Morley as governor.[13] That is not to say that Coloradans suddenly were blessed with liberality or a new enlightenment, for Adams was quite conservative. Rather, the decline of the white-sheet brigade was due more to internal squabbling and a diversion of the public's attention to such interesting things as the making of money in the new prosperity. Less than four months after the adjournment of the legislature, Grand Dragon Locke became embroiled in a dispute with his organization's national headquarters. Amidst charges of mismanagement and financial irregularities he broke with the main body and commenced a new group known as the Minute Men. The *Rocky Mountain American* ceased its publication at the end of July 1925 with the explanation that henceforth readers would be deprived of its offerings "owing to recent difficulties that have arisen in the Klan organization." In this last issue the editor recommended the new Minute Men to those who shared the ideals of "a pure patriotism toward our country, expressed in a militant, patriotic, Protestant movement." It was an organization that promised to continue the unrelenting war against "the evil hand of the Roman hierarchy."[14]

With the passing of this ideological trade journal Coloradans would be obliged to remain in the dark as to the true nature of affairs in the state. In their ignorance they would not realize that increased smoking among women was the fault of the "Jew movies" whose producers inferentially had approved of the idea by depicting it as fashionable among society women in films. As a by-product, of course, "this meant millions of dollars for the Jewish tobacco manufacturers and owners of chain tobacco stores." The chain store remark was suggestive of a matter much larger than the mere sale of tobacco. The Klan years in Colorado coincided with the coming of big chains, and the passing of some of the smaller, individually owned shops. Consequently it was not difficult to convince the owner of a small store that big firms, said to be dominated by the Jews, now threatened his existence. Perhaps it was in defense against such prejudices that Boulder's J. C. Penney store advertised in *The American* "Spring Values in our White Goods Department," a sale that featured "Wizard Sheets and Cases" at ninety-eight cents and twenty-five cents, respectively. Reference to the "wizard," a Klan office, indicated not only that Penney's local manager was abreast of the times but that he knew a potential market when he saw one. Nor was the proprietor of the Paris Dry Cleaning Parlor unaware that a new fraternity was in town when he advertised Klothing Karefully Kleaned. Boulder at that time was said to have in its midst about a thousand Klansmen. Another feature that readers of the Klan newspaper were to miss was the educational verse the magazine had provided, an example of which assured the faithful that:

> "I would rather be a Klansman
> in a robe of snowy white,
> Than to be a Catholic Priest
> in a robe as black as night;
> For a Klansman is AMERICAN,
> and AMERICA is his home,
> But a priest owes his allegiance
> to a Dago Pope in Rome."[15]

In a sense the Colorado Klan was a harmless manifestation of the juvenile desire to participate in uniformed parades and to chant mindless slogans, an activity not unknown to Americans in other and less offensive organizations. Under the guise of patriotism it provided an opportunity for men and women to take emotional shelter in an exclusive, secret social group at a time of national and local unrest. "During the summer of 1924," recalled a resident of Steamboat Springs, "scarcely a week passed that did not witness the spooky nocturnal spectacle of a long column of men in hooded regalia, marching and counter marching four abreast for the purpose of burning a cross on top of one or another of Steamboat's numerous hills." Since the parades usually were staged on a weekend, he added, it was not difficult to ascertain Klan membership "by taking inventory of excessive numbers of sheets and pillow cases dangling from the town's multitudinous clotheslines on Monday morning."[16]

If the Klan had been guilty of nothing more than midnight marching and ritualistic mumbo jumbo its members might have been forgiven their fraternal tendencies, but in an era of personal insecurity their activities certainly made life more difficult for individuals whose own sense of well-being needed no additional threat, minority Coloradans in particular. Intellectuals who had fought for freedom of the oppressed also felt the influence of the Klan. George Creel, a crusading Denver newspaperman, later recalled that Judge Ben Lindsey became one of the targets. "Up to 1924 he held his own fairly well," wrote Creel, "but in that year the Ku Klux Klan swept the state, starting fires of bigotry in every town and village. Ben, with his usual courage, was one of the few officials to fight the hooded fanatics, speaking day and night at the risk of his life."[17] Ironically, it was the Catholics, on the other side of the fence, who gave the judge a great deal of trouble because of his views on marriage, and they contributed more to his downfall than did the Klan.

Just as Klan activity in Colorado reflected national postwar social turmoil, so did the local response to national Prohibition, which became effective in January 1920. Although the state anticipated the nation by four years in its decision to dry up the flow of liquor, the longer experience at enforcement did not appear to have solved the problem of illegal sales. As was true every place else in the nation, those who preferred not to break earlier habits always could find something to drink at the neighborhood speakeasy or by consulting their personal bootleggers. It was not that Coloradans were more disposed to lawbreaking than average Americans; illegal beer and whiskey were relatively easy to find, there was no penalty for the buyer, and the seller exposed himself to relatively light risks because convictions for the offense often were hard to come by. Adding to the difficulty of enforcement was the division of jurisdiction. National, state, and municipal authorities were supposed to cooperate, but all too frequently local authorities showed little interest in their work. Federal law enforcement officers, trying to carry out the provisions of a law that became increasingly unpopular, were regarded with hostility by householders whose western background nurtured the antipathy to such "foreigners."

In the manner of the day, bootleggers in Colorado proceeded apace, taking their risks, submitting to periodic arrests, and going to the penitentiary upon occasion. During the decade of the twenties there were never fewer than 500 arrests in the state each year for violations of the prohibition law; on two occasions the figures exceeded 1,000, but convictions did not approach this number. During that "dry decade" seizures of illegal beverages averaged over 125,000 gallons a year, and in 1926 they topped 200,000. In their "best" year the agents knocked over nearly 2,500 stills, an effort that slowed only slightly the flow of beer, wine, and whiskey.[18]

In some instances the moral issue transcended political considerations. Late in 1919 the membership of a Holyoke, Colorado, church was rent asunder, as the saying goes, over the imbibing of alcohol by the Sunday school superintendent, whose suppliers, he asserted, were members of the church board. The superintendent stood up in church one Sunday and made a public confession, after which he complied with the board's request that he resign, but the brethren who were accused of being the bootleggers refused to surrender their board memberships. Led by the ex-superintendent and his wife, ninety members of the church walked out. The departing group included the lady choir leader who only a week earlier had "walloped" one of the accused purveyors of strong drink for supplying her husband. After the indignant secessionists were gone only eleven persons remained in the house of the Lord. The minister viewed the remnants of his shattered following and wearily enjoined them to sing a hymn he had designated just before the schism; they complied. During the following week the former superintendent's wife tried to get the local district attorney to prosecute the alleged bootleggers. When he refused to act, a delegation went over to Fort Morgan, the seat of the judicial district, and laid the case before the district attorney in that city.[19] Aside from the action of the choir leader, who took a swing at one of the local liquor salesmen, there was no violence.

One of the big complaints Americans came to have about the Eighteenth Amendment was that it produced unhealthy side effects. As one of the nation's most widely violated laws, it tended to foster related lawlessness, such as gang warfare, gambling, prostitution, and the bribing of law enforcement officers. Although one immediately thinks of Chicago, New York, and some of the other large cities in this regard, evidences of these developments were seen in Colorado's more populated centers. For example, in the spring of 1925 six Denver policemen were fired for selling confiscated liquor. While police corruption was nothing new—in the years to come Denver would see far more of it—the case of the bootlegging cops further undermined public confidence in law enforcement officials.

Gangsterism, on the other hand, was a more serious matter. Public shooting to resolve personal differences certainly was not foreign to the West, and it had been only a few years since Denver had witnessed such episodes, but when the bootleggers started warring on each other city fathers thought of Chicago and began to worry about civic reputations. Indeed, the problem in Colorado was suggestive of difficulties elsewhere, for it was the attempted invasion of Denver by Pueblo liquor interests that brought out the revolvers. The first efforts to dissuade the visitors from southern Colorado came in February 1931, and while a message was conveyed, there was no bloodshed. Pete Carlino, the intended victim, was fired upon four times as he stood in front of a local garage, but the would-be executioners, who were shooting from a moving car, Chicago style, were just learning their trade and Carlino was untouched.

Not so lucky was a Denver moonshine merchant named Joe Barry who was wounded by anonymous assailants. Meantime, Carlino's enemies continued their efforts to discourage his activities. They kidnapped one of his business associates, bombed his residence, and gunned down his brother. Authorities handled the situation in a manner typical of this sort of problem by trying to take him out of circulation on charges that were not related to bootlegging. He was accused of burning down his own house to collect insurance, and while this avenue of retribution was being explored the possibility of deporting him to Italy was studied. Not surprisingly, a more informal answer to the problem came from within rum-running circles; in September Carlino's body was found by a roadside not far from Pueblo. As was customary in such feuds, the power now shifted, this time to Joe Roma of Denver, who reigned until 1933, when he, in turn, was "rubbed out" as he sat at home, peacefully plucking his mandolin. The question of his successor became a moot point, for Prohibition itself was about to be terminated.[20]

By this time Colorado shared the national view that the Prohibition experiment had been a failure. When a University of Denver graduate student interviewed local authorities in 1932, most of them expressed the opinion that the law had done more harm than good. The county jail warden thought that the liquor law stimulated organized crime, gangs, and corruption, while making petty criminals out of people who were not criminally inclined. As a member of the board of corrections remarked, "When one devil went out seven came in." He admitted that when sources of liquor were dried up, middle-class families may have benefited, but countering this was the increased amount of drinking in what he called the "smart alec class." Social service and welfare agencies in Denver shared the general belief that Prohibition increased the extent of criminality among people with whom they dealt.[21]

Colorado voters agreed that the effort to legislate morals had failed, and they voted to suspend any local laws relating to the sale of intoxicating liquors as of July 1, 1933. Shortly the city of Denver repealed any ordinances that dealt with this subject. It was not until December of 1933 that national prohibition was suspended by the repeal of the Eighteenth Amendment.[22]

During the so-called dry years, that frustrating period in which federal and state officials fruitlessly smashed stills and tried to enforce an unenforceable law, Coloradans looked ahead to the day when their state would be wetter in an agricultural sense. Irrigation, of course, was the ideal way to ensure such a condition, and in the years to come renewed efforts to conduct water onto the land would be carried out. But in these early postwar years the old temptation to "shotgun" in a crop with the hope that this would be the abnormal wet year in which the grain would grow induced many a Colorado farmer to try his luck again. High prices during the war had made the gamble look realistic, and during that brief period farmers on the plains tore up more sod so that they might increase their stakes in the game. In a single eastern Colorado county (Washington) the number of winter wheat acres leaped from a little over 30,000 in 1917 to 175,000 a mere three years later. Even corn again became an important crop, as farmers sold their livestock and tried to cash in on the grain bonanza.

As the Roaring Twenties sent the nation into a postwar boom after a violent but brief financial recession in the early part of the decade, Colorado made the discovery that its days of financial near-independence were approaching an end. Americans could drink bathtub gin and count their paper profits in this new day of skyrocketing stock prices, but stockmen and farmers had to contend with falling prices and rising rail and tax rates, not to mention increased costs of manufactured products. Now that the war was over Europeans made great efforts to regain a self-sufficiency of their own, while in other grain-producing countries of the world efforts were made to compete with the Americans. Dietary changes that favored nonstarch foods, a declining demand for heavy meals by a growing force of white-collar workers, and an increased grain productivity generated by the opening of new lands during the war years produced an oversupply of cereals. Additionally, the Eighteenth Amendment's prohibition of beer and alcoholic beverages subtracted from the annual consumption of various grains.

Forced to farm as cheaply as possible, the cultivators took higher risks, cultivated minimally, and skimmed off what crop was available by the least expensive means at hand. The emergence of the "suitcase farmer," who lived apart from the land and took his chances with the probability of little moisture and a highly variable yield, spoke of changes in attitudes and in agriculture. The suitcase-farming frontier has been described as covering the Kansas and Colorado section of what soon was to be known as the dust bowl, a semiarid region with less than twenty inches of rainfall each year. That frontier developed between 1921 and 1933. Although charges that this type of farming led to greater neglect of the land have been denied both by the "suitcasers" and by serious students, it is difficult to show that absenteeism has been healthy for any area of the West, Colorado included.[23]

Wartime prices for agricultural products gave impetus to a belated homesteader boom that probably was Colorado's last fling at proving up on free land. It did not occur out on the windswept eastern plains, because most of the land in that area already was under cultivation, but rather developed in northwestern Colorado; like earlier booms, it was the result of a promotional scheme that involved colony effort. Some fifty thousand acres of land were taken up during 1915, thanks mainly to the promotional efforts of

Frederick G. Bonfils of the *Denver Post* and an enterprising individual by the name of Volney T. Hoggatt. The effort of railroad builder David Moffat to send his Denver, Northwestern and Pacific Railroad across that area just prior to this time, and the passage of the Stock-Raising Homestead Act of 1916, whose provisions offered as much as 640 acres of land, further stimulated settlement in this sparsely peopled section of Colorado.

Once more the siren song of the promoters floated eastward and the fresh hordes of settlers listened, hoping for a chance to stake out a claim on yet another "last frontier." Hoggatt, an old-time promoter endowed with the zeal of a Billy Sunday and given the enthusiastic support of Bonfils, who literally donated a weekly magazine called *The Great Divide* to the cause, erupted with an advertising program that gave northwestern Colorado the aura of another Shangri-La. Through the magazine's 100,000 readers enough settlers were attracted to justify the formation of a colony in Moffat County. By the spring of 1916 the Craig area was experiencing a homesteader boom that recalled the land-rush excitement of an earlier day. The surge continued, and by 1920 the Covered Wagon Colony, near Parachute Creek, came into being. Then came the postwar slump, and homesteaders in this rugged land faltered and finally failed. The spirit had been there, and all the enthusiasm of earlier pioneers had kept the little agrarian ventures alive, but the economic facts of life in the postwar grain market made marginal farming too difficult even for colonists grimly determined to stick together and see it through.[24]

Although latter-day homesteaders were willing to try their hands at agricultural "wildcatting," there was increasing recognition of the need for a more stable supply of moisture and further efforts at diversification. The earliest settlers had recognized this, and all during the nineteenth century the "irrigation frontier" of Colorado had crept eastward across the plains country. Periodically the farmers had gotten restive and had tried to bypass this notion, but inevitably dry years and crop failures had turned them back and they had resorted to the ancient method of irrigation. By the early years of the twentieth century the search for additional supplies of water was under way, and one of the sources appeared to be diversion from the western slopes of the Rockies, where supplies were larger than needed at that time.

Cities along the mountain front, fearing that their growth might be limited by the lack of an adequate water supply, joined the campaign for diversion. Even before World War I some of these places enforced limited lawn-sprinkling hours, and Denver, whose boosters worked so industriously to broadcast its virtues, foresaw the need for additional water. There had been a day when Denver thought railroads were the answers to its prayers, and indeed the rails had brought growth, which, in turn, necessitated additional water. In 1920 Mayor Dewey C. Bailey displayed some of the bold imagination witnessed in an earlier generation when he sent water prospectors some seventy miles into the mountains to stake out claims along the westward-flowing Fraser River. He hoped to take advantage of the proposed Moffat Railroad tunnel to conduct water into Denver, and by the mid thirties, indeed, that project's pioneer bore was being used to siphon off water from the Fraser.[25] Shortly after this a second diversion, the Williams Fork Tunnel under Jones Pass, was commenced, and by 1939 it was being used by Denver's sewage disposal plant, the recycled water later utilized for irrigation purposes. Demands for more irrigation water led to yet another tunnel, this one bored under Independence Pass to carry water from the Roaring Fork Basin to Twin Lakes Reservoir, near Leadville, and thence down the Arkansas River for waiting farmers at Rocky Ford and Ordway. Perhaps best known of all is the Colorado–Big Thompson Project that draws water from Grand Lake, the Colorado River's source, eastward through a thirteen-mile tunnel into the Big Thompson River and into the South Platte Valley. Approved by Congress in 1937, it took a full decade before the first water flowed eastward toward waiting farmland.[26]

Ironically it was a case of too much rather than too little water that triggered the west-to-east water diversion projects. The proposed railroad tunnel that Mayor Bailey fixed his eye upon had been a subject of much debate in Colorado, and as late as 1920 voters had rejected the idea because of its cost and also because Pueblo and southern Colorado were jealous of Denver. Then nature came to the rescue with the Pueblo flood of June 1921, a deluge that put part of the steel city's business district under twelve feet of water. Residents of that stricken city now talked loudly about the necessity for a conservancy district. In answer to these demands Governor Oliver H. Shoup called a special session of the General Assembly, but when advocates of flood control discovered that package also included a Moffat Tunnel Bill there were complaints. However, southern Colorado understood that it was being presented with a deal, and both proposals passed. Tunnel construction was to be financed by means of a local improvement district whose taxpayers were supposed to pay the nearly seven-million-dollar cost. Howls of protest arose when they were handed a bill for more than double that amount, but some of the oratorical heat was cooled by the realization that western slope water sources would supply Denver and its environs. The need for additional water even soothed some of those who objected to subsidizing the Moffat Road with public funds.[27] Not only did the pioneer bore of the railroad tunnel open the possibilities for water diversion, but in the aftermath of the Pueblo deluge the notion of flood control along the eastern slope became a subject of great interest.

The postwar era was more than a time of innovative deployment of water by means of transmontane diversions; a series of "treaties" with other neighboring states during this period made history and set precedents. Since the U.S. Constitution did not permit actual treaties between states except in special instances, permission was sought and granted for them to make compacts or agreements with regard to water and timber. Much of the credit for this method, the chief virtue of which was that it avoided extensive and expensive litigation, has been given to a Greeley irrigation attorney named Delph Carpenter who believed that interstate water problems could be solved through cooperation.[28] It was Carpenter who represented Colorado as it worked out a division of the South Platte's waters with Commissioner Robert H. Willis of Nebraska in 1925. In a similar agreement Colorado and New Mexico made an amicable division of La Plata River water that flowed southward from the San Juan country.

The most far-reaching of the compacts emerged from the Colorado River conference held at Santa Fe in November 1922. Here the states of Colorado, Wyoming, New Mexico, Arizona, Utah, Nevada, and California joined with representatives of the federal government and of Mexico and sat down to discuss the equitable use of an increasingly vital western resource. Led by Commerce Secretary Herbert Hoover, the group concluded that the Colorado River drainage was to be divided into the upper and lower basins, the boundary to be at Lee's Ferry, in northern Arizona. The upper basin covered portions of Colorado, New Mexico, Utah, and Wyoming; the lower basin was carved from the remaining states. The two sections divided the available water, leaving a surplus for contingencies and for use by Mexico should that country later make demands for water that were recognized by the United States. The agreement, much of which was written by Delph Carpenter, was known as the Colorado River Compact or sometimes as the Santa Fe Compact, and although years passed before all its details were settled, this historic document not only led to the construction of Boulder Dam but was a landmark in western interstate diplomacy.[29]

By the 1920s another Colorado resource was in great demand. Oil, once regarded as useful principally for illumination or lubrication, now was useful as a fuel to provide home heat or, in the form of gasoline, to operate the internal combustion engines that powered automobiles, tractors, airplanes, and motorboats. Nationally, this was the decade of the automobile, an era that in 1924 saw Henry Ford drive down the price of his vehicle to an all-time record low of $290, and one in which General Motors moved into the automotive field in force. After producing fifteen million units of his famed Model T, Henry Ford turned to the equally famous Model A and outsold the combined efforts of General Motors. The family car came into such demand that in 1923 Walter Chrysler, who earlier had worked as a mechanic in the Denver and Rio Grande Railroad's Salt Lake City shops, organized his own company; within a few years he offered the public a rival to the Ford and Chevrolet—a small car called the Plymouth. In 1920 the American automotive industry produced just under two million cars annually; by 1929 the figure approached five million. It was this item of merchandise, one that became the favorite of American buyers, that was to present demands upon the domestic petroleum industry that one day would outstrip its ability to produce.

The sharply increased demand for petroleum products sent a whole new group of prospectors called petroleum geologists scurrying into the field. During the twenties major oil discoveries were made in a number of locations in the American West, some of them in Colorado. Of great interest was the Wellington dome, north of Fort Collins, brought in during 1923, and the Moffat and Iles domes developed near Craig. During that same period the Tow Creek field, in Routt County, began to produce.

Until that time Colorado's production had been small. Beginning in 1862, when the owner of a small "oil spring" near Canon City sold small quantities of oil to Denver, Pueblo, and Santa Fe for about five dollars a gallon, the local industry grew very slowly. By the mid 1860s between twenty-five and thirty barrels of oil were produced daily at Canon City and Denver businessmen were excited over the prospect of a strike near Golden. Such well-known Coloradans as Governor Cummings and W. A. H. Loveland became involved in the formation of an oil company to extract what the *Rocky Mountain News* called "the precious liquid."[30] This early oil excitement came to nothing, and even in what became known as the Florence field, near Canon City, the production was limited because of a small demand for the product at that time. By the 1880s that field had a number of producing wells and three refineries with a combined capacity of three thousand barrels a day, but little of the product was being sold outside the region. In 1911 the Florence field was said to be controlled by a Standard Oil subsidiary known as the United Oil Company of Denver. A few independents operated there, but lacking a market of their own they sold to United for a dollar a barrel. There was some talk that natural gas one day would prove to be an asset to Colorado, but in the early days of the twentieth century that product was far from developed in terms of practical use.[31]

Although there was talk of an oil boom in Colorado shortly after 1900, when a number of holes were put down in various sections of the state, there were at that time only two bona fide fields where oil was produced commercially: Florence and Boulder. At the latter place an oil well known as the McKenzie, drilled almost at random, gave such favorable results that by 1903 more than a hundred rigs sprouted just northeast of that quiet university town. When a two-hundred-and-fifty barrel "gusher" was brought in during 1908, the Boulder field attracted even more attention, but after that there was little to boast about. By 1917 the total production of the field amounted to no more than six thousand barrels and by 1923 perhaps a dozen wells were at work, producing only a few barrels a day.[32] About the time the Boulder field first made news, oil was discovered in far western Colorado, at De Beque, a find that produced more excitement than oil. The western slope's Rangely field dated from 1911, but by the mid-twenties it was producing only about a hundred barrels a week. Nevertheless, by that time Colorado petroleum production had hit an all time high of five million dollars, thanks to production in the Wellington and Moffat domes. Before the state's oil resources were able to contribute heavily to the economy, the Great Depression struck. By 1933 production had sunk to just over a half-million dollars' worth per year. Not until the years of World War II did the local industry recover.

For decades one of Colorado's much-talked-about petroleum potentials has been oil shale. Neither oil nor shale, but rather an organic marlstone from which an incompletely developed oil called kerogen is produced by applying heat, the substance is found in great quantity in the northwest corner of the state. One of the most commonly told stories about the early discovery of shale oil concerns Mike Calahan's housewarming party. The rancher, who had equipped his new home with a giant fireplace made of black rock found in the Rifle neighborhood, proudly lit the fire. The logs, then the fireplace itself, and finally the entire house went up in a spectacular blaze that quickly ended the evening's festivities.

Even before the 1920s, when more traditional oil extraction in Colorado grew rapidly, oil shale received considerable publicity. Between 1915 and 1920 a boom developed that saw some thirty thousand claims staked on about four million acres of Colorado. Based on the 1872 mining law, these claims were made so rapidly that sometimes they were piled one atop another on the same land. The 1920 Mineral Leasing Act tried to clear up the confusion by holding that publicly owned shale lands could be leased only from the Secretary of the Interior. But the initial momentum of the boom carried it forward, and by 1921 there were over two hundred and fifty companies in this country listed as oil shale firms. Only nineteen of them had erected experimental plants or had indicated that they were anything but "paper" organizations. A great many of the companies were formed for no other purpose than to defraud investors, and when it became apparent that this means of oil extraction was commercially unprofitable under the existing price structure, this aspect of oil prospecting earned a very unsavory name. Since ordinary oil, drilled in the traditional manner, found a declining market with the onset of the depression, the possible use of oil shale fell back into the realm of theory. The notion came out of hibernation from time to time in the coming years, but it was not until the "crunch" of the 1970s that much more than experimentation resulted from the talk this interesting phenomenon generated.[33]

The great demand among Americans for petroleum products reflected an increasing use of the automobile, not only for purposes of business or Sunday joyriding, but also as a means of traveling far afield on vacation trips enjoyed by the entire family. Almost overnight the nation plunged into what became known as the "gasoline age," and as the number of automobiles multiplied, the demand for better roads upon which to operate them increased. Supplied with his own vehicle, the average American longed for the open road and adventure in parts of the country unknown to him; frequently he headed for the Rocky Mountains and their fabled scenery. Coloradans, who had seen the possibilities of tourism since the days when recreational railroad travel had become popular, realized that the automobile held great promise for travelers who sought both independence and economy on their summer outings. The mountains and the "champagne air" long had been an attraction for those in more humid climates. These resources still beckoned.

It was the automobile and the rapid development of Colorado highways during these years that altered the nature of the seasonal invasion of tourists and caused it to grow to such proportions that one day the tourist industry would rank very close to the top in annual revenues.[34] But this turn of events did not happen by accident. As early as 1905 the state's Good Roads Association was organized, and in the ensuing years a great deal of effort was put into highway construction so that the new "tin-can" tourist could make his way to points of scenic interest. During 1913, for example, state penitentiary warden Tom Tynan's convicts were hard at work improving the road from Canon City to the Royal Gorge overlook, an eight-mile stretch that was cut out of solid rock. At that time there was talk of constructing a suspension bridge across the gorge, a plan that when carried out later made the area increasingly attractive as a tourist spot. For the moment, however, the road builders were concerned with building a feeder to what then was referred to as the "new Santa Fe speedway," an automobile highway that ran from Independence, Missouri, through Kansas, and to Pueblo, Colorado, along the old Santa Fe Trail.[35]

The efforts of Tom Tynan's "boys" typified the activity of Colorado road builders in general at that time. From 1914, when the state had just under twelve hundred miles of improved roads, construction was carried on so intensively that within little over a decade the mileage of improved roads jumped to more than eighty-five hundred. And, by that later date, more adventurous motorists could work their way into some of the less populated areas by means of nearly sixty thousand miles of unimproved passageways. In 1916 the federal government entered the picture, offering the states financial aid for such construction, and this support, augmented by subsequent legislation, lent an impetus to highway building for an increasing number of automobiles. As this new pleasure and business vehicle became cheaper, and consequently more readily available to the average family, rail passenger travel declined. The high point in that mode of travel was reached as early as 1910 and never again was approached except during such unusual periods as the two world wars. When authorization was granted for the operation of a bus line between Denver and Boulder in 1919, a new threat to rail travel appeared. Within the next six years more than fifty such permits were issued for similar lines that served some seventeen hundred miles of improved roads.[36] As new roads opened for private automobiles, buses, and trucks, Colorado's cool mountains beckoned to a wider group of tourists than ever before, and thousands answered the call.

To accommodate the new mechanized brigade that invaded the Rockies, some of the cities along the mountain front provided camps for the new species that one writer called the "migratory motorist." Starting in 1915 Denver provided a five-acre free camping ground where sawed and split firewood at first was given away. During the summer of 1917 over three thousand cars, carrying more than twelve thousand passengers, stopped at this campground. Apparently these "nomads of the steering wheel" were not concerned about wartime gasoline shortages, for they drifted in from thirty-eight different states. So great was the rush that the next year Denver set aside sixty acres and established a second camp, in Genesee Park. Cold showers were provided, but this year tourists had to pay five cents for enough firewood to cook a meal, so great had been the wastage the year before. However, bricks were provided for those who wanted to make small fireplaces, and even a row of electric cookers was set up for use by those who did not care for campfires. Hydrants provided free water, city water trucks sprinkled down dusty roadways, and at night arc lights suspended from tree branches illuminated the encampment. Fishing was available in adjacent Rocky Mountain Lake, and for the children there was a nearby playground. More seasoned campers usually chose to move into the mountains twenty to thirty-five miles westward where less sophisticated but still comfortable campgrounds were available.[37]

In the early autumn of 1918 a couple from Indiana drove out to Colorado and became one of the many auto tourists to invade the Rockies that season. In a series of four articles published in *Outing* the lady described road conditions and the adventures of climbing high mountain passes in an underpowered and frequently overheated car. She spent a great deal of her time hurrying a stone to one of the back wheels to keep the vehicle from rolling downhill while her husband ministered to the wants of the radiator. After repeating the process a number of times she confessed to feeling "like a worn-out emergency brake." The main challenge was revealed in the title of her series: "Storming Berthoud Pass." This barrier successfully overcome, they visited some of the cities in the area and then returned to Denver. The author was impressed by the former mining camps, places she found quiet but by no means desolated. At Idaho Springs, for example, she observed "the steep little quiet streets, the unhurried detached-looking inhabitants, everywhere there is an air of satisfied prosperity." She explained why this and similar little towns had not surrendered to decay. "Indeed why shouldn't they be prosperous? Every summer thousands of automobile tourists pass this way each day. And gasoline retails at something like forty cents a gallon!"[38]

Although travel to Europe would enjoy a great postwar boom, the "See America First" movement was under way in the West, and the main troops in the army of tourists to reinvade that part of the country were families traveling by car and frequently burdened down with camping equipment. "Why should Americans go abroad to see the sights of foreign lands, who have not the faintest conception of the wonders of our own land to be found by getting away from the regular lines of travel?" asked one of Colorado's naturalists.[39] The answer came in a new rush to the Rockies, this time carried out by thousands who wanted to see and to enjoy, not to dig. So great was the invasion that one of the more discriminating visitors complained about his inability to find some place in the state that "the tenderfoot had not yet profaned with the 'great American tin can.' " He found temporary refuge in the San Juan Mountains where both the geography and the musical Spanish names soothed his shattered nerves.[40]

Attitudes had changed much since the Anglo miners had mispronounced Spanish names purposely and had resented their use. Now the mountains were valuable not so much for what lay hidden in them as for the beauty of their forms and the music in their names. Hamlin Garland felt the poetry of those lofty peaks when he recalled his honeymoon days among them.[41] The lady motorist from Indiana also felt the magic as she stood at the top of Berthoud Pass and looked across endless miles at the panorama below. "There was an aching catch in my throat and tears of wonder and joy in my eyes," she wrote. "All outdoors to be had for the mere asking. Surely this is the very apotheosis of the pleasure that God can give to his creatures."[42] Her reaction to the massiveness of the Rockies and the distances that might be seen from these elevations was shared by one of the state's more renowned visitors. Sir Arthur Conan Doyle was surprised at the width of the mountain range in Colorado, remarking that "an enormous tuck seems to have been taken in the earth's outer garment at this spot."[43] It was this "tuck" that produced the high parks sought earlier by the miners, then by the cattlemen, and finally by those in search of recreation.

God's creatures, as the visiting Hoosier had called them, responded to the call of the Rockies in increasing numbers during the postwar years. As early as 1919, asserted a Denver newspaper, a million tourists visited Colorado; the national parks within its boundaries were becoming major American tourist attractions. Denver, of course, was pleased, for it now regarded itself as the "gateway to the gateways of the national parks." In 1915 about thirty-one thousand tourists had stopped at Rocky Mountain National Park, but by 1919 the figure had climbed to just under a hundred and seventy thousand, a number that exceeded the total of the visitors to Yellowstone, Yosemite, Glacier, and Sequoia parks combined. Even more encouraging to Denver was the length of time tourists were spending in the mile-high city. Instead of a few hours, many of them now stayed for two or three weeks, changing the classification of that city from a "stopover" to a "point of destination." In response to such interest almost a half-million pieces of descriptive literature, booklets, and postcards had been mailed to all parts of the nation. Almost forty-four thousand people came to the capital city's Tourist Bureau to make personal inquiries during the 1919 season, and more conventions were held in Denver that year than at any time since the bureau had kept records. The Queen City's hotels and rooming houses did a thriving business. So did the campsites in Rocky Mountain Park, where nearly forty-seven hundred automobiles turned up that season. Kansas and Nebraska license plates were the most numerous, but

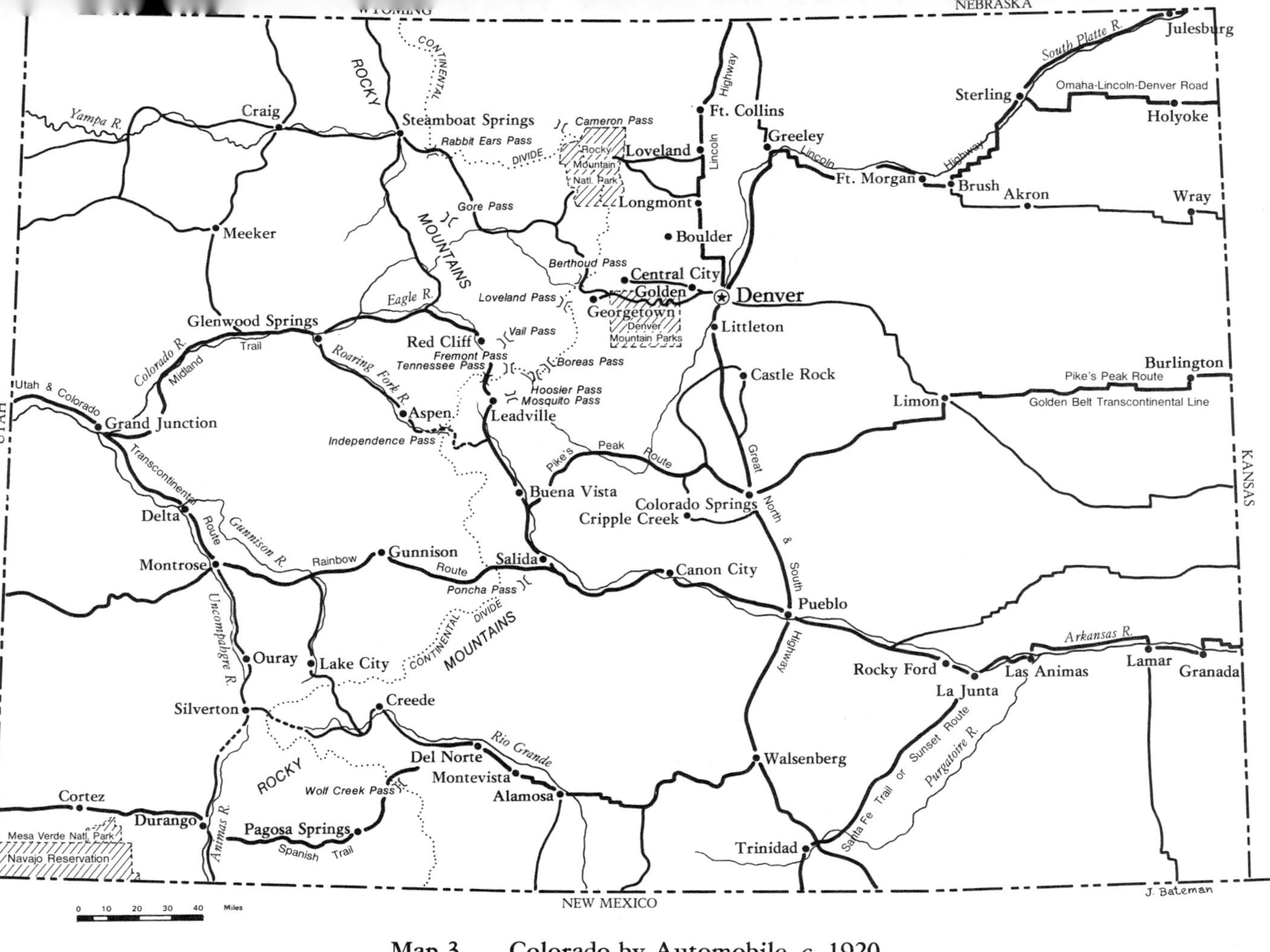


Map 3 Colorado by Automobile, c. 1920

there were a great many from as far away as New York, which led all the eastern states.

Colorado's national parks and their feeder cities were not the only points of interest for tourists in those early postwar years. In that same season of 1919 more than a million people came to the state's sixteen national forests, and it was estimated that they left some ten million dollars behind. These visitors came from every state in the Union and from twenty-three foreign countries. While many of them still came by rail, and then moved around by chartered or regularly scheduled modes of highway transportation, a significantly large number arrived in their own automobiles. Approximately one hundred eighty-five thousand automobiles, carrying six hundred sixty-five thousand passengers, made their way over mountain passes and through the forests. Head counts made at such places as Monarch Pass indicated that about 60 percent came from Colorado and the remainder from the other states and foreign countries. It was of great interest to Coloradans that the out-of-state count mounted steadily; it meant that increasing amounts of "outside" money were being left behind.[44]

In 1928 tourists were said to have left thirty-nine million dollars in Colorado. So said the Denver Tourist and Publicity Bureau, located on Seventeenth Street, with branch offices in six large American cities. Although rail travel slowly yielded to automobile traffic, the figures for that year indicated that of the total amount of tourist money spent in Colorado, railroad passengers accounted for twenty-two million. The other seventeen million were left by motorists who flocked to the forests and parks, some three hundred seventy-five thousand of them visiting the Rocky Mountain Park area that included Estes Park and Grand Lake. Over a half-million more viewed the Pike's Peak country, and almost seventeen thousand worked their way as far west in the state as Mesa Verde National Park. In the state's 350 auto parks some seven hundred fifty thousand tourists took their vacations, enjoying the climate and fishing the streams. Advertising in twelve national magazines and twenty-seven newspapers apparently was paying off.[45]

While the flow of visitors to Colorado poured in by train, bus, and automobile, a new means of transportation that one day would command a very large share of such travel made its appearance in the state. On a bright May morning in 1926 a small biplane flew in from the north, circled over Denver, and then came in for a precise landing at Don Hogan Airport. Piloting the craft was Erland L.

Curtis; he had just flown plane no. 14 of Colorado Airways, Inc., from Cheyenne to deliver the first airmail into Colorado. A mail bag was tossed out of the aircraft and whisked downtown to the post office, as other sacks were loaded into another plane that was bound for Colorado Springs and Pueblo. Denver's introduction to airmail service was momentarily marred by the refusal of that aircraft's motor to run smoothly, necessitating the use of a substitute plane, but despite this minor delay, history had been made. The events of that morning foreshadowed the coming of a day when not only mail, but passengers, would arrive at and depart from the capital city.[46]

Despite the pleasure experienced by the onlookers who watched Captain Curtis maneuver his airplane, there was irony in the situation. When the long-awaited airmail service had been announced in 1920, Coloradans learned that once again they had been bypassed in transcontinental transportation developments. Like the earlier Union Pacific Railroad, now the main air route was laid out from Omaha to Cheyenne and on to Utah. The mountain barrier, the "Apennines" of which Senator Sumner had spoken so long ago, still served as a great partition between eastern and western Colorado. Thus while the state was served early and well by railroads, both from the East and between Colorado cities themselves, the main range of the Rockies frequently made travel slow, particularly during the winter months. Commercial air service promised to alleviate the geographical problem of the continental divide, as well as that of poor north-south service and great distances from other major communities. The hope stayed alive during the thirties, but it was not until the close of World War II that direct service "over the hump" would straighten out some of Colorado's twisting transportation routes.

During the twenties, however, it was a moot point whether letters sent by air went over the Colorado Rockies or around them, for the system was faster than surface mail and gradually the public accepted it. During the remaining seven months of 1926, after that memorable day at Don Hogan Field, Colorado Airways flew seventy-five thousand miles on the Cheyenne-Pueblo run and carried over seventeen thousand pounds of cargo for which it received forty-seven thousand dollars. During the next year the line earned over sixty cents per revenue mile, being one of only four airmail carriers to report such earnings.

If Coloradans were willing to fly their letters, they showed no interest in risking their persons in these little two-cockpit biplanes. A few venturesome souls rode the front, or mail, cockpit at first, but the early passenger service boom died aborning. During the first six months of 1927 the total number of revenue passengers on Colorado Airways was two. It was not so much a lack of courage as it was the absence of convenience that prevented Coloradans from becoming airline-minded. "Residents of Pueblo or Colorado Springs who made a trip to Denver by air gained only a small saving in time over the train or automobile at extra cost and considerable hardship," wrote one historian who described the discomforts of a lumbering, open-cockpit biplane that offered gas fumes, noise, and blasts of icy wind in lieu of tea, coffee, or cocktails. A lack of passenger connections with other airlines cut into the potential for feeder lines. When a Chicago woman tried to bring her two children home by air from their Colorado vacation, she was told that only government mail flew between Cheyenne and her city. Undaunted, she asked the Colorado Springs postmaster to tag the youngsters and mail them back at the rate of $3.20 a pound, but the official had to refuse because regulations would not allow "perishable matter" to be carried in the mail planes.[47]

In 1927 Colorado Airways lost its mail contract and Boeing Air Transport, an operator serving the Chicago–San Francisco run, took over the Cheyenne-Pueblo branch until a new contract was awarded, this time to Western Air Express. United Air lines, successor to Boeing Air Transport, later gained the Cheyenne-Denver portion of the old mail route, succeeding a small outfit known as Varney Speed Lines. The loss of the mail route, coupled with the onset of the depression and some bad publicity resulting from crashes, put Colorado Airways out of business, but the seed had been planted and from it grew a number of successful air transport ventures that made Denver a major center for the new mode of travel.[48] By the thirties, a decade that was to be important in the development of commercial aviation in Colorado, the state had five commercial fields, one army field, and thirty-two airports. Of the commercial fields, Denver had two, Colorado Springs, Florence, and Salida each one. The facility at Colorado Springs was the Alexander Airport, named for the aircraft factory of the same name located at that city.[49]

The lack of public interest in Colorado Airways strongly suggested that there was no pressing necessity for such service at that time, yet the inauguration of these flights hinted at progress and placed Colorado on the nation's air map, if in name only. Such an inclusion during the prosperous, exuberant twenties was regarded as yet another indication of the state's economic well-being and a further example of its progressive thinking.

During these years the Coloradans, with the rest of the American people, plunged headlong toward the financial abyss known as the Great Depression, but in their innocence they thought they were simply preparing for an assault upon new and headier economic heights. Coloradans were very much in the mainstream of national thinking when they purred over the unprecedented prosperity and made elaborate predictions of future happiness and well-being. In its 1929 "Glory Edition," published as usual on New Year's Day, the *Denver Post* printed a "Sermon for the New Year" in which it announced, "The world's best year is closing. During 1928 God has given us His choicest blessings, material and spiritual, and today the world is better in every way than ever it has been before. And 1929 will be greater even than the year of 1928. What a blessed privilege it is to live in this age of the world's progress and advancement and spirituality and intelligence." It asked readers to be optimists, for there was no room for pessimists in the world. To show its own optimism the *Post* included a front-page story about a scientist who predicted a hundred-year life-span for earthly mortals who presently enjoyed a happiness and prosperity hitherto unknown to man.[50]

Evidence of prosperity appeared on all sides. Hoover's recent election, in November 1928, had sent the stock market soaring to new heights. "Dozen issues smash all-time records after Hoover victory," said a Denver newspaper. Locally the stockyards set a postwar record for volume, an achievement so encouraging that a hundred and fifty thousand dollars were set aside for improvements in anticipation of an even greater year in 1929. In this giddy period, when Americans cockily sang a tune called "My God How the Money Rolls In," they made almost embarrassed jokes about their financial successes. Denverites appreciated the *Post*'s anecdote in which Mrs. Housekeeper asked the applicant for a cooking job her reason for leaving her previous employment, to which the cook responded, "The poor simps were trying to live within their income."[51] It was a time when to attempt such a thing almost profaned the riches that poured in; to spend only the money one took in appeared to be unsporting. In the days that lay ahead such attitudes would be regarded as a form of madness, but during the twenties few people openly questioned personal deficit spending, known by its more popular title, installment buying. It all seemed to indicate an unbounded faith in America and an admission of the perfect ability of the American dream. Indeed, it appeared that to live in Colorado was a special kind of privilege.

# 14

# In the Valley of Doubt

Between the two world wars Colorado grew slowly and witnessed few significant changes. During these years California increased its population by 66 percent, Arizona by 30, and the nation by 16, but Colorado's advance was held to about 10 percent. The state's declining rate of growth—it would drop to about 8.5 percent during the 1930s—was not the result of any effort on the part of its people to control such statistics. During those years the mining and agricultural sectors showed signs of weakness and there was little expansion of manufacturing to take up the slack. It was a blow to civic pride to realize that fewer people than before were excited by the prospect of living among the privileged in Colorado.

The boosters knew that there were economic problems, but such things never were admitted publicly. At the beginning of the twenties predictions were made that Colorado was about to regain its title "the Silver State," that a healthy revival of mining was just around the corner. The basis for this false optimism was the presence of mineral experts in Colorado who were examining the possibilities of opening up some of the old mines at such places as Westcliff, Breckenridge, Aspen, and Leadville. The existing price of silver, $1.30 an ounce, was believed to be sufficient to justify such developments.[1] The hopeful talk did not subside during the remainder of the decade, and with the election of Herbert Hoover in 1928 it was argued further that the presence of the great engineer in the White House, plus recent advances in metallurgical science, somehow would put the state back at the top as a silver producer. The *Denver Post* commented that Colorado not only deserved such a reputation but was the only state in the union that had deposits of every kind of precious metals, base metals, and almost all of the nonferrous metals.[2] The optimists were whistling in the dark, for all during the decade the value of Colorado's precious metals output had sagged, with silver leading the decline. The white metal's production value had been reduced from about five million dollars to about a million and a half. Gold fell off by about a third. Even though copper, zinc, and lead showed an increase, the total value of all five of these metals diminished.[3]

Low prices for agricultural and mineral products during the twenties worried Coloradans, and they recalled the Populist message of economic salvation. In a strangely reminiscent mood the *Denver Post* made noises late in 1929 that sounded familiar. The spokesman for the idea, Frederick G. Bonfils, argued that high rail rates might have been necessary in an earlier day, when the roads had fought for their very existence in a thinly populated land, but now there was no justification for such high charges. Bonfils strongly suggested that the plains and mountain states should join in a Rocky Mountain League of States, the combined power of which could force the railroads to reduce rates. Local manufacturing, long desired, not only would help to free the region from outside financial control and broaden the local employment base, but the savings on transportation costs would be substantial. Calling for "justice" and a "square deal," the publisher promised that through collective action the West could demand and get its fair share of income. His comment, "We want our place in the sun," echoed a familiar western theme.[4]

It was an uncertain moment for Coloradans. While they understood that the wheels of economic activity had slowed during the twenties, and they looked forward as always to brighter and better days, there was an added cloud on the horizon. In October the stock market had reached dizzying heights and then had peeled off for a dive of breathtaking proportions. As 1929 closed no one yet knew what the result might be. In the presidential election of 1928 Coloradans had gone to the polls and had voted, as ever cautious white, Anglo-Saxon Protestants, to turn back the threat of papism and strong drink represented by Alfred E. Smith, whose Catholicism and indifference to the Prohibition law had generated strong criticism among the American hundred-percenters. The *Denver Post* praised the electorate for its presumed reaffirmation of faith in the Volstead Act, but it wisely refrained from agitating the religious issue in a state where the number of Catholics had shown a steady increase for several decades.

The *Post* not only expressed great happiness over the selection of Herbert Hoover, but in its postelection euphoria it went so far as to assert that the recent vote had destroyed the Democratic Party. If this were true the newspaper somehow had to account for the election of Democrat Billy Adams to the governorship. Its explanation was that he had not pardoned a single criminal, had not offered reprieves to any candidates for capital punishment, and that he had given the people an able and honest administration. It might have been mentioned, also, that the governor was a very conservative man. As such he and Representative Edward T. Taylor were the only candidates for major office to survive the Republican sweep.[5]

Despite the sluggishness of mining and agriculture, Colorado businessmen maintained their optimism, and as 1929 came to a close they took the traditional attitude that the next twelve months would be bigger and better. The *Post* talked of the golden dreams realized during the past year and stoutly maintained that the local economy was showing constant improvement. Denver, still regarded as the state's economic barometer, was said to be growing at a modest but healthy rate, a condition that promised both happiness and prosperity in the days that lay ahead.[6]

However, there were some discordant sounds in the Queen City of the Plains. Less than two months after the *Post* had issued its "all's well" bulletin, Arthur C. Johnson of Denver's *Record Stockman* noted that the price of sheep was the lowest since 1921, and within a few days anxious telegrams were on their way to Washington, D.C., complaining about depressed conditions among western stock growers. By mid March Johnson was listening to luncheon conversations terming Hoover a "dud," a charge he thought unfair so early in the new president's administration. But, he admitted, "there *is* depression and unemployment as there always is in the spring, it seems." By fall the situation was even worse. "Stock market dropping every day . . . where's the bottom," Johnson asked in September. "Hard times seem to be running throughout the world. Auto business, especially, is at low ebb." Puzzled, he noted that despite hard times miniature golf courses abounded. Already Americans were in search of diversions to take their minds off disturbing news from the business world. Theaters took advantage of the willingness of artists and musicians to work more cheaply and they began to offer stage shows in addition to films. Johnson, who thought this a good way to escape the gloom, remarked that he had attended a show at the Tabor where the management was "filling 'em up at 25 cts." As a Coloradan interested in the livestock industry he noticed that the desire for light entertainment apparently did not include Denver's famed stock show that was offered each January. As the economic picture darkened, that usually popular event drew fewer and fewer spectators and participants.[7]

Since economic difficulties traditionally create greater interest among the voters, the midterm elections of 1930 saw issues more sharply drawn than usual. The senatorial race between Democrat Edward P. Costigan and Republican George H. Shaw attracted particular attention. The *Denver Post* argued that to maintain the already "splendid business health of this state" Shaw should be elected. He was an advocate of high tariffs, and it was this barrier, the most recent of which was the Hawley-Smoot tariff, that the *Post* erroneously thought would ensure national prosperity through protection. Not only were Colorado sugar beets of vital importance to the local economy, said the *Post*, but the sugar factories were the second largest consumers of coal, and if the beet industry was ruined, coal mines would close.

Then there was the red menace to be considered. "Attempts of radical leaders, strike agitators, Communists, Russian Reds and others of that stripe to interfere in Colorado's selection of a United States Senator have aroused the wrath of the Colorado voters," announced Denver's leading proponent of red-blooded Americanism. As a result of this patriotic indignation, predicted the editor, Shaw was expected to win by at least fifty thousand votes. But the voters were not as wrathful as they were said to be and Costigan won by a margin of forty thousand votes. Billy Adams was returned to the governor's office because, as the Pueblo *Chieftain* remarked, the ensuing two years promised to be "years of much depression and distress during which a firm hand and an experienced hand will be needed at the helm of the state. It is no time to experiment." Yet, Coloradans must have been willing to experiment at the national level, for these traditionally conservative people were willing to send Costigan, a thoroughgoing Wilsonian liberal, a dedicated reformer, and a precursor of the New Deal, to Washington, D.C.[8]

The *Chieftain*'s gloomy view that the immediate future would be one of depression and distress was no outburst of unrealistic pessimism. After 1929 the state's petroleum output dropped sharply, and it showed no signs of recovery during the next ten years. Coal production fell off by nearly fifty percent during this period and the number of wage earners in the state declined by a third. There were no strikes in the state during the year 1930; their absence suggested the insecurity of workers in troublous times. Another unfavorable indicator was the sharp decline in visitors to Rocky Mountain National Park that year. The farmers, who had not fully recovered from the maladjustments that followed World War I, now suffered even more. Between 1929 and 1932 grain and hay prices dropped to new lows and apples were left rotting because their owners did not want to take forty-two cents a bushel for them. Twelve-dollar hogs now went for as little as three dollars. "Agriculture is in a desperate plight and must have some help," concluded a farm journal editor."[9]

As the economic situation deteriorated, money became tighter. By 1933 less than half as many banks were open than had functioned a decade earlier. "Banks are bursting right along," wrote one Denverite early that year. The financial drought was also reflected in declining college enrollments. As early as 1930 there were complaints from Boulder that if more of the students could not find some kind of work they would have to drop out. Their parents, many of whom lived in Colorado's numerous small towns, simply were not making enough to keep them in school. "Even in prosperous Boulder more money to provide for families of the unemployed is asked for—seems to be needed," said the editor of that university town's newspaper.[10]

For those whose wages had been cut, or whose income was reduced through falling prices, there were some compensations. In 1930 Arthur Johnson had commented that a new suit cost him sixty-three dollars, an article of merchandise that would have cost seventy-five or a hundred dollars a year earlier. Three years later he noted that a good suit of clothes could be bought for twenty dollars. By then Lucky Strike cigarettes were selling at eleven cents a pack and restaurant meals for twenty-five cents.[11]

Also relatively inexpensive were the means of whiling away the time until work was available or the depression slackened. As mentioned, movie theater admissions cost little. Thousands of people turned to books, and the many libraries across the state experienced sharply increased circulation figures. In addition there was a new means of communication and entertainment: the radio. The 1920s had been the big decade for the development of this household instrument and by 1930 every third American home had one. With the introduction of chain broadcasting, in the mid twenties, people in the most remote corners of the country were able to hear all types of programs, including news, sports, political events, and music.

Colorado approximated the national average for radio sets in 1930; about 38 percent of the homes owned one. The state's distribution, however, was quite uneven, with Jefferson County homes having nearly 55 percent of the total and Conejos County, in the southern part of the state, having only 4.5 percent. The state's radio broadcasting facilities originated in 1919 when a Colorado Springs doctor began to transmit on a special amateur's license. He moved to Denver the next year, where he expanded his services to include market and weather reports and Sunday sermons of local pastors. The first commercial license was issued to station KLZ in the spring of 1922, and two years later a second station, KOA, was on the air. As the depression worsened and the decade took on the name the "dirty thirties," more and more families turned to the radio as an opiate that would help to drown out the real world. "Radio, radio, all day," grumbled one inveterate reader. "The radio steals so much of our former reading time."[12]

But the real world was hard to wipe out. The coal industry, already sick, was struck a hard blow in the late twenties when a natural gas line was brought into Colorado from the Texas Panhandle. The only bright spot for the miners was the acquisition of control of the Rocky Mountain Fuel Company by Josephine Roche, who long had been interested in social problems. She shocked the business establishment by allowing her coal company to be the first to unionize, at the highest wages, in that state-wide industry. When rival companies struck back by cutting prices Miss Roche's employees placed with her three months of their pay as a loan. The principal opponent was the Rockefeller-owned Colorado Fuel and Iron Company, a nonunion firm. In 1932 the C.F.&I. attempted to reduce wages for a second time within two years, arguing that it no longer could compete with eastern steel manufacturers, but the State Industrial Commission disapproved, calling working conditions among miners "deplorable." The miners, said the commission, were slowly being driven into industrial slavery; it lamented the "human price" being exacted for the production of coal.[13]

As gloom pervaded the atmosphere, more and more people began to be affected. By the autumn of 1931 those who were still working at Colorado Springs were asked to give a half day's pay each month for a six-month period to alleviate suffering from cold and hunger among the city's poor. The call was issued in behalf of those "whose birth-right has been swept away by the winds of chance and circumstance," to use the expression of a local newspaper.[14] Representative of those whose birthright had been swept away were the members of a Denver family, a couple and their six children, who were taken into court and fined ten dollars for rummaging through the garbage cans of a local restaurant in search of a few bones and some crusts of bread. When a small-town editor read of this action he stated publicly that if he were the judge he would resign before imposing such a sentence.[15]

Colorado Springs faced yet another dilemma. For years it had advertised itself as a health spa, and a great deal of money had been collected from the "lungers," but not all who came were wealthy. The local economy had been able to aid some of the ailing of small means, and until the depression this had not become a serious civic problem. Now there were suggestions that the city, faced by declining municipal revenues, show a little restraint when advertising its salubrious climate. This raised objections from those who feared a loss of income from a business that had taken up slack when the mineral boom had faded. Unhappily, no means had been devised of formulating advertising read only by wealthy invalids.[16]

Efforts by cities such as Colorado Springs to provide relief money through salary donations underscored a problem that was to complicate the state's deteriorating economic situation. Colorado had neither a sales tax nor an income tax; its principal source of revenue was from property taxation. In 1931 farmers called upon Governor Adams for tax relief, but since he had been presented with a deficit of well over a million dollars when he assumed office four years earlier, and because he was determined to reduce that indebtedness, the petitioners had little hope of gaining relief from that direction. Meanwhile, farm prices remained low and the economy in general showed few signs of improvement; therefore, despite all efforts to trim governmental expenses, the deficit remained. Locked into the philosophy of watchful waiting, Colorado simply drifted, awaiting some fresh breeze to fill the fiscal sails and get things moving again.[17] In the meantime the state made no moves in the direction of relief.

Unable to get any aid from the state, some of Denver's business and civic leaders turned to the vaunted philosophy of self-help and private enterprise. In the spring of 1932 they resolved to reduce the city's unemployment through cooperative efforts. Led by Charles D. Strong, an architect whose practice had become a victim of the depression, a committee of unemployed professional men organized an Unemployed Citizens' League, copied from a similar effort at Seattle. Without funds, using only donated facilities and goods, the group set out to provide employment for the needy. The concept caught on, and by 1933 it reported some thirty-four thousand members. The league engaged in a number of activities, including the operation of a bakery, mining, timber cutting, shoe repairing, barbering, and the repair of unoccupied buildings tó provide housing. It even rehabilitated an old printing press and issued a weekly paper called *Dawn*. Employing the talents of some eighty-four different occupations, the organization credited its members with hours worked which, in turn, were convertible into an appropriate quantity of supplies. As it did in other sections of the nation, the old barter system temporarily replaced the use of money as a medium of exchange.[18]

Although the league's efforts were commendable, the resultant program was a stopgap measure and did not alleviate the basic frustration of the people. There was violence in the air, and early in 1932 a group of angry women voiced it when they milled about the Larimer County Courthouse, demanding lower taxes. A few weeks later some two hundred farmers staged a similar demonstration at Sedgwick, a performance that proved to be a mere prelude to a much more serious confrontation at Denver. Coloradans who watched or read about that disturbance, where shouting demonstrators surrounded the Capitol and angrily demanded relief from taxes, now began to understand some of the deeper implications of the general economic difficulty.

It was bad enough to witness mob action among householders who were presumed to be among the privileged in this mountain Utopia, but when nationally read journalists scorned the place as just another rotten borough, it cut to the quick. In two articles published in the spring of 1932 the *Atlantic Monthly* attacked the West, including Colorado, as a place where "sagebrush senators" voted along narrow, selfish, sectional lines and as a part of the nation supported by taxes of the more populous East. One of the authors dismissed "these miserable western states" as offering nothing but a drain on the rest of the country, and he called upon Colorado and its neighbors to relinquish their two senators each or get out of the Union. He thought one senator for the whole mountain West more than enough representation, for this was the least populated area of the civilized world. A defender of this presumably desolate part of the nation pointed out that when the mountain states watched their mineral wealth and other natural resources plundered by eastern corporations they were all too aware that the region had paid, and was paying, its fair share.[19] The scornful attacks were old ones, and the West would hear them again, but in the troublous times of 1932 it was particularly difficult to have one's home country dismissed as a place that had reverted to the Great American Desert.

Such was the situation as Colorado and the nation faced the 1932 presidential election. During the preceding decade the state had followed a traditional course of political conservatism, and even the election of a Democratic governor in 1926, a move that earlier might have been interpreted as indicating a desire for change, had produced no innovations. Cattleman Billy Adams was no spender, and his parsimony made him governor of Colorado three times. To complicate the situation the state's archaic administrative equipment was so wasteful and inefficient that even the most progressive of governors could not have made it function. Ever since 1915 administrative reform bills had been placed before the General Assembly, but other than a cursory examination of them by mildly curious legislators nothing had happened. Those representatives of the people feared executive power and they preferred to function in their own little power structures, the consensus of which controlled the state's gentle drift to nowhere. Even popular Billy Adams had no luck in his efforts to tighten up this administrative anarchy and convert it into a functioning entity.

The election of 1932 brought Franklin D. Roosevelt and his New Deal to the White House. It also put into the Colorado governor's chair Edwin C. ("Big Ed") Johnson, a Democrat who used his personal persuasiveness and the uncertainty of the times to make a final drive for the long sought-after administrative reorganization. He was able to consolidate some forty-four agencies into a five-man Executive Council, the principal responsibility of which was to streamline state fiscal policies. This group was composed of the elected major department heads, but when Johnson proposed that these be made appointive the voters turned down the proposed constitutional amendment. Thus, instead of having to deal with forty-four agencies pulling in different directions, the governor had to contend with an elected group that pulled in only five different directions. Certainly this was an improvement and occasionally Johnson was able to balance his budget, but there were enough limitations to the new arrangement to hobble the state's financial maneuverability.

In addition to the problem of a bureaucratic jungle overgrowth, Colorado was restricted by a fiscal rigidity that earmarked money for specific funds and did not allow transfer of money from one fund to the other. Governor Teller Ammons, who succeeded Johnson in 1937, struggled with a continuing problem of a deficit in the General Fund. Politicians were in the habit of circumventing the executive by earmarking money for certain funds by means of initiated measures, an example of which was a 1936 action that established an expensive pension program. Meantime, other funds suffered from the economy ax. Since the cry for administrative reorganization still was heard frequently, Ammons hired the firm of E. O. Griffenhagen & Associates, well known for their analyses of governmental problems, to make some suggestions for improvement. After a year's study, and the submission of detailed recommendations by the firm, the proposals languished and finally died. An administrative reform act of 1941 made a gesture at improvement by substituting a governor's Advisory Council for the Executive Council, but such a change barely acknowledged the Griffenhagen Report, the authors of which now had great difficulty in collecting their agreed-upon fee from the state.[20]

The people of Colorado undoubtedly were willing to share in at least some of the New Deal's efforts to do battle with the depression, but the antiquated legislative machinery with which their representatives had to work made it difficult. The Federal Emergency Relief Administration, headed by Roosevelt's right-hand man, Harry Hopkins, passed along about a third of a million dollars a month in pump-priming money, but Hopkins expected the state to match it. When the General Assembly failed to respond, he threatened to cut off the grant. Alarmed at the prospect of losing these funds, a group of angry depression victims, among them members of the United Front Organization, whose enemies called them "Communists," pushed their way into the Senate chamber, driving a covey of panic-stricken legislators before them. A national magazine screamed "Revolution!" and asserted that what followed was the first Communist meeting ever held under the dome of any capitol. A Boulder paper said that the visitors merely had knocked down the chamber door, after which there was no attempt to eject them and no disorder. Rather than being communistic, the newspaper thought the United Front was a successor to the KKK. A Denver journalist saw the event as a parade of five hundred hungry unemployed who marched to the Capitol in an orderly fashion and stated their grievances. The legislators may have accepted any or all of these views, but to them the message was clear: action was called for. By diverting highway appropriations and levying a tax on gasoline they were able to raise the matching funds.

An angry afterglow to the confrontation was reflected in Big Ed Johnson's war with Harry Hopkins, a bitter struggle that continued until the governor left office. One interpretation of this development was that Colorado simply was displaying a typically parochial western attitude toward the federal government. Another view held that it was just one more round in the feud between Johnson and Senator Edward P. Costigan, a New Dealer who opposed Colorado's political old guard. A national journal remarked that this group for some time had dominated state politics and that it had opposed almost every move the federal government had made to alleviate suffering and distress in Colorado. The Roosevelt administration, said the journal, might in the long run do Colorado a favor by helping to free it from the grip of conservative control.[21] Johnson merely sneered at the New Dealers and pronounced their program a fraud.

The rustic Colorado governor was a States' Rights man and showed no hesitancy in taking steps to prove it. For example, his reaction to labor's complaint that imported Mexican beet workers were depriving Colorado farm workers of their just due was to order a blockade of the state's southern boundary. In the spring of 1936 troopers from the National Guard set up barricades against possible incursions of migrant workers and began to stop trains, trucks, buses, and automobiles to inquire into the origins and assets of the occupants. Acting under martial law, they were instructed to "prevent and repel the further invasion of . . . aliens, indigent persons, or invaders." In more common parlance the barrier was referred to as the "bum blockade."

While those proscribed by the governor were to include indigents and invaders, the term "alien" was the operative word in the orders. Despite the business community's adherence to the "American way," the sugar companies preferred to use foreign labor because it was cheaper. They did not listen to Frederick Bonfils when he insisted that beet sugar was raised "in a white man's country, by white men, for white people. It isn't produced by cheap, white, black, or yellow foreign labor."[22] Rather the companies sought laborers from small Mexican communities and, after promising them lucrative employment, brought them in by the trainload. Once here, the head of the family often realized that to make a living he must contract for acreage so large that the entire family would have to work long hours. It meant a new peonage, but this time in a place where it was said to be a great privilege to live.

Despite enforced impoverishment, the families did their best to live as decently as possible. A Catholic seminarian who worked among them wrote that the children who came to school each morning were immaculately clean, and their much-patched clothing showed evidence of frequent washings. "The average Mexican mother is scrupulous in her cleanliness," he wrote. "Her house may have a dirt floor, but it is swept several times a day. There may be no other furniture than a stove and a bed, but the bed is made and the stove is polished."[23] Another missionary complained that while living conditions among the beet workers were poor and that the wages were pitifully small, it was difficult to be of much assistance to them because they moved about so much. She felt that they were in great need of educational assistance, for many of them were so ignorant that they had to be "looked after like little children." Automobile and radio salesmen had no trouble in persuading them that the installment plan was the answer to their prayers; soon repossessed autos and radios flooded the local market. As a Protestant, the missionary restated the old fear of her kind that the Catholic church had taken ruthless advantage of this ignorance to keep these people in a kind of religious bondage. She admitted that even with good educations many of the Spanish Americans had difficulty in finding acceptance outside their immediate communi-

Elaborately decorated interiors at the turn of the century invariably included a row of China dishes along the wall. *Denver Public Library, Western History Department*

These cabins, located near Chicago Creek, where George A. Jackson made his fabulous find in Fifty-Nine, were part of a little village about the turn of the century. It was called Burns-Moore Town. *Western History Collection, University of Colorado Libraries*

During the early years of the twentieth century, Denverites made special efforts to provide recreation for the young. These skaters are enjoying themselves in City Park, January 1903. *Denver Public Library, Western History Department*

Well past the mid twentieth century, visitors to Denver were familiar with the Navarre, one of the city's stylish downtown restaurants. On a winter night not long after 1900 it looked particulary inviting. *Library, The State Historical Society of Colorado*

Christmas Day, 1906, in a middle-class parlor. *Denver Public Library, Western History Department*

Early skiing lacked some of the refinements achieved later, but Coloradans enjoyed the slopes nevertheless. This picture was taken in March 1883 at Irwin, Gunnison County. *Library, The State Historical Society of Colorado*

The corner of 15th and Champa streets, Denver, early in the twentieth century. Both old and new modes of transportation were in use. *Denver Public Library, Western History Department*

The ruins at Mesa Verde remain one of Colorado's great tourist attractions. Here are some early visitors looking at Balcony House. *Denver Public Library, Western History Department*

Mountain climbers ascending the west side of Long's Peak. *Denver Public Library, Western History Department*

The annual Glenwood Springs Strawberry Festival, 1906. *Denver Public Library, Western History Department*

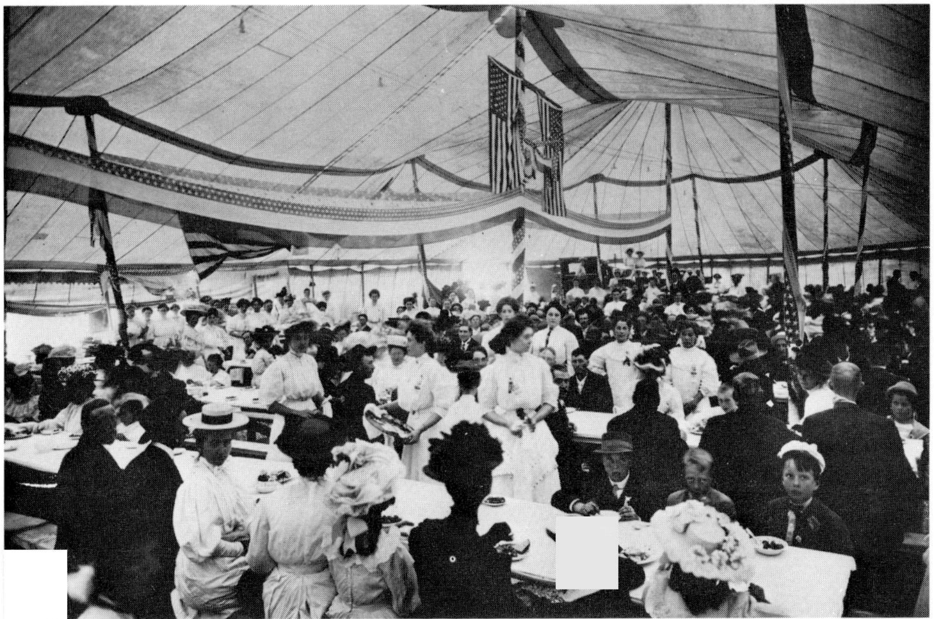

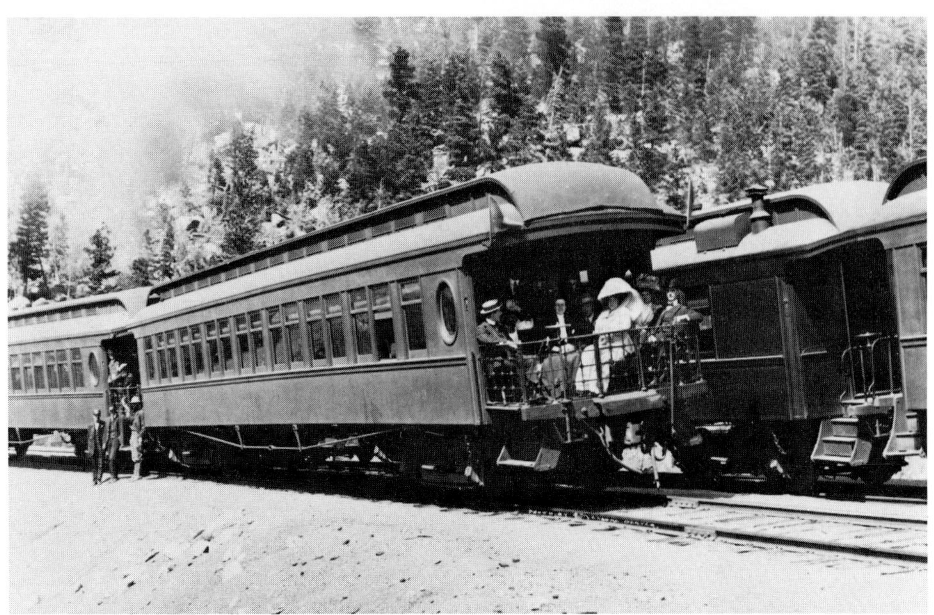

A private railroad car was the epitome of luxury. This is the car of Olga Nethersole, a well-known actress, halted near Colorado Springs. "I have taken to the rolling home since leaving the East," said Olga, " and I find it so delightful. . . .When I wish to rest I rest. When it pleases me to dine I dine, and my meals are prepared to please me." She concluded that it was "glorious traveling through the West." *Denver Public Library, Western History Department*

Auto caravans became popular when the new breed of tourist began to visit Colorado. This "See America First" caravan was photographed about 1920. *Western History Collection, University of Colorado Libraries*

Tent houses were much used by automobile tourists before the days of motels. *Library, The State Historical Society of Colorado*

The opening in the late 1920s of the suspension bridge over the Royal Gorge, or Grand Canyon of the Arkansas, attracted an enthusiastic crowd. *Library, The State Historical Society of Colorado*

During Prohibition, "moonshine" was often manufactured under rather primitive conditions. Here is a still in a Pueblo home, about 1918. *Denver Public Library, Western History Department*

These water nymphs are students at the Perry-Mansfield School of the Dance. The camp was located a mile north of Steamboat Springs in the 1920s, having been established in 1914 by Portia Mansfield and Charlotte Perry. As many as a hundred students a year were enrolled. *Library, The State Historical Society of Colorado*

From an early date, the "sell Colorado" advocates spread the good word about agriculture in this part of the West. As late as 1912, when this view was taken near Romeo, in the San Luis Valley, railroad agricultural exhibit cars visited the state's farming communities. *Library, The State Historical Society of Colorado*

Visitors to the agricultural trains were shown a number of examples of the local soil's productivity. This display was sponsored by the State Agricultural College. *Library, The State Historical Society of Colorado*

Oil company promoters often showed great imagination in naming their creations. Here is the Phenomenal Oil & Gas Company's well in the Boulder field. At the turn of the century this was one of the most important fields in the state. *University of Colorado Museum*

Shale oil, so popular a subject in the mid 1970s, was a matter of interest to Coloradans before 1920. Here is a group ready to leave Denver to study the possibilities of shale oil extraction in western Colorado. *Library, The State Historical Society of Colorado*

During the mid 1920s Coloradans watched the progress of the Moffat Tunnel with great interest. This view was taken in January 1926. *Denver Public Library, Western History Department*

The Great Depression produced many an irony. Here men are learning to pan gold in Denver as part of the federal government's relief and rehabilitation program. *Denver Public Library, Western History Department*

Travelers of the 1920s stuck to trains and buses, but the airplane was on its way to acceptance. By the 1930s the picture was to change rapidly, as would this Denver airport scene. *Library, The State Historical Society of Colorado*

Women participated more actively in World War I than in any previous conflict. Classes in auto mechanics at Denver's famed Opportunity School drew enthusiastic students. *Denver Public Library, Western History Department*

Colorado's enthusiasm for aviation bloomed as early as 1910. These Bleriot monoplanes, resting at Overland Park, in Denver, were among several shipped in by rail and assembled for demonstration purposes. Four of the French pilots, among them Roland Garros, later made names as aces in World War I. *Library, The State Historical Society of Colorado*

These two young Japanese Americans view their new wartime home with resignation. They have just become residents of Amache, Colorado, guests of the U.S. government. (1942) *Denver Public Library, Western History Department*

Captain William S. Fairchild explains to a group of Japanese-American internees at the Granada Relocation Center their opportunities to join a special U.S. combat unit. The reception is something less than enthusiastic. (1943) *Denver Public Library, Western History Department*

Americans preferred to think of their wartime internment camps as "relocation centers," as opposed to the concentration camps established by the Germans. Here are barracks under construction at the Granada Relocation Center, Amache, Colorado, 1942. *Denver Public Library, Western History Department*

The Brown Palace in the nineteenth century. *Library, The State Historical Society of Colorado*

In the post–World War II boom, Denver's skyline soared. The Brown Palace felt obliged to keep up, and across the street was built the Brown Palace West, a sterile stack of rooms that lacked the charm of the original building. *Library, The State Historical Society of Colorado*

A migrant worker. *Denver Public Library, Western History Department*

The children of migrant workers, housed in shanties like this one, may never have realized that " 'tis a privilege to live in Colorado." *Denver Public Library, Western History Department*

Celebrating Mexican Independence Day, 1968, at Colorado Grange Hall, Denver. *Denver Public Library, Western History Department*

Jeeps—and jeep rallies like the one shown here—became popular among mountain-climbing Coloradans in the post–World War II years. *Denver Public Library, Western History Department*

Hippies demonstrating before the Boulder County Courthouse, late 1960s. *Denver Public Library, Western History Department*

ties and that whether these people were so-called wetbacks or American citizens there was prejudice against them.[24]

It was the Mexican nationals, or temporary workers, that Governor Johnson had in mind when he originated the "bum blockade." For years they had worked in Colorado as beet thinners, sheepshearers, and truck-farm field hands. During ordinary times corporations did not encounter a great deal of opposition to these importations, but when residents of the state walked the streets in a vain search for work the situation was altered. New Mexico, of course, objected loudly when Johnson sealed off Colorado as if its neighbor to the south were infected by some dread disease, and the more northerly and western parts of Colorado felt that his action was discriminatory, but from places like Trinidad came praise and an acknowledgment that drastic action was necessary. Other contemporaries concluded that Big Ed merely was trying to do the right thing by his constituents in his own direct, western manner, and while they thought his methods somewhat extreme there were murmurs of approval for his motives. They pointed out that he was trying to protect the state from a flood of indigents. There was amusement among the critics of Anglo-Saxon supremacy when the troopers halted an attractive Spanish-American applicant for entry and questioned her financial status. Daintily turning aside, she stunned them by delving into her stocking top to produce a roll of bills totaling five thousand dollars. At once she was pronounced a desirable and was hurried on into the promised land.[25]

Rough-and-ready tactics by crusty state leaders were acceptable enough for purposes of building political images, or to amuse the locals, but for the moment, at least, the days of this brand of rugged individualism were over. While turning back cheap labor, even for a brief period, might have provided a little work for the hometown boys, it was no solution to a problem of such depth and seriousness. What the state needed was a massive financial injection, and the only source of that, as things stood during the thirties, was from the "enemy"—the federal government.

During Roosevelt's first two terms Colorado received approximately $396 million in federal relief and recovery funds. Part of the money was pumped into work projects to provide men with jobs. Roads were improved, bridges built, flood dams erected, schools, libraries, and hospitals built or renovated, and airports built. In an eight-year period $111 million went into Works

Progress Administration efforts; at one time as many as 43,000 Coloradans were employed by the WPA. The National Youth Administration spent more than $3 million to hire needy students in the state. Nearly $48 million more went into construction of buildings for schools, hospitals, courthouses, and post offices, filling a vacuum that had developed in the years immediately preceding the depression when economy measures curtailed such construction.

Yet another expediture of federal money was for the Civilian Conservation Corps, a program intended to furnish employment for young men in the fields of reforestation, fire-fighting, and reclamation. Because Colorado had more wooded land than many of its neighbors, it received a disproportionately large number of young men in this program. In some of their larger projects the young men worked for the Bureau of Reclamation, the National Park Service, the Division of Grazing, the U.S. Forest Service, and the Soil Conservation Service. Smaller groups cleaned up such recreational areas as Boulder's Green Mountain and Flagstaff Mountain parks; at the Garden of the Gods, near Colorado Springs, they constructed trails, bridle paths, and roads, built comfort stations, and improved facilities.[26] By the mid thirties some five thousand of them worked in forty-one camps; for this the federal government contributed fifty million dollars.

More millions went to the payment of benefits to farmers under the Agricultural Adjustment Acts.[27] Because of the economic first aid, because dry years across the plains elevated farm prices there and in Colorado, and thanks to an upturn in the national economy, the state began to come out of the slump by the end of the decade. Perhaps one measure of Colorado's improving economic picture was the figure representing those employed by such governmental agencies as the Works Progress Administration. At the close of 1935 just under thirty-eight thousand Coloradans were on the rolls of that agency; by mid 1941 that figure had dropped to approximately seventeen thousand.[28]

Widespread unemployment and a general atmosphere of insecurity turned many Coloradans of all ages in the direction of additional learning. In the autumn of 1936 some fifteen hundred people signed up for adult education classes in the Colorado Springs area. At nearby Peyton a vacant building was taken over for handicrafts, and students paid their tuition each time they came to class by offering a lump of coal or a few sticks of wood, the evening receipts at once going into the stove to keep the building warm. More than a hundred CCC boys took evening classes at Colorado College; at Boulder another group of them spent off-hours at the university.[29]

Denver's Opportunity School, founded in 1916 by Emily Griffith, attracted new interest during the depression years. Denver businessmen, who earlier had shown a reluctance to accept this unique institution because they thought it was pro-union or even union controlled, began to understand its value, and they cooperated with it. The school was open to all, with no tuition, no entrance requirement, and no graduation except for the high school students. Classes were offered in every imaginable subject, ranging from techniques of gold mining to preparing young girls for marriage. Although the courses ran alphabetically from advertising to welding and included a wide variety of fields, not all those who took advantage of them were able to find work upon completing their training. But many of them did, and a national magazine pointed to Denver's efforts to fight unemployment in this manner as being highly commendable, something that the federal government itself might imitate.[30]

Although Colorado's growth was relatively slow during the twenties, and the following decade was one of exceptionally hard times, interest in higher education did not languish; during these years several new, smaller colleges were founded. Adams State College, first known as the State Normal School at Alamosa, was authorized in 1921, followed four years later by Mesa Junior College at Grand Junction and Trinidad State Junior College. Several more institutions emerged during the depression years, among them Pueblo Junior College, shortly to be known as Southern Colorado Junior College, in 1933. That year Fort Lewis Agricultural and Mechanical College began offering higher education in the southwestern corner of the state, at the site of a nineteenth-century Indian school west of Durango. Later in the decade junior colleges were established at Lamar and La Junta, followed by Sterling Junior College in 1945.[31] Each of the schools illustrated the desire of Coloradans to give a greater geographical spread to the colleges and to serve more students at less expense.

Another side effect of the depression was the development of a pension program that, according to its critics, sent needy old people from a situation of famine to one of feast. In 1927 the state began to move away from the old poorhouse concept when it provided for a pension system, to be operated and paid for by the counties, that would allow a dollar a day to those who qualified. The legislation merely gave the counties permission to participate in this welfare; a new law, passed in 1931, made the system mandatory and reduced the age limit from seventy to sixty-five. Four years later the state allocated $100,000 a month from sales tax receipts to aid the counties. Shortly thereafter the federal government began its participation in the program. By the autumn of 1936 a constitutional amendment raised the minimum to forty-five dollars a month and lowered the age limit for beneficiaries to sixty years. From a position of having offered its needy senior citizens little or nothing during the twenties, in two decades Colorado had moved to a point where it could boast of the most generous state pension plan in the nation. Within two years of the passage of the amendment, the state was contributing to the support of approximately thirty-five thousand pensioners at a cost of more than $1 million a month.

Almost immediately there were complaints that the National Annuity League, whose local representatives had pushed through the amendment, had gone too far and that bankruptcy threatened the mountain commonwealth. Since the measure required that 85 percent of the state's excise taxes—that on liquor, for example—were to be earmarked for the pension fund, the new program absorbed a lion's share of income intended for other uses. O. Otto Moore of the National Annuity League had an answer for those who predicted dire financial problems for the state: "Nonsense. Balderdash. Piffle. Bunk." Colorado's problem, he said, was that since 1920 corporate and property taxes had declined steadily. What was gained from excise and sales taxes was taken primarily from the common man; therefore, why should his class not benefit from it? Asked where the money to support the state was to come from, he responded: "Well, let them go back to the fat boys. We got tired of paying their government bills."

The beneficiaries of the pension program formed a powerful pressure group, and all attempts to take allocated money away from them ran into severe opposition. At the time the amendment was passed, those who qualified looked forward to this new income with great anticipation. When a Loveland woman asked why she had not received her first forty-five-dollar check at once, it was explained to her that the program did not go into effect until the first of the year and that, at the moment, no funds were available for the program. Not to be put off, she challenged the statement, asking "Isn't the mint right there in Denver?" It was to such voters that those who wanted to place the matter in the hands of the General Assembly took their proposal in 1938. The "pension army" defeated it easily. When another attempt was made in 1940, this time to reduce the payments from forty-five to thirty dollars a month, it was rejected even more decisively. Midcentury would come and go before the electorate would approve an amendment that allowed state officials to use some of that jealously guarded money for other purposes.[32]

Transmontane water diversion was another issue that remained at the forefront as Colorado fought off the depression. The relatively small amounts of water diverted by such earlier projects as the Moffat Tunnel system and some of the ditch diversions across mountain passes had occasioned little real opposition in the state, but when the Big Thompson project was proposed, a number of interests felt endangered. Aside from the fact that the transfer of water from western to eastern slope was to be accomplished through federal largess, a situation that pleased some people and annoyed others, there were cries of apprehension from western Colorado. Traditionally the eastern power base, along the Rockies from Fort Collins to Pueblo, had tended to flex its muscles and shrug off outcries from the politically impotent western reaches of the state, but this time the westerners had some allies. The proposed shift of water from Grand Lake across the divide to the Big Thompson River was to be accomplished by a tunnel that ran through part of Rocky Mountain National Park, and when this information reached the nature lovers a verbal war erupted.

The National Parks Association and a variety of conservation groups loudly denounced the idea of defacing the park by boring holes in the mountains, constructing eight thousand feet of covered ditch within its limits, and erecting a maze of power transmission lines, not to mention the commotion to be caused by construction crews for an unknown number of years. Although opponents of the project admitted that the eastern slope needed more water, and even conceded that a diversion that did not enter the national park might be less offensive, the crusade upon which they embarked had more to do with environmental problems than with water. Fears that this one might set a precedent for other projects in environmentally sensitive areas were well founded, for in the next three or four decades the conservationist troops would be called upon many times. In this battle such important figures as Frederick A. Delano (President Roosevelt's uncle) and Frederick Law Olmsted, Jr., were asked for their assistance and raised their voices in protest. Colorado Senator Alva B. Adams defended the project on the ground that ultimately it would be the fourth largest power producer in the nation and that both the water and the power would be of great benefit to the people. He did not feel that a few piles of rock, "nice, clean rock" as he called it, could do irreparable damage to Rocky Mountain National Park.

Meanwhile western slope interests protested loudly that they were being robbed of their water to satisfy eastern Colorado farmers. Why, they asked, did these people need to raise bigger crops in a day when the New Deal was trying to reduce agricultural surpluses? When a Grand Junction editor spoke of such robbery, he was answered by a colleague from Boulder to the effect that it mattered not where in Colorado water originated because there was no ownership of water not used. He thought it more important that Coloradans use locally generated water in preference to its use by people of Arizona or California. To Grand Junction's complaint that the entire western slope had but one U.S. congressman to represent its interest in the matter, the Boulder journalist somewhat ungenerously pointed out that the individual involved—Edward T. Taylor—publicly favored the Big Thompson project. Undaunted, the westerner went to court, challenging the right of those living east of the mountains even to receive water passed through the Moffat Tunnel. Judge Charles E. Herrick, of Steamboat Springs, ruled that such a transmission was legal but that Denver could not sell any water so received. The city could use it for street sprinkling and to irrigate municipal parks, but not a drop was to be sold to truck gardens or for such other uses outside the city. But, since the legality of transporting water across mountains had been established as early as 1922, the judge from Steamboat merely was blowing his legal whistle, and to no avail. The project went forward and, as mentioned earlier, shortly after the close of World War II water began to flow out of Grand Lake onto the farms of eastern Colorado.[33]

Although the Colorado natives showed little sympathy for nature lovers who objected to having mountain areas defaced by the introduction of major waterworks, they were not unaware that scenery produced one of the state's better cash crops. As the depression deepened and tourism fell off, it became more obvious to them just how much they missed the flatlanders who brought their children and their money to the mountains each summer.

By the early thirties those interested in "selling" the state to visitors had become increasingly conscious of the need for further improvement of their highways. Aside from the paved road that connected cities along the mountain front from Fort Collins to Pueblo and ran a mile or so outside such cities as Trinidad, La Junta, and Grand Junction, the rest of the roads were judged to be atrocious. It was said at the time that there were not ten miles of continuous highway in the state, other than the strip along the eastern slope, where one dared to drive more than thirty miles an hour. The western slope, in particular, found this annoying and the Grand Junction *Sentinel* said that unless things improved the growth of that entire region would be hindered. "Millions for construction but not one cent for upkeep," roared one irate driver who predicted that visitors trying to make the Colorado passageway would have all the enthusiasm jounced out of them before they had gone very far. Here was a cash crop, he suggested, that was being allowed to die on the vine through neglect, inattention, and parsimony.[34]

Bitter complaint about the condition of the roads was an ancient habit among westerners; with some it was almost a way of life. But during the early thirties Colorado's situation improved rapidly, thanks, in part, to the efforts of State Highway Engineer Charles D. Vail. By the middle of that decade some six hundred miles of what one editor called "real paving" were in use, augmented by nearly two thousand miles of oiled surfaces. The earmarking of money raised by gasoline sales taxes, plus funds that Big Ed Johnson, now a United States senator, was able to wrest from the federal government, poured money into projects that had been starved for years. Western road building was expensive, particularly in the mountains, but it was generally agreed that in view of the great tourist potential the gamble would pay off handsomely.[35] When the sources of this gold mine, the all-important tourists, were asked what they thought Colorado needed in the way of improved facilities, they requested wider highways in the mountains, or at least wider shoulders, more camp sites, and lower gasoline prices. One of them caused shudders among the conservationists by the suggestion that the state ought to have more hamburger stands along the way, a wish that would come true with a vengeance in the years ahead.[36]

An eastern artist who visited Colorado about this time declared that the state had not been "properly sold to the nation." He thought the mountain country had everything, but east of the Mississippi River few people realized this and instead of coming to the Rockies they settled for such places as Michigan and Minnesota. He urged his western friends to present their case fully to the folks back east who then believed that Colorado was just a barren region somewhere near the Grand Canyon. Latter-day prospectors saw the point and responded with great energy. In the spring of 1937 a determined band of thirty-eight salesmen set out from Colorado Springs for Texas, where they hoped to extend to the more than six million souls living in that scenically impoverished place an invitation to spend the summer in Colorado. Ten cars and a truck upon whose side panels was emblazoned the message "Pike's Peak or Bust" set off for the Southwest in search of tourists with money. Another small group, representing the Colorado Springs Junior Chamber of Commerce, later scoured the plains of eastern Colorado and western Kansas with the hope that some of the plainsmen whom they visited would act as sentinels to direct tourists toward Pike's Peak when the weather warmed. As a Colorado Springs newspaper commented, in a tourist country a good summer meant a good winter and poor pickings during the travel season inevitably predicted a lean winter.[37]

As early as the 1920s there were signs that tourism could be a year-round proposition and that therefore the state might not have to depend exclusively upon the summer harvest of visitors. Late in 1929 a Denver paper noted that America's Switzerland was beginning to draw more people during the winter and that if facilities were developed winter sports promised to boom. By then Colorado boasted a half-dozen excellent ski courses, among them the one at Steamboat Springs where an annual tournament attracted nationally known skiers. Other courses, at Hot Sulphur Springs, Estes Park, Allen's Park, and the Homewood course at Deer Creek Canyon about thirty miles from Denver, also were drawing an increasing number of skiers. Homewood had a fine toboggan course, said to be the best in the state. In addition, Colorado's lakes were drawing the attention of ice skaters.[38] A decade later over a hundred thousand people were using the mountain slopes for winter sports. By then Berthoud Pass drew as many as fifty thousand skiers a season. To further publicize the possibilities of these western Alps a Universal newsreel feature presented the nation with pictures of sport scenes in the snow. A few sequences showing scantily clad girls playing badminton on ice were included to underscore the mildness of the winter climate.[39]

By 1940 Colorado Springs businessmen were complaining that the tourist business was falling off. It worried them that their city, renowned as a leading resort, was not benefiting sufficiently from the new tourism. Motorists now were stopping at roadside accommodations near other scenic spots that interested them more than did Pike's Peak or the Broadmoor Hotel. The city fathers resolved to make an even more aggressive bid for the trade because, they said, across the state a lot of competition was developing in the battle for tourists. "We live and grow and prosper on travel and that permanent residential development that grows out of travel," remarked the local editor. He thought the Chamber of Commerce should come forward at once with $25,000 to finance the needed search for tourists.[40]

Then came the war and gasoline rationing. By the summer of 1942 the usual seasonal travel was off by a third in the western states. Although Colorado was affected less than some of the others, the drop caused alarm among businessmen. It was recognized that to fund the state publicity bureau with its usual $50,000 appropriation might not be the most prudent course during wartime, but it was believed that the office ought to be kept open so that no time would be lost when peace came. As many as fifty inquiries a day were coming in from soldiers stationed in the state who wanted to tell their friends and relatives about its attractions. Looking back a few years, those interested in tourism had reason to be encouraged, for expenditures by visitors had risen from over $47 million in 1935 to $69 million by 1941; therefore hopes for the immediate postwar years were high.[41]

Somewhat ironically it was the depression that played a part in developing an improvement in public transportation that had been sought for nearly three-quarters of a century. Ever since the 1860s, when northern Colorado had had to swallow its disappointment at the Union Pacific's decision to build through Wyoming, Denver had looked longingly beyond the towering ranges that cut off its westward view. The Arkansas River route, utilized by the Denver and Rio Grande, had provided an early passageway to the west, but despite the later arrival of several major western railroads at Denver the capital city remained without a direct transcontinental connection until 1934.

Denver's hopes for a "window on the Pacific" rose when, in 1902, the Denver, Northwestern and Pacific Railway Company, commonly known as the Moffat Road, started construction crews for Rollins Pass and into the undeveloped country of northwestern Colorado, after which the company expected to reach Salt Lake City by means of a perfect beeline route. By 1911 David Moffat had spent all the money he had made in banking and mining, and in that year he died, his dream unfulfilled. William G. Evans, the son of territorial governor John Evans, took over, and, after a receivership, the line was reorganized as the Denver & Salt Lake Railroad. It became apparent that the enormous expense incurred in scaling the Rockies, complicated by snow-clogged winters, made a tunnel almost mandatory. Federal control of the road during World War I staved off financial disaster for the Colorado company, but in the years that followed its management became increasingly convinced that only a tunnel could keep the line solvent. With it, they hoped, the western slope's coal, oil, livestock, and agricultural products could be hauled economically enough to make a profit. After a long struggle, in which other major western railroads fought against the Denver interests, the Moffat Tunnel Act was signed into law in the spring of 1922. Now the mountain passage was lowered by twenty-four hundred feet, the trackage shortened by twenty-three miles, and the maximum grade reduced to 2 percent. The first train passed through the six-mile bore in 1928.

But the great engineering feat did not save the Moffat Road. As its backers had predicted, it helped materially to open up northwestern Colorado, but since it dead-ended at Craig, the road, in effect, went nowhere. Had it reached Salt Lake City, as did the Denver and Rio Grande, it could have picked up additional traffic and, as a shorter route, it would have attracted business from major roads from both east and west. As the depression continued and demands for coal, beef, and other products from northwestern Colorado fell off, so did the business of this stub-end railroad.

As the Moffat Road withered, the Rio Grande, whose managers once had fought the tunnel project, were tantalized by the fact that at one point the two roads passed within thirty-eight miles of each other; if the small gap could be bridged, the Rio Grande's route from Denver to Salt Lake City would be exactly what the Queen City had dreamed about for years. Moffat Road managers, who realized that the hard times threatened to strangle their road, were willing to talk business. The Reconstruction Finance Corporation, formed late in the Hoover period for the purpose of aiding floundering corporations, agreed to pump some money into depression-ridden Colorado. Thus the connecting link, called the Dotsero Cutoff, was commenced in the autumn of 1932 and completed in June 1934. Before the latter year was out the Denver and Rio Grande had bought out its former rival and the way west from Denver lay open and uncontested by any other road.[42]

The Rockies also had necessitated a detour west of Denver for airline traffic, but in 1937 United Air Lines, using their new DC-3s, offered two flights a day between Denver and cities on both coasts. Until that time travelers who wanted to go in these directions had to journey via Cheyenne or Albuquerque, both of which were on east-west routes. The coming of World War II delayed the full benefits of this new service to Colorado's capital city, but in the postwar years the air travel boom that the state so long had sought became a reality and very quickly Denver became one of the West's busiest and most important airline cities. As the war came to a close and pressurized aircraft came into more general use, the mountain wall that bisected Colorado was no longer a barrier to direct flights westward.[43]

Colorado's willingness to undertake great projects, such as that of major transmontane water diversion, and its aggressiveness in promoting both private and public transportation for the benefit of the state's economy, represented a go-getting spirit that businessmen liked to think of as being "progressive." When the word is transferred to the context of political liberalism or used to indicate advancement in such fields as social services or welfare, Colorado's picture becomes blurred. On the one hand the state could treat its poor and needy with almost criminal neglect during the 1920s; on the other it could then execute almost a complete flip-flop by introducing one of the most liberal old-age pension plans in the nation, one that threatened public bankruptcy.

Similar crosscurrents are noticeable in the state's response to the New Deal. That far-reaching program encountered a good many stumbling blocks in the West, including Colorado. Ed Johnson and Alva B. Adams, both Democrats, opposed both Roosevelt and his program, and by 1940 the state would go Republican. However, this did not mean that Coloradans rejected federal spending within their state; it was a kind of invasion of their privacy that they found they could get used to. Complain as they would about federal encroachment, Coloradans were not unhappy to hear Denver referred to as the "little Capital" nor were they embarrassed when the Denver Chamber of Commerce boasted that the city had more government offices than any other city except Washington, D.C.; yet they admired Ed Johnson's maverickism because he seemed to reflect what they thought was their own independence. Businessmen accepted the New Deal's National Recovery Administration and proudly flew the blue eagle as long as it seemed to be doing some good—after which they just as quickly abandoned that much-fired-upon bird. Colorado farmers joined the New Deal's agricultural program reluctantly; therefore they were not rescued from the depression until the coming of World War II and higher prices.[44]

# 15

# While the World Was at War

The Second World War affected Colorado much as it did other western states and the nation at large. A national draft to provide naval and military personnel had been created more than a year prior to the December 7, 1941, attack upon Pearl Harbor; now, consequently, it was only a matter of increasing requests for manpower and of accepting volunteers when war came. As draft boards made their calls and men began to depart for training camps, farewell dances, parades, and the issuance of patriotic municipal proclamations sent the young citizen soldiers on their way to war much in the manner of their fathers in World War I. Between 1941 and 1946 nearly 139,000 Coloradans of military age were drafted or volunteered for service, a figure that represented approximately 1 of every 8 residents, and during the course of the conflict approximately 2,700 of them would die from battle wounds or other causes.

Aside from the periodic send-offs, life in Colorado's little communities continued much as before. Rationing of various domestic items such as gasoline, tires, and sugar touched most of the homes, and before 1942 was out there was a coffee shortage, but it was attributed more to hoarding than to the exigencies of global war. With transportation restricted, families tended to stay at home growing victory gardens and participating in local scrap metal and used paper drives, Red Cross activities, and book collections for the troops. In the face of gasoline and tire shortages Glenwood Springs gave up its summer Strawberry Day celebration and Durango's fine arts festival was curtailed.

Although Colorado was far removed from any battlefront, there were the old concerns about enemy activities deep in America's heartland. For example, an Alamosa paper warned that any of the nine unguarded reservoir dams in the San Luis Valley would be choice targets for saboteurs, who could seriously diminish local agricultural production with a few well-placed sticks of dynamite. Or, said a Glenwood Springs editor, great damage could be done by pyromaniacs in the tinder-dry forests, particularly at a time when the manpower shortage made fire fighters hard to come by.[1]

While some feared that the state's natural resources thus might be jeopardized, Coloradans also saw the possibility that these gifts of nature could be in great demand by war industries. Memories of the World War I resurgence in mining had not faded and it took little imagination to project the prosperity that could be achieved if history repeated itself. By the summer of 1942 Leadville had cast off its near–ghost town reputation and had entered into a boom so brisk that it was placed under rent control by the federal government. At nearby Gilman the Empire Zinc Company took on more men. The Colorado Mining Association enthusiastically outlined a program for speeding up the extraction of zinc, lead, copper, and similar war materials; even the small, marginal mines were expected to get back into production.

But the war was demanding and selective, as Cripple Creek discovered when the gold mines there and at Victor were ordered closed by the federal government. Coloradans who had rejoiced at the new impetus for mining now complained vigorously that this was bureaucratic regimentation spawned at faraway Washington, D.C. Representative J. Edgar Chenowith, a Republican, argued that American boys were fighting and dying on the battlefields of the world so that they might come back to a nation that enjoyed freedom of opportunity and enterprise "rather than to state socialism."[2] The gold mines remained closed, and those producing war materials increased their production.

The state was willing to do all it could to stimulate the extraction of those minerals so much in demand by heavy industry. In the spring of 1942 it launched a $600,000 road-building program to make the vanadium deposits of southwestern Colorado more available, the Naturita and Uravan regions to be the principal beneficiaries. Western slope residents welcomed the improved transportation, something they long had desired, and they foresaw that the construction would aid not only future mining but farmers and stockmen as well. About this time the U.S. Vanadium Corporation opened a mill at Rifle that had a capacity of 200 tons a day, a supplement that increased the total daily output of that corporation in Colorado to 600 tons.[3]

During the war years Colorado produced nearly all of the world's supply of molybdenum and most of the vanadium found in this country. The mineral production for the year 1942 was worth nearly a hundred million dollars, of which the value of molybdenum alone reached twenty-nine million, outdistancing even the old standby, coal.

One of the early and obvious questions that occurred to Coloradans living in small and often remote agricultural communities was, What effect would the war have upon their neighborhood economies? From Montrose came the idea that although the Uncompahgre Valley was isolated, its agricultural and livestock production could be just as important to defense as the manufacture of airplanes or munitions. Despite wartime restrictions, residents of this and other thinly populated parts of the state felt that they would not suffer economically.[4] As it developed, the war brought rather early relief to farmers, stockmen, and woolgrowers, whose incomes generally had been low since the close of the First World War. By 1942 they were enjoying higher prices than many of them had seen since 1929, and the Secretary of Agriculture was urging them to raise all they could in behalf of the new war effort. Despite warnings that the overexpansion associated with World War I had led to the very problems from which they now were recovering, agriculturalists again responded to the call with enthusiasm. In the Gunnison Valley, for example, land recently drained by the Bureau of Reclamation was brought into production to meet the Food for Freedom campaign's annual quota and, incidentally, to bring new prosperity to that part of the state. The San Luis Valley farmers were urged to plant their full potato acreage allotments with the assistance of a price support level of $1.20 per hundred pounds produced. They responded with promises that they would make every effort to get the maximum from their lands.[5]

Sugar beets, a major crop, became increasingly important not only as a food but as a substitute for cane sugar, which was required for the manufacture of alcohol, explosives, and synthetic rubber. The Great Western Sugar Company told beet farmers that the firing of a sixteen-inch gun on a battleship required the sugar equivalent of seven-tenths of an acre of average beets. Since labor was in very short supply volunteers were called for. In the autumn of 1942 approximately 450 boys and girls from the Fort Morgan schools went into the fields to harvest the crop, and because of the emergency some of the Japanese Americans were permitted to join them, at going wages. A similar situation prevailed among potato growers; it was said that if students had not been made available as laborers the crop would have gone unharvested. Farmers complained bitterly that the draft and high wages in industry had drawn off most of their workers and that unless they gained relief their production would fall drastically. By November 1942, farm workers were being given deferments by selective service boards and agriculture was classified as one of the essential means of production, ranking with shipbuilding and other industrial efforts.[6]

While Colorado was not noted for its manufactures, its principal cities had factories that now gave first priority to war production. Western States Cutlery, at Boulder, turned out 1,200 to 1,500 knives per day, and during the war years Aircraft Mechanics, Inc., at Colorado Springs, produced about twelve million dollars' worth of aircraft parts. Denver's well-known luggage manufacturer, Shwayder Brothers, made lockers, ammunition boxes, and even incendiary bombs and grenades. Gates Rubber, also of Denver, manufactured tires, tubes, belts, hose, and other related products, the total value of which passed the million dollar mark. Stearns-Roger Manufacturing Company, Eaton Metal Products, and the Continental Can Company, all of Denver, contributed various metal containers, pumps, boilers, and the like.

Perhaps Colorado's most important industrial producer was the Denver Ordnance Plant operated by the Remington Arms Company, of Bridgeport, Connecticut. Contracts were let for the construction of about a hundred and twenty buildings early in 1941. It commenced production in October of that year, and when peak output was reached almost twenty thousand employees were at work turning out small arms ammunition. It was one of the largest establishments of its kind in the nation. So great was the output that by late 1943 the work force was reduced and at the end of July 1944 the plant was closed. At that point the Henry J. Kaiser Company, of California, moved in and began manufacturing heavy artillery shells, then much needed by the American forces in Europe. The Remington Company made artillery shell fuses in an adjacent location.[7] Other Denver wartime facilities included the

Rocky Mountain Arsenal, a producer of chemical warfare products, and a Medical Supply Depot. The Pueblo Ordnance Depot provided some twelve hundred storage magazines and a number of administrative buildings and barracks. It was ready for operation by the spring of 1942.

Another important contribution to the war effort came from Denver's widely known Opportunity School. During those years the school operated seven days a week, twenty-four hours a day, and by 1944 over sixteen thousand students were engaged in some kind of training, with over twenty-three thousand others participating in special war production programs. The school was awarded a Navy "E" pennant and it was dubbed the "Shipyard of the Rockies." So great was the demand for its services that by 1942 two additions to the school were under construction.[8]

From its earliest days Colorado had welcomed, and actively had sought, the presence of military establishments because of the income they generated for local labor and business. During World War II its leaders continued the quest, searching now for war plants and military bases. Since it was not one of America's industrial states, Colorado experienced an outflow of workers during the war; therefore, it was all the more important to attract what federal money it could in war-related projects.

During the depression Denver acquired what became Lowry Field after it purchased a local sanitarium for $200,000, along with 960 acres of land and an additional 64,000 acres for bombing practice, all of which it turned over to the government at no cost. Four years later Lowry took over Fort Logan and used it as a clerical training school for its growing staff. By the outbreak of the war the federal government had invested about $40 million in this important military complex. During 1942 Buckley Field, named in honor of a Longmont boy killed in the First World War, was begun a few miles from Lowry. Intended only for temporary use, it housed the staff and students of an armament school. Also in the Denver area was Fitzsimons military hospital, a World War I creation named for the first American medical officer killed in that war. This facility was so enlarged during World War II that it became not only Colorado's biggest hospital but one of the largest of its kind in the world.

In terms of size, Camp Carson, near Colorado Springs, ranked first among the state's military establishments. The creation of this post, named after Kit Carson, brought joy to local merchants.

Located on a reservation of 60,000 acres, about six miles south of the city, it was built at a cost of approximately thirty million dollars. As members of the city's Chamber of Commerce celebrated making a catch of this magnitude, the group's president cautioned his associates against taking advantage of the windfall by excessive profiteering. One of the members pointed out that the troops would attract a number of friends, family, and relatives, "camp followers" of a respectable stripe, and that these people would become an important segment of the shopping community.[9] He thought they should be treated with care. Also located at Colorado Springs, in 1942, was Peterson Field, used at first for training in photography and mapping. Very shortly the government had three million dollars invested in this war-born installation. During these months other communities, this time in southern Colorado, gained similar airfields. For example, one was laid out at La Junta, to be used primarily for the training of British flyers, and another five million dollars came into Colorado. Nine million more came to the Pueblo area when a large air base was put into operation near that community as a training facility for bombardiers.[10]

Some of the towns that did not have neighboring military-training establishments were given prisoner-of-war camps as consolation prizes in the hope that their payrolls would help to stimulate the local economy. Aside from Camp Carson's prisoner facility and its branch at Minturn, there were camps near Trinidad, Greeley, and other places. Camp Carson's prisoners had their own newspaper, *Die PW Woche* (*The PW Weekly*), the first issue of which appeared in August 1943.[11]

The enthusiasm with which Coloradans responded to the injections of money generated by the war had its limitations. When it was first announced in 1942 that a Japanese Relocation Center was to be established near Granada, in the eastern part of the state, the initial reaction was one of indifference. But as the plan was implemented, opinion hardened against the internees, and Governor Ralph Carr was obliged to defend his decision to welcome these unfortunate people to his bailiwick. In arguing that they had the same rights as other Americans he was literally a voice crying in the wilderness, for at a meeting of western state leaders held at Salt Lake City that spring he represented the only western state volunteering to accept the removed Japanese Americans.

The first contingent of those being "relocated," to employ the polite term then in vogue, arrived in Colorado during early September. There were about a thousand of them. The frightened, homesick families were brought in at night; since there was as yet no electricity they felt their way around by candlelight, seeking out their new homes in a flimsy, cardboard city located on what once was the eastern edge of the Great American Desert. A few of the camp's blocks had hot and cold water, but for the time being a good many of the residents had to walk some distance to bathe. There was but one mess hall for as many as four blocks, and it took three or four shifts to feed the population. Water to clean their dishes was hauled in from Granada because local water was impure. Such was Amache, a camp named after the daughter of Chief One-Eye, a Southern Cheyenne slaughtered at nearby Sand Creek nearly eighty years earlier. The instant city of Amache, said to be the tenth largest in Colorado when it reached its full population, was surrounded by nearly nine thousand acres of farm land, part of which had been operated by the American Crystal Sugar Company. About two-thirds of it was irrigated. On these acres relocation center occupants grew vegetables, melons, alfalfa, corn, and sorghum, as well as hogs and chickens.[12]

Although community leaders at nearby Lamar had wanted the camp, for which $5 million of federal money was appropriated to construct its nearly two hundred units, some of the local businessmen balked at the invasion of these "foreigners" and put signs in their windows reading "No Japs Wanted." When it was explained to them that the newcomers had not come of their own free will, and that they could bypass Lamar by making purchases through mail-order houses, the merchants liberalized their attitudes and voted to allow the strangers to enter their stores, hotels, and restaurants. Similar prejudices were seen at Greeley, where the city council, fearing that agents for West Coast Japanese intended to buy homes there, quickly passed a resolution opposing the acceptance of any of the evacuees in that community. Similar objections were heard from the people at La Junta and Swink, the residents of the latter place suggesting that violence would result if economic conditions in that community were thrown out of balance. Glenwood Springs, on the other hand, wanted such an establishment because its payroll promised to bring several thousand dollars into town each week.

As Amache's organizational machinery was perfected and day-to-day living within the camp became easier, the occupants participated in such cultural activities as the development of a library, adult night-school classes, and extension courses from the University of Colorado. Social activities included the establishment of a local YMCA, a YWCA, a Future Farmers of America chapter, and even an American Legion Post. With passable living conditions and opportunities to use their minds, the Japanese Americans found less and less need to take advantage of liberal offers to enter local stores and restaurants. Nor did they jump at the chance to go into the beet fields at the going wages; only a few hundred of them volunteered. There is some irony in the fact that a good deal of the opposition to them in the state arose from those who feared the introduction of cheap labor and another "California situation."

By the end of the 1943 harvest season, resentment of the Japanese mounted, particularly in the sugar beet and other irrigated areas. Old-time Klansmen figuratively suited up again and prepared to march. Farmers were warned that the yellow peril had arrived—in force. Some 3,000 alien Japanese—there were 2,214 of them in the state—were said to have bought land just north of Denver, but upon investigation it developed that only seven people, all Japanese Americans, had made such purchases. The alien landownership issue burned brightly, however, and when the General Assembly failed to protect the figurative Colorado hearth and home, the ancient constitutional amendment method was called forth and the question was placed upon the 1944 ballot.

The *Denver Post* did its civic best to alert voters to the dangers ahead. It warned of "a more serious Jap problem" than had existed in California before the war. Apparently a good many people listened, for the measure carried in Denver. It failed, however, across the state, due in part to the fact that the soldier vote opposed it three to one.[13] That the *Post* was unequivocal in its stand was seen in an editorial statement that "the Japs in this country are the same breed of rats that American boys are trying to exterminate in the Pacific." By that autumn more than six hundred of these "rodents" who lived at Amache had joined the armed services and forty-five of them had been killed in action. By the 1960s there would be some forty-four hundred Japanese Americans living in Colorado, the sixth highest total in the nation, and despite dire warnings to the contrary, they posed no problems to the reigning majority.

In general, antagonism toward the Japanese during the war appeared to stem more from the threat to agricultural labor and from the question of land tenure than from out-and-out racism. As a well-known Coloradan wrote, one of the few breaks the Japanese Americans received was the absence of the "subtle mountain form of Jim Crowism which excluded Negroes from restaurants, theatres, and the like." Not surprisingly, they found themselves ahead of the Spanish Americans in terms of social acceptance.[14]

The labor shortage forced some relaxation of Colorado's traditionally rigid attitudes toward its older minorities, and, as the demand grew, a number of them were belatedly called upon to aid in the great struggle for democracy. A good many of the Anglo-Saxons, particularly those with any skills, had migrated to the factories and shipyards. Now, said a Colorado Springs paper, there were places for black workers at the local army air base, laborers' jobs that paid up to $1,300 a year. But employment proved to be more difficult than advertised. Hearing that there was work in the area, a number of blacks began to filter into the community, only to find that the demand mysteriously had dried up. By a presidential order of May 27, 1943, discrimination was prohibited in government or defense industries, but management got around that in Colorado by hastily employing Mexican Americans whom they long had shunned. Patriotic blacks, of course, had any number of other opportunities. At Durango, for example, an army recruiting officer received instructions to sign up a company of them to be used in an ammunition unit, duty that was not always eagerly sought after. As was customary, they would be directed by white officers.[15]

Although Mexican Americans were taken on to fill minority requirements, their role in the Colorado labor force did not improve. As always, they were used as field workers. Joining them for the 1942 harvest were about two hundred Indians. When some three hundred Mexican Americans went to work on a construction project at Camp Hale, near Leadville, they soon experienced ethnic prejudice. Of the nine thousand workers they were the only ones not supplied with heated barracks and mess halls, and they had to drive nearly twenty miles each way to work over mountain roads. When the whole lot was summarily fired, the project engineer explained that they were all loafers. He cleared up the matter of the barracks and the food by saying that there were no quarters available for people of Mexican extraction and that meals were not provided because "Mexicans eat such different foods." When U.S. Senator Dennis Chávez, of New Mexico, heard about the case, he threatened to take it to the floor of the Senate unless immediate corrective action was taken. It was; the men went back to work, with equal facilities.[16]

Meanwhile, life among the majority of Coloradans proceeded in about the same way it did among other Americans under wartime conditions. When Colorado novelist Hal Borland visited his hometown of Flagler, he found a small community whose daily activities appeared to be representative of those in other little western towns. The wheat trucks that rolled into town driven by women underscored the shortage of labor caused by the war. As he said, one old lady who watched the exodus into the armed forces could remark, "I can't die now. All my pallbearers have gone to war!" Some of the high school boys filled gaps left by their older brothers, but those left behind felt restless. While not all of them wanted to hurry to the battlefield, there was a sense of guilt and of being out of place as a young, healthy civilian in time of war. Older people felt it, too. A rancher near Delta sold every piece of gasoline-burning equipment he had except an old Model-A Ford that took the cream to town twice a week, and he reverted to horse-drawn machinery—not because he was unable to get gasoline, but because he had a sense of doing something for the war effort and thought that perhaps the fuel would be needed to propel one of the tanks in which his son would ride across France with General Patton.[17] His sincere concern was by no means an isolated case, yet he might have felt self-conscious if anyone had labeled him patriotic.

Those who lived in towns near military bases contributed their time to assistance and entertainment of the troops in training. Colorado Springs formed a War Recreation Committee to coordinate services and to direct a force of over a thousand volunteers who participated in the program. Free refreshments, square dancing, bridge, and free portrait sketching were among the offerings. All servicemen were given reduced rates at the municipal golf course; at the public tennis courts, both balls and rackets were furnished to them free of charge. Two ten-team leagues played softball; of the total, sixteen of the teams were made up of military personnel.[18] On special holidays, such as Thanksgiving, free meals and refreshments were provided at the local auditorium.

Although the war affected the lives of Coloradans, as it did those of all Americans, the political and social outlook of these westerners remained very much the same during those years of great change. In 1943 the General Assembly passed what was termed a

Labor Peace Act, the restrictions of which were so severe that they canceled almost every gain labor had made since the days of Ludlow. It virtually invalidated the all-union shop, prohibited mass picketing and secondary boycotts, forbade the use of union funds for political action, compelled unions to keep all records open for inspection by the State Industrial Commission, and obliged the unions to have reviewed by the commission any punishments they doled out to their members. Governor John C. Vivian, who admitted that he had not read all of the final bill, signed it and pronounced its contents to be "progressive." Labor called it the worst law of its kind in the United States and went to court. Late in 1944 the Colorado Supreme Court invalidated portions of the act but allowed some rather severe restrictions to remain.[19] In the presidential election of that year Colorado voters further showed their hostility to political liberalism, and to the New Deal in particular, by giving Republican candidate Thomas E. Dewey a majority of 30,000 votes.[20]

The state's ultraconservative element reacted sharply when, in the spring of 1944, the University of Colorado invited Harry Bridges of the Longshoremen's Union to speak. Coming hard on the heels of a Labor Peace Act, the intent of which was to suppress any uprisings on the part of the workers, the invitation of a labor leader so radical in his views produced an immediate uproar. The American Legion demanded that the performance be called off, to which the university's acting president, R. G. Gustavson, responded that the institution would not be run by any one group, including the legion. The *Denver Post,* widely known for its right-wing policies, called the invitation a "stupid act" and some of the university regents agreed. One of them told the American Legion state commander that from time to time the faculty or students construed freedom of speech "as a license to invite any jackass to come and bray." Another regent charged that for the past twenty years the university had been teaching communism. As a national magazine pointed out, this elected molder of the university's policies believed the Communists occupied the White House, the Supreme Court, and other high places. His colleagues took a milder view and reprimanded President Gustavson while turning aside the demands that he be fired.[21] Meanwhile, "the notorious alien-Communist," as the *Post* described Bridges, made his appearance at Boulder.

By 1944 the outcome of the war was generally agreed upon; only the details of how it was to be concluded were yet to be revealed. By that time the output of the American industrial war machine had begun to level off, and some of the military establishments were closed in anticipation of dwindling requirements. Although Colorado had lost population to war plants rather than attracting it, the long glide toward peacetime activities did not seriously disrupt its employment stability. There was, however, an awareness that big changes lay just ahead. During that spring cattlemen were urged to reduce their herds, and an official from the Colorado Stock Growers and Feeders Association admitted, "We've got more cattle than we can handle." There was such a glut of eggs on the market that the government began guaranteeing producers a price of at least twenty-six cents a dozen and the press urged people to eat more poultry and eggs. On the other hand, petroleum products still were closely rationed, and in a further effort to conserve gasoline the state increased its limit of twenty fish a day to the possession of a two-day catch so that fishermen would not have to waste fuel by returning to the favorite spots for a second limited haul.[22]

As the war began to wind down, there were evidences that business interests both within and beyond Colorado's borders believed that in the near future the state would experience a resurgence of its tourist and commercial activity. During the spring of 1944 United Air Lines' application for a direct "over the hump" route to Los Angeles, via Grand Junction and Las Vegas, was tentatively approved. About that time T. E. Braniff visited the Colorado capital and outlined his plans for midcontinental service in Colorado, New Mexico, Wyoming, Kansas, and Nebraska. Already Continental Airlines served areas to the south, and, through a connection with American Air Lines at El Paso, one could obtain air passage to Mexico City. By 1947 Continental would have eighteen flights a day that originated or terminated in Denver. Local service grew rapidly in the early postwar years. By 1946 Monarch Airlines served western slope cities and the Denver-based Challenger Airlines flew routes to Montana and Utah. The subsequent merger of these two lines would produce Frontier Airlines, the largest company of its class. In an election held in the spring of 1947, Denver voters approved a $700,000 bond issue—to be matched by federal funds—for municipal airport improvement. It was the only one of several expansions that was to put Stapleton

Field on the air map as a principal stop along international routes.[23]

Optimism, so well known as a western characteristic, generally pervaded Colorado as it prepared itself for the postwar era, but even among some of the more aggressive communities there was an underlying concern that peacetime might not be as beneficial to the state's sometimes sensitive economy as was hoped. Colorado Springs, for example, once a mecca for wealthy invalids and a city that had benefited from neighboring mineral deposits, had gone into a slide during the late 1930s, much to the consternation of its business leaders. Thanks to the war, its population had increased from 37,000 in 1940 to an estimated 60,000 four years later, and that appeared to be a hopeful sign. While the city fathers were happy over the imminent fall of the Axis powers, they were concerned about what that event would do to local trade and population generated by the existence of neighboring military complexes, particularly one of such importance as Fort Carson. As they witnessed the closing of bases around the nation, these civic leaders resolved to fight with all their means any efforts to remove this golden egg that fortune had deposited at the foot of the Rockies.[24]

The sense that Colorado had reached a crossroads in its development was felt generally across the state. Once more its leadership peered into the future and concluded that growth was not only desirable but necessary. These people were not boomers or men of great speculative impulses but cautious, conservative individuals who wanted to creep ahead rather than trot or gallop. Critics harped on the fact that Colorado was a colonial appendage of the eastern business sector and that capital from this faraway and almost foreign place had enslaved the mountain residents. Business leaders had to agree, because some of them had felt the influence of this creeping financial ailment, but at the same time they felt that eastern money was a necessity even if it also was an evil. They knew that during the war the state's civilian population had diminished (perhaps by no more than the 5 percent the guessers claimed) and that the only counties showing any increase during the war were those having military establishments or war plants in or near them. It was hoped—and it turned out to be true—that some of the servicemen recently stationed in Colorado would want to return to make their homes in the state, but it also seemed possible that many who had been enticed away to shipyards and factories might not come back.[25]

But a number of those who had gone away did come back, along with a great many who first had seen the state as military trainees and had found its climate and social atmosphere pleasant. This infusion of new blood, mixed with some of that belonging to residents who were prone to be critical of the "establishment," produced a generation that began to question the "bigger is better" assumption. They challenged the notion so long held by the state's business leaders that growth was not only good but essential and that somehow strangers who found their way west and settled in the central Rockies inevitably would be valuable contributors to the economy. The new generation did not agree with community leaders that the flight of population during the war necessarily represented a statistical retrogression whose effects would mean a step backward for Colorado. While the critics of growth were as yet relatively small in number, and their notions of population control were regarded as somewhat visionary, nevertheless their growing presence forecast a day when some decisions would have to be made.

PART FIVE

# Colorado: Cool and Colorful

# 16

# The Rediscovery of Colorado

If Coloradans had reached a crossroads at the close of the war, it was by no means the first time; in fact, the state's history showed that since gold-rush days such occurrences had been periodic. During the intervening years, cautious, conservative Colorado had moved ahead haltingly, and then when crisis made its inevitable rounds, there was much stir and voluble outbursts of optimistic talk. It must have sounded familiar when a Denver city planner and landscape architect looked ahead from the vantage point of early 1945 and said that sackcloth and ashes were not the answer but that rather the sound of trumpets and aggressive action were called for. "We cannot sit down and moan. We will have to strike out and fight for the development of our own region, and we will do it vigorously," he wrote. He regretted that many a young Coloradan, attracted elsewhere by wartime industry, might not return to the state. If this occurred other young men would have to be brought here to work in agriculture, business, and government positions.[1]

Some residents of the Queen City were concerned by the indifference of their business leaders and by the apparent absence of promise for the days ahead. For approximately a quarter-century the look of Denver's central business district had remained virtually unchanged; almost no new construction had been undertaken nor was there any visible interest in the development of additional industries in the city and in its environs. Community leaders seemed almost proud that the war had brought so little change; they argued that it would make the transition to peace easier and that there would be less dislocation. Neither the governor nor the Manufacturers' Association showed concern about keeping the factory workers who had come during the war; they foresaw Denver as primarily a commercial city, an entrepôt of trade for a rich, irrigated agricultural country along the mountains and eastward. Business leaders banked on trade and tourism as sure things, and they resolved to move slowly but steadily. As some of them remarked, Denver's future might not add up to much "but it will be comfortable here and we're doing all right now."[2]

Much the same attitude had been evidenced when demands were made for temporary war housing. Although the need for it was painfully obvious, Denver was one of the few cities in America where almost no emergency housing was provided. Real estate men boasted that their city had the lowest amount of public housing per capita in the nation. They admitted freely that while other places were begging the government for temporary housing, they themselves were fighting just as hard to keep it out of their area. Since Denver's population was believed to have increased by nearly 20 percent during the war, the pressure for accommodations was enormous; since there were several ways in which rent controls could be eluded, property owners had a field day cashing in on a desperate situation.

Even if one takes the charitable view that Denver opposed cheap, temporary war housing on aesthetic grounds, as opposed to greed on the part of the landlords, the results were the same: a critical shortage not only during the war years but immediately afterward. Nor was it surprising that, architecturally speaking, Denver's chickens came home to roost in the immediate postwar years. An architect who drove along the city's tree-lined streets and viewed the solid brick houses, set off by lawns and foliage, remarked that when one entered the new suburbs the well-scrubbed appearance suddenly gave way to a treeless complex of boxlike structures thrown together of the cheapest material and with the least possible expenditure of money or imagination. "These houses are going to blight Denver for years," he correctly predicted.[3]

The housing problem did not exist only in Denver. All along the mountain front, from Fort Collins southward to Pueblo, a similar situation prevailed. At Boulder it was so severe that 200 trailers were brought in from Kansas to house the eruption of veteran-students that descended on the state university. Colorado College, at Colorado Springs, saw a Quonset-hut village sprout on its campus, and soon a little community of veterans and their families became a part of that scene. The demand was so great at Pueblo that families lived temporarily in some of the barns at the state fairgrounds. Since the Office of Price Administration had frozen prices at their previous levels, renters of a "one-horse apartment" paid only $2.50 a month, the price of equine rent. There were so many requests for these facilities that the management had to draw the line and reserve a reasonable number of the units for horses. Meanwhile, at Denver, some seven thousand veterans and their wives doubled up with friends or parents, or rented what they could and asked no indiscreet questions about rent ceilings.[4]

The flow of former servicemen, many of whom were non-Coloradans bound for campuses, was the beginning of a new rush to the Rockies that soon would outstrip in numbers the first assault upon Colorado almost a century earlier. Although a national business magazine charged that Denver had drowsed in the shadow of the Rockies during most of the intervening years, languidly presided over by a few old families who had put very little of their fortunes into its economic development, nevertheless outsiders had a hunch that there was great potential in the central Rockies. As early as the middle of the war *Life* magazine said that no matter which way it turned Colorado would exercise a quiet but firm influence on the other mountain states and that in its own way it was getting ready to welcome the world when the great commotion overseas had subsided. One of the key bits of evidence for such an assertion was Denver's announced desire to be a main hub for the world-girdling airlines that were expected to emerge with the coming of peace.[5]

Despite the apparent lack of interest in industrial growth manifested by business leaders in Denver and the state at large, there occurred a boom in postwar Colorado that appeared to defy not only the planners, but also the predicters. War veterans and their friends discovered the place boosters long had touted as "Cool, Colorful Colorado," and they flocked to it during these early postwar years. So did corporations, whose executives saw that the state offered them a number of advantages. It came as a mild surprise to the Seventeenth Street crowd when, at the close of the war, the New York real estate firm of Webb & Knapp purchased Denver's courthouse square and proposed to erect a large building there. Viewing the action with a mixture of flattery at such eastern attention and mild reservations about a new invasion of "foreign" capital, they concluded that it must have come about because of the old policy of steady but not sensational growth so faithfully followed over the years. The growing number of federal offices in Denver, the probable future of ordnance and other defense installations along the Rockies, the assurance of Big Thompson and other diverted water to the eastern plains, and the prospects of heavy tourist travel seemed to have convinced the "smart money" along the Atlantic Seaboard that Colorado was a place with a future.[6]

Thus potential investors looked at markets, materials, labor, available plant sites, and climate when they thought about branching out in Colorado. In general, they envisaged life in small to medium-sized cities situated in areas of high recreational potential as being highly desirable from the standpoint of worker morale. The state's ultraconservative attitude toward labor, as evinced in the recent act of 1943, made organized labor sufficiently weak to be attractive to management. Colorado's conservatism would work against the grain if financing proved necessary, for local bankers were notably cautious, but since most of the firms contemplating a relocation had other sources of money this was no real deterrent.[7]

If the new immigrants that now looked toward postwar Colorado believed that the state's highly regarded atmosphere had made it the sanatorium of the world and that invalids literally leaped out of the grave to enjoy additional years in this remarkable place, they must have found the public health statistics discouraging. Two-thirds of the states had better records for fatalities resulting from disease, and in some cases Colorado stood close to the bottom of the list. Its infant mortality rate was higher than those of all but seven other states. During the first half of the 1940s nearly 15,000 Coloradans had died from controllable or preventable causes. It was estimated that since half of that number could have been saved, more than 8,000 residents, or three times the Colorado fatalities suffered as a result of the war, had died needlessly.

In short, Colorado's public health record was one of the worst in the nation. Its expenditures for public health were less than half of those appropriated by Montana and less than a third of those provided by Utah. Dr. Florence R. Sabin, who had retired to her native state, was appalled by the situation, and during the early 1940s she campaigned vigorously to improve conditions. It was a long, hard journey, most of it uphill. Over the years the administrative machinery had rusted as the State Health Division, a politically controlled department, had deteriorated until six of the small department's principal administrative positions stood vacant. The general lack of education in the field of health had built up a barrier of indifference that only long and intensive educational programs would penetrate. As one unhappy rural school teacher lamented, "When kids laugh at you for having a cistern sterilized, just because a rat died in it, how are you going to conduct a class in health without implying that mama and papa belong on Tobacco Road?" By 1946 and 1947 Dr. Sabin's campaign had begun to show results and the state took action to correct some of the deficiencies.[8]

Rural areas, as always, were neglected in the realm of public health and education. In the immediate postwar years doctors began moving to Denver, but towns of 5,000 or fewer suffered, particularly those on the western slope. Small towns also found it hard to obtain teachers, many of whom had joined the armed services or had moved to better paying jobs in teaching or industry during the war. As a result just under 50 percent of all rural teachers in the state held emergency certificates in 1945. About 2,000 of them could not qualify for even a minimum certificate, but since replacements were almost impossible to find their jobs were in no immediate danger.

The president of the State College of Education, at Greeley, looked at the deteriorating situation and wondered if the state might not become famous as one where a billion-dollar highway ran past a $500 schoolhouse in which a $1,200 teacher with a handful of books and no equipment faced the students. One of those instructors, who worked with a minimum of aids or equipment pointed out that austerity did not end in the classroom. "My room has a clothes line crossing it thirteen times," she wrote. "On Monday evenings the landlord's heavy underwear is left to dry in my room. . . . There are twenty screen doors behind my bed; ten one-hundred pound sacks of flour against the wall; skiis and an old slop jar under my bed; surplus electric fans, boxes, suitcases and the smell of moth balls fill the room. The only place to eat is at the local beer joint. I have not been invited out to dinner once this year. Under no circumstances would I consider teaching in this place another year."[9]

Perhaps it was one of the great ironies of the era that the owners of the *Denver Post* were able to discern a beacon on the horizon and to lay a more liberal course in the very early postwar years. In the spring of 1946 the heirs of Bonfils and Tammen demonstrated a remarkable insight to the changes about to take place in Colorado when they brought in as editor E. Palmer Hoyt, of the Portland *Oregonian.* In a turnabout that was regarded as revolutionary, the "big brother," as smaller state newspapers called it, shed its reactionary image in exchange for one so enlightened that it amazed both friends and enemies of that widely read journal. Hoyt, who was given a five-year contract at $52,000 a year with no strings attached, wrought a number of changes, the more newsworthy of which were putting doors back on the toilets—Bonfils had removed them to keep the employees from loafing—allowing women reporters to smoke, raising wages, and shelving the "sonofabitch list" that so long had proscribed the paper's enemies. Of more significance were such changes as the innovation of a weekly roll of honor that drew attention to contributions made by Coloradans, and for the first time recognition was given to Negroes, Mexican Americans, and Nisei. As one Colorado journalist put it, at last the *Post* had accepted its social responsibility.

The changing of the guard at the *Post* was more noticeable for the suddenness with which it occurred and in the paper's altered appearance than in a ideological sense. Its front page, once described as a kind of puzzle that readers had mastered over the years, became less a journalistic jumble. News stories and editorials that formerly gave strangers a feeling of panic and impending doom now were less sensational. The political advance from the deepest realms of the far right to something approaching center lent the impression to faithful supporters of the old *Post* that radicals had seized the presses, while others regarded the change merely as an admission that the twentieth century had arrived. As it developed, the change made that spring foreshadowed a political upheaval in both Denver and the state in the elections held later that year.[10]

The first time Coloradans went to the polls in general postwar elections they indicated that significant changes were at hand by turning in some upsets that attracted national attention. In the autumn of 1946 Colorado was one of the few places where Democratic victories occurred, and when former district attorney John A. Carroll, a liberal who was supported by the gadfly journalist Gene Cervi, among others, was sent to Congress, there were hints that different days lay ahead for the central Rockies. Not only did Carroll unseat a Republican congressional candidate—a rare accomplishment in the nationwide elections of that year—but gubernatorial nominee W. Lee Knous performed a similar feat by taking the state's top executive office away from that party. These victories were modified considerably by the fact that Republicans retained control of both houses of the General Assembly and shared some of the other important elective offices with the Democrats, but the selection of Knous, in particular, indicated a growing concern among voters over the deterioration in the state's social services. In his campaign the new governor stressed the importance of such obvious needs as better highways, but there was also a call for better care of the sick and the needy, and for improvements in education.[11]

Perhaps more significant than the statewide elections of 1946 was the smashing defeat in 1947 of Denver's old-line politicians who for years had controlled the city. Although challenger Quigg Newton's supporters talked much of reform, the real issues were the incompetence and political encrustation that characterized the reign of Benjamin F. Stapleton, who had served as mayor since 1923 except for the 1931–35 period. By the war's end Denver's thirty-year-old charter was a fixture that had created a municipal autocracy. The mayor had almost unrestricted power to hire and fire city employees. He drew up a budget that was very difficult to contest, and his office let contracts without competitive bidding. Any regime of that age and strength was bound to generate rebellion eventually and in Denver's case it happened at a time when a good many people saw change as being not only desirable but necessary if the postwar years were to be a time of progress. When John Gunther stopped in the Queen City while gathering material for his *Inside U.S.A.* (1946), he remarked that most of the power lay with a tightly knit, old-family structure that was standpat, ultraconservative, and unenthusiastic about acquiring industries. The pressure of war had brought a certain amount of increased employment and capital equipment into Denver, as it had to other parts of the West, and now those who saw the acquisition as beneficial feared that shortsighted leadership might mar that encouraging development. As a young liberal Republican put it, the voters recognized that Denver was now a modern industrial city and no longer just a nice place in which retired western capitalists chose to spend their declining years. But it took more than the opinions of young liberals to sway the electorate.[12]

The "old" *Post* had quarrelled with Stapleton for years, and during the thirties it had helped to derail him, if only temporarily; now the "new" *Post* sought to repeat the performance once and for all. Its recently hired editor encouraged Quigg Newton, a young attorney, to lead the attack upon city hall. The *Rocky Mountain News* joined its journalistic archenemy, and between them they put on a campaign that produced almost eighty thousand votes for Newton, relegating Stapleton to a humiliating third-place spot with less than eighteen thousand. This "clear and vigorous young candidate," as the *Post* described their man, thus evicted the seventy-seven-year-old incumbent from a job paying an annual salary of only six thousand dollars, a figure that had not changed since 1916. Using some leftover campaign funds, Newton supplemented the proportionally low salaries of his chief administrators and thereby succeeded in attracting some decidedly competent people. Within months he upgraded city health services, greatly improving Denver General Hospital, and instituted a system of competitive bidding for city supplies that saved millions. Although he maintained a nonpartisan stance, there was no escaping the fact that the machinery the young man was asked to operate was antiquated; therefore, as he drove hard down the road that the *Post* had promised would be progressive, there were disappointments. But in spite of the reverses that inevitably confront any reform candidate, the innovative war veteran for eight years gave the capital city a new image of a place that welcomed the postwar world to Colorado. Suddenly Denver was young again.[13]

National magazines noted the political changes in Colorado and regarded them as revolutionary. One writer said that prior to the events of 1946 all of the state's four Republican congressmen dutifully had followed the line laid down by the National Association of Manufacturers, and that in Denver, where the Democratic Party was in the grip of the Stapleton machine, there had been little choice for liberal voters. John Carroll's victory, coupled with the Newton triumph a few months later, was seen as evidence that the young liberals were coming on strong. This appeared to be confirmed in 1948 when both Carroll and Knous were overwhelmingly returned to office and the Democrats occupied not only the remaining state elective offices but also controlled the legislature.

The reelection of Big Ed Johnson to the Senate that year signified nothing in terms of liberal or conservative thinking on the part of the voters because he was, as a maverick, by now almost a Colorado institution, unaffected by ordinary politics.[14]

When Harry Truman campaigned in Denver in 1948 he warned Coloradans that theirs was a state in which soil conservation, irrigation, and hydroelectric projects were important, suggesting that his party possessed the best record in these fields. He went on to say that the Republicans, whom he was sure were controlled by big business, wanted the West to furnish raw materials cheaply and then to buy back finished goods at high prices. He warned that if that party won the election it would try again to make the West an economic colony of eastern financiers.[15]

It was an ancient warning, one that westerners found difficult to heed. Theirs was an underdeveloped part of the nation, and without capital of their own to process extracted resources they had little choice but to turn elsewhere. Therefore, outside capital had been sought assiduously for nearly a century, and the desire for it was greater than the fear of its possible consequences. Truman's opponent, Thomas E. Dewey, also spoke in Denver. He, too, advocated conservation of resources, but he suggested a sufficient revision in federal tax laws to encourage the discovery and exploitation of new oil and mineral deposits. Certainly this had an appeal for a number of Coloradans, but it came at a time when the old, conservative element was coasting and a new, younger group already had commenced to talk about environmental problems. This did not account for Dewey's defeat in the state, but neither did the promise of further exploitation of resources result in much applause for the New Yorker.[16]

Truman carried the state heavily, and John Carroll went back to Congress with a two-to-one win over his opponent. Liberals, encouraged, told one another that theirs was the wave of the future in Colorado. Some of them were young and new to the state, so it was hard for them to understand that voters were not undergoing any reform but simply were in the midst of one of their periodic catch-up phases. During the next several years young Quigg Newton was to experience setbacks in Denver, to try unsuccessfully for the Democratic senatorial nomination, and finally to give up politics. His subsequent career in educational administration included posts with the Ford Foundation, the University of Colorado, where he served as president, and finally the Commonwealth Fund in New York City. After being defeated in a 1950 bid for the U.S. Senate, Carroll was successful six years later and served one term; failing reelection, he retired from politics. Meanwhile, in the Eisenhower election of 1952, the state's Republicans swept back into power and cautious Colorado resumed its old, carefully chosen pathway to the future.

As the traditionally conservative leadership resumed political control it looked around and found that much had happened since it had been away. Both Denver and the state were in the midst of an economic boom. During the 1950s the changes that had surfaced at the close of the war began to be more and more pronounced. Admittedly Quigg Newton had not lived up to his advanced billing as a reformer, and the *Denver Post*'s quest for respectability sometimes had shown indications of retrogression, but in the main these symbols told of gradual change; some even thought of it as progress.

Of the more obvious changes that were taking place, particularly in the capital city, few were more dramatic than those wrought by Webb & Knapp's face-lifting of downtown Denver. In a building splurge led by one of the firm's partners, a kind of latter-day Fifty-Niner type of financier named William Zeckendorf, the old twelve-story skyline was pierced by the city's first skyscrapers. The business district, said the New Yorker, was "too spread out to be quaint and too ugly to be pleasant"; in other words, he thought that Denver, a place he referred to as "the town that time forgot," needed modernizing. Some of the results of his wheeling and dealing efforts were the Hilton Hotel, a 2,200-car garage, quarters for the May D&F department store, and a skating rink. Down the street a few blocks, Texas promoter Clint Murchison's twenty-eight-story First National Bank building added another glittering piece to the Queen City's business-district crown.[17] Affecting the economy for miles along the mountain front was the establishment in 1957 of the twenty-seven-million-dollar Martin plant near Denver, built to turn out the Titan missile. In a five-year period the presence of this industry more than doubled the population of suburban Littleton and provided jobs for about twelve thousand Denverites.[18]

While Martin Marietta, as the firm came to be known, was welcomed because it had a large payroll and because it purchased some twenty million dollars' worth of supplies a year from other Colorado companies, the fact remained that it was a "single crop" type of industry; should the missile market became satiated, the resulting unemployment could hit hard at the community. As insurance against such an occurrence Coloradans looked to some of their older firms for growth and development. The Colorado Fuel and Iron Company began to show great vigor during the 1950s as it emerged from the role of a somewhat doddering old firm into that of an aggressive manufacturer prepared to branch out from its more traditional production of heavy steel manufactures into items that ranged from manhole covers to cigarette lighters. Other firms familiar to Coloradans were the Gates Rubber Company and Shwayder Brothers, the latter widely known for Samsonite luggage, card tables, and folding chairs. Ideal Cement, the American Crystal Sugar Company, and the Coors Brewery, at Golden, also were familiar names.[19]

The influx of new industries was due, in part, to the climate. The state's clean air and mild temperatures had been widely heralded for years, and now industry saw Colorado as a place where the scenery, the easily available recreational facilities, and the bracing atmosphere would attract employees. That the theory was correct was attested by the swarms of applications for transfers from other parts of the nation whenever an industry located in the state. Local firms knew that these advantages were important, but not without their price, because Colorado, in its remoteness, was an expensive place to operate. John Gates, of the Gates Rubber Company, pointed to this problem when he said, "Of course we have to fight the fact of being here. We get nothing from this area—we have to import everything and export everything." However, he admitted that he and his brother Charlie were not inclined to move because "this country of crisp nights is a great energizer." Jesse Shwayder, whose people had come all the way from Poland to locate in Central City and then in Denver, where he founded Shwayder Bros., Inc., agreed that it sounded impractical to try to manufacture in Colorado, because logistically the odds were against him. But, he sighed, "I'd rather make a dollar in Denver than three dollars in New York."[20]

When Coloradans pointed out to newcomers that the air and the mountains were worth an undetermined part of their income, it was regarded locally as poor taste to challenge such olympian thoughts. Labor, however, frequently argued that these benefits were costly, for families could not cash their "psychic paychecks" at grocery stores. As the saying went in Colorado Springs, "You can't eat Pike's Peak."[21] Additionally, labor found negotiations for better wages difficult in a state where the union movement was historically weak. Firms from other parts of the country were aware of this weakness, and frequently it played a significant part in their decision to locate in the central Rockies.

While climate and the availability of cheap, meek labor attracted industry, Colorado leaders tried to show some discrimination as to those who were invited. Colorado Springs, for example, acquired some sixty small firms in the postwar period, but it favored what was described as industry that kept its hair combed and its shoelaces tied, little factories that made small, easily shipped products. This, said the boosters, was intended to please everyone, even the retired millionaires who came to the mountains to forget why they needed a rest. Another example of "clean" industry was the establishment at Boulder of Esquire-Coronet's subscription department, a business that was nonpolluting and glad to get away from Chicago's unionism. The Triplex Corporation, makers of pistons, abandoned Chicago in favor of Pueblo. A number of familiar names turned up along the mountain base, among them Minneapolis-Honeywell Regulator, Hewlett-Packard, Beech Aircraft, Lionel Corporation, International Business Machines, Eastman Kodak, Monsanto, and others.[22] Less welcome was Dow Chemical's Rocky Flats plant, situated between Boulder and Golden, the output of which involved fissionable materials. By 1975 Dow would give up the operation, surrendering it to another company, but that did not alleviate the problem. However, when the boom was on, during the 1950s, environmental concerns were not the most important consideration among those who cherished growth; that problem would become more important later.

High priority was given even "cleaner" types of installations such as educational and scientific complexes that brought in large payrolls, talented people, and no smoke. The Air Force Academy near Colorado Springs, which graduated its first class in 1959, is a good example of federal largess that was eagerly sought by those who wanted to keep Colorado "green" in a financial sense. Similarly, Boulder made a spirited effort early in the fifties to land the Central Radio Propagation Laboratory of the National Bureau of Standards, and it was the winner of a contest that involved twenty-six other cities. With the addition of the Atomic Energy Commission's cryogenics engineering laboratory, the name of the complex was changed to read Boulder Laboratories of the National

Bureau of Standards. By the mid sixties it had an annual budget of about sixteen million dollars and its scientific personnel numbered almost seven hundred. Another instance of governmental scientific complexes locating in Colorado was the National Center for Atmospheric Research—popularly known as NCAR—established at Boulder in 1960. Five years later it had an operating budget of nearly eight million dollars and some three hundred fifty employees, and in 1964 ground was broken for the center's permanent home. Ball Brothers Research Corporation, a child of the old and well-known Muncie, Indiana, fruit jar firm, also located at Boulder in this period. It employed several hundred scientists and engineers who worked at the development of spacecraft systems.[23]

The objections to "growth at any price" were silenced for the moment by those who took pride in the results of the boom. Tract housing projects sprouted around cities in the growth areas, producing visual monotony and prospects for future slums, but this architectural fungus was regarded as part of Colorado's great leap forward. Into the boxlike homes moved the newcomers, who worked at their jobs, rushed to the nearby mountains at every opportunity, raised their families, and took reassurance from the *Denver Post* that indeed it was a privilege to live in such a place.

There was pride also in reclamation of more underdeveloped portions of the state. "Desert Dollars" was a national magazine's alliterative title for an article that described the boom in natural gas, oil, coal, silver, and uranium in the area known as the Four Corners. As always the measure of success was growth, and the fact that during the first half of the 1950s the population of the area trebled was taken as a satisfactory answer to its economic problems.[24] In just a few years loud complaints would be heard from those who objected to the pall of smoke drifting eastward from the coal-driven power-generating plants in that desert country.

By 1960 the latter-day promoters of Colorado could point with pride to their efforts at growth. The census of that year indicated a 31 percent increase, making the state the ninth fastest growing one in the nation and the fourth fastest since 1950. Colorado also ranked ninth in personal income. Theoretically everyone in the state ought to have been happy, for the growth was accompanied by a general economic upswing and most businesses prospered. One of the problems was that the old crowd—the miners, farmers, and ranchers who once ran things—no longer was in command.

Silver mining had faded, coal mining had been a sick industry for years, and even the farmers, whose incomes had risen, complained that inflation and a brief recession had lowered their net incomes. Also, the boom was spotty. A closer look at the much-advertised population gain showed that thirty-six of Colorado's sixty-three counties actually lost population during the 1950s and that more than 90 percent of the gain was confined to a narrow nine-county belt running between Fort Collins and Pueblo, an area that contained about 70 percent of the state's population. As an illustration of what was happening it may be noted that in 1960 thirty-one new companies opened plants in the state and that nineteen of them selected sites within the Fort Collins–Pueblo strip. Of those locating elsewhere, only one hired as many as fifty workers.[25]

Renewal of the establishment's ancient "sell Colorado" program brought complaints from planners, who predicted that reckless development would cost future generations part of their heritage. When the well-known writer and critic Bernard De Voto spoke at the University of Colorado's 1948 commencement exercises, he warned his listeners against throwing away western land and water resources. He stated that there were limitations to the sustenance capacities of the "desert," and he contended that nature's patrimony ought not be squandered by ambitious men whose rationale for their activity was the notion of progress. Governor Lee Knous agreed that conservation was a commendable ideal, but he thought the Utah-born writer had been in New York so long that he was out of touch with western problems. Former Governor Ralph L. Carr cried "bunk" and pointed to the vast development of the West over the preceding seventy-five years as proof that the desert had been conquered.[26] When the famed frontier historian Walter Prescott Webb offered a similar warning in a 1957 *Harper's* article, the response was much the same. He, too, talked of arid America and the chronic lack of moisture. The *Post* jeered at him, called him "Doc" as though he were some kind of quack, and expressed great indignation at his suggestion that mountain-front urbanization was a result of a flight from the desert. The title of the *Post's* article, "Us Desert Rats Is Doing Okay," was suggestive of the sensitivity felt by the boomers, and of a traditional inferiority complex that westerners still tried to cover with bombast.[27]

Fear that such talk would drive away potential industries did not apply to the tourist trade. Over the years it had been steady and important, so much so that it was regarded as an industry. One might even call it an extractive industry, because each season it separated millions of dollars from visitors who came to look at the scenery and to breathe Colorado's fabled invigorating air. The natives were perfectly aware that they were engaged in mining in reverse. "We still get the gold," remarked the mayor of Central City during the 1950s. "We get it from some 450,000 tourists a year."[28] He was right. That once charming little town was turned into the Coney Island of the Rockies and the one-time Queen of the Little Kingdom became a tired old bawd, painted up beyond recognition, selling her wares for any price to anyone. It stood out as the classic example of fakery in the world of tourist traps, and by the time Colorado's centennial year approached Central City had outdistanced all her rivals in this respect.

Complaints that Colorado was trying to get back its gold from the tourists in too brazen a manner began in the early 1950s. A travel magazine writer of that period wondered why the state needed phony atmosphere when it had so much to offer that was natural and beautiful. Neighboring Wyoming and Montana displayed their scenic attractions with a minimum of man-made embellishments, but Coloradans seemed to think that the state's complexion needed some kind of cosmetic aid. Thomas Hornsby Ferril, Colorado's internationally known poet and writer, complained about photographic deceptions such as the trick of pulling in mountains by means of telephoto lenses to make them appear higher and closer to the prospective viewer or buyer. The multiple sources of propaganda that deluged the eastern innocents bothered him, and he admitted that when anyone asked him how to spend a pleasant vacation in the Colorado Rockies, "My innards tie up into knots." As a native Coloradan he had come to loathe tourists and even to hate himself when "I get crowded into being one."[29]

A lot of Coloradans understood such sentiments. Yet they were proud of their state, privately pleased that others wanted to see it, and when given the opportunity to show it their hospitality was genuine. The people of Grand Junction were representative of those who wanted to attract tourists in a less flamboyant manner; they posted highway signs that offered tourists an opportunity to rest their children at one of the city's parks. Travelers were met by designated hosts who invited them to take part in a variety of locally sponsored programs. There was music, softball, basketball, a craft instructor, and a teacher of folk dancing to entertain the young. In the evening free movies and sometimes a pet show or a doll show provided further entertainment. There was no outward attempt to extract money from travelers, yet if the offerings kept them in the state one more day, local businessmen benefited.

In other cities visitors were able to study some of the old buildings and to see them much as they had been in the mining days. Frequently restaurants and bars had showcases containing ore samples that travelers were welcome to handle if they were curious. The once-famous town of Victor is an example of the "unrestored" mining metropolis, a place where one could—and still can—drive along streets of abandoned buildings without the feeling that these relics had been embalmed for viewing by paying customers. Ouray, in far western Colorado, was another such former mining town. Those who wanted to relive the day of the narrow-gauge took their families on the "trip into yesterday," riding the Denver and Rio Grande's old narrow-gauge between Durango and Silverton, a slightly "dolled up" old camp. As one observer put it, Colorado was not necessarily the place to go for history, even though the remnants of the state's brief past lay scattered about "as conspicuously as popcorn boxes after a ball game," but rather it was a part of the West refulgent with "instant nostalgia." Whatever the lure, by the mid fifties the "one more day in Colorado" program was keeping tourists in the state for an average of eight days.[30]

The dream of those who promoted tourism was to develop a year-round program, one that would keep merchants, innkeepers, and transportation facilities from suffering unnecessarily during the slack season. Winter sports dated back to the time of the Fifty-Niners, when the young miners, idled by the cold months, took to the slopes on sleds and toboggans. From that time forward men had moved around in the mountains on skis and snowshoes, but usually as a means of getting from one place to another as opposed to pure recreation. The question now was how to make playing in the snow safe, comfortable, and easily accessible to the outlanders.

Colorado, later to be hailed as "Ski Country, U.S.A.," began its campaign for that title before the outbreak of the First World War. In the winter of 1913 a Norwegian skier named Carl Howelsen helped to stage at Hot Sulphur Springs the first winter sports carnival and ski-jumping contest west of the Mississippi River. During the next summer he moved to Steamboat Springs and began to develop some ski slopes at nearby Strawberry Park, where he produced another carnival that winter. From that time the affair grew and its fame began to spread. By 1935 events such as the slalom and downhill racing were added to the earlier jumping events, so that when the postwar rush of skiers descended upon Colorado, Steamboat Springs was prepared to claim its share of the business.[31]

About the time Steamboat was graduating to the slalom and downhill racing classification, another skier was examining the possibilities at Aspen. André Roche, the Swiss expert, spent two weeks on the slopes above the town in 1934, and after he left a local cobbler named Mike Magnifico laid off a trail and built a crude tow out of abandoned mine equipment. The war, rather than constricting the new ski trade, actually was partially responsible for its later success. In 1942 the army sent its Tenth Mountain Division to train at Camp Hale, near Leadville, and before long its personnel discovered Aspen. It was during the following year that Friedl Pfeifer, a sergeant in the group, appraised the Roaring Fork country, and it did not take the Austrian-born skier long to see the possibilities. Later he declared that what he saw was the nearest thing to Switzerland in America. He and some of his friends vowed to return when the war was over to place their futures with the great snowy prospect. Pfeifer did return, and with the financial backing of Chicago financier Walter Paepcke the Aspen Ski Corporation was founded. Nearly twenty years later the Austrian, who meantime had founded Buttermilk, looked back at the Aspen adventure and said, "I never, never figured Aspen would get this big. . . . It is hard to believe it now, but in the early 1950s we had to pull investors in by their shoestrings."[32]

The Camp Hale troops found other attractive places to ski, and two of them agreed that one day they would come back and develop one of their favorite spots, Vail Valley. By 1962 Vail Village, the architecture of which was described as "instant Bavarian," was under construction, and before long a complete resort, plus ski trails and three large lifts, began operations. Not only were the after-skiing facilities attractive and reasonably priced, but the runs were widely acclaimed by experts who were familiar with the best of those in the United States and Europe. Colorado's dry, powdery snow generated much praise. So readily did the average skier take to the Vail facility that when an international ski competition was held there a few years later, only a few off-duty bartenders, some shivering reporters, and a handful of glum representatives of the U.S. Ski Association were said to have observed the action. "Thousands of people were in Vail," reported a sports writer, "but they were tumbling down the mountains themselves as if the whole of Chicago and Minneapolis had been parachuted into the Rockies."[33] During these years a quiet congressman from Michigan and his family used the slopes almost unnoticed during his Christmas vacation. Later, as president, Gerald Ford continued his visits to Vail, and the little village that had sprung from the imaginations of two mountain troopers took its place as the site of yet another "western White House."

By the early 1960s Coloradans, who had regarded the future with apprehension at the close of World War II, could look back upon a decade and a half of economic development and an accompanying population growth. The annual "sell Colorado" expeditions into eastern financial centers had yielded satisfactory hauls from capitalists; easterners readily accepted the notion that the West still was a land of opportunity, particularly that portion of it astraddle the central Rockies. Republican Dwight Eisenhower and his conservative advisers had occupied the White House during most of the 1950s and had given both hope and comfort to the business world. As financiers took advantage of the calm that prevailed, Coloradans did their best to profit from the situation, pausing only to take an occasional momentary glance at the upcoming "soaring sixties," a decade that promised even greater growth and economic rewards.

It was a stance that the optimists had taken before, but this time the voices crying out against untrammeled growth grew louder. As the 1960s came and passed the dissent would grow to significant proportions and lead to far-reaching political ramifications.

# 17

# Cultural Crosscurrents

When Colorado's business and political leaders struck off on a postwar course of continued growth and development for the state, they were following a path their predecessors had pursued for years. It was a long established maxim in American communities that not to move forward was to move backward and that census figures revealed the direction in which a given state was going. Coloradans had been aware from the beginning that theirs was a land well endowed by nature. While they had to concern themselves with the preservation of their heritage, they took the view that there were sufficient reserves of undeveloped resources to allow for the reasonable use of them without seriously damaging the environment. As late as 1945 it seemed clear to the planners that the state had room for more people, who, of course, would conduct new businesses or develop the old. And from them money would flow into the public coffers by way of the tax collectors' offices. It was a game that was entirely familiar; only the players were new.

Over the years the search for immigrants had been productive and Colorado had been lucky, or so it was said, in the kinds of people who had chosen it as their new home. Miners had come as laborers or entrepreneurs, and the quarrels of the two groups had left a history of strife and fumbling toward better working conditions that some appraisers liked to think of as progressive. Less controversial were the farmers, who stayed to themselves, worked the land, performed conservatively at the polls, paid their taxes, and were looked upon as satisfactory acquisitions.

The groups that arrived after World War II differed somewhat in their composition. A great many of them came as white-collar workers in the growing governmental complex at Denver, the scientific and research-oriented establishments such as those at Boulder, and as employees in the new "Swiss"-type industries. Blue-collar workers were a less important part of this mix. One result of the new migration was a growing awareness of the inequities suffered by minorities, of environmental ravishments, of mounting atmospheric and visual pollution, and alarm over what was held to be a declining quality of life in the land of the privileged. By the 1970s these concerns would be politically important.

To these changes "old" Colorado reacted with some vehemence. New blood inevitably meant new ideas, and these, in turn, suggested change. "Old" Colorado shared a national reluctance to accept change easily, and it was quick to voice its suspicions about any activities which looked likely to change the status quo. In the early postwar years there were cries for a housecleaning in the schools and demands for a purge of alleged efforts to indoctrinate youth with "alien ideologies of Socialist, Communist design," as one complainant at Colorado Springs put it. The red hunt after this war was not as violent as that of 1919 and after; nevertheless, as early as the spring of 1947, President Robert L. Stearns was obliged to exclude the American Youth for Democracy chapter from the University of Colorado campus on the ground that it was suspected of being a Communist-front organization.[1] By 1951, as national hysteria on the so-called Commie issue approached its zenith, the search for subversives on the university campus catapulted into high gear. A young philosophy professor named David Hawkins was, in effect, charged with *ex post facto* suspicion on the ground that former Communist Party membership made him unfit to teach his classes. That the investigators were on uncertain ground was suggested by the nature of their charges, that is, his failure to disclose prior party membership, "evasiveness" before the House Un-American Activities Committee, and the absence of a clearly defined withdrawal from the party. "Actually the issue was whether or not he should be ousted from his job because he once held ideas now heretical and had failed to recant in the socially acceptable . . . manner," said the *Nation*.

After failing to carry out the academic purging of Hawkins, who was a personable and popular member of the university community with a large following of students, the protectors of the realm went after easier game. Dr. Irving Goodman, an assistant professor of chemistry since 1939, was on a fellowship leave in Europe and therefore unable to appear before the university regents. After studying reports compiled by two former FBI agents, that governing body voted to fire Goodman because he was alleged to have lied about the termination of his membership in the Communist Party. Since they did not reveal why they found Goodman's case markedly different from that of David Hawkins, there lingered in some faculty minds the uncomfortable impression that the latter's unimpeachable WASP credentials had done him no harm. A similar case was that of philosophy instructor Morris Judd, who simply denied membership in the Communist Party and refused further information as to his political affiliations or beliefs. Unable to establish proof of any kind of subversive activity on his part, university officials discharged him on the grounds that he was a "pedestrian" teacher. The accusation generated considerable caustic comment among his colleagues, not a few of whom admitted that upon occasion they themselves had offered rather uninspired performances in the classroom. Some of them were even cynical enough to suggest that, given the presence of a campus red hunt, the university administration had felt a temptation to soothe the anxieties of a few clamorous legislators by tidying up the academic house a bit.[2]

The "Americanism" question, so pervasive in the early twenties, never had dropped out of sight in Colorado; it had smoldered quietly over the intervening years. From time to time some of the more easily frightened residents had made mention of its possible presence in the school system—for some reason this always appeared to be the home of subversion—but it had not been a political issue of any consequence. However, the post–World War II period that saw witch-hunting in the schools, and particularly at the university level, also witnessed its appearance in politics. This was not surprising, for in the late 1940s and early 1950s the nation writhed in the throes of McCarthyism, and Colorado, historically wired to the national ideological circuit, understandably felt the shocks generated in other parts of the land.

As early as 1950 men and women who had lived in Colorado for at least three decades began to hear familiar sounds. They came from political figures who expressed fears for the safety of the establishment—perhaps merely sought seats on a political bandwagon that was forming elsewhere. State Attorney General John W. Metzger sought public attention by warning that the Communist Party was prepared to undertake widespread sabotage of Colorado's radio stations, utilities, and various levels of government. He claimed to have unimpeachable information that seventy-five members of that sinister organization had specific assignments for blowing up designated facilities. To delay the coming of doomsday Metzger proposed a law that simply would outlaw both communism and subversion, and while Governor Walter W. Johnson (D.) was not willing to deny that such an act might be useful, he placed his faith in the FBI to save Colorado from terrorists.[3]

Disaster somehow was averted, and matters drifted along until the 1954 election, when the Communists were heard from again. The campaign, in which Gordon Allott defeated John A. Carroll, began quietly, but toward the end of October quarter-page advertisements appeared in newspapers around the state asking voters to send a "real American," Gordon Allott, to the Senate, where he could join the crusade to drive out communism and corruption. Carroll, while serving as a congressman, had voted against appropriations for the House Un-American Activities Committee. Both Carroll and Allott admitted that President Eisenhower's great popularity in Colorado—he was a frequent visitor—had a great deal to do with the outcome of the election. As Carroll himself suggested, this probably contributed more to Allott's victory than had the waving of the red banner, but he did not deny that this now-familiar threat once more had been dragged out to frighten voters all over the West, particularly in Colorado.[4]

By 1956 the ebb and flow of Colorado politics had shifted once more, and this time, despite the fact that Dwight Eisenhower picked up 60 percent of the vote in the presidential contest, the state's voters reverted to an old practice of independence at the polls. They sent a Democrat to the U.S. Senate and two to the House, and gave that party control of both houses of the General Assembly. Possibly some of senatorial candidate John Carroll's alleged weakness for red had faded into a hazy pinkness in the minds of the voters, or they regarded him as a man more experienced in national affairs than was his Republican opponent, former governor Dan Thornton. Of significance also was the conduct of the local Democratic Party, whose members were much given to in-fighting and a singular disregard for its possible consequences; for the moment they were united. Even Big Ed

Johnson submerged his long-time animosity toward Carroll long enough to serve his party's interests at election time. Stephen L. R. McNichols, a liberal Democrat who was to be very popular, succeeded Johnson and became the state's first Catholic governor. Two years later, in 1958, the independent conduct of the voters continued as Byron Johnson, an admitted pacifist, defeated his Republican opponent for a House seat. While it may seem strange that anyone advocating peace should have been in trouble at the polls, nevertheless it must be taken into account that in conservative postwar Colorado it was dangerous to be "soft" on almost anything, even peace.[5]

Any mention of political life in Colorado since the depression requires consideration of the "pension lobby," a disciplined group that was deadly to its enemies. Governor Thornton made this discovery in the mid fifties when he suggested reduction of payments. "Dan Thornton has sung his swan song," announced the secretary of the National Annuity League. "If he ever runs for office again, any office, we'll beat him. . . ." In 1956 the governor sought membership in that exclusive club, the U.S. Senate, and he lost; a good many of the negative votes came from the old people, who resented any threat to their pension checks. By that year the payments to this group—54,000 strong—represented 27 percent of the state's budget, and in some of the smaller counties the money constituted the area's biggest payroll. Therefore it was not just the old folks who were potent at the polls, but also the country storekeepers, the big food chains in the cities, and the pensioners' relatives, all of whom had a stake in the game.

Most Coloradans readily conceded that the elderly needed some kind of assistance; among the most enthusiastic supporters of this assumption were the children, who did not want to support their parents. From time to time, however, there were complaints that the program was too generous and that not all of the checks were being cashed locally. The law required that recipients spend at least twelve out of every twenty-four months in Colorado, but as of December 1956, nearly 1,800 monthly payments were being mailed to out-of-state addresses, 706 of which were in California. At one time welfare checks were being sent to points as far distant as Italy and Greece. When an aged woman pensioner at Fruita was found to have donated substantial sums to the local charities, money she claimed to have saved from her pension checks, an investigation followed. The results were indicative of the difficulties faced by those who attempted to prune the pension money tree. "Sure, we looked into it," said a welfare official. "But there it was. A little old lady, living all alone in a single room. She had everything—a Bible, a flag, a picture of Abraham Lincoln. How are you going to tell her, 'Look, you've got to pay us back or go to jail'?" So strong were the entrenched recipients of welfare benefits that it took the political know-how of that old-line conservative Big Ed Johnson, the incumbent governor, to achieve any measure of success in the welfare war. Through a compromise with the pension lobby it was agreed that the payments never should fall below $100 a month, minus outside income, and that a healthy reserve fund should be set up to guard against financial contingencies. In addition to that, a $10 million revolving fund was established to provide for hospital and medical care. Thus protected, the pensioners agreed that surplus money should go into the state's general fund, a provision that fiscal reformers long had sought. An amendment providing for such changes was approved by the voters.[6]

Despite the conservative tendencies of Coloradans during the early postwar years, their intellectual outlook remained one of curiosity and of interest in cultural matters. That music, drama, and the arts, in general, attracted both viewers and participants from among the people reflected either their broad interests or perhaps the "turning within" politically that prompted men and women to busy themselves with local affairs in order to shut out the realities of national pressures, or even those from abroad.

In keeping with Colorado's long, if somewhat irregular, support of the theater and other cultural endeavors, the years that followed World War II witnessed so sharp a resurgence that one critic said the place simply was "crawling with culture."[7] Red Rocks Theater, built during the depression by CCC boys, the National Park Service, and the city of Denver at a cost of about $750,000, provided a natural amphitheater in which any of the 20,000 spectators it held could hear without the use of amplifiers. It became an extremely popular location for outdoor performances, particularly after the war. Indoor facilities were provided for Denverites by a municipal auditorium; and by the early 1950s the Denver Symphony orchestra, directed by Saul Caston, was filling the auditorium's 3,200 seats. Only a few years earlier the poverty-stricken orchestra had performed before small, dutiful audiences and lost money regularly; Caston received much of the credit for the reversal of this situation. Since before the war the auditorium also had been used for operas conducted by Monsignor Joseph J. Bosetti to raise money for local Catholic charities. In commenting upon these productions *Time* magazine remarked that outside of these offerings local patrons of the arts had to content themselves with the performances of "bedraggled touring troupes" and a few free, open-air summer productions brought in by the *Denver Post.* Although the auditorium was criticized for its lack of acoustic properties, it came into much wider use during postwar years when top-line artists began to stop at Denver and also in Boulder, where the University Artists' Series drew appreciative audiences.[8]

In earlier days the heavily populated mining camps had provided large audiences for visiting artists, making the plains portion of the state, by contrast, a veritable cultural desert. Similarly, during the 1950s the climate and scenic beauty of the high country attracted visitors who, substituting for the earlier mining population, constituted paying audiences for various performances. By the early fifties, the ski-oriented town of Steamboat Springs was attracting notice with its Perry-Mansfield School of the Dance and Theater, whose summer offerings attracted viewers. Similar productions sponsored by Colorado College, in Colorado Springs, were produced on a year-round basis.[9] Meanwhile, the once-famous opera house at Central City, reopened in 1932 under the sponsorship of some Denver socialites but closed during the war, now resumed operations. Although the rejuvenated opera festival provided Denver's burgeoning postwar society with an opportunity to display its aesthetic impulses, there were not enough supporters of classical productions to keep the program going. Obliged to "go commercial" by 1949, the old place took on a new look as Mae West, playing Diamond Lil, undulated across the venerable stage. Despite moans from Denver society matrons, one of whom remarked that she had slaved to preserve Central City from the machinations of promoter Frank Ricketson, whom she called the "greatest *arriviste* this town has ever seen," the Central City opera house now pandered to the *hoi polloi* who happily paid the asking price to see Broadway performances high in the Rockies.[10]

As Central City's cultural efforts surrendered to the promoters' touch, the stage in other Colorado locations kept busy without the aid of Mae West. Denver University's School of Theatre produced a variety of plays each year as well as touring the Rocky Mountain region with traveling companies that played to both adult and children's audiences. At the University of Colorado the annual Shakespeare festival began to attract crowds in the late 1950s, its first effort playing to some seven thousand patrons during a two-week run. So popular was the program that in its second season (1959) admissions exceeded twelve thousand and there were three over-capacity performances in the Mary Rippon Theater.[11]

The outburst of uplifting programs that made Colorado appear to be crawling with culture was epitomized by the injection of culture into the former mining camp of Aspen. The old place had lazed along during the first three decades of the twentieth century, unable to live, unwilling to die, but with no hope for survival except, perhaps, the tourist or the ski industry as a savior. Once during the depression one of the community's businessmen stopped before an aged prospector who was drowsing in front of the old Jerome Hotel, and asked: "Pop, what makes this town so slow?" Opening his eyes the old man peered at the questioner and growled: "The people's mineralized, that's what. They got silver in their hair and lead in their pants."[12]

Then the virtual ghost town was "discovered" by Walter Paepcke, the Chicago manufacturer who conceived the idea not only of developing a major ski area there but also of converting the town into a location where a combination of climate and culture could offer families a better life. "When I saw Aspen," he said, "I wasn't just thinking of starting a place that would attract tourists. Here was a town, an old established place, that had had bad luck because its fortunes were all tied up in one thing—silver. Yet, it still possessed all the attributes of a wonderful place to live." With this in mind, Paepcke and his employees set out to restore the dowdy old camp, offering free paint to residents who would use colors that blended into an overall scheme of things, but there were few takers.

Aspen's era of culture was inaugurated in 1949 with a festival that celebrated the Goethe bicentennial. Into the town swarmed seekers of culture, garbed in attire that ranged from gabardines and prints to Levis and sport shirts. "Outwardly, the crowds might have been heading for any rodeo or county fair," wrote one newsman. "Instead, visitors arriving to double Aspen's normal 1,200 population were trekking thousands of miles to hear sonatas and symphonies, lieder and concerti—not a circus band. They ascended to Aspen to hear, not carnival pitchmen, but the world's best-informed disciples of Johann Wolfgang von Goethe." Among the dignitaries were Dimitri Mitropoulos, Artur Rubinstein, Gregor Piatigorsky, Nathan Milstein, and Albert Schweitzer, who served as the program's principal speaker. "Ideologically, we feel safer with winter skiing than summer civilizing," remarked one participant, but he added his hope that the idea would take hold.[13] For the optimists the Salzburg of America had been born.

The great Goethe festival came and went. Celebrities overran the place. The natives ogled as the chairlift broke down, marooning one passenger in space—he turned out to be Rubinstein—and as Igor Stravinsky strode down the street, *High Noon* fashion, wearing a ten-gallon hat and satisfactorily faded blue jeans. Then the bloom faded from the rose, and the natives began to weary of the inundation of culture. "First of all," wrote one observer, "there is a language barrier; the natives don't dig that long-hair jive. Most of them have been absorbed in the souvenir and sight-seeing economy, but they don't buy season tickets to operas and seminars." Tensions grew and the situation approached an outbreak of ideological warfare in the mid fifties when the "unreconstructed element" put on a rodeo at one end of town while a learned seminar was in progress at the other end. The matter was resolved when local mediators ruled that the events were noncompetitive.[14]

But this was no more than a surface confrontation. Deeper lay the antagonisms of the old-timers to a financial avant garde that apparently was determined to turn culture into cash in this quaint old mining village. Even at the time of the Goethe festival criticism was leveled at its promoters on the ground that it was a "fill-in" for the ski season, a summer promotion to lure visitors that took advantage of poor old Wolfgang's two-hundredth birthday to keep the floating population large enough to satisfy the innkeepers and merchants. Goethe unquestionably meant "culture" but, as one commentator put it, "The great but obscure Albert Schweitzer, coming to Colorado all the way from French Equatorial Africa, did not make it clearer."[15] Schweitzer had no argument with this. He spoke to his listeners humbly and affectionately, if in some bewilderment at his new surroundings, and he cheerfully shared the local newspaper's front page with an account of a burro race over Mosquito Pass and such competing attractions as that offered by the Isis Theater, then showing *Ma and Pa Kettle.*

What troubled the critic who favored winter skiing over summer civilizing was the uncomfortable feeling that promoting the ski slopes was an acceptable means of utilizing the terrain and the scenery in the off-season, and even that luring unsuspecting tourists into decaying mining camps during the warm months was well within the rules of tourist hunting, but that the idea of collecting spectators for an intellectual Roman holiday in a rejuvenated ghost town went beyond the bounds of the respectable hustle. This discomfiture, combined with the antagonism of the handful of natives who had lingered on at Aspen throughout the depression years, generated continuous friction between them and the Chicago philanthropist. It was yet another example of outside capital and outside promotion being simultaneously welcomed and resented in a Colorado community. But it was more than this. Even Paepcke's musicians finally fell out with their patron and began to offer festivals on their own. One of the town's old-timers spoke for many a native when he confessed: "I'm for all Walter has done for this town. But we're still hoping to bring in something more substantial."[16] He was thinking of uranium.

As the fifties passed and the sixties witnessed a further influx, the "I'm for Walter" crowd experienced a further diminution. In the sixties, when the economy was supposed to "soar," Aspen indeed saw a great deal of activity. Into the sleepy village came trucks, bulldozers, and beady-eyed speculators with somebody else's money, determined to cash in on this latest bonanza in the high country. Controls were thrown to the winds and amidst the blasting and the clouds of dust there arose an architectural mishmash that blighted a once beautiful part of the Rockies and shattered the dream of a midwestern container manufacturer. Beyond the defacement of an old mining camp—it was not as crude as that carried out at Central City—the clash of the old and new Colorado mentalities was brought into sharp focus at Aspen. "Gallons of printer's ink to lure the tourist! And not a drop of ink to tell the world where we stood, back in the Eighties. . . ," complained one old miner who remembered the silver years. "They only want Aspen's heavens to be murky with the smoke of mill and smelter!" replied one of the newcomers. And in those two comments lay the theme for a whole chapter of Colorado history, one that would be apparent not only in the "soaring sixties" but also in the "sagging seventies."[17] During the latter decade city planners, at Aspen as well as in other Colorado cities, would begin to tighten building codes.

In the new rush to this part of the Rockies, "beautiful people" mixed with ski bums and hippies, and an ersatz European mountain architecture was intended to effect a Hansel and Gretel atmosphere, but the earnest effort to establish an American Salzburg was continued. A national news magazine had proclaimed that as of 1950 America's intellectual center was to be found at Aspen, Colorado, some seventy-nine hundred feet above sea level. In that high, clear atmosphere, thinkers would have great thoughts at the Aspen Institute for Humanistic Studies. To this oasis in a culturally deprived portion of the land would come not only those blessed with capacious brain cells but also tired executives whose harried mental facilities could be plugged in for a quick recharge. The students were handed a ten-pound package of reading material that included classical works from many ages, and dutifully they went to work, figuratively gnawing away at this potent mass of brain food. In an effort to further enhance the institute's prestige it was announced in 1963 that Colorado's answer to the Nobel prize—in this case $30,000—would be awarded each year to the person making the greatest contribution to the humanities. The first recipient of the prize was a leading British composer. Despite this all-out effort, the flowering of the institute was slow, and by the mid 1970s efforts were being made to dispose of it. Culture, it seemed, just was not a paying proposition in old Rocky Mountain mining camps.[18]

While Aspen's cultural rehabilitation was in progress, Coloradans were dismayed to learn that in their capital city civic matters had relapsed into a situation far less praiseworthy. Denver, the old Queen of the Plains, had stepped forward into the postwar era proud and confident, led by the youthful, energetic, and progressive Quigg Newton and his freshly scrubbed young assistants. For the moment reform pervaded the atmosphere, sprayed in all directions from journalistic aerosol cans operated by the Palmer Hoyts and others, but beneath the surface the old rot festered, unchanged by the perfume that lingered above. Community leaders had put the "sell Colorado" campaign into high gear, using the word "clean" to describe not only the well-known "champagne air," but also Colorado's moral and intellectual climate. All the sordid characteristics of the eastern urban sprawl had been purged from or never had been permitted to take root in this privileged place. Then, as it inevitably does, came the word that there is no Santa Claus. This time the message was conveyed by the Denver Police Department.

One day in 1961 Denver residents learned that some of the boys in blue, far from being their protectors, had turned to systematized robbery of the local merchants. The causes, of course, were multiple. Starting salaries as low as $393.00 a month, a loose attitude by supervisory personnel that permitted highly informal garb and conduct, and poor selection of officers resulted in the accumulation of a number of young men on the force who ought not to have been hired. As one observer put it, "In Denver almost any able-bodied young man who is not a certifiable moron can join the force." As the scandal unfolded it was revealed that at least 36 "burglars in blue," as they were dubbed, had perfected their operations to a point where they could pull off burglaries netting as much as $40,000. It was theorized that, in all, as many as 150 officers were in one way or another involved, and the total amount of their take was said to be in the neighborhood of $150,000.

Embarrassed, ashamed, humiliated, Coloradans tried to pass the matter off with a grim humor reminiscent of earlier western responses. Stories abounded. When a police cruiser pulled up to a housing project, some of the workmen immediately warned others: "We got to lock up our cars. Cops are in the neighborhood." Another joke involved a housewife who told a neighborhood desk sergeant, "There's a burglar in my basement." Quickly he reassured her: "Okay, lady. Get his badge number. We'll pick him up at morning roll call." Even the youngsters, it was said, now played a game called "Cops and Cops."[19] An investigator, called in by Governor Stephen McNichols, concluded that far from being hardened criminals, the after-hours thieves were primarily simple farm boys from modest, low-income families who accepted police force assignments after a token orientation and no training, to be paired with older officers who may well have been thoroughly crooked. In short, no attempt was made to excuse such conduct, but at the same time there was the strong implication that Denver's "finest" were in serious need of upgrading. Although that housecleaning took place very shortly, the milk had been spilled and Coloradans were confronted with a stain upon an image they had worked hard to keep clean.

Other changes were taking place in Denver, changes for the better, during those early days of the 1960s. The Mexican-American population, for so many years "with us, but not of us," at last began to receive recognition and acceptance. But not without a struggle, and not because of any sudden outburst of liberality on the part of the Anglo-Saxon establishment. National pressures from the federal government for equal rights for minorities, plus militant action by Denver's Mexican Americans that derived, in part, from outside influences, resulted in some dramatic alterations in old attitudes.

Historically, most long overdue reforms have come hard, and they have been achieved through militant action by extremists willing to endure harsh criticism by the establishment. In Denver's case, the Spanish-speaking group's leader was Rodolfo "Corky" Gonzales, a one-time boxer who had become involved in the politics of minorities. Unsuccessful in his efforts to achieve election to municipal or state office, he served as Denver director of the War on Poverty until the mayor fired him. Then he blossomed as the Anglo community's gadfly. In Castro style, he made verbal war upon the majority, disclaiming any desire to live in the world of the "gringo," and he demanded that Mexican-American teachers be hired to teach Mexican Americans something of their own past. In general he and his restless young followers frightened the ruling class—that combination of old families and more recently arrived upper-middle-class white collars—but in the end they were obliged to listen.[20]

The Chicano "uprising" in the Denver area was noticeable largely because of the very rapid growth of the Hispano population during the 1960s—it more than doubled, reaching a figure that exceeded 86,000 or nearly 17 percent of the city's population—and because of the publicity given it by the metropolitan press. The sharp increase in numbers came during a decade that saw the city's population increase by slightly over 4 percent, a ratio difference that tended to exacerbate the problems of this long-time Colorado minority. As a result of the clash the Spanish-speaking element of the Denver area for the first time in the state's history assumed a significant role in an Anglo-dominated Colorado community.

If the resident Mexican-American population may be said to have arrived, it must be mentioned that it had been a long trip. For more than a century after the Anglo-American army of prospectors had set up camp in 1859, the people from Mexico and New Mexico had been the victims of Colorado's most virulent form of racism. That this condition occasioned relatively few open clashes between the groups was due largely to the fact that up to about 1918 the state's Spanish-speaking population was concentrated in the southern counties; then came a dilution that, by 1960, left only Costilla and Conejos counties predominantly Hispano.

Colorado agriculture dates back almost to the days of Fifty-Nine, but for about four decades thereafter farming was carried on by individual families much in the manner of their pioneer forefathers on earlier frontiers. Then, around 1900, sugar beets became important, first in the Grand Valley, where, by the turn of the century, a beet factory was built, and shortly thereafter on farms along the eastern slope. Suddenly there was a demand for cheap, easily managed "stoop" labor. German Russians, who were experienced in growing sugar beets, were not the answer because they tended to become growers, rather than laborers; the same was true of the Japanese, who next were put into the fields. Railroad workers imported from Mexico began to be used by sugar beet corporations, and, following the first World War, recruitment was carried on in New Mexico. Because transportation was expensive for the employers, they encouraged the temporary workers to stay on, usually in labor colonies located near agricultural towns. Thus the transplantation was complete, and ready-built ghettoes awaited the migrant workers, who moved into segregated dwelling areas, remained unassimilated, and became the victims of discrimination. They had to accustom themselves to exclusion from barbershops, theaters, swimming pools, and such, much as had the Negro in the American South, and their status remained unchanged until the new Coloradans of the post–World War II era began to voice objections. The gains of the sixties were due not so much to the victories of Corky Gonzales and his young militants as to the accumulation of equal opportunity sentiments that spread across America during that decade and spilled over into Colorado.[21]

Less spectacular than the Crusade for Justice, as the Chicano drive for recognition came to be called, was the changing status of blacks in both Denver and the state. Their situation was somewhat different from that of the Mexican Americans in that Colorado's black population was largely concentrated in the Denver area—by 1970 more than two-thirds of the state's 66,411 blacks lived there—with the remainder scattered thinly through the small towns. Prejudice against them long since had been incorporated into local laws but in many cases there had been so little need to invoke it that such legislation had been forgotten. An example of this development came to light in 1952 when the Melvin Minter family, of Louisiana, became involved in an automobile accident at Fruita in which the mother was injured and one of the children killed. The townspeople at once came to their aid, offering the family a house, a job for the father, and care for the children until their mother had recovered. Then it was discovered that Fruita had an ancient ordinance that made it illegal for blacks to remain in town after sundown. Embarrassed and indignant, the local judge at first declined to enforce the law, but since that might lead to further complications the city council met in an emergency session and expunged the offensive law from the books. "I never had such treatment in my life before," said the amazed Minter. "Why would a man leave a place like this?"[22]

There were other signs of enlightenment in Colorado during the 1950s. In the middle of that decade the University of Colorado Regents decreed that seven of the campus fraternities must, within a given period, clean up their constitutions and remove racially discriminatory clauses that barred membership to all but Caucasians.[23] The action was not taken to exemplify any landmark decisions in racial relationships or to show Coloradans once again that Boulder was a hotbed of liberalism, but rather it served as a weathervane. Days of change lay ahead for the whole state, much of it to be wrought through pressures by the federal government, but here were indications that Colorado's conscience was experiencing minor vibrations. The fact that the regents' vote was four to two revealed an old reluctance to tamper with the status quo and showed that the establishment still had its voice in matters that concerned social change. Not surprisingly there was resistance among fraternities and sororities to the edict handed down by the ruling body, but the ultraliberal members of the student body itself took much of the sting out of the decision. During the 1960s the social pressures against joining these organizations became so great that not only minorities but students in general shunned them. Regardless of one's color, to join simply was not the "in" thing to do. Within a decade the boycott appeared to be softening.

Another instance of national pressures that were reflected in Colorado was the question of black integration into traditionally white communities, particularly that of Denver. The number of blacks there grew by more than 55 percent during the 1960s, thus putting pressures of expansion into predominantly white neighborhoods. One of the early targets of integration efforts was the suburb of Park Hill where, after some street violence and a few racial incidents at East High School, the mix took place. So great was the movement into the area that the firstcomers tried to persuade others not to make the move for fear that part of the city would turn all black. Through the efforts of the Park Hill Action Committee the change took place in a more orderly fashion until, by 1972, a national magazine could state that greater Park Hill probably came as close to being genuinely integrated as any community in the United States.[24] The battle over forced busing of school children to achieve integration would go on, as it did in other major American cities, and thus keep alive an issue that obscured the great advances made between the races in the Queen City of the Plains. The fact remains, however, that Denver made its peace very well with minority problems that flared in the sixties. The development gave further evidence that at least the city's residents had come to grips with some of the important social problems of the day.

Efforts by politicians to unite the important minorities, particularly those in the larger Colorado cities, were not entirely successful. Except during political uprisings such as that led by Corky Gonzales, Denver Hispanos tended to be silent politically, and in their occasional appearances at the polling booths they favored the Democrats. When Herrick Roth founded the Colorado Coalition in 1966, it represented an effort to ally labor, pensioners, Chicanos, and blacks. The romance was short-lived. Labor was unhappy with Lyndon Johnson's lassitude over the Taft-Hartley act, and despite such efforts as those carried out in Park Hill the blacks were dissatisfied over delays in other sectors of reform in their lives. The Hispanic groups generally shunned such partnerships, Corky Gonzales holding that black pressure for integration was just another evidence of the inferiority complexes of these people, and members of the influential New Hispanic Movement did not even attend Colorado Coalition meetings.[25] Spanish-speaking voters preferred to steer their own course, and by the 1970 election they would field a political party of their own, La Raza Unida, and put before the voters for the first time a third party based upon an ethnic foundation. The party, organized by the Gonzales Crusade for Justice group, received only 1.8 percent of the gubernatorial vote, but three Mexican Americans who ran for the General Assembly on the Democratic ticket were victorious.[26]

During the years when Colorado's minorities showed evidence of coming into their own, and the state's leaders could point with pride to advances in the field of racial relationships, there were mounting concerns that the community at large was not making satisfactory progress in other areas, specifically education. The University of Denver, the University of Colorado, and other institutions of higher learning were obliged to offer courses in "dumb-bell" English in order to improve the literary abilities of high school graduates enough to carry on university-level work. Critics complained about the teaching of such courses as hypnotism, contract bridge, and other peripheral subjects to young men and women who could neither count nor spell.[27]

Part of the problem at these universities, as well as at other institutions of higher learning in the state, was the rapid growth they experienced in the immediate postwar years. By the 1950s definite efforts were being made to match size with excellence, a program whose success was reflected in the growing reputations of these schools. National, and in this case international, events had their influence upon those who were willing to spend money to upgrade higher education. The Russian space program, and the launching into orbit of the first earth satellite "Sputnik," in 1957, suggested that American scientific education and expertise were falling behind, and there was an immediate nationwide response. Universities across the country commenced to strengthen their science programs, aided by government funds and other forms of encouragement. One of the tangible contributions Colorado was to make from this acceleration was the participation of several of its young men in the successful space program America now launched. Astronauts Malcolm Scott Carpenter, of Boulder, John L. Swigert, Jr., of Denver, Stuart Roosa, of Durango, and Vance Brand, of Longmont, all did their college-level work at the University of Colorado.

The appointment of Quigg Newton to the presidency of the university coincided with the drive for improvement at the institution, and although conservatives complained bitterly that the place had been taken over by "ritualistic liberals," the changes that took place during his administration were felt for years afterward. By a happy circumstance Stephen L. R. McNichols was governor during part of Newton's tenure; in him, higher education throughout the state had a friend and supporter. The result of the joint effort was a general elevation of academic standards, an expansion of research and publication, and increased efforts to persuade the best faculty members not to seek greener academic pastures. Unfortunately Coloradans could not set aside the old temptations of political retrogression, and when an ultraconservative regent who had sworn to "get" the president was reelected by a heavy majority, Newton resigned and became head of the Commonwealth Fund of New York City.[28]

As the older schools sought to improve the quality of their instruction, the state's latest collegiate establishment indicated an equal desire to excel in all areas. The U.S. Air Force Academy, considered another of the "plums" that the business community had acquired as a means of attracting attention to Colorado, required a stiffer course than that offered at the older academies, institutions often sarcastically referred to in the academic world as "trade schools." Despite the growls from hardened old fliers that that "humanities stuff is all bologna" and that if the school ever found itself in need of a Ph.D. it could always fly one in, the curriculum was equally divided between the sciences and the humanities, and 25 percent more credits were required for graduation from the school than were needed at the sister academies. "Aluminum U," as it was teasingly called because of its architecture, not only kept pace academically with other state and nationally known institutions but set standards and adopted innovations that suggested the presence of a forward-looking, progressive-minded staff.[29]

The rapid growth of Colorado's institutions of higher learning during the postwar era was a reflection of the state's population growth and of the national attention that it attracted. While the legislators usually responded favorably to pleas for more money to meet the needs of academic communities, and they showed a sincere interest in advancing the reputations of the state's colleges and universities, they were not unaware that institutions of this kind were beneficial to the state's business sector. Aside from educating Colorado's young, the schools attracted students from all over the nation, and from a good many foreign countries. The unusually large number of out-of-state students bothered some of the legislators, who complained about paying for the education of outsiders, but this objection was met by raising tuition and by pointing out that these temporary residents brought considerable money into the community. For example, by the mid seventies it was estimated that, overall, higher education in Colorado had a total financial impact of more than $1.3 billion each year.[30] Governmental contracts to the schools accounted for millions of dollars brought in from the outside. Additionally, universities have been prime attractions for companies desiring to locate in the high, dry climate of Colorado where they could at the same time take advantage of the skills and learning of the academic world. The governmental and privately owned scientific complexes that clustered around Boulder illustrated that contention.

Granted that institutions of higher learning have served as bait for industry and population, the possibility of employing other, if somewhat less intellectually oriented, lures has not been overlooked. For example, Denver acquired a professional football team in 1960, and one of the thoughts of those who promoted it was the theory that it would help advertise the city and state, thus attracting industry. One of the principal stockholders, Gerald Phipps, admitted this motive when he commented to reporters, "We're not kidding ourselves that this will ever be a gold mine here. But we're trying to attract industry to this community." After some dismal seasons there was talk of moving the franchise, but, although Phipps could have sold out at a profit, he declined, with the remark: "Nothing would hurt us more than headlines around the country saying Denver had lost its football team."

Whether or not the Broncos lured westward their assigned share of industry may never be known, but few would argue that the team had not made a contribution to Colorado folklore. As was expected of most expansion teams, they lost; but it was the continuation of this habit and the flair the players developed for it that made the group newsworthy. As one writer said of the members, they usually came out for the kickoff "like ladies surprised at their bath," after which they purported to play football. Without playbooks and with the quarterback occasionally diagraming the next play in the ground with his forefinger, they maintained an unrivaled reputation as losers. It was said that after Denver's first point-after-touchdown conversion the team's general manager galloped into the stands and wrestled with a fan for possession of the historic ball.

While some ticketholders viewed the proceedings with ill-disguised bad humor and others made light of the team's antics, there were a few who took matters seriously. One man, no longer able to endure the weekly blundering, turned to thoughts of suicide. The event that precipitated the action was a game between the Broncos and the Chicago Bears in which the Colorado team turned over the ball seven times in one afternoon. Leaving a farewell note, the despairing spectator explained: "I have been a Bronco fan since the Broncos were first organized, and I can't stand their fumbling any more." His effort to shoot himself in the head proved not to be fatal and the unhappy fan lived to endure yet another agonizing season.

Time passed, migrating coaches and players arrived to replace those let go, good players were traded off for poor ones, and the Broncos escalated their losing streak to a point where other representatives of the American Football League complained that the team was a detriment to the league.[31] But the Broncos endured, the management refusing to let the team go to some other city, and gradually success came as the season's results soared past .500 percent. When the win side of the ledger surpassed the loss column Denver went wild with joy; unsuspecting visitors might have imagined that the team had just won the Super Bowl. Ticket sales improved and preparations were made to enlarge the stadium, but the whimsy did not end. In behalf of frustrated fans a measure was jokingly introduced into the Colorado legislature asking the Bronco management to contribute a portion of the season's profits for the rehabilitation of alcoholics driven to drink by the team's occasional maddening retreats to mediocrity.[32] In any event, it cannot be denied that the Broncos had made a name for themselves, locally and nationally, and that win or lose, football fans across the country came to know where Denver was. It was all that the original owners had asked for; their advertising campaign had paid off.

Thus for a quarter of a century after the close of World War II Coloradans employed the old formula that equated growth with progress and prosperity, convinced like their predecessors that it was the answer to future well-being. By then the concept had been in use for more than a hundred years, and, at least up to that time, there appeared to be no evidence to show it was not working.

In fact, the "sell Colorado" concept appeared to be functioning better than ever, if material results were the measure of success. During the 1960s the influx emphasized research and development organizations and featured space-age types of industry; the result was a new boom in the state that made old timers think of the gold strike at Cripple Creek or the excitement at Creede. Into Colorado came the scientific and Swiss-type industries already discussed, and ready to welcome them were the subdividers who offered to house their employees' families in this land of sunshine and historically clean air. During the latter half of the sixties the number of these developers jumped from thirty to over three hundred and by the early seventies they had laid out enough tracts to accommodate some twelve million latter-day settlers, or about five times the state's existing population.[33]

So successful was the drive to acquire new Coloradans that the program became self-defeating. "The strip" from Fort Collins to Pueblo threatened to become a continuous suburb where water was in short supply, the air was polluted, and urban problems the newcomers thought they had left in the East sprouted along the foot of the Rockies. The new Coloradans, in particular, reacted negatively to this possibility, and it was they, rather than the old-timers, who began to talk of controls and "Zero Population Growth." This thinking, by people who lived in the most heavily populated part of the state, would dominate local politics for the next few years. When those who called for controlled growth began to make themselves heard and showed some power at the polls, there were cries that Colorado had "turned to the left." Some people believed this; others understood that it simply was a case of promotional chickens coming home to roost.

# 18

# The Recycling of "Sell Colorado"

Signs of a possible turnaround in the "sell Colorado" campaign began to be noticed as the boom in the late 1960s crested. At first they came from the relatively quiet chirpings of a dedicated few who foresaw disaster to the environment if the subdivision culture blanketed the state. Their protests barely were heard amidst the cacophony of bulldozers, falling hammers, and the shouts of latter-day hucksters masquerading under the name of developers, whose combined efforts appeared to be the creation of border-to-border tract housing, embryonic slums. By the early 1970s about a thousand land development companies were operating in the state. Deaf to protest, indifferent to demands for caution, these purveyors of progress scoured the countryside, convinced that a new gold rush had thrust itself upon Colorado.[1]

When the Rocky Mountain Power Company sought to build a dam in the Flattops Primitive Area during the mid sixties, there were protests from the Colorado Mountain Club, the Izaak Walton League, and lesser known groups who called themselves conservationists, the words *environmental* and *ecological* not yet having come into wide use. The Forest Service also voiced its opposition. Those who objected to the dam were worried about the disruption of wilderness streams and lakes that would result from converting waterways into large, muddy, polluted reservoirs. At that relatively early date, well before the onset of the well-known "energy crisis," they called for alternative sources of power. Advocates of electric power thought such arguments weak in the face of the demand for electricity, and they regarded the protests as objections emanating

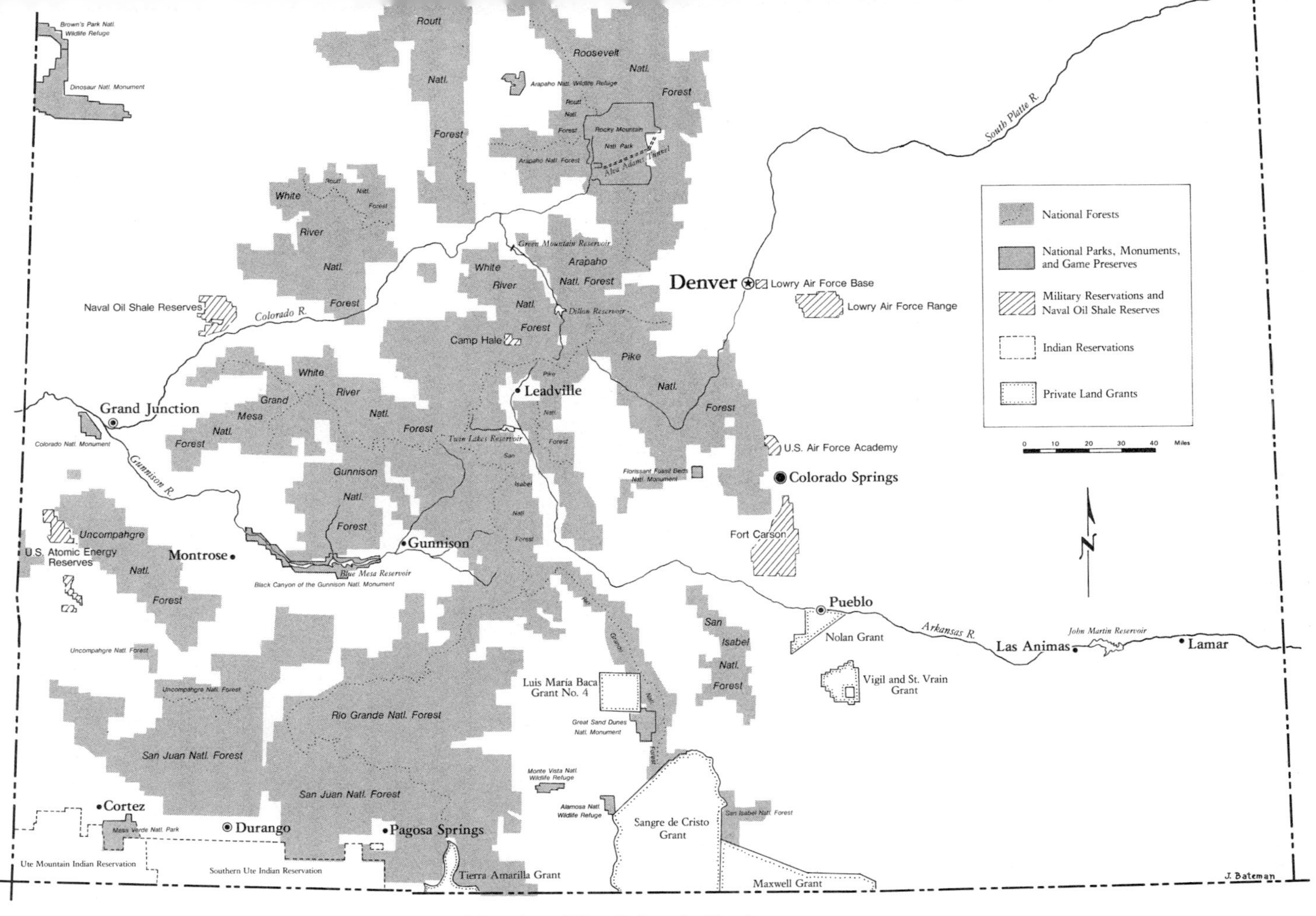


Map 4 The Colorado Environment

from old, familiar sources, critics who earlier had opposed projects such as the Big Thompson diversion. In this particular case the matter was of interstate interest, since the generated electricity was to be sold principally in Nebraska.[2]

Those who had lived in Colorado for some years or were—in a diminishing number of cases—natives were not immediately sympathetic to complaints about damming up streams. For years they had believed that hydroelectric power, if properly generated, was the cleanest kind of energy and that it represented the use of nature's gifts in the best sense. Even less understandable to them was the uproar that was heard in the late 1960s over the damage highway construction might inflict upon the environment. For generations westerners had regarded transportation of all kinds as not only desirable but absolutely essential to their economy. It was difficult for them to understand arguments against cutting a minute pathway through a vast and frequently undeveloped portion of the countryside. Therefore the battle over plans to build Interstate 70 through the Gore Range–Eagles Nest Primitive Area was another of the familiar contests waged between those seeking tourists' dollars and the conservationists who set a high priority upon preservation. Chambers of Commerce on the western slope naturally opted for divided highways, easy grades, and tunnels where necessary. Those living in Grand Junction or Gunnison thought tourists frequently avoided high mountain passes over twisting roads. The conservationists, on the other hand, argued that to hack out roads and drill holes in the mountains amounted to acts of vandalism.[3]

Some of the noisiest of those who voiced their environmental concerns and stressed the values of "back to nature" were the young transients who flooded Colorado during these years. Referred to as "street people" or, more frequently, as "hippies," they hung around small towns by day and spent their nights in rural communes, often situated in national forest areas. Their culture embraced drugs of varying degrees of potency, paid little attention to the accepted niceties of civilization such as clean clothing, baths, and trimmed hair, and made much of their affection for mother earth and all that was hers. Politically nonconformist, and frequently rebellious, they were well known to law enforcement officers. As part of the flow of newcomers that entered Colorado, these strangers brought in surprising amounts of cash. They were objects of animosity to the more conservative residents, but, on the whole, the majority showed them a remarkable tolerance.

Cultural centers where the young and presumably the tolerant lived seemed to attract the long-haired migrants. Signs posted as far away as Europe reading "See you in Boulder, Colorado" were not the kind of advertising the establishment found helpful or even amusing. Boulder was inundated with these transients to a degree that tested the patience and understanding of even its most liberal residents.

Aspen, more recently endowed with "culture," barely had accustomed itself to long-haired composers before the hippie invasion overran that quiet mountain town. In the mid sixties the "skiniks"—as in "beatniks"—made this mountain town their off-season habitat, an alternative to Laguna, Fort Lauderdale, or Mazatlán. Mixing with movie actors, wealthy singers, television stars, and young liberal political figures—the "beautiful people" —these modern ski bums street-fought, broke into homes and businesses, were thrown out of restaurants that tried to preserve a modicum of decorum, used liquor and drugs freely, and talked loudly of environmental preservation as they abandoned filthy campsites, left untended fires to burn countless acres, and ignored the ecological impact. Long-time Coloradans, as well as the more traditional recent arrivals, watched this aspect of population growth with a mixture of distaste and concern, wondering how one went about making advertising more discriminating.[4]

There were other concerns. In the late sixties a small group comprised mainly of scientists and calling itself the Colorado Committee for Environmental Information began to issue warnings about the potential dangers of air pollution emanating from sources such as the Atomic Energy Commission's Rocky Flats plant near Boulder, and the army's supply of nerve gas stored at the Rocky Mountain Arsenal. A serious fire at Rocky Flats, one that the AEC admitted was a near catastrophe, and the relevation that as many as 3,000 homes in Grand Junction might be standing on radon-gas-containing earth fill taken from uranium mine tailings, drew national publicity. So did a forty-kiloton nuclear blast set off in 1969 some two hundred miles west of Denver as part of an effort to free natural gas deep in the earth. Project Rulison, as it was named, was Colorado's first participation in the so-called Plowshare program designed to increase the nation's available gas supply.

Governor John Love was criticized by environmentally minded residents for not showing what they regarded as the proper degree of concern for such dangerous activities. Groups such as the Environmental Information Committee drew an annoyed reaction from the "sell Colorado" faction, the leaders of which did not appreciate warnings from strangers to the effect that Colorado's management was not doing a proper job. The recent arrivals argued that many of them had undergone some sacrifices to make the move, that they had done so because of the state's desirable environment, and they intended to fight to preserve the atmosphere in which they had made their investment.[5]

Objections to potential leaks in nuclear plants, or to blowing parts of the Rockies to pieces by miners looking for energy sources, were matters that drew a certain amount of publicity and obligated people in office, or those seeking office, to make some kind of response. Of wider interest was another kind of danger to the countryside: visual pollution. Unlike the complaints of a handful of scientists and a scattering of doom-sayers, this was a gut issue, for it touched directly upon the question of growth. The search for "clean" industry continued, but added to it was the suggestion that some of the industrial newcomers seek less heavily populated settings and avoid complicating the problems of the rapidly growing cities. The Eastman Kodak decision to locate a $100 million plant near the little town of Windsor was an example of this tendency and it was one that Governor Love could endorse. He wanted to achieve cluster cities as opposed to urban sprawl, cities that were suitably separated yet adequately served by an efficient and economical means of transportation.[6]

The reasonable use of land for residential or industrial purposes was a goal that the builders of Colorado had sought for over a century, and, as an ideal, it had a good many supporters, even among newcomers. But somehow the ideal became lost when land booms hit the state, as happened in the surge of the late sixties. When, early in the decade, the well-known commentator and author Eric Sevareid shouted "to hell with all the would-be Zeckendorfs now building all over the West" and alleged that he would join those who might take the law into their own hands to combat visual pollution, he was not speaking for the average Coloradan but rather as an angry outsider who foresaw the spoilage of western America by overdevelopment.[7]

In 1973 the completion of the Eisenhower Tunnel as an

alternative highway route over Loveland Pass generated complaints both from those who did not want holes drilled in the mountains and from residents who feared the resultant overcrowding of their neighborhoods. The tunnel, meant to speed trucks and cars on their way, caused such a new rush into the Rockies that at times traffic was backed up for miles as drivers impatiently awaited their turn. One of the first results of the single shaft was the demand for another, just like it, to provide for an increased vehicular flow.

Another result was a land boom in Summit County that made old-timers wonder if some miners again had not hit pay dirt in a big way. Dillon Reservoir's twenty-five mile shoreline and the presence of three nearby ski areas were attractions that quickened the pulses of even the more conservative developers. Although one of the local environmentalists admitted that "we don't want to kill Santa Claus," it was hard to control the land boom that ensued without bringing such charges against anyone who even so much as mentioned caution. The year the tunnel opened, the value of building permits doubled the $20 million figure of the previous year and, in terms of construction, Summit became known as the "hottest county in the state." Pessimists took the gloomy view that such growth foresaw a rash of houses and condominiums covering the surrounding hills, and the only comfort they could find in this incipient sequin-covered slum was the hope that the resultant density would discourage any more people from coming there. Another rationalization argued that old-timers need not worry, for the onrush of newcomers was escalating prices so fast that landowners could not turn down a chance to cash in on the rush, and after they had sold out they would have no alternative but to move elsewhere and try to forget what was going on in the new Eldorado.[8]

Aspen experienced a similar real estate crunch, and from that old mining town came the familiar outcries against wildly overinflated prices and mindless building. Here the original division between old-timers and newcomers had taken place shortly after the war, with the coming of Walter Paepcke and his plans for the American Salzburg, but during the intervening years there had arrived a new and younger group of "old-timers," those who now had been around for perhaps a decade, and they had begun to complain about growth. Many of them had come to get away from the very situation that now confronted them. Leon Uris, for example, the internationally known author who had made his stake and therefore had earned the right to live wherever he chose, had selected Aspen because it offered a quality of life a great many Americans cherished but one that was rapidly disappearing.

Aspen's growing pains puzzled Robert O. Anderson, of the Institute for Humanistic Studies, because there appeared to be as many points of view about its solution as there were people. On paper, he said, Aspen had everything: a wilderness setting, highly educated people, superior skiing, and a small-town atmosphere. He concluded that if this group of intelligent residents could not resolve the matter, surely no other community could. He may have been studying the problem too closely. Questions of a similar nature then faced other Colorado communities, places that did not possess "think tanks," and if there was a general diffusion of opinion it was because a group of highly individualistic people were confronted by an old western dilemma: What happens if we do not grow? As one of Aspen's shopkeepers put it: "Sure, I'm concerned about growth. But, dammit, it used to be that a man couldn't make a living here. The guys that really make me mad are the Johnny-come-latelies who don't want to let anyone else in." He predicted that if the newcomers shut off all growth the town would wither away.[9]

Just as early mining camps sprang up, flourished, and then encountered problems as the mineral frontier made its way deeper into the Colorado mountains, so did the boomtowns born of the tourist and ski industries. The growing pains of Aspen, Breckenridge, Vail, and other ski resorts were duplicated as modern prospectors probed more remote areas to ferret out hitherto untouched old mining towns considered to be fit subjects for restoration as vacation spots.

Telluride is a good illustration of the fact that conditions changed as rapidly in the new boom as they had in an earlier day. That old, forgotten mining camp, in full flight toward tourist riches by the beginning of the seventies, had begun to experience the pangs of plenty by mid decade. Some of the recently arrived "old-timers" were convinced that the developers were about to deflower their newfound garden spot. Particularly annoyed were those who had moved out of such places as Aspen in the belief that it had surrendered to the din of civilization and the disfiguring effects of crass commercialism. An outburst of condominium building just southwest of Telluride so alarmed residents that a Historical Preservation Commission was established, the purpose of which was to try to save some of the area's early-day charm. The building control group was joined by some of the town's long-time residents who now were having difficulty coping with the inflation that resulted from being "discovered." Soaring real estate prices meant that it was a place for the young, the active, or the rich, as an old miner discovered when he came down out of the hills to retire but found that he could not afford to live in Telluride.

When action was taken to limit development, however, there were the usual howls of complaint. The rejection of plans to build a sixty-five-unit four-story lodge because it involved the expansion of an old and historic structure to such a degree that it enveloped, and in effect destroyed, the older building generated the complaint that a community whose ski lifts could carry 6,000 skiers an hour needed more than the 650 beds it possessed. The old dilemma raised its head again. In the words of a young housewife who had come from California with her husband to enjoy the peace and quiet of an old mining town, "We've got to decide whether we're going to keep our town quaint or if we're going to build. Obviously, we want those tourist dollars, but. . . ."[10] The California transplant had come to a fork in the road contemplated by Coloradans for nearly a century.

The land boom of the late 1960s involved more than the crowding of Colorado's ghost towns with condominiums and mass housing projects. Attracted by mountain living, an increasing number of buyers sought property along tree-covered slopes where, unfortunately, domestic water sources were scarce, septic tanks frequently did not function—or, if they did, a neighbor's drinking water might be polluted—and there was a danger that the site selected might be a firetrap because forest fires could roar up hillsides as the draft of a chimney fans the flames of a fireplace. In the Crystal River Valley, near Marble, one developer undertook to provide up to 20,000 people with homes in an area of falling boulders that might threaten individuals, where a school was to be located at the base of an avalanche run, and homesites were located where floods of water and mud frequently occurred.

This emerging problem—plus the fact that developers all too often were of the transient type, men who took advantage of Colorado's loosely drawn laws to sell such property, complete with promises, only to leave the county the problems of drainage, roads, and other services after they had decamped—led to the passage of a basic land use act in 1970. In that year Governor John Love appointed a seven-man land use commission the report of which the General Assembly used in formulating a program that required each of the state's sixty-three counties to create planning groups, aided by state funds, and to make regulations based upon the commission's master plan to control the creation of rural and mountain subdivisions. Like those of most other initial programs, the rules were fairly loose, and within two years the governor was pressing for a strengthening of the codes obliging developers to obtain official certification that water and sewage facilities were available for their proposed projects before they would be allowed to proceed.

Most complaints about growth tended to come from burgeoning cities that were not prepared for the suddenness with which the boom struck their part of the West. As residents of the eighth largest state, they had for years accustomed themselves to the notion that growth was essential to commercial life, and even though Colorado grew by some 28 percent during the sixties and early seventies, population figures reached only about 2.4 million. Surely, said the boosters, this was not excessive for a western commonwealth of such a vast geographic expanse. Complainants pointed out that about 65 percent of the total lived along the Fort Collins–Pueblo strip and that, as a consequence, the frequent temperature inversions over that crowded belt of land produced a noxious smog that inspired bumper stickers reading "Don't Californicate Colorado." Those who feared further assaults by real estate developers thought state controls over bedroom-community expansion to be far from effective.

Although the provisions of the land use act of 1970 were bland, the rural response to it was not. Cattlemen and farmers, fearful that the big city legislators, particularly those from the Fort Collins–Pueblo strip, were about to abuse the power they long since had seized, complained vigorously about the inequities of Colorado's voting distribution. Developers alerted both the residents and the officials of mountain counties then feeding off the ski boom to the danger, as witness the sign posted in a county administrator's office warning flatlanders: "The hell with how they do it in Denver, this is Summit!" But the farmers, the ranchers, and the rural folk, once a power in the statehouse, were far outnumbered by the newcomers who had flooded the state after World War II; their cries of anguish barely were heard amidst the blasts of ecological bugles echoing across the state at election time.[11]

Dissatisfied with the relatively weak land use act of 1970, and concerned over creeping urban sprawl, smog, water pollution, and other blights induced by rapid growth, an increasingly powerful environmentalist group threw down the gauntlet and challenged the old establishment in the election of 1972. The manner in which members of the antigrowth forces chose to combat the "sell Colorado" advocates did not attack the central problem; rather it zeroed in on a particular proposal that, to many people, symbolized the issue. The immediate question was whether or not Colorado ought to host the 1976 Winter Olympics.

Presumably the honor of having such a notable event take place within the state's borders was something that no loyal Coloradan could regard with anything but pride and joy. However, to those who saw it otherwise, and who regarded it as yet one more ploy in the selling game, the effort to land yet another prize constituted no more than further aggression on the part of promoters who seemed to have more regard for money than for the environment.

The news that Colorado's offer had been accepted was followed by an outcry that negotiators had made false, or at least foolish, promises with regard to facilities; that the sponsorship would cost at least $25 million; and—the final disappointment—that local people would not be able to see the contests on television, except by paying for piped-in broadcasts at local theaters. Suspicions that the invitation was pregnant with financial expectations were not set at rest by statements such as that made by a Denver Olympics Committee member who discounted the cost to taxpayers with the remark, "I feel personally if Denver and Colorado spend $50 million on the Olympics even without a return, it's the best advertising . . . that's ever been done." Nor were ruffled feathers at Evergreen smoothed when residents who objected to the prospect of having their community torn up for ski-run construction were told that unless an acceptable alternative site was found they were "just going to have to eat it."

The notion that the state at large was going to have an expensive program foisted upon it for the sake of prestige, advertising, and consequent growth fueled the anti-Olympics drive. Colorado, already a speculator's paradise, now faced the prospect of paying heavily to broadcast that message to the rest of the country, and for a good many whose concern about the headlong plunge into congestion was mounting, this was the time to stand and fight. The matter went to the voters via the initiative and they said no by a vote of 537,440 to 358,906. It was a disappointment to supporters such as Denver Mayor William McNichols, Governor John Love, both U.S. senators, all of Colorado's congressmen, and the business establishment in general. It was a blow also to the pro-Olympics group that pumped $175,000 into a high-pressure campaign urging Coloradans to "light the torch now," and to the Denver *Post*, the management of which saw fit to allot five times more space to boosters of the winter events than it did to critics during the final days of that emotional contest.[12]

For the losers in the Winter Olympics battle the result was a short-term deprivation of potential profits. For the winners it meant possible savings for taxpayers but, more importantly, it signified a turning of the corner in the struggle over resource preservation. Meanwhile, the campaign for cleaner air, an undefiled landscape, and beautification of urban areas accelerated. City dwellers, who often were accused of having a great interest in preserving someone else's natural heritage while neglecting their own neighborhoods, tried to refute such charges by doing some municipal face-lifting.

One means of sprucing up decaying downtown areas was to employ the delightful device of going backward, to recapture some of the charm of old buildings now hidden by past efforts at progress. Merchants began to tear off the chromium and neon storefronts to reveal an earlier and more attractive architecture. They took their cue from such places as Aspen and Central City, believing that if these old camps could cash in on the nostalgia mania, so could they.

The effort at restoration was evident in Denver as early as the mid sixties. At that time steps were taken to revive a rundown, seedy part of the business district, the once-famous Larimer Street. By sandblasting, painting, and decorating the scene with street clocks, gaslights, and attractive courtyards, the merchants brought an old part of the city back to life. The locals responded favorably and joined out-of-town tourists in patronizing a neighborhood they now regarded as quaint and even historic. Here was the perfect blending of the environmentalists, who were obliged to admit that this indeed was preservation, and the enterprising merchants, who had no objections if Clio came to their aid in pursuit of the elusive dollar.[13]

Less constructive, at least from the standpoint of the commercial community, was Denver's drive to clear up visual clutter by making war upon signboards. A group calling itself Consumers for Better Signs flooded every public information outlet in the city with its message, picketed meetings, nagged officials with phone calls, and made so much noise in behalf of the cause that the city fathers had to respond if only out of sheer embarrassment. A powerful billboard lobby fought back, arguing that Denver's landscape needed a little color to offset the blandness of mere mountains and trees, but such an argument in the midst of the citizenry's environmental binge was not very convincing. In May 1971, the city council passed an ordinance banning the more garish and offensive types of signs, but the war went on, the billboard companies unwilling to admit that theirs was a lost cause.[14]

The Denver billboard war was a warning flag flying in the winds of change, an indicator that new days were ahead both for the capital city and for the state. In 1972 Denver's voters rather unexpectedly rejected a bond issue that proposed to finance more downtown parking, after which the city water board was defeated in its efforts to divert more water from the western slope in the interest of a bigger and more prosperous city. These apparent retreats from the commonly accepted roads to progress were underscored that autumn by the rejection of the Olympics, a scheme from which Denver merchants and innkeepers had expected to be the heaviest beneficiaries.

Even more surprising than this turnaround was the defeat suffered in the Democratic primary by the veteran congressman Wayne Aspinall. His tight control over the House Interior Committee, a body that dealt with legislation concerning the use of natural resources on federal lands, irritated conservationists, who charged that his views in these matters represented nineteenth-century thinking. Their annoyance was increased by the belief that the congressman intentionally had tied up wilderness and national parks legislation in committees for years while at the same time promoting dams in such places as the Grand Canyon area. When election time rolled around in 1972 Aspinall was opposed by Alan Merson in the party primary. Thanks to generous financial assistance from environmentalist groups the challenger was able to spend some $41,000, a sum considered to be large in a rural district and in a preliminary election. As it turned out, the money purchased only the retirement from public office of Aspinall, for Merson was narrowly defeated by Republican James P. Johnson in November.[15]

Merson's defeat did not mean that the electorate had turned back the conservationists—far from it. In fact, the trend in favor of such thinking was so strong, both in Colorado and in other states, that the *Rocky Mountain News* could label one of its postelection stories "Environmentalists Hail Election Victories." Other signs of change were discernible in the voting patterns of that year. In 1972, for the first time in history, Colorado voters sent a woman to Congress; her name was Patricia Schroeder. In the same election Boulder's Geraldine Bean, who had earned a doctorate in history at the university, was given strong support by the liberal element in her successful bid for a seat on the university's board of regents. Neither of these candidates stressed either women's liberation or liberal issues in their campaigns, yet the fact that they were women and happened to be generally sympathetic to environmental concerns was regarded by some political pundits as further evidence that Colorado's course had veered slightly to the left. A similar impression was left by the election to the Senate of Democrat Floyd Haskell, who had been a Republican as late as 1970. He hammered away at the "right-wing conservatism" of the veteran senior senator, Gordon Allott, whom he defeated in a surprising upset. Although Allott shared the concern of many Coloradans over threats to the environment, young voters thought the Senator, at sixty-five, too old and therefore too intellectually encrusted to understand their concerns. The youthful voters, supported by a significant body of recent arrivals from other parts of the country, were under the impression that the old guard had not watched over nature's treasure house in the central Rockies zealously enough in recent years.[16]

The feeling persisted, and as time for a statewide election approached two years later it became more apparent that the voters' desire for change was less transitory than some of the observers earlier had imagined. In 1974, in what must go down in Colorado history as the great environmental election, candidates for the U.S. Senate and House of Representatives, as well as for various state offices, stressed ecological issues in their respective campaigns. During the two years that followed the historic "Olympics election" of 1972 there developed a growing public concern over increasingly reckless land use, the greater possibility of the rape of Colorado's natural resources, and the implications of further gas-prospecting nuclear blasts. The latter particularly disturbed the voters, many of whom were newcomers who vowed that they had not moved to a state where it was said to be such a privilege in which to live just to risk absorbing radiation from that fabled mountain air.

The heating up of the atomic energy issue in the 1974 election grew out of renewed subterranean searches by gas hunters in western Colorado. The earlier effort, Project Rulison, still was being argued when, in May of 1973, three more explosions were set off. Project Rio Blanco, as the most recent effort was named, brought forth a storm of protest that radioactive materials would be transmitted to the users of gas so released. Environmentalist groups once more took to the field at election time, and Colorado voters were presented with a constitutional amendment that dealt with such methods of prospecting. The proposal called for the establishment of procedures to be complied with before any similar underground experiments could be launched. Although it was opposed, in principle, by the Colorado Association of Commerce and Industry, on the ground that like restraints might be employed against other efforts to develop energy, and that to place so complex a question on the ballot constituted a misuse of the initiative process, the voters approved the amendment by a margin of 60 percent.[17]

It was at this point, because Coloradans were increasingly concerned about environmental problems, that the voters undertook another of their occasional rebellions against the conservative establishment. The ticket that the Democrats fielded that year was one of the most liberal in the country. Gary Hart, who opposed the right-wing senator, Peter Dominick, had served as George McGovern's campaign manager in the disastrous presidential election of 1972. Gubernatorial candidate Richard Lamm, a relative newcomer from Wisconsin who had taken an important part in the Olympics battle, and sometimes was referred to even by his supporters as an "eco-freak," launched an environmentally oriented campaign by walking around the state, shaking hands, and praising Colorado's natural resources, which he promised to protect. His opponent, John Vanderhoof, had inherited the governorship when John Love was called to Washington to serve a brief, unhappy stint as Richard Nixon's "energy czar." Lamm's running mate was George Brown, a former Denver newspaperman and a long-time member of the General Assembly who drew national attention as the only black ever to run for a major Colorado office. At the time only about 3 percent of the state's population was black. Attracting notice also was young Sam Brown, a one-time divinity student who had earned the disapproval of the established order by promoting anti–Vietnam war demonstrations at Washington; to the undisguised horror of businessmen he asked to be elected state treasurer.[18]

Richard Lamm paced his campaign with a heavy attack upon the century-old "sell Colorado" program. Charging that land developers had captured the state's Republican Party, he told one group of developers that if he were elected they would be "on the outside looking in." He denied that he opposed growth, maintaining that there was such a thing as regulated development in which a better balance might be achieved, and he argued for much stronger land-use laws. Lamm made a wide appeal to voters when he implied that this was no visionary scheme got up by liberals but rather that it exemplified a kind of States' Rights doctrine in which energy-hungry easterners and ruthless land speculators would be prevented from looting another western commonwealth. The electorate, weighted more than ever by a group of politically active newcomers combined with an old cadre of local liberals, listened to the new Populists, pulled Democratic levers on the voting machines, and swept Republicans from the major offices.

A good many of these recent arrivals had come from the East and from the West Coast—California was a heavy contributor—to get away from urban sprawl, smog, and bumper-to-bumper Sundays in state and national parks. As they observed the tightening international energy crunch and saw extractive industries eye Colorado with renewed interest, these newer residents found little appeal in local candidates who talked of making the state the new energy capital of the nation. Although national pundits regarded the outcome of the vote as a swing toward the left for Colorado, a brief period of time would show that it was merely another evidence of independence at the polls, witnessed on and off for decades, and that the newly elected men were not, because they could not be, radical or even very "leftish."[19]

What the Colorado voters were trying to say in 1974 was that possibly their patrimony was being expended too rapidly, too recklessly, and sometimes for the wrong reasons. As always, events tended to bring matters to a head, and in this case widespread shortages of natural resources in the nation, underscored by the manipulation of energy resources abroad, drove home points that conservationists had been making for years. Suddenly their warnings sounded more like signals of clear and present danger than at any time before in American history.

When Richard Lamm promised, "We're not going to let exploiters rip us up and rip us off," his remarks sounded less iconoclastic than would have been the case a few years earlier. He elaborated: "I know that just as soon as some Eastern politician's constituents get cold in the winter, he's going to say 'screw Colorado.'" This was plain talk; westerners understood it. The threat to "control the big boys" once had been regarded as the program of a few misguided liberals, but now these warnings came out sounding more like "Colorado first," and therefore the response among old-timers was less hostile.

States' rights advocates nodded approvingly when the young governor pointed to the obvious geographic fact that no rivers flowed into Colorado, but rather they all ran out, and that nineteen states depended upon such a functioning of the law of gravity for their water supplies.[20] In the late 1940s John Gunther had reminded Coloradans of this when he wrote, "Water is blood in Colorado." About that time Bernard De Voto irritated the natives by saying much the same thing in his commencement address at the university. Outsiders always have upset Coloradans by referring to the problem, but in the meantime they have kept each other aware of it by continuing the eastern slope–western slope water diversion vendetta. Perhaps Governor Lamm inadvertently invoked the "foreign war panacea" when he talked about other states using what Coloradans had come to think of as Colorado water, thereby diverting their minds momentarily from the local water usage squabble. But not entirely. As one bitter western sloper put it: "The only return we get from their Eastern Slope water schemes is in the form of twelve-ounce Coors [beer] cans." He was referring to the fact that by 1974 approximately half of the water used by eastern slope cities came from across the mountains, and that the passageway was a one-way street.[21]

The water problem that faced Coloradans by the mid seventies was both practical and environmental. Colorado River Basin production of that dwindling resource could not promise places like California or Arizona the amount their growing needs would require; for that matter, they might not be able to get as much water as had been supplied earlier. At the same time studies indicated that the state itself might suffer if water-gobbling oil shale production was carried out to any great extent. Additionally, coal strip-mining could threaten water resources by interrupting normal drainage patterns and increasing stream pollution. Environmentalists argued that further water diversion for municipal use and oil shale development eventually could threaten not only the state's fishing—so tied to tourism—but even local agriculture. Cloud seeding, the introduction of new outside sources of water, and the recycling of water for use in irrigation suggested the possibility of long-range relief, but all of these possibilities were bound to be expensive.[22]

Accelerating demands upon energy resources, brought on in part by the international "crisis" of the mid seventies, were of great concern to western governors. In the Rocky Mountain region lay over 40 percent of America's coal deposits and about 60 percent of the national total that could be strip-mined economically. It also contained most of the country's known uranium sources and all of its oil shale. From the day of the Fifty-Niners Colorado had produced crude oil; this industry had developed rapidly throughout the mountain region ever since. A companion resource, natural gas, was more widely exploited as twentieth-century demands for that product increased. All of these resources made a cluster of states that included about a quarter of the nation's area, but only 4 percent of its population, worry about the final chapter in a history of exploitation that had begun well over a century earlier. As Governor Lamm commented at mid decade, "We don't want to be a national sacrifice area."[23]

The "go slowly" attitude was not espoused solely by the environmentalists. It is true that such groups were quick to go to court, and in some of the western states their actions temporarily halted the opening of new coal mines, but other interests dragged their feet when it came to all-out energy development. Farmers, for example, were not enthusiastic about diverting irrigation water to oil shale projects or even to such water-consuming operations as that of nuclear power plants. Others argued that a sudden return of boom days in energy resource neighborhoods would cause some painful problems in small towns. Coloradans who watched the population explosion at Rock Springs, Wyoming, and saw a life-style change almost overnight foresaw a similar plight befalling some of the small towns in the minerally rich western portions of their own state.

Somewhat modifying this general concern over resource exploitation was the feeling that if the pendulum was allowed to swing too far in the direction of preservation dire economic consequences could result. In some instances, enormous and expensive projects that would have provided local employment were stalled by the legal maneuvers of environmentalist organizations, and this made some of those who were genuinely concerned about the future disposition of natural resources back away from the "eco-maniacs," as their enemies called them. Also, an old, potentially dangerous sentiment reemerged: the strict control of development threatened the extinction of the traditional frontier ways so long and so jealously guarded by the establishment. Although Colorado always had been somewhat less "western" in its habits than some of its neighbors, the notion of internal expansion, and that more was better, had taken such a firm grip in the minds of its leaders that its momentum was hard to slow.[24]

Another factor that calmed apprehensions over Colorado's potential role as a supplier of energy was the reaction of Americans when threatened shortages did not materialize. All that happened was a rise in energy prices. The public accepted this development with amazingly little complaint, and the great urge to tap western resources began to fade. The great oil shale hunt and subsequent disenchantment with its results offered further evidence of Colorado's uncertain reaction to the energy crisis. For example, in 1974 the state was being referred to as "America's Persian Gulf," and at that time several of the big oil companies entered into expensive agreements to process oil shale. The idea was far from new—there had been a "rush" for leases on the western slope a half-century earlier and an attempt to develop oil shale during World War II—but now, with sharp price increases for petroleum products and avowals from the Nixon administration that America intended to become energy independent, there appeared to be a possibility that oil extraction of this kind could be made economically feasible. Yet by 1975 foreign oil imports were on the increase and old doubts about oil shale again emerged. In that year two of the four partners in a petroleum consortium withdrew from the Colorado project. Tosco, the Oil Shale Corporation of Los Angeles, and Atlantic Richfield explained that the federal government's refusal to guarantee $6 billion in loans meant that there was not sufficient incentive to continue the expensive projects. Shell Oil Company and Ashland Oil, Inc., retained their leases, but company representatives warned of a withdrawal if governmental roadblocks or other complications persisted. The tone of editorial comments in Colorado on the shaky future of oil shale suggested that, for the moment at least, the fear of environmental rape in that area had abated. The outcries subsided. Even former governor John Vanderhoof was forgiven for a remark attributed to him: "As my wife says, what difference does it make if they move that god-forsaken earth around? It couldn't look any worse." As the big oil companies began to retreat and the wooing of western Colorado showed signs of abating, the opinions of "Johnny Van" now echoed the sentiments of an earlier day when environmentalists were not quite so tall in the saddle.[25]

If the immediate prospect of having the countryside torn up in a search for oil shale began to recede, so did fears that strip-mining for coal would wreak the same kind of damage. When bids were opened in the fall of 1974 at Colorado's first coal-lease auction, there was general surprise and disappointment among officials; only one bid topped the minimum price of one dollar per acre per year, and no bids were received for over half of the 20,000 acres of state land offered. Although calls for greater western coal production were made by federal officials, who hinted strongly that environmental standards would be relaxed, industries were slow to make the necessary reconversion to that ancient form of energy. Homeowners showed almost no interest in returning to coal-burning furnaces but clung to natural gas service while toying with the idea of heating with solar energy. Colorado, whose boosters long had bragged about its three hundred days of sunshine a year, immediately claimed the honor of being a leader in this new field. By the mid seventies solar-heated homes began to appear and enterprising businessmen turned to the production of the rather expensive units necessary for such a conversion.[26]

As Coloradans emerged from their latest fright over the perils of the future and resolved, as they had done upon various past occasions, not only to stay afloat economically but to prosper while living the good life, the environmentalist crusaders discovered that audiences made up of apprehensives were getting harder to come by. Political indicators, both local and national, seemed to suggest this. Governor Lamm, who, said a Boulder newspaper, once had "swathed himself in the robes of an environmental savior" and had sallied forth as "a defender of the Earth and all the beasts and little children thereon," began to be condemned as an apostate by the more dedicated of his once-faithful followers. In pointing out that the governor was becoming more partial to tourists and that he now looked more favorably upon mining, a national magazine suggested that while political dogma was one thing, real life was something else.[27]

Alarmed by the apparent renewal of "sell Colorado," a concerned Colorado journalist objected to the warblings of such a harmless figure as singer John Denver, who, it seemed, was drawing too much attention to the state and who was advised, therefore, to sing the praises of Sandpoint, Idaho, if he felt inclined to advertise some section of the West in song.[28] But one did not have to be a modern minstrel to laud the grandeur of the central Rockies, as a well-known novelist demonstrated. In sugared prose James A. Michener, author of the best-selling *Centennial*, told readers of *Business Week* that this, indeed, was "the place." That is, he shared this information with most Americans, for the special advertising section dedicated to Colorado was aimed primarily at out-of-state industrialists who might be lured to the central Rockies, where, it was hoped, local people might become their employees. Those who were treated to the encomiums were told that, with certain limitations, this indeed would be a great state in which to settle. Accompanying the article were advertisements paid for by resorts, hotels, a land development company, a chamber of commerce group, and an oil shale development company that announced itself as working "for the good of mankind."[29]

There were other indications that the figurative No Trespassing signs, erected to warn away the new prospectors of Colorado, had begun to come down. The so-called liberals elected in 1974 were under heavy attack, and some of them had given indications of hedging their bets. Senator Gary Hart, who once had referred to nuclear power generators as the Edsels of the nuclear field, concluded that a proposed nuclear enrichment plant at Pueblo would possess the twin virtues of low radiation danger and higher employment possibilities in a city to which the mid-decade recession had brought economic woes. Similarly, Governor Lamm, the one-time challenger of Rulison, favored the Pueblo project, much to the dismay of his earlier followers. One of them, actor Robert Redford, who considered the governor's conversion something of a sellout, remarked: "It's like finding out you've been saving Confederate money all along."[30] Perhaps.

But Hart and Lamm, as well as Representatives Timothy Wirth and Patricia Schroeder, were aware that the tables had turned slightly in the other direction. An ultraconservative group calling itself the Committee for the Survival of a Free Congress had turned its guns on these and other members of Congress for earning exceedingly poor grades on that organization's voting report card. Aware of the independent nature of Colorado voters, and of constantly shifting political sands, the young Democratic incumbents felt obliged to take into account Colorado's traditionally Republican complexion and some recent economic changes that were certain to be important at balloting time. The change of mood was felt also in the Colorado legislature, where environmental bills found the going increasingly hard.[31] Preliminary indications appeared to support the contention that the predicted energy crisis had not yet become so serious as the doom sayers had forecast and that "business as usual" again was the order of the day. Critics of this view could only bide their time and warn, "Wait and see."

Thus as the state passed its hundredth birthday there were disagreements among its people as to the proper course to follow in the days that lay ahead. Schooled in the frontier tradition that the Lord had placed resources on earth to be used by the chosen, yet continuously influenced for decades by the philosophy of eastern nature lovers who long had regarded the place as a national scenic and natural preserve, Coloradans in more recent years had felt an increasing pressure from the latter group. A good many of the new immigrants were refugees from more heavily congested portions of the nation, both East and West, who had become disenchanted with what they regarded as the "rat race" of their daily lives, of crowded conditions, of polluted air, of a dwindling sense of individuality. It was the growing weight of their numbers, combined with that of residents who long had cherished the "champagne air" of Colorado, that had struck a new balance, the first real fruits of which were seen in the 1974 statewide election. As the implications of that contest began to be understood, it appeared that some kind of a consensus would have to be reached, a "use but not abuse" program, and that it would serve as a working plan for the immediate future.

Meantime, the Coloradans, both of the immigrant and the native variety, displayed a growing interest in their commonwealth, a fascination that was tinged with a curiosity about its past, and they entertained hope that it would prove to fulfill the promise that so many of the young Fifty-Niners had predicted for it.

In many ways the dreams of those firstcomers had been realized; in others, they had not. Many of the physical developments the founding fathers had dreamed of had been available for some time. The state had prospered for well over a century; it had achieved a more-than-satisfactory transportation connection with the rest of the nation; it had produced artists, writers, musicians, scientists, jurists, and political leaders whose names had become nationally and internationally famous. In short, Colorado had taken its place among its sister states in a manner that the pioneers would have approved.

Denver had become well known around the world as the Mile-High City, a bright, clean, modern western metropolis at the foot of the Rocky Mountain front. While it prided itself as being up-to-the-minute, Denver retained much of its earlier rusticity. It was, as one observer put it, charmingly schizophrenic—an overgrown cowtown where cowboy boots and hats did not look glaringly out of place, yet one that showed flashes of sophistication when the merchants were not trying to beguile easterners with their put-on roles as shrewd rubes just trying to make a living in the sticks. The capital city's women reflected some of this paradox; they made great efforts to show their awareness of things current yet, as any knowledgeable merchant knew, women's fashions invariably lagged between six months and a year behind eastern styles, or for that matter, those of Dallas or San Francisco. "We can get in trouble buying new fashions," said the head of one of Denver's better stores. "There aren't enough people interested in buying them. We can mark something down to sell, only to have it get really big the next season." Nor were the men fashion conscious. Local executives dressed informally, sometimes a little flamboyantly, their attire frequently reflecting an individualism that was apparent to visitors.[32]

The conservatism in women's dress and the casual garb of the men revealed something about Denver and about Colorado. While it hinted at regionalism, and caused eastern reporters to think in terms of cowboys, it was not so much a frontier spirit as it was an inherent independence that Coloradans had come to develop on their own, quite naturally. If Denver was thought to be schizophrenic in the 1970s, it had been equally so a hundred years earlier, and in that respect the city and the state itself had changed little, if at all, during the century, for both the capital and its outlying domain often had left observers with the feeling that the Coloradans were still trying to make up their minds where they were going and what they hoped to be.

This apparent indecisiveness was really a sense of selectivity, and it represented a people who from the outset had decided what kind of a society they wanted. That they were still debating the matter more than a century later perhaps spoke more for their discrimination and their high standards than it did for any inability to come to a decision. The "great debate" of the 1970s, one that posed questions as to the shape of things to come, was suggestive of a people whose minds remained open and who took the position that the heritage they hoped to pass on to future generations was still in their hands, as it had been in the days of the original builders. The Coloradans were on record as having recognized that responsibility.

# Notes

## Chapter 1

1. William B. Parsons, "Pike's Peak Fourteen Years Ago," *Kansas Magazine,* June 1872, p. 560; idem, "Report on the Gold Mines of Colorado, 1858," *Colorado Magazine* 13, no. 6 (November 1936):215–18.

2. Henry L. Pitzer, *Three Frontiers* (Muscatine, Iowa, 1938), p. 81.

3. Clifford C. Hill, "Wagon Roads in Colorado, 1858–1876" (M.A. thesis, University of Colorado, 1949), pp. 9–14.

4. *Harper's Weekly,* June 18, 1859, p. 390; *New York Times,* June 11, 1859; Libeus Barney, *Letters of The Pike's Peak Gold Rush* (San Jose, Calif., 1959), pp. 23–25; Chicago *Press and Tribune,* May 26, 1859.

5. Henry Villard, *The Past and Present of the Pike's Peak Gold Regions* (St. Louis, 1860), pp. 22, 23, quoted in Carla E. Neuhaus, "Transportation to Colorado, 1858–1869" (M.A. thesis, University of Colorado, 1926), p. 37.

6. Horace Greeley, *An Overland Journey from New York to San Francisco in the Summer of 1859* (Duncan edition: New York, 1963), p. 57; Villard, *Pike's Peak Gold Regions,* p. 153.

7. Emma Shepard Hill, *A Dangerous Crossing and What Happened on the Other Side* (Denver, 1924), p. 10.

8. *Rocky Mountain News,* April 24, 1861, quoting Galena *Courier.*

9. *New York Times,* May 24, June 13, 1859; *Harper's Weekly,* July 16, 1859, p. 459; E. H. N. Patterson Diary, in LeRoy R. Hafen, ed., *Overland Routes to the Gold Fields, 1859, From Contemporary Diaries* (Glendale, Calif.: 1942), pp. 99, 116, 127, 144.

10. Agnes Wright Spring, "Rush to the Rockies, 1859," *Colorado Magazine* 36, no. 2 (April 1959):100–103; Ovando J. Hollister, *The Mines of Colorado* (Springfield, Mass., 1867), p. 69.

11. Hollister, *Mines of Colorado,* pp. 59–63; Villard, *Pike's Peak Gold Regions,* pp. 38–39; Alice P. Hill, *Tales of the Colorado Pioneers* (Denver, 1884), p. 102.

12. Hollister, *Mines of Colorado,* p. 71.

13. Greeley, *Overland Journey,* p. 128.

14. Hollister, *Mines of Colorado,* p. 86; *New York Times,* August 26, 1859.

15. Sam Hawken to the *Missouri Democrat,* August 29, 1859, in LeRoy R. Hafen and Ann W. Hafen, eds., *Reports from Colorado: The Wildman Letters, 1859–1865* (Glendale, Calif., 1961), pp. 168–72.

16. Letter of H. G. Clark, July 24, in *New York Times,* August 16, 1859.

17. For a detailed discussion of population development see Colin B. Goodykoontz, "The People of Colorado," in LeRoy R. Hafen, ed., *Colorado and Its People* (New York, 1948), pp. 77–120. See also U.S., Department of the Interior, Census Office, *Population of the United States in 1860* (Washington, 1864), p. 549.

18. Parsons, "Pike's Peak Fourteen Years Ago," p. 557.

19. Augusta Tabor, "Cabin Life in Colorado," *Colorado Magazine* 4, no. 2 (March 1927), reprinted ibid. 36, no. 2 (April 1959):152.

20. A. A. Hayes, Jr., "Grub-Stakes and Millions in Colorado," *Harper's New Monthly Magazine,* February 1880, p. 380.

21. J. A. D., "The Wonderland of America: The Queen City of the Plains," *Potter's American Monthly,* February 1879, p. 82; Villard, *Pike's Peak Gold Regions,* p. 124.

## Chapter 2

1. Henry Villard, *The Past and Present of the Pike's Peak Gold Regions* (St. Louis, 1860), p. 122.

2. William Larimer, *Reminiscences of General William Larimer and His Son William H. H. Larimer* (Lancaster, Pa., 1918), pp. 88–89; Wilbur Fisk Stone, *History of Colorado,* 4 vols. (Chicago, 1918–19), 1:134–43.

3. Albert D. Richardson, *Beyond the Mississippi: From the Great River to the Great Ocean* (Hartford, 1867), p. 186; Villard, *Pike's Peak Gold Regions,* p. 27.

4. Horace Greeley, *An Overland Journey from New York to San Francisco in the Summer of 1859* (Duncan edition: New York, 1963), pp. 135–36; Richardson, *Beyond the Mississippi,* p. 187.

5. Libeus Barney, *Letters of the Pike's Peak Gold Rush* (San Jose, Calif., 1959), pp. 33–34, 41.

6. Thomas Wildman to Augustus Wildman, June 20, 1859 in LeRoy R. Hafen and Ann W. Hafen, eds., *Reports from Colorado: The Wildman Letters, 1859–1865* (Glendale, Calif., 1961), p. 39; Villard, *Pike's Peak Gold Regions,* p. 56.

7. Greeley, *Overland Journey,* p. 97; Villard, *Pike's Peak Gold Regions,* pp. 121–22; Hafen, *Reports from Colorado,* pp. 145–46.

8. For some prices see Villard, Barney, Greeley, and Wildman, all previously cited. The Wootton material is from Howard Louis Conard, *"Uncle Dick" Wootton* (Chicago, 1890), pp. 372–74.

9. *New York Times,* August 24, September 24, October 1, 21, 1859; reports from St. Louis papers in Hafen, *Reports from Colorado,* pp. 217, 227; *Harper's Weekly,* October 1, 8, 1859.

10. Thomas Wildman to his sister, August 6, 1859, in Hafen, *Reports from Colorado,* p. 52; Samuel Hawken to *Missouri Democrat,* August 29, 1859, in ibid., p. 172; Barney, *Gold Rush Letters,* p. 41.

11. Villard, *Pike's Peak Gold Regions,* pp. 131–32; Barney, *Gold Rush Letters,* pp. 53, 65.

12. See letters of November 10 and December 15, 1859 in Hafen, *Reports from Colorado,* pp. 190, 234.

13. Thomas Wildman as "Gregory" in *New York Times,* September 12, 1859. See Hafen, *Reports from Colorado,* pp. 234, 272.

14. Correspondent to the *Missouri Democrat,* from Denver, December 15, 1859, in Hafen, *Reports from Colorado,* p. 224 and Thomas Wildman to his sister, January 4, 1860, from Denver, ibid., p. 240.

15. Thomas Wildman to his sister from Denver, May 17, 1860 in Hafen, *Reports from Colorado,* p. 258; Augustus Wildman to his father, October 1, 1860, ibid., p. 263; Augustus Wildman to his sister, December 16, 1860, ibid., p. 271.

16. Correspondent to the *Missouri Democrat,* writing from Denver, December 15, 1859 in Hafen, *Reports from Colorado,* p. 229.

17. Correspondent to the *Missouri Republican,* November 10, 1859, ibid., p. 194.

18. Arthur J. Markley, "Colorado's Early-Day Doctors," in *Denver Westerners' Brand Book for 1946* (Denver, 1947), pp. 225–31.

19. Allen D. Breck, *The Centennial History of the Jews of Colorado 1859–1959* (Denver, 1960), p. 24; see also Ida Libert Uchill, *Pioneers, Peddlers, and Tsadikim* (Denver, 1957), p. 71.

20. William M. Kramer, ed., "The Western Journal of Isaac Mayer Wise," *Western States Jewish Historical Quarterly* 5, no. 2 (January 1973):121.

21. *Rocky Mountain News,* September 4, 1882.

22. Hafen, *Reports from Colorado,* pp. 200, 240. See also Thomas J. Noel, "The Multifunctional Frontier Saloon: Denver, 1858–1876," *Colorado Magazine* 52, no. 2 (Spring 1975):124.

23. *Rocky Mountain News,* August 2, 1864 and April 17, 1865. See also Eugene H.

Berwanger, "William J. Hardin: Colorado Spokesman for Racial Justice, 1863–1873," *Colorado Magazine* 52, no. 1 (Winter 1975):52–65.

24. William H. Rideing, *A-saddle in the Wild West* (London, 1870), pp. 26–27.

25. Barney, *Gold Rush Letters,* p. 59.

26. *Rocky Mountain News,* May 16, 1864.

27. Barney, *Gold Rush Letters,* p. 70; *Rocky Mountain News,* March 21, 1860.

28. Percy S. Fritz, *Colorado: The Centennial State* (New York, 1941), p. 176; Stone, *History of Colorado,* 1:393–94; Ovando J. Hollister, *The Mines of Colorado* (Springfield, Mass., 1867), p. 125.

29. *New York Times,* November 18, 1859; Stone, *History of Colorado,* 1:144; Frank Hall, *History of the State of Colorado* (Chicago, 1889), p. 250; LeRoy R. Hafen, *Colorado: The Story of a Western Commonwealth* (Denver, 1933), p. 128; Hollister, *Mines of Colorado,* p. 127.

30. Barney, *Gold Rush Letters,* pp. 66, 88.

31. Irving Howbert, *Memories of a Lifetime in the Pike's Peak Region* (New York, 1925), pp. 18, 19.

## Chapter 3

1. Correspondent for the *Missouri Democrat,* issue of December 12, 1859, in LeRoy R. Hafen and Ann W. Hafen, eds., *Reports from Colorado: The Wildman Letters, 1859–1865* (Glendale, Calif., 1961), p. 220.

2. A. A. Hayes, Jr., "Grub-Stakes and Millions in Colorado," *Harper's New Monthly Magazine,* February 1880, p. 380.

3. Alice P. Hill, *Tales of the Colorado Pioneers* (Denver, 1884), p. 20.

4. Emma Shepard Hill, *A Dangerous Crossing and What Happened on the Other Side* (Denver, 1924), p. 55.

5. Duane A. Smith, *Horace Tabor: His Life and the Legend* (Boulder, Colo., 1973), pp. 17–19; Augusta Tabor, "Cabin Life in Colorado," *Colorado Magazine* 4, no. 2 (March 1927), reprinted ibid. 36, no. 2 (April 1959):149–52. Henry L. Pitzer, *Three Frontiers* (Muscatine, Iowa, 1938), p. 97; *Rocky Mountain News,* August 8, 1860.

6. Libeus Barney, *Letters of The Pike's Peak Gold Rush* (San Jose, Calif., 1959 ed.), p. 40.

7. William Hepworth Dixon, *New America,* 2 vols. (London, 1867), 1:130.

8. Agnes Wright Spring, ed. *A Bloomer Girl on Pike's Peak, 1858: Julia Archibald Holmes, First Woman to Climb Pike's Peak* (Denver, 1949), p. 39. This equal rights advocate, who often used her maiden name to illustrate her beliefs, wrote from the top of the peak, August 5, 1858, "I have now accomplished the task which I marked out for myself, and now I feel amply repaid for all my toil and fatigue."

9. *Rocky Mountain News,* September 10, 1859. See also *Mountain Charley; or the Adventures of Mrs. E. J. Guerin, Who Was Thirteen Years in Male Attire* (Reprint: Norman, Okla., 1968).

10. Daniel Ellis Conner, *A Confederate in the Colorado Gold Fields,* ed. Donald J. Berthrong and Odessa Davenport (Norman, Okla., 1970), p. 98.

11. Pitzer, *Three Frontiers,* p. 97.

12. Barney, *Gold Rush Letters,* p. 81.

13. Corresondent to the *Missouri Democrat,* writing from Denver, December 1, 1859, in Hafen, *Reports from Colorado,* p. 222.

14. Dixon, *New America,* 1:125.

15. Hafen, *Reports from Colorado,* pp. 181–94, 202, 230.

16. Written from Denver on December 15, 1859, in Hafen, *Reports from Colorado,* pp. 231–32.

17. Thomas Wildman to his family, ibid., p. 247. *Rocky Mountain News,* March 7, 1866.

18. Samuel Bowles, *Across the Continent: A Summer's Journey to the Rocky Mountains,*

*the Mormons, and the Pacific States* (Springfield, Mass., 1866), p. 62. See also *Rocky Mountain News*, July 18, 1866.

19. Ovando J. Hollister, *The Mines of Colorado* (Springfield, Mass., 1867), pp. 447–48.
20. *Rocky Mountain News*, April 24, 1861.
21. *Rocky Mountain News*, December 12, 1860.
22. Augusta Tabor, "Cabin Life in Colorado" (1959 ed.), pp. 149–53.
23. Conner, *A Confederate*, p. 117.
24. Henry Villard, *The Past and Present of the Pike's Peak Gold Regions* (St. Louis, 1860), pp. 131–32; Barney, *Gold Rush Letters*, p. 65.
25. Melvin Schoberlin, *From Candles to Footlights* (Denver, 1941), pp. 19–20.
26. Schoberlin, *From Candles to Footlights*, pp. 21–23; Hafen, *Reports from Colorado*, p. 194; Villard, *Pike's Peak Gold Regions*, note, p. 123; Barney, *Gold Rush Letters*, pp. 49–50; *Rocky Mountain News*, September 29, 1859. See also Virginia McConnell, "A Gauge of Popular Taste in Early Colorado," *Colorado Magazine* 46, no. 4 (Fall 1969):338–50 and Alice Cochran, "Jack Langrishe and the Theater of the Mining Frontier," ibid., pp. 324–37.
27. Villard, *Pike's Peak Gold Regions*, p. 123.
28. Hafen, *Reports from Colorado*, p. 223.
29. *Weekly Rocky Mountain News*, December 12, 1860.
30. Ibid., December 7, 1861.
31. Ibid., October 30, 1861.
32. Ibid., April 19, 1869.
33. Harold E. Briggs, "Early Variety Theaters in the Trans-Mississippi West," *Mid-America* 34, n.s. 23, no. 3 (July 1952):193–94.
34. *Weekly Rocky Mountain News*, March 15, 1862.
35. Ibid., June 14 and October 23, 1862.
36. Ibid., April 16, 1863.
37. Ibid., October 7, 1868 and June 5, 1869.
38. By far the best book concerning Colorado journalism is Robert L. Perkin, *The First Hundred Years: An Informal History of Denver and* The Rocky Mountain News (New York, 1959). See also Neil W. Kimball, "George West," *Colorado Magazine* 27, no. 3 (July 1950):198–208.
39. D. W. Working, "Some Forgotten Pioneer Newspapers," *Colorado Magazine* 4, no. 3 (May 1927):93–100; Anson S. Rudd (interview), "Early Days in Canon City," ibid. 7, no. 3 (May 1930):109–13; Edwin A. Bemis, "Journalism in Colorado," in LeRoy R. Hafen, ed., *Colorado and Its People*, 4 vols. (New York, 1948), 2:247–48; Jennie R. Aultman, "I Remember Doctor Beshoar, Pioneer," *Colorado Magazine* 30, no. 2 (April 1953):150.
40. Maurice Frink, *The Boulder Story: Historical Portrait of a Colorado Town* (Boulder, 1965), pp. 54–55; Lynn I. Perrigo, "A Condensed History of Boulder, Colorado," *Colorado Magazine* 26, no. 1 (January 1949):37–49.

## Chapter 4

1. John Nicolson, ed., *The Arizona of Joseph Pratt Allyn* (Tucson, 1974), p. 12.
2. Robert G. Athearn, ed., "Life in the Pike's Peak Region: The Letters of Matthew H. Dale," *Colorado Magazine* 32, no. 2 (April 1955):18, 19.
3. Norman John Bender, "The Crusade of the Blue Banner: Rocky Mountain Presbyterianism, 1870–1900" (Ph.D. diss., University of Colorado, 1971), chap. 9, "Onward Christian Soldiers." See also Frank Hall, *History of the State of Colorado*, 4 vols. (Chicago, 1889–95), 1:403–8.
4. Colin B. Goodykoontz, "Colorado as Seen by a Home Missionary, 1863–1868," *Colorado Magazine* 12, no. 2 (March 1935):64.
5. Libeus Barney, *Letters of the Pike's Peak Gold Rush* (San Jose, Calif., 1959), p. 73.

6. Correspondent for the *Missouri Democrat,* writing from Denver, November 24, 1859, in LeRoy R. Hafen and Ann W. Hafen, eds., *Reports from Colorado: The Wildman Letters, 1859–65* (Glendale, Calif., 1961), p. 212.

7. Wilbur Fisk Stone, *History of Colorado,* 4 vols. (Chicago, 1918–19), 1:661–63.

8. Irving Howbert, *Memories of a Lifetime in the Pike's Peak Region* (New York, 1925), p. 24.

9. Wilson Rockwell, *New Frontier: Saga of the North Fork* (Denver, 1938), p. 66.

10. Barney, *Gold Rush Letters,* p. 73.

11. For more on Bishop Randall see Allen D. Breck, *The Episcopal Church in Colorado, 1860–1963* (Denver, 1963), chap. 1. The bishop's own report is to be found in *First Report of Bishop Randall of Colorado to the Board of the Protestant Episcopal Church, October, 1866* (New York, 1866).

12. Wilbur F. Stone, "Early Pueblo and the Men Who Made It," *Colorado Magazine* 6, no. 6 (November 1929):209.

13. LeRoy R. Hafen, ed., *Colorado and Its People,* 4 vols. (New York, 1948), 2:211; Stone, *History of Colorado,* 1:677–80. See also Rev. W. J. Howlett, *Life of the Right Reverend Joseph P. Machebeuf, D.D.* (Pueblo, 1908), pp. 288–301.

14. Frank Hall, *History of Colorado,* 1:218; correspondent for the *Missouri Democrat,* November 24, 1859, in Hafen, *Reports from Colorado,* p. 212.

15. O. J. Goldrick, "The First School in Denver," *Colorado Magazine* 6, no. 2 (March 1929):72–74. See also A. J. Fynn and L. R. Hafen, "Early Education in Colorado," *Colorado Magazine* 12, no. 1 (January 1935):16–19.

16. James H. Baker and LeRoy R. Hafen, *History of Colorado,* 3 vols. (Denver, 1927), 3:1153–54.

17. Correspondent to the *Missouri Democrat,* writing from Denver, December 1, 1859, in Hafen, *Reports from Colorado,* p. 226.

18. *Rocky Mountain News,* November 28, 1866; " 'School Days in Early Denver' by An Old School Boy," *The Trail* 1, no. 6 (November 1908):25.

19. *Rocky Mountain News,* September 18, 1867.

20. Ibid., January 31, 1866.

21. Lynn I. Perrigo, "The First Decade of Public Schools at Central City," *Colorado Magazine* 12, no. 3 (May 1935):86–87. See also idem, "A Social History of Central City, Colorado, 1859–1900" (Ph.D. diss., University of Colorado, 1939), p. 180.

22. *Rocky Mountain News,* September 18, 1867.

23. *Leadville Herald,* March 7, 1882.

24. *Rocky Mountain News,* September 18, 1867, and November 3, 1869. For the "surplus" item see ibid., July 18, 1866.

25. *Rocky Mountain News,* September 16, 1868. See also Alice P. Hill, *Tales of Colorado Pioneers* (Denver, 1884), p. 124. For Bishop Randall's comments on Jarvis Hall see his *Report,* p. 6.

26. Baker and Hafen, *History of Colorado,* 3:1156.

27. Athearn, "Dale Letters," p. 15.

28. Barney, *Gold Rush Letters,* p. 54; *New York Times,* September 10, 1859.

29. Letter of Thomas Wildman, September 8, 1859 in Hafen, *Reports from Colorado,* p. 60; *Rocky Mountain News,* September 10, 1859. See Howard Louis Conard, *"Uncle Dick" Wootton* (Chicago, 1890), p. 380, and letter of A. C. Smith in *Chicago Press and Tribune,* May 8, 1859, for comments of witnesses to public hangings.

30. Central City *Daily Register-Call,* June 9, 1882, quoted in Lynn I. Perrigo, "Law and Order in Early Colorado Mining Camps," *Mississippi Valley Historical Review* 28, no. 1 (June 1941):46–61.

31. *Rocky Mountain News,* July 9, 1861.

32. Ibid., May 15, 30, 1862.

33. John D. W. Guice, "Colorado's Territorial Courts," *Colorado Magazine* 45, no. 3

(Summer 1968):204–24; idem, "The Territorial Supreme Courts of Colorado, Montana and Wyoming, 1861–1890" (Ph.D., diss., University of Colorado, 1969). See also Peter Wikoff, "The Bar and Bench of Denver and Colorado," *Magazine of Western History* 9, nos. 5 and 6 (March and April 1889):605–10 and 764–73.

34. M. L. Crimmins, "Fort Massachusetts, First United States Military Post in Colorado," *Colorado Magazine* 14, no. 4 (July 1937):128; Morris F. Taylor, "Fort Massachusetts," ibid. 45, no. 2 (Spring 1968):120–42. A fort built by the Spanish northeast of Sangre de Cristo Pass in 1819 was the first of the forts in the area.

35. John Nankivell, "Fort Garland, Colorado," *Colorado Magazine* 16, no. 1 (January 1939):13–28; Duane Vandenbusche, "Life at a Frontier Post: Fort Garland," ibid. 43, no. 2 (Spring 1966):132–48.

## Chapter 5

1. Jerome C. Smiley, *Semi-Centennial History of the State of Colorado,* 2 vols. (Chicago, 1913), 1:327–62; Robert G. Athearn, ed., "Life in the Pike's Peak Region: The Letters of Matthew H. Dale," *Colorado Magazine* 32, no. 2 (April 1955):12; *New York Times,* September 24, October 31, November 5, 26, December 6, 24, 1859; Irving Howbert, *Memories of a Lifetime in the Pike's Peak Region* (New York, 1925), p. 46; Libeus Barney, *Letters of the Pike's Peak Gold Rush* (San Jose, Calif., 1959), p. 63. See also LeRoy R. Hafen, "Jefferson Territory and Its Competitors," in *Denver Westerners Brand Book for 1945* (Denver, 1946), pp. 145–70. An older, but scholarly, treatment may be found in Frederic L. Paxson, "Territory of Colorado," *American Historical Review* 12, no. 1 (October 1906):53–65.

2. Athearn, "Dale Letters," p. 12; Gus Wildman to his father, February 14, 1862, in LeRoy R. Hafen and Ann W. Hafen, eds., *Reports from Colorado: The Wildman Letters, 1859–1865* (Glendale, Calif., 1961), p. 306.

3. For more about southern sympathizers see Morris F. Taylor, "Confederate Guerrillas in Southern Colorado," *Colorado Magazine* 46, no. 4 (Fall 1969):304–23.

4. Ovando J. Hollister, *Boldly They Rode: A History of the First Colorado Regiment* (Lakewood, 1949); Sheldon Zweig, "William Gilpin: First Territorial Governor of Colorado" (M.A. thesis, University of Colorado, 1950), chaps. 4 and 5. See also Blanche V. Adams, "Colorado in the Civil War" (M.A. thesis, University of Colorado, 1930). William Clarke Whitford, *Colorado Volunteers in the Civil War: The New Mexico Campaign of 1862* (Denver, 1906; reprint, Lakewood, 1963) is the standard reference to this campaign.

5. For examples of irregularities among the troops see Stanley W. Zamonski and Teddy Keller, *The Fifty Niners* (Denver, 1961), p. 259, and *Colorado Republican* (Denver), October 12, 1861.

6. Thomas L. Karnes, *William Gilpin: Western Nationalist* (Austin, Texas, 1970), chap. 9; Zweig, "William Gilpin," chap. 5.

7. *Rocky Mountain News,* April 2, 1863.

8. Ibid., April 23, 1863.

9. Quoted by William M. Thayer, *Marvels of the New West* (Norwich, Conn., 1887), p. 521.

10. *New York Times,* May 2, August 24, and December 6, 1859.

11. C. M. Clark, *A Trip to Pike's Peak and Notes by the Way* (1861; reprint, San Jose, Calif., 1958), p. 110; Howbert, *Memories,* pp. 30, 59.

12. Correspondent to the *Missouri Democrat,* writing from Denver, December 1, 1859, in Hafen, *Reports from Colorado,* pp. 220–21.

13. "The Nebraska and Kansas Territories," *The Illustrated London News,* June 21, 1856.

14. When Emma Shepard Hill wrote her *Foundation Stones* (Denver, 1926) her interviews with pioneers indicated that there were many Indian "scares" but relatively little

violence. For contemporary evidence see letter of Gus Wildman to his father, April 29, 1861, in Hafen, *Reports from Colorado,* p. 285.

15. Horace Greeley, *An Overland Journey from New York to San Francisco in the Summer of 1859* (Duncan edition: New York, 1963), pp. 119, 121.

16. Henry Villard, *The Past and Present of the Pike's Peak Gold Regions* (St. Louis, 1860), p. 142.

17. John H. Edwards, in LeRoy R. Hafen, ed., *Overland Routes to the Gold Fields, 1859, From Contemporary Diaries* (Glendale, Calif., 1942), pp. 311–12.

18. George E. Hyde, *Life of George Bent* (Norman, Okla., 1968), p. 106.

19. Hyde, *Life of George Bent,* p. 114. See also Donald J. Berthrong, *The Southern Cheyennes* (Norman, Okla., 1963).

20. Howard Louis Conard, *"Uncle Dick" Wootton* (Chicago, 1890), p. 119.

21. See *Rocky Mountain News,* May 1, 1861; March 29, 1862; April 9, 1863; August 31, 1864.

22. Ovando J. Hollister, *The Mines of Colorado* (Springfield, Mass., 1867), p. 129.

23. Smiley, *Semi-Centennial History,* 1:426. See also David Lavender, *Bent's Fort* (New York, 1954), pp. 356–64. Irving Howbert, in *Memories,* p. 134, defended the action. For a general picture of Indian relations in eastern Colorado during the war years see Edmund Jefferson Danziger, Jr., *Indians and Bureaucrats: Administering the Reservation Policy during the Civil War* (Urbana, Ill., 1974), chap. 1, "The Struggle for Eastern Colorado." A balanced account of the Sand Creek affair is to be found in Berthrong, *The Southern Cheyennes,* chap. 9.

24. John Tice, *Over the Plains and on the Mountains or, Kansas and Colorado* (St. Louis, 1872), p. 207.

25. Mollie Dorsey Sanford, *Mollie: The Journal of Mollie Dorsey Sanford in Nebraska and Colorado Territories 1856–1866* (Lincoln, Neb., 1959), p. 188.

26. For an account of diffculties in 1868 see Robert G. Athearn, "Colorado and the Indian War of 1868," *Colorado Magazine* 33, no. 1 (January 1956):42-51.

27. George A. Custer, *My Life on the Plains* (Lincoln, Neb., 1966); see chap. 10, "The Battle of Washita."

28. *Rocky Mountain News,* December 19, 1866.

29. Harry E. Kelsey, Jr., *Frontier Capitalist: The Life of John Evans* (Boulder, Colo., 1969), pp. 169–207; Glenn C. Quiett, *They Built the West* (New York, 1934), pp. 143–81; Thomas J. Noel, "All Hail the Denver Pacific: Denver's First Railroad," *Colorado Magazine* 50, no. 2 (Spring 1973):91–116. For more on D.P.–K.P. relations see William Robinson Petrowski, "The Kansas Pacific: A Study in Railroad Promotion" (Ph.D. diss., University of Wisconsin, 1966).

30. For a comment on ballot box stuffing in the election see *New York Times,* January 9, 1866, in the article by "Croquis." See also Elmer Ellis, "Colorado's First Fight for Statehood, 1865–1868," *Colorado Magazine* 8, no. 1 (January, 1931):23–30.

31. *Rocky Mountain News,* January 17, 1866.

32. U.S., Congress, Senate, *Congressional Globe,* 39th Cong., 1st sess., April 24, 1866, pp. 2135–36. See also *New York Times,* January 30, 1866.

33. Kelsey, *Frontier Capitalist,* pp. 166–67; Smiley, *Semi-Centennial History,* 1:476-79. See also Harmon Mothershead, "Negro Rights in Colorado Territory," *Colorado Magazine* 40, no. 3 (July 1963):212-23.

34. Irving W. Stanton, *Sixty Years in Colorado* (Denver, 1922), p. 145.

35. *Rocky Mountain News,* January 16, April 10, 1867, and June 24, 1868.

36. For some pro-Colorado articles see *New York Times,* January 6, 1863, and February 14, July 12, and December 12, 1864.

37. Samuel Bowles, *Across the Continent: A Summer's Journey to the Rocky Mountains, the Mormons and the Pacific States* (Springfield, Mass., 1866), pp. 35, 44, 59–60.

38. A. W. Hoyt, "Over the Plains to Colorado," *Harper's New Monthly Magazine,* June 1867, p. 1.

39. J. A. Church, "The Disappointed Sister," *The Galaxy,* June 15, 1866, p. 296.

40. *The Great West* (Bloomington, Ill., 1880), p. 153.

41. *Rocky Mountain News,* June 13 and October 17, 1866.

42. Samuel Bowles, *Our New West* (Hartford, Conn., 1869), pp. 88–93, 179–87.

43. James F. Rusling, *Across America: Or, the Great West and the Pacific Coast* (New York, 1874), pp. 61, 71.

44. Ibid., p. 81.

45. Bowles, *Our New West,* pp. 141–42, 148–49.

46. William H. Brewer, *Rocky Mountain Letters* (1869; Denver, 1930), p. 43.

47. Bowles, *Our New West,* pp. 76–77.

## Chapter 6

1. *Weekly Rocky Mountain News,* April 13, 1864; Edward Bliss, "Colorado Territory," *New York Times,* February 14, 1864.

2. Clark C. Spence, *British Investments and the American Mining Frontier, 1860–1901* (Ithaca, N.Y., 1958), pp. 44, 45. For more on British participation later on, see Alfred P. Tischendorf, "British Investments in Colorado Mines," *Colorado Magazine* 30, no. 4 (October 1953):243–46.

3. Louis L. Simonin, *The Rocky Mountain West in 1867,* trans. Wilson O. Clough (Lincoln, Neb., 1966), chap. 5 See also Liston E. Leyendecker, "Colorado and the Paris Universal Exposition, 1867," *Colorado Magazine* 46, no. 1 (Winter 1969):1–15.

4. *Denver Daily Tribune,* September 4, 1871. See also James F. Willard and Colin B. Goodykoontz, eds., *Experiments in Colorado Colonization, 1869–1872* (Boulder, 1926), pp. 451–59; Frank Hall, *History of the State of Colorado,* 4 vols. (Chicago, 1889–95), 1:504–5.

5. Robert G. Athearn, *Rebel of the Rockies: A History of the Denver and Rio Grande Western Railroad* (New Haven, 1962), p. 9.

6. Ralph E. Blodgett, "The Colorado Territorial Board of Immigration," *Colorado Magazine* 46, no. 3 (Summer 1969):245–56.

7. Hall, *History of the State of Colorado,* 1:518; Jerome C. Smiley, *Semi-Centennial History of the State of Colorado,* 2 vols. (Chicago, 1913), 1:454–55.

8. Blodgett, "Colorado Territorial Board of Immigration," p. 256; Wilbur Fisk Stone, *History of Colorado,* 4 vols. (Chicago, 1918–19), 1:215.

9. The term was widely used but for one example, circa 1900, see Emma Abbot Gage, *Western Wanderings and Summer Saunterings through Picturesque Colorado* (Baltimore, 1900), chap. 7, "The Switzerland of America."

10. John Myers Myers, *Doc Holliday* (Boston, 1955), p. 210.

11. William A. Baillie-Grohman, *Camps in the Rockies* (1882; New York, 1905), p. 4; Samuel Nugent Townshend, *Colorado: Its Agriculture, Stockfeeding, Scenery, and Shooting* (London, 1879), p. 19; James Burnley, *Two Sides of the Atlantic* (Bradford, England, 1880), p. 141.

12. Quoted by John Baur, "The Health Seekers in the Westward Movement, 1830–1890," *Mississippi Valley Historical Review* 46 (June 1959):106. The "burying ground" quote was by George W. Pine and is found in ibid., p. 104.

13. LeRoy R. Hafen and Ann W. Hafen, eds., *Reports from Colorado: The Wildman Letters, 1859–1865* (Glendale, Calif., 1961), pp. 135, 152; C. M. Clark, *A Trip to Pike's Peak and Notes by the Way* (1861; reprint, San Jose, Calif., 1958), p. 88.

14. John Codman, *The Round Trip by Way of Panama through California, Oregon, Nevada, Utah, Idaho and Colorado* (New York, 1879), p. 289.

15. Billy M. Jones, *Health-Seekers in the Southwest, 1817–1900* (Norman, Okla., 1967), pp. 88–98.

16. Baur, "The Health Seekers," p. 105. See also Robert G. Athearn, *Westward the Briton* (Lincoln, Neb., 1962), p. 118.

17. Robert L. Perkin, *The First Hundred Years: An Informal History of Denver and the Rocky Mountain News* (New York, 1959), p. 304; Jones, *Health-Seekers,* p. 157. For a contemporary view see Frank Fossett, *Colorado: Its Gold and Silver Mines* (New York, 1879), chap. 11.

18. Gage, *Western Wanderings,* p. 100; Marshall Sprague, *Newport in the Rockies* (Denver, 1961), p. 72. See also Earl Pomeroy, *In Search of the Golden West: The Tourist in Western America* (New York, 1957), pp. 20–22. The Colorado Springs area received additional national publicity from Eliza Greatorex, *Summer Etchings in Colorado* (New York, 1873).

19. Frank Fossett, *Colorado,* pp. 107–11; George Charles Roche III, "Mt. Princeton Hot Springs; A Brief History," *Colorado Magazine* 37, no. 1 (January 1960):21–22.

20. Jane Furey, "Tourism in the Pike's Peak Area, 1870–1880" (M.A. thesis, University of Colorado, 1958), pp. 14–16. The newspaper quoted was the Colorado Springs *Gazette* for August 6, 1896.

21. R. B. Townshend, *A Tenderfoot in Colorado* (Norman, Okla., 1968 ed.), p. 187.

22. Furey, "Tourism," pp. 16, 21, 30, 48, 67. The newspaper quoted is the *Denver Tribune* for August 16, 1871.

23. Furey, "Tourism," p. 43, quoting *Out West* (Colorado Springs), July 4, 1872, and *Denver Daily Times,* September 24, 1873.

24. *Greeley Tribune,* August 4, 1874.

25. *Colorado Springs Gazette,* June 14, 1873.

26. Furey, "Tourism," pp. 22, 26–27.

27. Rose Georgina Kingsley, *South by West or Winter in the Rocky Mountains and Spring in Mexico* (London, 1874), pp. 132, 133.

28. Townshend, *Colorado,* p. 59; *Denver Weekly Times,* April 14, 1875.

29. Smiley, *Semi-Centennial History,* p. 450.

30. Furey, "Tourism," p. 34.

31. For a complete discussion of the statehood fight and Colorado's constitution see Donald Wayne Hensel, "A History of the Colorado Constitution in the Nineteenth Century" (Ph.D. diss., University of Colorado, 1957).

32. For a more detailed discussion of the convention see Colin B. Goodykoontz, "Some Controversial Questions before the Colorado Constitutional Convention of 1876," *Colorado Magazine* 17, no. 1 (January 1940):1–17.

33. Frank Hall, *History of Colorado,* 1:521.

34. *Colorado Springs Gazette,* February 20, 1875.

35. Quoted in Hensel, "A History of the Colorado Constitution," p. 225.

36. For the above material I have leaned heavily upon Colin B. Goodykoontz, "Some Controversial Questions before the Colorado Constitutional Convention of 1876," pp. 8–10. See also Hensel, "A History of the Colorado Constitution," pp. 349–60, and idem, "Religion and the Writing of the Colorado Constitution," *Church History* 30, no. 3 (September 1961):349–60.

37. Smiley, *Semi-Centennial History,* 1:487. See *Denver Times,* February 27, 1875, for Woodbury's editorial.

## Chapter 7

1. C. W. Upham, "Kansas and Nebraska," *North American Review,* January 1855, pp. 91–116; J. W. Scott, "The Great West," *DeBow's Review,* July 1853, p. 52; "Nebraska and

Kansas Territories," *Illustrated London News,* June 21, 1856; William Gilpin, "Pastoral Region of the West," *Littell's Living Age,* September 12, 1857, pp. 676–79; Horace Greeley, "Across the Continent," *Continental Monthly,* January 1862, pp. 81–83; idem, "On the Plains," ibid., February 1862, p. 171; idem, "The Plains as I Crossed Them Ten Years Ago," *Harper's New Monthly Magazine,* May 1869, pp. 789–95; idem, *An Overland Journey from New York to San Francisco in the Summer of 1859* (Duncan edition: New York, 1963), pp. 114–15.

2. Howard Louis Conard, *"Uncle Dick" Wootton* (Chicago, 1890), p. 316.

3. LeRoy R. Hafen and Ann W. Hafen, eds., *Reports from Colorado: The Wildman Letters, 1859–1865* (Glendale, Calif., 1961), p. 181; Henry Villard, *The Past and Present of the Pike's Peak Gold Regions* (St. Louis, 1860), p. 112.

4. Irving Howbert, *Memories of a Lifetime in the Pike's Peak Region* (New York, 1925), pp. 51, 59, 67, 92, 259.

5. Gus Wildman to his father, April 29, 1861, and to his mother in August 1861, in Hafen, *Reports from Colorado,* pp. 284, 297; Samuel Bowles, *Across the Continent: A Summer's Journey to the Rocky Mountains, the Mormons, and the Pacific States* (Springfield, Mass., 1866), p. 65; Albert D. Richardson, *Beyond the Mississippi: From the Great River to the Great Ocean* (Hartford, 1867), p. 333.

6. Samuel Bowles, *Our New West* (Hartford, Conn., 1869), pp. 180–89, 191–92.

7. *Rocky Mountain News,* May 20, 21, 29, 1868; Alvin T. Steinel, *History of Agriculture in Colorado* (Fort Collins, 1926), pp. 64–66.

8. *Rocky Mountain News,* June 17, 26, 1868; Steinel, *History of Agriculture,* pp. 65–66.

9. *Rocky Mountain News,* June 12, 1868.

10. Deryl V. Gease, "William N. Byers and the Colorado Agricultural Society," *Colorado Magazine* 43, no. 4 (Fall 1966):325–38.

11. James F. Willard and Colin B. Goodykoontz, eds., *Experiments in Colorado Colonization, 1869–1872* (Boulder, 1926), pp. xvii–xx.

12. "Colorado Place Names," *Colorado Magazine* 17, no. 4 (July 1940):135.

13. See Pueblo *Chieftain,* February 24, 1870.

14. Willard and Goodykoontz, *Experiments,* pp. xii, 99–132.

15. Willard and Goodykoontz, *Experiments,* pp. xx–xxiv.

16. Meliton Velasquez, "Guadalupe Colony Was Founded 1854," *Colorado Magazine* 34, no. 4 (October 1957):264–67.

17. James F. Willard, *The Union Colony at Greeley, Colorado, 1869–1871* (Boulder, 1918), pp. xx, xxi; David Boyd, *A History: Greeley and the Union Colony of Colorado* (Greeley, 1890), pp. 11–44.

18. Willard, *Union Colony,* pp. xxii–xxiii; Boyd, *Greeley,* p. 55; Robert L. Perkin, *The First Hundred Years: An Informal History of Denver and the Rocky Mountain News* (New York, 1959), p. 283.

19. Frank Hall, *History of the State of Colorado,* 4 vols. (Chicago, 1889), 1:535.

20. Willard, *Union Colony,* pp. xxx, xxxi.

21. Boyd, *Greeley,* p. 294.

22. Ibid., p. 52.

23. Alice P. Hill, *Tales of the Colorado Pioneers* (Denver, 1884), p. 138.

24. Willard and Goodykoontz, *Experiments,* xxiv–xxvii; Hall, *History of the State of Colorado,* 1:546–47; R. A. Puffer, "The Organization and Early History of Longmont" (M.A. thesis, University of Colorado, 1914), p. 6.

25. Boyd, *Greeley,* p. 185.

26. Esther Gunnison Kingdon, "Ryssby, the First Swedish Settlement in Colorado," *Colorado Magazine* 10, no. 4 (July 1933):121–30.

27. Willard and Goodykoontz, *Experiments,* pp. xxi–xxiii; Boyd, *Greeley,* p. 180.

28. Willard and Goodykoontz, *Experiments,* pp. xxxiii–xxxvi; Boyd, *Greeley,* pp. 188–90;

Hubert Howe Bancroft, *The Works of Hubert Howe Bancroft,* vol. 25, *History of Nevada, Colorado and Wyoming, 1540–1888* (San Francisco, 1890), p. 638.

29. Willard and Goodykoontz, *Experiments,* pp. 425–27.

30. Ibid., pp. 429–31, 446–49.

31. Jerome C. Smiley, *Semi-Centennial History of the State of Colorado,* 2 vols. (Chicago, 1913), 1:457; Hall, *History of the State of Colorado,* 1:526; Wilbur Fisk Stone, *History of Colorado,* 4 vols. (Chicago, 1918–19), 1:166. See also Agnes Wright Spring, "The Founding of Fort Collins, United States Military Post," *Colorado Magazine* 10, no. 2 (March 1933):47–55.

32. Nicholas G. Morgan, "Mormon Colonization in the San Luis Valley," *Colorado Magazine* 27, no. 4 (October 1950):271, 272.

33. Morgan, "Mormon Colonization," p. 274.

34. Colorado Mission, manuscript histories, vol. 1, Church of Jesus Christ of Latterday Saints, Salt Lake City, Utah; Robert G. Athearn, *Rebel of the Rockies: The Denver and Rio Grande Railroad* (New Haven, 1962), p. 20.

35. Colorado Mission, manuscript histories, vol. 1; *Deseret News,* May 14, 1878.

36. *Deseret News,* December 3, 1878, and January 20, 1879.

37. Andrew Jenson in *Deseret News,* November 29, 1930.

38. Morgan, "Mormon Colonization," p. 290; *Deseret News,* May 5, 1880.

39. Andrew Jenson, "The Founding of Mormon Settlements in the San Luis Valley, Colorado," *Colorado Magazine* 17, no. 5 (September 1940):178; *Deseret News,* July 2, 1879.

40. Jenson, "The Founding of Mormon Settlements," p. 179.

41. *Journal History,* L.D.S. Church Library, Salt Lake City, March 22, 1879; *Deseret News,* March 27, April 19, 1879.

42. *Journal History,* L.D.S. Church Library, December 31, 1880; *Deseret News,* December 31, 1880, February 15, March 25, 1881.

43. *Salt Lake Herald,* October 6, 1880; *Deseret News,* July 14, October 23, 1880; *Journal History,* L.D.S. Church Library, November 7, 1880.

44. H. W. Barnett to *Deseret News,* April 29, 1880, published in the May 5 issue; John Morgan to the *Deseret News,* April 2, 1880, published in the April 9 issue; Morgan, "Mormon Colonization," p. 286.

45. Morgan, "Mormon Colonization," p. 291; *Deseret News,* September 15, 1886 and September 5, 1888; William A. Braiden as told to Irma S. Harvey, "Early Days in the San Luis Valley," *Colorado Magazine* 21, no. 2 (March 1944):48. See also Alvar Ward Carlson, "Rural Settlement Patterns in the San Luis Valley: A Comparative Study," *Colorado Magazine* 44, no. 2 (Spring 1967):111–28.

## Chapter 8

1. Richard A. Bartlett, *Great Surveys of the American West* (Norman, Okla., 1962), see chap. 3.

2. Edmund B. Rogers, "Notes on the Establishment of Mesa Verde National Park," *Colorado Magazine* 29, no. 1 (January 1952):10–17.

3. Arthur W. Monroe, *San Juan Silver* (n.p., 1940), pp. 15, 17.

4. Rodman W. Paul, *Mining Frontiers of the Far West, 1848–1880* (New York, 1963), p. 124. See also James Edward Fell, "The Boston and Colorado Smelting Company: A Study in Western Industrialism" (M.A. thesis, University of Colorado, 1972). Briefer is Jesse D. Hale, "The First Successful Smelter in Colorado," *Colorado Magazine* 13, no. 5 (September 1936):161–67.

5. Wolfe Londoner, "Western Experiences and Colorado Mining Camps," *Colorado Magazine* 6, no. 2 (March 1929):69–70; Allen D. Breck, *Centennial History of the Jews of*

*Colorado, 1859–1959* (Denver, 1960), p. 124; Sewall Thomas, *Silhouettes of Charles S. Thomas* (Caldwell, Idaho, 1959), pp. 26–27.

6. Frank Fossett, *Colorado: Its Gold and Silver Mines* (New York, 1879), chaps. 18–22; Eugene F. Irey, "A Social History of Leadville, Colorado, during the Boom Days, 1877–1881" (Ph.D. diss., University of Minnesota, 1951), see foreword; Jerome C. Smiley, *Semi-Centennial History of the State of Colorado,* 2 vols. (Chicago, 1913), 1:538–41; Paul, *Mining Frontiers,* pp. 127–32.

7. Eddie Foy and Alvin F. Harlow, *Clowning through Life* (New York, 1928), pp. 119–22, 135–37.

8. Eugene F. Irey, "Social History of Leadville," pp. 278–81; Duane A. Smith, *Rocky Mountain Mining Camps: The Urban Frontier* (Bloomington, Ind., 1967), pp. 173–74; Wilbur Fisk Stone, *History of Colorado,* 4 vols. (Chicago, 1918–19), 1:388.

9. This charming account was related by Eugene Irey in "A Social History of Leadville," pp. 256–59. His sources included minutes of Leadville's Board of Trustees.

10. Foy, *Clowning through Life,* p. 141.

11. Quoted in Robert G. Athearn, *Rebel of the Rockies: A History of the Denver and Rio Grande Western Railroad* (New Haven, 1962), p. 98.

12. Carl L. Haase, "Gothic, Colorado: City of Silver Wires," *Colorado Magazine* 51, no. 4 (Fall 1974):295–96.

13. Athearn, *Rebel of the Rockies,* chap. 8; Herbert O. Brayer, "History of Colorado Railroads" in LeRoy R. Hafen, ed., *Colorado and Its People,* 4 vols. (New York, 1948), chap. 24.

14. Helen Hunt Jackson, "A New Anvil Chorus," *Scribner's Monthly,* January 1878, pp. 388–89.

15. Athearn, *Rebel of the Rockies,* pp. 160–63.

16. Walker D. Wyman, "Grand Junction's First Year, 1882," *Colorado Magazine* 13, no. 4 (July 1936):127–31; James H. Rankin, "The Founding and Early Years of Grand Junction," *Colorado Magazine* 6, no. 2 (March 1929):34–45. For a detailed discussion see Georgina Norman, "The White Settlement of the Ute Reservation, 1880–1885" (M.A. thesis, University of Colorado, 1957). The agricultural development of the area is discussed in Mary Rait, "Development of Grand Junction and the Colorado River Valley to Palisade from 1881 to 1931" (M.A. thesis, University of Colorado, 1931).

17. *Rocky Mountain News,* April 8, 1868.

18. *Denver Republican,* July 23, 1882.

19. L. P. Brockett, *Our Western Empire: Or the New West beyond the Mississippi* (Philadelphia, 1881), p. 706.

20. Walker D. Wyman, "Grand Junction's First Year," pp. 127–37; Lois Borland, "Ho for the Reservation: Settlement of the Western Slope," *Colorado Magazine* 29, no. 1 (January 1952):56–75.

21. *Deseret Evening News,* April 5, 1880.

22. Bernard J. Byrne, *A Frontier Army Surgeon: Life in Colorado in the Eighties* (New York, 1935), pp. 132–34.

23. Wilson Rockwell, *New Frontier: Saga of the North Fork* (Denver, 1938) pp. 41, 42.

24. For further discussion see Robert G. Athearn, *Union Pacific Country* (Chicago, 1971); Richard C. Overton, *Burlington Route* (New York, 1965); Julius Grodinsky, *Transcontinental Railway Strategy, 1869–1893: A Study of Businessmen* (Philadelphia, 1962).

25. David William Lantis, "The San Luis Valley, Colorado: Sequent Rural Occupance in an Intermontane Basin" (Ph.D. diss., Ohio State University, 1950), pp. 242, 250–51.

26. M. D. Johnston, "Eastern Colorado Fifty-Seven Years Ago," *Colorado Magazine,* 21, no. 3 (May 1944):117.

27. Smiley, *Semi-Centennial History,* 1:562.

28. Quoted by Robert G. Athearn, *Westward the Briton,* (Lincoln, Neb., 1962), p. 122.

29. Fossett, *Colorado,* pp. 175–94.

30. Henry Villard, *The Past and Present of the Pike's Peak Gold Regions* (St. Louis, 1860), pp. 114–15; Robert G. Athearn, ed., "Across the Plains in 1863: The Diary of Peter Winne," *Iowa Journal of History,* July 1951, p. 19; Irving Howbert, *Memories of a Lifetime in the Pike's Peak Region* (New York, 1925), p. 82.

31. See Maurice Frink, W. Turrentine Jackson, and Agnes Wright Spring, *When Grass Was King* (Boulder, 1956) pp. 345–94.

32. William Thayer, *Marvels of the New West* (Norwich, Conn., 1887).

33. Earl of Arlie, "The United States as a Field for Agricultural Settlers," *The Nineteenth Century,* February 1881, pp. 292–301. See also W. Turrentine Jackson, *The Enterprising Scot* (Edinburgh, 1968), W. M. Pearce, *The Matador Land and Cattle Company* (Norman, Okla., 1964); and Lewis Atherton, *The Cattle Kings* (Bloomington, Ind., 1961).

34. See William Ross Collier and Edwin Victor Westrate, *Dave Cook of the Rockies* (New York, 1963), chap. 9.

35. Ora B. Peake, *The Colorado Range Cattle Industry* (Glendale, Calif., 1937), pp. 126, 128, 145.

36. Smiley, *Semi-Centennial History,* 1:608.

37. S. L. Caldwell, "Ranching on the Colorado Plains Sixty-One Years Ago," *Colorado Magazine* 16, no. 4 (July 1939):148–56.

38. H. C. Cornwall, "Ranching on Ohio Creek, 1881–1886," *Colorado Magazine* 32, no. 1 (January 1955):16–27. See also J. W. Neal, "Ranching in Rio Blanca County," *Colorado Magazine* 34, no. 2 (April 1957):108–20.

## Chapter 9

1. William Elliott West, "Dry Crusade: The Prohibition Movement in Colorado, 1858–1933" (Ph.D. diss., University of Colorado, 1971), p. 145.

2. Douglas Jerome Ernest, "Origins of Libraries in Boulder, Central City, Colorado City, Colorado Springs, and Denver During the Period 1860–1905," manuscript in the possession of the author; *Rocky Mountain News,* December 15, 1872; Boulder *Daily Camera,* December 11, 1899.

3. Malcolm G. Wyer, "Colorado Libraries," in LeRoy R. Hafen, ed., *Colorado and Its People,* 4 vols. (New York, 1948), 2:chap. 20.

4. David Shaw Duncan, "Higher Education in Colorado," *Colorado Magazine* 14, no. 1 (January 1937):3–5. See also Stephen Carroll, "Territorial Attempts to Establish a University of Colorado at Boulder," *Red River Valley Historical Review* 1, no. 4 (Winter 1974):351–66.

5. *Rocky Mountain News,* October 24, 1866, September 18, 1867.

6. Harry E. Kelsey, Jr., *Frontier Capitalist: The Life of John Evans* (Boulder, 1969), pp. 221–22. Wilbur Fisk Stone, *History of Colorado,* 4 vols. (Chicago, 1918–19), 1:611.

7. Stone, *History of Colorado,* 1:611. See also Ann W. and LeRoy R. Hafen, "The Beginnings of Denver University," *Colorado Magazine* 24, no. 2 (March 1947):58–66.

8. Charlie Brown Hershey, *Colorado College 1874–1949* (Colorado Springs, 1952) is the standard work, but for an entertaining essay on the school see Marshall Sprague, *Newport in the Rockies* (Denver, 1961), chap. 19. Also see James H. Baker and LeRoy R. Hafen, *History of Colorado,* 5 vols. (Denver, 1927), 1:1170, and Stone, *History of Colorado,* 1:703. Irving Howbert, *Memories of a Lifetime in the Pike's Peak Region* (New York, 1925), contains some reminiscent material about Colorado College. See pages 287–88 in particular.

9. Robert V. Hine, *The American West: An Interpretive History* (Boston, 1973), p. 245.

10. Harry M. Barrett, "Education in Colorado," in Junius Henderson, et al., *Colorado: Short Studies of Its Past and Present* (Boulder, 1927), p. 134. See also James F. Willard, "The Early Days of the University of Colorado," *The Trail* 7, no. 12 (May 1915):5–16.

11. Colorado Board of Agriculture, Reports. See 1878 Report for details of the school's origins.

12. Stone, *History of Colorado,* 1:620–26; Barrett, "Education in Colorado," pp. 136–37.

13. Hafen, *Colorado and Its People,* 2:478–80; Stone, *History of Colorado,* 1:629–30.

14. A good general discussion of higher education in Colorado may be found in Michael McGiffert, *The Higher Learning in Colorado: An Historical Study, 1860–1940* (Denver, 1964).

15. Duane A. Smith, *Horace Tabor: His Life and the Legend* (Boulder, 1973), pp. 106–8, 150–51, 171–73. See also Hal Sayre, "Early Central City Theatricals and Other Reminiscences," *Colorado Magazine* 6, no. 2 (March 1929):47–53.

16. Howbert, *Memories,* pp. 253–54.

17. Alma Strettell, "A Little Western Town," *Macmillan's Magazine,* December 1881, p. 121.

18. The best thing written so far on this subject is West, "Dry Crusade."

19. West, "Dry Crusade," see chaps. 9 and 10.

20. *Rocky Mountain News* (Weekly), January 31, 1866.

21. Billie Barnes Jensen, "The Woman Suffrage Movement in Colorado" (M.A. thesis, University of Colorado, 1959), pp. 13–25. See also idem, "Let the Women Vote," *Colorado Magazine* 41, no. 1 (Winter 1964):13–25.

22. Quoted in Jensen, "The Woman Suffrage Movement," p. 33.

23. See ibid., chap. 3, "1877 and Failure."

24. John R. Morris, "The Women and Governor Waite," *Colorado Magazine* 44, no. 1 (Winter 1967):12–16; see also idem, "Davis Hanson Waite: The Ideology of a Western Populist" (Ph.D. diss., University of Colorado, 1965).

25. *Denver Republican,* November 5, 1893.

26. Elizabeth Cady Stanton, et al., eds. *History of Woman Suffrage,* 6 vols. (New York, 1881–1922) contains the suggestion. See vol. 4, p. 518. Quoted by Jensen, "The Woman Suffrage Movement," p. 83.

27. *Rocky Mountain News,* January 1, 1894. See also Mary C. C. Bradford, "The Equal Suffrage Victory in Colorado," *The Outlook,* December 23, 1893, pp. 1205–6.

28. Marion Foster Washburne, "Women in the Great West," *Harper's Bazaar,* May 1906, pp. 404–7.

29. David Shannon, ed., *Beatrice Webb's American Diary, 1898* (Madison, Wis., 1963), pp. 122–23.

30. Priscilla Leonard, "Woman Suffrage in Colorado," *The Outlook,* March 20, 1897, 789–92.

31. See William Macleod Raine, "Woman Suffrage in Colorado," *The Chautauquan,* February 1902, pp. 482–84. For further discussion see Elizabeth McCracken, "The Women of America—Fourth Paper—Women's Suffrage in Colorado," *The Outlook,* November 28, 1903, pp. 737–44, and Mary G. Slocum, "Women in Colorado under Suffrage: Another Point of View," *The Outlook,* December 26, 1903, pp. 997–1000. Mary Slocum was the wife of the president of Colorado College.

32. Gunnison *News-Champion,* May 4, 1939.

33. The most comprehensive study of Mears to date is Michael Kaplan, "Otto Mears: Colorado's Transportation King" (Ph.D. diss., University of Colorado, 1975).

34. Edwin Price, "Recollections of Grand Junction's First Newspaper Editor," *Colorado Magazine* 30, no. 3 (July 1953):225–33.

35. S. F. Stacher, "Ouray and the Utes," *Colorado Magazine* 27, no. 2 (April 1950):139.

36. Millard Fillmore Vance, "Pioneering at Akron, Colorado," *Colorado Magazine* 8, no. 5 (September 1931):176.

37. George B. Merrill, "Early History of Lamar, Colorado," *Colorado Magazine* 6, no. 4 (July 1929):122.

38. Leon W. Fuller, "A Populist Newspaper of the Nineties," *Colorado Magazine* 9, no. 3 (May 1932):81–87; John R. Morris, "Davis Hanson Waite: The Ideology of a Western Populist" (Ph.D. diss., University of Colorado, 1965), p. 43.

39. Levette Jay Davidson, "Out West, A Pioneer Weekly and Monthly," *Colorado Magazine* 14, no. 4 (July 1937):135–42.

40. Edwin A. Bemis, "Journalism in Colorado," in Hafen, *Colorado and Its People,* 2:256–58.

41. See "The Press in Colorado" in vol. 1 of Stone's *History of Colorado.*

42. Stone, *History of Colorado,* 1:chap. 29; Bemis, "Journalism in Colorado."

## Chapter 10

1. "Place Names in Colorado," *Colorado Magazine* 17, no. 5 (September 1940):190.

2. Henry Villard, *The Past and Present of the Pike's Peak Gold Regions* (St. Louis, 1860), p. 113; Samuel Bowles, *Our New West* (Hartford, Conn., 1869), p. 190; LeRoy R. Hafen and Ann W. Hafen, eds., *Reports from Colorado: The Wildman Letters, 1859–1865* (Glendale, Calif., 1961), p. 200.

3. "Trinidad War," *Rocky Mountain News,* January 15, 22, 1868.

4. *Rocky Mountain News,* September 10, 1869, quoting the *Chieftain.*

5. E. P. Tenney, *Colorado: And Homes in the New West* (Boston, 1880), p. 84.

6. Bowles, *Our New West,* p. 194.

7. L. I. Dupre, "Glimpses of Colorado, First Paper" and "Glimpses of Colorado, Second Paper," *Appleton's Journal,* March 15 and 22, 1873, pp. 368–71 and 399–402.

8. John Codman, *The Round Trip by Way of Panama through California, Oregon, Nevada, Utah, Idaho, and Colorado* (New York, 1879), pp. 283, 307–8.

9. Irving Howbert, *Memories of a Lifetime in the Pike's Peak Region* (New York, 1925), p. 167; Samuel Bowles, *Across the Continent: A Summer's Journey to the Rocky Mountains, the Mormons, and the Pacific States* (Springfield, Mass., 1866), p. 21; William H. Thayer, *Marvels of the New West* (Norwich, Conn., 1887), pp. 210–11.

10. Ernest Ingersoll, "Heart of Colorado," part 1, *The Cosmopolitan,* September 1888, p. 434; idem, *The Crest of the Continent* (Chicago, 1885), p. 79.

11. William E. Pabor, *Colorado as an Agricultural State* (New York, 1883), p. 131; Helen Hunt Jackson, *Bits of Travel at Home* (Boston, 1909), p. 359; S. N. Townshend, *Colorado: Its Agriculture, Stockfeeding, Scenery, and Shooting* (London, 1879), pp. 20–21; N. S. Shaler, "Winter Journey in Colorado," *Atlantic Monthly,* January 1881, p. 51.

12. See Frank Hall, *History of the State of Colorado,* 4 vols. (Chicago, 1889–95), 1:510.

13. Bowles, *Our New West,* pp. 123, 156.

14. Mrs. F. D. Bridges, *A Journal of a Lady's Travels Round the World* (London, 1883), p. 408.

15. Ernest Ingersoll, "Camp of the Carbonates," *Scribner's Monthly,* October 1879, p. 821. See also Eugene F. Irey, "A Social History of Leadville, Colorado, During the Boom Days, 1877–1881" (Ph.D. diss., University of Minnesota, 1951), and Gerald E. Rudolph. "The Chinese in Colorado, 1869–1911" (M.A. thesis, University of Denver, 1964). The Gothic item is from Carl L. Haase, "Gothic, Colorado: City of Silver Wires," *Colorado Magazine* 51, no. 4 (Fall 1974):308.

16. Duane Smith, *Silver Saga* (Boulder, 1974), p. 97.

17. Roy E. Wortman, "Denver's Anti-Chinese Riot, 1880," *Colorado Magazine* 42, no. 4 (Fall 1965):276–91.

18. Codman, *The Round Trip,* p. 286.

19. Richard Sallet, *Russian-German Settlements in the United States* (Fargo, N.D., 1974); Emma D. Schwabenland, "German-Russians on the Volga and in the United States" (M.A. thesis, University of Colorado, 1929); David J. Miller, "German-Russians in Colorado," *Colorado Magazine* 21, no. 4 (July 1944):129–32.

20. For a good discussion of life among the German-Russians in the West, see chap. 7 of Sallet, *Russian-German Settlements.*

21. For most of the material in this section I leaned heavily upon the excellent M.A. thesis "The Cotopaxi Colony," by Flora Jane Satt, (University of Colorado, 1950). Ida Libert Uchill, in her *Pioneers, Peddlers, and Tsadikim* (Denver, 1957) also used Satt's thesis in discussing Cotopaxi, with a few minor variations of interpretation.

22. Dorothy Roberts, "The Jewish Colony at Cotopaxi," *Colorado Magazine* 18, no. 4 (July 1941):125.

23. Ibid., p. 127.

24. Helen Hunt Jackson, "O-Be-Joyful Creek and Poverty Gulch," *Atlantic Monthly,* December 1883, pp. 754–60.

25. George W. Romspert, *The Western Echo: A Description of the Western States and Territories of the United States as Gathered in a Tour by Wagon* (Dayton, O., 1881), pp. 293–94.

26. Elinor Bluemel, *One Hundred Years of Colorado Women* (n.p., 1973), pp. 10–11.

27. S. C. Clarke, "Colorado and the South Park," *Lippincott's Magazine,* September 1873, p. 337.

28. Grace Greenwood (Mrs. Sara Jane Lippincott), *New Life in New Lands: Notes of Travel* (New York, 1873), p. 63.

29. J. Max Clark, *Colonial Days* (Denver, 1902), pp. 58–60.

30. Quotation by Byron Shelton in Charles H. Leckenby, comp., *The Tread of Pioneers* (Steamboat Springs, 1944), p. 45.

31. Mary E. Blake, *On the Wing; Rambling Notes of a Trip to the Pacific* (Boston, 1883), pp. 46–47.

32. *Gunnison News Champion,* August 15, 1946.

## Chapter 11

1. LeRoy R. Hafen, *Colorado: The Story of a Western Commonwealth* (Denver, 1933), p. 244; idem, ed., *Colorado and Its People,* 4 vols. (New York, 1948), 1:581, 2:460; Jerome C. Smiley, *Semi-Centennial History of the State of Colorado,* 2 vols. (Chicago, 1913), 1:709.

2. *Rocky Mountain News,* June 27, 1893.

3. Smiley, *Semi-Centennial History,* 1:710–12.

4. For a good discussion of the changing role of the miner see James Edward Wright, *The Politics of Populism: Dissent in Colorado* (New Haven, 1974), pp. 22–29.

5. Charles Merrill Hough, "Leadville, Colorado, 1878 to 1898: A Study in Unionism" (M.A. thesis, University of Colorado, 1958). See pp. 57–60 for comments on the outcome of the strike. For a brief account see Paul T. Bechtol, Jr., "The 1880 Labor Dispute in Leadville," *Colorado Magazine* 47, no. 4 (Fall 1970):312–25.

6. A. A. Hayes, Jr., "Pioneers of the Sierra Madre," *International Review* 10 (June 1881):519.

7. Irving Howbert, *Memories of a Lifetime in the Pike's Peak Region* (New York, 1925), p. 271.

8. David L. Lonsdale, "The Fight for an Eight-Hour Day," *Colorado Magazine* 43, no. 4 (Autumn 1966):339–53. See also Lonsdale's doctoral dissertation on this subject (University of Colorado, 1963).

9. Emma F. Langdon, *The Cripple Creek Strike* (Denver, 1904), gives a prolabor view. A more readable and more recent work is Stewart H. Holbrook, *The Rocky Mountain Revolution* (New York, 1956). The 1896 difficulty at Leadville is described by Merrill Hough, "Leadville and the Western Federation of Miners," *Colorado Magazine* 49, no. 1 (Winter 1972):19–35.

10. Wilbur Fisk Stone, *History of Colorado,* 4 vols. (Chicago, 1918–19), 1:chap. 41; Hafen,

*Colorado and Its People,* 2:chap. 11. For a prolabor view of the Ludlow affair see Barron B. Beshoar, *Out of the Depths* (Denver, 1942), chap. 12.

11. One of the best sources for information about the A.P.A. is Carla Joan Atchison, "Nativism in Colorado Politics: The American Protective Association and the Ku Klux Klan" (M.A. thesis, University of Colorado, 1972). See chapter 4.

12. Albert Shaw, "A Successful Farm Colony in the Irrigation Country," *Review of Reviews* 26 (November 1902):561–66.

13. H. Rider Haggard, *The Poor and the Land* (New York, 1905), p. 73; Dorothy Roberts, "Fort Amity, The Salvation Army Colony in Colorado," *Colorado Magazine* 17, no. 5 (September 1940):168.

14. Roberts, "Fort Amity," p. 170.

15. J. D. Whelpley, "Salvation Army Colonies," *Harper's Weekly,* September 7, 1901, p. 902.

16. Shaw, "A Successful Farming Colony," p. 566.

17. Roberts, "Fort Amity," pp. 170–74; Haggard, *The Poor and the Land,* pp. 77–82.

18. Haggard, *The Poor and the Land,* pp. xxxix–xli, 1–27.

19. Ellen Z. Peterson, "Origin of the Town of Nucla," *Colorado Magazine* 26, no. 4 (October 1949):252; Agnes Wright Spring, "Experiment in Utopia," *Denver Post* magazine section, May 1, 1949.

20. Dorothy Roberts, "A Dutch Colony in Colorado," *Colorado Magazine* 17, no. 6 (November 1940):229–30.

21. *Denver Republican,* December 19, 1892; Roberts, "A Dutch Colony," p. 232.

22. Ida Libert Uchill, *Pioneers, Peddlers, and Tsadikim* (Denver, 1957), p. 177.

23. Ibid., pp. 178–82. As Uchill pointed out, not only is there a dearth of information about the Atwood Colony, but much of it is contradictory.

24. Allen D. Breck, *The Centennial History of the Jews of Colorado, 1859–1959* (Denver, 1960), pp. 156–160, briefly discusses Atwood and corroborates Uchill's assertion that information about the colony is contradictory by using different figures and some different dates, although his general conclusions are about the same.

25. For material concerning Colorado's correctional institutions I have borrowed freely from George Thomson, "The History of Penal Institutions in the Rocky Mountain West, 1864–1900" (Ph.D. diss., University of Colorado, 1965), one of the very few good sources of information available on this subject.

26. *Rocky Mountain News,* January 1, 1897.

27. Robert Pfanner, "Highlights in the History of Fort Logan," *Colorado Magazine* 19, no. 3 (May 1942):81–91; Albert B. Sanford, "Life at Camp Weld and Fort Lyon in 1961–62," *Colorado Magazine* 7, no. 4 (July 1930:132–39; Mrs. C. F. Parker, "Old Julesburg and Fort Sedgwick," ibid., pp. 139–46.

28. Mary C. Ayres, "History of Fort Lewis, Colorado," *Colorado Magazine* 8, no. 3 (May 1931):81–92; John H. Nankivell, "Fort Crawford, Colorado, 1880–1890," *Colorado Magazine* 11, no. 2 (March 1934):54–64; Patrick H. Gorman, "Town and Fort: Civil-Military Relations in Colorado, 1880–1891," manuscript, in possession of the author.

29. Quoted by Clifford P. Westermeier, *Who Rush To Glory* (Caldwell, Idaho, 1958), pp. 41–43.

30. James H. Baker and LeRoy R. Hafen, eds., *History of Colorado,* 5 vols. (Denver, 1927), 3:980; Westermeier, *Who Rush To Glory,* pp. 226–32.

31. Baker and Hafen, *History of Colorado,* 3:982–90.

32. Sewall Thomas, *Silhouettes of Charles S. Thomas* (Caldwell, Idaho, 1959), p. 70.

## Chapter 12

1. *The Denver Post* (Glory Edition), December 13, 1900.
2. Ibid., December 31, 1903.

3. Ibid., January 1, 1904.
4. Ibid., January 2, 1900, and January 2, 3, 4, 1901.
5. Ibid., January 2, 1900.
6. Roland L. DeLorme, "Turn-of-the-Century Denver: An Invitation to Reform," *Colorado Magazine* 45, no. 1 (Winter 1968):1–15. J. Paul Mitchell, "Municipal Reform in Denver: The Defeat of Mayor Speer," ibid., pp. 42–60. See also Robert L. Perkin, *The First Hundred Years* (New York: 1959), pp. 409–10. For a personalized view of this period of reform see George Creel, *Rebel at Large* (New York, 1947), chaps. 13, 14. Comments on Denver's abandonment of the commission form of government may be found in H. S. Gilbertson, "Denver 'Goes Back,' " *The American City,* June 1916, pp. 577–78. Details of the campaign for an eight-hour day are found in David L. Lonsdale, "The Fight for an Eight-Hour Day," *Colorado Magazine* 43, no. 4 (Fall, 1966):339–53.
7. John F. Shafroth, "The New Campaign Expense Law in Colorado," *The Independent,* July 8, 1909, pp. 83–84.
8. Quoted in Mitchell, "Municipal Reform in Denver," p. 42.
9. Arthur Chapman, "A Colorado Prison Reformer: Tom Tynan and His Convict Boys," *Harper's Weekly,* August 2, 1913, pp. 18–19, 22–23.
10. Charles M. Harvey, "The Pike Exploration Centennial," *The American Monthly Review of Reviews,* September 1906, 333–37.
11. *Denver Times,* September 3, 1911. See also Edmund B. Rogers, "Notes on the Establishment of Mesa Verde National Park," *Colorado Magazine* 29, no. 1 (January 1952):16 and Virginia McClurg, "The Making of Mesa Verde into a National Park," *Colorado Magazine* 7, no. 6 (November 1930):216–19. Mrs. McClurg was one of the active two hundred ladies who strove to save the ruins at Mesa Verde.
12. Eva Mills Anderson, "A Tenderfoot at the Cliff Dwellings of the Mesa Verde," *The Chautauquan,* July 1908, p. 203.
13. Mrs. Crawford Hill, "East vs. West," *Harper's Bazaar,* May 1910, p. 314.
14. Arthur Chapman, "Denver, A Typical American City," *The World Today,* September 1906, pp. 982–83.
15. Hill, "East vs. West," p. 314.
16. Emily Post, *By Motor to the Golden Gate* (New York, 1916), see chap. 18.
17. Walter A. Wyckoff, "The Rampart Range: Ten Years After," *Scribner's Magazine,* October 1908, pp. 491–502.
18. Julian Street, "Colorado Springs and Cripple Creek," *Collier's,* November 7, 1914, pp. 16–17, 29–33.
19. Forbes Parkhill, *The Wildest of the West* (1951; Denver, 1957), p. 281.
20. "Licensing of Dance Halls in Denver," *The Survey,* September 28, 1912, pp. 787–89.
21. Creel, *Rebel at Large,* pp. 119–24; John Gunther, *Inside U.S.A.* (New York, 1947), p. 217; Julian Street, "Hitting a High Spot Denver," *Collier's Weekly,* November 7, 1914, pp. 16–17, 29–33; *Denver Post,* January 2, 1901. A personal account of Lindsey's work may be found in Ben B. Lindsey and Harvey J. O'Higgins, *The Beast* (New York, 1911). For his version of the disbarment case see Ben B. Lindsey and Rube Borough, *The Dangerous Life* (New York, 1931), part 3. A more recent biography of the famous judge is Charles Larsen, *The Good Fight: Life and Times of Ben B. Lindsey* (Chicago, 1972).
22. Edward Keating, *The Gentleman from Colorado: A Memoir* (Denver, 1964), chap. 39.
23. Larsen, *The Good Fight,* pp. 96–97.
24. James E. Hansen II, "Moonshine and Murder: Prohibition in Denver," *Colorado Magazine* 50, no. 1 (Winter 1973):1–8.
25. Arthur Chapman, "Mountain Camps for a City's Children," *The Playground,* November 1916, pp. 283–85.
26. Richard Detrano, "The Grand Old Man of Estes," Boulder *Daily Camera,* Focus section, August 17, 1975.
27. Guy Elliott Mitchell, "The Rocky Mountain National Park," *Review of Reviews,* July

1913, pp. 51–55; Enos A. Mills, *The Story of Estes Park, Grand Lake and Rocky Mountain National Park* (Estes Park, 1905, 1917), pp. 102–3; Merlin K. Potts, "Rocky Mountain National Park," *Colorado Magazine* 42, no. 3 (Summer 1965):217–23.

28. Chapman, "Denver," pp. 982–88.

29. *Rocky Mountain News,* January 1, 1901; J. D. L., "Where to Go," *Good Housekeeping Magazine,* June 1911, pp. 750–51.

30. LeRoy R. Hafen, ed., *The Diaries of William Henry Jackson: Frontier Photographer* (Glendale, Calif., 1959), p. 270; Horace Greeley, *An Overland Journey from New York to San Francisco in the Summer of 1859* (Duncan edition: New York, 1963), p. 100; Samuel Bowles, *Across the Continent: A Summer's Journey to the Rocky Mountains, the Mormons, and the Pacific States* (Springfield, Mass., 1866), pp. 31–32.

31. Donald W. Hensel, "A History of the Colorado Constitution in the Nineteenth Century" (Ph.D. diss., University of Colorado, 1957), p. 176.

32. LeRoy R. Hafen, ed., *Colorado and Its People,* 4 vols. (New York, 1948), 1:517–19. G. Michael McCarthy, "White River Forest Reserve: The Conservation Conflict," *Colorado Magazine* 49, no. 1 (Winter 1972):55–68. For greater detail consult idem, "Colorado Confronts the Conservation Impulse, 1891–1907" (Ph.D. diss., University of Denver, 1969) or Walter Andrew Voss, "Colorado and Forest Conservation" (M.A. thesis, University of Colorado, 1931).

33. Donald N. Baldwin, "Wilderness: Concept and Challenge," *Colorado Magazine* 44, no. 3 (Summer 1967):224–40. For a general discussion of forest reserves see Bernard Frank, *Our National Forests* (Norman, Okla., 1955) sections of chaps. 2 and 3.

34. Albert N. Williams, *The Water and the Power* (New York, 1951). See chap. 2.

35. James W. McKenna, "The Geology of the Conger Mine, Boulder County, Colorado" (M.A. thesis, University of Colorado, 1940); Victor G. Hills, "Tungsten Mining and Milling," *Proceedings of the Colorado Scientific Society* 10 (1908–10):135–53; R. D. George, *The Main Tungsten Area of Boulder County, Colorado* (Denver, 1909), p. 182. See also Percy S. Fritz, "The Tungsten Boom," in Carl Ubbelohde, ed., *A Colorado Reader* (Boulder, 1962), pp. 292–301.

36. Percy S. Fritz, *Colorado: The Centennial State* (New York, 1941), pp. 409–15.

37. Hafen, *Colorado and Its People,* 1:537–43. *The Colorado Yearbook* for 1927, p. 237 gives 42,898 as the number of Coloradans serving in all branches of the armed forces.

38. For items concerning Colorado's wartime hysteria I have leaned heavily upon Lyle W. Dorsett, "The Ordeal of Colorado's Germans during World War I," *Colorado Magazine* 51, no. 4 (Fall 1974):277–93. The Wyoming material came from T. A. Larson, *History of Wyoming* (Lincoln, Neb., 1965), pp. 400–401.

## Chapter 13

1. For comments on the "Blue Menace" see Charles Larsen, *The Good Fight: Life and Times of Ben B. Lindsey* (Chicago, 1972), p. 183. Another recent work is Kenneth T. Jackson, *The Ku Klux Klan and the City: 1915–1930* (New York, 1967).

2. *Denver Catholic Register,* September 11, 1919, quoted in Philip L. Cook, "Red Scare in Denver," *Colorado Magazine* 43, no. 4 (Fall 1966):313.

3. *Denver Post,* November 8, 1919.

4. Cook, "Red Scare," pp. 314–15.

5. *Denver Post,* January 1, 1920.

6. I have drawn heavily upon Cook's "Red Scare" article for most of this material. But see also Edward Keating, *The Story of "Labor"* (Washington, D.C., 1953), pp. 70–71. Keating served as editor of this, one of America's most influential labor papers, for over thirty years. The sacking of the *Post's* building is described in Bill Hosokawa, *Thunder in the Rockies: The Incredible* Denver Post (New York, 1976), pp. 116–19.

7. *Denver Post,* January 1, 1920.

8. Ibid., Sec. 3, p. 2.

9. David M. Chalmers, *Hooded Americanism: The First Century of the Ku Klux Klan, 1865–1965* (New York, 1965), p. 126. See all of chap. 18, "Pike's Peak or Bust."

10. Ibid., p. 127.

11. James H. Davis, "Colorado under the Klan," *Colorado Magazine* 42, no. 2 (Spring 1965):93–94. See also John Rolfe Burroughs, *Steamboat in the Rockies* (Fort Collins, 1974), pp. 179–80. Carla Joan Atchison, "Nativism in Colorado Politics" (M.A. thesis, University of Colorado, 1970) has some interesting material on the Colorado Klan. See chap. 6.

12. Dixon Wector, "Norlin," *Atlantic Monthly,* June 1939, pp. 785–89.

13. Davis, "Colorado under the Klan," pp. 95–108.

14. *The Rocky Mountain American,* July 31, 1925.

15. Ibid., April 24, June 12, 1925.

16. Burroughs, *Steamboat in the Rockies,* pp. 179–80.

17. George Creel, *Rebel at Large* (New York, 1947), p. 122.

18. Figures for 1921 through 1930 taken from *Colorado Year Book,* 1932, p. 298. See also *Denver Post,* December 31, 1928.

19. *Denver Post,* January 1, 1920. See page 8 of section 1.

20. James E. Hansen II, "Moonshine and Murder: Prohibition in Denver," *Colorado Magazine* 50, no. 1 (Winter 1973):7–12.

21. Robert N. Annand, "A Study of the Prohibition Situation in Denver" (M.A. thesis, University of Denver, 1932).

22. Hansen, "Moonshine and Murder," p. 23.

23. For comments on the "satchel farmers" see Leslie Hewes, *The Suitcase Farming Frontier* (Lincoln, Neb., 1973), especially the introduction and the conclusion on pages 173–74.

24. A very interesting account of the Great Divide Colony may be found in John Rolfe Burroughs, *Where the Old West Stayed Young* (New York, 1962), pp. 320–37.

25. Albert N. Williams, *The Water and the Power: Development of Five Great Rivers of the West* (New York, 1951), pp. 105–6; Donald Barnard Cole, "Transmountain Water Diversion in Colorado," *Colorado Magazine* 25, no. 2 (March 1948):49–65.

26. Williams, *The Water and the Power,* pp. 106–11; Percy S. Fritz, *Colorado: The Centennial State* (New York, 1941), pp. 469–70.

27. Robert G. Athearn, *Rebel of the Rockies: A History of the Denver and Rio Grande Western Railroad* (New Haven, 1962), pp. 269–71.

28. For more about Carpenter see Ralph Carr, "Delph Carpenter and River Compacts Between Western States," *Colorado Magazine* 21, no. 1 (January 1944):5–14. A more recent study is Norris Hundley, Jr., *Water and the West: The Colorado River Compact and the Politics of Water in the American West* (Berkeley, 1975), chap. 4.

29. Williams, *The Water and the Power,* p. 83.

30. *Rocky Mountain News,* January 24, 1866; John Ise, *The United States Oil Policy* (New Haven, 1926), p. 98.

31. Julian Ralph, *Our Great West* (New York, 1893) discussed Colorado's young oil industry as of 1893; see pages 339–40. Also see Ise, *United States Oil Policy,* pp. 98–99, and Arthur Lakes, "The Present Oil Situation," *Mines and Minerals,* April 1903, pp. 399–401.

32. Lakes, "The Present Oil Situation," p. 399; Ise, *United States Oil Policy,* p. 99.

33. Ise, *United States Oil Policy,* p. 427; Chris Welles, *The Elusive Bonanza: The Story of Oil Shale—America's Richest and Most Neglected Natural Resource* (New York, 1970), p. 25. Drawing upon this work, among others, is a series of articles by Ted Blankenship of the Ridder News Service, 1974. See, for example, the Boulder *Daily Camera,* August 25, 1974.

34. For a discussion of early Colorado automotive history see LeRoy R. Hafen, "The Coming of the Automobile and Improved Roads to Colorado," *Colorado Magazine* 8, no. 1 (January 1931):1–16.

35. Arthur Chapman, "A Colorado Prison Reformer: Tom Tynan and His Convict Boys," *Harper's Weekly,* August 2, 1913, p. 18.

36. James H. Baker and LeRoy R. Hafen, eds., *History of Colorado,* 5 vols. (Denver, 1927), 2:858–61.

37. Edgar C. McMechen, "A Home for the Migratory Motorist," *Outing,* June 1918, pp. 161–63.

38. Lillian Habich Lennox, "Storming Berthoud Pass," *Outing,* November, December, 1918, January, February, 1919. See December 1918, p. 142.

39. Junius Henderson, "A Colorado Glacier," *Harper's Monthly Magazine,* March 1906, pp. 609–13.

40. H. P. Ufford, "Out of Doors in Colorado," *The Century Magazine,* June 1899, pp. 313–14.

41. Hamlin Garland, *Daughter of the Middle Border* (New York, 1922), p. 146.

42. Lennox, "Storming Berthoud Pass," p. 194 of January 1919 *Outing.*

43. Arthur Conan Doyle, *Our Second American Adventure* (Boston, 1924), p. 83.

44. Most of the abovementioned statistical information came from the January 1, 1920 issue of the *Denver Post.*

45. *Denver Post,* December 31, 1928.

46. Emerson N. Barker, "Colorado Mail Takes Wings," *Colorado Magazine* 20, no. 3 (May 1943):95–99.

47. Lee Scamehorn, *Colorado's First Airline,* University of Colorado Studies, Series in History, no. 3 (January 1964), pp. 30–31. See also Ed Mack Miller, "Castor Oil, Kerosene and Contrails," *Colorful Colorado* 1, no. 3 (Winter 1966):24–31 and 106–10.

48. Scamehorn, *Colorado's First Airline,* pp. 33–37.

49. *Colorado Year Book,* 1931, p. 328.

50. *Denver Post,* December 28, 1928, and January 1, 1929.

51. *Denver Post,* November 7, December 31, 1928.

## Chapter 14

1. *Denver Post,* January 1, 1920.

2. Ibid., December 31, 1928.

3. *Colorado Year Book,* 1939–40.

4. *Denver Post,* December 31, 1929.

5. Ibid., November 7, December 12, 1928.

6. Ibid., December 31, 1929.

7. Arthur C. Johnson Papers, Western History Collections, University of Colorado, Boulder. Diary entries for February 17, March 18, September 12, 29, 1930; January 14, February 14, 26, 1933.

8. *Denver Post,* October 27, 29, 31, November 3, 1930; Pueblo *Chieftain,* quoted by *Daily Camera,* October 28, 1930. See also Ronald S. Brockway, Jr., "Edward P. Costigan: A Study of a Progressive and the New Deal" (Ph.D. diss., University of Colorado, 1974).

9. Johnson Papers, diary entry for January 8, 1933; LeRoy R. Hafen, ed., *Colorado and Its People,* 4 vols. (New York, 1948), 1:chap. 29.

10. Boulder *Daily Camera,* October 1, 1930.

11. Johnson Papers, diary entries for November 7, 1930, January 25, 1933.

12. Johnson Papers, diary entries for March 30, April 5, 1930; *Colorado Year Book,* 1926, 1930, 1931; *Denver Post,* November 17, 1974, for a reminiscent article about KOA.

13. R.M.F., *Time,* July 10, 1939; "Colorado Tries a New Strategy," *Christian Century,* January 28, 1931; "Union Angel," *Business Week,* June 17, 1944; "Coal Miners Enter," *New Republic,* September 23, 1931; Oswald Garrison Villard, "Josephine Roche for Governor of Colorado," *Nation,* June 13, 1934; *Monthly Labor Review,* August 1932.

14. Colorado Springs *Gazette-Telegraph,* September 20, 1931.

15. Boulder *Daily Camera,* October 14, 1933.

16. Colorado Springs *Gazette-Telegraph,* September 20, 1931.

17. Colorado Springs *Gazette-Telegraph,* August 23, 1931.

18. For a very good discussion of the league see Bernard Mergen, "Denver and the War on Unemployment," *Colorado Magazine* 47, no. 4 (Fall 1970):326–37. See also "Unemployed" in *Monthly Labor Review,* March 1933.

19. Bernhard Knollenberg, "Sagebrush Rule," *Atlantic Monthly,* March 1932, pp. 289–95; Edward A. Newton, "Westward," ibid., May 1932, p. 527; B. H. Kizer, "In Defense of the Sagebrush States," ibid., June 1932, pp. 746–52.

20. James F. Wickens, "Tightening the Colorado Purse Strings," *Colorado Magazine* 46, no. 4 (Fall 1969):271–86.

21. For comments on Johnson's attitudes see James T. Patterson, "The New Deal in the West," *Pacific Historical Review* 38, no. 3 (August 1969):317–27. See also Johnson Papers, diary, January 23, 1933; Frank Clay Cross, "Revolution in Colorado," *Nation,* February 7, 1934, pp. 152–53; Boulder *Daily Camera,* January 4, 1934.

22. *Denver Post,* December 31, 1929.

23. W. J. Canavan, "I Was a Vacation School Teacher," *Catholic World,* July 1939, pp. 478–82.

24. Laura Makepeace, "Among Migrant Spanish-Americans," *Missionary Review,* November 1933, pp. 536–38.

25. "Barricading Jobs: Troops Guard Colorado Borders to Keep Out the Indigent," *Literary Digest,* May 2, 1936, p. 5; see also Durango *Herald-Democrat,* as quoted by the Colorado Springs *Gazette-Telegraph,* August 25, 1935, for a criticism of Johnson.

26. Boulder *Daily Camera,* October 25, 1935; Colorado Springs *Gazette-Telegraph,* August 25, 1935, April 25, 1937.

27. James F. Wickens, "The New Deal in Colorado," *Pacific Historical Review* 38, no. 3 (August 1969):275–91; Hafen, *Colorado and Its People,* 1:chap. 29.

28. *Colorado Year Book,* 1941–42, p. 462.

29. Colorado Springs *Gazette-Telegraph,* September 26, 1935, October 11, 1936; Boulder *Daily Camera,* October 26, 1935.

30. Marc A. Rose, "For All Who Wish to Learn: Denver's Amazing Opportunity School, Which Teaches Anybody Anything," *Reader's Digest,* February 1939, pp. 6–9; "Opportunity," *Fortune,* November 1939, pp. 71, 150–53.

31. George W. Frasier and William Hartman, "History of Higher Education in Colorado," in Hafen, *Colorado and Its People,* 2:chap. 17; *Colorado Year Book,* 1941–42, p. 348.

32. Boulder *Daily Camera,* February 13, 1937, November 3, 4, 1938; Walter Davenport, "Good Intentions Won't Pay Pensions," *Collier's,* October 29, 1938, p. 28; Farnsworth Crowder, "Who Pays the Pensions? Colorado's Pensions for Everyone over Sixty," *Survey Graphic,* July 1938, pp. 376–80; *Newsweek,* August 22, 1938, February 13, 1939.

33. Arthur A. Matthews, "Trans-Mountain Water Diversion for Denver," *American City,* November 1937, pp. 58–60; "Irrigation Project Threatens Rocky Mountain Park," *Nature Magazine,* August 1937, pp. 109–10; "Protest Against the Exploitation of the Rocky Mountain Park," *Science,* April 24, 1936, p. 385; Boulder *Daily Camera* quoting Grand Junction *Sentinel,* November 13, 15, 1937; see also *Camera* for January 11, 23, February 20, October 2, November 8, 1937, November 4, 1938.

34. Boulder *Daily Camera,* October 28, 1932, quoting *Sentinel;* see also *Camera* for October 14, 1933, and October 27, 1936.

35. Boulder *Daily Camera,* January 9, March 15, October 27, 1937.

36. Colorado Springs *Gazette-Telegraph,* June 20, 1937.

37. Colorado Springs *Gazette-Telegraph,* April 11, 1937; April 23, May 21, 1939.

38. *Denver Post,* December 31, 1929.

39. Colorado Springs *Gazette-Telegraph,* April 14, 1937, May 28, 1939.

40. Ibid., November 10, 1940.

41. Colorado Springs *Gazette-Telegraph,* October 4, November 24, 1942; *Colorado Year Book,* 1941–42, pp. 388, 425–26.

42. Robert G. Athearn, *Rebel of the Rockies: A History of the Denver and Rio Grande Western Railroad* (New Haven, 1962), chaps. 12–14; see also Hafen, *Colorado and Its People,* 2:68–90, and Edgar C. McMechen, *The Moffat Tunnel of Colorado,* 2 vols. (Denver, 1927).

43. *Denver Post,* December 31, 1929; *Time,* May 10, 1937; Lee Scamehorn, "The Air Transport Industry in Colorado," in Carl Ubbelohde, ed., *A Colorado Reader* (Boulder, 1962), pp. 312–15.

44. Wickens, "New Deal in Colorado," pp. 285–89. For a more optimistic view of the West's liberalism about this time see Edward G. Costigan, "The Maverick Far West," *Nation,* July 29, 1939, pp. 123–26.

## Chapter 15

1. *Alamosa Daily Courier,* March 6, 1942; *Glenwood Post,* October 22, 1942.

2. "Leadville's Comeback," *Business Week,* August 22, 1942; Colorado Springs *Gazette-Telegraph,* October 25, November 15, 1942, October 29, 1944.

3. *Durango Herald-Democrat,* April 4, 25, 1942; *Montrose Daily Press,* February 4, 1942; Colorado Springs *Gazette-Telegraph,* November 1, 1942; *Colorado Year Book,* 1943–44, p. 161.

4. *Montrose Daily Press,* February 19, 1942.

5. *Montrose Daily Press,* February 6, 9, 1942; *Alamosa Daily Courier,* March 12, 22, 1942.

6. *Fort Morgan Herald,* October 15, 22, 29; November 5, 12, 19; December 3, 1942.

7. *The Denver Post,* January 15, 1941; May 15, December 13, 1944; LeRoy R. Hafen, ed., *Colorado and Its People,* 4 vols. (New York, 1948), 1:620–21.

8. Elinor Bluemel, *The Golden Opportunity: The Story of the Emily Griffith Opportunity School of Denver* (Denver, 1965), pp. 52–53; Lyle A. Ashby, "Denver Schools and the War," *Journal of the National Education Association,* April 1942, p. 113.

9. Colorado Springs *Gazette-Telegraph,* January 7, 21, 1942.

10. Hafen, *Colorado and Its People,* 1:591–95.

11. *Colorado Year Book,* 1943–44, p. 510; Hafen, *Colorado and Its People,* 1:597.

12. "Amache, Colorado," a 24-page typed description of the camp dated April 5, 1943. Held in R. E. Bennett Collection, Western History Collections, University of Colorado, Boulder.

13. *Colorado Year Book,* 1943–44, pp. 28, 519–20; Clarence W. Kemper, "Colorado Girds for Race Fight," *Christian Century,* November 1, 1944, p. 1262; "Alien Land Ban Asked," *Business Week,* March 4, 1944, p. 22; M. Paul Holsinger, "Amache" *Colorado Magazine* 44, no. 1 (Winter 1964):50–60; Barron Beshoar, "When Goodwill is Organized," *Common Ground* 5, no. 3 (1945):19–20, 29; *Denver Post,* April 14, 16, 1944; *Lamar Register,* September 13, 1944; Colorado Springs *Gazette-Telegraph,* October 4, 11, December 6, 1942, November 9, 26, 1944; *Alamosa Daily Courier,* March 24, 26, 1942; *Glenwood Post,* May 14, 1942; *Durango Herald-Democrat,* April 22, 1942.

14. Barron Beshoar, "Report from the Mountain States," *Common Ground* 4, no. 3 (1944):23–30.

15. Colorado Springs *Gazette-Telegraph,* October 18, 1942; *Durango Herald-Democrat,* April 9, 1942.

16. Beshoar, "Report from the Mountain States," pp. 24, 25, 27, 29; *Glenwood Post,* June 25, August 13, 1942.

17. Hal Borland, "Home Town Makes Good," *New York Times Magazine,* December 26, 1943, p. 13; interview with Robert Ruble, Boulder, Colorado, July 10, 1975.

18. George L. Nichols, "War Recreation in Colorado Springs," *American City*, November 1943, pp. 44, 45.

19. *Denver Post*, April 4, 1943; December 21, 1944.

20. "Curbs Removed," *Business Week*, December 30, 1944, pp. 84–86; Colorado Springs *Gazette-Telegraph*, November 9, 1944.

21. "Legion Carries On," *Nation*, April 15, 1944, p. 459; *Denver Post*, April 2, 1944.

22. *Denver Post*, April 5, 6, 7, 1944.

23. Ibid., April 4, 13, 1944; May 1, 21, 1947; Colorado Springs *Gazette-Telegraph*, November 26, 1946; *Colorado Year Book*, 1943–44. For further information on the general subject I am much indebted to Howard Lee Scamehorn for the loan of his manuscript, "Air Transportation in the Mountain West."

24. Fred R. Baker, Jr., "Colorado Springs Plans for Postwar Jobs and Public Improvements," *American City*, November 1944, pp. 74–76; "Rockies Town Copies the Swiss," *Business Week*, May 27, 1950, p. 66; Colorado Springs *Gazette-Telegraph*, October 1, 1944.

25. *Colorado Year Book*, 1943–44, p. 27; S. R. De Boer in *Denver Post*, January 7, 1945. One of the critics was University of Colorado Professor Morris E. Garnsey. See his article "Future of the Mountain States" in *Harper's*, October 1945, pp. 329–36.

## Chapter 16

1. S. R. De Boer in *Denver Post*, January 7, 1945.

2. A. G. Mezerik, "Journey in America," *New Republic*, December 11, 1944, pp. 794–95.

3. Velie, "Housing" *Colliers*, December 21, 1946, pp. 18–19.

4. Clarence W. Kemper, "Colorado," *The Christian Century*, October 17, 1945, p. 1190; Colorado Springs *Gazette-Telegraph*, October 6, November 13, 17, 27, 1946.

5. "Colorado: It Stands Aloof amid Its Mountain Beauties," *Life*, October 23, 1943, pp. 95–103; "Denver's Commercial Building Surge Is Started by Outsider," *Business Week*, September 19, 1943, pp. 80–82.

6. "Pushing Skyward," *Business Week*, September 1, 1945, p. 36; "Denver," *House and Garden*, September 1956, p. 148. William Zeckendorf (with Edward McCreary), *The Autobiography of William Zeckendorf* (New York, 1970), chaps. 9 and 10.

7. John D. Garwood, "Analysis of Postwar Industrial Migration to Utah and Colorado," *Economic Geography*, January 1953, pp. 79–88.

8. Albert Q. Maisel, "Dr. Sabin's Second Career," *Survey Graphic*, February 1947, pp. 138–40; Elinor Richey, *Eminent Women of the West* (Berkeley, 1975), pp. 66–70; D. H. Cooper, "Lest We Forget: Pitiful Situations in Rural Schools," *Elementary School Journal*, March 1948, pp. 358–61; Colorado Springs *Gazette-Telegraph*, November 21, 1946.

9. Cooper, "Lest We Forget," p. 360.

10. Ralph G. Martin, "Changes on Champa Street," *New Republic*, October 7, 1946, pp. 449–50; A. Gayle Waldrop, "A Chinook Blows on Champa Street," *Journalism Quarterly*, June 1947, pp. 109–15; Roscoe Fleming, "Revolution in Denver," *Nation*, June 29, 1946, pp. 780–81; Mary Ellen Murphy and Mark Murphy, "Papa's Girl" (Helen Bonfils), *Saturday Evening Post*, December 23, 1944, pp. 14–15.

11. *Rocky Mountain News*, November 7, 1946; interview with John A. Carroll, July 25, 1975.

12. Don Eddy, "Uprising in Denver," *American Magazine*, October 1947, pp. 30–31; "Landslide in the Rockies," *Time*, June 2, 1947, p. 28; Carey McWilliams, "Bright Spot in the West," *Nation*, June 14, 1947, pp. 709–10; John Gunther, *Inside U.S.A.* (New York, 1947), pp. 223–26; *New York Times*, May 18, 1947, sec. iv, p. 6.

13. *Denver Post*, May 1, 6, 8, 21, 1947; George V. Kelly, *The Old Gray Mayors of Denver* (Boulder, 1974), pp. 23–54. See also Marshall Sprague, "Mayor of Denver, etc.," *New York Times*, November 30, 1946, sec. iv, p. 8.

14. William E. Leuchtenburg, "Revolt in Colorado," *Nation,* September 4, 1948, pp. 260–61; *Denver Post,* November 3, 4, 1948.

15. *New York Times,* September 21, 1948, pp. 1, 22.

16. Ibid., September 22, 1948, p. 1. More on "colonial bondage" may be found in Bernard De Voto, "West Against Itself," *Harper's Magazine,* January 1947, pp. 1–13; see also comment in the *Denver Post,* May 13, 1947.

17. Neil Morgan, *Westward Tilt: The American West Today* (New York, 1961), p. 272. Zeckendorf, *Autobiography,* p. 107.

18. Morgan, *Westward Tilt,* p. 272.

19. "Pride of Pueblo," *Time,* October 12, 1953, p. 98; "Colorado's Boom Problem," *Business Week,* November 25, 1961, p. 48.

20. Ralph G. Martin, "Sky-High Empire," *Newsweek,* July 26, 1954, p. 77; Walter B. and Walter S. Lovelace, *Jesse Shwayder and the Golden Rule* (Denver, 1960), chap. 7.

21. Gunther, *Inside U.S.A.,* p. 213.

22. Colorado's Boom Problem," p. 48; "Rockies Town Copies the Swiss," *Business Week,* May 27, 1950, p. 64.

23. Maurice Frink, *The Boulder Story: Historical Portrait of a Colorado Town* (Boulder, 1965), pp. 73–81.

24. "Desert Dollars," *Business Week,* March 24, 1956, p. 96.

25. "Colorado's Boom Problem," pp. 46–47.

26. *Denver Post,* June 14, 1948. See also De Voto, "The West Against Itself," pp. 8–9. Morris E. Garnsey, "The 'Great Literary Battle': A Footnote to Bernard De Voto's Uneasy Chair" is a reminiscence of the stir De Voto caused in Colorado circles in 1948. It is found in the *Silver and Gold Record* (University of Colorado), January 27, 1976.

27. *Denver Post* Sunday *Roundup* section, April 28, 1957, p. 4. For the controversial Webb article see Walter Prescott Webb; "The American West: Perpetual Mirage," *Harper's Magazine,* May 1957, pp. 25–31.

28. Martin, "Sky-High Empire," p. 78.

29. Debs Myers, "Colorado," *Holiday,* September 1952, pp. 34–51; Marshall Sprague, "Doing the Rockies," *New York Times,* May 7, 1950, section x, p. 29; Thomas Hornsby Ferril, "Tourists, Stay Away from My Door," *Harper's Magazine,* May 1954, pp. 77–81.

30. Eugene Hansen, "Welcome Hand for Tourists," *Recreation,* February 1954, p. 83; "Colorado Spa" (Ouray), *Sunset,* July 1955, pp. 33–34; Colorado Springs *Gazette-Telegraph,* October 10, 1954. The "nostalgia" remark is found in William Houseman, "Going Places, Finding Ghosts in Colorado's Nostalgic Mining Towns," *House and Garden,* June 1966, p. 48.

31. The best account of early skiing in Steamboat Springs is to be found in John Rolfe Burroughs, *Steamboat in the Rockies* (Ft. Collins, 1974). See chaps. 13 and 14.

32. Evan M. Wylie, "Ghost Town on Skis," *Collier's,* February 7, 1948, pp. 24–26; Jill Durrance and Dick Durrance II, "A Town . . . a Mountain . . . a Way of Life," *National Geographic,* December 1973, p. 793.

33. Dan Jenkins, "Our Problem: How to Beat the Ski Ennui," *Sports Illustrated,* March 17, 1969, pp. 58–59; E. Ward McCray, "The Many Faces of Vail," *Travel,* January 1969, pp. 54–57; "Too Cold Colorado for the Joys of Powder Skiing," *Sunset,* February 1969, pp. 62–69.

## Chapter 17

1. Colorado Springs *Gazette-Telegraph,* October 3, 1948; *New York Times,* March 16, 1947; interviews with Robert L. Stearns and Eugene H. Wilson, September 7, 1975. Wilson, then librarian, later became vice-president and interim president of the university.

2. *Nation,* May 26, July 28, 1951, November 29, 1952; letter from David Hawkins to the author April 21, 1976.

3. *New York Times,* September 16, 1950, p. 8.

4. *U.S. News and World Report,* November 12, 1954, pp. 77–78; *New Republic,* November 15, 1954.

5. *The Rocky Mountain News,* November 7, 8, 1956; Curtis Martin, "1956 Election in Colorado," *Western Political Science Quarterly* 10 (March 1957):117–21; Curtis Martin, "Political Behavior in Colorado," *Colorado Quarterly* 6 (Summer 1957):63–78; Charles Oxton, "Colorado's Champion of Good Government" (Stephen McNichols), *Catholic World,* June 1957, pp. 180–85; William P. Irwin, "Peace Wins an Election," *Nation,* December 6, 1958, pp. 419–22. For Ed Johnson's role in the election see Patrick F. McCarty, "Big Ed Johnson of Colorado—A Political Portrait" (M.A. thesis, University of Colorado, 1958), pp. 251–55.

6. "Pensions That Rise," *U.S. News and World Report,* April 19, 1957, pp. 51, 52; "Too Big Pensions," *Business Week,* January 21, 1956, p. 71; Roscoe Fleming, "Welfare State of Colorado," *Nation,* September 6, 1958, pp. 101, 120. Colorado Constitution, Revised to March 1, 1969, pp. 75–77.

7. "After Hours," *Harper's Magazine,* July 1949, p. 99.

8. "Denver's Red Rocks," *Time,* June 23, 1941, p. 51; "*Carmen* in Denver," *Time,* May 5, 1941, p. 89; "Denver's Happy Orchestra," *Time,* October 29, 1951, p. 71.

9. Beatrice Gottlieb, "Dancing in the Hills," *Theatre Arts,* June 1951, p. 97.

10. Charles F. Collisson, "Opera Revived in the Heart of the 1859 Gold Rush," *Etude,* January 1947, p. 20; Roger Angell, "Denver," *Holiday,* August 1949, p. 114; John Chapman, "Well-Heeled Ghost" (Central City), *Theatre Arts,* June 1952, p. 35; Robert Stapp, "Perils of Living in Tourist Land," *House and Garden,* September 1956, p. 160.

11. Campton Bell, "University Theatre in Operation," *Theatre Arts,* April 1950, p. 54; Robert L. Perkin, "Shakespeare in the Rockies," *Shakespeare Quarterly,* Fall 1958, p. 555; ibid., Fall 1959, p. 587.

12. Joe Alex Morris, "Aspen, Colorado," *Saturday Evening Post,* October 14, 1950, p. 172.

13. "Goethe in Colorado," *Newsweek,* July 11, 1949, p. 64; "Aspen, America," *Commonweal,* July 22, 1949, p. 347. "After Hours," *Harper's Magazine,* July 1949, p. 99. A fuller treatment of efforts to bring culture to Aspen and to Colorado may be found in Sidney Hyman, *The Aspen Idea* (Norman, Okla., 1975).

14. Stapp, "Perils," p. 160.

15. "Aspen, America," p. 357; Curtis W. Casewit, "Aspen and the Snowmen," *Saturday Review,* February 3, 1968, pp. 42–44.

16. William Harlan Hale, "Culture with a Suntan High in the Rockies," *The Reporter,* August 8, 1957, pp. 24–28.

17. P. G. Ernst, "Will Success Spoil Aspen," *Nation,* July 25, 1966, p. 72; Casewit, "Aspen and the Snowmen," p. 44.

18. *Newsweek,* July 3, 1950, p. 66, and August 9, 1954, p. 71; Hale, "Culture with a Suntan," p. 27; *Time,* November 29, 1963, p. 79; *The Economist,* August 15, 1964, p. 646; John Scanlon, "Aspen: A New Day for the Humanities," *Saturday Review,* December 21, 1963, p. 40; Boulder *Daily Camera,* October 23, December 16, 1975, January 14, February 12, 1976. For a further account of doubts raised over the institute see H. B. Rouse, "Questions about Aspen," *Saturday Review,* January 18, 1964, p. 56.

19. *Time,* October 13, November 3, 1961, p. 17; *Life,* November 3, 1961, p. 18, and May 18, 1962, pp. 110–13; *U.S. News and World Report,* October 16, 1961, pp. 65–66.

20. For more about Corky Gonzales see Christine Marin, "Rodolfo 'Corky' Gonzales: The Mexican-American Movement Spokesman, 1966–1972," *Journal of the West* 14, no. 4 (October 1975):107–19.

21. Bernard Valdez, "The History of Spanish Americans," typescript provided by the

Denver Department of Welfare, of which Mr. Valdez is the manager; William J. May, "The Grand Valley Sugar Beet Industry," Montrose *Daily Sentinel*, September 7, 14, 28, November 9, 1975.

22. *Time*, May 12, 1952, p. 27.

23. Edward L. Whittemore, "Colorado U. Ends Fraternity Bias," *Christian Century*, April 18, 1956, p. 494.

24. *Business Week*, May 13, 1972, p. 167. See also *U.S. News and World Report*, October 18, 1965; *Time*, May 30, 1969; and the *New Yorker*, May 31, 1969, p. 88.

25. Calvin Trillin, "U.S. Journal: Denver," *New Yorker*, May 31, 1969, pp. 85–89; Conrad L. McBride, "1966 Election in Colorado," *Western Political Quarterly*, June 1967, pp. 555–62.

26. Rudolph Gómez and Robert L. Eckelberry, "1970 Election in Colorado," *Western Political Quarterly* 24 (June 1971):274–78.

27. Lawrence Martin, "Public School Crisis," *Saturday Review*, September 8, 1951, pp. 9–10.

28. Lawrence G. Weiss, "Goldwater and Colorado U.," *Nation*, December 8, 1962, pp. 402–4; Warren H. Carroll, "Counterattack at Colorado," *National Review*, June 18, 1963, pp. 494–95; *Newsweek*, May 20, 1963, p. 88, and February 13, 1967, p. 95.

29. "Rarified Air," *Economist*, June 8, 1963, p. 1014.

30. Boulder *Daily Camera*, May 8, 1975.

31. Edwin Shrake, "Love Affair With a Loser: Denver Broncos," *Sports Illustrated*, March 29, 1965, p. 67. The story of the football fan's attempted suicide is found in Michael Roberts, "The Vicarious Heroism of the Sports Spectator," *New Republic*, November 23, 1974, p. 17.

32. Boulder *Daily Camera*, February 8, 1976.

33. Edward J. Linehan, "The Rockies' Pot of Gold: Colorado," *National Geographic*, August 1969, p. 166; Hugh Gardner, "Good-Bye, Colorado: The Transformation from Dreamland to Nightmare," *Harper's Magazine*, April 1974, p. 14.

## Chapter 18

1. Juan Cameron, "Growth Is a Fighting Word in Colorado's Mountain Wonderland," *Fortune*, October 1973, p. 158.

2. Lois Phillips Hudson, "Battle in the Wilderness," *Nation*, April 4, 1966, pp. 393–96. Stream pollution became a cause of the Izaak Walton League shortly after the close of World War II. For an example see complaints in Colorado Springs *Gazette-Telegraph*, September 9, 1945, p. 7.

3. "Wilderness vs. I-70," *National Parks Magazine*, November 1967, p. 21.

4. Robert Bradford, "Aspen's Awful Problem: Surfers on Skis," *Life*, March 12, 1965, pp. 42–44; Roger Rapoport, "Explosion in a Boom Town," (Aspen), *Sports Illustrated*, September 14, 1970, pp. 26–27; Curtis W. Casewit, "Aspen and the Snowmen," *Saturday Review*, February 3, 1968, p. 44; "Who Needs Skis?" *Life*, January 18, 1963, p. 97; "Ski People," *Time*, January 11, 1963, p. 38.

5. Bryce Nelson, "Colorado Environmentalists: Scientists Battle AEC and Army," *Science*, June 12, 1970, pp. 1324–28; Steve Gascoyne, "How I Learned to Live with Radioactivity and Love It in Colorado," *Commonweal*, March 13, 1970, p. 7; "Colorado Committee," *Environment*, May 1970, p. 15; Hugh Gardner, "Good-Bye Colorado: The Transformation from Dreamland to Nightmare," *Harper's Magazine*, April 1974, p. 20; Linda Harvey, "Colorado's Nuclear Contamination: What You're Not Told," *Denver*, March 1976, pp. 34–39, 62.

6. Edward J. Linehan, "The Rockies' Pot of Gold: Colorado," *National Geographic*, August 1969, p. 167.

7. Eric Sevareid, "Why the Aspens Quake," *Saturday Review*, October 20, 1962, p. 45.

8. "Colorado Tunnel Triggers a Battle," *Business Week*, October 6, 1973, pp. 67–70.

9. Jill Durrance and Dick Durrance II, "A Town . . . a Mountain . . . a Way of Life," *National Geographic*, December 1973, pp. 797–806. See also Neal R. Peirce, *The Mountain States of America* (New York, 1972), pp. 52–54.

10. Jerry Hulse, "Telluride is the New Rage of the Rockies," Boulder *Daily Camera*, November 23, 1975; Jakki Savan, "Newcomers Fight to Save Telluride Charm," St. Louis *Post-Dispatch*, January 25, 1976.

11. "Saving the Slopes," *Time*, January 10, 1972, pp. 62–63; Gardner, "Good-Bye Colorado," pp. 19–21.

12. Roger Rapoport, "Olympian Snafu at Sniktau," *Sports Illustrated*, February 15, 1971, pp. 60–61, Jerry Kirschenbaum, "Voting to Snuff the Torch," ibid., November 20, 1972, pp. 44–46; Milton Viorst, "Bumpy Course for the Denver Olympics," *Saturday Review*, October 21, 1972, pp. 12–17; Sam W. Brown, Jr., "Snow-job in Colorado: The '76 Winter Olympics," *New Republic*, January 29, 1972, pp. 15–19; " '76 Olympics: Quarreling Already," *Business Week*, p. 30.

13. "Denver's Old Larimer Square Is Making a Comeback," *Sunset*, January 1971, p. 32.

14. "Sign Busters," *Newsweek*, June 7, 1971, p. 116.

15. "How the Ecologists Defeated Aspinall," *Business Week*, September 23, 1972, p. 27; Gardner, "Good-Bye, Colorado," p. 20; *Rocky Mountain News*, November 9, 1972. See also Aspinall's comments in an article "Scenery or Minerals," *Denver Post* Empire Magazine section, April 12, 1970, p. 16.

16. *Denver Post*, November 8, 1972; *Rocky Mountain News*, November 9, 1972.

17. James A. Goodman, "No Radiation without Representation," *New Republic*, December 14, 1974, pp. 11–12.

18. "New-Style Politicians," *Economist*, November 2, 1974, p. 49; Winthrop Griffith, "An Eco-Freak for Governor?" *New York Times Magazine*, October 27, 1974, pp. 34–35, 37–46.

19. Paul R. Wieck, "Chance for Democrats," *New Republic*, August 24, 1974, pp. 11–13; idem, "How They Won in Colorado," ibid., November 23, 1974, p. 8; *Time*, November 18, 1974, p. 12; *Denver Post*, October 9, 1974; Boulder *Daily Camera*, July 30, 1974.

20. Boulder *Daily Camera*, December 22, 1974.

21. Gardner, "Good-Bye Colorado," p. 18.

22. Ibid., p. 22; Boulder *Daily Camera*, October 17, 1975, March 7, 1976.

23. "Warning from the Rockies: Go Slow in Exploiting Our Fuel," *U.S. News and World Report*, December 22, 1975.

24. Toba J. Cohen, "Colorado's New Governor Wages a War for Ecological Survival," *Today's Health*, October 1975, p. 23.

25. "Shale Oil Rush," *Economist*, August 15, 1965; Roscoe Fleming, "Oil Rush," *New Republic*, September 18, 1965, p. 11; Ronald Schiller, "Biggest Buried Treasure on Earth," *Reader's Digest*, September 1971, pp. 160–62; "Slowdown on Oil Shale," *Economist*, November 2, 1974, p. 53; Linehan, "The Rockies," p. 190; Gardner, "Good-Bye, Colorado," p. 22; Boulder *Daily Camera*, August 24–29, 1974; February 7, May 8, October 28, December 20, 1975; advertisement, Standard Oil Company, *U.S. News and World Report*, September 9, 1974, p. 61; Annual Report, Texaco Company, 1975, p. 11.

26. *Denver Post*, October 17, 1974; Boulder *Daily Camera*, January 25, 1975. Comments on solar energy may be found in "Colorado Shows How to Put the Sun to Work," *U.S. News and World Report*, June 2, 1975, p. 66.

27. Phil Gruis, "The Capitol Is Haunted," Boulder *Daily Camera*, Sunday "Focus" section, February 29, 1976; *U.S. News and World Report*, March 29, 1976, p. 12; *Denver Post*, October 22, 1975.

28. Phil Gruis, "Scram, John," Boulder *Daily Camera*, Sunday "Focus" section, March 21, 1976.

29. James A. Michener, "Colorado," *Business Week,* February 23, 1976, special advertising section.

30. Linda Harvey, "Colorado's Nuclear Contamination: What You're Not Told," *Denver,* March 1976, p. 39.

31. *Colorado Daily,* December 3, 1975; Boulder *Daily Camera,* April 11, 1976.

32. W. Cyrus Wilson, president of Gano-Downs clothing store. "Denver Peaks," *Business Week,* September 25, 1965, p. 192; "Denver: A Cow Town," ibid., January 27, 1973, p. 71.

# Acknowledgments

One of the real pleasures of preparing a manuscript for publication, "putting it to bed," is the opportunity to say "thanks" in print to people who have been helpful. So many debts are incurred along the line, from the first research down to the laying out of maps, selecting photographs, and checking final points that may be in doubt, that these are obligations most pleasant to discharge. Yet it seems so little to do for those who have done so much.

My principal debt is to Eugene H. Wilson, to whom this book is most affectionately and warmly dedicated, for it was he who conceived the idea for it and encouraged the writing process all the way. He and my wife, who also is an experienced editor, outvoted me a number of times and saved me from countless pitfalls.

Two extremely able graduate students, Douglas J. Ernest and Edward G. Agran, did much of the legwork, digging up obscure bibliographical references and searching newspapers for color and richer background material. They sat with me for hours as we combed the findings, refined them, and made evaluations of the harvest. I owe much to both of them.

As always my colleagues have been willing to lend their talents and experience as advisers. Professors Clifford Westermeier, University of Colorado, Lyle Dorsett, University of Denver, and Liston E. Leyendecker, Colorado State University, all read the entire manuscript and each of them made suggestions, found small slips of the typewriter, and made evaluations of my concepts. Professor Howard Lee Scamehorn, the University of Colorado, allowed me the advance use of his manuscript material for *Pioneer Steelmaker in the West: The Colorado Fuel and Iron Company, 1870–1903*, published in mid 1976 by the Pruett Publishing Company of Boulder.

Others read portions of this manuscript. Former Governor John A. Love took time from a busy life to comment on some things I had written about more recent Colorado history, in which he played an important part. My old friend Lawrence G. Weiss, of the incumbent governor's staff, read some of the pages that dealt with environmental ideas and more recent politics, and he steered me away from some small mistakes.

Robert L. Stearns, former president of the University of Colorado, whom I have known for three decades, helped me to remember some of the events that took place during the years both of us were associated with the university. John A. Carroll, who served the state as a member of both the U.S. House of Representatives and the U.S. Senate, was another longtime friend upon whom I called for, and received most willingly, the help I needed.

Professor David Hawkins of the University of Colorado read and commented upon my interpretations of the "red scare" that disturbed the academic community after World War II. Walter Lovelace of Boulder provided me with a copy of his book on Jesse Shwayder and offered his assistance with materials related to early business leaders. Marshall Sprague, one of Colorado's best-known authors, who has written the Colorado volume of the Bicentennial series, gave his time for some long talks over refreshments in the book-lined study of his Colorado Springs home. Professor Duane A. Smith of Fort Lewis College at Durango, one of the authors of *A Colorado History*, made some very good suggestions and let me read part of the manuscript of an upcoming revision of that book. Professor Richard N. Ellis of the University of New Mexico helped me in my quest for a publisher, and he led me to the right place. Frederic J. Athearn of the Bureau of Land Management not only provided material from the publications of that excellent organization but lent his skills to the graphics sections of the book. Timothy J. Kloberdanz of Sterling, Colorado, who knows a great deal about the German Russians, generously provided me with some of his written work on that subject. My thanks also to Albin Wagner of the Brighton Publishing Company, of Brighton, Colorado, for the use of his centennial pamphlet about that city. Robert Ruble, who grew up at Delta, referred me to people who could be of help on the project and also lent some of his background and experiences to it. Harold Morse of the Denver Department of Social Services offered his assistance with information about minorities in the later period.

My university backed the project all the way. The University of Colorado Centennial Commission, of which Eugene Wilson was the chairman, supported the work, and I want to thank members H. H. "Bud" Arnold and Geraldine Bean, in particular, for their help. Additionally, the University of Colorado Council on Research and Creative Work provided faculty leave time without which the on-schedule completion of the study, commenced fairly late in the game, would have been an impossibility. Other members of the university community to whom I owe thanks are John Brennan and Cassandra Tiberio of the University of Colorado Western Historical Collections Library, as well as Peter Robinson of the university's fine museum.

Denver librarians Eleanor M. Gehres, of the Denver Public Library's Western History Department, and Ellen Wagner and Maxine Benson, of the State Historical Society, were very helpful to me and I owe them the warmest of thanks.

Much of the dull, hard work came from those who typed and retyped the manuscript. Carolyn Dill, Carol Watson, Ruth Major, and Aladeen Smith carried the burden cheerfully, and in addition to producing great numbers of pages of manuscript, they made some very good suggestions for improvement of style and grammar. For them I have very special thanks. And I don't blame them for expressing relief that the thing finally was finished. In that, I join them.

# Bibliographical Essay

### About the Bibliography

In a book of this kind, one that attempts to synthesize for the general reader and interested students rather than to offer all-inclusive factual material, the preparation of a long, formal bibliography usually does not serve any good purpose. Those who want to know where the author found his material, something every reader has the right to demand, may consult the numerous footnotes. For others, who want some broad guidelines for further reading, there is a body of basic materials available in the better libraries, and in the following pages some of the more useful items are mentioned. These are intended as samples only, representative of past writings about the Centennial State.

As with most states there are old, monumental histories of Colorado that no longer are read by anyone except writers and historians. Among those most widely used are Wilbur Fisk Stone, *History of Colorado,* 4 volumes (Chicago: S. J. Clark Publishing Co., 1918–19); Jerome C. Smiley, *Semi-Centennial History of the State of Colorado,* 2 volumes (Chicago: Lewis Publishing Co., 1913) by a former state historian; and Frank Hall, *History of the State of Colorado,* 4 volumes (Chicago: Blakely Printing Co., 1889–95), by an early newspaperman and territorial secretary. A frequently used reference work by another of Colorado's pioneers is William N. Byers, *Encyclopedia of Biography of Colorado* (Chicago: Century Publishing and Engraving Co., 1901). The O. L. Baskin Publishing Company, of Chicago, produced three early works that now are regarded as sources for material otherwise hard to find: *History of Clear Creek and Boulder Valleys, Colorado* (1880); *History of the Arkansas Valley, Colorado* (1881); and *History of the City of Denver, Arapahoe County, and Colorado* (1880). A more particularized history of the capital city is Jerome C. Smiley, *History of Denver* (Denver: Denver Times, 1901). All of the above fit Webster's definition of "tome" and are useful principally for encyclopedic purposes, certainly not for ordinary reading.

Among more modern multivolume studies, and heavily factual in content, are LeRoy R. Hafen, ed., *Colorado and Its People,* 4 volumes (New York: Lewis Publishing Co., 1948) and an earlier but somewhat similar effort, James H. Baker and LeRoy R. Hafen, eds., *History of Colorado,* 5 volumes (Denver: Linderman Co., 1927).

A smaller and more readable book is LeRoy R. Hafen, *Colorado: The Story of a Western Commonwealth* (Denver: Peerless Publishing Co., 1933) by a former director of the state historical society and a widely known Colorado historian. Now dated but once widely read is *Colorado: A Guide to the Highest State,* compiled by workers of the Writers' Program of the Work Projects Administration of the State of Colorado (New York: Hastings House, 1941).

Surprisingly few one-volume general histories of Colorado have been written since Hafen's *Colorado* (1933), perhaps because studies of this kind came to have a reputation for being narrow and parochial. In recent years scholars have shaken off this feeling and have taken another look at state and local history. Percy S. Fritz wrote his *Colorado: The Centennial State* (New York: Prentice-Hall, 1941) primarily for college students, and it was so used for a quarter-century, or until Carl W. Ubbelohde, *A Colorado History* (Boulder: Pruett Publishing Co., 1965) replaced it. Later editions of the latter work included as authors Maxine Benson of the state historical society and Professor Duane A. Smith of Fort Lewis College. Then came the centennial year and a rash of books, the more general of which were Carl Abbott, *Colorado: A History of the Centennial State* (Boulder: Colorado Associated University Press, 1976), Marshall Sprague, *Colorado: A Bicentennial History* (New York: W. W. Norton, 1976), and *The Coloradans.*

Finally, worthy of mention among the general works are some excellent pictorial volumes that provide a third dimension when viewing Colorado's past. An excellent example of the use to which historians have put the work of artists is Clifford P. Westermeier, *Colorado's First Portrait: Scenes by Early Artists* (Albuquerque: University of New Mexico Press, 1970), a book of some five hundred drawings, sketches, engravings, and lithographs. Representative of the work done by early photographers is Terry William Mangan, *Colorado on Glass: Colorado's First Half Century As Seen by the Camera* (Denver: Sundance, 1976). See also Carl Akers, *Carl Akers' Colorado* (Ft. Collins, Colo.: Old Army Press, 1975).

A good combination of western art and history applied to early Colorado are the books of Muriel Sibell Wolle. Her volume *Stampede to Timberline: The Ghost Towns and Mining Camps of Colorado* (Boulder: published by the author, 1949) has gone through several editions, so popularly was it received. Her latest book, *Timberline Tailings* (Chicago: Swallow Press, 1976) is one of the many spin-offs of *Stampede,* a work that adds considerably to the original effort.

Closely related to the abovementioned works are the travel guides heavily used by local history buffs. An example is Robert L. Brown, *Jeep Trails to Colorado Ghost Towns* (Caldwell, Idaho: Caxton Printers, 1963) and the same author's *Ghost Towns of the Colorado Rockies* (Caldwell, Idaho: Caxton Printers, 1968). Another widely consulted volume, one that has seen a number of editions, is Perry Eberhart, *Guide to the Colorado Ghost Towns and Mining Camps* (Denver: Sage Books, 1959).

## Part 1: The Invasion

Some contemporary accounts of the Fifty-Niner rush are as interesting today as they were when they were written. Henry Villard, *The Past and Present of the Pike's Peak Gold Regions* (St. Louis, 1860; reprinted by Princeton University Press, 1932, with notes by LeRoy R. Hafen), by a correspondent to the *Cincinnati*

*Daily Commercial;* Horace Greeley, *An Overland Journey from New York to San Francisco in the Summer of 1859* (New York, 1860; reprinted by Alfred A. Knopf in 1963 with an introduction by Charles T. Duncan, then dean of the School of Journalism, University of Colorado); and Albert D. Richardson, *Beyond the Mississippi* (Hartford: American Publishing Co., 1867) all are accounts by eastern newspapermen.

The way west in 1859 is well described in LeRoy R. Hafen, ed., *Overland Routes to the Gold Fields, 1859, Contemporary Diaries* (Glendale: Arthur H. Clark Co., 1942) and LeRoy R. Hafen, ed., *Pike's Peak Gold Rush Guidebooks of 1859* (Glendale: Arthur H. Clark Co., 1941). Engrossing reading about experiences in the mining region are two contemporary accounts by young gold hunters: Henry L. Pitzer, *Three Frontiers* (Muscatine, Iowa: Prairie Press, 1938) and Libeus Barney, *Letters of the Pike's Peak Gold Rush* (San Jose: Talisman Press, 1959), a compilation of letters written form Denver to a Bennington, Vermont, newspaper in 1859–60. Pitzer went home fairly early; Barney stayed on. Less engrossing but informative for its statistical information and for its contemporary point of view is Ovando J. Hollister, *The Mines of Colorado* (Springfield, Mass., 1867; reprinted by Promontory Press, of New York City, 1974). A good picture of a young man's reaction to the miners' society is Robert G. Athearn's "Life in the Pike's Peak Region: The Letters of Matthew H. Dale," *Colorado Magazine* 32, no. 2 (April 1955):1–25.

Accounts by women who made early crossings of the plains are Emma Shepard Hill, *A Dangerous Crossing and What Happened on the Other Side* (Denver: Bradford-Robinson Printing Co., 1924) and Mrs. H. A. W. (Augusta) Tabor, "Cabin Life in Colorado," *Colorado Magazine* 4, no. 2 (March 1927):71–75, and reprinted ibid. 36, no. 2 (April 1959):149–53. Another good account is that of Susan Riley Ashley, "Reminiscences of Colorado in the Early 'Sixties," *Colorado Magazine* 13, no. 6 (November 1936):219–30. The enjoyable story of a Fifty-Niner "women's libber" may be read in Agnes Wright Spring, ed., *A Bloomer Girl on Pike's Peak, 1858: Julia Archibald Holmes, First Woman to Climb Pike's Peak* (Denver: Western History Department, Denver Public Library, 1949).

A widely used contemporary account of municipal beginnings at the foot of the Rockies is William Larimer, *Reminiscences of General William Larimer and His Son William H. H. Larimer* (Lancaster, Pennsylvania: New Era Printing Co., 1918). Valuable, too, are the letters of Thomas Wildman and others, in LeRoy R. and Ann W. Hafen, eds., *Reports from Colorado: The Wildman Letters, 1859–1865* (Glendale: Arthur H. Clark Co., 1961). Of interest also is LeRoy R. Hafen, ed., *Colorado Gold Rush: Contemporary Letters and Reports, 1858–59* (Glendale: Arthur H. Clark Co., 1941).

For a look at the role of minorities in the early towns, especially Denver, see Eugene H. Berwanger, "William J. Hardin: Colorado Spokesman for Racial Justice, 1863–1873," *Colorado Magazine* 52, no. 1 (Winter 1975):52–65, and Harmon Mothershead, "Negro Rights in Colorado Territory," *Colorado Magazine* 40, no. 3 (July 1963):212–23. Allen D. Breck, *The Centennial History of the Jews of Colorado, 1859–1959* (Denver: Hirschfeld Press, 1960) is very informative for this period, as is Ida Libert Uchill, *Pioneers, Peddlers, and Tsadikim* (Denver: Sage Books, 1957).

The spread of Colorado's placer mining frontier is outlined in Rodman W. Paul,

*Mining Frontiers of the Far West, 1848–80* (New York: Holt, Rinehart & Winston, 1963), one of the finest works of its kind in recent years. Daniel Ellis Conner, *A Confederate in the Colorado Gold Fields,* edited by Donald J. Berthrong and Odessa Davenport (Norman: University of Oklahoma Press, 1970) describes vividly the life of a young miner in South Park.

Social life in these rapidly multiplying mining camps, as in Denver, is portrayed in Melvin Schoberlin, *From Candles to Footlights* (Denver: Old West Publishing Co., 1941), Virginia McConnell, "A Gauge of Popular Taste in Early Colorado," *Colorado Magazine* 46, no. 4 (Fall 1969):338–50, and Alice Cochran, "Jack Langrishe and the Theater of the Mining Frontier," ibid., 324–37.

The newspapers and the highly individualistic men who ran them were important elements in the development of the territory. Unsurpassed on this subject is Robert L. Perkin's *The First Hundred Years: An Informal History of Denver and the Rocky Mountain News* (New York: Doubleday and Co., 1959). A good brief general account is Edwin A. Bemis, "Journalism in Colorado," in LeRoy R. Hafen, ed., *Colorado and Its People,* 2:246–78. A number of articles about journalists have appeared in the *Colorado Magazine,* among them D. W. Working, "Some Forgotten Pioneer Newspapers," in vol. 4, no. 3 (May 1927):93–100, and Neil W. Kimball, "George West," in vol. 27, no. 3 (July 1950):198–208.

Off-duty diversions of soldiers stationed at some of Colorado's army posts are treated by Duane Vandenbusche, "Life at a Frontier Post: Fort Garland," *Colorado Magazine* 43, no. 2 (Spring 1966):132–48 and Morris F. Taylor, "Fort Massachusetts," *Colorado Magazine* 45, no. 2 (Spring 1968):120–42.

The difficulties faced by early Colorado jurists are set forth by John D. W. Guice in *The Rocky Mountain Bench: The Territorial Supreme Courts of Colorado, Montana, and Wyoming, 1861–1890* (New Haven: Yale University Press, 1972) and Guice's article "Colorado's Territorial Courts," *Colorado Magazine* 45, no. 3 (Summer 1968):204–24. Much older, but worth digging out for scholarly purposes, is Peter Wikoff, "The Bar and Bench of Denver and Colorado," *Magazine of Western History* 9, nos. 5 and 6 (March and April 1889):605–10 and 764–73.

Education, of enduring interest to Coloradans, has not been treated in sufficient depth, but there are a few helpful articles about it. O. J. Goldrick, the pioneer educator, wrote of his experiences in "The First School in Denver," *Colorado Magazine* 6, no. 2 (March 1929):72–74. A companion piece is by A. J. Fynn and L. R. Hafen, "Early Education in Colorado," *Colorado Magazine* 12, no. 1 (January 1935):16–19. Central City's early schools are the subject of Lynn Perrigo, "The First Decade of Public Schools at Central City," *Colorado Magazine* 12, no. 3 (May 1935):86–87. More on the same subject is found in Perrigo's "A Social History of Central City, Colorado, 1859–1900" (Ph.D. dissertation, University of Colorado, 1939).

**Part 2: The Age of Acquisition**

A great deal has been written about Colorado during the Civil War years, but much of it concerns the campaign in New Mexico, and not enough is about life in the territory during that period. For a firsthand account of the military activity see Ovando J. Hollister, *Boldly They Rode: A History of the First Colorado Regiment* (Lakewood, Colo.: Golden Press, 1949) and William Clarke Whitford, *Colorado Volunteers in the Civil War: The New Mexico Campaign of 1862* (Denver, 1906; reprinted by Golden Press, Lakewood, Colo., 1963). Sheldon Zweig, "William Gilpin: First Territorial Governor of Colorado" (M.A. thesis, University of Colorado, 1950), describes Gilpin's role, as does Thomas L. Karnes, *William Gilpin: Western Nationalist* (Austin: University of Texas Press, 1970), chap. 9. A good picture of the problems faced by Gilpin's successor is set forth in Harry E. Kelsey, Jr., *Frontier Capitalist: The Life of John Evans* (Boulder: Pruett Publishing Co., 1969).

Indian affairs during these early years will be better understood by reading Donald J. Berthrong, *The Southern Cheyennes* (Norman: University of Oklahoma Press, 1963), and some chapters in Kelsey's book on John Evans, referred to above. Nothing worth reading about John Chivington has been published in book length studies. The difficulties of 1868 need further study, but until then, see Robert G. Athearn, "Colorado and the Indian War of 1868," *Colorado Magazine* 33, no. 1 (January 1956):42–51.

The coming of the railroads, an event of great significance to Colorado, has been widely covered. A brief, general discussion is by Herbert O. Brayer, "History of Colorado Railroads," in LeRoy R. Hafen, ed., *Colorado and Its People,* vol. 2. Little has been done on the history of the Kansas Pacific. One of the better unpublished works is William R. Petrowski, "The Kansas Pacific: A Study in Railroad Promotion" (Ph.D. dissertation, University of Wisconsin, 1966). Elmer O. Davis, *The First Five Years of the Railroad Era in Colorado* (Golden, Colo.: Sage Books, 1948) treats the early years. For information about a principal Colorado railroad read Robert G. Athearn, *Rebel of the Rockies: A History of the Denver and Rio Grande Railroad* (New Haven: Yale University Press, 1962). *Union Pacific Country* (Chicago: Rand McNally and Co., 1971), by the same author, involves Colorado, particularly in chapter 11. Numerous books have been written about the little narrow-gauge roads that prospected the Colorado Rockies in search of minerals, one of the most interesting of which is Morris Cafky, *The Colorado Midland* (Denver: Rocky Mountain Railroad Club, 1965). Another example is Forest Crossen, *The Switzerland Trail of America* (Boulder: Pruett Press, 1962).

More should be written about early efforts to "sell" Colorado to settlers and investors. Nineteenth-century "puff pieces" such as Frank Fossett, *Colorado, Its Gold and Silver Mines* (New York: C. G. Crawford, Printer, 1879) is illustrative of the enthusiasm with which the promotion was undertaken. It should be read with Ovando Hollister's *Mines of Colorado,* mentioned above. Liston E. Leyendecker wrote an interesting article about such advertising: "Colorado and the Paris Universal Exposition, 1867," *Colorado Magazine* 46, no. 1 (Winter 1969):1–15. Ralph E. Blodgett's "Colorado Territorial Board of Immigration," *Colorado Magazine* 46, no. 3 (Summer 1969):245–56 deals with a phase of "sell Colorado."

A great deal of the capital used to develop Colorado came from foreign sources; in addition to the financial aid given, the practice benefited Colorado by advertising the new state among prospective emigrants. The best work on this subject is Clark C. Spence, *British Investments and the American Mining Frontier 1860–1901* (Ithaca, N.Y.: Cornell University Press, 1958). Spence's M.A. thesis

(University of Colorado, 1951), entitled "Robert Orchard Old and The British and Colorado Mining Bureau," provides an excellent description of publicizing efforts. For the later nineteenth century see Alfred P. Tischendorf, "British Investments in Colorado Mines," *Colorado Magazine* 30, no. 4 (October 1953):243–46.

Colorado, the tourists' paradise, is in need of fuller treatment. Earl Pomeroy, *In Search of the Golden West: The Tourist in Western America* (New York: Alfred A. Knopf, 1957) is an excellent study, part of which deals with Colorado. More specifically, one may consult Jane Furey, "Tourism in the Pike's Peak Area, 1870–80" (M.A. thesis, University of Colorado, 1958). Marshall Sprague's delightful *Newport in the Rockies* (Denver: Sage Books, 1961) describes "the life and good times of Colorado Springs," one of the state's early resort towns.

Statehood and the constitutional convention are discussed in most of the older histories. Somewhat more recent is Colin B. Goodykoontz, "Some Controversial Questions Before the Colorado Constitutional Convention of 1876," *Colorado Magazine* 17, no. 1 (January 1940):1–17. One of the most extensive studies is Donald W. Hensel "A History of the Colorado Constitution in the Nineteenth Century" (Ph.D. dissertation, University of Colorado, 1957).

The development of agriculture and the colony towns, so important to the development of the state, is a subject much in need of updating. Alvin T. Steinel, *History of Agriculture in Colorado* (Fort Collins: State Agricultural College, 1926), written as a part of the semicentennial observance, is a solid piece of work but it is old. Unfortunately nothing has superseded it. Some comments about Byers and his interest in Colorado agriculture may be found in Deryl V. Gease, "William N. Byers and the Colorado Agricultural Society," *Colorado Magazine* 43, no. 4 (Fall 1966):325–38.

More has been written about the agricultural colonies. James F. Willard and Colin B. Goodykoontz, eds., *Experiments in Colorado Colonization* (Boulder: University of Colorado Historical Collections, 1926) is old but is not apt to be outdated because it consists largely of original documents. Another of Willard's edited contributions was *The Union Colony at Greeley, Colorado, 1969–71* (Boulder: University of Colorado Historical Collections, 1918). An old, biased, and frequently acerbic account of northern Colorado colonies is David Boyd, *A History of Greeley and the Union Colony of Colorado* (Greeley: Greeley Tribune Press, 1890), a work that is broader than its title indicates, and one that is useful for its contemporary view. Colonization in southern Colorado is treated in Nicholas G. Morgan, "Mormon Colonization in the San Luis Valley," *Colorado Magazine* 27, no. 4 (October 1950):269–93, and Andrew Jenson, "The Founding of Mormon Settlements in the San Luis Valley, Colorado," *Colorado Magazine* 17, no. 5 (September 1940):174–80, both articles by Mormons.

The spread of Colorado's mineral frontier and the development of mining technology are well described by Rodman Paul, *Mining Frontiers of the Far West,* already mentioned. More specific are Jesse D. Hale, "The First Successful Smelter in Colorado," *Colorado Magazine* 13, no. 5 (September 1936):161–67, and James Edward Fell, "The Boston and Colorado Smelting Company: A Study in Western Industrialism" (M.A. thesis, University of Colorado, 1972).

For an appreciation of the social life in these boom towns see Duane A. Smith, *Rocky Mountain Mining Camps: The Urban Frontier* (Bloomington: Indiana

University Press, 1967). Life in one of the towns is the subject of Eugene F. Irey, "A Social History of Leadville, Colorado, During the Boom Days, 1877–1881" (Ph.D. dissertation, University of Minnesota, 1951). Briefer is Carl L. Haase, "Gothic, Colorado: City of Silver Wires," *Colorado Magazine* 51, no. 4 (Fall 1974):294–316. A firsthand account may be read in portions of Eddie Foy and Alvin F. Harlow, *Clowning through Life* (New York: E. P. Dutton, 1928), the memoirs of a well-known nineteenth-century comedian.

Colorado's western slope, frequently neglected by historians, felt the full pressure of settlement in the early 1880s. Several articles describe aspects of this development, among them Walker D. Wyman, "Grand Junction's Year, 1882," *Colorado Magazine* 13, no. 4 (July 1936):127–31, James H. Rankin, "The Founding and Early Years of Grand Junction," *Colorado Magazine* 6, no. 2 (March 1929):39–45, and Lois Borland, "Ho for the Reservation: Settlement of the Western Slope," *Colorado Magazine* 29, no. 1 (January 1952):56–75. "Solving" the Ute problem is the subject of Georgina Norman, "The White Settlement of the Ute Reservation, 1880–1885" (M.A. thesis, University of Colorado, 1957). Focusing more upon the coming of the farmers to the western slope is Mary Rait, "Development of Grand Junction and the Colorado River Valley to Palisade from 1881 to 1931" (M.A. thesis, University of Colorado, 1931).

Southern Colorado's agricultural development is detailed in David William Lantis, "The San Luis Valley, Colorado: Sequent Rural Occupance in an Intermontane Basin" (Ph.D. dissertation, Ohio State University, 1950). A settler's life in eastern Colorado is recalled by M. D. Johnston, "Eastern Colorado Fifty-Seven Years Ago," *Colorado Magazine* 21, no. 3 (May 1944):116–18.

The cattle business, about which so much has been written, became important to the Colorado economy at an early date. For some sample works describing activity in this state see W. M. Pearce, *The Matador Land and Cattle Company* (Norman: University of Oklahoma Press, 1964), Lewis Atherton, *The Cattle Kings* (Bloomington: Indiana University Press, 1961), and Mari Sandoz, *The Cattlemen* (New York: Hastings House, 1958). Dealing more directly with Colorado is Ora B. Peake, *The Colorado Range Cattle Industry* (Glendale: Arthur H. Clark Co., 1937). Gene M. Gressley, *Bankers and Cattlemen* (New York: Alfred A. Knopf, 1966) and W. Turrentine Jackson, *The Enterprising Scot* (Edinburgh: Edinburgh University Press, 1968) are concerned with the financing of the industry.

For a feel of ranch life in early Colorado read S. L. Caldwell, "Ranching on the Colorado Plains Sixty-One Years Ago," *Colorado Magazine* 16, no. 4 (July 1939):148–56; H. C. Cornwall, "Ranching on Ohio Creek, 1881–1886," *Colorado Magazine* 32, no. 1 (January 1955):16–27, and J. W. Neal, "Ranching in Rio Blanca County," *Colorado Magazine* 34, no. 2 (April 1957):108–20.

## Part 3: In Search of Maturity

Nineteenth-century "cultural Colorado" is a rich field for further research. Some good studies have been made by graduate students in theses and dissertations, but until they are published they are available to relatively few readers.

More has been written about higher education than about some of the allied subjects. Michael McGiffert, *The Higher Learning in Colorado: An Historical Study, 1860–1940* (Denver: Sage Books, 1964) is one of the serious efforts to deal with the entire field. Some works deal with specific institutions, such as Charlie Brown Hershey, *Colorado College, 1874–1949* (Colorado Springs: Colorado College, 1952) and William E. Davis, *Glory Colorado! A History of the University of Colorado* (Boulder: Pruett Press, 1965), a somewhat rollicking account. More recent and more concerned with administration as opposed to student life is Frederick S. Allen, et al., *The University of Colorado: 1876–1976* (New York: Harcourt, Brace, Jovanovich, 1976). A brief treatment of early desires for higher education is Stephen Carroll, "Territorial Attempts to Establish a University of Colorado at Boulder," *Red River Valley Historical Review* 1, no. 4 (Winter 1974):351–66.

A good brief account of the regard Coloradans had for books is Malcolm G. Wyer, "Colorado Libraries," in Hafen, *Colorado and Its People,* 2:541–56. Also well worth examining is W. Storrs Lee, ed., *Colorado: A Literary Chronicle* (New York: Funk & Wagnalls, 1970).

Extending the franchise to women is the subject of Billie Barnes Jensen, "The Woman Suffrage Movement in Colorado" (M.A. thesis, University of Colorado, 1959). For published matter see Billie Barnes Jensen, "Let the Women Vote," *Colorado Magazine* 41, no. 1 (Winter 1964):13–25, taken from her thesis. Another brief piece is John R. Morris, "The Women and Governor Waite," *Colorado Magazine* 44, no. 1 (Winter 1967):11–19. More detail may be found in the same author's "Davis Hanson Waite: The Ideology of a Western Populist" (Ph.D. dissertation, University of Colorado, 1965). For more about the role of women see Elinor Bluemel, *One Hundred Years of Colorado Women* (n. p., 1973).

Not only did Colorado women fight for the right to vote, but they were prominent also in the battle against John Barleycorn. Not much has been published on this interesting subject but there is available to scholars William Elliott West, "Dry Crusade: The Prohibition Movement in Colorado, 1858–1933" (Ph.D. dissertation, University of Colorado, 1971), the best thing turned out so far.

Accounts dealing with Colorado's "other people," those not belonging to the dominant Anglo majority, usually are brief and somewhat inconclusive. However, there are some good articles available, among them Roy E. Wortman, "Denver's Anti-Chinese Riot, 1880," *Colorado Magazine* 42, no. 4 (Fall 1965):276–91. The German Russians, about whom much will be written in the near future, are discussed briefly in David J. Miller, "The German-Russians in Colorado," *Colorado Magazine* 21, no. 4 (July 1944):129–32. More may be found in Emma D. Schwabenland, "German Russians on the Volga and in the United States" (M.A. thesis, University of Colorado, 1929) and in Richard Sallet, *Russian-German Settlements in the United States* (Fargo, N.D., 1974). The sad story of some of the Jewish settlers is the subject of Flora Jane Satt, "The Cotopaxi Colony" (M.A. thesis, University of Colorado, 1950), and Dorothy Roberts, "The Jewish Colony at Cotopaxi," *Colorado Magazine* 18, no. 4 (July 1941):124–31. Ida Libert Uchill, *Pioneers, Peddlers and Tsadikim,* mentioned above, treats the Colorado Jewish element more broadly.

The emergence of labor problems in Colorado mining has been dealt with rather extensively by historians. Emma F. Langdon, *The Cripple Creek Strike* (Denver: Great Western Publishing Co., 1904) is one of the old classics. More recent is Charles Merrill Hough, "Leadville, Colorado, 1878 to 1898: A Study in Unionism" (M.A. thesis, Univeristy of Colorado, 1958). Hough's article "Leadville and the Western Federation of Miners," *Colorado Magazine* 49, no. 1 (Winter 1972):19–35, and Paul T. Bechtol, Jr., "The 1880 Labor Dispute in Leadville," ibid., vol. 47, no. 4 (Fall 1970):312–25 are briefer accounts of difficulties in the "Cloud City." David L. Lonsdale, "The Fight for an Eight-Hour Day," *Colorado Magazine* 43, no. 4 (Autumn 1966):339–53 is a distillation of his doctoral dissertation written at the University of Colorado in 1963. A detailed, serious study of labor relations is George G. Suggs, Jr., *Colorado's War on Militant Unionism* (Detroit: Wayne State University Press, 1972), a work that also emerged from the author's "Colorado Conservatives Versus Organized Labor: A Study of the James Hamilton Peabody Administration, 1903–05" (Ph.D. dissertation, University of Colorado, 1964). A rather popularized account, and easy reading, is Stewart H. Holbrook, *The Rocky Mountain Revolution* (New York: Henry Holt and Co., 1956), a work that touches frequently upon the labor turmoil in Colorado mining circles.

The contribution to Colorado society made by the military is touched upon in several articles, but, as yet, no lengthy studies have appeared. Some of the articles available are Robert Pfanner, "Highlights in the History of Fort Logan," *Colorado Magazine* 19, no. 3 (May 1942):81–91; Mrs. C. F. Parker, "Old Julesburg and Fort Sedgwick," ibid., pp. 139–46; Mary C. Ayres, "History of Fort Lewis, Colorado," ibid., vol. 8, no. 3 (May 1931):81–92; and John H. Nankivell, "Fort Crawford," ibid., vol. 11, no. 2 (March 1934):54–64.

Colorado and the Spanish-American War is a subject no one has found sufficiently interesting to write about. Baker and Hafen, *History of Colorado,* vol. 3, give it some attention. A book that does not deal with Colorado specifically, but which contains some very interesting material about the state's contribution to this "splendid little war," is Clifford P. Westermeier, *Who Rush to Glory* (Caldwell, Idaho: Caxton Printers, 1958), which offers an account of Colorado's cowboy warriors.

## Part 4: Colorado in Midpassage

Populism, early twentieth-century reform movements and the influence of progressivism have interested scholars sufficiently to generate some good work in this area of the state's history. James Edward Wright's *The Politics of Populism: Dissent in Colorado* (New Haven: Yale University Press, 1974) is an excellent place to begin reading. John Morris's doctoral dissertation about Davis Hanson Waite, already mentioned, should be looked at in conjunction with the Wright volume.

Municipal reform, so popular around the nation in the early 1900s, was a subject of much concern to the Coloradans. For further reading about it see Roland L. DeLorme, "Turn-of-the-Century Denver: An Invitation to Reform," *Colorado Magazine* 45, no. 1 (Winter 1968):1–15, and J. Paul Mitchell, "Municipal Reform in Denver: The Defeat of Mayor Speer," ibid., pp. 42–60. George Creel's *Rebel at Large* (New York: G. P. Putnam's Sons, 1947) and Ben B. Lindsey and Harvey J. O'Higgins, *The Beast* (New York: Doubleday, Page and Co., 1911) provide some firsthand views. More about Lindsey may be found in Charles Larsen, *The Good Fight: Life and Times of Ben B. Lindsey* (Chicago: Quadrangle Books, 1972). Prison reform is the subject of Arthur Chapman, "A Colorado Prison Reformer: Tom Tynan and His Convict Boys," *Harper's Weekly,* August 2, 1913, pp. 18–19, 22–23. A longer study of the Colorado prison system is found in George Thompson, "The History of Penal Institutions in the Rocky Mountain West, 1864–1900" (Ph.D. dissertation, University of Colorado, 1965).

Outdoor recreation, so popular among Coloradans and their friends who come to visit them, has a long history in the state. However, it was not until the twentieth century that parts of the state became national parks. Edmund B. Rogers, "Notes on the Establishment of Mesa Verde National Park" *Colorado Magazine* 29, no. 1 (January 1952):10–17 and Virginia McClurg, "The Making of Mesa Verde Into a National Park," ibid., vol. 7, no. 6 (November 1930):216–19 tell the early story of one of the parks. For the origins of another see "Guy Elliott Mitchell, "The Rocky Mountain National Park," *Review of Reviews,* July, 1913, pp. 51–55 and Enos A. Mills, *The Story of Estes Park, Grand Lake and Rocky Mountain National Park,* (Estes Park: published by the author, 1905). A brief piece about this park is Merlin K. Potts, "Rocky Mountain National Park," *Colorado Magazine* 42, no. 3 (Summer 1965):217–23.

Forbes Parkhill's colorful study of Denver's demimonde about the turn of the century, *The Wildest of the West* (Denver: Sage Books, 1951), is highly entertaining. Briefer is Fred M. Mazzulla, *Brass Checks and Red Lights* (Denver: published by the author, 1966), an illustrated account of parlor houses and prostitutes.

Arguments over usage of forests and the creation of wilderness areas are covered in Bernard Frank, *Our National Forests* (Norman: University of Oklahoma Press, 1955), particularly in chapters 2 and 3, and in Donald N. Baldwin, "Wilderness: Concept and Challenge," *Colorado Magazine* 44, no. 3 (Summer 1967):224–40.

As is the case with the Spanish-American War, little has been written on Colorado's participation in World War I apart from talk about the numbers who served, war bond drives, and so forth. A refreshing view of life in the state during the time the boys were "over there" is Lyle W. Dorsett, "The Ordeal of Colorado's Germans During World War I," *Colorado Magazine* 51, no. 4 (Fall 1974):277–94.

For Coloradans the years immediately following the close of World War I were flawed by a mixture of economic uncertainty and deep suspicions of each other that grew out of the national "red scare" of that period. A better understanding of the difficulty will be gained by reading Charles Larsen's *The Good Fight,* mentioned above, especially his comments on the "Blue Menace." More general, but essential reading, is Kenneth T. Jackson, *The Ku Klux Klan and the City: 1915–1930* (New York: Oxford University Press, 1967) and David M. Chalmers, *Hooded Americanism: The First Century of the Ku Klux Klan, 1865–1965* (New York: Doubleday and Co., 1965). Philip L. Cook, "Red Scare in Denver," *Colorado Magazine* 43, no. 4 (Fall 1966):309–26, is the best short account in print. Another good article is James H. Davis, "Colorado Under the Klan," *Colorado Magazine* 42, no. 2 (Spring 1965):93–108. More details of the turmoil, particularly in Denver, are in Edward Keating, *The Story of Labor* (Washington, D.C.:

privately printed, 1953) and Bill Hosokawa, *Thunder in the Rockies: The Incredible Denver Post* (New York: William Morrow & Co., 1976).

The search for water was an important part of Colorado's economic efforts during the 1920s. The best of the recent general works on the subject is Norris Hundley, Jr., *Water and the West: The Colorado River Compact and the Politics of Water in the American West* (Berkeley: University of California Press, 1975); see chapter 4. Older but still pertinent is Albert N. Williams, *The Water and the Power: Development of Five Great Rivers of the West* (New York: Duell, Sloan and Pearce, 1951). For more specific information consult Donald Barnard Cole, "Transmontane Water Diversion in Colorado," *Colorado Magazine* 25, no. 2 (March 1948):49–65 and Ralph Carr, "Delph Carpenter and River Compacts Between Western States," ibid., vol. 21, no. 1 (January 1944):5–14.

The search for other natural resources, oil in particular, is generally treated in John Ise, *The United States Oil Policy* (New Haven: Yale University Press, 1926) and in Chris Welles, *The Elusive Bonanza: The Story of Oil Shale, America's Richest and Most Neglected Natural Resource* (New York: E. P. Dutton and Co., 1970). The oil shale excitement of the 1970s generated considerable comment in the periodicals. See, for example, "Shale Oil Rush," *The Economist,* August 15, 1965; Ronald Schiller, "Biggest Buried Treasure on Earth," *Reader's Digest,* September 1971; and "Slowdown on Oil Shale," *The Economist,* November 2, 1974.

Tourism, another promising "industry," continued to be important as the development of the automobile and better highways opened more of Colorado's mountain country to the public. A good brief account is LeRoy R. Hafen, "The Coming of the Automobile and Improved Roads to Colorado," *Colorado Magazine* 8, no. 1 (January 1931):1–16. Air travel, so important to Colorado tourism later, particularly to ski resorts, had slow beginnings. For a discussion of this period read Lee Scamehorn, *Colorado's First Airline,* University of Colorado Studies, Series in History, no. 3 (January 1964) and Ed Mack Miller, "Castor Oil, Kerosene and Contrails," *Colorful Colorado* 1, no. 3 (Winter 1966):24–31, 106–10.

The years of the Great Depression, so critical to the nation, saw great changes in Colorado. Since few books deal with this very extensively, the best source of information is in scattered articles. For example, "Colorado Tries a New Strategy," *Christian Century,* January 28, 1931; Bernard Mergen, "Denver and the War on Unemployment," *Colorado Magazine* 47, no. 4 (Fall 1970):326–37; James F. Wickens, "Tightening the Colorado Purse Strings," *Colorado Magazine* 46, no. 4 (Fall 1969):271–86; and Wickens, "The New Deal in Colorado," *Pacific Historical Review* 38, no. 3 (August 1969):275–91.

More extensive work has been done on Colorado and the New Deal. Ronald S. Brockway, Jr., "Edward P. Costigan: A Study of a Progressive and the New Deal" (Ph.D. dissertation, University of Colorado, 1974), a portrait of a leading Colorado liberal, dovetails state and national politics well. Colorado's role, compared to that of neighboring states, may be found in James T. Patterson, "The New Deal in the West," *Pacific Historical Review* 38, no. 3 (August 1969):317–27. For a contemporary view see Frank Clay Cross, "Revolution in Colorado," *The Nation,* February 7, 1934, pp. 152–53.

Nothing of consequence about Colorado's role in World War II has found its way into print, other than the usual accounts of manpower offerings to the armed forces and bond-raising efforts similar to those of the First World War. Interesting, however, and different, is the story of internees in Colorado, particularly the Japanese. M. Paul Holsinger, "Amache," *Colorado Magazine* 44, no. 1 (Winter 1964):50–60 is the best thing in print on this subject. Colorado author Barron Beshoar provided some assessments of his home state during the war years, such as "When Goodwill is Organized," *Common Ground* 5, no. 3 (1945):19–20, 29, and his earlier "Report from the Mountain States," ibid., vol. 4, no. 3 (1944):23–30. Another well-known Colorado writer, Hal Borland, gave his impressions in "Home Town Makes Good," *New York Times Magazine*, December 26, 1943, p. 13.

## Part 5: Colorado: Cool and Colorful

Several post–World War II national and regional "report" books included chapters on Colorado. John Gunther, *Inside U.S.A.* (New York: Harper and Brothers, 1947) was first, followed by Neil Morgan, *Westward Tilt: The American West Today* (New York: Random House, 1961) and Neal R. Peirce, *The Mountain States of America* (New York: W. W. Norton, 1972). In general they provide brief summaries of the state's past followed by descriptions of existing conditions, frequently based upon interviews with leading political and business figures. While they became outdated quickly, nevertheless they offer insights into Colorado's progress and problems at intervals of about ten years each after the war.

In the early postwar years national magazines gave attention to Colorado's economic resurgence and changes that took place in the capital city, Denver; specific references to these are found in the notes to chapter 16. A good deal of interesting information on the subject may be had by reading William Zeckendorf (with Edward McCreary), *The Autobiography of William Zeckendorf* (New York: Holt, Rinehart and Winston, 1970), whose flamboyant financial "prospecting" in Colorado drew wide attention. Changes in old patterns, such as the face-lifting given the *Denver Post* with the acquisition of Palmer Hoyt, are to be found in A. Gayle Waldrop, "A Chinook Blows on Champa Street," *Journalism Quarterly*, June 1947, pp. 109–15 and Roscoe Fleming, "Revolution in Denver," *Nation*, June 29, 1946, pp. 180–81. Political changes were described by Carey McWilliams in "Bright Spot in the West," ibid., June 14, 1947, pp. 709–10, and in Gunther's *Inside U.S.A.*, pp. 223–26. An "inside view" of Denver politics, written in an engaging manner, is George V. Kelly, *The Old Gray Mayors of Denver* (Boulder: Pruett Publishing Co., 1974).

An interesting, and at the time a controversial, antigrowth article is Walter Prescott Webb, "The American West: Perpetual Mirage," *Harper's*, May 1957, pp. 25–31; its references to Colorado had local editors and chambers of commerce up in arms. Companion reading to the Webb article is Bernard De Voto, "The West Against Itself," ibid., January 1947, pp. 1–13.

Colorado's postwar political history has been followed by such people as Professor Curtis Martin of the University of Colorado. Two of his articles of particular interest are "1956 Election in Colorado," *Western Political Science Quarterly* 10 (March 1957):117–21 and "Political Behavior in Colorado,"

*Colorado Quarterly* 6 (Summer 1957):63–78. A good study of a well-known political figure is Patrick F. McCarty, "Big Ed Johnson of Colorado—A Political Portrait" (M.A. thesis, University of Colorado, 1958).

Life in Aspen, the recreational and cultural center, has been followed closely by journalists, and there are a number of contemporary articles about it (see the notes to chapter 17). In a book-length effort Sidney Hyman, *The Aspen Idea* (Norman: University of Oklahoma Press, 1975) described the efforts of Walter Paepcke.

Numerous articles about Colorado's growth problems have appeared in national opinion magazines, probably the best of them being Hugh Gardner, "Goodbye, Colorado: The Transformation from Dreamland to Nightmare," *Harper's*, April 1974, pp. 14–23. Lois Phillips Hudson, "Battle in the Wilderness," *Nation*, April 4, 1966, pp. 393–96 discussed the growing concern of Coloradans over land use during post–World War II years. The well-known journalist and television personality Eric Severeid gave his opinion in "Why the Aspens Quake," *Saturday Review*, October 20, 1962, pp. 45–46. The environmentalists' view was set forth by Toba J. Cohen, "Colorado's New Governor Wages a War for Ecological Survival," *Today's Health*, October 1975, pp. 22–25. James Michener's "Colorado" in *Business Week*, February 23, 1976, a special advertising section, described the attractions of Colorado to prospective latter-day settlers.

# Index


Adams, Alva, 205, 286, 291
Adams, James Barton: poem by, 217
Adams, William H. ("Billy"), 245, 271–72, 275, 277
Adams State College, 283
Adriance, Jacob, 49
agriculture, 106–27 passim, 136, 137–42, 180–84, 189, 199, 200, 204, 234, 286, 287, 290, 340, 356; early efforts at, 3, 77, 90, 92, 106–9, 173, 177; Great Depression influences, 273, 282; in 1920s, 251–53; sugar beets, 272; suitcase farmers, 252; World War II, 295, 296, 299, 300. *See also* colonies
Aircraft Mechanics, Inc., 296
Airlie, Earl of, 144
air travel: early flights at Denver, 264–65; passenger service established, 291
Akron, 167
Alamosa, 294; Dutch colonists at, 203
Albuquerque, N. Mex., 291
Alder Gulch, Mont., 69
Alexander Airport, Colorado Springs, 266
Allen's Park, 288
Allott, Gordon, 330, 360
Alma, 132
Amache. *See* Japanese Relocation Center
American Crystal Sugar Company, 299, 319
American Legion, 300, 303; of Denver, 241
American Protective Association, 197
American Smelting & Refining Company, 132
American Youth for Democracy, 328
Amity Land and Irrigation Company, 199
Ammons, Teller, 278
Anderson, Robert O., 354
Animas City, 138
Anthony, Susan B., 163
Anti-Saloon League, 229
anti-Semitism, 27. *See also* Jews
Antonito, 176
Apollo Hall, 36, 42
Arapahoe County, 20
Arapahoe Indians, 3, 23, 35, 72, 76
architecture: attempts to copy East, 30; Denver homes, 224, 310
Arizona, 71, 234, 286, 363; growth compared to Colorado's, 269
Arkansas River, 67, 73, 121, 134, 181, 199, 201, 254, 289
Arkansas Valley, 109, 141, 167, 181
Armour, Charles Lee, 58
Arnett, R. E., 160
Ashland Oil, Inc. *See* oil
Ashley, William H., 2
Aspen, 135, 269, 325, 334–37, 351, 354, 358
Aspen Institute for Humanistic Studies, 337, 354
Aspen Ski Corporation, 325
*Aspen Union Era*, 167
Aspinall, Wayne, 359
Associated Cycle Club, 207
Atchison, Topeka & Santa Fe Railroad, 134, 135, 167
*Atlantic Monthly*, 276–77
Atlantic Richfield Oil Company. *See* oil
Atomic Energy Commission, Rocky Flats Plant, 320, 351
Atwood colony, 204–5
Auraria, 20, 31
Auraria-Denver, 33, 49, 56; declining business activity, 22; early business district, 23, 24
Autobees, Charles, 3
automobile: influence on tourism, 256

Bailey, Dewey C., 254
Ball Brothers Research Corporation, 321
Bank of England, 88
Bannack, Mont., 69
Baptists, 154
Barney, Libeus, 29, 35, 36
Barnum, P. T., 93
Barry, Joe, 250
baseball, 209; in early Denver, 43
Bean, Geraldine, 360
Bear Creek Valley, 109
Beaver Creek, 109
Beckwourth, Jim, 29
Beech Aircraft Company, 320
Beecher's Island, battle at, 76
Beeger, Hermann, 129
Belt, W. M., 27
Benevolent and Protective Order of Elks, Leadville, 133
Bent, George, 72, 74

Bent, William, 3, 74
Bent's Fort, 2, 3, 8
Berthoud Pass, 261
Beshoar, Michael, 45
bicycling, 207
Big Sandy Creek, 10
Big Thompson Project. *See* Colorado–Big Thompson Project
Bijou Canal, 140
Black Hawk, 55, 70, 117, 129
Black Kettle, 74, 76
blacks. *See* Negroes
Blake, Charles, 41
Blake, Mary, 186
Bliss, Edward, 87–88
Blue River, 70, 134
Boeing Air Transport Company, 266
Bonfils, Frederick G., 270, 280, 314; and *Denver Post,* 169; interest in colony, 253
Borland, Hal, 302
Bosetti, Joseph J., 333
Boston, Mass., 89, 153, 154
Boston and Colorado Smelter, 129
Boulder, 59, 100, 107, 150, 151, 155, 172, 236, 243, 244, 247, 260, 273, 279, 283, 286, 296, 303, 310, 320, 321, 328, 333, 341, 343, 345, 351, 366; Colorado Chautauqua at, 232; in depression, 281; oil at, 257; press of, 45
Boulder Creek, 13, 70
Boulder Valley, 116
Bowles, Samuel, 175, 232; on agriculture, 108, 109; on Colorado's prospects, 82, 83, 84, 85; on Indians, 178; on Mexican Americans, 176
boxing: in early Denver, 44
Boyd, David, 115, 117, 118
Bradford, R. R., 24, 25
Brand, Vance, 343
Braniff, T. E.: plans airline, 304
Breckenridge, 40, 269, 354
Bridger, Jim, 2
Bridges, Harry, 303
British and Colorado Mining Bureau, 88
Broadmoor Hotel, Colorado Springs, 289
Broadwell Hotel, Denver, 24, 42
Brown, Abner R., 53
Brown, George, 361
Brown, John L., 4
Brown, Sam, 362
Brown Palace Hotel, Denver, 189
Brown University, 129
Brush, 144, 204
Brush, Jared L., 143
Buckley Field, 297
Buckskin Joe, 71, 85
Buena Vista, 206
"bum blockade," 280, 281
Bureau of Reclamation, 295
Burlington, 116, 117, 155, 180
Byers, William, 12, 15, 35, 36, 39, 43, 45, 55, 58, 68, 70, 73, 82, 87, 95, 109, 110, 114, 116, 117, 120, 157, 158, 161, 162. *See also Rocky Mountain News*

Cache la Poudre Valley, 113
Calahan, Mike, 258
California, 4, 10, 18, 32, 57, 61, 179, 200, 228, 286, 300, 331, 355, 356, 362, 363; growth compared to Colorado's, 269
California Gulch, 35, 71, 130
California Trail, 78
Cameron, Robert A., 113, 120
Camp Carson, 297, 298
Camp Collins, 208
Camp Hale, 301, 325
Camp Weld, 68
Canada: Fifty-Niners from, 17
Canon City, 58, 111, 112, 181, 205, 206, 220; oil at, 256, 257; penitentiary at, 59
Cantrell, John, 7
capital punishment, 205, 206
Carhart, Arthur H., 233
Caribou, 179
Carlino, Pete, 250
Carpenter, Delph, 255, 256
Carpenter, Malcolm Scott, 343
Carr, Ralph, 298, 322
Carroll, John A., 331; in Congress, 314–18; defeated, 330
Castello, Dan, 44
Caston, Saul, 332
Catholic Club, Young Men's, 150
Catholics, 49, 51, 52, 115, 197, 198, 240, 241, 243, 244, 245, 246, 247, 248, 270, 271, 280, 331, 333; anti-Mormon, 123; attitudes toward, 104, 163, 164; clubs of, 150; and higher education, 154; and Mexican Americans, 173; in territorial era, 48; on proposed constitution, 103. *See also* religion
Catholic Library Association, 150
cattle industry, 143–46, 233; Jews in, 183; in World War II, 304
"Centennial State": term suggested, 105; term used, 212, 216, 237
Central City, 58, 70, 84, 100, 150, 319, 333, 336, 358; branch mint at, 30; early theater in, 43; low crime rate, 57; post–World War II, 323; press of, 45; religion in, 49, 51; schools in, 54; theater at, 158
Cervi, Gene, 315
Chaffee, Jerome B., 81, 82; "elected" senator, 79; elected to Senate, 105
Challenger Airlines. *See* Frontier Airlines
Chapman, Arthur, 224
Charles River, 109
Charpiot, Frederick J.: and restaurant, 89

Chávez, Dennis, 301
Chávez, Salvador, 123
Chenowith, J. Edgar, 294
Cherokee Trail, 8
Cherry Creek, 13, 20, 21, 24, 31, 52, 65, 78, 82, 109; gold discovery at, 7; settlement at, 20
*Cherry Creek Pioneer*, 45
Cherry Tree Home, Fort Amity, 200
Cheyenne, Wyo., 78, 79, 229, 265, 266, 291
Cheyenne Indians, 3, 23, 72, 73, 114
Cheyennes, Southern, 73–75, 76, 299
Chicago, Ill., 116, 134, 325, 336, 345; colony from, 111, 199
Chicago, Burlington & Quincy Railroad, 140
Chicago-Colorado Colony, 116, 117
Chicago, Rock Island and Pacific Railroad, 140
Chicano movement, 339–40
Chinese, 175, 178; anti-Chinese riots, 179
Chinese Exclusion Act, 179
Chivington, John M.: as officer of volunteers, 67; as religious leader, 50; at Sand Creek, 74, 75
Chrysler, Walter, 256
Churchill, Mrs. C. M., 163
Church of Jesus Christ of Latter-Day Saints, 125. *See also* Mormons
Cibola Hall, 41
Cibola Minstrels, 41
circuses, 44
Civil War, 38, 45, 58, 60, 65, 67, 68, 71, 82, 108
Civilian Conservation Corps, 282, 332
Clark, Gruber and Company, 30
Clark, Max, 185
Clear Creek, 34, 232; agriculture along, 107; strikes on, 13, 22, 70
Cleveland, Grover, 169
Cliff Palace. *See* Mesa Verde
climate, 108; early praise of, 25, 92, 93, 95, 228
coal, 192, 195, 196–97, 226, 234, 274–75, 321, 322; strip mining of, 364, 366
Colfax, 112
Colfax, Schuyler, 76, 111
Collyer, Robert, 116
Colona (proposed territorial name), 66
colonies: Atwood, 204–5; Chicago-Colorado (Longmont), 116, 117; Colfax, 112; Corona, 119; Covered Wagon, 253; Cotopaxi, 181, 184; Dearfield, 172; Fort Amity, 141, 198, 201, 205; Fort Collins Agricultural Colony, 120; Fountain Colony, 90, 120; Georgia Colony, 120; Great Divide Colony, 253; Green City (Southwestern), 119; Mormon colonies, 123, 124, 138; Pinon, 202; Platteville, 120; Ryssby settlement, 117, 118; St. Louis–Western colony, 118; Union Colony (Greeley), 115, 117. *See also* agriculture; Dutch immigrants
Colorado Agricultural College. *See* Colorado State University
Colorado Airways, Inc., 265, 266
Colorado Association of Commerce and Industry, 361
Colorado–Big Thompson Project, 254, 285, 286, 312, 350
Colorado Central Railroad, 78, 134
Colorado Chautauqua, Boulder, 232
*Colorado Chieftain* (Pueblo), 112, 174, 272; founded, 45; on women's suffrage, 163
Colorado City, 71, 107; as capital, 66; decline of, 85, 90; founded, 35
Colorado Coal & Iron Company. *See* Colorado Fuel & Iron Company
Colorado Coalition, 342
Colorado College, 153, 157, 283, 310, 333
Colorado Committee for Environmental Information, 351, 352
Colorado Cooperative Company, 201
Colorado Federation of Women's Clubs, 222
Colorado Fuel Company. *See* Colorado Fuel & Iron Company
Colorado Fuel & Iron Company, 189, 195, 196, 274; post–World War II development of, 319
Colorado Grange, 160
Colorado Midland Railroad Company, 135
Colorado Mining Association, 294
Colorado Mountain Club, 348
Colorado River, 138
Colorado River Conference and Compact (1922), 255–56
Colorado School of Mines, 156
Colorado Seminary, 50, 153. *See also* University of Denver
Colorado Springs, 97, 98, 140, 150, 153, 154, 158, 168, 184, 207, 265, 266, 274, 282, 297, 298, 305, 319, 328; beginnings of, 90, 96; during depression, 275, 281; health resort, 95; promotional efforts by, 288; in World War II, 302; at turn of century, 224, 225
Colorado Springs *Gazette*, 98, 102, 103
Colorado Springs Town Company, 96
Colorado State College of Education. *See* University of Northern Colorado
Colorado State Historical Society, 152
Colorado State Teachers College. *See* University of Northern Colorado
Colorado State University, 155, 156
Colorado Stock Growers Association, 144, 304
Colorado Territory: created, 65
*Colorado Transcript* (Golden), 45, 103
Colorado Volunteers, 66

Colorado Women's College, 154
Comanche Indians, 3
Committee for the Survival of a Free Congress, 368
Communists, 279, 303, 328, 329. *See also* "red menace"
Conejos, 52, 122, 123
Confederate invasion of New Mexico, 67
Conger, Samuel P., 234
Congregationalists: and Colorado College, 153
Conner, Daniel, 36, 40
Continental Airlines, 304
Continental Can Company, 296
Cook, Dave, 144
Coors Brewing Company, 319, 363
copper, 234, 270, 294
Corona, 119
Coronado, Francisco Vásquez de, 1
Cornwall, Harry, 146
Costigan, Edward P., 272, 279
Cotopaxi, 181, 184, 204
courts. *See* law and order
Covered Wagon Colony, 253
Craig, 253, 256, 290
Crawford, Emmet, 137
Crawford, William, 49
Creede, 59, 189, 346; newspaper, 168
Creel, George, 248
Cricket Hall, 43
Cripple Creek, 197, 294, 346; gold at, 190, 191; at turn of century, 225, 227; 1896 strike, 196
Criterion music hall, 36
Crofutt, George A., 101
Crook, 203, 204
Crusade for Justice, 342
Crystal River Valley, 355
Cummings, Alexander, 102; on black franchise, 80; as governor, 77, 79; interest in oil, 257
Curtis, Erland L., 264–65
Curtis, S. R., 74
Custer, George A., 76

Davis, Carlyle Channing, 168
*Dawn*, 276
Day, David F., 168
Deadwood Gulch, 13
Dearfield Colony, 172
DeBeque, 257
Deer Park Canyon, 288
Delano, Frederick A., 286
Delmonico's of the West. *See* Charpiot, F. J.
Del Norte, 141; newspaper at, 167
Delta, 138, 302
Dempsey, Jack, 242
Dempsey, John (father of Jack), 124
Denver, 19, 20, 33, 35, 38, 41, 43, 44, 45, 53, 67, 71, 73, 74, 75, 76, 77, 78, 83, 84, 89, 90, 94, 97, 100, 101, 103, 104, 105, 108, 113, 114, 119, 120, 137, 140, 143, 150, 152, 154, 157, 164, 167, 169, 171, 172, 174, 179, 180, 185, 189, 190, 193, 195, 197, 205, 207, 208, 210, 215, 216, 219, 221, 223, 224, 227, 228, 229, 231, 236, 241, 248, 250, 251, 253, 260, 262, 265, 273, 274, 285, 286, 288, 290, 300, 304, 309, 310, 311, 312, 313, 314, 315, 318, 319, 328, 332, 333, 337, 341, 343, 345, 351, 356, 358, 359, 368; air travel to, 291; business decline at, 31; as capital, 66; during Civil War, 67, 68; concern about Montana gold fields, 69; during depression, 275, 276; early night life, 36; early settlement of, 7; fire and flood in, 30, 82; future of, 15, 26; home rule for, 218; newspapers of, 169; Opportunity School at, 283; parks of, 230, 260; police scandal in, 338; possible railroad terminus, 25; propaganda from, 16; rivalry with Auraria, 30; schools in, 55; in World War II, 296, 297; post–World War II, 309, 310, 311
Denver, James W., 20
Denver, John, 367
Denver and Auraria Library and Reading Room Association, 151
Denver-Auraria. *See* Auraria-Denver
Denver and Rio Grande Railway, 98, 101, 121, 122, 124, 134, 135, 138, 182, 183, 203, 280, 290, 291, 324; origins, 90, 95, 97; reading rooms of, 150
Denver and Salt Lake Railroad, 253, 255, 290
Denver Board of Trade, 88
Denver Broncos, 345–46
Denver Club, 223
*Denver Daily Times*, 169
Denver *Democrat*, 169
*Denver Evening Post. See Denver Post*
Denver General Hospital, 316
Denver Guards, 67
Denver Hall, 41
Denver Library Association, 151
Denver Medical Association, 27. *See also* Jefferson Medical Society
Denver Northwestern and Pacific Railroad. *See* Denver and Salt Lake Railroad
Denver Olympics Committee, 357–60 passim
Denver Ordnance Plant. *See* Remington Arms Company
Denver Pacific Railroad, 78, 79, 113, 114, 116
*Denver Post*, 216, 218, 240, 241, 243, 251,

267, 269, 270, 271, 272, 300, 303, 316, 321, 322, 333, 358; founded, 169; post–World War II changes, 314
Denver Public Library, 151, 152
Denver *Republican*, 169
Denver, South Park and Pacific Railroad, 135
*Denver Times*, 105
Denver *Tribune*, 169
*Deseret News* (Salt Lake City), 124
De Voto, Bernard, 363; on resources, 322
Dewey, Thomas E., 303, 317
Dillon Reservoir, 353
Dominick, Peter, 361
Dotsero Cutoff, 291
Dougherty, Michael J., 43
Dow, Justin E., 155
Dow Chemical Company, 320, 350. *See also* Atomic Energy Commission
Doyle, Arthur Conan, 262
Durango, 134, 138, 168, 195, 208, 209, 283, 293, 301, 343; tourism in, 324
Dutch immigrants, 202–4

Eagle River, 134
Eagles Nest Primitive Area, 350
Eastman Kodak Company, 320, 352
Eaton Metal Products Company, 296
Ebert, Frederick J., 232
education, 52, 53, 55; by churchmen, 51; Colorado Seminary (University of Denver) founded, 50; higher, 153–57 passim, 343, 344; post–World War II, 312, 313; school lands in San Luis Valley, 124; schools at Ryssby settlement, 111
Eisenhower, Dwight D., 318, 326, 330
Eisenhower Tunnel, 352
Elbert, Mount, 130
Elbert, Samuel H., 79
Empire Land and Canal Company, 203
Empire Zinc Company, 294
England, 88, 96, 190; and Colorado, 201, 202
entertainment: in Denver, 40; movie houses, 227, 272; music among Fifty-Niners, 34
environmental concerns, 327, 328, 336, 348–64 passim
Environmental Information Committee. *See* Colorado Committee for Environmental Information
Ephraim (Mormon colony), 124
Episcopalians, 156
Equitable Building, Denver, 189
Esquire-Coronet Company, 320
Estes Park, 230, 231, 264, 288
Evans, 79, 113, 118, 120
Evans, John, 78, 81, 82, 135, 154, 161, 290; railroad president, 78, 79; territorial governor, 59; and University of Denver, 153

Fairplay, 71
Fashion Saloon, 30
Federal Bureau of Investigation, 329, 330
Ferril, Thomas Hornsby, 323
Field, Marshall, 131
Fifty-Niners, 87, 92, 100, 106, 107, 109, 152, 187, 364, 368; attracted to Rockies, 8, 10; composition of, 26; discouragement of, 16; efforts at intellectual improvement, 48; second wave of, 23; trail life of, 10–12; types of, 19
Fine, Louis, 204
First Colorado Regiment, in Spanish American War, 211–12
First National Bank of Denver, 31, 79, 318
Fisher, George W., 50
Fitzsimons Hospital, 297
Flagler, 302
Flattops Primitive Area, 348
Florence, 257, 266
Ford, Barney, 28
Ford, Gerald R., 326
Forest, Elsa Jane ("Charley"), 35
forest reserves, White River, 233
Fort Amity, 141, 188–201, 205
Fort Collins, 100, 156, 256, 285, 286, 310, 322, 347, 356
Fort Collins Agricultural Colony, 120
Fort Lewis College, 283
Fort Lyon Canal, 141
Fort Morgan, 249, 296
Fort Morgan Canal, 141, 204
forts: Bent's, 2, 3, 8; Carson, 297, 305; Crawford, 137, 208; Davy Crockett, 3; Garland, 4, 60, 67, 121, 122, 208; Jackson, 2; Lewis, 138, 208; Logan, 208, 297; Lupton, 2; Lyon, 74, 208; Massachusetts, 4, 60, 174; Reynolds, 208; Roubidoux, 3; Sedgwick, 208; St. Vrain, 2; Vasquez, 2; Wallace, 111; Wise, 3, 67
Fort Wise Treaty, 73
Forty-Niners, 8
Fossett, Frank, 105, 143
Fountain Colony, 90, 120
Fountain Creek, 107
Fountain Valley, 109
Four Corners area, 321
Foy, Eddie, 131
Francis, William, 244
Francisco, J. M., 174
Fraser River, 254
Frémont, John C., 2
Frontier Airlines, 304
Fruita, 341
fur traders, 2
Future Farmers of America, 300

gambling, 41, 48, 138, 225, 229

gangsters, 250
Garland, Hamlin, 262
Garland City, 135
gas, natural, 274, 321, 360–61, 364. *See also* Project Rio Blanco; Project Rulison
Gates, Charles, 319
Gates, John, 319
Gates Rubber Company, 296, 319
Gay, Sidney H., 116
General Assembly, 37, 58, 155, 156, 162, 164, 165, 169, 196, 205, 235, 285, 300, 302, 315, 342, 356; Board of Immigration, 91; charters college, 153; during depression, 277, 278; first session of, 66; flood control actions of, 254; resolution on Sand Creek, 75
Georgetown, 84, 88
Georgia, 4, 7, 13, 18, 21, 120, 130
"Georgia Colony," 120
German Americans, 236
German colonists, 111–13
German Colonization Company, 111, 113
German Russians: religion of, 51; role of, 180, 181; as sugar beet raisers, 340
Gibson, Thomas, 45
Gilman, 294
Gilpin, William, 66; arrives Colorado, 65; establishes judicial districts, 58; removed, 68; and Volunteers, 67
Gilpin census (1860), 28
Gilpin County, 134
Gilpin drafts, 67, 68, 76
Gilpin's Pet Lambs, 67
Glenwood Springs, 93, 293, 294, 299
Glorieta Pass, battle of, 67, 68
go-backers, 12, 13, 16, 22, 92, 115, 190
Goethe Bicentennial, Aspen, 334
gold, 2, 4, 7–19 passim, 23, 30–31, 32, 69–71, 108, 129–30, 141, 170, 190–91, 226, 234, 270, 294
Golden, 31, 70, 78, 206, 319, 320; as capital, 66; oil near, 256; press of, 45; school at, 51, 53, 55
Golden, Tom, 31
Golden Fleece Mine, 129, 139
Gold Hill, 70
Goldrick, O. J.: journalist, 53, 169; schoolmaster, 52
Gold Run, 13
Gonzales, Rodolfo ("Corky"), 339, 340, 342
Goode, H. W., 49
Goodman, Irving, 329
Goodnight, Charles, 143
Good Roads Association, 259
Gore Range, 350. *See also* Eagles Nest Primitive Area
Gothic (city), 134, 178, 179
Governor's Guard, 158; library of, 151
Graham, Hiram J., 66
Granada, 298, 299
Grand Junction, 135, 167, 283, 286, 350, 351; air service to, 304; platted, 138; tourism in, 323
Grand Lake, 264, 285, 286; diversion from 254
Grand River. *See* Colorado River
Grand Valley, 138, 234, 340
Grant, James B., 131
Grant, Ulysses S, 102, 104, 105
Great American Desert, 2, 10, 17, 60, 92, 106, 107, 108, 116, 198, 200, 277, 298
Great Depression, 267, 271–76 passim, 290, 297
*Great Divide, The*, 253
Great Divide colony, 253
Great Western Sugar Company, 295
Greeley, 97, 113, 114, 116–19, 120, 204, 298, 299; newspaper at, 168; as temperance town, 159
Greeley, Horace, 114, 232; on agriculture, 106; trip to Colorado, 14, 15, 72
Green City colony, 119
Green, David S., 119
Greenhorn Creek, 3
Green River, 3
Gregory Gulch (Gregory Diggings), 14, 16, 50
Gregory, John H., 13, 16, 22
Griffenhagen Report, 278
Griffith, Emily, 283
Guadalupe colony, 113
Guggenheim, Meyer, 132
guidebooks, 12
Gunnison, 135, 156, 350
Gunnison, John, 2
Gunnison area, 137, 146, 186, 295
Gunnison River, 138
Gunther, John, 315, 363

Hagerman, James John, 94, 135
Haggard, H. Rider, 201
Hall, Benjamin F., 58
Hall, Frank, 92, 114, 177
Hallett, Moses, 58
Hamilton, 50, 71, 85
Hardin, William J., 28, 80
Hardscrabble Creek, 3, 109
Harrison Hook and Ladder Company, Leadville, 132
Hart, Gary, 361, 367
Haskell, Floyd, 360
Hawken, Sam, 15, 16, 18
Hawkins, David, 328, 329
Hawley-Smoot Tariff, 272
Hayden, Ferdinand V., 128
Hayes, Rutherford B., 105

Head, Lafayette, 105
health seekers, 93–95, 225
Hebrew Immigrant Aid Society, 181, 182
Henry, T. C., 141, 204
Herrick, Charles E., 286
Hewes, Charles Edwin, 243
Hewlett-Packard Company, 320
High Line Canal, 140
Hill, Mrs. Crawford, 223
Hill, Nathaniel P., 129
Hilton Hotel, Denver, 318
hippies, 350–51
Historical Preservation Commission of Telluride. *See* Telluride
historic preservation, in Colorado cities, 358, 359
Hobbs, George A., 115
Hoggatt, Volney T., 253
Holladay Overland Mail and Express Company, 79
Holland American Land and Immigration Company, 202, 203
Holliday, John Henry ("Doc"), 93
Hollister, Ovando, 15, 38, 39
Holly, 201
Holmes, Julia Archibald, 35
Holyoke, 249
Homestead Act, 107, 112
Hoover, Herbert, 271, 291; and Colorado River Compact, 255; election of, 267, 269
Hopkins, Harry, 278, 279
horseracing, 44, 209
Hotchkiss, 139
Hotchkiss, Enos, 129, 139
hotels, 24, 289, 309; Broadmoor, 289; Broadwell, 24, 42; Denver Hilton, 318; at Estes Park, 230; at Georgetown, 84, 100; H. Greeley on, 21
Hot Sulphur Springs, 95, 288, 324
Howbert, Irving, 107, 158, 194
Howelson, Carl, 324
Hoyt, E. Palmer, 314, 337
Huerfano River, 106, 107
Huerfano Valley, 110
Hughes, Bela M., 78, 79
Hugo, 145
Hunt, Alexander C., 76, 122

Idaho, 81; name proposed for Colorado, 66
Idaho Springs, 13, 96, 173, 261
Ideal Cement Company, 319
Iles Dome, 256
Illinois, 11, 102, 116, 120; colonists from, 199; Fifty-Niners from, 17
Immigration, Board of, 91
Immigration, Denver Board of, 100
Indiana, 107; colonists from, 199; Fifty-Niners from, 17
Indians: attacks by, 24, 72, 76; attitudes toward, 94, 177, 178; passing of, 223, 224, relations with whites, 3, 69, 108, 121, 136, 208, 301; views of Fifty-Niners, 72, 73; warfare, 73–75
Indian Territory, 76
Independence Pass, 254
Ingersoll, Ernest, 101, 176, 178
International Business Machines Company, 320
Irish Americans, 17, 180
irrigation, 140–41, 202, 203, 233, 251, 253, 286, 364
Irwin, 134
Irwin, D. W., 167
Italian Americans, 179, 250
Izaak Walton League, 348

Jack, Ellen E., 185
Jackson, George A., 13, 16
Jackson, Helen Hunt, 94, 135, 177, 184
Jackson, O. T., 172
Jackson, William, 101, 128, 232
Jackson Diggings, 13
Jácquez, José María, 113
jails, 59. *See also* penitentiary
Japanese Americans, 178, 296, 298–99, 301, 314; post–World War II role of, 300; sugar beet workers, 340; World War II role of, 298–300
Japanese Relocation Center, 298–99
Jarvis Hall, 55, 156
Jefferson, 36, 71
Jefferson, Thomas, 1, 4
Jefferson House, 24, 36
Jefferson Medical Society, 26
Jefferson Rangers, 67
Jefferson State (proposed), 66
Jefferson Territory, 1, 66, 67; unites Auraria and Denver, 31
Jensen, Hans, 123, 124
Jesuits, 154
Jews, 138, 204, 241, 244, 245, 246, 247; as colonists, 181, 182, 204, 205; among Fifty-Niners, 27; as merchants, 29
Jicarilla Apaches, 3
Johnson, Andrew, 81, 82
Johnson, Arthur C., 271, 273
Johnson, Byron, 331
Johnson, Edwin C., 281, 291, 292, 331, 332; as governor, 277, 278, 279; as senator, 287, 317
Johnson, Irving P., 242
Johnson, James, P., 359
Johnson, Lyndon B., 342; Wilderness Bill (1964), 233
Johnson, Walter W., 330
Jones Pass, 254

journalism, 56, 98, 100, 101, 166, 167, 168, 169, 220, 248, 287, 314, 315; early role of, 44–46; in politics, 102–3, 163, 169, 194. *See also names of individual communities, editors, and newspapers*
Judd, Morris, 329
Julesburg, 75

Kaiser, Henry J., 296
Kansas, 7, 17, 23, 65, 78, 111, 131, 141
Kansas City, Mo., 8, 78
Kansas Pacific Railway, 78, 90, 111
Keating, Edward, 228, 229
Kehler, John, 51
Kingsley, Charles, 98, 168
Kingsley, Rose, 98, 168
Kiowa Apaches, 3
Knight, John H., 235
Knights of Labor, 194; library of, 150
Knous, W. Lee, 315
Kokomo, 134
Kroenig, William, 107
Ku Klux Klan, 243–48 passim, 279, 300

labor, 241, 242–43; eight-hour day, 195; Labor Peace Act, 303; post–World War II, 319–20; strife in mining camps, 191–97, 234; trade unions, 194
La Jara, 124
La Junta, 283, 287, 298, 299
Lake City, 129, 139, 186, 196
*Lake City Silver World,* 166
Lake County, 130
Lamar, 167, 283, 299
Lamar, L. Q. C., 167
Lambert, J. J., 45
Lamm, Richard, 361–63, 364, 366–67
Lamy, Jean Baptiste, 52
land use, 348–70 passim
Land Use Act (1970), 357
Langrishe, John, 43, 158
La Plata River, 255
La Porte, 120
La Raza Unida, 342
Laramie and Fort Bridger stage route, 71
Larimer, General William, 20, 21, 24, 41
Larimer and Weld Canal, 140
Larimer Street, Denver, 37, 51
La Salle, 180
Last Chance Gulch, Mont., 69
La Veta Pass, 134
law and order, 217, 337–38; in early Colorado, 29, 34; early courts, 47, 57–59; and prohibition, 250–51
Lawrence, Kans., 14, 20
lead, 234, 270, 294
Leadville, 92, 100, 128, 130–35, 168, 178, 191, 193, 269, 301, 325; 1880 strike at, 192; theater at, 158; World War II role, 294
Leavenworth, Kans., 10, 13, 41
Leavenworth and Pike's Peak Express Company, 10
Leavenworth City, St. Joseph and Pike's Peak Railroad, 37
Lee, Abe, 130
Left Hand, and Arapahoe Indians, 74
legislature. *See* General Assembly
Lewis and Clark Expedition, 2
libraries: early efforts for, 56; private, 149–51; public 152
*Life* magazine, 311
Liller, J. E., 98, 168
Limon, 217
Lincoln, Abraham, 29, 58, 78, 332
Lincoln Land Company, 167
Lindsey, Ben B., 216, 227–28, 229, 248
Locke, John Galen, 245, 246
Logan, Samuel M., 66
London, England, 88, 97, 130
Londonér, Wolfe, 130, 167
Long, Stephen H., 2
Longmont, 120, 155, 230, 297, 343; founded, 116–17; newspaper at, 168; social control, 159
Long's Peak, 116, 231
Loretto Heights College, 154
Louisiana Purchase, 1, 2, 33
Love, John, 352, 355, 358, 361
Loveland, 180, 284
Loveland, W. A. H., 78, 257
Loveland and Greeley Canal, 140
Loving, Oliver, 143
Lowry Field, 297
Ludlow massacre, 196, 197
lynchings. *See* law and order
Lyons, 231

McBride, Sam, 112
McCarthyism, 329. *See also* "red menace"
McCook, Edward M., 102, 161, 162
McCourt, "Baby Doe." *See* Tabor, "Baby Doe"
McDonough, William, 44
McGovern, George, 361
Machebeuf, Joseph P., 52, 103, 154, 163
Macky, A. J., 155
McIntire, Albert, 197, 210
McNichols, Stephen L. R., 331, 338, 343
McNichols, William, 358
McMurtry, J. S., 201
Magnifico, Mike, 325
Manassa, 123–24
Mancos, 138, 222
Manitou Springs, 95, 96
Marble, 355

Marshall, Robert B., 231
Marshall Pass, 134
Martin-Marietta Company, 318
Massachusetts, 37, 49, 82, 116, 137
Massive, Mount, 130
Masters, 119
Matthews Hall, 51
May, David, 131
May D & F Company, Denver, 318
Mears, Otto, 138, 167
medicine, 93, 94, 209, 313
Medicine Bow Mountains, 70
Meeker, Nathan C., 113, 137
Mercantile Library of Denver, 151
Merrick, John L., 45
Merson, Alan, 359, 360
Mesa Junior College, 283
Mesa Verde National Park, 129, 221–22, 264
Methodist Episcopal Church, 49, 50, 67
Methodists, 49, 50, 153
Metzger, John W., 330
Mexican Americans, 106, 110, 122, 123, 125–26, 163, 175–77, 236, 301, 314, 338–40; attitudes toward, 173–74; in beet fields, 279–80; early drift into Colorado, 48, 60, 173; political action by, 342
Mexican cession (1848), 1
Mexican War, 3
Michener, James A., 367
Middle Park, 70, 95, 96
Miles, Nelson, 210
Millet, H. S., 45
Mills, Enos, 231
Milstein, Jacob, 181
Miners and Mechanics Institute, Central City, 150
mining, 1, 4, 7–19 passim, 22, 69–71, 77, 83–84, 85, 87, 128–34, 146, 181, 184–85, 190–92, 225–26, 234–35, 269–70, 274–75, 294. *See also* coal, copper, gold, lead, molybdenum, silver, tungsten, uranium, vanadium, zinc
Minneapolis-Honeywell Regulator Company, 320
Minter, Melvin, 340
Minturn, 298
Minute Men, 237, 246
Mississippi Valley, 15
Missouri, 24, 78; Fifty-Niners from, 17
Missouri River Valley, 7, 14, 23, 87
Mitropoulos, Dimitri, 335
Moffat, David H., 78, 79, 131, 252, 290
Moffat Dome, 256, 257
Moffat Road. *See* Denver and Salt Lake Railroad
molybdenum, 234, 295
Monarch Airlines. *See* Frontier Airlines
Monarch Pass, 264
Monsanto Company, 320
Montana, 51, 81, 107, 108, 142, 170, 323; gold strikes, 69–70, 71
Montana City, 20
Monte Vista, 159
Montgomery, 7, 85
Montrose, 137, 163, 208, 295
Moore, O. Otto, 284
Moore, William H., 51
Morgan, John, 120–23, 125
Morley, Clarence J., 245, 246
Mormons, 110, 120–27, 135, 138–39, 200, 202, 204; Mormon "war," 8; opposed by Presbyterians, 49
Morrison, 154
Morrison Springs, 96
Mosquito Pass, 132
Mountain City, 70
Mount Princeton Hot Springs, 96
Murchison, Clint, 318
music halls, 36

Nathan Hale Volunteers, World War I, 237
National Annuity League, 284, 331
National Association of Manufacturers, 316
National Bureau of Standards, 320
National Center for Atmospheric Research, 321
National Guard, 235, 279
National Land Company, 109, 114, 116–18, 120
National Livestock Association, 145
natural gas. *See* gas
Naturita, 202, 294
Navajo Indians, 211
Nebraska, 65, 77, 78, 81, 141, 350; Fifty-Niners from, 17
Nederland, 234
Negroes, 115, 161, 172, 174, 197, 211, 217, 243, 244, 301, 314, 361; in Denver, 54, 340, 341–42; in early mining towns, 28, 29; franchise question, 80–82; women Fifty-Niners, 35
Nevada City (Nevadaville), 53, 55, 70
Nevada, 81, 102
Newton, Quigg, 337; Denver mayor, 315, 316, 318; tries for Senate, 317; university president, 317, 343, 344
New Deal, 277, 278, 279, 281–82, 283, 286, 291, 293, 303
New England, 49, 123, 154
New Hispanic movement, 342
New Mexico, 48, 67, 84, 103, 121, 134, 173, 174, 281, 301, 339, 340; as a part of Colorado, 17, 65
New York City, 87, 88, 89, 113, 133, 181, 199, 221, 224, 311, 319, 322, 344
New York *Times*, 15

New York *Tribune,* 14, 15, 113
Nichols, David, 155
Nisei. *See* Japanese Americans
Nixon, Richard, administration of, 361, 365
Noce, Angelo, 179
Norlin, George, 243, 246
North Fork country, 139; religion in, 50–51
Nucla, 202

Oakes, D. C., 12
Ohio, 80, 94, 110, 120; Fifty-Niners from, 17
Ohio Creek, 146
oil, 256–59, 321; oil shale, 258, 363–66, 367
Old, Robert O., 88
*Olden Times in Colorado* (Davis), 168
Olmsted, Frederick Law, Jr., 286
Olympic Games. *See* Denver Olympics Committee
Opportunity School, 283, 297
Ordway, 254
Oro City, 130
Osage (proposed territorial name), 66
Ouray, 136, 138, 149; newspaper, 168
Our Lady of Guadalupe Church, Conejos, 52
*Out West,* 98
Owen, Robert L., 228

Pabor, William, 177
Packer, Alfred, 205
Paepcke, Walter, 325, 334, 336, 353
Pagosa Springs, 96
Palisade, 234
Palmer, A. Mitchell, 240
Palmer, William Jackson, 154, 158, 168; and education, 153; promoter of Colorado, 89–90, 95–96, 97, 101, 134–35, 138
Panic of 1873, 135, 191
Panic of 1893, 189–91
Paonia, 139
Paris Exposition (1867), 88
Parkville, 40
Parson, William B., 7
Payne, Bill, 29
Pearce, Richard, 129
penitentiary, 59; conditions at, 206–7; reforms at, 219–20
pension system, 284–85, 331
People's Theater, 42
Perry-Mansfield School of Dance, 333
Peterson Field, 298
Pettis, E. Newton, 58
Peyton, 282
Pfeifer, Friedl, 325
Phipps, Gerald, 345
Piatigorsky, Gregor, 335
Pickett, Horace Greeley, 167
Pike, Zebulon M., 2, 18, 221
Pike's Peak region, 32, 33, 70, 71, 98, 107, 165, 190, 264, 288; gold rush to, 8, 11, 15, 16, 18, 19
*Pioneer Press* (Akron), 167
Pinon, 202
Pitkin, 134
Pitkin, Frederick, 193
placer mining. *See* mining
Platte Valley Theater, 42
Platteville, 120
Plowshare program, 351
Polk, James K., 4
population: blacks (Denver), 340; Colorado Springs, 305; Denver, 219; Hispanos (Denver), 339; mining, 22; post–World War II, 321, 356, 364, 365; women (1860), 34
Populism, 163, 164, 168, 169, 191, 270
Post, Emily, 225
Pratt, C. N., 116
Presbyterians, 123; missionary activities of, 48–49, 50
Price, Edwin, 167
Progressive movement, 216, 219, 233
Progressive music hall, 36
prohibition, 244, 245, 248–50; 1916 and 1918 acts of, 229; failure of, 251, 252. *See also* temperance.
Project Rio Blanco, 361
Project Rulison, 351, 361
promotional efforts, 87–105 passim, 137, 231, 232, 269, 288, 305–6, 311, 321–26, 345–47, 348–70 passim
prostitution, 229; at Cripple Creek, 226–27; at Denver, 227; in territorial era, 36, 41
Protestant Episcopal Church, 51
Protestants, 48–49, 171. *See also names of individual denominations*
Public health, post–World War II, 312–13
Pueblo, 8, 103, 109, 112, 121, 122, 141, 150, 175, 240, 250, 256, 265, 266, 285, 286, 310, 320, 322, 347, 356, 367; education at, 51, 53, 55; flood at, 254, 255; military air field at, 298; ordnance depot at, 297; post–World War II conditions, 311
Pueblo *Chieftain. See Colorado Chieftain*

radio broadcasting, 274
Raffles, James, 44
railroads, 77, 90, 108, 134, 135–36, 207, 224, 260, 239, 324; early plans for, 24–25; influence of, 100; in San Luis Valley, 125. *See also* Atchison, Topeka & Santa Fe Railroad; Chicago, Burlington & Quincy Railroad; Chicago, Rock Island and Pacific Railroad; Colorado Central Railroad; Colorado Midland Railroad Company; Denver and Rio Grande Railway; Denver and Salt Lake Railroad; Denver Pacific Railroad; Denver, South Park and

Pacific Railroad; Kansas Pacific Railway; Leavenworth City, St. Joseph and Pike's Peak Railroad; Union Pacific Railroad
Randall, George M., 51, 156
Rangely oil field, 257
Raton Pass, 134
Raverdy, John B., 52
Ray, Sallie, 184–85
Reconstruction Finance Corporation, 291
*Record Stockman*, 271
Redcliff, 134
Redford, Robert, 367
"red menace," 239–43, 272, 328–30
Regis College, 154
Reid, James, 41
religion, 48, 49, 89. *See also* Baptists; Catholics; Congregationalists; Episcopalians; Jews; Methodist Episcopal Church; Methodists; Mormons; Presbyterians; Protestant Episcopal Church; Protestants
Remington Arms Company, 296
Republican River, 10, 76
Richardson, Albert D., 14
Richfield, 124
Ricketson, Frank, 333
Rifle, 295
Rinehart, Mrs. A. E., 207, 208
Rio Blanco, 361
Rio Grande Canal, 141
Rio Grande Valley, 67, 173
Roaring Fork River, 325
Roberts, William, 133
Robinson, 134
Roche, André, 325
Roche, Josephine, 274
Rock Springs, Wyo., 364
Rocky Flats Plant. *See* Atomic Energy Commission
Rocky Ford, 141, 254
*Rocky Mountain American*, 244, 246, 247
Rocky Mountain Arsenal, 297, 351
Rocky Mountain Fuel Company, 274
Rocky Mountain League of States, 270
Rocky Mountain National Park, 231, 262, 273, 285, 286
*Rocky Mountain Herald*, 169
*Rocky Mountain News*, 12, 14, 15, 27, 29, 35, 42, 43, 52, 53, 54, 55, 58, 73, 74, 80, 83, 87, 90, 95, 114, 136, 151, 153, 155, 157, 161, 162, 165, 168, 174, 190, 208, 257, 316, 360; on agriculture, 109; boosts Colorado, 69; founded, 45; as political force, 79; works for libraries, 69. *See also* Byers, William
Rocky Mountain Power Company, 348
Rocky Mountain Railroad, 24
Roma, Joe, 251
Roman Catholics. *See* Catholics
Rocky Mountain Power Company, 348
Rocky Mountain Railroad, 24
Roma, Joe, 251
Roman Catholics. *See* Catholics
Roosa, Stuart, 343
Roosevelt, Franklin D., 229, 277, 281, 291
Roosevelt, Theodore, 211, 212, 233
Roth, Herrick, 342
Routt, John L., 102, 105
Royal Gorge, 134, 259
Rubinstein, Artur, 335
Rudd, Anson, 45, 59
Rulison, 351, 361
Rusling, James F., 84
Russell, Levi J., 21
Russell, William Green, 7, 8, 13, 16, 119
Russell Gulch, 39, 143
Russian Germans. *See* German Russians
Ryssby settlement, 117–18

Sabin, Florence R., 312, 313
Sacred Heart College, 154
Saguache *Chronicle*, 167
St. Charles, 20, 21
St. Louis, Mo., 16, 36, 37, 118
St. Louis–Western colony, 118
St. Mary's Academy, Denver, 154
St. Patrick's Benevolent Society, library of, 150
Salida, 181, 266
Saltiel, Emanuel H., 181
Salt Lake City, 37, 71, 121, 123, 135, 256, 290, 298
Salvation Army. *See* Fort Amity
San Cristobal, Lake, 129
Sand Creek, 76, 81, 299; battle at, 74–75
Sanderlin, Ed, 28
Sands, Obediah B., 134
Sanford, 124
Sanford, Mollie, 75, 76
Sangre de Cristo Mountains, 112
San Juan country, 134, 255
San Juan Mountains, 71, 137
San Luis, 56
San Luis, Province of, 1
San Luis Valley, 1, 3, 4, 60, 65, 67, 105, 107, 113, 120, 141, 167, 174, 177, 202, 203, 204, 294, 295; Mormon colonies in, 122–24
San Miguel River, 202
Santa Fe, 1, 67, 173
Santa Fe Compact, 256
Santa Fe Trail, 8
Schroeder, Patricia, 360, 367
Schwartz, Julius, 182, 183
Schweitzer, Albert, 335
Scott, William E., 211
Scott, Tully, 241
Selig, Joseph, 138
"sell Colorado." *See* promotional efforts

Sevareid, Eric, 352
"Seventy-Niners," 131
Sewall, Joseph A., 155
Seward, William, 80
Shafroth, John F., 172, 218, 219
shale oil. *See* oil
Shaw, George, 272
sheep raising, 143
Shoup, Oliver H., 254
Shwayder brothers, 319, 296
silver, 84, 130, 132, 134, 141, 181, 189–90, 198, 215, 234, 269–70, 321, 322
Silver Cliff, 112
Silverton, 129, 138, 324
Simonin, Louis, 88, 89
Sims, J. G., 28
Singleton, Judson, 217
Sioux Indians, 3
skiing, 288, 324, 325, 326, 351
Slough, John P., 67
Smiley, Jerome, 75, 81, 100
Smithsonian Institution, 222
Smoky Hill route, 10
social control, 47–48, 91, 149
Solly, Samuel E., 95
Sons of Colorado, 242
South Boulder Creek, 13
Southern Colorado State College, 283
South Park, 71, 72, 85, 96, 130, 185
South Platte River, 2, 4, 7, 8, 119, 120, 140, 141, 143, 203, 204, 254
South St. Vrain River, 117
Southwestern Colony. *See* Green City
Spanish American War, 208, 210–12, 215
Spanish exploration, 2, 4
stagelines, to Colorado, 10
Stanley, Freelan O., 230, 231
Stapleton, Ben, 245, 315, 316
Stapleton Field, Denver, 304, 305
*Star of Empire,* 115
statehood, 79, 82, 83, 101; demands for, 66; realization of, 102, 104, 232
State Industrial School, Golden, 206
State Normal School, Alamosa. *See* Adams State College
State Normal School, Greeley. *See* University of Northern Colorado
State Normal School, Gunnison. *See* Western State College
Steamboat Springs, 286, 333; Klan in, 248; skiing at, 288, 324–25
Stearns, Robert L., 328
Stearns-Roger Manufacturing Company, 296
Steinberger, A. B., 42
Sterling, 159, 160
Sterling Junior College, 283
Stevens, William H., 130
Stewart, James Z., 12, 122, 125
Stone, Lucy, 163
Stone, Wilbur Fisk, 153, 168
Strahorn, Robert, 232
Street, Julian, 226
Strong, Charles D., 276
sugar beet industry, 279, 280, 340
Summers and Dorsett livery stable, 30
Summit County, 353, 356
Sumner, Charles, 80–81, 82, 103
Swedish Americans: in Denver, 180; Ryssby group, 117
Swigert, John L., 343
Swink, 299
Sylvanite mine, Gothic, 134

Tabaguache Park, 202
Tabor, Augusta, 18, 35, 39, 40, 131, 163
Tabor, "Baby Doe," 131, 163
Tabor, Horace A. W., 18, 35, 39, 40, 131, 158, 163
Tabor Grand Opera House, Denver, 158
Talbot, Joseph C., 51
Tammen, Harry H., 196, 314
Tarryall, 71, 85
Taylor, Bayard, 70
Taylor, Edward T., 271, 286
Taylor, John, 121, 122, 123
telegraph service, 25
telephones, at Leadville, 132
Teller, Henry M., 79, 81, 105
Telluride, 354–55; labor trouble at, 196
temperance, 117, 118, 159–61, 229. *See also* prohibition
Tenney, Edward P., 153, 174
Terrill, Green, 29
Texas, invasion from, 67. *See also* Civil War
theaters, 36–37, 41–43, 85, 121, 157, 159, 209
Thespian Theater, 121
Thomas, Charles S., 131, 205, 212, 215
Thomas, Henry (Gold Tom), 181
Thomas, William R., 109
Thorne, Charles R., 41–42
Thornton, Dan, 330, 331
*Time* magazine, 333
Tin Cup, 134
Todd, Andrew C., 118, 119
Torrey, Jay, 211
tourism, 230–33; by automobile, 259, 264, 288; early, 128; highway improvement, 260, 261
Tow Creek oil field, 256
Travelers Insurance Company, 140, 141
Trinidad, 55, 176, 196, 281, 287, 298; racial violence in, 174
Trinidad State Junior College, 283
Triplex Corporation, 320
Truman, Harry, 317

Tucker, Booth, 198, 199
tungsten, 234–35
Twin Lakes Reservoir, 254
Tynan, Thomas J., 219–20, 259

Uncompahgre Utes, 136
Uncompahgre Valley, 138, 295
Unemployed Citizens' League, 276
Union Colony, 116, 117, 119. *See also* Greeley
Union Pacific, Eastern Division, 78. *See also* Kansas Pacific Railway
Union Pacific Railroad, 77, 78, 108, 109, 125, 135, 140, 143, 193, 204, 265, 289
United Airlines, 269, 291, 304
United Front Organization, 279
United Mine Workers, 196
United Oil Company, Denver, 257
United States Air Force Academy, 320, 344
United States Mint, 30
University of Colorado, 116, 151, 153, 300, 303, 310, 317, 322, 333, 334, 343; racial discrimination at, 341
University of Denver, 50, 143, 153, 333, 343
University of Northern Colorado, 156, 313
U.S. Vanadium. *See* Vanadium Corporation of America
uranium, 235, 321, 351
Uravan, 235, 294
Uris, Leon, 353
Utah, 71, 110, 123, 125, 139, 187, 195, 265; as part of Colorado, 17, 65
Ute Indians, 3, 35, 95, 102, 136, 178, 185, 208, 222, 224; land cession (1882), 137; removal of, 139
Ute treaty (1868), 136
Ute war (1879), 137

Vail, 325, 326, 354
Vail, Charles D., 287
Valmont, 45
vanadium, 235, 295
Vanadium Corporation of America, 235, 295
Vanderhoof, John, 361, 366
Vanover, Edgar, 57
Varney Speed Lines, 266
Vasquez House, 24
Victor, 294, 324
Villard, Henry, 14, 72
Vivian, Charles, 133
Vivian, John C., 303
Volunteers, First Regiment of, 67, 74

Wade, Benjamin F., 80
Wade, Sam, 139
Wagon Creek, 135
Wagoner, Henry O., 28
Waite, Davis H., 197, 205; founds newspaper, 167, 168; governor, 195; on women's suffrage, 164
Wall, David N., 107
Wallingford and Murphy (store), 66
Walsenburg, 196
Walsh, Thomas F., 191
Warman, Cy, 168
Washington, D.C., 65, 66, 72, 76, 79, 81, 83, 112, 271, 292, 294
Washington Territory, 38
Washita, battle of, 76
water diversion, 253–56, 285, 363
Webb, Beatrice, 165, 166
Webb, Sidney, 165
Webb, Walter Prescott, 322
Webb & Knapp, Inc., 311, 318
Weld, Lewis, 68
Wellington Dome, oil at, 256, 257
West, George, 45
West, Mae, 333
Westcliff, 269
Western Air Express, 266
Western Colony. *See* St. Louis–Western Colony
Western Federation of Miners, 196
Western State College, 156
Western States Cutlery, 296
Western Union Company, 132
Wet Mountains, 3, 112
Wet Mountain Valley, 111, 112, 113
Wheeler, George M., 29
whiskey, 22
White River Utes, 136
Whitney, J. P., 88
Wildman, Gus, 107
Williams Fork Tunnel, 254
Willis, Robert H., 255
Wilson, Woodrow, 228
Windsor, 180, 352
Wirth, Timothy, 367
Wolfe Hall, 55
Womack, Bob, 190
women, 34–40, 53, 89, 94, 146, 149, 161, 162, 171, 184–86, 187, 211; in education, 55; among Fifty-Niners, 11, 18, 21, 24, 34; in journalism, 163, 167; in mining, 185; suffrage for, 161–66
Women's Christian Temperance Union, 149, 150, 160, 165, 229
Woodbury, R. W., 105
Woods, H. M., 166
Wootton, Richens ("Uncle Dick"), 3, 23, 73, 106
World War I, 208, 233, 234–38 passim, 239, 274, 290, 293, 294, 295, 297, 340
World War II, 177, 258, 265, 286, 289, 291, 292, 293–306 passim, 345, 356, 365
Wulsten, Carl, 111–13

Wyckoff, Walter, 224–25
Wyer, Malcolm G., 152
Wyoming, 70, 142, 164, 187, 236, 289, 323, 364

Young, Brigham, 111, 120
Young Men's Christian Association, 150, 300
Young Women's Christian Association, 300

Zeckendorf, William, 318
zinc, 181, 234, 270, 294

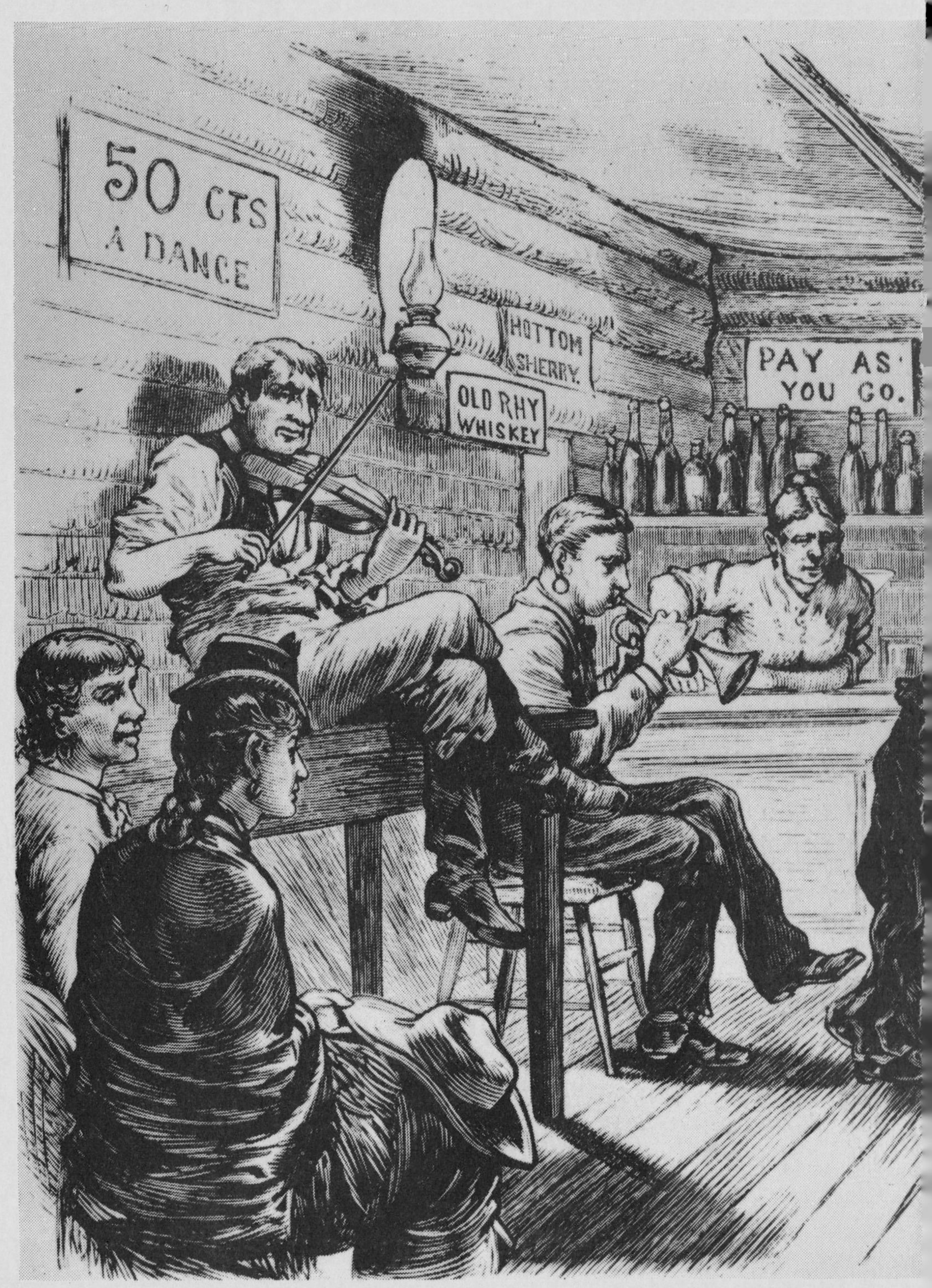
50 CTS
A DANCE
HOTTOM
SHERRY.
OLD RHY
WHISKEY
PAY AS
YOU GO.